Filmmakers' YEARBOOK 2008

Edited by Tricia Tuttle and Briony Hanson

A & C Black • London

Second edition 2007
A & C Black Publishers Limited
38 Soho Square, London W1D 3HB
www.acblack.com

ISBN: 978–0–7136–8470–4

A CIP catalogue record for this book is available from the British Library.

This book is produced using paper that is made from wood grown in managed, sustainable forests. It is natural, renewable and recyclable. The logging and manufacturing processes conform to the environmental regulations of the country of origin.

Typeset by QPM from David Lewis XML Associates Ltd
Printed and bound in Great Britain by William Clowes, Beccles

Contents

Exhibition:

Resources

Foreword

Sir Richard Eyre

I became a filmmaker almost by accident. I was running a theatre in Nottingham in the 1970s and made a reputation for directing and commissioning new plays by new writers (David Hare, Trevor Griffiths, Howard Brenton, Stephen Lowe, Ken Campbell) when I was offered a job by the BBC producing *Play for Today*, its contemporary drama strand.

I agreed to become a producer on condition that I would be able to direct, and I started to learn about directing films by employing good directors – in particular my friend, Stephen Frears. From watching and talking to film directors I acquired some basic film wisdom: that the director needs to hold the film in his or her head while shooting; that s/he needs to know what shot s/he is coming from and going to; that a film needs to move – if you can't move the camera, move the actor; that a film is not made in the cutting room; that photography captures everything it sees – what you see through the lens is what you get on the screen; that there is no alchemical transformation when the film is processed; and that light, as Fellini says, is "the miracle worker, adding, blotting out, reducing, enriching, shading, emphasising, hinting, making the fantastic and the substance of dreams acceptable, or, on the contrary, adding quivering transparent effects and making an illusion out of the greyest everyday reality".

When I say I learned these things, it was more that I observed them to be true without experiencing them. That came later, as I struggled to rid myself of the habits of years of working in the theatre, where at least you learn the most important elements of filmmaking: how to work with actors and how to tell stories.

The tendency of the theatre director coming to film is to duplicate sound and vision – to show the audience who is speaking, to be reluctant to assume the power of being able to change the audience's perspective by changing the size of the shot, by cutting, by music, by sound effects. It's all too easy, too, to assume that the visual image is paramount, and to ignore the capacity of film to exploit the dynamic of what you see and what you hear; sometimes complementary, sometimes in opposition. Theatre is a linear medium, and the physical relationship between the actors and the audience is essentially static. Film is mobile; the audience's point of view is always being changed by the camera. All the experience of a theatre director is to take the text as the unalterable given, and illuminate it, not shape it, carve it up, mould it, reconstruct it as a director does in editing a film. What film and theatre have in common is this: they both have to live from moment to moment, and to achieve this their essence has to be distilled from the raw material. That it's incomparably harder to achieve this in the theatre doesn't, of course, make either a superior medium, and blaming theatre for not being film is as foolish blaming a melon for not being an orange.

Unquestionably, making a film is more complicated, more time-consuming, more labour-intensive – and incomparably more expensive. That's probably what inspires the indignation that bubbles just beneath the surface when a film crew appears on a street. An unwieldy procession – trucks, trailers, caravans, generators, cherry-pickers – invades like an occupying army and departs as suddenly as it arrives, leaving behind, in spite of scrupulous clearing-up, the spoor of polystyrene coffee cups and strips of gaffer tape.

In London the public are sated with the sight of pavements bulging with people in anoraks who divert their traffic and rob them of parking spaces. Or they're saturated with knowledge of the process of filmmaking either from DVD 'making-of' extras or from their own efforts at home with video-cams. In spite of this, however, they remain forever mystified at the effort that it takes to record a fraction of a fragment of a scene in a film: the most frequent words that you hear when you're filming in a street are not "tosser" or "wanker" but "Why does it take so many people to make a film?"

I find myself time after time asking myself the same question, and even though I'm only too aware of the essential role of each member of the crew, I'm still awed by the extraordinary degree of artifice that is required to simulate reality in order, paradoxically, to make fiction. We cosmeticise streets and houses. We make them look dirtier or older than they are – disguising their TV aerials, changing the profile of their chimneys, 'breaking down' their paintwork, 'distressing' their facades (and often their owners). We populate the streets with extras (to avoid the legal and physical peril of being accused of filming people without their consent); we introduce huge lamps when nature fails to provide sunlight; we make rain and snow. In short, we play God.

At the tip of this colossal inverted pyramid, stuffed with technology and manpower, there is a camera at the end of whose lens, perhaps no more than a few inches in diameter, is a small, vulnerable, variable, gifted person – an actor, whose image will be recorded on a rectangular piece of film a few centimetres wide, 24 times a second. At this point – the sharp end filmmaking, if you like – everything the director does is an attempt to confound or subvert the artifice of it all.

In Truffaut's (very romantic) film about filmmaking, *La Nuit Americaine*, the director (played by Truffaut) lies awake, racked with pain and doubt. "Is my film alive?" he asks himself, and every film director confronts the same question. In an attempt to give life to their film, directors of drama often mimic documentary; they make actors mumble to simulate the incoherence of real speech, the camera shakes and wobbles, the picture slips in and out of focus, the editing is raw. These are all devices which conspire to give the impression that events have occurred spontaneously and a film crew has been lucky enough to be there to film them.

But pretty soon these efforts to create a heightened sense of realism decline into mannered stylistic tricks and directors are forced to find another way to suggest the appearance of reality. They have to confront the immutable truth that reality will always mock the way that fiction seeks to tidy up chaos. And that's true whether it's film, theatre or literature. Real life will always rebuke its fictional counterfeit.

Richard Eyre, April 2007

Screenwriting and project development
The screenwriter and script development

Lucy Scher

"That's a great idea for a film...!"

There is no market for good ideas – or, to put it another way, you can only buy something once it has been turned into a product. Writers of novels, poems, songs, comedy sketches and plays may self-publish or self-produce their creations, and this method of cultural production has delivered some fine work, often to huge and appreciative audiences. But the screenwriter must engage at some level with the established industry to reach an audience. The point at which the new screenwriter engages with the industry varies, but it is always *after* a script or a treatment is written.

The sector of the film industry in which the screenwriter usually operates is called *development*. This introduction aims (1) to clarify the role and function of development for the new screenwriter in his/her journey to having a script produced, and (2) to explore the processes of professional development for future script readers and developers, and for other new professionals who are likely to work with writers – such as producers and directors. The terms 'screenwriting' and 'screenwriters' are self-explanatory, but it may be less clear what 'script development' involves.

Why does my screenplay need to go through script development?

As a screenwriter, your work is likely to be the foundation on which the whole production process rests. It is therefore essential, for the future success of the project, that the screenplay be sound and well realised at the development and pre-production stages (although this isn't to say that a screenwriter shouldn't expect changes to be made to their work throughout the production and post-production process as well!). Whereas the writer working in other media – such as literature, theatre and even television – can expect a certain degree of autonomy, the film screenwriter must recognise that they are a part of a much larger creative team. Feature filmmaking is an extremely expensive endeavour, and if the film is being funded by more than the screenwriter's friends/family/credit card, s/he should expect to have to 'develop' their script with input from a range of sources: the producer and director of the project; the development team at a production company; and perhaps even the financiers. If you are a screenwriter reading this, you will need to learn how to use this input constructively (and know when to politely ignore some advice). If you are a potential developer, you will need to learn when, and how, to engage with the writer productively. To these ends, it is hoped that this introduction and Emma Berkofsky's article, *The role of the developer* (see page 29) will be of use.

Development of the screenwriter

Before we consider development, it is helpful to define the screenwriter as 'the author of a story for the screen'. The story can be original; it can be based on a 'slice of life' or adapted from another fictional source; it can be written in the form of a script or as a treatment; there can be one or more screenwriters working on any one project. A professional screenwriter has developed the necessary creative and technical skills to do the job well: as with any other creative production, inspiration alone is not enough.

New screenwriters might well ask: 'How do writers learn to write?' The single most important way for any writer to learn their craft is by reading and digesting good examples. Unlike authors working in other areas, would-be screenwriters may not have ready access to scripts and treatments ... but reading them is essential. Consider the possibility of a novelist sitting down to write a novel without ever having read one! So it falls to the screenwriter to actively seek out routes to basic learning. Watching films and reading books about screenwriting are no substitute for, or shortcut to, learning specific script-writing skills; many new screenwriters seem to be trying to do professional work without having first acquired the basics.

There are some very good courses for new screenwriters, and a number of organisations that can provide assistance. In addition to committing time and money to these, a new screenwriter should start reading good produced screenplays. This is essential if s/he is to acquire skills comparable to that of the novelist, for example, who has been absorbing books ever since learning to read.

What is the development sector?

Development is difficult to define. It comprises everything to do with finding and nurturing screenwriters, and reading and responding to their work. At the same time we must have an eye on the wider field of current film production. While it is generally accepted that 'getting the script right' is important, there are in fact very few recognised methods and working practices in the development sector that help achieve this directly. There is no industry-wide, structured training path into development; nor is there a clear career progression. Jobs in development are rarely advertised; there are no standard definitions of the documents existing in this sector (such as a script report, for instance); and development takes neither credit nor blame for the films that have *all* travelled through the sector.

The Script Factory defines development as the process whereby the developer finds that which is meaningful in the project to the writer, and in turn assists the writer to make that meaningful to the audience. Understanding how the development sector works will advantage the new screenwriter, aspirant script reader or developer.

The process

The journey of a script through this sector for *a new screenwriter* is something like this:

- The writer sends a script to be considered for development or production to a public fund or a production company (for the developer's perspective on this process, see Emma Berkofsky's article later in this section).
- The script is then sent to a script reader for a script report, otherwise known as a coverage. The summary conclusion of the coverage is to reject; to second-read; or to recommend. In the case of rejection, the script is likely to be returned with a standard letter (usually without detailed comments). If however a script is recommended (either first time round, or after a second read), the writer will be invited to a meeting with the development executive or the producer. At this stage the writer as well as the script will be under scrutiny, and it is advisable to rehearse extensively so that both self-confidence and confidence in the project are demonstrated at the meeting.

Development tools

Here are some of the tools of development, covered in more detail.

The script report

This should be a summary, in sections, of the strengths and weaknesses of the script. It will usually start with a synopsis to relate the main beats of the story to someone who hasn't read the script; this can be anything from three paragraphs to two pages. The reader tries to convey the story in its best light in the synopsis, but it is also the beginning of the reader's analysis of the script. For example, if the main character changes or the conflict alters during the course of the screenplay, the reader will notice this in trying to write a coherent synopsis. This will inform the rest of the script report – so obviously, the simpler the story, the easier it will be to put into synopsis. A good exercise for both new writer and new reader/developer is to practise writing a script report on available films. Condense each one to the main story outline to learn how films that seem very complex can be reduced to quite simple synopses.

There is no standard industry format for a script report, but at The Script Factory we try to teach readers to analyse scripts or other proposals using the following structure:

• **Premise** – this is also called the idea, the concept, or the story. Avoid abstractions and think of the premise as the main conflict and where it is set to generate a clear and tangible perception. In a screenplay it is crucial that there is a conflict to resolve, whether this manifests as interpersonal conflict, internal personal conflict or a conflict within the social or environmental situation of the characters.

• **Structure** – this is the order of the story or the form the story takes, rather than its essential premise. The reader is analysing the way in which the writer has presented the information in the story so that 'who knows what and when' creates or contributes to the tension, pathos, humour, etc. This will provide evidence of the writer's skill in rendering a story for the screen.

• **Characters** – these are specific constructs rather than abstract concepts. The reader is looking for compelling characters that are integral to the story they are making. Characters are revealed by their appearance, what they say and what they do. This requires emotional truth and consistency; the script will be more interesting if the characters are not stereotypes, nor their actions entirely predictable.

• **Dialogue** – the reader is trying to establish whether this sounds authentic and believable. Does it reveal character and necessary back-story successfully? Is there too much?

• **Visual grammar** – the reader assesses whether or not the writer has command and control of the various cinematic techniques available in the writing, and whether or not they have been deployed effectively. The key question here is: Why is this story being told as a film? Do we need to see it rather than read it? Assured visual grammar must be evident in the script for affirmative answers to such questions.

• **Pace** – under this heading the reader is observing whether the writer has a sophisticated understanding of the economy of screen time and of the efficient construction of scenes. Knowing how to engage the audience emotionally by using real time appropriately is another important element of this technique.

There may be other headings in a report, such as 'plot'; some also include a 'log-line' (a one-sentence summary). However, the sections outlined above are the key story elements and craft skills that need to be mastered by screenwriters and understood by readers and developers in preparing a script for production.

As a screenwriter working independently, you may find that using some of these same tools in your own work will help you to refine your own screenplay, and to better understand if you are achieving your own creative aims. Most writers might also find an objective perspective on their script useful. New writers can access script reports *designed for the writer* to help in the development of their project from The Script Factory. To gain a greater understanding of these principles in practice, and in application to a particular script, it is well worthwhile to commission a script report.

The treatment

This is the other key document that exists in the development sector. At some point in a screenwriter's career, s/he will be asked to produce a treatment of their screenplay. Incredibly, this document too has no standardised form in the industry; it should be shorter than a script and written in prose, but there is no agreement as to how extensive it should be, or what should be in it, or how to write or assess a treatment.

The practical response to this of course is to ensure that the treatment delivers *whatever serves the story best*, and this is a good maxim to have as a screensaver. It requires the writer to know the story and convey it in such a way that the reader knows it too – though this is easier said than done!

There are four different functions for which a treatment may be needed:

- as a document to sell the merits of a script already written;
- as a document setting out an idea for a script not yet written;
- as a treatment for an adaptation to the screen of material from another source;
- as a document to be used as a tool in developing the script between drafts.

When and why may a writer be asked to produce a treatment? In most circumstances a treatment will be requested by a developer or producer, who either wants to take a view on reading a script or commissioning a script, or wishes to clarify development for the next draft of a script. Increasingly, treatments are requested as part of an application or course work for screenwriting training or education programmes.

Where the treatment is part of the development process, for the eyes of the writer and those intimately involved in the script, its purpose is likely to be one of clarification. (To try out new ideas, new endings, new events, a new structure.) The style of writing is less important than for the other specific development function. If however the treatment is in any way a sales document, or a document intended to excite the reader about the possibility of a film, it is imperative that it be very carefully composed for that purpose.

If as a writer you have been asked for a treatment and are not sure what is required of you, request clarification (if at all possible). Similarly, a developer or producer asking a writer for a treatment should be clear about what they expect the document to deliver, to make the assessment easier and fairer.

Any treatment which is to serve as a sales document must render the story in a concise and dramatic way, using visual language to engage the reader. The worst treatments are the ones that attempt to follow or describe the structure of the script, and in so doing become impenetrable. The best ones rethink the story for its new medium – the prose version. In single- or dual-protagonist stories, the situation which gives rise to the goals (or needs) of the characters will be in the foreground, and interest focused on whether/how the characters take on their particular challenges (or fail to). In multi-strand stories, the connection between the different strands needs to be clear – whether this is an event, a theme, a location, and so on. Interest must be in the more significant idea underlying the choices and actions of the characters, as readers place themselves within that continuum.

Finally ...

Finding out about script reading and development is still hard, and it is very gratifying that The Script Factory has been asked to provide the introduction to this section of this valuable resource book. For some time, one explicit aim of The Script Factory has been to explain the development sector of the UK film industry; to champion screenwriters, script readers and developers as the best investment in the future of cinema here; and to give the people in these key creative roles, confidence through knowledge of the craft as well as of the industry. It is the current indeterminate character of the development sector that presents this opportunity to attempt to define it usefully.

Never forget that a good film starts with a good story. If you are reading this book, once upon a time a good story, well told on a cinema screen, may have touched your heart and soul – and led you to want to be a filmmaker. Good luck on your journey.

Lucy Scher is co-director of the filmmakers' organisation, The Script Factory, which she helped to establish in 1996. Lucy oversees The Script Factory's training programme where she trains screenwriters and developers, and she has acted as a development mentor for many short- and feature-film writers. In addition she has devised and delivered many short courses and workshops on screenwriting and script development for film funds, production companies, media-funded training courses and the UK Film Council, both in the UK and internationally. Lucy established the first Diploma in Script Development in partnership with the National Film and Television School; she is a regular contributor to screenwriting publications.

Writers' organisations

It's an oft-stated fact that screenwriting is the loneliest of the film disciplines. Screenwriters spend countless hours honing their craft in solitude; unless you are part of a writing team, you will usually work without much creative interaction until you've spent months developing something that is ready for feedback. Screenwriters' groups and organisations can offer much-needed creative communion with other writers who are puzzling over the same questions that you are, and many offer short courses, events and networking opportunities which can help to make your work better, easier and more enjoyable.

BBC Writersroom

Grafton House, 379-381 Euston Road,
London NW1 3AU
website www.bbc.co.uk/writersroom

BBC Writersroom finds and develops new writers across BBC drama and comedy programmes, covering all networks and platforms. Accepts and reads unsolicited scripts for film, TV and Radio drama, TV and Radio narrative comedy, Children's and Online. Submissions must be original and not 'spec' scripts for existing shows. The website features other writing opportunities inside and outside the BBC, an archive of produced scripts, free script formatting software and interviews with writers and industry professionals. Full submission details are available on the website and writers are encouraged to check the guidelines before submitting work.

Euroscript

Suffolk House, 1-8 Whitfield Place, London W1P 5SF
mobile (07803) 369414
email enquiries@euroscript.co.uk
website www.euroscript.co.uk

Euroscript is an independent, UK-based script development organisation for film and television, which offers analysis of screenplays by a team of screenwriters, producers and experienced teachers in the field. It also offers day-long training workshops focusing on different aspects of screenwriting and development. Course details are posted on the website when available.

Filmmakers' Alliance

The American Cinematheque, The Egyptian Theater, 6712 Hollywood Blvd, Los Angeles, CA 90028, USA
tel +1 310 568 0633
email info@filmmakersalliance.com
website www.filmmakersalliance.com

This Los Angeles-based organisation hosts monthly meetings and seminars, and encourages members to share resources.

The London Script Consultancy (LSC)

1 Penpoll Road, London E8 1EX
tel 020-8510 0674
email info@londonscriptconsultancy.com
website www.londonscriptconsultancy.com

LSC offers training and support to writers seeking to work professionally in the film industry. Organises weekly seminars and workshops for writers, directors and producers looking to develop scripts and skills. Also offers a number of development services, including: script coverage (script report); development report (a more extensive script report); treatment analysis services; and development consultation.

NPA

See New Producers Alliance (NPA) on page 96.

Rocliffe

PO Box 37344, London N1 8YB
email scripts@rocliffe.com
website www.rocliffe.com

A production company providing a series of events, such as the New Film Forums and the New Writing Forums. Created in 2000, the Rocliffe New Writing Forum is a platform for new writing and a networking event; 3 x 7- or 8-minute script extracts are selected, which are then rehearsed by professional actors and directors. Following each performance the writer receives feedback from a co-chair, who is an established professional in the industry, and answers questions from the audience. The evening rounds off with an open Q&A with the co-chair, and a networking session in the bar.

Screenwriters' Festival

tel (01453) 753440
email info@screenwritersfestival.com
website www.screenwritersfestival.com

Held in July at Cheltenham Film Studios, and dedicated to the art, craft, and business of writing for the screen. Brings together professional industry delegates, high-profile guests and new talent for forums to debate and discuss writing dramatic scripts for film, television and new media.

The Script Factory

Welbeck House 66/67 Wells Street,
London W1T 3PY

tel 020-7323 1414 *fax* 020-7323 9464
email general@scriptfactory.co.uk
website www.scriptfactory.co.uk
Co-directors Briony Hanson, Charlotte Macleod, Lucy Scher

The Script Factory was established in 1996 to stage readings of unproduced screenplays for a live audience. As the open submissions for screenplays began to generate an influx of scripts, the company started to train people to read and comment on scripts – and The Script Factory Training Department was born. The company has become one of Europe's leading screenwriter and development organisations, providing training for both writers and the people who work with writers. It also offers a year-round public events programme with some of the industry's top filmmakers, producers and developers, and has a large Training Centre available for rent suitable for meetings, away-days, training courses and receptions.

For details on The Script Factory's development services, see page 38.

The Society of Authors' Broadcasting Group

84 Drayton Gardens, London SW10 9SB
tel 020-7373 6642 *fax* 020-7373 5768
email info@societyofauthors.org
website www.societyofauthors.org
Chairman Tracy Chevalier, *General Secretary* Mark Le Fanu

The Society of Authors has been serving the interests of professional writers since 1885. Today it has more than 7500 members writing in all areas of the profession, from novelists to doctors, textbook writers to ghost writers, broadcasters to academics, illustrators to translators. Staff help members with any query relating to the business of writing. Services include the confidential, individual vetting of contracts, and help with professional disputes. The Society also holds meetings and seminars, publishes a quarterly journal, *The Author*, and maintains a database of members' specialisations. It administers a wide range of prizes, as well as the Authors' Foundation, which is one of the very few bodies making grants to help with work in progress for established writers.

The Broadcasting Group represents all Society members working in radio, television, film and other such broadcasting media within the UK (and, where possible, abroad). To be eligible for membership you need to have written and had broadcast at least 2 scripts for radio or television of at least 20 minutes' duration. The aim of the Group is to support members by negotiating minimum-terms agreements with organisations such as the BBC; by promoting legislation for the benefit of members; by providing day-to-day professional advice; and by holding seminars and meetings on matters of concern to broadcasting writers.

A committee of 10 elected members runs the Group; their term of office lasts for 3 years.

The annual subscription for Society membership (which is tax-deductible) is £80 (£75 by direct debit after the first year). Authors under 35 not yet earning a significant income from writing, may pay a lower subscription of £56. Authors over 65 may pay at the reduced rate after their first year of membership.

Sundance Institute

8530 Wilshire Blvd, 3rd Floor, Beverly Hills, CA 90211-3114, USA
tel ++1 310 360 1981
email la@sundance.org
website www.sundance.org

The Institute is most famous for the Sundance Film Festival, but also runs a biannual Screenwriters' Lab, which brings in 12 feature writers for extensive script development work. The Institute offers financial support via its Documentary fund.

Writers' Guild of America, East

555 West 57th Street, Suite 1230, New York, NY 10019, USA
tel ++ 1 212 767 7800
website www.wgaeast.org

Represents writers from the east of the US on trade matters.

Writers' Guild of America, West

7000 West Third Street, Los Angeles, CA 90048, USA
tel ++ 1 323 951 4000
website www.wga.org

Trade organisation for writers in the west of the US.

Writers' Guild of Great Britain (WGGB)

15 Britannia Street, London WC1X 9JN
tel 020-7833 0777 *fax* 020-7833 4777
email admin@writersguild.org.uk
website www.writersguild.org.uk
General Secretary Bernie Corbett

The Writers' Guild of Great Britain is the trade union representing writers in TV, radio, theatre, books, poetry, film and video games. It campaigns and lobbies on behalf of all writers. In the film and broadcasting industries, WGGB is the recognised body for negotiating minimum terms on behalf of writers.

Full membership is open to writers who have at least 1 contract at or above WGGB minimum terms. Fees are £150 + 1% of earnings from writing over £15,000, up to a maximum fee of £1500. Benefits include free phone advice, contract vetting, access to a pension scheme, and inclusion in the 'Find a Writer' database.

The Guild also offers Candidate and Student memberships for writers who do not yet qualify for Full membership; fees range from £20 to £90 per year.

The Writers' Workshop

Pritchards Cottage, Steeple Barton,
Oxfordshire OX25 4QP
tel (01869) 347040
email info@writersworkshop.co.uk
website www.writersworkshop.co.uk

Offers editorial advice to writers, screenwriters and poets. All editors are writers themselves, and aim to help the writer bring their work to the standard needed for publication. Feedback for scripts generally takes 4-6 weeks and the fees are £250 for a feature-length screenplay.

The pitch

Producer and Pitch guru **Eileen Quinn** gives an expert's guide to getting the pitch for your film just right.

Remember the day your film was born? A title, a first image, an outline? Gradually it grew fingers, toes, and started kicking inside. This is the magical part of the filmmaking process, when the idea for a film first takes shape; enjoy it. The next leaps from Development (those tricky infant years) to Financing (those terrible volatile teens) and on to Production/ Distribution (the grown-up stuff) are the hard yards.

The bridge between those different phases of growth is known as *pitching*. Without it, a project is stillborn, or dies young; nobody knows what you've got. Pitching is as vital as air or food to your embryonic idea.

What is pitching? Hollywood, thanks in part to wonderful films like *The Player,* has mystified and demonised the pitch to the point of derision. But it's very simple, really: pitching is just selling. It's telling someone else your story, handing him or her a baton they can run with and hand along to the next vital person in the 'food chain' of the filmmaking process. The best advice I've ever had is to keep it simple and to communicate your passion for the project in such a way that it ignites the other person's.

Easier said than done, eh?

Over the years, I've developed a few practical tools which should help you with this process, based on interviews with and experience of many hundreds of buyers and sellers. The most useful tool is the 'PFC' or Pitch Format Card. This will not make your work of art formulaic – nor will it make a good project bad or a bad one good. It simply distils stories for the sake of clarity. I suggest that you get out a small index card and read on. The PFC is not by any means the whole pitch; it provides the basis for an introduction; the beginning of your pitch meeting. Jot down the following along the left-hand side of your index card:

Title
Time/Place
Genre
Protagonist
What s/he wants (goal)
What is stopping them from getting it (obstacles)?
What happens in the end (do they get the goal or not) – by doing what?
What does the protagonist learn from this journey – what do we learn?

Can you fill this in for your current project? It may seem a tall order, but the shortlist above encompasses the key elements of a story that will decide whether your 'pitchee' would like to develop the conversation beyond this intro and find out more. For many buyers, as soon as you tell them just the first three elements they may know if they want to stop you right there (a painful but time-saving kind of rejection). This is often because their company brand or strategy may be circumscribed by things like genre and setting of films (for example, an Irish company maximising subsidy and tax benefits locally may not be open to a project that can't be shot there – a tropical romance, perhaps!). One buyer I know described the PFC as the way to get quickly to 'the story melody' – the bare bones of the piece. The 'harmony' comes later, when you expand the conversation or even read the script.

Why put this on an index card? Because you can tuck it away in your wallet or purse and double-check it every time you go out to pitch. I do it every time – and not one buyer that I've encountered, no matter what their job title, has queried the elements on the list. These are the core elements they want to know first, whether they are an agent, a director, a producer, a sales agent, a broadcaster or a distributor. If anything, most buyers would be glad to hear *less* – and to be allowed to press 'pause' if there is no point in going further down the list. Brutal? Maybe, but as you try to get films made, you'll soon become grateful for time saved, even if you get a 'no'. There are many ports of call, and time is your most valuable resource. Better this than a vague 'maybe' that stretches on for months, or even years.

Going back to the Hollywood cliché of the pitch meeting, one of the core myths to debunk is the idea that all pitches must be summed up by X meets X – as in 'this is *Pretty Woman* meets *Out of Africa*'. While that kind of 'movie algebra' may have its place in a some LA offices, particularly with moneymen who can only look at the gross of the two successful films you've just deftly united and imagine their lucrative offspring, it won't work well in the UK or Europe.

For one thing, it's not as easy as it looks to choose your Xs, and the wrong choices can be very off-putting, for creative or financial reasons. All it takes is for the pitchee to have hated one or both of the Xs you proffer, or for them to dryly point out (as has happened to me) that one of the Xs didn't do that well at the box office, great work of art though it may be. If you're determined to bandy comparisons around, go ahead on a single basis (as in 'this film is a British *Brokeback Mountain*'), but make sure that you are referring to films that are fairly widely known (a risky guess sometimes) – and which didn't lose money. Another problem with 'X meets X pitching' is that sometimes the people we are pitching to in the UK haven't seen all that many films. Sounds crazy? It's true – we don't live in a nation of cinephiles, and while there are the odd pockets of true enthusiasts, many buyers here are not steeped in the art or history of their field, and will therefore look blank or lie to save face when you introduce a title they don't know. Neither result will cause them to warm to your idea; resentment and feelings of inadequacy are not common preludes to expenditure.

When you are busily checking the gross of the film(s) you wish to reference if appropriate, take the time to do some other research. One of the top reasons for failed pitches are mistaken assumptions; you may think they will like something that they don't, or that they made a film actually done by the competition. This can kill a pitch stone-dead. So, if you are a writer pitching to an agent to get representation, find out who else they look after and whether your work fits with that profile. If you are a producer pitching to a sales agent, how does your film fill a gap in their slate, and does it sit well alongside the rest of their catalogue? In other words, ask not what they can do for you, so much as what you bring to them. The successful pitcher is the one who can prove that s/he is bringing value to the buyer.

All of this advice assumes that you've actually got a pitch meeting to go to – that you've secured someone's time for a proper discussion. Needless to say, that's not always so easy to get. There are other pitch opportunities, as we all know; I offer the following cautions and suggestions for those here:

(1) The elevator pitch: heard of this? This is the one where you get in a lift at the Carlton Hotel in Cannes and find you are standing next to the Big Cheese who could just finance your whole movie. You have eight floors to make your pitch. Whole books have been written in Hollywood about the art of the elevator pitch, much to my amusement and horror. Imagine that you're the Big Cheese, just slipping out of the dreadful cocktail party to nip upstairs to phone the kids before bed/go to the loo/fix your toupee, etc. Do you really want some nutter in the lift rattling out a story idea? Not me! Bad idea. Personally I'd be respectful, make eye contact, perhaps make some kind of brief but witty comment about the lift décor or something, and then catch the Cheese when s/he's back in party mode. As a general rule, I'd suggest you don't pitch anyone in an 'off duty' setting, be that the elevator ('I was only trying to dive up to my room!'), the loo, a funeral, a wedding, or an airplane.
(2) The event pitch: this is when you are networking at a film industry event (note: an 'on duty' setting!) such as a market or festival and find an opportunity to speak to that selfsame Big Cheese. Maybe s/he remembers your face from the lift – that's no bad thing. My advice here is to stay general. If you get to speak to 'the Man' (or 'the Woman'), you don't want to regurgitate your whole film story, harmony, melody and album cover. You may want to just establish that you have a project that could interest them (because? Have a reason – they just did a romcom and have publicly stated that they are looking for more/have made another film by the same director which did well at the box office, etc.) … and briefly state the title and genre. That's it. Ask if you could send it to them (or to whom you could send it in their company to be read). Follow up with a meeting if it's of interest. This is likely to provoke gratitude, especially in a festival setting. Most buyers will want to embrace you for not taking up much of their canapé-eating time, and not shoving a 200-page first-draft screenplay into their hands (which will inevitably be left in their hotel room unread). Once you've established the reply, thank them, and move away. Many buyers I've talked to feel stalked at these events, and while they are happy to 'show their face' and network with the best (after all they need to meet talent), they don't like the hard sell. This is especially true in the UK and Europe.
(3) The sales letter: a sales letter is just 'you in an envelope'; it should therefore be worked on very carefully, not dashed off as a hasty email. Hone each word and hack out the dead wood; be brief and to the point. A good tip is to mention the first three or four elements on the PFC along with any unique selling point you may have, which could be that your project has hot talent attached, or is based on a bestselling novel, for example.

However you manage to pitch, not everyone's going to love your 'baby'. When you go out to pitch, prepare yourself for a lot of rejection. Tenacity is the soul of producing, so get out there and try, then try again. Preparation and passion will take you a long way. When the going gets tough, in your darkest hour, remind yourself of the love and excitement you felt at the outset. Hold onto that feeling and ultimately, it is my experience that you will infuse others with it too, and get your film made. It's worth all the difficulties along the way; there is nothing like the feeling of pride when you see your fully grown offspring step out alone onto the screen, ready to face the world.

Eileen Quinn is a producer of 20 years' experience in UK film and TV. Currently Head of Drama at IWC Media, she is the co-author of *The Pitch*, written with Judy Counihan for Faber and Faber, published in 2006. For your copy, go to **www.faber.co.uk/film**, **www.amazon.co.uk**, or to a good bookstore.

Getting an agent

Sayle Screen's **Matthew Bates** explains the role of the screenwriters' agent – and offers some advice on how to get one.

This article is based on a talk I give to newer writers, and I will start with the same disclaimer that I give to them. The thoughts and advice I offer are not definitive; others may well see things differently. I hope you find the advice useful, but beware of taking it as gospel, carved-in-stone truth.

To keep things simple I'm just going to discuss an agent's role when working with screenwriters – writers of drama for film and TV. However, many agents who represent screenwriters also represent drama directors, and much of what I say below can be applied to directors too.

Writers' agents – a brief introduction

People who work freelance in creative fields very often employ agents. Authors, actors, even artists and musicians use agents, as do screenwriters and film and television directors. Viewed at its most basic, the role of all these types of agents is to help look after the business affairs of their creative clients – although I'll examine this description in more detail later.

In the UK a writers' agent will represent a list of their own clients. They may look after their list as part of a larger organisation with many agents under one roof; they may work in smaller companies; or they may work alone. Bigger agencies are not necessarily better than smaller ones: in the end it's often the effectiveness of the individual agent that counts, together with the strength of the relationship between client and agent.

Agents make a living by taking a percentage (generally 10-15%) of any money generated from contracts they negotiate on behalf of their clients. So if an agent doesn't generate any contracts for a client, they won't make any money from them (this may be something they stomach in the early days in the expectation of many and significant contracts to come in the future).

What do writers' agents do?

1) *They negotiate contracts.* This involves negotiating the best payment for a writer as well as ensuring that all other contractual terms are as good as they can be. It also involves 'running' a contract – making sure, for example, that any payments made are correct and are made on time.

2) *They give career guidance.* Every writer will be confronted with choices and decisions, and it's an agent's job to help with these choices – building a solid, sustainable career for their client.

3) *They give creative feedback.* Different agents give different levels of creative feedback, but generally a writer can rely on their agent to read and comment on their work. I work quite closely with clients on any new pieces of original writing before allowing them to be sent out, my philosophy being that it's important for me to have a reputation for sending out good stuff.

4) *They promote clients.* Agents do this actively by submitting material to producers, and by discussing clients and their projects with producers. And we do this reactively by being on the end of a phone or email inbox when producers contact us looking for writers or for new projects.

Why use an agent to do these things?

1) *For their technical expertise.* Agents understand the intricacies of contracts: which terms are fair and acceptable, and which are not. Writers' contracts (particularly those selling original stories and ideas) can be very complex and there are significant dangers in getting the detail wrong.
2) *For their role as a buffer between writer and producer.* In an ideal world, a writer should have a very easy, creative relationship with a producer. They do not want this relationship marred by, for example, having to enter into tough negotiations with their producer, particularly negotiations over money. Tricky business matters can be passed to an agent to handle in the background.
3) *For their knowledge of who's who and what's going on.* We have to know – it's our job! We spend our days in the thick of it anyway and we're interested. And this kind of knowledge is invaluable; screenwriters are not, say, literary novelists, who might be able to write in a kind of vacuum without having to consider the 'industry' they are writing for.
4) *For their extra pair of eyes and ears.* Screenwriters have a responsibility to keep tabs on the industry in which they've chosen to work, but if you've got an agent, you've got someone else to do it too. Suddenly there are two of you watching out for news, trends and opportunities.

And producers often rely on agents as a kind of filter system. Of course, there are some producers who will consider material sent directly by writers, but there are some who don't – and even those who do will probably look more quickly and more seriously at work sent to them by an agent they trust.

How to get an agent

At the start of your search for an agent, you have to face some facts. Good agents are busy: they're busy *because* they are good. And because they are busy they will not be frantically searching for new clients.

So be patient. Be ready for a certain amount of rejection and be realistic (not downhearted) about why you're rejected. If agents write to you and say, "I can't take you on because I'm very busy with the clients I already look after," then that's what they mean – they're not pretending.

That said, hundreds of writers have agents, so it obviously isn't impossible to find one. How do you go about it?

Make sure you really are ready to start approaching agents

Be strict with yourself about this. Have you got a body of good work that will impress an agent? Remember that it needs to impress the agent, because the agent will need it to impress people who can actually pay you. I rarely take on writers unless I've read at least two pieces of their work, one of which should be the length of a feature script. If you haven't written very much, and if you know that what you've written isn't as good as you can make it, then wait – write more and keep working on what you've already written.

You may be ready to approach agents because you've actually made some things happen yourself. This is, in fact, the case with most writers who do find representation. Maybe you've managed to get a commission to write an episode of a TV series, or you've got a film producer interested in your feature script. Like it or not, agents are going to take more notice of you if you approach them saying: "I've got a deal that needs negotiating."

Do it right

If you are sure that now's the time to start the search, then here are some suggestions as to how.

• Select, say, a dozen agencies, getting their details from one of the useful publications on the market that list UK agencies and give brief descriptions of them.

• Phone the agencies on your list. Ask: "Do you consider submissions from new writers looking for an agent?" If the answer is yes, then follow up with: "Is there someone specific I should write to?"

• Send a feature-length script, a brief CV and a brief covering letter to the agencies who have said they accept submissions. Anything shorter than a feature-length script will probably not be enough. There's no point sending more than one script at this point – if the agent likes it then they'll ask to see more.

• Sit back and wait. Possibly months. It's a bit cheeky, but you could ring after about three or four months just in case the script never arrived or just in case it pushes your script further up the reading pile. This is a risky tactic, though – agents may think, "If they're putting pressure on me now, what on earth would they be like as a client?"

Various tips: Presentation is important; it shows that you care about being taken seriously as a professional. Don't bang on in your covering letter, either about yourself or about your script. Your CV should only deal with information relevant to your writing experience; agents aren't interested in your GSCE grades or whether you have a clean driver's licence.

What agents look for in new clients

1) *Talent.* That impossible-to-define (and utterly objective) quality which makes an agent think, "This person's got it," and, "Other people are going to see that this person's got it, too."

2) *Commitment.* A sense that a new client is going to last the course. Making a living as a screenwriter is extremely tough, particularly in the early days when money will be tight. There's no point in an agent taking on a new writer unless they are confident that s/he will work hard and keep bashing away.

3) Personality. The agent will want to feel that they are going to get on well on a personal level with a new client, and – just as importantly – that the client is going to work well with others in the industry. Screenwriting is about collaboration. A brilliant writer who has no interest in collaboration should probably be writing books.

Getting on without an agent

There is a chicken and egg problem which can't be denied. Many producers (of both TV and film) won't consider work from writers who don't have an agent, and many agents won't consider writers who haven't had something produced. It's a challenge to break the cycle, but it can be done. The main thing is to keep writing and keep working hard to make your writing as good as it can be.

Then send scripts to people. If you want to write film, target producers and production companies whose work you know and like. The same is true for TV – track down the producers making the shows you enjoy and post a script to them. And if anyone opens the door just a little bit, then jam your foot in it; you need all the help and advice you can get.

Keep an eye out for initiatives and schemes for new writers, and consider some of the writing courses on offer. Apart from anything else they're good places to meet people.

If possible, club together with other writers: read each others' scripts and share information.

If you're good, persistent and lucky then something will give.

Matthew Bates qualified as a lawyer in 1991, then became a writers' and directors' agent. He has been at Sayle Screen since 1995, where he represents film and television writers as well as drama directors and writer/directors. Clients include Emily Woof, Martin Stellman, Paul Morrison and Andrea Arnold, who won an Oscar for her short film *Wasp* and whose first feature *Red Road* was highly acclaimed at its 2006 Cannes Film Festival premiere.

Screenwriters' agents

In this section you will find a list of agents who represent writers across a range of media, but who all have some association with the film and television industries. For the ease of screenwriters looking for an agent, we have noted where an agency specialises in representing screenwriters.

A & B Personal Management Ltd

Suite 330, Linen Hall, 162-168 Regent Street, London W1B 5TD
tel 020-7434 4262 *fax* 020-7038 3699
email billellis@aandb.co.uk

Represents screenwriters. Founded in 1982. Agents cover film, TV and theatre as well as literature. Fees range between 12.5% and 15%. Does not welcome unsolicited material, but enquiries are accepted in writing.

The Agency (London) Ltd*

24 Pottery Lane, London W11 4LZ
tel 020-7727 1346 *fax* 020-7727 9037
email info@theagency.co.uk

Represents screenwriters. Founded in 1995. Agents cover film, TV, radio, theatre and literature. Also represents non-fiction for film and TV rights. *Commission*: 10%. Does not accept unsolicited material, but enquiries are accepted in writing. Founded 1995.

Aitken Alexander Associates Ltd*

18–21 Cavaye Place, London SW10 9PT
tel 020-7373 8672 *fax* 020-7373 6002
email reception@aitkenalexander.co.uk
website www.aitkenalexander.co.uk
Film and TV Agent Lesley Thorne

Represents screenwriters. Agency represents existing book clients in the fields of film and television, and is now building a list of high-end television and feature-film screenwriters. While emphasis is on writing, it also represents writer/directors. Please send a short covering letter and biography, with list of credits if applicable, or other relevant information, plus sample script and sae. Submissions should be sent to Lesley Thorne. *UK commission*: 10%, or 15% if a US sub-agent is used. Showreels also welcome.

Clients include: Clare Allan, Pat Barker, Nicholas Blincoe, Gordon Burn, Jung Chang, John Cornwell, Josephine Cox, Sarah Dunant, Susan Elderkin, Diana Evans, Roopa Farooki, Sebastian Faulks, Helen Fielding, Germaine Greer, Mark Haddon, Susan Howatch, Liz Jensen, John Keegan, VS Naipaul, Jonathan Raban, Anna Ralph, Piers Paul Read, Louise Rennison, Michèle Roberts, Nicholas Shakespeare, Gillian Slovo, Rory Stewart, Matt Thorne, Colin Thubron, Salley Vickers, Penny Vincenzi, Willy Vlautin, AN Wilson, Robert Wilson. Founded 1977.

Darley Anderson Literary, TV and Film Agency*

Estelle House, 11 Eustace Road, London SW6 1JB
tel 020-7385 6652 *fax* 020-7386 5571
email enquiries@darleyanderson.com
website www.darleyanderson.com, www.darleyandersonchildrens.com
Contacts Darley Anderson (crime, mystery, thrillers, women's fiction), Julia Churchill (children's fiction), Emma White (US, foreign, TV rights, film), Rosi Bridge (finance), Zoe King, Ella Andrews

Represents selected scripts for film and TV, but primarily deals with commercial fiction and non-fiction. *Commission*: 20% for film/TV/radio. Has an association with APA Talent & Literary Agency in Hollywood. Send preliminary letter and synopsis by post, with sae for reply.

Blake Friedmann Literary, TV & Film Agency Ltd*

122 Arlington Road, London NW1 7HP
tel 020-7284 0408 *fax* 020-7284 0442
email firstname@blakefriedmann.co.uk
Directors Carole Blake, Julian Friedmann, Isobel Dixon

Represents screenwriters and specialises in film and TV rights. Fiction, film and TV scripts, but no plays (home 15%, overseas 20%). Founded 1977. Preliminary letter preferred. Authors include: Gilbert Adair, Jane Asher and Tim Sebastian.

Alan Brodie Representation Ltd

6th Floor, Fairgate House, 78 New Oxford Street, London WC1A 1HB
tel 020-7079 7990 *fax* 020-7079 7999
email info@alanbrodie.com
website www.alanbrodie.com
Contacts Lisa Foster, Sarah McNair, Hariett Pennigton Leigh

Represents screenwriters and specialises in film and TV rights. Also represents stage and radio plays (home 10%, overseas 15%). No unsolicited scripts; recommendation from known professional required.

Brie Burkeman*

14 Neville Court, Abbey Road, London NW8 9DD
tel 0870-199 5002 *fax* 0870-199 1029

email brie.burkeman@mail.com
Proprietor Brie Burkeman *Contact* Brie Burkeman, Isabel White

Highly selective boutique agency, founded in 2000, representing commercial and literary fiction and non-fiction, playwrights, and screenwriters. No academic text, poetry, short stories, musicals or short films. Sample scripts may be sent by post with covering letter; no reading fee but return postage essential. Any emails with attachments are deleted without opening. Also associated with Serafina Clarke Ltd and independent film/TV consultant to literary agents. *Commission*: Books/Plays: home 15%, overseas 20%; Films: 15% worldwide.

Capel & Land Ltd*

29 Wardour Street, London W1D 6PS
tel 020-7734 2414 *fax* 020-7734 8101
email rosie@capelland.co.uk
Agents Georgina Capel (literary), Yvonne Anderson (film), Anita Land (TV)

Literary and commercial fiction, history, biography; film and TV (home/overseas 15%). No reading fee; will suggest revision.

Represents screenwriters and specialises in film and TV rights. Also literary and commercial fiction, history, biography (home/overseas 15%). No reading fee; will suggest revision. Founded 1999. Clients include: Julie Burchill, Louis Theroux, and Jeremy Paxman.

Casarotto Ramsay & Associates Ltd

(formerly Margaret Ramsay Ltd and Casarotto Company Ltd)
Waverley House, 7–12 Noel Street, London W1F 8GQ
tel 020-7287 4450 *fax* 020-7287 9128
email agents@casarotto.co.uk
Directors Jenne Casarotto, Giorgio Casarotto, Tom Erhardt, Sara Pritchard, Mel Kenyon, Charlotte Kelly, Jodi Shields, Rachel Holroyd

Represents screenwriters, directors, DoP, designers and editors, and specialises in film and TV. *Commission*: 10%. Preliminary letter essential. Clients include: Lynne Ramsay, Christopher Hampton, David Hare, Shane Meadows, Stephen Frears, Neil Jordan, and Seamus McGarvey.

Jonathan Clowes Ltd*

10 Iron Bridge House, Bridge Approach, London NW1 8BD
tel 020-7722 7674 *fax* 020-7722 7677
Directors Jonathan Clowes, Ann Evans, Lisa Thompson

Represents screenwriters. Fiction, non-fiction, film, TV, theatre and radio. *Commission*: 15% home, 20% overseas. Preliminary letter required. No unsolicited scripts. Clients include: Doris Lessing and Kingsley Amis.

Rosica Colin Ltd

1 Clareville Grove Mews, London SW7 5AH
tel 020-7370 1080 *fax* 020-7244 6441
Directors Sylvie Marston, Joanna Marston

Represents screenwriters in film and TV; also all other forms excluding science fiction and poetry. *Commission*: home 10%, overseas 10-20%. Send synopsis only in the first instance, with letter outlining writing credits and whether script has been previously submitted, plus return postage. Clients include: Wim Wenders (UK only), and work of Rainer Werner Fassbinder (in UK).

Curtis Brown Group Ltd*

Haymarket House, 28–29 Haymarket, London SW1Y 4SP
tel 020-7393 4400 *fax* 020-7393 4401
email cb@curtisbrown.co.uk
website www.curtisbrown.co.uk
Actors Sarah Spear (Head of Acting Dept), Grace Clissold, Maxine Hoffman, Sarah MacCormick, Kate Staddon, Olivia Woodward

Represents screenwriters and specialises in film and TV. *Commission*: 15-20%. Website includes submission guidelines. Also represents directors, designers and actors. Founded 1914.

Judy Daish Associates Ltd

2 St Charles Place, London W10 6EG
tel 020-8964 8811 *fax* 020-8964 8966
Agents Judy Daish, Howard Gooding, Tracey Elliston

Represents screenwriters and specialises in film and TV. Also represents directors, designers and producers. Rates by negotiation; no reading fee. No unsolicited MSS. Founded 1978.

Bryan Drew Ltd

Quadrant House, 80-82 Regent Street, London W1B 5AU
tel 020-7437 2293 *fax* 020-7437 0561
email bryan@bryandrewltd.com
Literary Manager Bryan Drew

Represents screenwriters and specialises in film and TV; also fiction and thrillers. No reading fee. Enclose sae.

Janet Fillingham Associates

52 Lowther Road, London SW13 9NU
tel 020-8748 5594 *fax* 020-8748 7374
email info@jfillassoc.co.uk
website www.janetfillingham.com
Director Janet Fillingham

Represents screenwriters and specialises in film and TV only. Represents a range of writers and directors working in film and television, including family entertainment markets. *Commission*: 10% home, 15-20% overseas. No unsolicited submissions; professional recommendation required. Founded 1992.

Film Rights Ltd

Mezzanine, Quadrant House, 80-82 Regent Street, London W1B 5AU
tel 020-7734 9911 *fax* 020-7734 0044
email information@filmrights.ltd.uk
website www.filmrights.ltd.uk
Directors Brendan Davis, Joan Potts

Represents screenwriters and specialises in film, TV and sound broadcasting. *Commission*: 10% home, 15% overseas. No unsolicited submissions; professional recommendation required. Founded in 1932. Owns rights in a number of classic cinema scripts. Represented in the USA and abroad.

Laurence Fitch Ltd

(incorporating The London Play Company 1922)
Mezzanine, Quadrant House, 80-82 Regent Street, London W1B 5AU
tel 020-7734 9911 *fax* 020-7437 0561
email information@laurencefitch.com
website www.laurencefitch.com
Directors F.H.L. Fitch, Joan Potts, Brendan Davis

Represents screenwriters and specialises in film and TV. *Commission*: home 10%, overseas 15%. Also affiliated with Film Rights Ltd; works with several agencies in USA and in Europe.

Jill Foster Ltd (JFL)

9 Barb Mews, Brook Green, London W6 7PA
tel 020-7602 1263 *fax* 020-7602 9336
Agents Jill Foster, Alison Finch, Simon Williamson, Dominic Lord, Gary Wild

Represents screenwriters and specialises in film and TV. Particularly interested in film and TV comedy and drama. No novels or short stories. No reading fee. Preliminary letter essential – no submissions by email, and do not send material in the first instance. Founded 1978.

Futerman, Rose & Associates*

17 Deanhill Road, London SW14 7DQ
tel 020-8255 7755 *fax* 020-8286 4860
website www.futermanrose.co.uk
Contact Guy Rose

Represents screenwriters. Writers' agency representing approximately 20 writers in film, television and theatre, as well as 30 authors. Send a preliminary letter with brief résumé, detailed synopsis, first 20pp and sae. No materials will be accepted via email. *Commission*: 20%

Jüri Gabriel

35 Camberwell Grove, London SE5 8JA
tel 020-7703 6186

Authors include Maurice Caldera, Diana Constance, Gerry and Joanne Dryansky, Miriam Dunne, Matt Fox, Paul Genney, Pat Gray, Mikka Haugaard, Robert Irwin, John Lucas, 'David Madsen', Richard Mankiewicz, Karina Mellinger, David Miller, Andy Oakes, John Outram, Philip Roberts, Stefan Szymanski, Adisakdi Tantimedh, Dr Terence White, Chris Wilkins, Dr Robert Youngson.

The Rod Hall Agency Ltd

6th Floor, Fairgate House, 78 New Oxford Street, London WC1A 1HB
tel 020-7079 7987 *fax* (0845) 6384094
email office@rodhallagency.com
website www.rodhallagency.com
Director Charlotte Knight, Martin Knight, *Contact* Tanya Tillett

Specialises in writers for stage, screen and radio. Also deals in TV and film rights in novels and non-fiction (home 10%, overseas 15%), and represents writer/directors. Email synopsis and intro in first instance, with a showreel if you are a writer/director. No reading fee.

Clients include: Simon Beaufoy, Jeremy Brock, Martin McDonagh, Simon Nye, Ol Parker, Lucy Prebble, Richard Smith, Laura Wade. Founded 1997.

Valerie Hoskins Associates Ltd

20 Charlotte Street, London W1T 2NA
tel 020-7637 4490 *fax* 020-7637 4493
email vha@vhassociates.co.uk
Proprietor Valerie Hoskins, *Agent* Rebecca Watson

Represents writers in film and TV, and specialises in animation (12.5%). Does not accept unsolicited submissions, but writers may send a letter of introduction about their work by email, or by post with an sae.

Michelle Kass Associates*

85 Charing Cross Road, London WC2H 0AA
tel 020-7439 1624 *fax* 020-7734 3394
Proprietor Michelle Kass

Represents writers for film. Full-length MSS. Literary fiction and drama scripts for film (home 10%, overseas 15-20%). Will suggest revision where appropriate. Works with agents overseas. No reading fee. Absolutely no unsolicited MSS without a preliminary phone call. Founded 1991.

Frances Kelly Agency*

111 Clifton Road, Kingston-upon-Thames, Surrey KT2 6PL
tel 020-8549 7830 *fax* 020-8547 0051

Primarily non-fiction: general and academic, reference and professional books, all subjects (home 10%, overseas 20%). Handles rights for radio and TV (10%). No reading fee, but no unsolicited MSS; preliminary letter with synopsis, CV and return postage essential. Founded 1978.

Andrew Mann Ltd*

(in association with Jane Conway-Gordon)
1 Old Compton Street, London W1D 5JA

tel 020-7734 4751 *fax* 020-7287 9264
email info@manscript.co.uk
Contacts Anne Dewe, Tina Betts, Louise Burns

Represents scripts for TV, radio, theatre and film. *Commission*: home 15%. Preliminary enquiry essential; email with synopsis. Founded 1968.

Marjacq Scripts

34 Devonshire Place, London W1G 6JW
tel 020-7935 9499 *fax* 020-7935 9115
email enquiries@marjacq.com
website www.marjacq.com
Contact Philip Patterson (books), Luke Speed (film/TV)

Represents scripts for TV, radio, theatre and film. *Commission*: home 10%, USA and Europe 20%. Send full script with 1- or 2-page short synopsis/outline. Strong interest in writer/directors: send showreel with script. Also looking for documentary concepts and will accept proposals from writer/directors. Sae essential for return of submissions. Most other writers' media represented as well.

MBA Literary Agents Ltd*

(incorporating Merric Davidson Literary Agency)
62 Grafton Way, London W1T 5DW
tel 020-7387 2076 *fax* 020-7387 2042
email firstname@mbalit.co.uk
website www.mbalit.co.uk
Contacts Diana Tyler, John Richard Parker, Meg Davis, Laura Longrigg, David Riding, Susan Smith, Sophie Gorell Barnes

Represents scripts for TV, radio, theatre and film. *Commission*: home 15%, overseas 20%. No unsolicited submissions. Founded in 1971.

William Morris Agency (UK) Ltd*

Centre Point, 103 New Oxford Street, London SW1A 1DD
tel 020-7534 6800 *fax* 020-7534 6900
website www.wma.com
Managing Director Caroline Michel *Books* Eugenie Furniss, Lucinda Prain, Rowan Lawton *TV* Holly Pye, Isabella Zoltowski

Specialises in film and TV. Influential worldwide talent agency representing writers, directors and actors from offices in London, New York, Beverly Hills, Nashville, Miami and Shanghai. Handles film and TV scripts; TV formats; fiction and general non-fiction (film/TV 10%, UK books 15%, USA books and translation 20%). No science fiction or fantasy; send MSS sample of approx. 30-50pp with letter and 1-page synopsis. No reading fee. London office founded 1965.

PFD (The Peters Fraser & Dunlop Group Ltd)*

Drury House, 34–43 Russell Street, London WC2B 5HA
tel 020-7344 1000 *fax* 020-7836 9539
website www.pfd.co.uk
Film/TV Agents Hannah Begbie, Tim Corrie, St John Donald, Jago Irwin, Anthony Jones, Lynda Mamy, Andrew Naylor, Charles Walker, Alice Dunne, Natasha Galloway

Specialises in film and TV. Represents writers, directors, actors and technicians. Has 75 years of international experience in all media. Screenplays/TV scripts should be addressed to the 'Film & Script Dept.' – material submitted on an exclusive basis preferred; in any event, it should be disclosed if material is being submitted to other agencies or publishers. Return postage essential. No reading fee. No guaranteed response to submissions by email. See website for detailed submission guidelines.

Clients include: Mark Herman, Mike Leigh, and Pawel Pawlikowski.

The Lisa Richards Agency

108 Upper Leeson Street, Dublin 4, Republic of Ireland
tel (01) 637 5000 *fax* (01) 667 1256
email faith@lisarichards.ie
website www.lisarichards.ie
Contact Faith O'Grady

Fiction and non-fiction, but represents these for film/TV rights as well. Also represents actors and playrights.

Sayle Screen Ltd

11 Jubilee Place, London SW3 3TD
tel 020-7823 3883 *fax* 020-7823 3363
email info@saylescreen.com
website www.saylescreen.com
Agents Jane Villiers, Matthew Bates, Toby Moorcroft

Specialises in film, TV, theatre and radio. Approximately 100 writers; the agency also represents directors for both film and television. Clients include: Andrea Arnold, Marc Evans, John Forte, Mark Haddon, Sue Townsend.

The Sharland Organisation Ltd

The Manor House, Manor Street, Raunds, Northants NN9 6JW
tel (01933) 626600 *fax* (01933) 624860
email tsoshar@aol.com
website www.sharlandorganisation.co.uk
Directors Mike Sharland, Alice Sharland

Specialises in film, TV, stage and radio rights throughout the world (home 15%, overseas 20%). Preliminary letter and return postage essential. No reading fee. Works in conjunction with overseas agents. Founded 1988.

Sheil Land Associates Ltd*

(incorporating Richard Scott Simon Ltd 1971 and Christy & Moore Ltd 1912)
52 Doughty Street, London WC1N 2LS

tel 020-7405 9351 *fax* 020-7831 2127
email info@sheilland.co.uk
Agents UK & US Sonia Land, Vivien Green, Ben Mason, *Film/theatre/TV* Sophie Janson, Emily Hayward, *Foreign* Gaia Banks

Specialises in theatre, film, radio and TV scripts. Welcomes approaches from new clients, either to start or to develop their careers. Preliminary letter with sae essential. No reading fee. Overseas associates: Georges Borchardt, Inc (Richard Scott Simon). US film and TV representation: CAA, APA and others. Clients include: Rose Tremain, Paul Wilson, and Bonnie Greer.

Robert Smith Literary Agency Ltd*

12 Bridge Wharf, 156 Caledonian Road, London N1 9UU
tel 020-7278 2444 *fax* 020-7833 5680
email robertsmith.literaryagency@virgin.net
Directors Robert Smith, Anne Smith

The agency does not represent screenwriters, but rather sells rights for books to film and television industries.

Authors include Kate Adie (serialisations), Martin Allen, Amanda Barrie (serialisations), Kevin Booth, Judy Cook, Stewart Evans, Neil and Christine Hamilton, James Haspiel, Nikola T. James, Lois Jenkins, Roberta Kray, Jean MacColl, Ann Ming, Theo Paphitis, Mike Reid, Frances Reilly, Prof. William Rubinstein, Keith Skinner. Founded 1997.

Rochelle Stevens & Co

2 Terretts Place, Upper Street, London N1 1QZ
tel 020-7359 3900 *fax* 020-7354 5729
email info@rochellestevens.com
Proprietor Rochelle Stevens, *Associates* Frances Arnold, Lucy Fawcett

Specialises in film and TV. Agent represents approximately 70 writers working in film, TV and theatre, as well as directors. Unsolicited enquiries welcome. Please send CV or showreel, covering letter and synopsis along with an sae.

Talent Media Group t/a ICM

Oxford House, 76 Oxford Street, London W1D 1BS
tel 020-7636 6565 *fax* 020-7323 0101
email writers@icmlondon.co.uk
Directors Duncan Heath, Susan Rodgers, Lyndsey Posner, Sally Long-Innes, Paul Lyon-Maris, *Literary Agents* Susan Rodgers, Jessica Sykes, Catherine King, Greg Hunt, Hugo Young, Michael McCoy, Duncan Heath, Paul Lyon-Maris

Specialises in scripts for film, theatre, TV and radio (home 10%, overseas 10%).

The Tennyson Agency

10 Cleveland Avenue, London SW20 9EW
tel 020-8543 5939
email submissions@tenagy.co.uk
website www.tenagy.co.uk
Theatre, TV & Film Scripts Christopher Oxford, *Arts/Humanities* Adam Sheldon

Specialises in film and TV. Scripts and related material for theatre, film and TV (15-20%). No reading fee. Founded 2002.

JM Thurley Management

Archery House, 33 Archery Square, Walmer, Deal, Kent CT14 7JA
tel (01304) 371721 *fax* (01304) 371416
email JMThurley@aol.com
website www.thecuttingedge.biz
Contact Jon Thurley

Specialises in commercial work for film and TV. No reading fee, but preliminary letter and sae essential. Editorial/creative advice provided to clients (home 15%, overseas 20%). Links with leading US and European agents. Founded 1976.

United Authors Ltd

11–15 Betterton Street, London WC2H 9BP
tel 020-7470 8886 *fax* 020-7470 8887
email editorial@unitedauthors.co.uk

Works across a range of media, but doesn't generally represent screenwriters who *only* work in film. *Commission*: 12-15%. Send writing samples by email, or by post with sae.

AP Watt Ltd*

20 John Street, London WC1N 2DR
tel 020-7405 6774
fax 020-7831 2154 (books), 020-7430 1952 (drama)
email apw@apwatt.co.uk
website www.apwatt.co.uk
Directors Caradoc King, Linda Shaughnessy, Derek Johns, Georgia Garrett, Natasha Fairweather, Sheila Crowley, Rob Kraitt (associate)

Represents screenwriters in film and TV. Also represents writers in other media (home 10%, USA and foreign 20% – including commission to foreign agent). No poetry. No reading fee. No unsolicited materials and will not accept responsibility for any which are sent in.

Other agents

Caroline Cornish Management Ltd
12 Shinfield Street, London W12 0HN
Agent's tel 020-8743 7337 *tel* 020-8580 0693
fax 020-8743 7887
email carolinecornish@btconnect.com
website www.carolinecornish.co.uk

Represents technical heads of departments for film and TV (home 10%, overseas 10%). Welcomes CVs.

Casarotto Marsh Ltd – see page 21 for contact details. Represents DoPs, production designers, costume designers and editors.

Casarotto Ramsay & Assoc
Waverley House, 7-12 Noel Street,
London W1F 8GQ
tel 020-7287 4450 *fax* 020-7287 5644
email info@casarotto.co.uk
website www.casarotto.uk.com
Agents Jenne Casarotto, Sara Pritchard (film), Emma Trounson (television), Lucie Llewellyn (commercials, promos and short film), Kate Bloxham (documentaries & assistant to Sara Pritchard)

Casarotto is one of the UK's leading creative agencies representing a large number of award-winning writers, directors, directors of photography, production designers, costume designers and editors working in film, television and theatre. Casarotto Ramsay & Associates Ltd represents writers, directors, estates, translators and producers.

Creative Media Management
3b Walpole Court, Ealing Studios, London W5 5ED
tel 020-8584 5363 *fax* 020-8566 5554
email enquiries@creativemediamanagement.com
website www.creativemediamanagement.com

Leading technical and literary agents for film, theatre and TV.

The Dench Arnold Agency
10 Newburgh Street, London W1F 7RN
tel 020-7437 4551 *fax* 020-7439 1355
email contact@dencharnold.com
website www.dencharnold.com
Agent Michelle Arnold

Created by Elizabeth Dench and Michelle Arnold, who are renowned, both domestically and internationally, for their carefully selected client list of award-winning writers, directors and heads of department.

Dinedor Management
81 Oxford Street, London W1D 2EU
tel 020-7851 3575 *fax* 020-7851 3576
email info@dinedor.com
website www.dinedormanagement.co.uk

Representing DoPs, specialist operators, production and costume designers, hair and make-up designers, and editors.

Exec Management
tel (01753) 646677 *tel* 020-7402 2788
email sue@execmanagement.co.uk
website www.execmanagement.co.uk

Technical management agency.

Faber Music Media
3 Queen Square, London WC1N 3AU
tel 020-7833 7922 *fax* 020-7833 7939
email richard.paine@fabermusic.com
website www.fabermusicmedia.com

Represents composers.

International Creative Management (ICM)
ICM London, Oxford House, 76 Oxford Street, London W1D 1BS
tel 020-7432 0800
website www.icmtalent.com
CEO Jeffrey Berg

One of the world's largest talent and literary agencies, with offices in Beverly Hills, New York and London. Formed in 1975 by the merger of Creative Management Associates and The International Famous Agency, the company is a cornerstone in the entertainment community under the leadership of its Chairman and CEO Jeffrey Berg. ICM is wholly owned by management and agents, and has been privately held since 1988.

The agency represents creative and technical talent in the fields of motion pictures, television, publishing, music, comedy, commercials, new media and live theatre. ICM agents negotiate agreements and work closely with creators and distributors worldwide, which include television networks, movie studios, independent producers, concert promoters, publishers and Internet site creators.

Manners McDade Artist Management
4th Floor, 18 Broadwick Street, London W1F 8HS
tel 020-7277 8194 *fax* 020-7277 7630
email info@mannersmcdade.co.uk
website www.mannersmcdade.co.uk

Composers' agency.

McKinney Macartney Management
The Barley Mow Centre, 10 Barley Mow Passage, London W4 4PH

tel 020-8995 4747 *fax* 020-8995 2414
email mail@mckinneymacartney.com
website www.mckinneymacartney.com

McKinney Macartney Management has been one of the leading technicians' agencies for the past 10 years. Representing some of the best and most accomplished technicians in the world of film, television, commercials, and music promos, its client list is extensive and its clients highly skilled. Established by Flic McKinney and Kim Macartney, the agency represents freelance DoPs, production designers, directors, assistant directors, producers, line producers, costume designers, make-Up and hair designers, editors and sound mixers.

PFD

Drury House, 34-43 Russell Street,
London WC2B 5HA
tel 020-7344 1000 *fax* 020-7836 9543
website www.pfd.co.uk

One of Europe's leading literary and talent agencies, both in terms of turnover and breadth of representation. An acknowledged leader in many of its specialist areas, acting as agent to writers, directors, producers, actors, technicians, composers, sportsmen and women, public speakers and illustrators across a wide variety of media – including books, plays, television, film productions and multimedia projects. PFD represents its clients both domestically and internationally, in English and foreign-language markets, over a broad range of copyright media.

Sara Putt Associates

Room 923, The Old House, Shepperton Studios, Studios Road, Shepperton, Middlesex TW17 0QD
tel (01932) 571044 *fax* (01932) 571109
email info@saraputt.co.uk
website www.saraputt.co.uk

Over the last decade Sara Putt Associates has established itself at the forefront of UK agencies. Based at Shepperton Studios, the company represents directors, producers and HoDs in all areas of feature films and television, offering a service tailored to the needs of each individual production and client. With sister companies Carlin Crew and ADS, the agency can provide a full range of personnel.

The Screen Talent Agency

58 Speed House, Barbican, London EC2Y 8AT
tel 020-7628 5180 *fax* 020-7861 3588
email info@screen-talent.com
website www.screen-talent.com
Director James Little

Primarily represents behind-the-camera talent and creative Heads of Departments.

Yellow Inc.

email email.mail@yellowinc.co.uk
website www.yellowinc.co.uk

Group agency for production designers, costume designers, producers, hair and make-up artists, and DoPs.

Degree and postgraduate courses for screenwriting

These courses are designed to equip screenwriters with the craft skills and industrial knowledge to help prepare for a career in film and television. For a more extensive list of film courses, see Filmmaking degrees in the Resources section of this book.

American Film Institute Conservatory – see page 343 for contact details.

This 2-year screenwriting MA focuses on narrative storytelling in an environment designed to simulate the world of the professional screenwriter. Screenwriting Fellows find their voices, while learning the essence of working as part of a creative team. Professionals serve as faculty, acting as mentors to guide and support each writer's development in an intimate workshop setting.

The first year begins with an immersion in the production process in order for writers to learn how screenplays are visualised – initially writing short screenplays, one of which will be the basis for a First Year production with other filmmaking fellows. Screenwriting Fellows collaborate with Producing and Directing Fellows to see their work move from page to screen. By the end of the first year, Fellows write a feature-length screenplay.

Second Year Fellows may develop material for television, including biopics, television movies and spec scripts for sitcoms or 1-hour dramas, in addition to writing theatrical films. They also have the opportunity to work closely with their peers from other disciplines.

Course fees: available on request. *Entry requirements*: BA or equivalent. Application details and deadlines can be downloaded from the website.

Bournemouth University

MA/Pg Diploma Screenwriting, The Media School, Bournemouth University, Fern Barrow, Poole, Dorset BH12 5BB
tel (01202) 524111
email media@bournemouth.ac.uk
website www.bournemouth.ac.uk/media

This part-time MA Screenwriting course is part of The Media School that is accredited by Skillset. Starting in June, it is taught entirely by residential/attendance periods combined with distance-learning. Students are on campus for approximately 3 weeks during the entire 2-year course, in a total of 6 residentials. Periods on campus comprise an intensive course in writing for the screen, with lectures, presentations, seminars, analysed screenings, exercises and discussions together with group meetings and 1:1 tutorials. These form the core of the course, and all script assignments are fully prepared during these meetings.

Throughout the rest of the course students work through a range of scripts, with close supervision and guidance from their tutors, who are all professional working writers. Students are allocated to a different tutor for each assignment, so that during the 2-year programme each individual has the experience of working with a variety of styles and methods. In addition the course has a dedicated Internet chat room, which acts as a continuous monitoring and discussion forum for students and tutors.

The course is designed for members of the media industry and those seeking such careers. The normal requirement is an Honours degree or comparable qualification, but appropriate experience will also be taken into account.

Course fees: available on request. *Entry requirements*: BA or professional equivalent.

Columbia University

Film Division, 513 Dodge Hall,
116th Street & Broadway, New York 10027, USA
tel ++1 212 854 2815
email film@columbia.edu
website www.columbia.edu

One of the USA's best-regarded film programmes, Columbia University's MFA in Film emphasises film as a storytelling medium. Instruction combines directing, writing and producing with technical training and history/theory, to provide students with understanding of the principles and practice of dramatic narrative. In the first year, all students take a required programme of workshops and lectures before selecting a specialised concentration in screenwriting, directing, or producing.

Faculty combines veteran and new members of the New York and Hollywood film communities, including professionals such as Philip Seymour Hoffman and James Schamus; alumni include some of the biggest names in American independent cinema.

Course fees: available on request. *Entry requirements*: BA or professional equivalent.

Leeds Metropolitan University

School of Film, Television & Performing Arts,
Faculty of Arts & Society, Room H505,
Civic Quarter, Calverly Street, Leeds LS1 3HE
tel 0113-283 2600 (ext 3860) *fax* 0113-244 3927
email c.j.pugh@leedsmet.ac.uk
website www.leedsmet.ac.uk

This MA and Pg Dip in Screenwriting is 1-year full-time, followed by an additional year part-time. The course aims to prepare students for careers as professional screenwriters, or to develop writing skills so that they might work as development personnel, creative producers, directors, writer/directors, and literary agents. MA course graduates may expect to have not only a coherent understanding of the business and the principles and practice of screenwriting and development, but also a strong portfolio of work to assist them in entering the industry in their preferred arena.

Course fees: £4000 for Year 1 and £2000 for Year 2, for UK residents. *Entry requirements*: applicants are normally expected to have a first degree, but original creative writing of a suitable standard may be sufficient instead. All applicants need to submit evidence of their previous work.

London College of Communication

MA in Screenwriting,
London College of Communication,
Elephant & Castle, London SE1 6SB
tel 020-7514 6800 *fax* 020-7514 6848
email s.paskell@lcc.arts.ac.uk
website www.lcc.arts.ac.uk
Postgraduate Administrator Simeon Paskell

The MA in Screenwriting is a project-based course, one of the UK's leading film and television screenwriting courses. It develops writing skills through a programme of lectures, seminars and tutorials, preparing students to pursue careers as screenwriters in film and television. Its workshop and portfolio creation programme provides a sound basis for work as a script editor or reader. Projects include taking a short film, television episode, or adaptation for a feature film or television series/serial from concept to first draft.

The course has extensive industry links; past students have won the Palm D'Or, Orange Screenwriting Prize and Oscar nominations. Others currently write for *Eastenders, Coronation Street, Family Affairs, Taggart* and *Casualty*, and many maintain their links with the course as visiting tutors. The MA is 1 day per week during term-time, plus a minimum of 10 hours' individual study for 2 years (Jan-Dec).

Course fees: £1495 per year (home); 5 full-fee scholarships are available through Skillset. *Entry requirements*: BA or professional equivalent.

London Film School – see page 353 for contact details.

The LFS MA Screenwriting course is an intensive 1-year programme which aims to: develop the writer's voice through small-group and 1:1 mentoring from industry professionals; encourage writing as a continuous practice; stimulate reflective and critical approaches to screenwriting; and provide a specific historical background to film narrative, genre, and dramaturgy.

The course aims to develop screenwriting skills in the context of a filmmaking community, where writing is a collaborative process involving actors, directors, musicians, editors and producers. Regular screenings of classic and contemporary films, and visits by contemporary filmmakers, complement the core practical work of developing a feature screenplay.

Course fees: there is an application fee of £25 which is non-refundable; course tuition is £8321 for the 1-year course. *Entry requirements*: BA or professional equivalent.

London South Bank University

BA Writing for Media Arts,
Faculty of Arts and Human Sciences,
103 Borough Road, London SE1 0AA
tel 020-7815 5702
email harveycb@lsbu.ac.uk
website www.lsbu.ac.uk
Pathway Leader for BA (Hons) Writing for Media Arts Colin Harvey

The BA (Hons) Writing for Media Arts is a 3-year full-time BA programme which aims to prepare people for a career in journalism, and creative and commercial writing for television, radio advertising, and interactive multimedia.

The course is 50% practice and 50% theory and aims to develop a knowledge and understanding of contemporary media and literature in their historical and political contexts, while teaching students the basics of writing for different media. Throughout the degree, students produce a portfolio of their own work; in the final year they may specialise in journalism or scriptwriting to produce an independent practical project.

Course fees and entry requirements: available on request.

Screen Academy Scotland, Napier University

61 Marchmont Road, Edinburgh EH9 1HU
tel 0131-455 5203 *fax* 0131-455 5224
email screen@napier.ac.uk
website www.napier.ac.uk
Programme Leader Robin MacPherson

The Screen Academy Scotland is one of 7 UK Screen Academies endorsed by Skillset and the UK Film Council as an industry-recognised centre of excellence.

The MA in Screenwriting offers aspiring film, television and interactive screenwriters the opportunity to develop their creative skills through taught and project-based modules. It combines professional tuition in the craft of screenwriting with understanding of the professional and business issues that writers need in order to work within the screen industry. The programme interacts with the MA Screen Project Development – one of the only development degrees in the UK – so writers have the opportunity to meet up-and-coming producers, development executives and script editors.

The full-time route is 3 trimesters (45 weeks); part-time, 6 trimesters (90 weeks). Students can also undertake distance learning online.

Course fees: £3100 for full-time EU students. *Entry requirements*: Honours BA in appropriate degree; in some cases a high professional equivalent will be accepted.

Royal Holloway, University of London

Media Arts Centre, Arts Building, Royal Holloway, University of London, Egham, Surrey TW20 0EX
tel (01784) 443734 *fax* (01784) 443832
email MediaArts@rhul.ac.uk
website www.rhul.ac.uk/media-arts
Programme Director Susan Rogers

The MA in Feature Film Screenwriting at Royal Holloway is very highly regarded in the UK, and is accredited by Skillset. It was devised in 1999 with input from the film development and production sectors of the industry. The programme is aimed at creative professionals – people already employed in film and television, or writers in other media who may have an interest in writing for film. The tuition and coursework are pitched to provide students with a thorough understanding of the film industry, and to help students develop skills to tell strong stories with cinematic language. The course is offered part-time over 2 years in central London. The programme also operates an exchange with UCLA.

Southampton Solent University

Media, Arts and Society Faculty,
Southampton Solent University, East Park Terrace, Southampton, Hampshire SO14 0YN
fax 023-8031 9653
email fmas@solent.ac.uk
website www.solent.ac.uk

Taught by experts from the film and television industry, this BA in Screenwriting specialises in writing for all major screen formats, including drama documentary, soap opera, comedy and feature film. Through outside links, students get work placements in the screenwriting industry. Academic study combines with practical coursework.

Full time for 3 years (part-time study is also available). Information about course fees is available from the website.

University of Salford

School of Media, Music & Performance,
Adelphi Building, Peru Street, Salford M3 6EQ
tel 0161-295 5000
email course-enquiries@salford.ac.uk
website www.smmp.salford.ac.uk
Head of School of Media, Music & Performance Walt Denning

Runs MA courses in Fiction Film Production and Documentary Production (both full-time) and a part-time MA in Radio and TV Scriptwriting. In 2007 launched a joint-venture MA in Screenwriting with Tampere Polytechnic in Finland. Also has a large range of undergraduate degrees relevant to filmmaking activity.

University of Wales, Newport

Caerleon Campus, PO Box 101, Newport NP18 3YG
tel (01633) 432432 *fax* (01633)432046
email uic@newport.ac.uk
website www.newport.ac.uk

This BA in Cinema Studies and Scriptwriting explores current and developing practices and theories of world cinemas, as well as critical writing, screenwriting, distribution and exhibition. The first year gives students a general background in film studies and history before allowing them to choose specialised areas of study, including screenwriting, critical writing and film journalism. Screenwriting projects are developed in collaboration with students on other production-based programmes. Final-year projects include a dissertation and/or screenwriting project. The course is 3 years full-time.

University of Westminster

The School of Media, Arts & Design, Watford Road, Northwick Park, Harrow, Middlesex HA1 3TP
tel 020-7911 5000 (ext 4293)
email mays@wmin.ac.uk
website www.wmin.ac.uk
Course Leader Steve May

The University of Westminster's MA in Screenwriting and Producing builds on the successful BA in Film and TV Production. It is designed to develop skills in screenwriting as well as in producing and script editing, and to create for students an experience akin to that which they will experience professionally. The university works in partnership with the film industry and hosts seminars with sales agents, distributors and other professionals. Also teaches through workshops, pitching ideas, script readings and much writing and rewriting. Partnerships between writer and producer students are encouraged. The course is 1 year full-time or 2 years part-time.

Short courses in screenwriting

As with the degree courses, most of the short courses listed below are designed for the serious aspiring or already-established professional screenwriter. Also see Short courses in filmmaking.

Arista Development

11 Wells Mews, London W1T 3HD
tel 020-7323 1775 *fax* 020-7323 1772
email arista@aristotle.co.uk
website www.aristadevelopment.co.uk
Director Stephen Cleary

Arista Development was created in 1996 by Stephen Cleary, then Head of Development at British Screen, to provide the first serious script development skills training for development executives, producers and writers in Europe.

Among its other activities, Arista hosts a series of courses for writers and developers, called Arista Specials. These 2-day short courses are in-depth, practical and industry-focused seminars on aspects of screenwriting craft and the business of film and TV development. The courses include:

- Writing & Developing Horror
- Writing & Developing Thrillers
- Writing & Developing Romantic Comedy
- Writing & Developing Adaptations
- Understanding Genre
- Short Documents, Treatments and Other Hellish Innovations
- Low-budget High+Quality

Course fees: vary; approx. £250 + VAT. Seminars take place regularly in Central London.

The Arvon Foundation

42a Buckingham Palace Road, London SW1W 0RE
website www.arvonfoundation.org
National Director Stephanie Anderson

These residential courses are held at one of 4 houses located in the Devon, Inverness-shire, Shropshire or West Yorkshire countryside, and give participants the opportunity to spend time writing, discussing the process of writing, and receiving guidance and advice from experienced professional writers. The centres are: The Hurst – The John Osborne Arvon Centre; Lumb Bank – The Ted Hughes Arvon Centre; Moniack Mhor; and Totleigh Barton.

Screenwriting courses are geared towards writers new to screenwriting, and cover some foundation areas such as story genres, premise and structure, character and craft. They also look at what makes a good 'film treatment'. As well as facilitating a writers' retreat which focuses on screenwriting, the centres also run many creative writing courses. *Course fees*: available on request.

Binger Filmlab

Nieuwezijds Voorburgwal 4-10,
1012 RZ Amsterdam, The Netherlands
tel ++31 (0)20 530 9630 *fax* ++31 (0)20 530 9631
email info@binger.nl
website www.binger.nl
Director Ido Abram

Maurits Binger Film Institute, also known as Binger Filmlab, was established in 1996 to provide screenwriters, script editors, directors and producers with the opportunity to upgrade their skills under the guidance of prominent filmmakers and experienced tutors from around the world. It is now one of the best-respected film teaching institutions in Europe. The Filmlab's philosophy is based on the conviction that script development is essential for the success of a film project. Its programmes are flexible and led by some of the best tutors in their subjects. All programmes are project-based – each student coming to the Institute learns using his/her film project. Students also gain the real-world experience of a film market at either Rotterdam or Cannes, depending on which term they are enrolled.

Binger Filmlab offers 5 key programmes for scriptwriters, script editors, directors, producers and documentary filmmakers. All of the programmes are aimed at filmmakers who already possess some experience and skill.

Course fees: the 5-month screenwriting programme costs €1250-€1450.

Central Saint Martin's College of Art and Design (Short Courses) – see page 357 for contact details.

FOCAL (Fondation de formation continue pour le cinéma et l'audiovisuel)

2 rue du Maupas, 1004 Lausanne, Switzerland
tel +41 21 312 6817 *fax* +41 21 323 5945
email info@focal.ch
website www.focal.ch

FOCAL is not a school in a traditional sense; its Foundation organises further training for professionals in all fields of cinema, and participants should already have some professional experience. Courses generally take between 2 days and 1 week and are usually held in German and/or French.

Detailed information on Focal workshops can be found at www.focal.ch.

London College of Communication– see page 24.

Short courses for screenwriters include: a film & TV vacation course; and 1-day courses on genre studies for writers. *Course fees*: available on request.

MFI Script Workshops

Mediterranean Film Institute, Varvaki 38 114 74, Athens, Greece
tel ++30 210 6457223 or ++30 6974 796098
fax ++30 210 6457223
email info@mfi.gr
website www.mfi.gr

An intensive, project-oriented screenwriting training programme for writers, directors, producers and script editors. It aims to fully develop the participating projects, from extensive outline to final draft. The course takes place over 12 months, with 2 residential workshops in Europe plus further online teaching sessions. Writing, script analysis, and rewriting are all focused on developing the essential elements of story, theme, character and circumstance through dramatic action.

Course fees: €1000 for participants with a project, and €500 for 8 further observers (script editors, teachers). Participation fee includes tuition, accommodation and meals during residential weeks. Applications are open to anyone from the EU, but southern Europeans are given priority.

Moonstone International Screenwriters' Lab – see page 349 for contact details.

The Screenwriters' Lab runs over 6 days. It offers screenwriters the opportunity to work on their projects in a series of 1:1 meetings with a team of award-winning screenwriter advisers selected from the Sundance Institute and throughout Europe. The Lab provides participant screenwriters with an analysis of the nature and structure of their project, and its creative possibilities. Open to applications from experienced screenwriters or writer/directors; participants are selected on the originality and viability of project, and their track record.

Course fees: £750 + VAT.

North by Northwest – Danish Film Institute

c/o Danish Film Institute, Vognmagergade 10, 1120 Copenhagen, Denmark
tel ++45 337 43528 *fax* ++45 337 43604
email n.nw@dfi.dk
website www.n-nw.com

Offers 2 MEDIA-supported screenwriter training programmes for professional European writers of feature film and television drama. Also offers a parallel programme which teaches development skills to the people who work with screenwriters (developers, producers, directors, etc.). All programmes are structured as 3 workshops over the course of 7 months.

PAL (Performing Arts Labs) – PAL Screenwriters Labs

6 Flitcroft Street, London WC2H 8DJ
tel 020-7240 8040
email office@pallabs.org
website www.pallabs.org
Director Susan Benn

PAL Labs aim to stimulate creative development and growth by bringing together small groups of talented people, of differing ages and professional backgrounds, to work in residential workshops or 'labs'. The goal of these sessions is to help participants discover new ways of working. After an intensive Lab experience, the process continues with online development of ideas and non-residential Minilabs. These sessions cover many disciplines, but PAL regularly runs Screenwriting Labs and has recently developed a newer programme, PYGMALION – a European Lab for makers of family film, TV and interactive media.

sagas – Writing Interactive Fiction

c/o Bayerisches Filmzentrum, Bavariafilmplatz 7,82031 München-Grünwald, Germany
tel +49 (89) 64 98 11 30 *fax* +49 (89) 64 98 13 30
email e-mail: sagas@sagasnet.de

sagas Writing Interactive Fiction is a joint initiative of the European MEDIA Plus Programme Training & Hochschule für Fernsehen und Film München aimed at furthering fiction writing skills for the interactive media market. sagas focuses on the most fundamental and creative level: the stage of developing storytelling ideas and organizing them into workable interactive concepts. sagas is an ongoing cross-disciplinary project encouraging a professional knowledge transfer between the audio-visual industry and the interactive market. Innovative, creative and team-oriented workshops address scriptwriters, directors, producers, artists and designers as well as developers, programmers, conceptors.

Short Courses@ NFTS – see page 359 for contact details.

Sources 2

Köthener Str. 44, 10963 Berlin, Germany
tel ++49 30 886 0211 *fax* ++49 30 886 0213
email info@sources2.de
website www.sources2.de

Offers advanced training and professional script development workshops in the European

Community for screenwriters and writer/producer/director teams, by organising the following activities:

SOURCES 2 Script Development Workshops focus the development of the participants' feature film or creative documentary projects. During a seven-day session, participants work in small groups with four or five projects each. The following period of approximately three months is dedicated to re-writes, and is coached by the script advisers involved. The second session is either an individual or a small group consultation of one day per project.

SOURCES 2 compact is an abbreviated format of the basic workshop focusing drama and mini-series for television, short films and other genres: The initial four-day session is followed by a coached rewriting period of approximately three months and a final feed-back from the advisers to the participants' latest draft by e-mail.

SOURCES 2 Projects & Process: Training Mentors for European Screenwriters is an intense training programme making the SOURCES 2 methodology transparent and is specifically created to enhance the skills of professional practising scriptwriters, developers and trainers working as mentors for screenwriters in the field of script and story development. The three-day sesiosion is follwoed by a three-month coaching and final round-up.

Course fees: these and further details are available from the website.

Spark (Screen Yorkshire) – see page 56 for contact details.

Spark is Screen Yorkshire's multi-stage development programme, offering new writers in the region the opportunity to develop their script idea through a series of workshops and residential tutorials. There is the future possibility of additional development funding after the programme, to take the script to draft stage. Writers must first attend a series of open workshops before submitting a treatment to be considered for the more extensive development programme. Refer to the website for full application details.

Sundance Screenwriters' Lab – see page 7 for details of the programme.

UEE (Université Européenne d'Ecriture Audiovisuelle et Créative)

489 Av. Brugman, 1180 Bruxelles, Belgium
tel ++02 344 65 70 *fax* ++02 347 22 01
email uee@skynet.be
website www.uee.be

UEE provides a wide variety of viewpoints on writing, via workshops on feature films, TV series, soaps, sitcoms, storyboards, film music, novels, short stories, stage and radio plays, poetry, comic strips and commercials.

The full curriculum takes 2 years but it is also possible to register for 1-2 semesters or to select a few courses.

Course fees: range from €2000 for a 2-semester year to €325 for a 20-hour workshop.

Writers Factory at Scottish Screen – see page 52 for contact details.

The Writers' Factory comprises four new initiatives, supported by lottery funding: to support training for screenwriters in radio, television and film; to explore the feasibility of a development agency supporting writers and publishers in the Highlands, as a model which could be used in other parts of Scotland; to explore and meet the development needs of writers in all literary communities. The Writers' Factory also provides development grants to publishers and magazines to commission and publish new writing in all the languages of Scotland.

The role of the developer

Say "development" to many screenwriters, and they will conjure images of demoralising meetings at which countless producers and financiers tear apart their careful work, and give conflicting script notes about how to make it better. Here **Emma Berkofsky** explores a better development scenario – one in which writer and developer build a mutual trust.

Development – taking an idea and turning it into a screenplay – can be a challenging experience for writers and developers alike. This is because the development process is not governed by a mathematical formula of, say, good developer + talented writer = great draft; rather, the point of the process is for the writer to find out or explore what their story is, and this will very likely happen over the course of several drafts. In order to make any meaningful change to a story, you have to understand how the story works: in other words, what characteristics it has, how it is configured, what makes it tick – all of which is a bit like finding the blueprint for the story. If you don't understand how the story functions, you usually end up plugging the holes rather than truly making it better. However, it is not easy to arrive at this point of enlightenment!

The developer's role is to help the writer through this process, mainly by asking questions to establish how well he or she understands their own story and their intention for writing it. These questions are integral to the process, for they often shed light on where the story problems lie, and will help the writer find the answers. If the writer doesn't or can't confront these problems, the idea is likely to stall. Although it's possible to still get to the finish line, the script will be much better if you face the obstacles it throws at you rather than look the other way.

There are also other factors outside of the script itself which can affect its progress. For example, is it the right time for the writer to be telling this particular story? Does it really work for the big screen? Will the story be what the market wants right now? Even if the writer writes a good script, it's much easier for a financier to say no than yes. Most financiers don't want to spend money unless there are exceptional conditions for them to do so, which are just as likely to do with the director or the cast as the script you and the writer have spent years honing. The reality of the film world is that it's not just about the script. If this easily puts you off, then screenwriting or development is probably not for you! You have to be prepared for the fact that as a writer or developer, you may work passionately on a project for years only to find it doesn't ever see the light of day through no fault of your own. And if you are lucky enough to get something made, it may be that your efforts go unrecognised.

The outlook in the UK

In the UK there are companies that invest significantly in development, such as Working Title, but generally the market is much more fragmented than the US market and development money in Britain can be hard to come by. This lack of infrastructure means that British projects get made on an *ad hoc* basis, with producers struggling to pay the bills. The Film Council has tried to address this imbalance by helping companies to sustain themselves financially. The lack of funding in the UK also means that there is not much money for rewrites, whereas rewriting is an industry in itself in the US. Some US-based writers only ever rewrite others' work.

In fact, one of the main reasons why it is so difficult for British films to be successful is the dominance of the US studios. The apathy of British audiences to British films only makes it harder for producers to run sustainable businesses that make money. What does tend to work is when a film offers an audience something different from a studio film, and instead says something unique about our own culture in a universal way – as with *The Full Monty* or *Bend It Like Beckham*. However, there is a paradox here because often a commercially minded organisation will turn down a project if it's perceived to be too 'novel'.

Like many other companies, Lionsgate UK appreciates the importance of development, but finds it hard to commit significantly to British projects because of the difficulty in making British films work even in their own market. Therefore, when we develop material we have to have a clear idea of the intended audience, and how we are going to reach them. This means thinking about the concept: whether it's strong enough to get across to an audience quickly, and whether we can encapsulate the idea in one line, in an image, on a poster or a trailer. During the development process, the script can change considerably and we have to be aware of how these changes will affect the way in which we sell the film. Our involvement in any project always comes down to the risk/reward ratio: how much money are we risking for what we would expect to get back if the film performs below average? We always have to consider the worst-case scenario.

This is actually good advice for writers, developers and producers as well. Know your audience, and try to understand how to reach them. Cinema has gone from a relatively cheap form of entertainment to a fairly expensive one when compared to watching a DVD at home. When you write your story, you have to be able to justify why someone would shell out £10-20 (with concessions) to go and see your film.

What to expect in the development process

Once a writer gets into development, s/he will have to learn to take criticism and communicate with others in order to progress. A writer will usually be working with a developer, and often a producer; there may also be financiers involved, and therefore many voices to factor in – and this can be challenging. Very often the script does not get better straight away. Draft two can be a step sideways, and it might not be until a couple of drafts later that writer and developer start to feel they are getting anywhere. As daunting as it may sound, there may be as many as 10-15 drafts in all. Screenwriting is an exacting discipline which can take time to get right.

In general, the writer and the developer need to build a relationship whereby they understand and respect one another's roles and differences. They must also develop a shared insight into the story, otherwise it is difficult to move it forwards. Sometimes a producer can feel left out of this process, particularly if they are not confident about development. If this is the case, the developer has to make sure that the producer is not alienated during the development process.

Although there is no tried and tested formula to make a script better, there is at least good practice, as follows.

For the developer

As a developer working closely with a writer, you will have to earn the writer's trust and respect. If a developer is any good, they will most likely work extremely hard to achieve this. A writer has usually written something that is personal to them in some way, and will be questioning why they should trust you with all this information. A good developer will, among other things, make the writer feel comfortable, be excited about their work, and have interesting and insightful things to say about it.

Before meeting a writer you must know the material as well as, if not better than, they do. You also need to prepare what you are going to talk about in the meeting and be able to communicate your ideas clearly and respectfully. It's helpful to have a list of questions to hand, in case the conversation stalls.

The biggest mistake a new developer makes is to get carried away. You should be able to get through everything you need to discuss in an hour or so, but the temptation is to spend double that in order to prove that you can be trusted. A writer would love you to spend hours on end discussing the intricacies of their script – but you must be disciplined and keep the meetings to the point, otherwise you run the risk of losing your objectivity and the writer's respect in the long run.

As a developer you do have to be objective, but this doesn't mean that you have to act as if you don't have any feelings of your own. When you've seen a film, or are in the process of watching a film, you are constantly responding to the material. The same process goes on when you read a script; it's your own response to the material which forms the basis of your opinion. You just need to work out why you feel the way you do, how that relates to what the writer intends, and whether s/he has in fact achieved that. In this way you remain objective but you are not denying that you are also human. If you don't like something, you need to work out why: there is probably a good reason for it.

Sometimes developers need to be reminded that they are not the writer. You may have lots of ideas about the material and feel excited by it, but try not to impose them on the writer. You can make suggestions or give examples, but if the writer is any good they will find a better solution than you anyway. The idea is that you draw the story out of the writer rather than tell it to him or her yourself.

For the writer

Be wary of producers or developers who have no notes on your script. Every script can be better, even if you are a complete genius. As a writer, it might be tempting to work with someone who agrees with every last thing you say, but if they do, they're probably not experienced in this field and may therefore not be the best person to help you get your film made.

When you are having meetings with a developer and you don't agree with them, say so and explain why. Don't think that because they've got the money you have to do everything they say, or that they are always right. If you are unclear about what someone is saying, don't be afraid to ask for clarification. Never leave a meeting unsure about what has been said.

Don't write something you don't believe in. Developers can quickly tell if you are not passionate about your material.

Writing can be a long, difficult process and sometimes you will feel like you'll never find the solutions to your script problems. Keep in mind that the difference between success and failure is having the tenacity and self-belief to write through your problems.

Don't deliver something you're not happy with, because you will be found out. It's better to ask for help, and for more time if you need it.

Emma Berkofsky began her career in film production before moving into script development. She has developed more than 20 produced features, including the Palme d'Or nominee *Wonderland* (Michael Winterbottom), and *Grand Theft Parsons* (David Caffrey), which was selected for Sundance. She spent five years at British Screen (including two as Head of Development) where she focused on spotting new talent, working with filmmakers such as Marc Evans, Nick Love, David Mackenzie and Asif Kapadia on their first projects, as well as Oscar-winners Gavin Hood and Andrea Arnold. Emma is currently Head of Development at Lionsgate UK (formerly Redbus Pictures, and co-producer of *Bend It Like Beckham* and *Good Night and Good Luck*), working on projects from directors Jeff Wadlow (*Cry Wolf*), and Neil LaBute (*Nurse Betty*), among others.

Public funding for development

Listed below are the regional screen agencies who had published development funds at the time of print. However, it is always worth checking with yours if it does not appear here: staff may be able to tell you about available development funds – either within the agency itself, or from the local arts board.

EM Media – see page 53 for contact details.

Offers some project development funding for script and games development to filmmakers and companies located in the East Midlands.

MEDIA Funding for Development – see page 57 for contact details and funding schemes.

North West Vision – see page 54 for contact details.

Offers script development funding and training for feature film scripts and scriptwriters from the region, in the following categories:

- **Feature Script Development** awards are made to writers for script development twice a year; writers can apply individually or with a producer (£5000 max. for next draft).
- **New Feature Film Writers' Development Scheme** aims to develop screenwriting skills and equip writers with the tools to write more accomplished feature film scripts. Takes a group of writers through a multi-stage development process. See **www.northwestvision.co.uk** for full course details.
- **Development Plus** is a short course for writers who have little or no experience in feature film writing. Teaches development skills and tools to help with the writing process.

Screen East – see page 55 for contact details.

Offers the following development support:

- **Project and script development fund** – investments range from £1000 to £12,000 max. in treatments, first and subsequent script drafts and revisions, rehearsed readings, packaging, casting, budgets, schedules and pilots. Investments made at the maximum level are likely to apply only where a writer of some experience is working closely with industry contacts. All investments are geared towards filmmakers in the East of England.

Screen West Midlands – see page 56 for contact details.

The following funds are for West Midlands-based filmmakers:

- **Lottery Script Grants scheme** supports individual writers and production teams from the region looking to develop first- or second-draft screenplays for feature films from treatment or first-draft stage. Writers and producers can apply for a maximum grant of £5000 to support writing costs, and application rounds take place on average twice a year. An additional £2000 may be made available towards script editor costs for successful applications.
- **Advantage Development Fund** is intended to enable applicants to develop projects to a higher standard before taking them to market. Normally scripts submitted for feature film or one-off broadcast projects for this fund should be at least at second-draft stage. Applicants with treatments or first-draft scripts seeking development should refer to the Lottery Script Grants scheme above. Applicants can apply for between £5000 and £30,000. All awards are made on a loan basis.

UK Film Council Development Fund – see UK Film Council for contact details.

The UK Film Council's Development Fund, newly headed by producer Tanya Seghatchian, has an annual budget of £4million to help to raise the quality of screenplays from the UK through targeted development initiatives for individuals and for companies. There are 2 different initiatives for individual projects:

25 Words or Less

Offers up to 12 writers each year a fixed sum of £10,000 to develop a first-draft script in a specific genre. Applications are run 3 times a year; at each entry point different genres are selected (for example, 'Comic Odd Couple', 'Fighting the System', and 'Teen'). The Development Fund will assign a script editor to the project to help the writer take a story idea from concept to first draft (completed screenplays are ineligible for this fund).

Applicants must have secured the services of a literary agent and/or be a member of the Writers' Guild of Great Britain with 'Full Membership' status (as such term is defined by WGGB) before applying for this scheme. Projects are selected based on story outline, 10 pages of sample scenes and a strong pitch of '25 words or less'.

Single Development Projects

Available to individuals or a company, to develop a UK feature film project which will reach the broadest range of cinema audiences both inside and outside the UK. Individuals will be offered a maximum of £10,000. There are 3 types of funding:

• **Seed Funding** is for projects at a very early stage of development, such as treatment or first-draft stage, or for options over published works. The purpose of this funding is to shape development projects in order to make them more attractive in the marketplace.
• **Partnered Development Funding** is for projects which require funding for the full development process, or where a project has already been developed beyond first-draft stage. Applicants should seek third-party partnership funding of a minimum of 25% of the 'hard' costs.
• **Pre-pre production Funding** is considered at the discretion of the Development Fund, provided that you can provide documentary evidence of interest from potential investors in the production of the film. You will be required to provide an element of partnership funding of approximately 50% of the pre-pre-production costs.

Extensive details of what these funds cover and how to apply are available on the UK Film Council website, **www.ukfilmcouncil.org.uk**.

Courses on development

These courses are primarily aimed at core feature film development teams (either writer alone or some combination of writer/director/producer), and are designed to help take feature projects through several stages of script development.

ACE (Ateliers du Cinéma Européen) – see page 95 for contact details.

Producers' organisation which puts the producer at the helm of the filmmaking process. Runs an extended project-development training programme aimed at producers who already have a track record and who come with a specific feature film project. The selected producers on the programme begin by taking part in a pre-workshop, which consists of in-depth project analysis with several consultants: this session focuses principally on the script but also serves to establish a possible financing plan. The day-long discussion also aims to establish a development strategy for the project before the producers take part in a longer residential workshop, at which they interact with professionals from the wider industry.

Arista – see page 26 for contact details.

Arista Story Development Workshops are intensive 6-day residential courses providing advanced training in all aspects of film and TV script development for writers, directors, producers and executives. This MEDIA-supported programme offers filmmakers the opportunity to work with experienced tutors to get to the heart of creative, production and collaborative issues in developing a project.

Applicants may apply as a writer/producer team that already has a project, or as a developer. Workshops are held in Italy. *Course fees*: the programme costs between £1500 and £3000 + VAT. Deadlines and details are available from the website.

EAVE – European Audiovisual Entrepreneurs

238c rue de Luxembourg, L-8077 Bertrange
tel ++352 44 52 10 1 *fax* ++352 44 52 10 70
email eave@eave.org
website www.eave.org

Offers a 'package-based' development programme aimed at experienced European producers. The EAVE workshops take place over a year-long period with 3 intensive residential modules of 1 week each (conducted in English) in different European countries, linked together by long-distance monitoring and tutoring.

During the workshops some 50 participants work in 4 groups, each led by an experienced producer. The group work is complemented by individual meetings with analysts and experts. Training focuses on development, financing, packaging and distribution as well as strategic business management and planning. Producers attend with their author/scriptwriter for workshop 1 and 2, at which they will work on developing the script, and also on refining the budget and package. *Course fees*: €2500 with project, or €1500 without.

EKRAN

Andrzej Wajda Master School of Film Directing, ul.Chelmska 21, 00-724 Warsaw, Poland
tel ++48 22 851 10 56 *fax* ++48 22 851 10 57
email info@wajdaschool.pl
website www.ekran.info.pl, www.wajdaschool.pl

EKRAN is a European training programme for film professionals that focuses on the creative pre-production process. Key members of the creative team attend 3 sessions over 4 months to test narrative ideas, discuss casting, and work on tone and visual strategies for the project. The team may be made up of a director (or writer/director), a writer, a producer, and optionally, a director of photography. To be eligible, filmmakers should have made a first feature or several short films, and must be working on a script.

Katapult – European Script Centre

Logodi u.31, Budapest, 1012, Hungary
tel ++36 1 30 26 287 *fax* ++36 1 30 26 287
email office@katapultfilm.hu
website www.katapultfilm.hu/workshop

The European Script Centre consists of 3 workshops over 12 months for a targeted group of EU-based screenwriters, directors and producers who will have the opportunity to develop their own projects. Sessions are in Budapest and Prague. *Course fees*: the programme costs €600; filmmakers should be active in the audiovisual industry.

Napier University (MA in Screen Project Development) – see page 24 for details on the linked MA in Screenwriting programme.

The MA in Screen Project Development offers aspiring film, television and interactive media producers the opportunity to develop their creative and business skills and take a live project in drama, documentary or interactive media through an intensive, supported development process. The programme combines professional tuition in creative skills – such as documentary research, story development and script editing – with the business of producing: securing rights, pitching projects, raising finance, doing deals and finding an audience. *Course fees*: £3100 for full-time, EU students. *Entry requirements*: Honours BA in appropriate degree; in some cases a high professional equivalent will be accepted.

The Script Factory (Courses on Development) – see page 6 for contact details.

The Script Factory offers an annual programme of short development training courses such as Script Reading and Television Drama Script Reading. They also offer a part-time Diploma in Script Development in partnership with the NFTS; for European film professionals, they offer a MEDIA-supported training and networking programme called SCENE Insiders.

Script registration services

While the messy court case over *The Da Vinci Code* shows that it is not always easy to prove a creative copyright, there are things you can do to protect your script or programme ideas.

If you are at the stage where you are sending out a script, treatment or programme proposal for other people to read, then it's a good idea to register the documents you send. It may be stating the obvious to say that a creative 'idea' which exists only in your head is not copyright-protected, but once you write it down in material form, according to the *Copyright, Designs and Patents Act 1988*, it is.

The services below work for the screenwriter, by 'registering' a copy of a script or treatment in a dated and sealed envelope, or on a write-protected CD-ROM. In the case of a future dispute, these registered documents might help the artist to establish the date at which copyright first existed. As a general rule, the more specific and detailed a document is, the more protection this service will offer you – so a script is better protected than a 150-word synopsis or programme idea. Unfortunately, copyright does not protect titles to a work, so if yours is very important to you, you may have to legally make it a trademark.

BECTU (Registration) – see page 160 for contact details.

BECTU Script Registration is a free service offered to members – but note that copies are not kept on file. Members send their script to BECTU head office, where it is logged, sealed, and returned to the member for safekeeping.

Raindance – see page 359 for contact details.

Raindance's Script Registration scheme costs £6.25 (Members) or £20 (Non-Members). Writers put a hard copy of their script or a write-protected CD-ROM in an envelope bearing the title of the script, name and address of writer, draft number and number of pages. They then send it with a cheque to Raindance, where it is held for safekeeping.

The Script Factory (Script Registration) – see The Script Factory for contact details.

The Script Factory Registration Service costs £30 + VAT (total £35.25). Refer to **www.scriptfactory.co.uk** for full details of how to submit a script.

The Script Vault

PO Box 36, Todmorden, Lancashire OL14 7WZ
email info@thescriptvault.com
website www.thescriptvault.com

The Script Vault offers the only UK registration service which is endorsed by The Writers' Guild (see page 7). It is not necessary to become a Script Vault member to use the registration service; however, members are entitled to several free registrations. Bronze members can register 1 free script every year; Silver members, 4; and Gold members, 10. Scripts may be sent at any time during the membership period. Otherwise each script is £10.

Membership costs: Bronze £30 per year; Silver £45 per year; Gold £60 per year.

Development services

It used to be the case that unless you were part of a writing team, or unless your film was being developed commercially, you would work alone without much creative interaction for months until you had something to send out to companies and agents. Rather frighteningly, at that point, you might send your script to be read 'blind' by people who could have a major impact on your future career.

There are now increasing opportunities for writers to get early independent professional feedback before starting to submit a script for commercial consideration. Some of the regional Screen Agencies offer script reading services, such as Northern Film & Media (see page 55) who will read up to three scripts per year from writers living in their area.

Alternatively, you can commission script reports from one of the companies listed below – or even work in collaboration with an experienced professional developer for hire; someone who will read drafts of your script and meet you to give verbal and/or written feedback on your script. While these services are generally reasonably priced – you can find them for under £300 for a programme of meetings and written reports – you should investigate the credentials of the people offering the service. There is nothing wrong with speaking to the person who will be working as your developer to better understand how the service works, and to try to get a sense of whether you will be comfortable working with them. You can also ask to be put into contact with other writers who have used the service, or ask your regional Screen Agency if they are familiar with the company. You may even want to start by commissioning a Treatment Report from the company: this should reveal much about the reliability and professionalism of their services. Development is a sensitive process and one built on trust, so it's hugely important that you have confidence in the developer!

Euroscript – see page 6 for contact details.

Euroscript's feedback and script-reading service provides writers with a personal, in-depth report, highlighting the strengths and weaknesses of the script. A report for a feature-length screenplay or single TV drama (up to 120 pages) costs £75; a report on a full-story treatment (up to 15 pages) costs £35. Turnaround is 2-4 weeks. Euroscript also offers a project development consultancy. For fee details, contact the company.

Raindance (Development Services) – see page 359 for contact details.

For its Script Analysis service, Raindance recommends that you send 2 copies of your script – 1 for the reader, and 1 for Raindance to register (this can be on CD). The company will then register the script for free before sending it out to a reader. If you choose not to do this, the script will be sent out at your own risk.

Costs are as follows:

- Feature length: £100 (£80 for members) up to 120pp – please call for a quote if your script is over 120pp
- Short: £55 (£45 for members) up to 30pp – please call for a quote if your script is over 30pp
- Treatment: £55 (£45 for members) up to 15pp – please call for a quote if your script is over 15pp

The Screenwriters' Store

website www.thescreenwritersstore.net

This online store for filmmakers also offers script consultancy services in written or verbal form. The developer reads the writer's script and then gives extensive notes. Verbal feedback costs £109.95; written feedback costs £239.95 and includes notes written onto the actual page using Final Draft.

Script Consultancy services are provided by Pilar Alessandra, who has worked as Senior Story Analyst for Dreamworks and Radar pictures, and taught screenwriting at UCLA's Writers' Program.

The Script Factory (Development Services) – see page 6 for contact details.

The Script Factory's development services include: Script Feedback, which provides industry-level feedback reports on feature screenplays, shorts and treatments (£50–£70 + VAT); Draft to Draft, which offers the opportunity for individual writers to discuss their project with a script consultant to help move a feature screenplay from one draft to the next (£250 + VAT); and Private Readings for writers and production companies whose feature and short film projects are at an advanced stage of development with some finance in place (POA).

The Writers' Workshop – see page 8 for contact details.

Magazines

Creative Screenwriting

6404 Hollywood Blvd, Suite 415, Los Angeles, CA 90028, USA
tel ++ 1 323 957 1405
email info@creativescreenwriting.com
website www.creativescreenwriting.com

American magazine combining industry news relevant to screenwriters with interviews with some of the industry's key writers, and articles on craft. Widely considered to be the best US screenwriting magazine. *International subscription*: $49.95 per year incl. postage.

Hollywood Scriptwriter

PO Box 11163, Carson, CA 90746, USA
tel ++1 310 283 1630
website www.hollywoodscriptwriter.com

An online subscription magazine, providing resource tools for screenwriters, producers and directors. Coverage includes articles on screenwriting, profiles and Q&As with industry professionals. *International subscription*: $55.50 per year.

MovieScope Magazine

802 Capital Tower, 91 Waterloo Road, London SE1 8RT
tel (0845) 094 6263 *fax* (0845) 094 3846
website www.moviescopemag.com
Editor Eric Lilleør
Publisher Rinaldo Quacquarini, *Editor-in-Chief* Eric Lilleor

MovieScope Magazine provides a fresh perspective on the collaborative nature of filmmaking. Each full-colour issue features contributions by key industry professionals, established journalists and filmmakers from Hollywood, the UK/Europe, the Indie film scene and other global movie hotspots. The result is an informative and entertaining read filled with practical advice, encouragement and behind-the-scenes information: invaluable and entertaining in equal measure. Ideal for filmmakers and serious movie-lovers. *Subscription*: Normal price £29.70, but often has introductory offers (e.g. £20.79 for 6 issues).

Script Magazine

5638 Sweet Air Road Baldwin, MD 21013-0007, USA
email shelly@scriptmag.com
website www.scriptmag.com
Editor-in-Chief Shelly Mellott

American magazine featuring articles written by screenwriters currently working in the industry – such as Jim Sheridan, Nicole Kassell, Guillermo Arriaga. Also includes craft articles and development news/advice. *International subscription*: $49.95 per year.

ScriptWriter Magazine

email info@scriptwritermagazine.com
website www.scriptwritermagazine.com

Bi-monthly UK print magazine for people who work with television and film scripts, including producers, writers and developers. Includes interviews, reviews and articles on craft and ones which contextualise the writer's place within the industry. Has a strong accompanying website detailing current and previous articles and with a useful FAQ section at **www.scriptwritermagazine.com**. *Subscription*: £36 incl. postage.

Finance

House of cards: putting the project together

Robert Jones makes the observation that assembling the finance for an independently produced film could be likened to building a house of cards in a high wind. The most likely outcome is that, at some point, it will collapse ...

That said, the number of independently financed films that do go before the camera is surely testament in no small part to the efforts of a doggedly single-minded breed – the independent producer.

The journey to production can be every bit as dramatic as the film itself, and sometimes with a larger cast of characters. When the cameras do roll, all eyes are on the director to deliver the goods. But before anyone gets to shout "Action!", all hopes rest on the producer or producing team. It is his/her/their ambition, entrepreneurial know-how and plain cunning that must combine to deliver the necessary resources to move forward to production.

The producer is the link between the art and the commerce of filmmaking. From the birth of an idea, through the development, packaging, financing, physical production, and even marketing and distribution of a movie, there's only one seat in the house with a grandstand panoramic view of it all. The producer's decisions and actions at even the earliest stages of a putative project's life can have significant consequences when it comes to raising the finance. And, in turn, the choice of financing partners and types of finance can themselves be determining factors on the production process and even the marketing and distribution of a movie.

Financing a project

At its simplest, the act of financing can be expressed as a transaction in which money is exchanged for rights in and ownership of a property or project.

When first committing to a project, producers must acquire ownership of all the rights (usually by way of an option) that will be required by distributors and financiers. The 'chain of title' is the litany of documentation that evidences how ownership has passed through various hands (e.g. novelists and writers) and ended with the producers. A clean or complete chain of title is required to make a financing deal.

The way in which the financing transaction works depends on several factors – not least market economics. In North America it is understood that with few exceptions, the studios want complete ownership of the films they finance. Budgets can be substantial; competition for producing jobs is fierce; and all but the most powerful producers generally accept that in return for decent producer fees they must relinquish ownership and work as (albeit creative) hired guns.

In non-English-speaking Europe, producers tend to work for much lower fees. However, home-territory markets are often buoyed by generous box-office subsidy systems and (in France, for example) quotas that favour local and European product. By taking advantage of domestic and European subsidies, and working with budgets that can be wholly or majority financed from their home territory, producers are often able to retain a substantial part of the ownership of a film and build an asset base for their businesses.

Historically, UK producers have enjoyed the worst of both worlds. Limited budgets make available modest producer fees in comparison with those of US counterparts. The weakness of the home market for domestic (i.e. UK) pictures, combined with an absence of protectionist film policies, increases the difficulty in financing all but the cheapest of pictures without selling international rights as well as UK ones. So generally the rights and ownership of a project end up somewhere other than with the UK producer.

Of course there are a small handful of exceptions – producers who, through previous successes and/or current access to their own finance, can stay more firmly in the driving seat when ownership is at stake. But they are still few and far between and it will be interesting to observe whether the new tax credit that has superseded the Section 48 sale and leaseback provision sees a shift in the balance of ownership.

If the world of film financing seems complicated, it is useful to start with a few simple questions. Who are the major suppliers of finance for film? How does one approach them, and what do they expect from a producer in order to evaluate a project? Why would a financier choose to invest in a particular film? When is the right time to raise money for a particular project? Where are the most appropriate sources of money in each case? What deal terms might an investor expect? Who else is involved in the pursuit of financing, and how can they help? Should the search be conducted in the UK or further afield?

Types of film investment

As with any market, the film financing market comprises many and varied players, some of whom are compatible with each other (i.e. their respective investments will sit happily together in a deal), and others who are in direct or indirect competition.

Fundamentally, there are four categories of film investment.

- Firstly, there is investment that is made as or against a purchase of distribution rights in the film. Such investors sit closer to the consumer in the value chain, and include single or multi-territory distributors, international sales companies, television broadcasters, foreign co-production companies, webcasters and games companies.
- Secondly, there is equity finance: money that is invested against a share in the overall receipts and profits of a film. In this category one would find private equity investors, tax funds and government subsidies.
- Thirdly, loan finance. Largely provided by banks or specifically designed loan funds, it is often the most expensive money in terms of fees and interest charged to the budget of the production – and usually occupies the lowest-risk, 'last in, first out' recoupment position.
- Lastly, non-repayable money is available in the form of local or national tax legislation, incentives to encourage use of certain locations and studios, and in-kind investment in the form of production facilities.

The extent to which these monies are available either separately or as partnership funding fluctuates over time and place, according to a variety of factors including both legislative change and technological innovation. For example, the favourable tax regime in Germany in the 1990s led to the rise of numerous funds comprising private investors seeking tax relief. The funds invested aggressively in both US studio and indie movies. However, changes of late in tax legislation have seen a dramatic contraction (and in many cases overnight disappearance) of such funds.

The boom in DVD sales in the last five years has increased the desire of theatrical and DVD distributors to invest in film – whereas the concurrent proliferation of new digital TV channels has resulted in a dilution of audiences in television markets, and a stagnation or downward movement in European television investment in film.

Producers who keep themselves as closely connected as possible with global market conditions and changes, with the names of those financiers who keep cropping up on the credits of local and international films, and with developments in local and national government film policies and incentives, will find themselves one step ahead of the pack when it comes to devising creative financing strategies.

Certain financiers are motivated entirely by the deal; others will have a more discernible profile in terms of the films they back. There are no absolutes where taste is concerned, but knowledge such as this will identify particular places and may eliminate others as potentially suitable homes for a project.

Presenting the package

Most financiers will evaluate a potential investment on the basis of a 'package'. This is the combination of material, project attachments and arguments that will hopefully persuade an investor to jump on board.

The package can include anything from a film treatment or outline, to a screenplay, a director's involvement, headshots of actors (intended or attached), a trailer or showreel, poster ideas, examples of the creative team's previous work, an idea of the market and genre of the film, a budget and schedule, proposed financing plan and recoupment structure, sales estimates from a reputable international sales agent, examples of success of films in the same genre, identities of key crew, music and mood references, storyboards, location shots – and last but not least, a convincing story pitch and logline.

The value of a good pitch can't be underplayed. Like films themselves, good pitches get passed around the industry by word of mouth and can result in a project becoming 'hot' and fought over.

The content, presentation and timing of delivery of the package is a matter for the judgement of the producer. With so many projects vying for finite amounts of money, one should assume a limited attention-span on the part of a financier. How much more important, then, is the need to go in first time round with 'all guns blazing': a second chance may not arise.

The strength of each existing element in the package will give a feel as to its readiness for presentation. For instance, a screenplay may be deemed so powerful that it could be submitted without any additional elements, not even a director.

Establishing credibility

Financiers will look closely at the credibility of what is on offer. Even with the financial guarantees afforded by bond and insurance companies, they rely on a producing team to deliver on their creative promise, and their confidence is determined as much by first impressions as it is by subsequent due diligence.

The financier might consider the following questions: Does the producer have a reliable track record? If there is no track record, has the producer taken the initiative and recruited a more experienced producing partner? Is the budget set at a realistic level, both in line with the commercial potential and to deliver a film in the proposed genre with the suggested elements? Does the producer have a clear sense of what the film is, who the audience is, and how the project might bring a financial return?

Above all, the presentation needs to be passionate, entertaining, and memorable. Don't forget that it's called *show*business. Financiers may want a return on investment, but they're not immune to the glamour and magic either.

Many producers will find that the best time to pitch new projects is at major film markets and festivals. At least those events provide an opportunity to contact many companies in a short period. But beware: distributors and sales agents are generally concentrating on films they are trying to sell or acquire, and are too busy to hear a pitch or read a screenplay for something away on the horizon. Smaller local festivals or periods in between festivals can be more productive times for raising finance.

Perhaps the best use of such events is as an opportunity to network. The more comprehensive the list of a producer's contacts, the more financing options will present themselves.

Confronting and overcoming the hurdles

Once the package has been presented, the rejections will begin. There are always rejections – it's a subjective business and there is no such thing as a sure thing in movies. Financiers that do express interest will expect to see a budget, schedule and cashflow sooner rather than later.

Even with financiers willing to commit, a producer must still confront and overcome one of the biggest hurdles going forward to production. How to keep the wheels greased on the creative front while financing and other deals are being closed?

Most financiers are not willing to risk advancing money to a production until all documents are signed and the completion guarantor is officially 'on risk'. Prior to such 'closing', as it is known, a film could collapse for a variety of reasons and the money be lost. Indeed, many financiers are not structured to cashflow even after closing. The producer will have to borrow (from a bank) against their contract, incurring often burdensome fees, interest and expenses on top of the basic production budget.

The difficulties faced at this stage constitute possibly the biggest blight on independent production. There are dedicated funds that provide limited pre-production funds at a high premium, but inevitably many films cannot afford this option and collapse because of inadequate funding, or (perhaps worse still) limp towards production without adequate preparation.

With crew being hired, actors committing, a director preparing with heads of department, and financiers vying for pole position on the starting grid of the deal, dependence on the producer is never greater than during pre-production. Someone once characterised a producer as the glue that holds everything together – and if ever there is such a defining moment, it occurs at this point.

Consequently, many producers will structure financing around a cornerstone financier who is more open to the concept of advancing money before 'closing'. The choice of this first piece of the puzzle is crucial. A cornerstone partner with a great reputation and industry contacts (as well as money, and hopefully the ability to cashflow) can become an ambassador for the project to other potential financiers, and reduce the size of the headache leading up to principal photography.

The assistance of a seasoned film-financing lawyer in negotiating and closing film deals is most definitely money well spent. Many will agree fee caps depending on film budget at the time of engagement, and their knowledge of deal structures, and of potential partners both at home and abroad, can pay for itself many times over.

Moreover, financiers will expect a producer to be represented by an entertainment lawyer who will negotiate the deal. Deal-making is a time-consuming and expensive business – even more so if one of the parties is still learning to walk, as it were. Many deals are scuppered by the endless prevarication of inexperience or fixation on hair-splitting irrelevances. The window of opportunity can close as quickly as it opens.

When all is said and done, despite the hitches and glitches of bankrolling dreams, those films that make it through their gestation generally do so because of a common commitment, enthusiasm and desire on the part of all involved – including the financiers. Like filmmaking itself, financing is a collaboration in which each player must play their role to make the whole greater than the sum of its parts: to make the house of cards that much stronger against the wind.

During 24 years in the film industry, **Robert Jones** has worked as producer, distributor, international acquisitions executive and film funder. He is now President of Material Entertainment, a production outfit owned and distributed worldwide by New Line Cinema and top UK distributor Entertainment. Previous to this, he worked as Head of Acquisitions for UK indie Palace Pictures, and was Head of the UK Film Council's Premiere Fund. He has built a proven track record, working with established filmmakers and identifying and developing new film talent. His production credits include Oscar-winners *The Usual Suspects* (from *X-Men* director Bryan Singer) and Robert Altman's *Gosford Park*, Stephen Frears' Oscar- and BAFTA-nominated thriller *Dirty Pretty Things*, Paul Thomas Anderson's *Hard Eight* starring Gwyneth Paltrow and Samuel L Jackson, Mike Leigh's multi-Oscar- and BAFTA-nominated *Vera Drake*, and *Run, Fat Boy, Run.*

The core strands of film finance

Partner at Lee & Thompson, **Reno Antoniades** examines the main areas of finance available to UK producers.

In his introduction to this section of the *Yearbook*, Robert Jones identifies the four main categories of film investment. My aim in this article is to expand a bit on these four categories, hopefully giving a more full understanding of how they work – both on their own and in conjunction with each other.

To recap, the four main areas of film financing, are: (i) pre-sale of sales and distribution (and other) rights; (ii) equity finance (i.e. where an investor provides recoupable finance and buys a 'stake' in the film and in its earning potential); (iii) loan/debt finance; and (iv) non-repayable money (including government subsidies, tax breaks and so on). I will look at each of these in turn and try to give you some tips on how to fit them together as different pieces of a financing 'puzzle'.

Pre-sales

For a number of years, it has generally – and certainly in the UK – become more difficult to raise production finance through pre-sales, as distributors have become increasingly risk-averse and competition has grown. At the same time, it is common for loan/debt finance and even equity finance to require evidence of pre-sales as an indicator of a project's value in the marketplace. This quite often includes the local territory, i.e. the 'home market' of the producer, which in the UK is notoriously difficult to pre-sell at a premium. Producers will either seek to pre-sell rights directly or through an appointed sales agent. Direct deals are more likely to be done for a producer's home market.

There are of course all sorts of rights in a film project that can be pre-sold. The most 'mainstream' examples are the sale of the theatrical, non-theatrical (e.g. airlines, etc.), television and video/DVD rights in a film for a particular territory or territories. It will depend entirely on the nature of the project, but some distributors may not insist on acquiring all allied and ancillary rights, such as merchandising or computer games rights: indeed, some of these more specialist rights may not be their field. Others may want to acquire (or at least have the option to acquire) as many rights as possible. The producer has to look carefully at how valuable all of these different rights are, and take a commercial view. Television rights may also have been separately pre-sold as part of the financing (see below), and appropriate holdbacks on the timing of the exploitation of certain rights may need to be negotiated. Increasingly, the exploitation of online and Internet rights have become the source of much negotiation. For a producer, reassurance is needed that there will be no overspill in respect of Internet exploitation outside of a distributor's agreed territory.

The key players

So who are the key players, and how (as Robert asked in his introduction to this section) does one approach them?

Distributors

In the independent distribution sector in the UK, the key players are Entertainment, Pathé, Lionsgate, Momentum, Icon and Optimum. There are many smaller and niche operators such as Metrodome, Revolver, Verve, Artificial Eye and Tartan. It is key for producers to develop relationships with the acquisitions executives at these organisations, in order to build knowledge of the type of product they regularly distribute and the point at which a project is ready to be submitted to the distributor – that is to say, how developed the package has to be. There are no quick or correct answers to this, but experience is a great thing to have or to seek out as a producer. The ultimate 'deal' a producer can do is likely to be circumscribed by the requirements of the other financiers in the case of a local sale (for example, the UK Film Council has specific requirements, such as a guarantee of theatrical release) and the particular circumstances of a project. If in doubt, advice should always be sought before committing to any deal.

Sales agents

As well as distributors, we should look briefly at the concept of sales agents. As the name would suggest, these are 'middle-men' who are often better placed than the producer to pitch and sell projects to distributors internationally.

Once appointed, a sales agent will provide sales estimates; these are key for loan/debt financiers and equity investors as an indicator of a project's commercial value. It is important for a sales agent to be pre-approved by other financiers – both in terms of the estimates they provide, and their credentials for selling the film. Just as pre-sales have suffered over the last few years, so have sales agents, whose business is dependent on both pre- and post-sales: their resulting inability to provide 'pre-sales advances' has also pushed down their commission rates from around the 25% level to closer to 10-15%. So, while it may not be as easy as it once was for a producer to raise money for their film's budget from appointing a sales agent at an early stage, the producer will in theory see more money more quickly as a result of these lower commission rates.

Broadcasters

Another key pre-sale category is the sale of television rights. Over recent years the amount of money that the 'big player' broadcasters, such as Channel 4 and the BBC, will pay to pre-buy territorial exclusivity in respect of TV rights has been falling in real terms. Yet it still tends to far outstrip any post-sale of UK TV rights, the value of which tends to be measured by the box-office success of a film. TV licence fees are therefore a major contributor to the budgets of many British independent films. A broadcaster will often also mix its pre-sale licence fee with an equity investment, which in the aggregate can be between £400,000 and £1,000,000, dependent on a number of factors. While TV pre-sales can bring much-needed money to the producer's finance plan – especially with the added equity investment – the downside is that all TV rights in perpetuity tend to be sold as part of the package, which can of course be before the true value of such rights has been ascertained.

Equity finance

Equity finance can take many different forms, but a particularly common and key distinction is that between public funding and private-sector finance.

Public funding

Looking first at public funding, the biggest single funder in the UK is the UK Film Council, which is responsible for administering and allocating Lottery money to film projects on a national basis. There are also a number of regional bodies, including Scottish Screen, the Northern Ireland Screen, and the Arts Council of Wales – as well as a number of more specifically local bodies which have been established in the last few years, including North West Vision, Screen West Midlands, Screen East, Screen Yorkshire and Screen East Midlands.

One thing the regional bodies all have in common, in terms of their *raison d'etre*, is the promotion of local culture through film. They also have a much more practical justification, being the promotion of general economic wellbeing in their regions, including in particular the generation of jobs and the encouragement of 'outsiders' to come in and spend money in their locality. This means that at least a certain amount of film production work needs to be carried out in the geographical area. (Obviously, when it comes to things like shooting a film in a particular geographical area, there is only so much a producer can do to compromise ... but it is the ability to cleverly fit things into seemingly odd-shaped boxes that can sometimes separate the astute producer who is likely to get his/her film made, from the rigid idealist who never gets theirs off the ground.)

All these public funders have well-publicised application procedures. Whether or not they will select the project for funding is of course another matter, particularly given the volume of applicants.

Private-sector finance

There are a whole range of different companies, organisations, individuals and tax funds who offer equity investment. I have already mentioned the BBC and Channel 4 in relation to TV pre-sales; both these bodies are also significant equity investors in many British films. Certain distributors will also invest by way of equity, must notably Pathé in the UK. Some tax-driven funds will invest equity finance, as distinct from the now defunct regime of 'sale and leaseback' and the new tax credit system. These tax funders include Scion, Ingenious Films, Baker Street and Future Film. However, producers should beware, as these deals – while providing invaluable finance – can add significant costs to a budget in terms of fees. It is key to have an overall knowledge of the marketplace in terms of equity financiers, and to source relevant relationships.

Working out the deal

Whoever the financier – whether private, public, British or foreign – in terms of equity investment there are always certain key issues for the producer to consider when working out the deal.

Firstly, one needs to consider the level of investment. It is not necessarily the case that the more equity finance raised, the better – although traditionally UK films have high proportions of equity investment. The level of equity investment required will depend on what other funding is available from other sources. The key is to endeavour to keep a finance plan as simple as possible. From the investor's point of view, a critical issue is its recoupment position. It can be very difficult to get all equity financiers to agree to recoupment structures and this is therefore a tricky area for producers. One financier putting in the same amount or type of money as another will not necessarily agree to equality in terms of recoupment.

Another thing to bear in mind is what premiums and/or interest a particular equity financier (normally a private equity investor) will want, on and in return for its investment. Equity investors by definition will assume a profit share in terms of the net profits of the film: while it is common for them to accept a share which is proportionate to the level of their investment, this is not always the case. The traditional split of net profits in the UK between financier(s)/producer is 50/50.

Equity financiers may also charge executive producer fees; will usually expect executive producer credits for the relevant key individuals from their organisations; and will of course require various editorial rights and approvals to do with the production of the film – although this will depend upon the level of their investment. All these are important points for a producer to consider: remember that whatever is given away to one financier can dictate what is left to offer to another.

As with any other type of financing, it is necessary to consider the cash flow of equity investments, and the order of cashflowing. For example, a bank may wish to see other financing invested first; other financiers may not wish to take a credit risk on a particular financier in the absence of concrete evidence of available funding. This is more pertinent to individual investors.

Debt/loan finance

As Robert has already said, this is certainly often the most 'expensive' money a producer can raise. Although certain banks have developed a specialisation for film finance (examples include Bank of Ireland, Allied Irish Bank, Royal Bank of Scotland and Comerica in the USA), they are still, after all, banks and the producer should expect them to be very conservative in terms of minimising their own exposure and risk. There will therefore be a lot of documentation, which will mean more legal fees for the budget as well as arrangement fees and the cost of the money.

This type of finance is not particularly creative, at least compared to the other sources that I have talked about – but money is money and it can sometimes be an easy (if not the only!), albeit expensive, way of filling a smaller 'gap' in a producer's finance plan. Typically these gaps will be between 8% and 20% of a film's budget. The cost of this money can be as high as 20% of the money borrowed.

While banks do not take equity positions on a film, they do expect to recoup first, see sales agents defer part of their commissions, and inevitably push back the investments of the equity investors. The 'numbers' have therefore to be able to support a finance plan and the proposed recoupment structure.

Non-repayable money

It is certainly true that UK-based producers are at a relative disadvantage, compared to some of their European counterparts, in terms of the amount of 'soft money' that they are able to raise. However, there are still plenty of opportunities here. The ever-changing new tax-credit regime is always anticipated as being of great value for the British film producer, but only time will tell. Producers can also, of course, team up with their peers in other countries for international co-productions. Co-production is an altogether different subject and not something I have focused on directly in this note, but international co-producers tend to be categorised as providing pre-sales finance or equity investment.

Independent film finance is constantly in a state of flux. Ever-changing financiers, tax initiatives, market trends and personnel make it a minefield for both new and experienced producers. There are rules of engagement, and there is help to be had: the trick is to learn the rules and take the offer of help – or to seek it out.

Reno Antoniades trained at the City firm, Herbert Smith, qualifying in 1991. After two years spent in the corporate department he joined a specialist entertainment practice acting principally for independent production companies, sales companies and distributors within the film and television industries. In 1994, Reno joined Lee & Thompson to work with Jeremy Gawade in building up the firm's film and television department, becoming a partner in April 1997. Reno represents a wide range of US- and European-based independent film and television production companies, international sales agents and UK distributors as well as talent-based production companies. He has developed a particular expertise in independent feature film financing (including tax-based financing) and in production, television animation projects and music programming. Lee & Thompson's current clients include some of the leading independent film and television production companies, including Revolution Films, Kudos Film & Television and Red Production Company. Reno has tutored extensively on the Media II-sponsored training course, Arista, participating in workshops throughout Europe.

UK and European funding bodies

This section lists the key sources of public funding for UK film producers, and gives information on the leading legal firms and financial advisers for the UK film industry. Additional contacts for sales and distribution companies can be found in the Distribution and exhibition section of this *Yearbook*.

NATIONAL AGENCIES

Finance Wales

Creative IP Fund, Finance Wales, Oakleigh House, Cardiff CF10 3DQ
tel (02920) 338146 *fax* (02920) 338198
email creativefund@financewales.co.uk
website www.financewales.co.uk

The funding body established by the Welsh Assembly Government, Finance Wales administers the £7 million Creative IP Fund, which provides gap finance for projects within the creative industries, including feature films. Investment of between £50K and £700K can be provided for projects which have secured at least 60% of the budget from other funding providers. Investment is made in the intellectual property of the film, not in the production company itself. The fund operates on a commercial basis and is not a form of soft loan or grant. Contact Finance Wales to find out more about what it has to offer, and about eligibility criteria.

NESTA (The National Endowment for Science, Technology and the Arts)

Fishmongers' Chambers, 110 Upper Thames Street, London EC4R 3TW
tel 020-7645 9500 *fax* 020-7645 9500
website www.nesta.org.uk

NESTA is a public endowment which supports creators who are making truly innovative advances at the 'meeting place' of science, technology and the arts. While its awards must go to cross-disciplinary innovators, Dream Time may be appropriate for some filmmakers. The award offers support for talented and accomplished individuals. Over the last 3 years, NESTA has awarded 31 Dream Time Fellowships to the value of £1.2 million: these have enabled individuals from across science, technology and the arts to pursue ideas and activities which benefit their own development and achieve impacts within their sectors. The award is currently under review; updated details should be posted on the website shortly. It is worth noting that NESTA will only fund projects in the moving image if they are truly innovative and working at the crossroads of other disciplines.

Northern Ireland Film and Television Commission (NIFTC)

Alfred House, 21 Alfred Street, Belfast BT2 8ED
tel 028-9023 2444 *fax* 028-9023 9918
email info@niftc.co.uk
website www.niftc.co.uk

NIFTC has a wide range of funding schemes for filmmakers working in Northern Ireland, and for projects benefiting the Northern Irish media industries. These include specific funds for animation, factual, feature film and TV drama, low-budget production support, several development funds, and skills development bursaries.

The following feature film funds are available to filmmakers or companies living in Northern Ireland:

• **Project Development (Lottery)** NIFTC will fund up to £40,000, or 50% of the total development costs. Funding is available for single features, single television films, television series and serial dramas.
• **Feature Film and Television Drama Production Fund (Lottery)** The NIFTC Lottery fund will not usually contribute more than £150,000 to any one production. Its contribution to a feature film or television drama production budget can be no more than 50% of the total cost of the production. Funding is available towards the cost of pre-production, production and post-production.
• **Low Budget Feature Film Production** Priority for this fund is given to: films which have a strong cultural resonance for Northern Ireland; films which develop talent from Northern Ireland; films which use digital formats; and films which have broadcasters or sales agents attached. NIFTC's Lottery fund will not contribute more than £150,000 to any one production, and the contribution to a low-budget feature film can be no more than 75% of the total cost of the production.
• **Northern Ireland Film Production Fund** NIFTC will invest between £150,000 and £600,000, or 25% of the overall project costs in a live action or animated feature film, or a live action or animated television drama single, series or serial where the production has a strong cultural relevance to Northern Ireland.

The following short film schemes are available:
• **MINI Individuals** These are available for short narrative films, short experimental films, short animations, or single documentaries. They are for productions with a total budget of less than £2500; up to 90% of the budget may be awarded. NIFTC's maximum cash contribution will therefore be £2250.
• **MINI Small Awards** Similarly geared towards the above formats, but aimed at small groups rather than

at individuals. They are for productions with a total budget of less than £5001; up to 90% of the budget may be awarded. NIFTC's maximum cash contribution will therefore be £4500.

Both MINI schemes are generally non-recoupable.

For details on other schemes, refer to the website.

Scottish Screen

249 West George Street, Glasgow G2 4QE
tel 0141-302 1700 *fax* 0141-302 1711
email info@scottishscreen.com
website www.scottishscreen.com
Chief Executive Ken Hay

Scottish Screen is the national body responsible for developing every aspect of film, television and broadcast new media in Scotland. The organisation allocates National Lottery funds to support the screen industries through training, education, funding support and development opportunities designed for applicants at all stages of their careers. The Entrant Training Scheme has been established for 27 years and has seen all its graduates go on to work in the industry. Also offers locations services for anyone thinking of shooting in Scotland. Scottish Screen publishes a weekly e-bulletin, *e-roughcuts*, to keep the industry up to date with all the latest news and events; every 2 months it also publishes the magazine *Roughcuts*, with interviews and features about all aspects of the moving image industry.

Skillset

Prospect House, 80-110 New Oxford Street, London WC1A 1HB
tel 020-7520 5757 *fax* 020-7520 5758
email info@skillset.org
website www.skillset.org

Skillset does not offer production funding, but does support training for filmmakers – and in some cases offers bursaries for training courses through the Skillset Film Futures scheme. The website features a brilliant introductory storyboard guide to understanding filmmaking, which includes a clear reference guide to finance and pre-production.

UK Film Council

10 Little Portland Street, London W1W 7JG
tel 020-7861 7861 *fax* 020-7861 7862
email premiere@ukfilmcouncil.org.uk, newcinemafund@ukfilmcouncil.org.uk, development@ukfilmcouncil.org.uk
website www.ukfilmcouncil.org.uk
Fund Heads – *Premiere* Sally Caplan *New Cinema* Lenny Crooks *Development* Tanya Seghatchian

The UK Film Council is the Government-backed strategic agency for film in the UK. Its main aim is to stimulate a competitive, successful and vibrant UK film industry and culture, and to promote the widest possible enjoyment and understanding of cinema throughout the nations and regions of the UK. It delivers these aims through targeted national programmes which focus on different aspects of the industry – professional training, export promotion, distribution and exhibition, filmmaking education in schools, and production funding. Feature film production support is divided into 3 main funds: Development, New Cinema and Premiere. Details of the Development Fund can be found on page 33. The 2 UK-wide feature film production funds are detailed below.

The New Cinema Fund (£5 million per annum)

Designed to support fresh, original and dynamic work in any style or genre. Previous investments have included: Kevin MacDonald's *Touching the Void*, Paul Greengrass' *Bloody Sunday*, and Saul Dibb's *Bullet Boy*. The fund prioritises work which might be described as follows:

- films from diverse innovative and cutting-edge filmmaking talent
- films from black, Asian and other ethnic minority filmmakers
- films that utilise the benefits offered by digital

What is available? The New Cinema Fund will usually contribute between 15% and 50% of a feature film's production budget. Funding will usually be provided by way of an equity investment in the film.

Who can apply? Any company registered in the UK or EU, or a UK-based individual (although you would be expected to form a limited company, should your application be successful) with a script which is ready to go into production. The New Cinema Fund would also expect that much of the cast and principal crew would be in place, and that a deal with a UK distributor or web broadcaster would be in place or likely.

The Premiere Fund (£8 million per annum)

Aims to invest in inventive, dynamic, commercially viable feature films – ones typically associated with the private sector – as a means developing a greater breadth of experience and expertise across the UK film industry. Investment is designed to assist the development of sustainable British film businesses capable of long-term growth. The Premiere Fund is looking for projects that can find cinema audiences in the UK and around the world across a full range of budgets and genres. Previous investments have included: *Young Adam* (David McKenzie), *Code 46* (Michael Winterbottom), and *Vera Drake* (Mike Leigh).

What is available? The Premiere Fund will usually contribute up to 35% of a feature film's production budget, but will consider a higher level of investment where the balance of the funding is from commercial sector sources (pre-sales, distribution guarantees, broadcasters, etc.). Funding will usually be provided by way of an equity investment in the film.

Who can apply? Only companies that are registered in the UK or EU are eligible to apply (no individuals may do so). The project should be for a feature-length English-language film intended for theatrical release; you must be able to demonstrate that it is commercially viable.

ARTS COUNCILS

Criteria for Arts Council funding differ greatly across the national offices. While we give a broad sense of the criteria here, you should speak to someone at the relevant Arts Council before submitting an application, to make sure that your project is eligible for an award.

Arts Council England

14 Great Peter Street, London SW1P 3NQ
tel 0845-300 6200 *fax* 020-7973 6590
email enquiries@artscouncil.org.uk
website www.artscouncil.org.uk
Chief Executive Peter Hewitt

Arts Council England is the national development agency for the arts in England, distributing public money from Government and the National Lottery. Grants are for individuals, arts organisations and other people who use the arts in their work. The Arts Council will only fund film projects if they are in support of an artist's work in the moving image. Conventional commercial feature film and video production are not eligible (the organisation publishes a document detailing exactly what types of film and video are eligible; this is available to download from the website).

Arts Council of Northern Ireland

MacNeice House, 77 Malone Road, Belfast BT9 5JW
tel 028-9038 5200 *fax* 028-9066 1715
website www.artscouncil-ni.org
Chief Executive Roisín McDonough *Visual Arts Officers* Iain Davidson, Suzanne Lyle

The lead development agency for the arts in Northern Ireland. Funding is available to artists in all disciplines, and the Arts Council calls for applications on a rolling basis with deadlines updated on the website. Grants for individuals can either be General Art Awards or Travel Grants. Special priority for General Art Awards is given to artists whose work is challenging and innovative, especially in areas of new technology.

Arts Council of Wales

9 Museum Place, Cardiff CF10 3NX
tel 029-20 376500 *fax* 029-20 221447
website www.artswales.org.uk

The national development and funding body for the arts in Wales, established in 1994 by Royal Charter. It has 4 key objectives:

- To develop and improve the knowledge, understanding and practice of the arts
- To increase the accessibility of the arts to the public
- To advise and cooperate with other public bodies
- To work through the medium of Welsh and English

As this *Yearbook* went to print, the Arts Council of Wales and the Welsh Development Agency were in the process of establishing a new film agency for Wales. Please refer to the website for further details of new funds and guidelines.

Scottish Arts Council

12 Manor Place, Edinburgh EH3 7DD
tel 0131-226 6051 *fax* 0131-225 9833
email help.desk@scottisharts.org.uk
website www.scottisharts.org.uk
Chief Executive Graham Berry

The lead body for the funding, development and advocacy of the arts in Scotland. For the most part, Scottish Arts Council works to support the art forms which Scottish Screen does not support (i.e. craft, dance, drama, music, etc.). Filmmakers are only eligible for funding if the films they are making develop the understanding of, or have a benefit to, one of the other art forms that Scottish Arts Council supports.

REGIONAL SCREEN AGENCIES

The nine Screen Agencies listed in this section are responsible for developing and supporting the film and television industries and professionals in their region. The funds they manage will primarily be for filmmakers and companies from the region, but in a few cases feature film awards may be made to projects which are located in the region with heavy investment in the local industry and the use of key talent from the area. Please contact the film officer at the relevant agency before submitting an application.

EM Media

35-37 St Mary's Gate, Nottingham NG1 1PU
tel 0115-934 9090 *fax* 0115-950 0988
email info@em-media.org.uk
website www.em-media.org.uk
Chief Executive Debbie Williams *Film Development Executive* Paul Welsh *Executive Producer* Lizzie Francke

EM Media invests in the development and production of films, broadcast media and interactive media – including computer games – which benefit the development of the film and media industries in the East Midlands. By 2009, the organisation aims to double its support for the region's feature filmmakers: investment will see at least 6 new feature films hitting the screens.

Instead of operating specific feature schemes, EM Media has a more open application process. It asks that filmmakers call its offices to discuss the project for which they need funding support. Filmmakers will then be advised as to whether the funds are appropriate for the project(s) in question.

In aiming to nurture the region's media talent and develop the media sector, EM Media will support:

- **Product Development** (including script and games development)
- **Individual Production Awards**
- **Slate Development**
- **Co-Production**

Investment will vary according to the type of project. For example, individual production awards for short films could range from £500 to £5000, and are unlikely to exceed £10,000; investment in the development of larger-scale projects (feature films, projects for television, games development, etc.) is likely to range from a very small initial investment up to a maximum of £95,000 for the development of slates. Production co-finance for features and large-scale projects will be up to a maximum of £250,000. EM Media's investment will be up to 50% of product development and production costs.

In addition to this rolling funding, EM Media also runs a DV Shorts scheme.

Areas covered: Derbyshire, Leicestershire, Lincolnshire, Northamptonshire, Nottinghamshire, Rutland.

Film London

Suite 6.10, The Tea Building,
56 Shoreditch High Street, London E1 6JJ
tel 020-7613 7676 *fax* 020-7613 7677
email info@filmlondon.org.uk
website www.filmlondon.org.uk
Chief Executive Adrian Wootton *Film Commissioner* Sue Hayes *Head of Production* Maggie Ellis

Screen agency aiming to develop and support London's film and media culture and industries. Film London offers the following production schemes:

- **London Artists' Film and Video Awards** (LAFVA) is an open-submission awards scheme for artists living and working in the London region. Funds are available to artists producing work in the context of the fine art moving image, or work that is intended for exhibition in galleries, at festivals, at specialist venues and as site-specific installations. The scheme offers awards from £2000 up to a maximum of £20,000. Awards are intended for fully developed projects with a realisable exhibition and distribution plan.
- **PULSE** is Film London's low-budget digital shorts scheme, run in partnership with the UK Film Council's New Cinema Fund. PULSE is open to new talent in London, and offers filmmakers an opportunity to make short digital films of 1-10 minutes' duration. At least 8 films will be commissioned every year, and filmmakers may receive between £2000 and £10,000 depending on the nature of the project.
- **Microwave: Micro-budget Feature Film Fund** is a new project to develop 10 micro-budget feature film projects in the capital. Microwave challenges filmmakers to shoot a full-length film for up to £75,000, with the option of raising additional in-kind support to take the budget to a maximum of £100,000. The scheme aims to provide an intensive approach to filmmaking, with an emphasis on tightly focused scripts, short production schedules and commercial potential. Backed by the BBC, the scheme provides up to £75,000 of direct funding per project, together with a professional mentoring scheme from leading industry figures such as directors Stephen Frears and Gurinder Chadha, and producers Sandy Lieberson and Jeremy Thomas. This scheme is for filmmaking teams with practical experience in making films.
- **Borough Funds** are available through many of the London boroughs, and aim to provide a 'first step on the ladder' for newer filmmakers. These funds are detailed under Additional funding schemes and awards – Film London East.

Film London is also an indispensable resource for anyone planning to shoot a film in London. Its offices can help with everything from location information and crew to whom you need to speak to for permission to shoot in the capital.

Area covered: Greater London.

North West Vision

c/o BBC, Oxford Road, Manchester M60 1SJ
tel 0870-609 4481 *fax* 0151-708 2984
email info@northwestvision.co.uk
website www.northwestvision.co.uk
Chief Executive Alice Morrison

North West Vision is one of 9 regional screen agencies that form part of Screen England. Over the last 3 years NWV has been busy behind the scenes, supporting, funding and promoting TV and film production in the North West – and has achieved a great deal. North West Vision's team of experienced and committed staff provide film and TV makers and media professionals with a range of services, including:

- FREE film office liaison service for all production filming enquiries, large or small, across England's North West
- Funding advice and support for new filmmakers through to established production companies
- Events calendar and information on industry events
- Exciting news updates
- Advice and tips on working in the industry

- Crew database
- Facilities database

Visit **www.northwestvision.co.uk** for further information regarding available funding.

Areas covered: Cumbria, Cheshire, Greater Manchester, Lancashire, Merseyside.

Northern Film & Media

Central Square, Forth Street,
Newcastle-upon-Tyne NE1 3PJ
tel 0191-269 9200 *fax* 0191-269 9213
email info@northernmedia.org
website www.northernmedia.org
Chief Executive Tom Harvey

Northern Film & Media is the Regional Screen Agency covering the North-East of England. At the time this *Yearbook* went to print, the organisation was restructuring all of its funding schemes for filmmakers; please refer to the website for further details and updates.

During the restructuring period, Northern Film & Media will continue to offer a free script reading service to writers in the area. You may submit up to 3 projects during a 12-month period for assessment by script assessor, Gorel Halstrom. There is no application form to complete for this procedure. If you live in one of the areas listed below, simply send your script, by post, with a covering letter and sae to the address above, marked with the reference 'Script Service'. The company aims to return your script report within 10 weeks.

Areas covered: Durham, Tees Valley, Tyne & Wear, Northumberland.

Screen East

2 Millennium Plain, Norwich NR1 1TF
tel (01603) 776920 *fax* (01603) 767191
email info@screeneast.co.uk, funding@screeneast.co.uk
website www.screeneast.co.uk
CEO Laurie Hayward, *Funding Officer* Annabel Grundy

Screen East's remit is to encourage talent and content development within the East of England, with the potential to make an impact on the wider film industry. It is committed to supporting films which have a commercial and cultural value. Screen East offers funding support in the following areas:

- **Project and Script Development** Investments range from £1000 to £12,000 in project and script development, including treatments, first and subsequent script drafts and revisions, rehearsed readings, packaging, casting, budgets, schedules and pilots. Investments made at the maximum level are likely to apply only where a writer of some experience is working closely with industry contacts.
- **Production Investment Finance** Screen East will invest a maximum of £75,000 (for total production budgets from £50,000 to £3m) in 2-3 films per year. These funds will either be invested in companies based within the East of England who have strong relationships with the wider film industry, or in companies from outside the region whose scripts have a strong local story element and who are working with talent from the region. The overall aim is to encourage distinctive regional stories with international appeal. For a full list of criteria, refer to application guidelines on the website.
- **Short Films** Screen East supports short film through its Digital Shorts scheme. It will not provide full production funding for short films outside of the official schemes, but will consider completion funding for short films made in the region on a case-by-case basis.
- **Small Awards Funds** These aim to support and encourage small-scale projects that develop industry skills and talent throughout the region. 20 small-scale awards of up to £500 each are available for individuals across Talent and Content Devlopment, Audience Development, and Enterprise and Skills Development.

Areas covered: Bedfordshire, Essex, Cambridgeshire, Hertfordshire, Norfolk, Suffolk.

Screen South

Folkestone Enterprise Centre, Shearway Road, Folkestone, Kent CT19 4RH
tel (01303) 298222
email info@screensouth.org
website www.screensouth.org
Chief Executive Jo Nolan

Screen South is responsible for developing and nurturing talent and industry in the South of England. It operates the following funds:

- **Open Fund** A scheme with a rolling deadline; includes *Small Awards* (up to £500) and *Large Awards* (over £500). As an individual you can apply for a maximum of £5000 per project; organisations can apply for a maximum of £10,000. These funds are for projects which support Screen South's aims and priorities of talent and industry development in the region, and they cover a diverse range of activities in addition to production and development, such as film festivals, training, and distribution activities.

Short films are not eligible for the Open Fund, but makers may apply for the following:

- **Digital Shorts** Screen South and the UK Film Council's New Cinema Fund commissions 10 films from the South East of England for the Digital Shorts Scheme. Shorts must be no longer than 10 minutes, including credits, and can be drama, documentary, or animation. All films must be shot digitally. Screen South runs 2 strands: *Long Shots* – 5 shorts of 5-10 minutes' duration, with a cash budget of £7250 each; and *Close Ups* – 5 shorts of 1-3 minutes' duration, with a cash budget of £2250 each.

The total cash budget awards above will be actual production spend. The schemes are intended for newer filmmakers.

Screen South will also provide and/or meet the costs of the following: basic production insurance, training workshops, script development executive, production executive and executive producer. At least 1 of the key people – writer, producer or director – must live or work in the region.

Areas covered: Berkshire, Buckinghamshire, Oxfordshire, Hampshire, Isle of Wight, Kent, Surrey, Sussex, Channel Islands.

Screen West Midlands

9 Regent Place, Birmingham B1 3NJ
tel 0121-265 7120 *fax* 0121-265 7180
email info@screenwm.co.uk, production@screenwm.co.uk
website www.screenwm.co.uk
Production & Development Executive Dan Lawson

Screen West Midlands' mission is to create a thriving screen media industry in the region (Birmingham and The Black Country, Herefordshire, Shropshire, Staffordshire, Warwickshire and Worcestershire). Programmes are designed to support, promote and develop the screen media industry through areas such as production, education, exhibition, archive and skills development. Funded through the UK Film Council, Advantage West Midlands and The Learning and Skills Council.

SWM manages a number of production funds:

• **Film & Media Production Fund** May invest up to £300,000 or 25% of a feature film project's budget (whichever is less). The aim is to invest in productions that contribute to building a sustainable screen media economy in the region. The fund will support filmmakers from the West Midlands, as well as encouraging those outside the region to relocate part or all of their production there. The fund can also invest in interactive games production, single TV dramas, and feature-length documentaries. Short films are not eligible for this fund.
• **Digital Shorts** Supports 8 filmmakers in developing and producing a short film that is shot or originated in a digital format and no longer than 10 minutes. Filmmakers may apply for a maximum of £9000. The application will ask for a showreel, so filmmakers are expected to have some experience.
• **Digital Shorts Extreme** Joint-funded by Screen West Midlands and the UK Film Council's New Cinema Fund. Aimed at further supporting and developing filmmakers who have previously made a film through the digital shorts scheme. One film will be produced at a maximum budget of £20,000. The film must be a maximum of 10 minutes' duration, including all credits, and originated on a digital format. Filmmakers must have made a short through the previous programme.

SWM also regularly supports other production schemes in the region for entry-level filmmakers, and encourages filmmakers to join the mailing list to be kept abreast of such schemes.

Areas covered: Herefordshire, Shropshire, Warwickshire, Staffordshire, West Midlands, Worcestershire.

Screen Yorkshire

Studio 22, 46 The Calls, Leeds LS2 7EY
tel 0113-294 4410 *fax* 0113-294 4989
email info@screenyorkshire.co.uk
website www.screenyorkshire.co.uk
Chief Executive Sally Joynson *Head of Production* Hugo Heppell

Established in 2002, Screen Yorkshire is the Regional Screen Agency responsible for inspiring, promoting and supporting a successful and sustainable film, broadcast and interactive media sector for the region. In May 2006, it was awarded £10.2m by Regional Development Agency Yorkshire Forward to deliver its Digital Media Content Programme. Screen Yorkshire's Production Fund is a digital media content development and production fund aimed at developing a long-term and successful production sector in the Yorkshire and Humber region. Screen Yorkshire sees film as an integral part of its programme; develops and supports regional talent in all areas of media; and is committed to attracting key productions to Yorkshire. Recent credits include: *Mrs Ratcliffe's Revolution, Mischief Night, This Is England* and *Like Minds*.

Screen Yorkshire offers a free bespoke production liaison service to filmmakers shooting in the region. It can provide expert advice, liaise with local authorities on filmmakers' behalf; and has an extensive online database of locations, and crew and facilities.

Screen Yorkshire distributes Regional Investment Fund for England (RIFE) Lottery and Grant in Aid awards on behalf of the UK Film Council; these are aimed at developing a sustainable screen industry and culture for the region. It offers 2 different levels of lottery funding to short filmmakers, with the purpose of developing emerging talent, and also offers a professional script reading service to companies and individuals in the Yorkshire and Humber region. This service is available for feature film scripts, television projects and detailed treatments.

Areas covered: Yorkshire, Humberside.

South West Screen

St Bartholomews, Lewins Mead, Bristol BS1 5BT
tel 0117-952 9982 *fax* 0117-952 9988
email info@swscreen.co.uk
website www.swscreen.co.uk
Chief Executive Caroline Norbury

The film, television and digital media agency for the South West of England, South West Screen offers a number of production development awards to filmmakers and films teams. These include: Production Alliance, which rewards teams who come up with innovative new ways to make programmes;

and Screen Shift, aimed at African and Caribbean artists working in the South West. South West Screen also runs a 2-tiered Digital Shorts scheme in partnership with the UK Film Council. Details of new schemes and deadlines will be announced on the website as soon as they are available.

Areas covered: Cornwall, Devon, Dorset, Gloucestershire, Somerset, Wiltshire.

EUROPE-WIDE AGENCIES

EU funding for filmmakers is available through MEDIA and Eurimages; however, there are also countless regional and national funds set up specifically to encourage co-productions which invest in local economies and help to develop regional film industries. KORDA, listed below, is an extensive database set up to help producers learn more about these funds.

Eurimages

Council of Europe, F-67075 Strasbourg Cedex, France
tel ++33 (0)3 88 41 26 40 *fax* ++33 (0)3 88 41 27 60
email eurimages@coe.int
website www.coe.int/Eurimages

Eurimages is the Council of Europe's fund for the co-production, distribution and exhibition of European films. The fund aims to promote the European film industry by encouraging the production and distribution of films from the member countries, and fostering co-operation and co-productions. Since it was set up in 1988, Eurimages has supported the production of more than 1000 features films (fiction, documentary and animation).

All projects submitted must have producers from at least 2 member states. The project must be 'of European origin and character' and the director of the film must have a European passport. Eurimages' financial support cannot exceed 15% of a film's overall budget and/or more than €700,000.

KORDA

website http://korda.obs.coe.int

The KORDA database provides an extensive collection of available information on public funding for film and audiovisual production and distribution in Europe. The database is the result of collaboration between the European Audiovisual Observatory, the funding bodies concerned, and with various specialised national sources.

UK MEDIA Desk

10 Little Portland Street, London W1W 7JG
tel 020-7861 7511 *fax* 020-7861 7950
email England@mediadesk.co.uk
website www.mediadesk.co.uk
Director Agnieszka Moody

An information and promotion office of the European Union's MEDIA programme in the UK, providing advice to UK film professionals on how to access available funding. The MEDIA programme offers a range of support schemes for training, project development, distribution, and promotion of European films and TV programmes. UK MEDIA Desk helps potential applicants assess their eligibility and assists them in the application process. Also offers advice on a range of MEDIA-supported training courses, markets and events.

MEDIA Plus funding schemes for film & TV projects

All MEDIA funding is distributed based on published 'Calls for Proposals'. These consist of a set of guidelines and official application forms to complete. Each call is published on an annual basis and can have 1 or more deadlines. The following information provides the basic outline of funds available for film and television projects and their producers:

- **Development** Funding towards development costs of film, television and multimedia projects is available for European production companies with a track record (no applications are considered from individuals). Companies can apply for support for a single project or a slate of projects (3 and above). Grants of up to 50% of the development costs are available. Sums available range from €10,000 to €150,000.
- **TV Broadcasting** Funding is available for television productions not intended for theatrical release. At least 2 broadcasters from MEDIA member states and 2 different language zones must be involved. Companies can apply for 12.5% of the production budget for animation and drama. For creative documentaries, applications can be made for up to 20% of the budget. The money is awarded as a non-repayable grant and is capped at €500,000.
- **i2i Audiovisual** Support available for producers to facilitate access to bank financing. Subsidies are up to 50% of the costs of insurance, completion bond and financing costs of the loan.

For up-to-date information, deadlines, and funds available for distribution, festivals and training, please visit **www.mediadesk.co.uk**.

OTHER

Isle of Man Film

Department of Trade and Industry, Hamilton House, Peel Road, Douglas, Isle of Man IM1 5EP
tel (01624) 687173 *fax* (01624) 687171
email iomfilm@dti.gov.im
website www.gov.im/dti/iomfilm/
Development Manager (Film & Media) Ms H Dugdale

The Isle of Man Media Development Fund has been established to make available equity investment to film and television productions shooting on the Isle of Man. It can offer 25% of the budget as direct equity investment.

To be considered for investment, a project should: be able to be filmed wholly or in part on the Isle of Man (at least 50% of all principal photography must take place on the Island); be capable of spending at least the equivalent of 20% of the below-the-line budget with local service providers; be otherwise fully funded; and have a completion bond in place. Applications should be submitted as early as possible. In all cases, emphasis will be placed on the commercial aspect of the project. Sales and distribution prospects will be considered as a vital element in the decision-making process. This is a rolling scheme, so applications may be made at any time with no deadlines. See the website for full details.

Tax credits explained

Mike Kelly demystifies the government's tax credit for film production.

You can't beat a good book (like this one!) or a magazine or a newspaper – but don't put too much faith in the headlines; for example, those which describe the UK tax credit as being worth 20% of a film's budget. In practice it is highly unlikely that a film will generate a tax credit exactly equal to 20% of its budget. So how *does* it work, and what is it worth?

It's probably important first to say what the tax credit isn't: it isn't a straightforward flat-rate reimbursement of qualifying production expenditure that someone with experience of, say, some of the North American incentives might expect. The UK tax relief is accessed by a two-stage process whereby it can only be claimed after a film is certified as officially 'British'. Yet, just because a film passes the first test doesn't necessarily mean that it can access any tax relief. Certification is, in effect, a door that leads to another test – whether the film meets the criteria of the 2006 Finance Act (FA 2006). Only after passing through this second gateway can the tax incentive be accessed.

Officially 'British'

Passing the first stage of eligibility for the tax credit is further complicated by there being two means of achieving certification. A film can qualify as British by being produced in accordance with one of the UK's Co-Production Treaties, or under Schedule 1 of the 1985 Films Act, which was recently amended to include a new 'Cultural Test' (see below).

Official co-productions

A co-production that is 'unofficial' may still pass the Cultural Test and proceed to FA 2006. However, if a film meets the requirements of a Co-Production Treaty or the European Convention on Cinematic Co-Production (the Convention), then it will not only qualify as British without the need to pass the Cultural Test; it will also normally be eligible for any equivalent tax break or state aid in the partner country or countries.

A whole book could be written on co-production, and it would probably be out of date as soon as it was published, given the number and complexity of co-production arrangements throughout the world. The UK's treaty network is currently in the middle of a particularly turbulent period. After a comprehensive review, several long-standing treaties have been ended and a number of new treaties are being put in place.

The websites of the UK Film Council (UKFC) and The Department of Culture, Media & Sport (DCMS) contain up-to-date information on the status of the various treaties. At the time of writing, in addition to the Convention, the UK is currently signed up to bilateral agreements with Australia, Canada, France, New Zealand and South Africa. It has signed but not yet ratified a bilateral agreement with Jamaica, and is in negotiation to establish new bilateral treaties with India, China and Morocco. The former treaties with Germany, Italy and Norway are no longer effective.

Applying for official co-production status is another two-stage process. First, an application must be made for provisional certification to the UKFC; a final application must then be made after the production is complete. Provisional certification is exactly what it says: it can be withdrawn, and as a consequence the tax credit will be lost. However, provisional certification is like a deal struck with the government; if you meet your side of the bargain then the government will generally meet its own. The UKFC will advise the producer on any areas of concern they may have regarding the application, so that they can be fixed before it is too late. The UKFC requires provisional applications to be made at least four weeks before principal photography commences, but you should submit the package of information they require as soon as you are able. This will help them help you.

Schedule 1 and the Cultural Test

The Cultural Test is an elaborate point system. If a film scores 16 out of a potential 31 points then it passes the Cultural Test and can be considered for relief under FA 2006. Simple? Well, in practice not quite so simple.

The intention is that films will be pre-certified and, as with provisional certification of co-productions, the earlier you apply, the earlier the UKFC will be able to advise you of any problems they foresee. As with co-productions, interim certification is like a deal struck with the government, but be sure to keep your side; even the Secretary of State hasn't got the authority to waive or relax the test, whatever the circumstances.

You can find a breakdown of the 31 points, together with detailed guidance notes on how they are scored, on the UKFC's website (**www.ukfilmcouncil.org.uk**), but here is an overview:

16 Content Points

• Up to 4 points are scored for the proportion of a screenplay's total pages set in the UK (1 point for a quarter, 2 for half, 3 for 66% and 4 for three-quarters). The guidance notes are not explicit, but they seem to imply that the custom of dividing pages of a screenplay into one-eighths for the purpose of scheduling a production would be an acceptable basis for determining whether each mark has been reached. It's important to emphasise that *set* does not mean *shot*: a scene set in a Scottish Glen can be shot in a valley in New Zealand and still be included with the 'good' pages, but a scene set in a bar in the Irish Republic won't count even if it is actually shot in a pub in Belfast.

• Up to 4 points are available depending on the number of principal characters who are, were or can be explained as British. Again, it is how this is written, not how it is shot, that counts at this stage. A US actor playing Winston Churchill would contribute to the point-scoring; a UK actor playing Eisenhower wouldn't. Where the nationality of the character isn't clear – for example, if the film were set in some unspecific future world – it might be possible to construct a perfectly good argument as to why they should be considered British, but there must be some rationale for the points to be claimed.

• 4 points are earned if the film's subject matter is British or the authorship of the underlying material is British. The underlying material does not have to be a book or play that has been formally optioned, though an option could give a direct link to a clearly British authored work to support an application.

• Up to 4 points are available depending on the proportion of the original dialogue that is English and/or a recognised regional or minority language (e.g. Welsh). Again, very crudely, a film earns 4 points for three-quarters, 3 points for 66%, 2 for a half, and 1 for a quarter. The guidance notes appear to be contradictory, but it seems best to assume that the test is ultimately applied against the language recorded (including any ADR), not the language written ... so a film that was highly improvised and mixed, say, English and Mandarin and depended on the points in this section would need to be carefully produced and edited.

4 Cultural Contribution Points

These points are earned if the film makes a significant cultural contribution over and above the cultural content marked out of 16 above. The cultural contribution is assessed under three key categories: creativity, heritage and diversity. One point is available if a significant contribution is made in the first two; for the latter, a point is earned if a film's subject or the portrayal of the subject reflects Britain's cultural diversity in a significant way, with a further point available if there are "other cultural diversity factors which can be shown to have an impact on the final content". If the contribution goes beyond being significant and can be classed as "outstanding", then the point(s) can be doubled, but a film can only score a maximum of 4 points in this section no matter how outstanding its contribution.

I believe it is fair to say that the official guidance notes struggle to outline a clear policy that can be objectively applied in this area, and, since the test is new, there are few precedents to inform filmmakers who are developing or preparing a film. That doesn't necessarily mean that these points should be ignored or written off; this particular glass is as likely to be half full as half empty. An applicant should perhaps claim as much as can reasonably be argued in this section. Whilst hoping for the best, they should, however, assume the worst until the interim certificate is issued. Even then, for a film that depends on scoring points in this section to pass the Cultural Test, the producer should make sure that the basis for the award of points in the interim certificate is very clear. Anyone lending against the value of the tax credit in such circumstances would be well advised to be particularly diligent.

3 Hub Points

Originally this section scored the highest number of points, but its importance to the test was drastically reduced during the process by which the tax credit gained EU approval, because its former dominance was seen to make the earlier version an *economic* not a *cultural* test.

Put very simply; 2 points can be earned if 50% of the visual or special-effects spend or 50% of principal photography is in the UK, and 1 can be earned if 50% of the music recording or sound or picture post-production expenditure is spent in the UK.

8 Practitioner Points

Forecasting the score on this section is fairly straightforward; it's essentially a matter of fact not opinion. The details are on the UKFC site, but the principle is: the more people involved in the film are ordinarily resident in the European Economic Area, the more likely the film will score these points.

The Golden Point

Whenever something is described as "golden", it's best to check the small print, and there is plenty to be found here. It is the UK film industry's answer to the Schleswig-Holstein question – though sensibly, before the DCMS's equivalent of Lord Palmerston forgot how it works, they summarised it in a flowchart and appended it to the guidelines on the UKFC website.

Distilled down, the Golden Point works something like this. If you're producing an English-language film that is set mainly outside the UK, and where Britons are in a minority amongst the lead characters, but you plan to spend enough money in the UK and hire enough EEA labour to score the maximum Hub and Practitioner points, then the subject matter, underlying material or authorship of the underlying material had better be British, because all those cultural contribution points don't count any more, no matter how outstanding the contribution.

And distilling that down even further; if you're thinking of shooting an essentially American film in the UK and are hoping to get the benefit of the tax credit, check out that flow-chart!

So the Golden Point is really the Golden No-Points – but at least there isn't a Platinum Point to worry about as well.

Animation, documentaries, other points

The points systems for documentary and animation films depart from the above on occasions, but follow the same broad pattern and a similar logic. There are some other requirements for certification under Schedule 1 in addition to the Cultural Test, such as who can apply (companies only, no individuals and no partnerships) and how much archive footage can be incorporated in a film submitted for certification (10%, but the definition of 'archive footage' is complex and worth checking out even if you don't think you have any).

FA 2006

Whether via Schedule 1 or by an official co-production, the film enters the chamber of secrets that is the 2006 Finance Act ... or rather the film production company enters, since, whilst certification is accorded to films, the tax relief is given to UK companies (not individuals, not partnerships).

To be eligible, the company must be largely responsible for the preparation, production and delivery of the film, and be the party most engaged in planning and decision-making and negotiating contracting and paying for rights, goods and services. If the film is a qualifying co-production, the UK co-producer can share these duties and does not have to take the lead, but must make "an effective creative, technical and artistic contribution" to the film.

All films must spend at least 25% of their *core expenditure* in the UK. This little phrase belies a myriad of details, but in simple terms core expenditure equals expenditure on pre-production, production and post-production, but not development. The cost of an option isn't core expenditure, but the cost of exercising it is. The costs of raising finance aren't core and whilst the costs of delivering the film can be included, the costs of marketing, distributing and exploiting it can't.

UK expenditure means goods supplied and services performed in the UK, but again there is an enormous amount of detail behind this headline statement. For example, whereas a visual effect is a service supplied in the UK because the work is performed in the UK, it appears that a special effect is determined to be UK or non-UK (or 'good' or 'bad' respectively), depending on where the scene incorporating the effect is shot. So even if the special effects and visual effects are used in the same scene and made in premises next door to each other in the UK, if the scene is shot outside of the UK the cost of the special effects will be bad spend but the costs of the visual effects will be good spend.

All companies claiming a tax credit must intend that their film will generate a significant proportion of its revenues from commercial cinema exhibition, and this has to be the intention at the end of each accounting period for which the credit is claimed. It is not good enough, for example, to have intended that the film will generate box office revenues when the film is developed or produced (or when the application for certification is sent to the UKFC).

So, if at the end of the accounting period the company is in serious negotiation with a distributor who intends to take their film straight to DVD, then, *prima facie*, there is no intention and there will be no tax credit? Well, perhaps not, since it isn't clear whose intention it has to be, nor does a film have to be intended to be theatrically released worldwide for it to be eligible. So a film might go straight to DVD in a number of territories and still be intended to be released theatrically in others, though HM Revenue and Customs (HMRC) expects the film to be at least intended to be released in Britain. Film production companies might want to retain any correspondence with distributors and similar parties to evidence the intention to theatrically release the film.

Provided that the intent is still valid and the 25% spend threshold is met, a film certified as British is then able to generate an additional deduction that may reduce profits or create a trading loss.

The additional deduction is like an artificial expense added to the final cost statement, but one that you didn't actually pay for. In other circumstances, the directors of a company which accounted like that could end up in jail, but under FA 2006 it is a legitimate entry in the company's tax return.

The additional deduction for films with total core expenditure less than £20m (limited budget films) is the lower of core UK expenditure or 80% of total core expenditure. If (and remember that if; we'll be coming back to it) this creates a loss, it can surrender the loss for a cash payment equivalent to 25% of the losses surrendered. It is this cash payment that is generally referred to as the 'tax credit'.

The headlines declared the value of this credit as 20% of a film's budget (i.e. 25% x 80%), but this oversimplifies the calculation. First the percentage (and the £20m threshold for consideration as a limited budget film) only applies to core expenditure and not to the total budget. Second, and most important, the tax credit should be viewed incrementally not absolutely.

Imagine a co-production with core expenditure budgeted at £10m but with zero 'good' spend. Gradually the producer decides to increase the planned core expenditure in the UK; the first £1 to be spent in the UK will earn nothing from the tax credit (the 25% threshold has not been reached) nor will the next £1 or the next ... in fact, even if the producers plan to spend £2,499,999 in the UK and the film is capable of qualifying as British via a co-production treaty, the tax credit is still worth £nothing because the threshold of spending 25% of the film's core expenditure in the UK hasn't been met. The next pound of UK spend is money well spent, however, for the percentage clicks over from 24.99999% to the magic 25% and suddenly the tax credit is worth £625,000 (i.e. the film now clears the FA2006 threshold and the tax credit is worth 25% of the whole £2.5m of UK spend). Perhaps *that* should be called the platinum pound?.

Each subsequent £1 of good spend generates a tax credit of 25p, until the core expenditure in the UK reaches £8m. At this point the tax credit is worth £2m, but the incremental benefit of spending further money in the UK drops down to £nil again and, since the final £2m generates no further tax credit, if all £10m of core expenditure was spent in the UK the total tax credit would still be worth £2m, or, on average, 20%.

For films with core expenditure greater than £20m, lower rates apply, but the principle is the same.

Remember that the tax credit is not a straight rebate of production expenditure? Remember that 'if' from above? It is important to highlight that it is only *if* the film production company and the transactions it enters into are structured correctly that a loss that can be surrendered for a cash payment can be assured. Getting the structure right needs to be done from the outset. Restructuring the arrangements mid-way through the production to secure the tax credit will be extremely difficult. Now that's what I call a golden *if*!

Cashin-in

Provided that everything is in order, HMRC is obliged to pay the tax credit on the later of the completion of their enquiries or nine months after the end of the company's accounting period, which can be a long time after the wrap party.

In practice, tax credits are typically being paid within a matter of weeks after being claimed, but this depends on which office the claim is sent to. Unlike certification by the UKFC, there is no central unit within HMRC to deal with the tax credit and to dispense advice, so whether a claim is processed quickly may depend on whether the tax inspector assigned to the production company is familiar with the relief. Tax inspectors and companies are normally married up on the basis of postcodes, so it may be an advantage to have a registered office address in an area where a relatively large number of other film companies are registered.

Signing-off

The process has been presented above as sequential steps: first get certification, then proceed to FA 2006, then collect your cash. There are however two important practical considerations that you should bear in mind.

First, the tests are not completely distinct and apply over periods that overlap, so a producer can't afford to ignore the requirements of FA 2006 and focus exclusively on the Cultural Test or qualifying under a treaty; decisions made before even interim or provisional certification is received can scupper the ability to claim the tax credit months or even years further down the line. If you're not confident about your understanding of both certification and FA 2006, get appropriate advice, and get it early. A brief dialogue with a good accountant who knows about filmmaking before you prep the film can save a lot of time and money after the film is in the can.

Second, who pays the sparks whilst all this is going on? There may be exceptions (animation, perhaps), but the reality is that the tax credit is paid too late to be used to fund the film it relates to. For most independent productions, a third party will have to be found that has the resources to lend against the prospective value of the tax credit, and this changes the rules of the game. In particular, it is highly unlikely that any financier is going to be comfortable lending against a tax credit on a film that only scores 16 out of 31 points on the Cultural Test, or one that is willing to cash-flow a film that is spending the bare minimum 25% of core expenditure in the UK.

Financiers will tend to limit their risk. Even if a film has enough points and core UK expenditure to satisfy them that there is a margin for error, a producer may find that they are only offered a percentage of the potential tax credit. Financiers will discount the tax credit's value to allow for unforeseen reductions in its ultimate value, and the interest cost or fees that they are likely to charge.

Against that, there are ways that can be used to leverage the tax credit into more sophisticated offerings to investors, perhaps using another tax break such as an Enterprise Investment Scheme, but that increases the complexity even further.

Even taken on its own, this is still a very new, very complex relief and I've only covered a fraction of the detail associated with it. I've also tried to focus on those points that are relevant to filmmakers with projects in development, for when a film reaches the preparation stage and is taking shape, the UKFC, accountants, lawyers, financiers and even tax inspectors can represent good sources of advice and can help to fine-tune the arrangements. Use them, but bear in mind that everyone is still in the tax credit learning curve, and don't put too much faith in those headlines!

Mike Kelly established the Chartered Accountancy firm Northern Alliance in 2006, having previously gained a range of public and private sector experience in Film – including assisting in planning and executing the extension of Warner Bros' local language production throughout Europe and Asia, and helping with the establishment of the UK Film Council's long-term financial plans, its finance and accounting processes and the creation of the nine Regional Screen Agencies in England. Mike is also a guest lecturer at the Film Business Academy at Cass Business School. He began his career at Price Waterhouse, worked throughout Europe, Japan and the USA for the international logistics firm TNT, and was Group Accountant at Thames Television PLC prior to working in the film industry. If you have any queries regarding the tax credit, Mike can be reached via info@northern-alliance.co.uk.

Film finance companies and accountancy firms

To state the obvious, major financial funds and private investments of this kind are generally not geared towards the new filmmaker, but rather towards producers and filmmakers with proven track records and developed projects.

Aurelius

3 Lower James Street, Soho, London W1F 9EH
tel 020-7287 1900 *fax* 020-7287 2314
website www.aureliuscapital.com
Group Director Kaspar Strandskov

Specialist banking adviser and deal broker in the entertainment and media industries. Aurelius uses an international network of film financiers, equity, banks, national subsidies and other financing methods to provide production finance for film. The company works with producers with proven track records and strong established connections across the film industry who have developed projects. Aurelius also works with games producers and companies.

Baker Street Media Finance

96 Baker Street, London W1U 6TJ
tel 020-7487 3677 *fax* 020-7487-5667
email enquiries@bakerstreetfinance.tv
website www.bakerstreetfinance.tv

Specialises in the co-production, financing and structuring of British feature films, and British qualifying international co-productions. Baker Street arranges and manages a series of private investor funds for film and television production. The funds are structured to utilise income tax reliefs whereby investors can obtain a tax deduction in the first year of investment. Along with numerous television productions, the company has co-produced some 27 feature films alongside major production companies and studios as well as industry bodies such as the UK Film Council, Scottish Screen, and the Australian Film Finance Corporation.

Draft finance plans must be submitted with scripts. Supporting materials such as draft budgets and schedules should also be included, and projects should be commercially viable. See website for further information.

Credits include: *My Summer of Love*, *Green Street*, *Bloody Sunday*.

Film Finances Limited

15 Conduit Street, London W1S 2XJ
tel 020-7629 6557 *fax* 020-7491 7530
email contact@filmfinances.co.uk
website www.ffi.com
UK Managing Director Graham Easton

Film Finances was formed in the UK in the 1950s, to provide Completion Guarantees (which protect investors against films which overrun or go over budget). Now has offices all over the world.

Future Films Group

25 Noel Street, London W1F 8GX
tel 020-7434 6600 *fax* 020-7434 6633
website www.futurefilmgroup.com
Chief Executive Tim Levy *Business Development Manager* Carla Ash

Film financing partner for feature film production. Future Film Group prefers to work with producers on films which already have partial finance attached, and can help source remaining non-recoupable financing through the investment community. They can also help producers to integrate funds through new financing methods, co-production, distribution and development activity, post-production facilities and equity funding.

Grosvenor Park Media Limited

53-54 Grosvenor Street, London W1K 3HU
tel 020-7529 2500 *fax* 020-7529 2511
email dan.taylor@grosvenorpark.com
website www.grosvenorpark.com
Managing Director Daniel JB Taylor

A leading provider of tax-based film finance to producers in the UK and around the world. In more than 20 years in film and television financing and international co-productions, Grosvenor Park has raised more than $5 billion for over 400 film and television productions. Co-production services include: structuring and management (from script analysis, travel and shooting logistics, to creative elements); knowledge of and compliance with treaties and European Convention; application and lobbying for government certification and subsidies; budget and cost report management; post-production supervision and management; and a full range of financing services.

Ingenious Film & Television Limited

100 Pall Mall, London SW1Y 5NQ
tel 020-7024 3600 *fax* 020-7024 3601
email enquiries@ingeniousmedia.co.uk
website www.ingeniousmedia.co.uk

Commercial Director Duncan Reid *CEO* Thomas Gardiner

A fully integrated group of companies that advises and invests solely in the media and entertainment sectors. Founded in 1998, Ingenious is one of the UK's leading investors in these sectors. Services include: private equity investments; project financing; and a range of media consultancy services on strategy, finance and operations.

International Film Guarantors

19 Margaret Street, London W1W 8RR
tel 020-7636 8855 *fax* 020-7323 9356
email ukinfo@ifgbonds.co.uk
website www.ifgbonds.co.uk

One of the leading providers of completion bonds for feature films in the USA and UK. Work ranges from major studio films to smaller indie productions.

Invicta Capital

33 St James' Square, London SW1Y 4JS
tel 020-7661 9376 *fax* 020-7661 9892
website www.invictacapital.co.uk
Managing Director Neil Bamford

Invicta advises private clients and corporations on equity and tax-efficient investments in film production and distribution. It has a strong track record in helping put together complex international financing packages.

MagicGate

c/o StarGate Capital Management Limited,
62-65 Trafalgar Square, London WC2N 5DY
tel 020-7024 9740
email david.kraftman@magicgate.co.uk
website www.magicgate.co.uk

Offers film investment services for the investor community that minimise investment risk by demanding that a film have many of the qualities which contribute to typically successful films: star actors, filmmakers with proven track records, good scripts (as judged by an advisory committee). Producers may complete a pre-application through the website, but *no unsolicited scripts will be received* whatsoever. Only applications that meet the necessary criteria will be seriously considered.

Matrix Film Finance LLP

1 Jermyn Street, London SW1Y 4UH
tel 020-7925 3300
email info@matrix-film-finance.co.uk
website www.matrixgroup.co.uk

Offers financial services to film producers; also offers to UK investors, film partnerships as a way of investing in British feature films. Previous credits include: *Ae Fond Kiss*, *Where the Truth Lies* and *Alexander*.

Movision Entertainment Ltd

Kingfisher House, Hurstwood Grange,
Hurstwood Lane, Haywards Heath,
West Sussex RH17 7QX
tel 0870-389 1415 *fax* 0870-389 1410
website www.movision.co.uk

Film partnerships for UK investors to invest in a wide range of British feature films. Credits include: *Beowulf and Grendel*, *Head in the Clouds*.

Northern Alliance Ltd

131-151 Great Titchfield Street, London W1W 5BB
tel 020-3008 5887
email info@northern-alliance.co.uk
website www.northern-alliance.co.uk
Contact Mike Kelly (Director)

A Chartered Accountancy firm providing accounting, tax, financial, management and business consulting services to private and public sector organisations and individuals, especially to those operating in the media, entertainment and creative industries. The company has substantial practical knowledge of how the private and public sectors work. Its range of experience extends throughout Europe, Asia and North America. Northern Alliance Ltd is a member of the Institute of Chartered Accountants Practice Assurance Scheme, which has been designed to demonstrate to the business community and the wider public the Institute's commitment to upholding and developing public standards that command public confidence. Although Northern Alliance does not provide finance for filmmaking, it can assist producers with their finance plans including advising on how to maximise the benefit of the tax credit and how to establish Enterprise Investment Schemes.

Park Caledonia Media Ltd

4 Park Gardens, Glasgow G3 7YE
tel 0141-332 9100 *fax* 0141-332 5641
email wstevenson@parkcaledonia.biz
website www.parkcaledonia.biz

Handles film finance for the The Park Caledonian Associates.

Prescience Film Finance

Marlborough House, 45 Wycombe End,
Beaconsfield, Buckinghamshire HP9 1LZ
tel (01494) 670737 *fax* (01494) 670740
email info@presciencefilmfinance.co.uk
website www.presciencefilmfinance.co.uk

Prescience is a specialist film company that works with producers, distributors and sales agents to make quality specialist feature films. Has ongoing relationships with companies such as Archer Films, Ecosse Films and Gruber Films.

Random Harvest Pictures – see entry for AMC Pictures on page 132.

Scion Films

tel 020-7025 8003 *fax* 020-7025 8133
email info@scionfilms.com
website www.scionfilms.com

Co-Chairmen & Founders Jeff Abberley, Julia Blackman

Scion Films is a member of the Scion family of businesses, which encompass structured finance, asset management, film finance and production and legal services. The company has produced, co-produced or provided financial backing for some of the most prestigious and critically acclaimed British films, including: *Pride & Prejudice*, *Tristram Shandy: A Cock and Bull Story* and *The Constant Gardener*. Opportunities for investment are provided through sister company, Scion Financial Partners Limited.

Scotts Atlantic

3 De Walden Court, 85 New Cavendish Street, London W1W 6XD
tel 020-7307 9300 *fax* 020-7307 9292
email info@scottsatlantic.com
website www.scottsatlantic.com

Scotts Atlantic raises finance for feature films and structures international co-productions. Key executives of the company have structured more than 30 co-productions in the last 4 years and completed £600m of film finance in this time.

UKFS

7 Marlborough Place, Brighton BN1 1UB
tel (01273) 690285 *fax* (01273) 679954
email into@ukfs-online.co.uk
website www.ukfsfilms.com

Budgeting a film for the market

Chris Collins gives new producers and director/producers an experienced insider's tips for drafting realistic film budgets.

Filmmaking is a mysterious art. It's at once a combination of very practical things (how much things actually cost and how to use them) and very intangible ones (the effect and value of talent), so that experience of the process can seem to be a bit like bargaining in a souk – the actual value and cost of the project appears to be whatever can be negotiated at any one time depending on the mood and skill or stubbornness of the people making the transaction. Trying to unravel the mystery and therefore giving your project a marketability and consequent viability is the critical part of the process for a producer; it's the part which determines whether that beautiful script remains 'in development' or makes it into production.

Films and their market value

Knowing how and at what value to pitch a project is a delicate combination of several things, all of which have an important part to play in the process. In an ideal world the process would be simple: a script would be written; it would be costed; then the producer would raise the money and the project would get made. Unfortunately, it's almost always at the juncture of script completion and costing that the trouble starts. One of the most frustrating features of filmmaking is that films always seem to cost more to make than there is money available, or more than the market values the project.

What is the market?

The market varies at different stages of the journey of any film. At the point of raising finance, potential investors are its market. Your sales agent will assess the film's commercial prospects to another market: international distributors. Then finally, when your film is distributed, the box office revenue determines value to the public – the ultimate market for the film.

But how does a producer assess the market value of the project? This can depend on the nature of the project. For instance, there is a general consensus amongst financiers and the industry that a first feature by an unproven filmmaker should cost a million pounds. It doesn't matter what is written on the 100 script pages or what the aesthetic or casting ambitions of the project are; the expectation is that it should cost a million pounds. Many new writers, producers and directors waste a lot of time developing projects that are too ambitious for these market expectations, and so the projects flounder.

To a filmmaker who has made a couple of self-financed or very low-budget shorts, this may sound like an amazing amount of money. But the truth is that at a million pounds,very few feature films can be made with adequate production values, and the time and freedom that allow a filmmaker to establish a worthwhile creative vision. Micro-budget films notwithstanding, this is very much the bottom rung of the film financing ladder.

The top of the ladder is relatively high, although very few UK films would go higher than £20 million. At that level, the market of potential investors in the UK is generally small, and films with budgets on a higher level would inevitably have a high proportion of their finance from a US-based studio, or through a US-backed subsidiary such as Working Title or DNA. These would have to be very strong commercial projects with a high level of talent attached. To finance a film solely from the UK market inevitably means involving a combination of a broadcaster, the UK Film Council, possibly a regional fund, a bank, a distributor and, until in recent years, an equity fund; often more than five different parties who all have to be cajoled and persuaded into position in a delicate operation that can take years to complete.

The key to bringing the finance together is the co-operation of a sales agent, and the real piece of magic in the operation is the set of figures or sales estimates that is produced by them, and which places a value for the project on each territory in the world. Their total on all of the territories will determine the theoretical value of the project, and therefore show the investors the likelihood of getting their money back should they come on board. These figures are often conservative because not all UK films achieve the quality, and therefore the sales results, that they could in the international marketplace. More importantly, the estimated figures always fall short of what the producer needs to raise in order to make the project in the way that the script and the director's ambitions require. Even at low-budget levels, these figures become the sacred object before which all parties bow down and worship – even though experience tells everyone involved that they are often wildly inaccurate and relate only remotely to actual sales achieved. Faced with the value of the estimated sales figures, the producer will often enter into a painful process of trying to reduce the budget while maintaining the ambitions of the package – a process in which everything can get fatally compromised.

How to achieve money/value synthesis

Quite quickly, a producer should be able to develop an instinctive and holistic overview of the process, and get a real feel for how to balance the cost/value dialectic. Yet it is surprising how often even very experienced industry practitioners will be shocked and amazed that the project which they have been developing with you for the last two years works out to a budget level twice what they thought it should be (or wanted it to be). Oh, and even at half the value, you'd better think of casting it with much higher-level actors than the ones you believe you can get, otherwise it's not even worth discussing. As a producer, you've really got to get a feel for the parameters that will ultimately determine your project, or it's going to be a difficult process. Naivety goes a long way – especially with your first feature project – but if you've done some background work along the way, then you'll find it easier to get the project financed and made, and be better able to manage the expectations of all involved.

For me, most of the difficulties originate in the development process. There is a widespread feeling that the ideas and writing stage should not be limited; that one should be able to think freely in order not to constrain the creative process. To a point, that's true. Writers loathe the idea of having to contemplate how much that nightclub scene with its 1000 extras might cost, or whether it might even be achievable. Of course, it's very important in development for the producer to keep everyone motivated and happy. However, without setting some basic parameters, it's easy to find yourself with a script full of very expensive and ambitious situations and scenes that everybody has invested a lot of time and creative energy in, and that is very difficult to change.

For a new producer, getting an idea of what the money will buy you at one million, two million, four million, etc. is essential. It's easy enough to find out what UK films cost from other producers (although remember that everyone fudges the actual figures downwards), and to watch similar films and talk to the people involved so that you get a good overview of what the current practice is. Knowing the details of other films – how many shooting days took place, what the format was, the number of crew members involved – really gives you a base of knowledge that can inform the approach to your own film, and help you guide the development process in the right direction. Once you've got an idea of different scales, then you can select the one that is right for you and your project, and drive it towards that goal.

It's easy to be seduced into saying that you can make a project for the figure people want to hear. Remember, though: you have then got to deliver. Since you are going to invest up to two years of your hard work in the film, you really must give yourself the resources to make it well and to give it a real chance in its final marketplace. It's critical that you don't pitch too low, and that you are realistic. I've had many discussions in the last few years about how to reduce the budget of a project which has been developed in, say, the two to three million budget range. Inevitably, someone will have a revelation and say, "Let's shoot it digitally – then we can make it for a million," whereas the actual cost benefit of changing formats is only a relatively small amount. *Real* budget reduction can only be achieved by rewriting to scale and a radical rethink of the aesthetic ambitions of the director. Once a project has found its form, its very hard to reduce the budget by a substantial amount. It's easy to shave thousands from a budget, but millions are very difficult without starting from scratch.

Producers sometimes seem to think that the cost of the film is not their responsibility, and that their role is simply creative – developing the script and the package and then turning the film over to a line producer to make the numbers work. Yet without a really good knowledge of the practical aspects of the process and the costs, it's very hard to control a film through the critical decision-making moments in production, and to effectively engage in discussions about how to do things and how to shape the film in the most cost-effective way.

A good way for a new producer to find the right path for their project is to enlist the support of an experienced executive producer who can guide them through the process. With this in mind, it is important to try and get someone with expertise at the right budget level. Experience comes at a cost, and people get used to doing things in a particular way with a lot of support which – if you are trying to make a low-budget first film – doesn't help. Equally, there are a lot of very experienced and sympathetic people who have made all of the mistakes that you will also make and have learned from them and really want to share their expertise in a helpful way. Producers are often very approachable and will give a lot of their time to advise new filmmakers without requiring payment.

For those people who want to get a really good overview of the ultimate market potential for their film, it's possible to access box-office statistics via websites such as **www.imdb.com**. Subscription costs a small amount but offers a wealth of detail on many aspects of a film – from the budget through to really detailed box-office revenues. But beware. Fascinating as these statistics are, it can be dispiriting to work back to the revenues that you as a producer might receive: few films go into profit. The stats nevertheless can be useful in helping you to develop the film that you are making into a more audience-friendly one ... one which just might give you more of a chance of success.

Chris Collins has 15 years of experience in trying to square the circle of director's expectations, available resources and the goal of making films at the appropriate scale. He has worked in development, as a line producer, producer and executive producer. Among the films he has guided to fruition are John Maybury's *Love is the Devil*, Jasmin Dizdar's *Beautiful People*, Pawel Pawlikowski's *Last Resort* and *My Summer of Love* (BAFTA for Best British Film in 2004), and Francesca Joseph's *Tomorrow La Scala*. He has recently produced (with Alison Owen) the eagerly awaited adaptation of *Brick Lane*, directed by Sarah Gavron. He is Executive Producer on Duane Hopkins' debut feature, *Better Things*.

Additional funding schemes and awards

The following organisations manange funds that have very specific targets, and limited eligibility criteria based on an applicant's local or social group, or the relevance of the project to a wider community.

Awards for All

2 St James' Gate, Newcastle Upon Tyne NE1 4BE
tel 0845-600 2040
email general.enquiries@awardsforall.org.uk
Apex House, 3 Embassy Drive, Calthorpe Road, Edgbaston, Birmingham B15 1TR
website www.awardsforall.org.uk

A Lottery grants scheme for local communities. Programmes differ across the 4 countries of the UK, but range from £500 to £10,000. Grants are for projects which benefit the community and increase access to arts, culture and sport for a wider range of people. Film projects supported generally must be for the good of the wider community. Newcastle office deals with projects from the Eastern, North East, North West, South East or Yorkshire and the Humber regions. Birmingham office deals with projects based in the East Midlands, West Midlands, London or South West regions.

Big Lottery Fund

1 Plough Place, London EC4A 1DE
tel 0845-410 2030 (Advice Line)
website www.biglotteryfund.org.uk

Big Lottery Fund was established in 2004 to manage Lottery funds that support a wide range of activities which are of benefit to communities and to health, education and the environment. Awards for All is one of the open application funding schemes, as is the Young People's Fund, which is partially aimed at getting young people more involved in the development of their communities. Funds would not be appropriate for most filmmakers, but if a project has strong community benefits, it would be worth seeking further information.

Borough Production Funds

website www.filmlondon.org.uk

Film London (listed on page 54) supports production schemes in a number of London's Boroughs. In addition to the funds for Hackney, Newham and Tower Hamlets mentioned in the listing for Film London East (see page 73), Wandsworth, Greenwich, Enfield and Westminster also have awards for filmmakers living or working in the Borough:

Greenwich fund@greenwichfilms.demon.co.uk
Enfield julia.harriman@enfield.gov.uk
Wandsworth srusso@wandsworth.gov.uk
Westminster paula@cwac.org.uk

The Channel Four British Documentary Foundation Fund

PO Box 51376, London N1 6WX
tel 020-7366 5650 *fax* 020-7366 5652
email info@britdoc.org
website www.britdoc.org
Chief Executive Jess Search

The Foundation was set up in part by ex-Channel 4 commissioners with funds from Channel 4. It forms part of Channel 4's mission to support documentary both on and off TV, and sits alongside other new initiatives from Channel 4 – such as FourDocs, a new broadband channel, and More4, the digital channel launched in October 2005. The Foundation has a firstlook deal with Channel 4 on all films funded by the Foundation.

The Foundation takes all applications for funding for documentary shorts and features through the website above, with an easy submission process for filmmakers. It also runs a special fund in conjunction with the ICA and Channel 4 called BRITDOCARTS, which is for visual artists who want to make documentary work of between 3 and 30 minutes and for up to £30,000. The fund is for any artist working in visual, video, performance or installation art.

Film London East

tel 020-7613 7676
email ambur.beg@filmlondon.org.uk
website www.east.filmlondon.org.uk

Set up to support the development of the moving image industries in East London through training, networking, skills development and funding schemes. Production funds are available to filmmakers who live or work in Tower Hamlets, Hackney and Newham. Funds usually range from £1000 to £5000, with the Newham Short Production Scheme going up to £7500 for a short film.

First Light

Unit 6, Third Floor, The Bond,
180–182 Fazeley Street, Birmingham B5 5SE
tel 0121-753 4866

email info@firstlightmovies.com
website www.firstlightmovies.com
Chief Executive Pip Eldridge

First Light is the Lottery-funded body set up to fund and inspire films made in the UK by people aged 5–18 years. It has helped fund the production of more than 600 films involving more than 9000 young people. First Light will fund films of any genre of 5–10 minutes' duration (depending on the scheme) where young people take an active role in all aspects of the production process. Films must be mainly digital productions, should be shot entirely in the UK, and must be for the benefit of teaching the young people who work on the film about the production process. First Light also holds an annual Awards Ceremony in London each year.

Glasgow Media Access Centre

3rd Floor, 34 Albion Street, Glasgow, Lanarkshire G1 1LH
tel 0141-553 2620 *fax* 0141-553 2660
website www.g-mac.co.uk

An open-access facility for young Scottish filmmakers; runs 2 short film production initiatives – Cineworks and Digicult – as well as Little Pictures for new filmmakers. The schemes are supported by BBC Scotland, Scottish Screen and UK Film Council.

- **Cineworks** Entry-level scheme with funds of £8000 to £10,000
- **Digicult** A Talent Development Pool which can support projects to the tune of £6000-£8000
- **Little Pictures** Can offer new filmmakers up to £1000 plus in-kind support

Heritage Lottery Fund (HLF)

7 Holbein Place, London SW1W 8NR
tel 020-7591 6000 *fax* 020-7591 6001
email enquire@hlf.org.uk
website www.hlf.org.uk

HLF enables communities to celebrate, look after and learn more about the UK's diverse heritage. More than £3.6 billion has been awarded to projects which attempt to achieve these aims. HLF awards grants to not-for-profit organisations seeking to fund relevant projects: archives may receive funding if projects improve access, while filmmaking projects can only be supported if they are part of a wider aim to increase understanding of and knowledge about heritage within the community. Application guidelines are available on the website.

The Jerwood Charitable Trust

website www.jerwood.org

Charity dedicated to funding visual arts and education. The Jerwood Foundation is responsible for the capital grants of the organisation. Funding is *not* open to individuals. See the website for details of the Documentary Award, which Jerwood presents with Sheffield International Film Festival.The Jerwood Charitable Foundation was established by the Jerwood Foundation in 1999 and awards the Jerwood Painting Prize, Jerwood Applied Arts Prize and Jerwood Choreography Award. In 2005 the Jerwood Foundation completed a capital endowment to the Jerwood Charitable Foundation, making it totally independent.

Pocket Shorts

c/o BLINK, The Old Caretaker's House, JL Brierley Mill, Quay Street, Huddersfield, West Yorkshire HD1 6QT
tel (01484) 301805
email lisa@blinkmedia.org
website www.pocketshorts.co.uk

Pocket Shorts is an innovative production funding scheme started in 2002, and giving early-career filmmakers the opportunity to make original content for mobile phones. Working with a sister company in Scotland, Pocket Shorts has commissioned more than 30 films since its launch. Commissions are designed to be easily shared between mobile phones, and so the duration is limited to 60 seconds. Bluevend, the scheme's Bluetooth 'vending machine', allows for the wireless distribution of free content and is set up at key international film festivals. Pocket Shorts is dependent on annual funding; refer to www.pocketshorts.co.uk and www.blinkmedia.org for updates about submission procedures and deadlines.

The Prince's Trust

18 Park Square East, London NW1 4LH
tel 0800-842842
website www.princes-trust.org.uk

A UK charity set up to help people aged between 14 and 30 develop skills and realise potential. The charity aims to help people who have previously struggled in school, been young offenders, or been in care. Offers a number of development awards which are designed to help its target group of young people to fund training, education or skills development.

UnLtd

c/o Head Office, 123 Whitecross Street, London EC1Y 8JJ
tel 0845-850 1122
email info@unltd.org.uk
website www.unltd.org.uk
Chief Executive John Rafferty

UnLtd is supported by the Millennium Awards Trust, and funds projects by 'social entrepreneurs', or people who make a major difference in their community. There are separate awards for start-up projects (Level 1) and for projects which are already established (Level 2). Level 1 awards range from £500 to £5000, and Level 2 awards from £10,000 to £20,000. Funds are for individuals, rather than organisations, whose projects have a clear benefit to the community. Projects should not promote political or religious beliefs.

Warp X

email submissions@warpx.co.uk, info@warpx.co.uk
website www.warpx.co.uk
Directors Robin Gutch, Mark Herbert

Low-budget feature film slate managed by Warp X with £3m from the Lottery via UK Film Council's New Cinema Fund, and in collaboration with Film Four; also with support from EM Media and Screen Yorkshire.

Warp X is an offshoot of Warp Films, and has a distribution alliance with Optimum Releasing. Warp X intends to produce 7 films over 3 years; the films are made digitally and on budgets of between £400,000 and £800,000. Warp X intends to build on Warp's previous successes, such as Shane Meadows' *Dead Man's Shoes*, and Chris Cunningham's *Rubber Johnny*. Warp X is looking for films which aim to "use cutting-edge digital technology and low-budget production methods to make high-value movies that can reach cinema audiences across the world".

Filmmakers must have a high level of experience in making films to be eligible for the scheme. If your project has already been rejected by UK Film Council or Film Four, then Warp X is unlikely to consider it. The joint objectives of the New Cinema Fund and FilmFour for Warp X are:

• to source a diverse range of filmmaking talent and mentors;
• to provide new opportunities to increase participation of groups currently under-represented in the UK film industry, such as writers, directors, producers and actors who are disabled, female and/or from black and visible minority ethnic groups;
• to encourage filmmakers to explore social issues of disability, cultural/ethnic diversity and social exclusion;
• to create progression routes into the UK film industry for identified filmmaking talent;
• to encourage established filmmaking talent to reinvest their expertise in helping develop new talent.

To apply, send a 1-2 page outline pitch for your film, and also attach a short biography of the key members of the creative team to the email above. Screenplays will not be accepted at first stage.

The Wellcome Trust

Gibbs Building, 215 Euston Road, London NW1 2BE
tel 020-7611 8888 *fax* 020-7611 8545
email contact@wellcome.ac.uk
website www.wellcome.ac.uk

The Wellcome Trust is an independent charity funding research to improve human and animal health. Established in 1936 and with an endowment of around £13 billion, it is the UK's largest non-governmental source of funds for biomedical research. It contributes to Science and Art initiatives encouraging interactions with biomedical science through visual art, music, digital media, film, creative writing and the performing arts.

Overseas funding

Australian Film Commission

Level 4, 150 William Street, Woolloomooloo, Sydney NSW 2011, Australia
tel ++61 2 9321 6444 *fax* ++61 2 9357 3737
email info@afc.gov.au
website www.afc.gov.au

The Australian Government has entered into official co-production arrangements with the United Kingdom and Northern Ireland, and Ireland. A film or television programme approved as an official co-production is regarded as a national production of each of the co-producing countries, and is therefore eligible to apply for any benefits or programmes of assistance available.

An official international co-production must be made under the terms of one of the arrangements in place between Australia and the co-producing countries. There must be a producer from each of the countries, and a balance between the Australian financial equity in the project and the Australian creative components.

HAF – Hong Kong-Asia Film Financing Forum

7/F, United Chinese Bank Building, 31-37 Des Voeux Road Central, Hong Kong
tel (852) 2970 3300 *fax* (852) 2970 3011
email info@haf.org.hk
website www.haf.org.hk/haf

A film project market that aims to bring the most exciting Asian filmmakers with upcoming film projects to Hong Kong for international co-production ventures, by meeting some of the world's premier film financiers, producers, bankers, distributors, buyers and funding bodies.

IFC Productions

The Independent Film Channel LLC, 11 Penn Plaza, 15th Floor, New York, NY 10001, USA
fax ++1 516 803 4506
website www.ifc.com

The production arm of the Independent Film Channel in the US, IFC Productions acts as an equity partner with *established* indie talent to produce low-budget ($500K to $4M total) films. IFC Productions considers *only* fully packaged projects. To submit a feature project proposal, send a 2-3 page proposal to the fax number above, containing a synopsis of the script/story and with brief bios of the primary people attached to the project (producers, writer, director or other talent), along with an outline of your total budget and the amount of financing you are seeking.

Japan Foundation

Russell Square House, 10-12 Russell Square, London WC1B 5EH
tel 020-7436 6695 *fax* 020-7323 4888
email junko.takekawa@jpf.org.uk
website www.jpf.org.uk
Cineaste Programme Officer Junko Takekawa

Japan Foundation has a Film and TV Production Support Programme which offers financial support for the production of films, TV programmes and other audio-visual materials that promote a deeper understanding of Japan and Japanese culture abroad. Grant assistance takes the form of subsidies towards the production costs and will not be more than 5 million yen (£25,000), and not more than 50% of total production costs. Projects must be viable (for example, those with a television commission or match funding will be preferred), and the fund is open to companies only (not individuals). The application deadline is in November of each year; details can be obtained from the website but applicants *must* contact The Japan Foundation before submitting an application, to make sure that the project is appropriate for this fund.

Roy W Dean Grants

c/o From the Heart Productions, 1455 Mandalay Beach Road, Oxnard, California 93035-2845, USA
tel ++1 805-984 009
email Caroleedean@att.net
website www.fromtheheartproductions.com

The Roy W Dean Grants are run through From the Heart Productions, a not-for-profit organisation dedicated to funding films that are "unique and make a contribution to society". Started in 1992 by Carole Dean, the fund was named after her late father and is open to filmmakers from all over the world. The Writers' Grant gives screenwriters 4-6 weeks away in rural New Zealand, with a stipend for living expenses, to work on developing a project or project ideas. The organisation offers a similar grant for people with a film/video project to edit. Deadlines are posted on the website homepage.

Sundance Documentary Fund

8530 Wiltshire Blvd, 3rd Floor, Beverly Hills, California 90211, USA
tel ++ 1 310 360 1981 *fax* ++ 1 310 360 1969
email sdf@sundance.org
website www.sundance.org
Programme Leader Cara Mertes

Dedicated to supporting US and international documentary films and videos focused on current and significant issues in contemporary human rights, freedom of expression, social justice and civil liberties. The fund accepts projects dealing with contemporary issues, but cannot accept historical projects, biographies or series. Individuals from around the world can apply, with projects ranging from hour-long to long-format features. Applicants must have creative and budgetary control over the proposed documentary. There are 2 categories: Development funding, with grants up to $15,000; and Work in Progress, with grants normally ranging from $20,000 to $50,000.

World Cinema Fund

c/o Berlin International Film Festival,
Potsdamer Strasse 5, 10785 Berlin, Germany
tel 49 30 259 20 516 *fax* 49 30 259 20 529
website www.berlinale.de

Launched in co-operation with the German Federal Cultural Foundation, the World Cinema Fund supports filmmakers from transition countries. Up until 2007 the focus has been on Latin America, Africa, the Middle East and Central Asia. The fund offers an annual budget of up to €600,000 to help realise feature-length films and creative documentaries with a strong cultural identity. Production companies working with a director from one of the specified regions can apply for a maximum of €100,000, but must have a German partner. Distribution funds are also available for up to €15,0000 per project.

Getting a documentary commission for TV

Executive producer and former commissioner **Jacquie Lawrence** gives new filmmakers an introduction to getting a factual project made in the UK.

Be realistic about today's factual commissioning

Chances are, if you are passionate about the documentary form, you will have had many a heated debate about the distinctions between documentary and reality television. For the purposes of this article, the definition of factual programming will include any genre that is (to use an American term) 'non-scripted'. This includes documentaries, factual formats, current affairs and reality television. The reason I have used such a broad definition is because the main broadcasters – BBC, ITV, C4 and five – tend to umbrella these genres under the heading 'factual programming'. In the same way, most independent factual producers will produce a veritable smorgasbord of factual fare.

It is rare for anyone to limit themselves to the pure documentary form. To put it bluntly, you cannot be too snobbish or purist about documentary production if you want to get commissioned by European or American broadcasters. Take, for example, Morgan Spurlock and his highly authored film *Supersize Me*. Although it was a 'pure' documentary, it spawned a successful and lucrative factual format that was commissioned by FX in the US and subsequently sold to numerous international territories. There was nothing precious about his approach to the documentary commissioning process; in collaboration with a broadcaster, he took the premise of his documentary and applied to it a factual format that both entertained and informed.

Getting a 'pure' documentary project off the ground can take years, and commissioners and producers are more likely to get involved with a filmmaker who has a track record. Ben Gale, BBC Commissioning Editor for Factual Features and Formats, advises directors

Channels and commissioning – insider's wisdom

We spoke with several of the UK's top factual commissioners to get their advice for filmmakers wishing to submit a proposal. See full contact information in the listings at the end of this article.

Channel Four Factual Commissioning

Channel Four's factual programming remains a gateway for emerging filmmakers, whether they are at assistant level in television production or film/art school graduates. At an open day, Angus McQueen Head of C4 Documentaries said: "Part of the department's role is to nurture talent. We are not frightened of taking a first-time director. If nobody at the Channel knows them, we will think harder about giving them a 120-minute film, but we have a ladder of programme slots so we can try people out".

Two particularly good starting points for new filmmakers are the New Talent Strand commissioned by Sarah Mulvey and 3 Minute Wonder commissioned by Kate Vogal.

More4 Factual Commissioning

The factual commissioning teams across Channel 4 commission programmes for the More4 schedule so you should direct your idea to the relevant department and specify that it is for More4 via the online proposal system. The More4 commissioners do not receive any proposals directly themselves but will communicate regularly with the commissioning editors across the channel about More4's programming requirements. They are looking for factual programming ideas that have an innovative and challenging take on the world.

www.channel4.com/corporate/4producers/commissioning

to seek realistic introductory routes into television documentary. Working on an existing programme such as *Airport* or *Children's Hospital*, he says, is like the 'nursery slope' on which to learn one's craft (see **www.dfgdocs.com/Resources/Articles/10.aspx** for more tips from commissioners).

Many commissioners agree that these shows are also good places to hone your own sense of style and voice. Adam Barker, ex-C4 Commissioner and now Head of Factual at Diverse Productions, adds: "Just because the market is flooded with format and reality shows right now, doesn't mean you give up on your own unique authorship. Find a way to smuggle it into the everyday work you do, and keep your pet projects alive until someone agrees to make them." Bridget Deane was a jobbing Assistant Producer who was given the chance to direct an episode of *Wife Swap*. She did so, infusing it with her idiosyncratic observational eye, and it became the award-winning episode of the series. This got her noticed, and she has since been encouraged to develop her own documentary ideas.

What are the commissioning opportunities for UK filmmakers?

If you apply yourself to the marketplace with an understanding of the needs of the commissioners, alongside passion and tenacity, there is a wealth of opportunity in domestic and international factual programming. Literally thousands of hours of factual programming are transmitted every year on the UK's terrestrial and non-terrestrial channels.

Think in broad terms. Don't just consider documentary and factual departments; familiarise yourself with the features, education, history, science, arts and religion departments. All the major broadcasters have these dedicated teams.

Don't limit yourself to the terrestrial channels either. There is now a whole host of cable/satellite broadcasters that commission factual programmes. Some of these, like the History Channel, National Geographic, Discovery and UK Documentary, are specifically created to transmit specialist factual fare only.

Other, more entertainment-driven cable/satellite broadcasters like Sky One and Living have made the foray into commissioning populist documentaries. Commissioning Editor for Factual at Sky One, Emma Read is convinced that cable/satellite broadcasters are able to take more risks with smaller companies and newer talent: "Non-terrestrials can work with smaller and newer companies because they are much more nimble, both with ideas and budgets. Their size means that they have lower overheads and much less dependence on having to clear large profit margins. They seem more imaginative with budgets and costs. I also think that smaller companies are less entrenched in particular and overly clichéd ways of thinking about programme ideas. They aren't always

Channels and commissioning – insider's wisdom

BBC One, Two, Three and Four Factual Commissioning

The BBC's website outlines each commissioner's programming priorities and offers links to factual programming departments across all BBC Channels. It is also a coherent guide to their independent commissioning process.

Todd Austin (Series Editor, *ONE Life*) gives advice to filmmakers looking to submit programme ideas: "a unique approach or a new methodology and a total dedication and passion for an idea always inspires commissioners and helps the new filmmaker to stand out from the many other bright, young things who want to make films. It's important for new filmmakers to find their own voice and to be able to show the commissioner they will bring something fresh".

www.bbc.co.uk/commissioning

thinking, 'Can I sell this format to other countries? Will I be able to make a profit out of the rights?'"

Each broadcaster has its own particular commissioning process, but all have the same aim: to get the most compelling factual programming on air. However, they also have specific schedule and remit needs. C4 and BBC2 and BBC3 tend to be more risky than BBC1, ITV and five, but all are looking for mainstream documentaries and factual formats that will attract 'volume' audiences. Every commissioner will expect any producer or filmmaker to make themselves aware of the output needs of the channel they are approaching before coming to them with programming ideas.

This intelligence is easy to come by; just watch their output! You can also log onto the commissioning websites. Commissioners are not shy about outlining exactly what works for them and what doesn't. Many of them have given us further information about what they look for, which we have included in the insets in this article. All broadcasters, including the non-terrestrials, have websites for producers, outlining their annual needs. At the risk of becoming a stalker, you can never know enough about a commissioning editor and his/her programming interests.

Can first-time filmmakers get original ideas commissioned?

The reality is that unless you have submitted your project through an initiative for first-time filmmakers, then you will be more successful in the commissioning process if you take your idea to a production company. This may be the company you are already working for – say, in an assistant capacity. Or it may be a company whose portfolio you admire. Most companies have a development department and may be open to your ideas. This book's useful inventory of production companies endeavours to note which ones are willing to listen to unsolicited ideas (see page 131).

Some channels *will* meet and greet new filmmakers. Richard Melman at the History Channel says, "I am happy to match good ideas and people with production companies," – but, as his comments suggest, most commissioners would expect a new filmmaker to be aligned with an experienced producer. Fenton Bailey, Managing Director of World of Wonder Productions, adds: "Go in with a production company who has relationships with and access to broadcasters and funding. But beware, the bigger ones cut hard 'take-it-or-leave-it' deals. It may be better to go with a smaller outfit with whom you can have a personal ongoing relationship and who has nurtured several first-time filmmakers."

Channels and commissioning – insider's wisdom

ITV Factual Commissioning

ITV's website provides information about how the commissioning teams work. There is no formal online submission system at ITV, so the best way to get your idea to the Channel is to email the commissioning editor directly, copying in their PA to be sure the idea won't get lost in the hundreds of emails they get every day.

Jane Rogerson (ITV Factual Features Controller) says, "most ideas which standout are those which have a clear premise and a clever grabby title. Those that feel fresh, 'of the moment' and with a strong character journey, are the ones most likely to get read. Don't waste time on a ten-page document - we just don't have the time to read it. I always look for something that reads like a compelling Radio Times billing in the first two paragraphs and then gives a sense of the journey's beginning, middle and end. That can usually be done in two pages. It's also best to channel your idea through someone who has an existing relationship with a commissioning editor; relationships where people trust each other are invaluable".

www.ITV.com

International markets and international co-production

Finally, do not forget the international market. Award-winning documentary producer Andre Singer, MD of West Park Pictures, points out: "There are many examples of projects that have succeeded on the international circuit, where the new talent has worked out that an idea might get a more sympathetic hearing abroad. They have been able to start a snowball effect by getting a little support from a number of broadcasters until the numbers make sense. It's not easy, but it has often worked and there are places and organisations that can help. An established production company with an existing chain of international contacts can help make it work on your behalf, or go it solo and invest in attending workshops, festivals and the occasional forum. There are many active ways of collaborating, such as the European Documentary Network, the Discovery Campus, Hot Docs, Sunny Side of the Doc, BritDoc, the Sheffield Documentary Film Festival, International Documentary Festival of Amsterdam."

The successful exportation of British factual formats like *Wife Swap* and *Brat Camp* to the American market has had a positive effect on the procurement of documentary funding from American broadcasters. Cable channel CINEMAX will license documentaries at the rough or fine-cut stage. The other main single-documentary funders in the USA are Discovery and HBO, although they primarily commission bigger, expensive films. A&E Films have a $50K annual prize award for documentaries in progress, whilst The Learning Channel Films is also a potential funder. PBS (public broadcasting) is another route; the best way in is via their funding body, ITVS.

five Factual Commissioning

five's programme controllers have clear remits on commissioning. Before submitting a programme idea, it's worth familiarising yourself with each individual controller's requirements to ensure that your proposal won't be dismissed out of hand. Visit their 'controller pages' to find out more about their remits and the type of programme ideas they are looking for. Once you have identified the relevant controller and are satisfied that your programme idea meets their basic requirements, submit your idea as instructed. They aim to respond within four weeks.

Chris Shaw, Senior Controller (News, Current Affairs and Docs) argues that, "as an new independent producer you have to persuade a relatively small number of commissioning editors that you alone can develop a particular idea and you can deliver that idea to the broadcaster as a quality programme or series of programmes. To compete with established suppliers and the big independents who have fairly unfettered access to broadcasting decision-makers, you would do well to note the following:

- have unique or exclusive access to an individual or organisation;
- bring total passion and commitment to the project;
- demonstrate a clear understanding of how this idea fits the broadcaster's needs and target audiences;
- and also, leave copycat ideas and reworking of existing formats to the big independents - smaller companies should focus on the original and unusual (that's why broadcasters cast their net wider)"

www.five.tv/aboutfive/producersnotes

Sky One Factual Commissioning

All factual programming submissions go through the Sky One website (there are no restrictions on length as long as you don't exceed 2.5MB). This system allows Sky One to keep a proper log of all ideas coming in.

Emma Read (Commissioning Editor for Factual at Sky One) advises, "ideas are the lifeblood of any channel so commissioning editors are glad to receive proposals from anyone. However, be prepared to be partnered with a production company that the commissioning editor trusts if you get the initial bite. They will know how to develop your idea further and be able to produce it for you, with the branding of the channel in mind, which is of stellar importance in a multi-channel universe".

www.skyone.co.uk/commissioning

At times, it can seem that the aspiring documentary filmmaker is merely joining with many others in an industry driven by so many ideas chasing limited funds and outlets. Of course, there are no guarantees of success in *any* kind of filmmaking, but don't be discouraged. The opportunities are out there. If you have a good idea, passion, and perseverance, then you also have the basic ingredients for success. Good luck.

UKTV Factual Commissioning

This site provides information about commissioning opportunities for UKTV and the BBC's international services. UKTV currently operates 11 commercial channels including UKTV People, UKTV Documentaries and UKTV History, all of which commission factual programming.

Charlotte Ashton (Director of Channels, Entertainment and Factual at UKTV) reiterates: "We'd need somebody to be linked with an existing company. The company can approach us quite speculatively with an idea from a new filmmaker - literally an email or one pager - to test the appetite but we'd need to know they had a strong independent behind them to progress. We have nothing against new talent; it's just that we have limited origination, which is all pretty strategic and no real slots dedicated to innovation or development in the way that say, C4 has".

www.bbc.co.uk/commissioning/tv/other

Living/Bravo Factual Commissioning

On this site you'll find in-depth information about Virgin Media Television channels' (including Living and Bravo) commissioning needs and requirements. Here you will find the sort of programmes each channel looks for, and the information you need to present your ideas.

www.virginmediatv.co.uk/commissioning

History Channel, Biography Channel and the Crime & Investigation Network Factual Commissioning

These channels commission throughout the year and treatments should be sent to Richard.Melman@bskyb.com or his deputy Martin.Morgan@bskyb.com. If they like it they will invite you in to discuss it in further detail. In the majority of cases, given the limitations of budgets, they prefer to co-produce. They have successfully co-produced with UK terrestrials, the ITV regions, major distributors such as RDF and international broadcasters like ZDF.

Richard Melman (Channel Director for the UK's The History Channel, The History Channel HD, The Biography Channel and the Crime & Investigation Network) gives his top tips for emerging filmmakers:

- A great title is the best start to getting a commission.
- If I haven't understood what your programme is about by the second paragraph, then "m going to have trouble telling the audience what it is I want them to watch?
- If you wouldn't want to watch it, I probably wouldn't want to commission it.
- Please don't just tell me the story, tell me how you are going to do it.
- Your Great Aunt may have lived a fascinating life, but unless she is already famous only your Great Uncle will watch the programme.
- Please try and watch my channels. If you can't, check out our websites, read the programme synopsis, have a look at the schedules. It saves you writing and me rejecting the programming we're showing tomorrow or your proposal on Grand Opera.
- Make sure your name and contact details are on the proposal. Sounds obvious? My desk is littered with unidentified documents.
- When I tell you how much money I have, I'm not lying and planning on spending the surplus on two weeks in the Caribbean. Coming back at £10k more than I said I had means I can't do it.
- A good 1-hour programme stretched to a 13 part series because it's more 'cost effective', means 13 hours of cost-effective bad programmes.
- Yes, I know he'd be great, but Stephen Fry is unlikely to be available for your 3-month trip to Egypt as he's apparently doing the other 57 proposals on my desk. Be realistic and imaginative in picking presenters, and if I haven't heard of them a show reel helps.

Jacquie Lawrence graduated from the North East Media Training Centre in 1989, with a Diploma in Scriptwriting and Producing. After a brief spell working for London-based production companies, she returned to Newcastle to set up My Aunt Fanny Films and Ipso Facto Films, out of which she produced and directed documentaries and dramas for ITV, Channel 4 and BBC. In 1995 she became a Commisssioning Editor for C4 Independent Film and Video, where she was responsible for C4's lesbian and gay programming and for new talent initiatives. In 2000 she became Head of Development for the indie World of Wonder, during which time she executively produced international and domestic documentaries for C4, HBO, A&E, Court TV, C5 and Sky One. In 2004 she returned to commissioning, this time for BSKYB, where she was charged with extending Sky One's factual slate. In 2005 she commissioned the BAFTA award-winning series, *Ross Kemp on Gangs*. During her career she has taught documentary producing at the Universities of Northumbria and Sheffield. She has also been involved with numerous regional production boards, documentray film festivals and television conferences. She is now a freelance executive producer, whilst commencing postgraduate study at the University of Oxford. She lives with her partner and their daughter in Oxford and in London.

Broadcasters/TV commissioners in the UK (factual)

BBC Daytime Entertainment & Out Of London Factual

Room 6239, BBC TV Centre, Wood Lane, London W12 7RJ
tel 020-8576 3199
Contact Sumi Connock

BBC Documentaries

Room 6060, BBC TV Centre, Wood Lane, London W12 7RJ
tel 020-8752 6608 *fax* 020-8752 6117
Contact Richard Klein, Commissioning Editor; Todd Austin, Commissioning Editor (ONE life strand)

BBC Documentaries (Storyville)

2nd Floor, BBC Grafton House, 379 Euston Road, London NW1 3AU
tel 020-7765 5211 *fax* 020-7765 5210
email storyville@bbc.co.uk
website www.bbc.co.uk/storyville
Contact Nick Fraser, Commissioning Editor

BBC Factual Features & Formats

Room 6060, BBC TV Centre, Wood Lane, London W12 7RJ
Contact Ben Gale, Commissioning Editor

BBC Northern Ireland (Entertainment & Events)

Room 229, BBC Northern Ireland, Broadcasting House, Ormeau Avenue, Belfast BT2 8HQ
tel (02890) 338375 *fax* (02890) 338175
email mike.edgar@bbc.co.uk
Contact Mike Edgar, Head of Programme Production

BBC Peak Time Entertainment

Room 6070, BBC TV Centre, Wood Lane, London W12 7RJ
tel 020-8225 9510 *fax* 020-8576 7328
Contact Pinki Chambers, Development Co-ordinator

BBC Scotland (Comedy & Entertainment)

Room 3160, BBC Scotland, Queen Margaret Drive, Glasgow G12 8DG
Contact Alan Tyler, Head of Comedy & Entertainment

BBC Scotland (Factual)

Room 3169, BBC Scotland, Queen Margaret Drive, Glasgow, G12 8DG
tel (0141) 338 3646
email andrea.miller.01@bbc.co.uk
Contact Andrea Miller, Head of Factual Programmes, Scotland

BBC Wales Arts, Classical Music/ Performance & Wales Entertainment

Room E411, BBC Wales, Broadcasting House, Llantrisant Road, Cardiff CF5 2YQ
tel (02920) 322 111 *fax* (02920) 322 544
email davidm.jackson@bbc.co.uk
Contact David Jackson, Head of Music

BBC Wales (Factual)

Room 4020, BBC Wales, Broadcasting House, Llantrisant Road, Cardiff CF5 2YQ
tel (02920) 322 976 *fax* (02920) 322 418
Contact Adrian Davies, Head of Factual Programmes

Channel 4

124 Horseferry Road, London SW1P 2TX
Contact Andrew Mackenzie, Head of Factual Entertainment; Dominique Walker, Commissioning Editor, Factual Entertainment; Angus Macqueen, Head of Documentaries; Simon Dickson, Deputy Head of Documentaries; Sarah Mulvey, Commissioning Editor Documentaries

ITV Factual

ITV Network Centre, 200 Gray's Inn Road, London WC1X 8HF
tel (084488) 18000 *fax* (084488) 16355
Contact Alison Sharman, Director of Factual & Daytime; Paul Jackson, Director of Entertainment & Comedy

Sky

Grant Way, Isleworth, Middlesex TW7 5QD
tel 020-7705 3000 *fax* 020-7705 3030
Contact Emma Read, Commissioning Editor, Specialist Factual & Factual Entertainment; Andrew O'Connell, Commissioning Editor, Factual

UKTV

2nd Floor, Flextech Building, 160 Great Portland Street, London W1W 5QA
tel 020-7299 6179
website www.uktv.co.uk
Contact Andy Whitman, Commissioning Executive Factual

UKTV is a partnership between BBC Worldwide and Flextech Television, the content division of Telewest

Communications. Currently operates 11 commercial channels: UKTV Gold, UK G2, UKTV People, UKTV Documentaries, UKTV Style, UKTV Style Gardens, UKTV Food, UKTV Drama, UKTV Bright Ideas, UKTV History, and UKTV Style +1. These channels commission programmes across a broad range of genres.

Virgin Media Television

Virgin Media Television Commissioning,
160 Great Portland Street, London W1W 5QA
email LivingCommissions@virginmediatv.co.uk, bravo_commissions@Virgin Media.co.uk
website www.virginmediatv.co.uk/commissioning
Contact (LIVING) Clare Hollywood, Head of Commissioning; Mark Sammon and Sophie Morgan, Commissioning Editors
Contact (Bravo) Rebecca Johnson, Commissioning Editor; Oliver Wilson, Commissioning Editor

Virgin Media TV commissions factual programming for LIVING and Bravo.

Getting a drama commission for TV

BAFTA-winning TV producer **Claire Parker** provides a guide to UK drama commissioning.

The way in which dramas are commissioned for TV is a frustratingly inexact science. An idea that one broadcaster thinks is a turkey can be snapped up just days later by another and become a ratings hit.

Every channel has a different process for selecting ideas, and every commissioner has their own personal tastes. What they want and when they want it can sometimes seem as changeable as the British weather. But if you get to know the basics, throwing yourself and your idea at the mercy of the drama commissioners will quickly become a lot less daunting.

What is a commissioner?

Every broadcaster has a team of commissioning editors who are responsible for the drama output. The BBC, for example, has separate commissioning teams in London, Scotland, Wales and Northern Ireland, each of which commissions projects from both independent and in-house producers. On the other hand, ITV handles all commissioning centrally.

The job of a commissioner is to anticipate what audiences want to watch, decide which are the best ideas from the thousands they receive, and, crucially, ensure that these are executed by the best writers and producers. Senior commissioners often have teams made up of readers, script editors and heads of development. These are the people who will usually be the first point of contact and often have most day-to-day contact with producers and writers.

How does a commission work?

Most channels commission a range of drama output – from returnable series, serials (anything with more than one part, which has a finite story) and single dramas. Commissioners will sometimes be looking to develop more of one type of drama than another; this changes on a regular basis depending on what they require for the channels.

Once an idea has been pitched to a broadcaster, they will decide if they want to pursue it. If they do, the project will enter a development period. You should expect that your commissioner will want to take an active role in the early evolution of an idea, for example helping to shape an idea from an initial notion into something more likely to succeed. This is useful and you should try not to see it as interfering – TV drama is highly collaborative. A process of submitting and resubmitting scripts to the commissioner goes on until a decision is made by the broadcaster to either reject the project or greenlight it for production.

The commissioner should be a guide to what is most likely to make it onto the screen, as well a critic and a support. Because they are not living and breathing the project like the writer or producer, their fresh perspective is often incredibly useful.

How should you approach them?

You need to start by establishing your credibility. Don't even think about contacting a commissioner until you have absolute faith in your idea and you are ready to persuade them that you and your team are the safe hands to deliver it.

Next, make sure that you have a writer on board. They will never say it, but no matter how good the idea, commissioners tend to reject those which do not have a good writer attached. It doesn't have to be a big name; a good spec script can be enough to clear this hurdle even if the writer is an unknown. Some of the channels have fewer resources and are therefore more reluctant to take risks on newer talent. But all are looking for the next big thing, so will never rule this out.

If you are a writer or director with a brilliant idea, it can help to have the backing of an established production company – even if it just acts as an umbrella to a newer writing/producing team. Though if you do gain the ear of an interested commissioner, they may team you up with a trusted production company anyway. Commissioners want to know that their money will be safe if it ever comes to spending millions on bringing your idea to the screen.

Each commissioner has a different set of guidelines about how they like to receive material and it's best to check directly with them before you submit. They usually like to be approached by the writer or the producer with the idea outlined on a short document.

What happens if they like your idea?

In all but the rarest cases where commissioners commit to making a programme on the basis of a pitch alone, the next step is development. This will usually trigger some funding to finance the writing and editing of sufficient scripts to give the commissioner an idea of whether to support the idea or to drop it.

Commissioners will demand to see material as it develops. First they will want an outline, then a more detailed treatment, a first draft script, and subsequent drafts.

The exception to this is ITV, which does not fund development. This makes life more difficult, but not impossible. You can either fund the development yourself, or approach an independent funding body – a sales company, for example. ITV will still want to see scripts during the development process to ensure that the project is something that they think is worth pursuing.

Development can be time-consuming and painful; hence the complaint heard from writers and producers everywhere: "I'm in development hell." Be prepared. It can take several years for a project to make it to the screen – even with active development for that whole period. And development hell spares no-one: new writers and established talent can suffer just the same (see the case study below).

On the plus side, development is often the time at which an idea really takes flight. You should value the criticism and guidance from the commissioners, who know what it takes to make sure your idea reaches the screen.

How does the funding structure work?

Typically, a broadcaster who is interested by your initial short pitch document will invite you in to discuss the idea and will then commission a treatment. For most of the broadcasters (ITV being the exception as mentioned), this will involve a contract and a small fee. If the idea progresses to the next stage, the commissioner is then likely to ask for a script, which triggers a larger fee.

Unlike in film, once a script is commissioned the writer needs to be prepared to continue working on as many drafts of the script as it takes, until it reaches a point where either it is rejected by the broadcaster, or moves forward to production.

The structure of the contracts usually reflects this, by being split into sections. A typical three-part development deal would involve one payment on signature of the agreement, one on delivery of first draft, and a third on acceptance of the script.

At its best, this thorough system can produce a highly polished and honed script before going into production. If the project is a series or serial rather than a single TV film, the broadcaster will often want to see scripts for a second and sometimes a third episode before moving to the green light for the whole series.

What happens once a project is greenlit?

Once a project is greenlit for production, the commissioner will not let go. In fact, some become more involved and remain heavily so in all the major decisions as the stakes rise. To keep progress as smooth as possible, the more communication you can have with your commissioner, the better.

During pre-production, they will expect to be consulted on the appointments of all writers, directors, and heads of departments. They will also want to be involved in significant casting decisions and script rewrites. During the shoot they will expect to see daily rushes; in post-production they will want to see several versions of the cut with final sign-off on the picture lock. In some cases they will attend the mix and online. After all, your programme is going out on their channel and their professional reputation depends on making sure it meets, and hopefully exceeds, the expectations of their audiences.

A case study: *Life on Mars*

The commissioning of *Life on Mars* is a lesson in never giving up.

The first episode was broadcast at 9pm on Monday 9 January 2006, but its development began eight years earlier when writers Matthew Graham, Tony Jordan and Ashley Pharoah were sent by Kudos, the production company, to a Blackpool hotel to brainstorm some ideas for a series. They came up with several, most of which they predicted were far more likely to get made than a show about a man from today who wakes up in the 1970s.

The BBC showed only a passing interest in the apparently left-field idea. They commissioned a script, written by Matthew Graham, but quickly rejected it, leaving the idea to languish in a drawer for several years.

When John Yorke joined Channel 4 as a commissioner in 2003, he remembered the idea and asked Matthew and Kudos to revisit it as an idea for Channel 4. Matthew, Jane Featherstone (joint Managing Director of Kudos) and I put our heads together to work out how to reshape the project for a Channel 4 audience. The idea had originally been conceived as a light, pre-watershed piece. For Channel 4, we wanted to add more layers and dig deeper into the darkness of the idea. Over the course of two years, we worked on the script, polishing and honing it, and each draft was received very positively by the channel – with notes towards the next draft.

It looked more and more likely that the series would be made at Channel 4, which spurred all of us on, even when it felt dispiriting to have to keep revisiting the script. Hopes rose further when a second script was commissioned. Eventually, just when it seemed like we were finally going to get the green light, the project was rejected. Life as a producer or a writer doesn't get much worse than this. Two years of toil lay in tatters.

At times like this you must fall back on any idea you have to save the day. Jane and I had just met with Julie Gardner, who had been recently appointed as Head of Drama for BBC Wales. She was fresh to the idea and we had a hunch that she might like it. We sent it straight to her and unbelievably, within days, we had a green light from the BBC. Then began the real hard work of bringing the idea to the screen …

Claire Parker is an executive producer at Kudos Film and Television. Claire started her career as a freelance script reader and then script editor for independent film and TV companies and broadcasters, including the BBC. In 2001, Claire was appointed as head of development at Kudos, and for three years was responsible for a large development slate which produced, amongst other things, the hit series *Hustle* (BBC), and the provocative singles *Comfortably Numb* (C4) and *Pleasureland* (C4). In her first role as producer in 2005 she made the Emmy award-winning *Life on Mars* (BBC), and in 2006 went on to executively produce the second series. Alongside this she also oversaw the critically acclaimed single drama *Wide Sargasso Sea* for BBC4 as executive producer.

The Big 5: the UK's main drama commissioners

Here we offer a very broad overview of the biggest commissioners of drama in the UK (terrestrial and non-terrestrial), and the departments within those channels. See contact information listed below.

BBC

The BBC has the largest drama output in the UK and is divided into Nations and Regions (BBC Wales, BBC Northern Ireland, BBC Scotland). All the nations and regions commission both from independents and in-house and all commissions are dealt with by the same team. Independent producers have the choice of whether to offer ideas to BBC Network via the Genre Controller/ Commissioning Editor or via the contact in individual Nations. Drama commissioning is London-based. There are separate teams to commission from independents and in-house. All drama commissioners commission for BBC1 (which has the largest remit for drama), as well as for BBC2, BBC3 and BBC4.

There is a separate comedy commissioning department. Both drama and comedy and all channels are now centralised through Jane Tranter (Controller of BBC Fiction). In the first instance it is best to contact the development teams of the individual departments.

www.bbc.co.uk/commissioning/tv/network/genres

Channel 4

Drama commissions for Channel 4 and E4 are centralised through Tessa Ross' Film and Drama department. There is a separate comedy department. Channel 4 has no in-house production. All their programmes are commissioned through independent production companies.

www.channel4.com/corporate/4producers

Channel Five

The channel has a small drama commissioning output but typically budgets are very low. It is currently seeking proposals for low-cost, returnable 60' series for a 9pm slot, aimed at the 16-34 demographic; Five is no longer developing one-off or two-part dramas. It is not looking to develop any period pieces, or issue-driven drama; ideas should be unashamedly entertaining, for a post-watershed audience.

www.five.tv/aboutfive/producersnotes/submitting

ITV

ITV has a large drama commissioning output. All new commissions are centralised are dealt with by the Drama department, Laura Mackie, Nick Elliot and Sally Hayne,s with Corinne Hollingworth responsible for long-running series.

http://about.itv.com

Sky

Sky has a small drama commissioning output, mainly focussed on Sky One.

www.skyone.co.uk/commissioning

Broadcasters/TV commissioners in the UK (drama)

BBC Acquisitions: Feature Films
Room 6023, BBC TV Centre, Wood Lane, London W12 7RJ
tel 020-8225 6052 *fax* 020-8749 0893
email steve.jenkins@bbc.co.uk
Contact Steve Jenkins, Head of Films

BBC Acquisitions: Series (Fiction)
Room 6023, BBC TV Centre, Wood Lane, London W12 7RJ
tel 020-8225 6048 *fax* 020-8749 0893
email sue.deeks@bbc.co.uk
Contact Sue Deeks, Head of Series

BBC Comedy
Room 6070, BBC TV Centre, Wood Lane, London W12 7RJ
tel 020-8576 7394 *fax* 020-8576 7328
Contact Michael Buchanan-Dunne, Development Co-ordinator

BBC Drama
Room 6027, BBC TV Centre, Wood Lane, London W12 7RJ
tel 020-8225 7500 *fax* 020-8225 7734
Contact Jane Tranter, Controller BBC Fiction; John Yorke, Head of Drama Serials; Kate Harwood, Head of Drama Series and Serials; Ben Stephenson, Head of Drama Commissioning; Sarah Brándist, Polly Hill, Lucy Richer, Commissioning Editors, Independent Drama

BBC Northern Ireland Drama
Room 3.07, Blackstaff House, Great Victoria Street, Belfast BT2 7BB
email tvdrama.ni@bbc.co.uk
Contact Patrick Spence, Head of Drama; Kate Evans, Executive Producer; Susan Carson, Programme Development Executive

BBC Scotland Drama & Films
Room 2170, BBC Scotland, Queen Margaret Drive, Glasgow G12 8DG
tel 0141-338 2517 *fax* 0141-338 2273
email anne.mensah@bbc.co.uk
Contact Anne Mensah, Head of Television Drama Scotland; Gaynor Holmes, Executive Producer for Drama

BBC Wales Drama & Films
Room E2106, BBC Wales, Broadcasting House, Llantrisant Road, Cardiff CF5 2YQ
tel (02920) 322935 *fax* (02920) 322668
Contact Julie Gardner, Head of Drama

BBC Writersroom – see page 6
The BBC Writersroom informs new writers and the public on how to develop and submit unsolicited drama scripts to the BBC.

Channel 4
124 Horseferry Road, London SW1P 2TX
tel 020-7306 8333
Contact Tessa Ross, Controller, Film and Drama; Liza Marshall, Head of Drama; Camilla Campbell , Sophie Gardiner, Commissioning Editors Drama

Channel Five (five): Comedy
22 Long Acre, London WC2E 9LY
tel 020-7421 7115
email graham.smith@five.tv
Contact Graham Smith, Controller of Comedy

Channel Five (five): Drama
22 Long Acre, London WC2E 9LY
tel 020-7550 5559
email abigail.webber@five.tv
Contact Abigail Webber, Commissioning Editor Drama

ITV Drama
ITV Network Centre, 200 Gray's Inn Road, London WC1X 8HF
tel (084488) 1800 *fax* (084488) 16355
Contact Laura Mackie, Controller of Drama; Sally Haynes, Deputy Controller of Drama; Nick Elliot, Director of Drama; Corinne Hollingworth, Head of Continuing Series

Sky
Grant Way, Isleworth, Middlesex TW7 5QD
tel 020-7705 3000 *fax* 020-7705 3030
Contact Elaine Pyke, Sarah Conroy, Commissioning Editors Drama

Pre-production
A practical guide to clearances and deliverables

Producer **Rachel Robey** talks us through the clearances, agreements, monies, plans and insurances a producer will need to have in place before starting a shoot, as well as the items the production will be expected to deliver to a sales agent and distributor for release.

When first committing to a project, producers must acquire ownership of all the rights in the film, demonstrating a clear 'chain of title' from the birth of the idea right up to the delivery of the finished movie. The process of clearances is an inescapable and inevitable part of filmmaking at all levels – from the smallest micro-budget masterpiece to the Hollywood blockbuster. Sort it out upfront and then stay on top of it, and you won't spend months backtracking over paperwork – or worse, find that an integral part of your film cannot be 'cleared', which will cost *you* big to fix. Using music tracks or original story material that hasn't been cleared is an all-too-frequent mistake made by new filmmakers.

Find a media lawyer you think you can work with and negotiate a fee for the production, Be clear about exactly which partners are involved and the size of the budget you are raising. They will draw up templates for your cast and crew and help you negotiate with financiers and literary agents. Don't forget that your financiers will want to approve the wording of all of these documents, so you need to start this process early. Most financiers won't release, or 'cashflow', a penny of your finance until your chain of title is approved and in place.

Financiers will need many assurances and clearances from you before they feel confident enough to start the flow of money into your production bank account; they are by their very nature 'risk averse'. The list below is pretty exhaustive and not all of these items will be required for *every* film: you or your lawyers will need to negotiate with the film's financiers on what, exactly, is needed to 'close' the film and release that all-important cashflow.

Checklist of standard clearances, agreements and additional items required in the course of prepping your film

(The items marked with a* are generally required for 'closing' – prior to the commencement of the production of the film):

Chain of title

- Source material*
- Screenplay*
- Option agreement (and proof of payment of option fee)*
- Proof of any extensions to the option*
- Development finance agreements*
- Screenwriters' agreement*
- Publishers' release (if an adaptation of a novel)*

• Chain of title legal review / opinion* – sometimes you will be asked for a lawyer to give an opinion that your chain of title is intact (it would depend on how complex the chain of title is, and who the financiers are)
• Clearance check on screenplay*
• Product clearances and releases
• Film clip clearances
• Music clearances and licenses

Reports and registrations

Register your script for copyright and confirm that nothing of the same title exists already.
• Copyright report*
• Title report*
• Copyright registration of screenplay and underlying rights*
• Copyright registration of finished film

Crew contracts

• Director*
• Individual producers*
• Co-producers*
• Executive Producer*
• Approved template for Heads of Departments and crew*
• Signed agreements from *all* Heads of Departments
• Signed Casting Director agreement
• Signed Composer agreement
• Signed Unit Publicist agreement
• Crew stop date issues / letters

Cast agreements

• Approved template for cast*
• Signed cast agreements
• Licences for child actors

Co-production

• Co-production agreement*
• Provisional co-production agreement*
• Provisional co-production status

Financing and distribution contracts

• Longform contracts with all of your financiers*
• International sales agent agreement & sales figures / projections*
• UK distribution agreement*
• Collection agent agreement*
• Bank mandate (original signatures required)*
• Laboratory pledgeholders' agreement and access letter* (this is a letter signed by the lab and the financiers, agreeing who has access to the neg / materials which are stored at the lab)
• Interparty agreement* (This is the 'daddy' of all the finance documents; although you sign agreements with all the financiers individually, all parties then sign up to the 'inter-

party' agreements which binds everyone together in a joint financial agreement: who will put how much money in, and when, and what their joint responsibilities are. Once this is signed you are 'closed'.)

Insurances

- Completion guarantee*
- Errors and ommissions insurance*
- Employer liability insurance*
- Public liability insurance*
- Production insurance*
- Action vehicle insurance

Production details

- Agreed / bonded budget*
- Agreed / bonded shooting schedule*
- Agreed / bonded post production schedule*
- Approved cast*
- Approved Heads of Department*

Deliverables required

There are numerous 'deliverables' required in filmmaking. These are the physical, tangible elements that make up a film. They can be as straightforward as the 35mm or digital print, or as strange and mysterious as the textless elements used in the production of the film's credits – and your financiers, sales agent and UK distributor will have an extensive list that will need to be reflected in your budget. Again, it's important to clarify exactly what they will each require very early in your pre-production process.

If money is tight, you can sometimes negotiate to provide access to certain elements, rather than physically delivering them to each party, but don't forget that anything you have granted access to will need to be professionally stored for years to come.

The following list should give you an idea of the sort thing you will be asked for.

Negative / picture elements

- Access / delivery of a 35mm cut negative (or digital intermediate alternative)
- Access / delivery of a 35mm optical soundtrack negative
- Showprint with sound (you may need more than one of these, depending on whether your financiers, distributor and sales agent request one each)
- Access / delivery of the 35mm interpositive
- Access / delivery of the 35mm internegative
- Access / delivery of any 35mm or digital 'textless elements' for credits / captioned shots

Sound elements

- Stereo master versions of the film's dialogue, music and effects (separately and mixed together)
- Digital Magnetic Optical Disk of the soundtrack to the film, suitable for the production of optical sound tracks

Videotape masters

HD D5 and Digi-beta are different tape formats; Digi-beta comes in PAL and NTSC – PAL being the broadcast system in the UK, and NTSC being American. The numbers reflect the 'aspect ratio' – the size the picture will be on a TV – so 4:3 is pan and scan, 16:9 is broadcast widescreen and 2.35:1 is cinema scope.

- HD D5 Master in 4:3
- HD D5 Master in 16:9
- HD D5 Master in 2.35:1
- Digi-Beta Pal copy in 4:3
- Digi-Beta Pal copy in 16:9
- Digi-Beta Pal copy in 2.35:1
- Digi-Beta NTSC copy in 4:3
- Digi-Beta NTSC copy in 16:9
- Digi-Beta NTSC in 2.35:1

Disability access materials

This is something that is becoming more commonly requested, particularly by the public funders, and makes your film accessible to people who are partially sighted and / or hard of hearing.

- Audio described track for use on 35mm and video copies (for the partially sighted)
- Subtitled track (for the hard of hearing)
- 35mm subtitled showprint (for the hard of hearing)

Publicity materials

- A selection of production stills at high resolution
- Materials for DVD 'making of' films and EPK
- Production notes, including biographies of key personnel

Paperwork

- Dialogue list / post production script
- Music cue sheet
- Audited set of accounts and final cost statement
- Complete list of all credits and credit obligations on the film

As a rule, each financier will usually want a digital master, and a few DVD copies for their archives; they may also request a 35mm showprint. A distributor will want a 35mm showprint, access to an internegative, and certain video copies for the DVD release. The sales agent will want an extensive amount of material to cover distribution in each territory across the globe. When you get your sales agency contract, brace yourself: the deliverables will run into tens of pages and can seem extremely daunting.

OK, so what are you waiting for? Get planning!

Rachel Robey produces for Wellington Films, the company she established in 2000 with Alastair Clark. Their debut feature film *London to Brighton* (Paul Andrew Williams) was released in 2006 to critical acclaim and received multiple awards, including Best Achievement in Production at the British Independent Film Awards and a nomination for the Carl Foreman Award at BAFTA. Their second feature film, *Better Things* (Duane Hopkins), received the MEDIA New Talent Award for screenwriting in 2004 and will be released during 2008 by Soda Pictures in the UK. In addition to producing, Rachel works in physical production, with credits including *Control*, *Dead Man's Shoes* and *Irina Palm*.

Producers' organisations

These organisations are set up to support producers in their creative and business roles. They offer a range of services, from script and project development programmes to extensive opportuinities to meet people in the wider industry who may be future partners or investors.

International Federation of Film Producers Associations (FIAPF)

9 rue de l'Echelle, 75001 Paris, France
tel ++33 1 44 77 97 50 *fax* ++33 1 44 77 97 55
email info@fiapf.org
website www.fiapf.org

FIAPF is an international alliance of producers' groups from around the world, with 31 member associations (such as PACT in the UK) from 25 countries. FIAPF's mandate is to represent the economic, legal and regulatory interests which the film and TV production industries in 4 continents have in common.

As an advocate for producers, FIAPF helps coordinate political action in key areas such as copyright and related intellectual property rights legislation; enforcement of anti-piracy legislation and action; deployment of digital technologies; and standardisation and trade-related issues. FIAPF is also a regulator of international film festivals.

EUROPE

European Audiovisual Entrepreneurs (EAVE) – see page 35 for contacts and details of EAVE's MEDIA-supported project development programme for producers.

EAVE primarily provides long and short media training seminars, workshops and forums for professionals in the UK media industries. However, it also offers continuous online services to European producers and professionals.

Ateliers du Cinéma Européen (ACE)

8 rue Mayran, 75009 Paris, France
tel ++33 1 53 25 00 01 *fax* ++33 1 53 32 76 94
email infos@ace-producers.com
website www.ace-producers.com
Head of Training Laura Gragg

Producers' organisation which puts the producer at the helm of the filmmaking process. In addition to offering producer training and a project development programme, ACE assists its producers by establishing contacts for them with potential partners, and providing them with advice regarding their needs – from scriptwriting to international sales.

– see page 35 for details of producer training and project development programmes run by ACE.

Austria

Fachverband der Audiovisions und Filmindustrie

Wiedner Hauptstraße 63, PO Box 3271045, Wien, Austria
tel ++ 43 (0)5 90 900 3010 ++ 43 (0)5 90 900 276
email mueller@fafo.at
website www.fafo.at

National producers' association of Austria.

Czech Republic

Audiovisual Producers' Association (APA)

Národní 28, 110 00 Praha 1, Czech Republic
tel ++ 420 221 105 302
email apa@asociaceproducentu.cz
website www.asociaceproducentu.cz

Czech national producers' association.

Denmark

Danish Producers Association (DPA)

Bernhard Bangs Allé 25, DK-2000 Frederiksberg, Denmark
tel ++ 45 33 86 28 80 *fax* ++ 45 33 86 28 88
email info@pro-f.dk
website www.pro-f.dk

National association of film and TV producers. Promotes the interests of Danish producers in trade and policy on a national level.

Finland

The Finnish Cinema Exhibitors' Association

Kaisaniemenkatu 3 B 29, 00100 Helsinki, Finland
email etunimi.sukunimi@filmikamari.fi, filmikamari@filmikamari.fi
website www.filmikamari.fi

Finnish national cinema producers' group.

Iceland

Association of Icelandic Film Producers

Tungötu 14, PO Box 5367, 125 Reykjavik, Iceland
tel ++354 5117060 *fax* ++354 5117061
email sik@producers.is
website www.producers.is

Association of Icelandic film production companies and producers of all types of film – Feature, Television, Documentary and Shorts.

Netherlands

Netherlands Association of Feature Film Producers (NVS)

Rokin 91, 1012 Kl Amsterdam, Holland
tel ++ 31 (0) 20 6270061
email info@speelfilmproducenten.nl
website www.speelfilmproducenten.nl

Association of Dutch feature film producers.

Norway

Norwegian Film and TV Producers' Association

Dronningens gt. 16, 0152 Oslo, Norway
tel ++ 47 23 11 93 11 *fax* ++ 47 23 11 93 16
email produsentforeningen@produsentforeningen.no
website www.produsentforeningen.no

National producers' organisation of Norway.

Russia

Film Producers' Guild of Russia

1 Mosfilmovskaya str., Moscow, Russia, 119992
tel ++ 7 095 143 90 28
email guild@kinoproducer.ru
website www.kinoproducer.ru

Spain

Spanish Federation of Audiovisual Producers

C/ Luis Buñuel,
2 - 2º-Izq. Ciudad de la Imagen Pozuelo de Alarcón
28223 Madrid, Spain
tel ++34 91 512 16 60 *fax* ++34 91 512 01 48
email web@fapae.es
website www.fapae.es

Umbrella body that integrates almost all the film and television production companies in Spain (approx. 400) and represents their interests in policy-making.

Sweden

Swedish Film Producers' Association

Box 27 183, SE-102 52 Stockholm, Sweden
tel ++ 46 8 665 12 55 *fax* ++ 46 8 666 37 48
email info@filmproducers.se
website www.swedishfilmproducers.com

National producers' trade organisation, with 35 members who produce 90% of Sweden's annual film output.

United Kingdom

New Producers Alliance (NPA)

NPA Film Centre, Unit 7.03 The TEA Building, 56 Shoreditch High Street, London E1 6JJ
tel 020-7613 0440
email queries@npa.org.uk
website www.npa.org.uk

Established in 1993, the NPA is a national membership organisation for film producers, screenwriters and directors, and a registered charity. The NPA is an international training and support provider for the production industry.

Producers Alliance for Cinema and Television (PACT)

Procter House, 1 Procter Street, Holborn, London WC1V 6DW
tel 020-7067 4367 *fax* 020-7067 4377
website www.pact.co.uk
Information Manager David Allen Mills

PACT is the UK trade association that represents and promotes the commercial interests of independent feature film, television, animation and interactive media companies. As a lobbying group, it has regular dialogues with government, regulators and public agencies on all issues affecting its members, participating in key public policy debates on the media industry, both in the UK and in Europe.

PACT negotiates terms of trade with all public service broadcasters and also lobbies for a properly structured and funded UK film industry. A range of support and information services is available to all members, including training, events, business affairs guidance, subsidised legal advice, web resources, the monthly PACT magazine and regular e-bulletins. PACT also administers the Independent Production Training Fund levy for television producers, and is a partner in the Skills Investment Fund – the feature-film training levy administered by Skillset.

Membership is for registered companies only; fees range from £353 to £10,000 (excluding VAT) depending on the annual turnover of the company.

Welsh Independent Producers (TAC)

33-35 West Bute Street, Cardiff CF10 5LH
tel (01286) 671123 *fax* (01286) 678890
website www.teledwyr.com

TAC (Welsh Independent Producers) is a trade association formed to represent the interests of independents producing mainly for broadcasters in Wales. It offers a range of services, including industrial relations, specialist contracts negotiated with trade unions, business and legal advice, and information services. It also acts as a lobbying and representative body in discussions with broadcasters, development agencies, government departments and various other bodies.

THE AMERICAS

Argentina

Asociacion General De Productores Cinematograficos / Instituto Nacional De Cine Y Artes Visuales

c/o ARIES – Fitz Roy 1940, 1414 Buenos Aires, Argentina
tel ++ 54 11 4 777 04 04
email aries@fibertel.com.ar

Argentina's national producers' association.

Canada

Canadian Film and Television Production Association

Toronto Office: 160 John Street, 5th Floor, Toronto M5V 2E5, Canada
tel ++ 1 416 304 0280 *fax* ++ 1 416 304 0499
website www.cftpa.ca

National producers' association of Canada, with a useful searchable guide to companies comprising the Canadian film and TV industries on its own website.

United States of America

Independent Film & Television Alliance

10850 Wilshire Boulevard, 9th Floor, Los Angeles, CA 90024-4321, USA
tel ++ 1 310 446 1000 *fax* ++ 1 310 446 1600
email info@ifta-online.org
website www.ifta-online.org

Trade association for the independent film and television industry in the US; represents the interests of film and TV producers and runs the American Film Market (see page 285).

ASIA AND THE MIDDLE-EAST

China

Chinese Filmmakers' Association

595 Cao Xi Road (N), Shanghai 200030, China
tel ++ 86 21 64396720
email sfscpc@online.sh.cn
website www.sfs-cn.com

Chinese producers' association (also known as Shanghai Film Group Corporation) charged with increasing international co-production.

Egypt

Egyptian Chamber of Cinema Industry

33 Orabi Street, PO Box Cairo 251, Eygpt
tel ++ 202 5741 638 *fax* ++ 202 5751 583
email egy_cinemachamber@hotmail.com
website www.g15.gov.eg
Chairman Mr Moneib Mahmoud Shafey

National producers' association of Eygpt.

India

National Film Development Corporation Ltd

Discovery of India Building, Nehru Centre, 6th Floor, Dr Annie Besant Road, Worli, Mumbai-400 018, India
email nfdc@nfdcindia.com
website www.nfdcindia.com

National organisation which provides support and trade promotion to Indian films and permissions for shooting in India.

Iran

The Iranian Alliance of Motion Picture Guilds

(Khaneh Cinema)
Seranan Street, South Bahar Avenue, Tehran 15617, Iran
tel ++ 98 21 7752 5967 or 5966
email intl@khanehcinema.ir
website www.khanehcinema.ir

National trade organisation.

Japan

Motion Picture Producers Association of Japan

website www.eiren.org

Japanese producers' organisation. Website includes Japanese Box Office data in English.

OCEANIA

Australia

Screen Producers Association of Australia (SPAA)

34 Fitzroy Street, Surry Hills NSW 2010, Australia
tel ++61 2 9360 8988 *fax* ++61 2 9360 8977
email spaa@spaa.org.au
website www.spaa.org.au

National producers' association of Australia.

New Zealand

Screen Production and Development Association (SPADA)

PO Box 9567, Wellington 6141, New Zealand
tel ++ 64 4 939 6934 *fax* ++ 64 4 939 6935
email info@spada.co.nz
website www.spada.co.nz

SPADA represents the interests of producers and production companies on all issues affecting the commercial and creative aspects of independent screen production in New Zealand.

Legal firms with film expertise

The firms listed in this section offer services covering all legal needs for professionals and companies working in the media industries – from contract negotiation to copyright protection. Many of the firms also offer production finance advice and deal-structuring services.

Addleshaw Goddard

150 Aldersgate Street, London EC1A 4EJ
tel 020-7880 5653
email david.engel@addleshawgoddard.com
website www.addleshawgoddard.com

A firm with specialist knowledge in media and the Internet; particular expertise includes: defamation on the web; recovery of domain names; illegal downloads; and unauthorised use of copyright material on websites. More broadly, clients include companies and organisations in a wide variety of sectors, such as financial services, media, insurance, manufacturing, travel and retail, as well as major rights owners like collecting societies, Hollywood studios, musicians and other entities and individuals from the worlds of politics, sport and the arts.

Ashurst

Broadwalk House, 5 Appold Street,
London EC2A 2HA
tel 020-7638 1111 *fax* 020-7638 1112
website www.ashurst.com

A large international firm whose success is built on extensive experience of working with clients on the complex legal and regulatory issues relating to cross-border transactions.

Berwin Leighton Paisner

Adelaide House, London Bridge, London EC4R 9HA
tel 020-7623 3144 *fax* 020-7760 1111
email david.newton@blplaw.com
website www.berwinleightonpaisner.com

Full-service firm that aims to employ media lawyers who are experienced in their specialist sectors, but who also understand how this fits into a wider context.

Bird & Bird

90 Fetter Lane, London EC4A 1JP
tel 020-7415 6000 *fax* 020-7415 6111
email peter.dally@twobirds.com
website www.twobirds.com

Established in 1846, Bird & Bird is a full-service legal firm which represents filmmakers and film companies in contract negotiations. The company has particular expertise in production, co-production and finance, and also offers advice on deal structuring and accessing finance.

Full services offered to the film industry include: production finance; production services such as agreements with principal cast and crew, script clearances, music licences and location agreements; international sales and distribution; international co-productions; employment and employee benefits and incentives; and e-commerce and dispute resolution. Offers some flexibility on rates for independent producers in a start-up situation.

Clintons Solicitors

55 Drury Lane, London WC2B 5RZ
tel 020-7379 6080 *fax* 020-7240 9310
email info@clintons.co.uk
website www.clintons.co.uk
Film & TV Team James Jones, Stephen Joelson, Paul March, Tom Frederikse

Clintons has an extensive department devoted to Entertainment and Media law, with a specialist film and television division which represents clients in the UK, Europe and North America. Clients include: studios, film and television production and distribution companies, as well as independents, film financiers, funding bodies and a range of other film and TV companies from all sectors of the industry. Provides commercial legal advice in all aspects of film and television, including: finance; development; copyright and format protection and exploitation; production; catalogue acquisition and disposal; distribution and exploitation; and rights clearance.

Davenport Lyons

1 Old Burlington Street, London W1S 3NL
tel 020-7468 2600 *fax* 020-7437 8216
email dl@davenportlyons.com
website www.davenportlyons.com
Head of Media Department Leon Morgan

A commercially focused law firm acting for businesses and entrepreneurial clients from a wide range of market sectors, including entertainment, media, retail and banking. It has grown to have one of the largest dedicated media entertainment practices in London, representing key businesses and individuals from all sectors of film, television and video, production, financing and distribution, book publishing and the performing arts generally. Services are extensive and cover specialties in copyright and contract law for film finance, production, post and distribution as well as expertise in new and interactive media law.

David Wineman

Craven House, 121 Kingsway, London WC2B 6NX
tel 020-7400 7800 *fax* 020-7400 7890
email law@davidwineman.co.uk
website www.davidwineman.co.uk
Founders Irving S David, Vivian Wineman

Specialist practice for commercial media law; represents clients across the music, film and broadcast industries. Areas of service include: co-production agreements; film and television software production agreements; sponsorship and employment contracts; and taxation.

Denton Wilde Sapte

One Fleet Place, London EC4M 7WS
tel 020-7242 1212 *fax* 020-7404 0087
email info@dentonwildesapte.com
website www.dentonwildesapte.com
Partner & Head of Department Catherine Bingham

Technology, Media and Telecoms is one of Denton Wilde Sapte's 4 areas of expertise. The firm aims to offer clients in this sector the full range of legal services that they might need – from finance to contracts and taxation.

Dorsey & Whitney LLP

21 Wilson Street, London EC2M 2TD
tel 020-7588 0800 *fax* 020-7588 0555
email london@dorsey.com
website www.dorsey.com

Huge international law firm with offices all over the world, and with expertise and services in almost every conceivable field, including media and entertainment.

Finers Stephens Innocent

179 Great Portland Street, London W1W 5LS
tel 020-7323 4000 *fax* 020-7580 7069
email enquiries@fsilaw.co.uk
website www.fsilaw.co.uk

An 80-lawyer practice based in Central London, and providing a full range of legal services to a broad spectrum of primarily business clients in a range of sectors, including media.

Hammonds

7 Devonshire Square, Cutlers Gardens, London EC2M 4YH
tel 0870-839 0000 *fax* 0870-839 0001
email enquiries@hammonds.com
website www.hammonds.com

Hammonds' specialist Media & Communications team has more than 50 lawyers with combined expertise in all aspects of media content production and delivery in the UK and internationally.

Harbottle & Lewis

Hanover House, 14 Hanover Square, London W1S 1HP
tel 020-7667 5000 *fax* 020-7667 5100
email adean@harbottle.com
website www.harbottle.com
Senior Partner Film & Television Robert Storer
Partners Film & Television Abigail Payne, Medwyn Jones

Harbottle & Lewis' work covers all aspects of film, including structuring co-productions, pre-sales, equity and tax-based funding, and bank finance arrangements throughout all stages in the lifecycle of a film, from development through to financing, production and distribution. Also has expertise in digital formats such as web TV and broadband delivery. The firm is ranked as one of the leading firms for TV and film production by both The Legal 500, 2005 and Chambers & Partners, 2006.

Howard Kennedy

Harcourt House, 19 Cavendish Square, London W1A 2AW
tel 020-7546 8889 *fax* 020-7664 4489
email b.eagles@howardkennedy.com
website www.howardkennedy.com

Howard Kennedy is a full-service legal firm with a strong media and entertainment department. Offers contract negotiations for filmmakers and production companies as well as film financing and talent representation. Clients include: producers of the films *Tsotsi, Keeping Mum* and *Control,* and film financiers Bank of Ireland, Bank of Scotland, Invicta Capital and Scotts. Rates are available on request.

Lee & Thompson

Green Garden House, 15-22 St Christopher's Place, London W1U 1NL
tel 020-7935 4665 *fax* 020-7563 4949
email mail@leeandthompson.com
website www.leeandthompson.com
Partners Robert Lee, Andrew Thompson, Robert Horsfall, Jeremy Gawade, Reno Antoniades, Gordon Williams, Mike Brookes, Nicki Parfitt, Richard Lever, Sonia Diwan, Mark Ashelford

A leading media and entertainment law firm established in 1983, with experience in all areas of the industry including the impact of Internet technology and e-commerce. Represents clients at all stages of their career – from established stars to emerging talent – and works for companies, individuals, corporations and independents. The firm's services in film range from finance-structuring to helping producers put packages together. Also see Reno Antoniades' article on page 46.

Marriot Harrison

12 Great James Street, London WC1N 3DR
tel 020-7209 2000 *fax* 020-7209 2001
email a.morris@marriottharrison.com
website www.marriottharrison.com

Marriot Harrison is an independent corporate and media law firm with expertise across all aspects of the industry, from finance to delivery. Partners also specialise in new media.

Michael Simkins LLP

45-51 Whitfield Street, London W1T 4HB
tel 020-7907 3000
email nigel.bennett@simkins.com
website www.simkins.co.uk

The Film & Television Group at Michael Simkins advises on all the legal and related issues involved in the development, production and exploitation of audiovisual material in all forms (traditional as well as developing media). Clients come from all areas of the film and broadcast industries, and range from individuals to multinational corporations.

Olswang

90 Long Acre, London WC2E 9TT
tel 020-7208 8888 *fax* 020-7208 8800
email olsmail@olswang.co.uk
website www.olswang.com

Specialises in Technology, Media, Telecoms and Property, and has a dedicated film practice which was set up in 1981. Team advises on all aspects of film process.

Osborne Clarke

One London Wall, London EC2Y 5EB
tel 020-7105 7000 *fax* 020-7105 7005
website www.osborneclarke.com

A European law firm that provides business-focused legal solutions. Voted UK Law Firm of the Year by Legal Week Awards 2006.

Richards Butler

Beaufort House, 15 St Botolph Street, London EC3A 7EE
tel 020-7247 6555 *fax* 020-7247 5091
email law@richardsbutler.com
website www.richardsbutler.com

Firm with particular strengths in film and television finance and production, and also in broadcasting. The film and media team's work includes services in: finance; production and distribution; intellectual property; resolution and litigation; freedom of expression and defamation; and advertising.

Schillings

Royalty House, 72-74 Dean Street, London W1D 3TL
tel 020-7453 2500 *fax* 020-7453 2600
email legal@schillings.co.uk
website www.schillings.co.uk

Simons Muirhead Burton

50 Broadwick Street, London W1F 7AG
tel 020-7734 4499 *fax* 020-7734 3263
email info@smab.co.uk
website www.smab.co.uk
Partners Simon Goldberg, Nicholas Lom

Has a full-service practice in film and media, with clients who work in all aspects of these industries. The firm offers services in everything from finance to distribution; also represents a number of independent production companies and distributors such as Tartan.

SJ Berwin

10 Queen Street Place, London EC4R 1BE
tel 020-7111 2222 *fax* 020-7111 2000
email info@sjberwin.com
website www.sjberwin.com

SJ Berwin represents filmmakers and film companies at all stages of the filmmaking process (development, financing, production and distribution). It is a full-service firm whose clients include studios, individual producers, production companies, distributors and sales agents as well as rights holders, and equity, bank and tax-based financiers. The department also works in other media sectors. Rates are available upon request.

Insurance and guarantors

Allan Chapman & James Ltd
7 Phoenix Square, Wyncolls Road,
Severalls Business Park, Colchester, Essex CO4 9AS
tel (01206) 500 000 *fax* (01206) 752216
email insurance@acjltd.co.uk
website www.acjltd.co.uk
MD Terry Austin, *FD* Les Marshall

Specialist insurance services to the Media Industry for more than 18 years.

Aon Entertainment & Media Team
4th Floor, Capital House, 1 Houndwell Place,
Southampton, Hampshire SO14 1HU
tel 0845-601 0380
email entertainment.media@ars.aon.co.uk
website www.aon.co.uk

A world leader in risk management, insurance broking, reinsurance, employee benefits and HR consulting services.

Butcher, Robinson & Staples International Ltd
Collegiate House, 9 St Thomas Street,
London SE1 9RY
tel 020-7397 5060 *fax* 020-7407 1076
email leech@brsint.com
website www.brsint.co.uk

Financial, travel and accident insurers.

Cadogan Hanover Park Commercial – Erinaceous
Phoenix House, 11 Wellesley Road,
Croydon CR0 2NW
tel 0845-345 0815 *fax* 0845-345 0816
email andrew.leen@chp-insurance.co.uk
website www.chp-insurance.co.uk/performance

Performance Media insurance for Production, Post-production and facilities companies, and for freelance filmmakers, cameramen, soundmen, etc. Annual or short-period policies available. The company insures a number of Production and Post-production companies, sound studios and freelancers throughout the UK.

FMW Risk Services Ltd
Farr House, Railway Street, Chelmsford CM1 1NR
tel (01245) 348500 *fax* (01245) 356653
email media@fmw.co.uk
website www.fmw.co.uk

One of the leading independent specialist insurance brokers and risk management consultants in the UK.

Working with actors

Director **Bille Eltringham** has worked with a wide range of actors, from Derek Jacobi, Catherine Tate and Ray Winstone to untrained actors and children. In this mini-interview, she shares some of her working methods.

What is the casting process like for you?

I've always worked with a casting director, but the process has depended on the nature of the piece. When I've worked with non-actors (by which I mean people with no previous experience of acting), and children, it tends to be a very long process involving accessing schools, youth clubs, etc. and then meeting literally hundreds of people. I usually do some drama exercise with them devised specifically for the film.

With professional actors, it depends on how grand they are. There's a mysterious etiquette to how casting works, and I rely on the casting director to guide me through the minefield. Basically, if the actor is 'very, very grand', they won't meet unless they've been absolutely offered the part. 'Very grand' might agree that the part is theirs subject to a mutually acceptable meeting between them and the director. 'Grand' will meet and chat about the script and the part (and may be prepared to read). But luckily, lots of hugely talented and experienced actors are happy to come and read, without any formal offer. Sometimes I meet them alone, or with the casting director; when I work in TV it's more usual for the producer to be present too. I like it to be a fairly casual conversation to see their take on the part and whether I feel we'll work well together.

What preparation do you do for casting?

I would expect to be extremely familiar with the script (you never know which way the conversation will go). I like to go through the script and pretend to be an actor looking at the role: it helps me check that the character arc is working. If they are going to read, I will have picked out the scene(s) I think will best serve the purpose. I will have checked through their CV, and if I don't know their work (and sometimes even if I do), I'll watch as much of it as I can.

How do you decide whether an actor is the right person for the part?

To answer this question, I'll leave aside questions of finance – there are often financial pressures to gather a 'name' cast – and answer as if I am trying just to cast the person who is right for the role ...

Casting is largely instinctive and based on personal opinion. I might just like the way the actor delivers some of the lines: maybe it's unexpected; maybe I like how they move as well. I'll also be interested in how they respond to me, because obviously our relationship will be important – we'll need to be good at listening to each other. But I will try to stay open-minded for as long as possible; I've sometimes had wonderful left-of-field surprises. I may also be considering the other roles around which this person has to fit, so matching them to another actor may come into play.

What kind of pre-shoot preparations do you do with your actors?

Again, that totally depends on a number of things. Experienced actors are often busy working on something else up until the shoot; sometimes, I have had no time at all to prepare with them. Frequently there are only a few minutes to rehearse and block a scene just before it's shot. But I don't tend to like to rehearse too much anyway. I prefer to talk through things and make sure we agree on the character, their back story, the nature of the scenes, the subtext, the crucial beats ... that kind of thing.

They may want to have some voice coaching if there's an accent involved. Sometimes either or both of us feel we should do some research, which could be anything from getting some hands-on experience with people who really do a particular job or have a particular skill, to ploughing through technical data about an unfamiliar subject. If I have time and I think it is appropriate, I may improvise around scenes – often other than those in the script. Or if there are two or more actors who are strangers, but are supposed to be familiar, I may ask them to have, say, a meal or an outing together in character ... But it really varies depending on the material.

On set, how do you like to give direction to your actors? How do you handle it if you aren't getting what you need from a performance?

I find this an incredibly intimate thing and I am rather shy about the conversations I have with actors. It's a real art and I am still slowly, slowly learning it. It so depends upon the personalities involved, and on what's gone wrong – and why, and how bad things are. Sometimes, when it's something minor – if I give a note too sensitively – I have found that an actor will think there's another subtext and worry that I'm hating more than I'm letting on. So for minor things, I tend to just breeze through. Mostly I would hope to give notes reasonably privately, although there's rarely time to take a break. It has to be done while the crew are busy with something else. It's not easy to do ... and not easy to get the result you hope for. That is one of the really mysterious arts of directing, I think.

Any final tips for new filmmakers when working with their actors?

Don't ignore them. Don't be frightened of them. Be kind – they are in a very vulnerable position. Don't spoil them. But take care of them – they are not only a valuable asset to the film, but sometimes we forget that they are not our dolls ...

Bille Eltringham graduated from Bournemouth Film School, where she met writer Simon Beaufoy (*The Full Monty*) and producer Mark Blaney. The three later set up Footprint Films, which made several short films and a feature film for BBC Films and Pathe, called *The Darkest Light* with Kerry Fox. Bille then directed a three-part drama for Channel 4, written by Tony Marchant, called *Kid in the Corner* before making a second feature in 2002 with Simon and Mark for the UK Film Council, *This is Not a Love Song*. The film was the first film to be distributed theatrically and on the Internet. Bille recently completed her third feature film, *Mrs Ratcliffe's Revolution*, a comedy drama starring Catherine Tate. Her work in television includes *The Long Firm*, the acclaimed four-part drama for BBC2 based on Jake Arnott's critically acclaimed novel, and an episode of the groundbreaking American series, *The L Word*. *Mrs Ratcliffe's Revolution* was released by Warner in the Autumn of 2007.

Actors' agents

While these agents primarily represent actors, we have tried to indicate where an agent also represents other film crafts (directors, writers, technicians). For a more complete list of agents who represent these other crafts, refer to the listings in the 'Crew' subsection of Production.

41 Management

3rd Floor, 74 Rose Street, North Lane,
Edinburgh EH2 3DX
tel 0131-225 3585 *fax* 0131-225 4535
email mhunwick@41man.co.uk
Agent Maryam Hunwick *Assistant* Amanda Stewart

Personal management agency established in 1999. One agent represents actors in all media including several BAFTA and BIFA award-winning stage, screen and television artists.

A&J Management

242A The Ridgeway, Botany Bay, Enfield EN2 8AP
tel 020-8342 0542 *fax* 020-8342 0842
email info@ajmanagement.co.uk
website www.ajmanagement.co.uk
Managing Director Jackie Michael *Key personnel* Joanne Michael, Hannah Liebeskind

Established in 1984. 3 agents represent actors. Areas of work include theatre, musicals, television, film, commercials, corporate and voice-overs.

Actors' recent credits range from *Eastenders* to *Kinky Boots*. Serious enquiries about actors may be made by phone or email and should be accompanied by a character breakdown, synopsis and shoot dates.

June Abbott Associates

55 East Road, London N1 6AH
tel 020-7251 6018
email jaa@thecourtyard.org.uk
website www.thecourtyard.org.uk
Agent June Abbott *Assistant Agent* Tanya Parkin

Established in 1994. 2 agents represent 50 actors. Areas of work include theatre, musicals, television, film, commercials, corporate and voice-overs.

Filmmakers should make contact by email and submit casting details, narrative breakdown, dates and fee information. Also open to short film work.

Acting Associates

71 Hartham Road, London N7 9JJ
tel 020-7607 3562 *fax* 020-7607 3562
email Fiona@actingassociates.co.uk
website www.actingassociates.co.uk
Agent Fiona Farley

Established in 1988. 1 agent represents 45-50 actors.

Actors Ireland

Crescent Arts Centre, 2-4 University Road,
Belfast BT7 1NH
tel 028-9024 8861 *fax* 028-9024 8861
email Geraldine@actorsireland.com
website www.actorsireland.com

Established in 2001. 2 agents represent 90 actors. Areas of work include theatre, musicals, television, film, commercials, corporate and voice-overs.

Actual Management

The Studio, 63a Ladbroke Road, London W11 3PD
tel 020-7243 1166 *fax* 0870-874 1149
email agents@actualmanagement.co.uk
website www.actualmanagement.co.uk

Established in 2002. 2 agents represent 50 actors. Areas of work include theatre, television, film and commercials.

Anita Alraun Representation

5th Floor, 28 Charing Cross Road,
London WC2H 0DB
tel 020-7379 6840 *fax* 020-7379 6865
Sole Proprietor/Agent Anita Alraun

1 agent represents a varying number of actors. Areas of work include theatre, musicals, film, television, commercials, radio drama, corporate and some voice-overs.

Alvarez Management

33 Ludlow Way, London N2 0JZ
tel 020-8883 2206 *fax* 020-8444 2646

Established in 1990. 2 agents represent 55 actors. Areas of work include theatre, musicals, television, film, commercials, corporate and voice-overs.

ALW Associates

1 Grafton Chambers, Grafton Place,
London NW1 1LN
tel 020-7388 7018 *fax* 020-7813 1398
email alweurope@onetel.com

Established in 1977 as Vernon Conway Ltd. Sole representation of 35 actors. Areas of work include theatre, musicals, television, film and commercials.

Amber Personal Management Ltd

189 Wardour Street, London W1F 8ZD
tel 020-7734 7887 *fax* 020-7734 9883
email info@amberltd.co.uk
website www.amberltd.co.uk

Established in 1986. 3 agents represent around 80 actors. Areas of work include theatre, musicals, television, film, commercials, corporate and voice-overs. Also represents directors and presenters (normally as an additional skill of actors already represented by the agency). Management has agents based in London as well as in Manchester.

Susan Angel & Kevin Francis Ltd

1st Floor, 12 D'Arblay Street, London W1F 8DU
tel 020-7439 3086 *fax* 020-7437 1712
email agents@angelandfrancis.co.uk
Director Kevin Francis

Established in 1976. 3 agents represent about 75 actors (including one disabled actor) and six major TV/film casting directors. Areas of work include theatre, television, film, and commercials.

APM Associates

PO Box 834, Hemel Hempstead,
Hertfordshire HP3 9ZP
tel (01442) 252907 *fax* (01442) 241099
email apm@apmassociates.net
website www.apmassociates.net
Managing Director Linda French

Established in 1989. Represents around 65 actors. Areas of work include theatre, musicals, television, film, commercials, corporate and voice-overs. Also represents actor-writers, presenters and directors.

Welcomes email enquiries from filmmakers/producers, giving a detailed breakdown of characters, shoot dates and fees.

Argyle Associates

St John's Buildings, 43 Clerkenwell Road,
London EC1M 5RS
tel 020-7608 2095 *fax* 020-7608 1642
email argyle.associates@virgin.net
Director Richard Linford *Key personnel* Geraldine Pryor

Established in 1995. 2 agents represent 30 actors. Areas of work include theatre, musicals, television, film, commercials and corporate.

Ash Personal Management

3 Spencer Road, Mitcham Common, Surrey CR4 15G
tel/fax 020-8646 0050
email ash-personal-mgmt@yahoo.co.uk
Agent Anthony Hyland

Established in 1986. 1 agent represents 15 actors working in theatre, musicals, television, film and commercials.

Associated International Management (AIM)

45-53 Sinclair Road, London W14 ONS
tel 020-7300 6506 *fax* 020-7300 6656
email info@aimagents.com
website www.aimagents.com
Key personnel Derek Webster, Stephen Gittins, Lisa-Marie Assenheim, Amy Jenkins

An international management established in 1984. 4 agents represent 90 actors. Areas of work include theatre, television, film and commercials. Also represents directors.

BAM Associates

Benets Cottage, Dolberrow, Churchill,
Bristol BS25 5NT
tel (01934) 852942
email casting@ebam.tv
website www.ebam.tv

2 agents represent 60 actors. Areas of work include theatre, musicals, television, film, commercials, corporate and voice-overs.

Gavin Barker Associates Ltd

2D Wimpole Street, London W1G 0EB
tel 020-7499 4777 *fax* 020-7499 3777
email amanda@gavinbarkerassociates.co.uk
website www.gavinbarkerassociates.co.uk
Managing Director Gavin Barker *Associate Director* Michelle Burke

Established in 1998. 2 agents represent 55 actors and a handful of creatives. Areas of work include theatre, musicals, television, film, commercials, corporate and voice-overs. Also represents directors and choreographers.

Filmmakers should send serious enquiries about actors by email. Short film work not prioritised.

Actors' credits include: *Doctor Who*, *Nip and Tuck*, and *Coronation Street*.

Olivia Bell Ltd

189 Wardour Street, London W1F 8ZD
tel 020-7439 3270 *fax* 020-7439 3485
email info@olivia-bell.co.uk
Managing Director Xania Segal

Established in 2001. 2 agents represent 90 actors. Areas of work include theatre, musicals, television, film and commercials.

Jorg Betts Associates

Gainsborough House, 81 Oxford Street,
London W1D 2EU
tel 020-7903 5300 *fax* 020-7903 5301
email jorg@jorgbetts.com

Established in 2001. Areas of work include theatre, musicals, television, film, commercials and corporate. Also represents directors and presenters.

Billboard Personal Management

Unit 5, 11 Mowll Street, London SW9 6BG
tel 020-7735 9956 *fax* 020-7793 0426
email billboardpm@btconnect.com
website www.billboardpm.com
Agent Daniel Tasker

Established in 1985. 1 agent represents 55 actors. Areas of work include theatre, musicals, television, film, commercials, corporate and voice-overs.

The Bridge Agency Ltd

PO Box 261, Loughton IG10 2WS
tel 0870-116 1388 *fax* 0870-116 1389
email the_bridge_agency@yahoo.co.uk
Agent Robert Stokvis

Established in 2002. 1 agent represents 10 actors. Areas of work include theatre, musicals, television, film, commercials, corporate and voice-overs.

BROOD

3 Queen's Garth, Taymount Rise, London SE23 3UF
tel 020-8699 1071 *mobile* (07932) 022635
email broodmanagement@aol.com
website www.broodmanagement.com
Director Brian Parsonage Kelly

Established in 2003. 1 agent represents 40 actors. Areas of work include theatre, musicals, television, film, commercials and corporate. Also represents models.

Website includes actor details. Please submit a synopsis and character breakdown with enquiries. Does consider short film work.

Valerie Brook Agency

10 Sandringham Road, Cheadle Hulme, Cheshire SK8 5NH
tel 0161-486 1631 *fax* 0161-488 4206
email colinbrook@freenetname.co.uk

Would consider short film work. Please send a breakdown of parts with enquiries by email or post.

Brown & Simcocks

1 Bridgehouse Court, 109 Blackfriars Road, London SE1 8HW
tel 020-7928 1229 *fax* 020-7928 1909
email mail@brownandsimcocks.co.uk
website www.brownandsimcocks.co.uk
Partners Carrie Simcocks, Peter Walmsley

Established in the 1970s; 2 agents represent 65-70 actors. Areas of work include theatre, musicals, television, film, commercials and corporate.

Brunskill Management Ltd

Suite 8A, 169 Queen's Gate, London SW7 5HE
tel 020-7581 3388 *fax* 020-7589 9460
email contact@brunskill.com
website www.brunskill.com
Agents Aude Powell, Geoff Stanton, Roger Davidson

In business for 45 years, the agency represents over 100 clients between 3 agents. Client actors work across film, television and theatre and have appeared in *Lord Of The Rings* among other top film, TV and theatre titles. Welcomes enquiries from filmmakers, who should email or phone for an informal chat.

Bronia Buchanan Associates Ltd

Nederlander House, 7 Great Russell Street, London WC1B 3NH
tel 020-7631 2004 *fax* 020-7631 2034
email info@buchanan-associates.co.uk
website www.buchanan-associates.co.uk
Agents Bronia Buchanan, Phil Belfield, Mark Ward

Sole representation of approximately 25 creatives and 150 actors. Areas of work include theatre, musicals, television, film and commercials.

Welcomes all enquiries. Actors are interested in short film work as well – send character breakdown and script.

Burnett Granger Associates Ltd

3 Clifford Street, London W1S 2LF
tel 020-7437 8008 *fax* 020-7287 3239
email associates@burnettgranger.co.uk
Agents Barry Burnett, Lindsay Granger, Lizanne Crowther

Established in 1965. 3 agents represent 140 actors.

CADS Management

209 Abbey Road, Bearwood, Birmingham B67 5NG
tel 0121-420 1996 *fax* 0121-434 4909
email info@cadsmanagement.co.uk
website www.cadsmanagement.co.uk
Manager T Smith *Coordinator/Key contact* Rosina Chaudry *IT/Administration* Ben Steel

Established in 1990. Sole representation of 60-70 actors. Areas of work include theatre, musicals, television, film, commercials, corporate, voice-overs and role-play. Also represents directors and presenters.

Jessica Carney Associates

4th Floor, 23 Golden Square, London W1F 9JP
tel 020-7434 4143 *fax* 020-7434 4175
email info@jcarneyassociates.co.uk

Established in 1950. Areas of work include theatre, television, films, commercials and musicals. Also represents technicians and directors.

Busy agency welcomes enquiries from filmmakers for paid work. Student film work should go through the casting director, rather than as a direct enquiry.

Casting Couch Productions Ltd

213 Trowbridge Road, Bradford-On-Avon, Wiltshire BA15 1EU
tel (01225) 869212 *fax* (01225) 869029
mobile (07932) 785807
email moiratownsend@yahoo.co.uk
Key personnel Moira Townsend

Established in 1991. Sole representation of 25 actors. Areas of work include theatre, musicals, television, film, commercials, corporate and voice-overs.

CFA Management

22 Church Street, Briston, Melton Constable, Norfolk NR24 2LE

tel (01263) 860650 *fax* (01263) 860650
email frances@cfamanagement.fsnet.co.uk
Key personnel Frances Ross

Established in 2000. 1 agent represents 30 actors. Areas of work include theatre, television, film and commercials.

Cinel Gabran Management

PO Box 5163, Cardiff CF5 9JB
tel 0845-066 6601 *fax* 0845-066 6605
email info@cinelgabran.co.uk
website www.cinelgabran.co.uk
Managing Director/Agent David Chance *Agent* Sioned James

Established in 1988. 2 agents represent 65 actors. Also represents presenters, singers who act, and actors who write. The company has a London client list, although 60% of clients are Wales-based and 75% bilingual. It works in both English and Welsh-language production.

Shane Collins Associates

11-15 Betterton Street, Covent Garden, London WC2H 9BP
tel 020-7470 8864 *fax* 0870-460 1983
website www.shanecollins.co.uk
Agents Shane Collins, Polly Andrews, Paul Martin

Established in 1986, the agency represents around 85 actors working in all areas of the industry.

Actors have appeared in short films and the agency does welcomes enquiries from up-and-coming directors. Please make initial contact by phone, email or fax. Recent film credits include: *Breakfast on Pluto, Oliver Twist, Batman Begins, The Business*, and *Song of Songs*.

Conway Van Gelder Grant

18-21 Jermyn Street, London SW1Y 6HP
tel 020-7287 0077 *fax* 020-7287 1940
Agents Jeremy Conway, Nicola van Gelder, John Grant, Liz Nelson

4 agents represent actors working in all areas of the industry.

Howard Cooke Associates (HCA)

19 Coulson Street, London SW3 3NA
tel 020-7591 0144
Managing Director/Senior Agent Howard Cooke
Junior Agent Bronwyn Sanders

2 agents represent 40 actors. Areas of work include theatre, musicals, television, film, commercials and corporate.

Filmmakers should submit cast breakdown and budget. No short films or student films.

Coulter Management Agency

333 Woodlands Road, Glasgow G3 6NG
tel 0141-357 6666 *fax* 0141-357 6676
email cmaglasgow@btconnect.com
Agent Anne Coulter *Assistant* S Bartram

2 agents represent 80 actors. Areas of work include theatre, television, film, commercials, corporate and voice-overs.

Filmmakers/producers should contact the agency by email or phone, and be prepared to submit script synopsis and character breakdown.

Covent Garden Management

5 Denmark Street, London WC2H 8LP
tel 020-7240 8400 *fax* 020-7240 8409
email agents@coventgardenmanagement.com

Established in 2002. The agency represents around 30 actors. Areas of work include theatre, musicals, television, film, commercials, corporate and voice-overs. Also represents directors.

CSM Artists

Honeysuckle Cottage, 93 Telford Way, Yeading, Middlesex UB4 9TH
tel 020-8839 8747
email csmartists@aol.com
Proprietor Angela Radford *Agent* Carole Deamer
Personal Assistant Anthea Francis

Personal management established in 1984. Sole representation of 40-50 actors. Areas of work include theatre, musicals, television, film, commercials and corporate.

Curtis Brown Ltd

Haymarket House, 28-29 Haymarket, London SW1Y 4SP
tel 020-7393 4400 *fax* 020-7393 4401
email info@curtisbrown.co.uk
website www.curtisbrown.co.uk
Agents Jacquie Drewe, Maxine Hoffman, Sarah MacCormick, Sarah Spear, Kate Staddon

One of Europe's oldest and largest independent literary and media agencies. Established over 100 years ago, there are now more than 20 agents within the Book, Media, Actors and Presenters Divisions, 5 of whom represent actors. Also represents writers, directors, playwrights and celebrities.

Dance UK

Battersea Arts Centre, Lavender Hill, London SW11 5TN
tel 020-7228 4990 *fax* 020-7223 0074
email francesca@danceuk.org
website www.danceuk.org

Resource that holds details of UK-based choreographers with experience in the film, television, theatre and entertainment industries. Online database.

Caroline Dawson Associates

125 Gloucester Road, London SW7 4TE
tel 020-7373 3323 *fax* 020-7373 1110

email cda@cdalondon.com

Represents 80 actors who work across a wide range of film and television. Roles have included: *Harry Potter*, *Bridget Jones*, *Calendar Girls*, *Emmerdale* and *Cracker*. Enquiries by phone or email are welcomed.

E15 Management

East 15 Acting School, Hatfields, Rectory Lane, Loughton, Essex IG10 3RY
tel 020-8508 3746 *fax* 020-8508 3746
email e15management@yahoo.com

1 agent represents around 60 East 15 graduates. The agency works in all fields of the acting industry.

Evolution Management

Studio 21, The Truman Brewery Building, 91 Brick Lane, London E1 6QB
tel 020-7053 2128 *fax* 020-7375 2752
email info@evolutionmngt.com
website www.evolutionmngt.com
Development Directors Loftus Burton, Henrik Bjork

Founded in 1999; 3 agents represent around 30 actors working in theatre, musicals, television, film and commercials. The agency also represents directors, make-up artists and presenters.

Fushion

27 Old Gloucester Street, London WC1N 3XX
tel (08700) 111100 *fax* (08700) 111020
email info@fushion-uk.com
website www.fushionpukkabosh.com
Key personnel Lawrence Endacott, Judy Oliver

Established in 1998 and re-branded in 2004, Fushion Pukka Bosh is a vibrant high-profile sole management agency based in London and New York with an intimate portfolio of 25 leading performing and recording artistes. Only deals with featured established artistes, so no unsolicited requests. Enquiries should submit casting details and script.

Garricks

5 The Old School House, The Lanterns, London SW11 3AD
tel 020-7738 1600 *fax* 020-7738 1881
email megan@garricks.net
Key personnel Megan Willis

Established in 1981. Areas of work include theatre, television, film, commercials and corporate. Also represents directors and presenters.

Gilbert & Payne Personal Management

Room 236, 2nd Floor, Linen Hall, 162-168 Regent Street, London W1B 5TB
tel 020-7734 7505 *fax* 020-7494 3787
email ee@gilbertandpayne.com
Director Elena Gilbert *Key personnel* Elaine Payne

Established in 1996. 2 agents represent 50 actors. Areas of work include theatre, musicals, television, film, commercials and corporate, with a particular emphasis on musical theatre. Also represents choreographers.

Global Artists

23 Haymarket, London SW1Y 4DG
tel 020-7839 4888 *fax* 020-7839 4555
email info@globalartists.co.uk
website www.globalartists.co.uk

A personal management company representing professional actors and actresses. Areas of work include theatre, musical theatre, television, film, commercials and corporate. Also represents a limited number of theatre designers, choreographers, directors and musical directors.

Darren Gray Management

2 Marston Lane, Portsmouth, Hampshire PO3 5TW
tel 023-9269 9973 *fax* 023-9267 7227
email darren.gray1@virgin.net
website www.darrengraymanagement.co.uk
Managing Director Darren Gray

Established in 1994. 2 agents represent 60 actors in both England and Australia. Agency mainly represents Australian actors, the majority of whom come from Australian soap operas. Areas of work include theatre, musicals, television, film, commercials, corporate and voice-overs. Also represents directors, producers, writers and presenters.

Film enquiries accepted by email. Please send casting breakdown, synopsis, fee information and filming dates.

Joan Gray Personal Management

29 Sudbury Court Island, Sunbury-on-Thames, Middlesex TW16 5PP

1 agent represents a small number of actors. Areas of work include theatre, musicals, television, film, commercials, corporate and voice-overs. Not looking to take on any new actors at the moment.
Commission: 10%

Grays Management Ltd

Panther House, 38 Mount Pleasant, London WC1X 0AP
tel 020-7278 1054 *fax* 020-7278 1091
email e-mail@graysmanagement.idps.co.uk
website www.graysman.com
Agent Mary Nelson

2 agents represent approximately 90 actors working in theatre, musicals, television, film, commercials and corporate role-play.

Hatton McEwan

PO Box 37385, London N1 7XF
tel 020-7253 4770 *fax* 020-7251 9081
email info@thetalent.biz
website www.thetalent.biz

Established in 1988, the agency represents actors working in theatre, musicals, television, film, commercials and corporate. Other clients include directors, composers and designers.

Actors will consider short film work if paid; submit a CV and script with enquiries.

Henry's Agency

53 Westbury, Rochford, Essex SS4 1UL
tel (01702) 541413 *fax* (01702) 541413
email info@henrysagency.co.uk
website www.henrysagency.co.uk

Established in 1995; 1 agent represents 35 actors. Areas of work include theatre, musicals, television, film, commercials and corporate.

Sandra Singer Associates

21 Cotswold Road, Westcliff-on-Sea, Essex SSO 8AA
tel (01702) 331616 *fax* (01702) 339393
email sandrasinger@btconnect.com
website www.sandrasinger.com
Key personnel Sandra Singer (MIEAM)

Main areas of work are feature films, film, TV, commercials and musical theatre. Also represents singers.

Williamson & Holmes

9 Hop Gardens, St Martin's Lane,
London WC2N 4EN
tel 020-7240 0407 *fax* 020-240 0408
email info@williamsonandholmes.co.uk
Agents Jackie Williamson, Michelle Holmes *Voice-over Agent* Sophie Reisch, *Children's Agent* Danica Pickett

Established in 2004, the agency represents 70 actors and 30 voice-over artists. Areas of work include theatre, musicals, television, film, commercials, corporate and voice-overs.

Casting directors

Joanne Adamson Casting

Northern Star Productions, 4 Pollard Lane, Leeds LS13 1EY
mobile (07787) 311270
email watts07@hotmail.com

Main areas of work are theatre, musicals, television, film and commercials. Casting credits include: *Flesh and Blood* and *Nice Guy Eddie* (BBC), and *Fat Friends II* (Rollem, Tiger Aspect and Yorkshire Television).

Dorothy Andrew Casting

Mersey TV, Campus Manor, Childwall Abbey Road, Childwall, Liverpool L16 OJP
tel 0151-737 4044 *fax* 0151-722 9079
email casting@merseytv.com

Casts mainly for television, film and commercials. Recent credits include: *Hollyoaks*, *Grange Hill* and *Court Room*.

Victoria Beattie

Big Fish, 27 Cranworth Street, Top Flat Right, Glasgow G12 8AD
tel 0141-339 1935 *fax* 0141-339 1935
email victoria@victoriabeattie.com

Casts for film. Credits include: *Yasmin*, *Blind Flight*, and *Dogging: A Love Story*.

Lucy Bevan

Twickenham Film Studios, The Barons, St Margarets, Twickenham TW1 2AW
tel 020-8607 8888 *fax* 020-8607 8701
email lucy@lucybevan.com

Credits include: *His Dark Materials: The Golden Compass* (New Line Cinema), *The Libertine* (Mr Mudd/Weinstein Co.), *Dirty War* (BBC Films) and *Camera Obscura* (Almeida Theatre).

Sarah Bird CDG

PO Box 32658, London W14 0XA
tel 020-7371 3248 *fax* 020-7602 8601

Casts for film, television, theatre and commercials. Casting credits include: *You Don't Have To Say You Love Me*, directed by Simon Shore (Samuelson Productions); *Ladies in Lavender*, directed by Charles Dance (Scala Productions); *Fortysomething* (Carlton TV); and *Calico*, directed by Edward Hall (Sonia Friedman Productions).

Lucy Boulting CDG

22 Montreal Road, Brighton BN2 9UY
email lucy@boultingcasting.wanadoo.co.uk

Casts mainly for film. Casting credits include: *Besieged* (Bernardo Bertolucci); *Shadowlands* (Richard Attenborough); and *Sexy Beast* (Jonathan Glazer).

Candid Casting

1st Floor, 32 Great Sutton Street, London EC1V 0NB
tel 020-7490 8882
email mail@candidcasting.co.uk
Casting Director Amanda Tabak CDG *Assistant Casting Directors* Brendan McNamara, Katie Needle

Main areas of work are television, film and commercials. Casting credits include: *The Low Down* (film) and *Is Harry on the Boat?* (television film), *WASP* (Oscar-winning short film), *Kidulthood*, and *Mr Harvey Lights a Candle* (TV).

Filmmakers may make enquiries by phone or email. Will consider short film work.

Cannon Dudley & Associates

43a Belsize Square, London NW3 4HN
tel 020-7433 3393 *fax* 020-7813 2048
email cdacasting@blueyonder.co.uk
Casting Director Carol Dudley CDG, CSA *Casting Associate* Helena Palmer

Main areas of work are theatre, television and film. Recent credits include: *The Third Mother – Mother of Tears* (Director: Dario Argento), *Master Harold and the Boys* (Director: Lonny Price), and theatre productions for Bath Theatre Royal, Nuffield Theatre, Southampton and Library Theatre, Manchester.

Anji Carroll CDG

tel (01270) 250240
email anjicarrollcdg@yahoo.co.uk

Main areas of work are film and television. Casting credits include: *The Sarah Jane Adventures*, New Year's Day Special (Dr Who Productions for BBC); *Mrs Ratcliffe's Revolution* (feature film directed by Bille Eltringham); *The Bill* (Talkback Thames); *Stir It Up*, *The Trial*, *The Window and Service* (IWC Media for C4); *Out of Depth* (feature film directed by Simon Marshall); and 4 x 90 min of *The Knock* and 32 x 60 min of *London's Burning* (LWT).

The Casting Angels (London and Paris)

Suite 4, 14 College Road, Bromley BR1 3NS
fax 020-8313 0443
Director Michael Ange

The company has 30 years' experience of working across theatre, television, film and commercials and is interested in any genre, as well as in short films. It has some international clients; also specialises in documentary subjects and welcomes enquiries from new filmmakers via letter or phone.

Casting UK

10 Coptic Street, London WC1A 1NH
tel 020-7580 3456
email drew@castinguk.com
Casting Director Andrew Mann

Casts mainly for film and commercials. Casting credits include: commercials for Bacardi, Acuview, DFS, ASDA and Maltesers; and pop videos for Placebo, Sugarbabes and Busted.

Contact by email or post.

Suzy Catliff CDG

PO Box 39492, London N10 3YX
tel 020-8442 0749
email soose@soose.co.uk

Casts mainly for television, film and theatre. Most recent credits include: for television, *Lifeline* (BBC1), *Empathy* (BBC1), *Silent Witness* (Series IX & X), *Blitz* (Channel 4), *D-Day* (BBC 1), and *Sir Gadabout* (ITV); for film, *Stormbreaker* (associate), *The Swimming Pool* (assistant), *Sense and Sensibility* (assistant), and *Wilde & Hackers*; and for theatre, *Life X 3* (No. 1 tour), *The Play What I Wrote*, *Ducktastic* (associate).

Does work on paid short films; filmmakers should make contact via post, phone or email in the first instance.

Alison Chard CDG

23 Groveside Court, 4 Lombard Road, London SW11 3RQ
tel 020-7223 9125
email alisonchard@castingdirector.freeserve.co.uk
website www.thecdg.co.uk

Main areas of work are theatre, television, film and commercials. Will consider paid short film projects; enquiries should be sent via email initially, with information about plot, casting breakdown, budgets/fees and contracts. Will request script and showreel in due course.

Sarah Crowe Casting

75 Amberley Road, London W9 2JL
tel 020-7286 5080 *fax* 020-7286 5030
email sarah@sarahcrowecasting.co.uk
website www.sarahcrowecasting.co.uk

Credits include: *Grow Your Own*, and *Hustle*.

Jane Davies Casting Ltd

PO Box 680, Sutton, Surrey SM1 3ZG
tel 020-8715 1036 *fax* 020-8644 9746
email info@janedaviescasting.co.uk
Casting Directors Jane Davies CDG, John Connor CDG

Casts mainly for television. Casting credits include: *My Family*, *The Green Green Grass*, and *Black Books*.

Leo Davis

Just Casting, 128 Talbot Road, London W11 1JA
tel 020-7229 3471 *fax* 020-7792 3043

Credits include: *The Queen*, *Mrs Henderson Presents*, *The Constant Gardener*, *Girl With A Pearl Earring*, *Dirty Pretty Things*, *The Deal*, *Wit*, *Croupier*, and *Felicia's Journey*.

Gary Davy CDG

1st Floor, 55-59 Shaftesbury Avenue, London W1D 6LD

Casts for film and television. Casting credits include: *Band of Brothers* (mini-series directed by Tom Hanks); *Revengers Tragedy* (Alex Cox); *Sweeney Todd* (starring Ray Winstone – BBC); Nick Cave's *The Proposition* (John Hillcoat); *The Business* (Nick Love, and his latest film, *Outlaws*). Also cast BAFTA-winning film, *Kiss of Life* (Emily Young). In 2006/07 worked for Ecosse TV, Company TV, Vertigo and Autonomous. Written submissions only.

The Denman Casting Agency

Burgess House, Main Street, Farnsfield, Notts NG22 8EF
Key personnel Jack Denman, FEAA

Main areas of work are theatre, musicals, television, film and commercials. Casting credits include: *Peak Practice*, *Doctors*, and *Crimewatch* (television); videos for PC World and Boots.

Lee Dennison CDA

Fushion, 27 Old Gloucester Street, London WC1N 3XX
tel 0870-011 1100 *fax* 0870-011 1020
email leedennison@fushion-uk.com
website www.ukscreen.com/crew/ldennison
website www.leedennisonassociates.com
Casting London/New York Lee Dennison, Chuck Harvey, Ram Tucker *Casting London/Paris* Lee Dennison, Will Baker, Jamie Lowe *Assistant* Dean Saunders

Casts mainly for film and television features as well as commercials and music promos. Recent credits include: *Vacancy* (Screen Gems), *Buttermilk Sky* (Charles R Leinenweber), *Echo Park LA* (Sony), *United 93* (Universal) and *Standoff* (Fox). Will consider film feature and television scripts, dependent on script and budget. Applicants should send script, budget and casting details and dates to London office, unless otherwise requested.

Malcom Drury CDG

34 Tabor Road, London W6 0BW
tel 020-8748 9232

Casts mainly for television. Casting credits include: *The Bill*, *Heartbeat*, *The Beiderbecke Affair* and Laurence Olivier's *King Lear*.

Enquiries welcomed in writing. Please send a script and/or synopsis.

Julia Duff CDG

73 Wells Street, London W1T 3QG
tel 020-7436 8860 *fax* 020-7436 8859

Casts mainly for film, television and commercials. Casting credits include: *Hamish Macbeth*, *Hotel Babylon* and *Lorna Doone* (for television), and UK casting for *The House of Mirth* (Terence Davies).

Welcomes enquiries via email from filmmakers with a synopsis, and will consider short film projects.

Irene East Casting CDG

40 Brookwood Avenue, Barnes, London SW13 0LR
tel 020-8876 5686 *fax* 020-8876 5686
email IrnEast@aol.com

Main areas of work are theatre and film. Casting credits include: *Distant Mirage*, *Big Claus, Little Claus*, *Pets*, and UK casting for *Scandinavian Features* (film); and *The Playboy of the Western World*, *Henry V*, *Wuthering Heights*, *Two Into War* and *Murder in Paris* (theatre).

Occasionally casts commercials. Drama is the preferred film genre; has cast several short film projects. Works in the UK and on foreign projects and welcomes enquiries. Please send Director CV and synopsis of the script by email or post.

EJ Casting

150 Tooley Street, London SE1 2TV
tel 020-7564 2688
email info@EJCasting.com
Director Edward James

Casts for theatre, musicals, film, commercials and corporate work. Casting credits include: *Into the Woods* and *Sweet Charity* (theatre); commercials for AOL, Lloyds Bank, Sony BMG, Universal Music, and Cadbury's Fingers; and *Air on a G String* (film).

All enquiries should be sent with cast breakdown, synopsis, and production details. Will consider short film work.

Chloe Emmerson

96 Portobello Road, London W11 2QG
tel 020-7792 8823
email c@ChloeEmmerson.com

Casts mainly for film, TV, theatre and commercials. Credits include: *Pure* (Gillies MacKinon), *The Last Resort* (Pavel Pawlikowski), *The Yellow House* (Chris Durlacher), *Nathan Barley* (Chris Morris), and *The Somme* (Carl Hindmarch). Also known for child casting, including for *Billy Elliot* (Stephen Daldry), and *The War Zone* (Tim Roth). Welcomes enquiries by email or phone, and will consider short film projects, dependent on script.

Richard Evans CDG

10 Shirley Road, London W4 1DD
tel 020-8994 6304
email info@evanscasting.co.uk
website www.evanscasting.co.uk
Key personnel Richard Evans CDG

Main areas of work are theatre, musicals, television, film and commercials. Casting credits include: *The Rat Pack – Live From Las Vegas* (theatre).

Welcomes enquiries from new filmmakers, but short-film/low-budget work only considered if not on deferred or no-payment fee basis. Make contact by email or post (please, no large attachments by email). Include information on project, shoot dates and details of cast requirements.

Bunny Fildes Casting CDG

56-60 Wigmore Street, London W1U 2RZ
tel 020-7935 1254 *fax* 020-7298 1871

Casts mainly for theatre, television, film and commercials.

Celestia Fox

5 Clapham Common, Northside, London SW4 0QW
tel 020-7720 6143 *fax* 020-7720 2734

Credits include: *Lassie*, *The White Countess*, and *Oliver Twist*.

Nina Gold CDG

117 Chevening Road, London NW6 6DU
tel 020-8960 6099 *fax* 020-8968 6777

Main areas of work are film, television and commercials. Casting credits include: *Vera Drake*, directed by Mike Leigh (Thin Man Films); *The Life and Death of Peter Sellers*, directed by Stephen Hopkins; *The Jacket*, directed by John Maybury (Warner Bros); *Daniel Deronda*, directed by Tom Hooper (BBC TV); *Amazing Grace* and *Rome* both directed by Michael Apted; *Starter for Ten* directed by Tom Vaughan; *The Illusionist* directed by Neil Burger; and *Brothers of the Head* directed by Keith Fulton and Louis Pepe.

Miranda Gooch

102 Leighton Gardens, London NW10 3RP

Casts mainly for feature films. Recent credits have included: *True Story* and *Tooth*.

Jill Green CDG

Cambridge Theatre, Earlham Street, Seven Dials, Covent Garden, London WC2H 9HV
tel 020-7379 4795 *fax* 020-7379 4796

Casts for theatre, musicals and film. Casting credits include: *The Producers* (Drury Lane Theatre); *Thoroughly Modern Millie* (Shaftesbury Theatre); *Contact* (Queens Theatre); and *Beyond the Sea* (film directed by Kevin Spacey).

Marcia Gresham CDG

3 Langthorne Street, London SW6 6JT
tel 020-7381 2876 *fax* 020-7381 4496
email marcia@greshamcast.com

Main area of work is television. Casting credits include: *The Debt*, *Walk Away and I Stumble*, *The Project* and *Innocents* (television).

All casting enquiries welcome, by phone or by email.

David Grindrod CDG

4th Floor, Palace Theatre, Shaftesbury Avenue, London W1D 5AY

tel 020-7437 2506 *fax* 020-7437 2507
email dga@grindrodcasting.co.uk

Casts for musicals and film. Casting credits include: *The Phantom of the Opera* (film directed by Joel Schumacher); and *The Woman in White*, *Brighton Rock*, *Jerry Springer the Opera* and *Chicago* (all West End musicals).

Michelle Guish

The Casting Company, 3rd Floor,
112-114 Wardour Street, London, W1F 0TS
tel 020-7734 4954 *fax* 020-7434 2346 (Fax)

Credits include: *Perfume*, *Goya's Ghosts*, and *Breaking and Entering*.

Janet Hall

69 Buckstones Road, Shaw, Oldham OL2 8DW

Main areas of work include television, film and commercials. Casting credits include: AXA commercial, and *The Sound of Music* (theatre).

Areas of specialism include casting children and young actors. Will consider short film work and welcomes enquiries by phone or email.

Louis Hammond

30-31 Peter Street, London W1F 0AR
tel 020-7734 0626 *fax* 020-7439 2522

Main areas of work are theatre, television and film. Casting credits include: *Mirrormask* and *Arsene Lupin* (films), and *The Bill* and *Rock 'N' Roll* (Royal Court/West End).

Gemma Hancock CDG

The Rosary, Broad Street, Cuckfield,
West Sussex RH17 5DL
tel (01444) 441398 *fax* (01444) 441398

Main areas of work are theatre, television and film. Casting credits include: *The Bill* (Talkback Thames); Peter Ackroyd's *London* (BBC 2); *Blithe Spirit* (West End and tour); and *The Dresser* (Bath Theatre Royal and tour).

Polly Hootkins CDG

PO Box 52480, London NW3 9DH
tel 020-7233 8724 *fax* 020-7828 5051
email phootkins@clara.net
website www.thecdg.co.uk
Key personnel Polly Hootkins

Main areas of work are theatre, television and film. Casting credits include: *A New Day in Old Sana'a* and *Captain Jack*.

Filmmakers should make contact by email and send script with enquiries. Will consider short film work.

Dan Hubbard CDG

24 Poland Street, London W1F 8QL
tel 020-7636 9991 *fax* 020-7636 7117
Casting Directors John Hubbard, Ros Hubbard, Dan Hubbard

Casts mainly for film, television, theatre and commercials. Casting credits include: *Murder Squad* (Granada television); *Paradise Heights* (BBC); *The Murder of Stephen Lawrence* (Granada); *Tomb Raider 1* and *2* (films for Paramount); and *Dracula 2000* (Miramax/Dimensions films).

Jennifer Jaffrey

136 Hicks Avenue, Greenford, Middlesex UB6 8HB
tel 020-8578 2899 *fax* 020-8575 0369
Key personnel Jennifer Jaffrey *(Proprietor)*

Main areas of work are theatre, musicals, television, film and commercials. Casting credits include: *Cross My Heart*, *Ten Minutes Older* and *Such a Long Journey*.

Jina Jay

2 Sound Centre, Twickenham Film Studios,
The Barons, St Margarets, Middlesex TW1 2AW
tel 020-8607 8888 *fax* 020-8607 8982

Credits include: *The Last King of Scotland*, *Atonement*, and *Munich*.

Lucy Jenkins CDG

Royal Shakespeare Company, 1 Earlham Street,
London WC2H 9LL
tel 020-8943 5328 *fax* 020-8977 0466

Casts mainly for film, television, theatre and commercials. Casting credits include: *Babyfather* (BBC), *The Bill* (television), *Top Dog* (short film) and *Emma* (theatre).

Doreen Jones

PO Box 22478, London W6 0WJ
tel 020-8746 3782 *fax* 020-8748 8533

Casts mainly for television and film. Recent credits include: *Fingersmith*, *Elizabeth*, *Instinct* and *The Palace*.

Sue Jones CDG

24 Nicoll Road, London NW10 9AB
tel 020-8838 5153 *fax* 020-8838 1130

Main areas of work are film, television, theatre and commercials. Casting credits include: *The Virgin of Liverpool*, starring Ricky Tomlinson and Imelda Staunton (MOB Films); *The Sound of Thunder*, with Ed Burns, Ben Kingsley and Catherine McCormack; *The Origins of Evil* (CBS/Alliance Atlantis); *Messiah* and *Coriolanus* (both plays directed by Stephen Berkoff); *The Vicar* (BBC television); and *The Politician's Wife* (Channel 4).

Anna Kennedy Casting

anna@kennedycasting.com
mobile (07973) 119269
tel 020-8673 6550

Credits include: *Daddy's Girl*.

Beverley Keogh

29 Ardwick Green North, Ardwick, Manchester M12 6DL
tel 0161-273 4400 *fax* 0161-273 4401
email Beverley@beverlykeogh.tv

Main areas of work are television, film and commercials. Casting credits include: *Fat Friends, Clocking Off* and *Second Coming.*

Sharon Levinson

30 Stratford Villas, London NW1 9SG

Main areas of work are theatre, television, film and commercials. Casting credits include: *Two Thousand Acres of Sky* and *A Christmas Carol* (television).

Karen Lindsay-Stewart CDG

PO Box 2301, London W1A 1PT

Main areas of work are television and film. Casting credits include: *Sylvia, Harry Potter and the Chamber of Secrets* and *Cambridge Spies.*

Carolyn McLeod

PO Box 26495, London SE10 0WO
tel + 44 (0)704 4001720
email actors@cmcasting.eclipse.co.uk

Main areas of work are film, television and promos. Casting director credits include: *The Bill, Pumpkinhead 3: Ashes to Ashes*, and *Pumpkinhead 4: Dark Hell.* Casting associate credits include: *Basic Instinct 2: Risk Addiction, Rottweiler*, and *Im Auftrag Des Vatikans.*

Sooki McShane CDG

8a Piermont Road, East Dulwich, London SE22 0LN
tel 020-8693 7411 *fax* 020-8693 7411

Works mainly in theatre, film and television. Casting credits include: *Rainbow Room* (Granada television); *My Brother Rob* (feature film); and casting for the Warehouse Theatre Croydon.

Carl Proctor CDG

66 Great Russell Street, London WC1B 3BN
tel 020-7405 0561 *fax* 020-7405 0564
email carlproctor@btconnect.com
website www.carlproctor.com

Casts mainly for film, television, theatre and commercials. Casting credits include: *Mrs Palfrey at the Claremont, Something Borrowed* and *Dead Cool.*

Andy Pryor CDG

Suite 3, 15 Broad Court, London WC2B 5QN
tel 020-7836 8298 *fax* 020-7836 8299

Casts mainly for film, television and commercials. Casting credits include: *Perfect Strangers* and *The Lost Prince* (both directed by Stephen Poliakoff for BBC television); and *Long Time Dead* (film directed by Marcus Adams).

Francesca Raftery CDG

51 Purley Vale, Purley, Surrey CR8 2DU
tel 020-8763 0105 *fax* 020-8763 0105
email info@francescaraftery.com
website www.fancescaraftery.com
Casting Director Francesca Raftery CDG

Casts mainly for commercials. Casting credits include: commercials for Grolsch, Knorr, Coca Cola, Volkswagon and Visa.

Welcomes enquiries from filmmakers and would consider short film projects. Send storyline, character breakdown and timing for casting.

Simone Reynolds CDG

60 Hebdon Road, London SW17 7NN

Main areas of work are film, television, theatre and commercials. Casting credits include: *The 39 Steps* (Olivier Award for Best Comedy); *The Vicar of Dibley* and *Turning Points: Emma's Story* (both for BBC television); *Jack and Sarah* (film for Granada); *Shining Through* (film for Twentieth Century Fox) and *Quicksand* (film).

Sasha Robertson Casting CDG

19 Wendell Road, London W12 9RS
tel 020-8740 0817 *fax* 020-8740 1396
email sasha@sasharobertson.com

Credits include: *The Mysti Show, Timewatch*, and *Born With Two Mothers.*

Laura Scott CDG

56 Rowena Crescent, London SW11 2PT
tel 020-7978 6336 *fax* 020-7924 1907

Main areas of work are film, television, theatre and commercials. Casting credits include: *William and Mary* (Series 1-3, TV), *Trial and Retribution XIV* (TV), and *The Time of Your Life* (TV).

The Searchers

70 Sylvia Court, Cavendish Street, London N1 7PG
Directors Wayne Waterson, Ian Sheppard

Casts mainly for television, film and commercials. Recent credits include: commercials for Pepsi, Nike, Kellogg's and Royal Mail. Has worked for directors including Terry Gillingham, Tarsem and Earl Morris.

Phil Shaw

Suite 476, 2 Old Brompton Road, South Kensington, London SW7 3DQ
tel 020-8715 8943 *mobile* (07702) 124935
fax 020-8408 1193
email shawcastlond@aol.com

Main areas of work are theatre, television, film and commercials. Casting credits include: *The Turn of the Screw* (theatre); *The Last Post* (film – BAFTA nominated); *When Harry Tries to Marry* (film); *La Mere Sauvage* (film); *Body Story* (TV documentary series); *Days in the Trees* (radio); *Love and Virtue* (feature); *Deckies* (TV series).

Preferred areas of work include period costume dramas, psychological thrillers, and drama-docs. Has worked on short films for leading film schools and welcomes enquiries from new filmmakers with a script, treatment and casting breakdown.

Michelle Smith CDG

220 Church Lane, Woodford, Stockport SK7 1PQ
tel 0161-439 6825 *fax* 0161-439 0622

Main areas of work are film, television and commercials. Casting credits include: *Steel River Blues* (ITV); *Max and Paddy* (Channel 4); *Phoenix Nights* (Channel 4); and *Cold Feet* (Series 1-5 – Granada).

Suzanne Smith CDG

33 Fitzroy Street, London W1T 6DU
tel 020-7436 9255 *fax* 020-7436 9690

Main areas of work are film, television, theatre and musicals. Casting credits include: UK casting for *Alien vs Predator* (directed by Paul Anderson for 20th Century Fox); *The Dark* (directed by John Fawcett for Impact Pictures); UK casting for *Black Hawk Down* (directed by Ridley Scott); and *Band of Brothers* (for television – HBO/Dreamworks).

Gail Stevens Casting CDG

Greenhill House, 90-93 Cowcross Street, London EC1M 6BF

Main areas of work are television, film and commercials. Casting credits include: *Twenty-Eight Days Later*, *Calendar Girls* and *Spooks.*

Sam Stevenson CDG

email sam@hancockstevenson.com
website www.hancockstevenson.com

Main areas of work are television, theatre and film. More details are available on the website.

Emma Style

c/o Ken McReddie Ltd, 21 Barrett Street, London W1U 1BD
tel 020-7701 7750
email emmastyle@lineone.net

Credits include: *Creep*, *Tea With Mussolini*, and *Our Friends in the North.*

Lucinda Syson CDG

1st Floor, 33 Old Compton Street, London W1D 5JT
tel 020-7287 5327 *fax* 020-7287 3629

Recent feature films include: *Children of Men*, directed by Alfonso Cuaron; *Syriana*, directed by Stephen Gagan; *Batman Begins*, directed by Chris Nolan; *Troy*, directed by Wolfgang Petersen; *Snatch*, directed by Guy Ritchie; *Spygame*, directed by Tony Scott; and *Fifth Element*, directed by Luc Besson.

Jill Trevellick CDG

92 Priory Road, London N8 7EY
tel 020-8340 2734 *fax* 020-8348 7400

Main areas of work are film and television. Casting credits include: *The Ruby In The Smoke*, *North and South*, and *The Canterbury Tales* (all BBC); *Primeval* (ITV); and *The Queen's Sister* and *The Hamburg Cell* (both Channel 4).

Sarah Trevis CDG

PO Box 47170, London W6 6BA
tel 020-7602 5552 *fax* 020-7602 8110

Main areas of work are television and film. Recent casting credits include: work for Granada television, the BBC and Twentieth Century Fox.

Vital Productions

PO Box 26441, London SE10 9GZ
tel 020-8316 4497 *fax* 020-8316 4497
email mail@vital-productions.co.uk
Key personnel Melissa Waudby

Main areas of work are theatre and television. Casting credits include: *BBC Crimewatch* and *The Great Dome Robbery* (television).

Anne Vosser CDG

Nederlander House, 7 Great Russell Street, London WC1B 3NH
tel 020-7079 0277 *fax* 020-7079 0276
email anne@vosser-casting.co.uk

Main areas of work are theatre and musicals but does some work in film. Producers are welcome to make contact by telephone or email.

Matt Western

59-61 Brewer Street, London W1F 9UN
tel 020-7434 1230 *fax* 020-7439 1941

Main areas of work are film, television, theatre and commercials. Casting credits include: *The Other Boleyn Girl* (film for BBC television); *The Night Detective* (series for Zenith/BBC); and *Essential Poems* (for Talkback Productions).

Will consider short film work. Email enquiries, or phone.

Toby Whale CDG

80 Shakespeare Road, London W3 6SN
tel 020-8993 2821 *fax* 020-8993 8096
website www.whalecasting.com

Head of Casting at the National Theatre 2003-06. Main areas of work are film, television and theatre. Casting credits include: *The History Boys*; *East is East* (Assassin Films/FilmFour); *The French Film* (Slingshot); *True Dare Kiss* (BBC); *Spoonface Steinberg* (BBC Films); *Wire in the Blood* (Series 1 & 2 – Coastal/ITV); and more than 40 theatre productions for the Royal Court Theatre, Out of Joint, the Almeida Theatre, English Touring Theatre and Sheffield Crucible, among others.

Tara Woodward

Top Flat, 93 Gloucester Avenue, Primrose Hill, London NW1 8LB

tel 020-7586 3487 *fax* 020-7681 8574

Main areas of work are film, television, theatre and commercials. Casting credits include: *The Early Days, Post* and *Hello Friend* (all for Shine/Film Four Lab); *Chasing Heaven* (for Venice Film Festival); *The Browning Version* and *Romeo and Juliet* (theatre); and commercials for Parmalat Aqua and Royal Danish Post. Has worked as Casting Assistant to Nina Gold on films including *All Or Nothing* (directed by Mike Leigh) and *Love's Labour's Lost* (directed by Kenneth Branagh).

Jeremy Zimmermann Casting

36 Marshall Street, London W1F 7EY
tel 020-7478 5161 *fax* 020-7437 4747

Main areas of work are film and television. Recent casting work includes: the films *Keeping Mum*, *The Contract, Van Wilder 2, Dog Soldiers* and *Blood And Chocolate.*

Casting resources

From websites that advertise roles in new productions to actors' organisations, these companies provide invaluable help in casting your film.

Actors' Centre (London)

1A Tower Street, Covent Garden,
London WC2H 9NP
tel 020-7240 3940
email act@actorscentre.co.uk
website www.actorscentre.co.uk

Full membership organisation that holds regular classes and workshops for actors.

Actors Inc.

FREEPOST NATW1128, Bracknell RG12 9BR
tel (01344) 449314
email info@actors-inc.co.uk
website www.actors-inc.co.uk

Actors' details are included in a fully searchable database that is accessible to casting professionals. Voice samples can also be incorporated. Casting breakdowns are delivered to actors via email. Members can search the website for information, advice and details of workshops and events, as well as the Jobs Notice Board, which is updated daily.

The Agents' Association

54 Keyes House, Dolphin Square,
London SW1V 3NA
tel 020-7834 0515 *fax* 020-7821 0261
email association@agents-uk.com
website www.agents-uk.com

Established in 1927 to represent and enhance the interests of entertainment agents in the UK. Membership includes more than 430 agencies, covering all fields of the entertainment industry.

British Academy of Dramatic Combat

3 Castle View, Helmsley, North Yorkshire Y062 5AU
email enquiries@badc.co.uk
website www.badc.co.uk

Trains actors in stage and screen combat.

Casting Directors' Guild

website www.thecdg.co.uk

A professional organisation that represents casting directors working in film, television, theatre and commercials. Members are listed on the website, with information about their areas of work and recent credits.

Casting People Ltd

PO Box 26736, London SW17 7FW
fax 020-8672 9738
email info@castingpeople.com
website www.castingpeople.com

Online information service with casting breakdown emails circulated to subscribers on a daily basis.

CastNet Ltd

20 Sparrows Herne, Bushey,
Hertfordshire WD23 1FU
tel 020-8420 4209 *fax* 020-8421 9666
email admin@castingnetwork.co.uk
website www.castingnetwork.co.uk

CastNet is a slightly more selective email casting information service; members need to meet minimum criteria in training and professional experience to join. Casting information is circulated to actor members by email every day. It is tailored to the exact requirements of the actor and is also filtered to the actor's physical characteristics. Also provides an online directory of actor members.

Castweb

7 St Luke's Avenue, London SW4 7LG
tel 020-7720 9002 *fax* 020-7720 3097
email castweb@netcomuk.co.uk
website www.castweb.co.uk

CastWeb is an online casting service designed for The Spotlight members only. Circulates casting notices to member actors.

Conference of Drama Schools

PO Box 34252, London NW5 1XJ
email info@cds.drama.ac.uk
website www.drama.ac.uk

Organisation of 22 member schools offering courses in Acting, Musical Theatre, Directing, and Technical Theatre training. Also produces the *Guide to Professional Training in Drama and Technical Theatre*, which is available free of charge as a download from the CDS website.

The Council for Dance Education and Training

Old Brewer's Yard, 17-19 Neal Street,
Covent Garden, London WC2H 9UY
tel 020-7240 5703 *fax* 020-7240 2547
email info@cdet.org.uk
website www.cdet.org.uk

The national standards body of the professional dance industry.

Dance UK

Battersea Arts Centre, Lavender Hill,
London SW11 5TN

tel 020-7728 4990 *fax* 020-7223 0074
email info@danceuk.org
website www.danceuk.org

Dance UK provides information, publications, networks, forums for debate and conferences around Dance. Corporate members include most of the major dance companies, venues, agencies, funders and educational institutions – as well as individual dance artists, choreographers, administrators, managers, technicians, teachers, students, writers and members of dance audiences.

Equity Job Information Service (JIS)

Guild House, Upper St Martin's Lane, London WC2H 9EG
website www.equity.org.uk

Free casting notice service for Equity members. Producers may post production casting information free of charge, but the work must be for a fee that Equity finds acceptable for them to publish details of the work.

International Federation of Actors (FIA)

Guild House, Upper St Martin's Lane, London WC2H 9EG
tel 020-7379 0900 *fax* 020-7379 8260
email office@fia-actors.com
website www.fia-actors.com

The FIA currently represents 103 performers' unions and guilds in 73 countries around the world.

National Association of Youth Theatres

Arts Centre, Vane Terrace, Darlington DL3 7AX
tel (01325) 363330 *fax* (01325) 363313
email nayt@btconnect.com
website www.nayt.org.uk

The leading development organisation for youth theatre practice in England and Wales. NAYT provides a variety of resources, information and support for registered groups, including training programmes and a monthly *Bulletin* containing the latest news on funding, training, performances and vacancies.

Production & Casting Report (PCR)

PO Box 11, London N1 7JZ
tel 020-7566 8282 *fax* 020-7566 8284
website www.pcrnewsletter.com

Available in print and online, *PCR* is a reliable weekly newsletter that carries details of casting and crew opportunities in film, television and theatre. Casting notices are published free of charge. The deadline for receiving copy is 12pm UK time every Thursday, for publication the following Monday. Student filmmakers have an earlier deadline of 5pm Wednesday, due to the high volume of student copy received. Send copy via fax on (44) 020 7566 82841 by email at info@pcrnewsletter.com; or through the post to *PCR*, PO Box 11, London N1 7JZ. *PCR* recommends that you ring the office after sending your submission to confirm that it was recieved. Also publishes *Filmlog*, which lists feature films in pre-production and development, with details of studios, locations, key people and addresses.

Shooting People's Casting Network

website www.shootingpeople.org

See page 351 for more information.

Provides daily email bulletins for film professionals, including a daily UK Casting Bulletin. The bulletin allows actors to receive casting calls from directors, producers and casting directors. Actors can create a public casting profile which can be viewed online.

Rehearsal spaces

These are useful spaces not only for rehearsing, but also for casting your film. Keep in mind that actors will expect a professional approach to casting. It should be too obvious to mention, but it's probably not a good idea to use an informal space like someone's home or a place which may have noise issues for a casting session. You will, of course, want to videotape your sessions to see how the actor works on film, so make sure the space you select is appropriate for this.

The Amadeus Centre

50 Shirland Road, London W9 2JA
tel 020-7286 1686 *fax* 020-7266 1225
email info@amadeuscentre.co.uk
website www.amadeuscentre.co.uk

Tastefully renovated in 1989 from a former 19th century Welsh Presbyterian chapel, the Amadeus Centre offers exclusive use of 2 unique halls for events, rehearsal and location use.

American Chruch in London

Whitefield Memorial Church,
79a Tottenham Court Road, London W1T 4TD
tel 020-7580 2791 *fax* 020-7580 5013
email Latchcourt@amchurch.fsnet.co.uk
website www.latchcourt.com
Hire contact Monty Strikes

A large rehearsal space adaptable for filming, conferences, meetings and rehearsals. Parquet floor, acoustic panels on walls, and full blackout capability. Seats 300, theatre style. Approximate size 57'x36'; ceiling height: 16' approximately. There is a Yamaha U3 upright piano available.

Aviv Dance Studios

Wren House, 1st Floor, 19-23 Exchange Road, Watford, Hertfordshire WD18 0JD
tel (01923) 250000
email nikki@avivdance.com
website www.avivdance.com

A 90m2 studio available for short- and long-term hire for rehearsals, workshops and classes. The studio offers air conditioning, mirrors and bars, a fully sprung Harlequin floor, a stereo system and facilities including a changing room, toilets, snack machine and viewing area. Located in the centre of Watford just off the High Street.

Big City Studios

Montgomery House, 159-161 Balls Pond Road, Islington, London N1 4BG
tel 020-7241 6601/6655 *fax* 020-7241 3006
website www.pineappleagency.com

In partnership with Pineapple Agency, Big City Studios provides audition and rehearsal facilities, choreographer-dancers, dancer/singers & dancer/models for the TV, theatre, music, film and advertising industries.

Candid Arts

Candid Arts Trust, 3 Torrens Street,
London EC1V 1NQ
tel 020-7837 4237
email info@candidarts.com
website www.candidarts.com

There are 20 studios in the Candid buildings, providing space for all kinds of artists including photographers, multimedia designers, jewellers, painters, illustrators, shoemakers and textile designers. Sizes range from small individual studios to larger shared work spaces.

Core Studio

7 Osbourne Street, Glasgow G1 5QN

Danceworks

16 Balderton Street, London W1K 6TN
tel 020-7318 4100
website www.danceworks.co.uk

High-quality professional studios available most days and hours for rehearsals, auditions, workshops, photoshoots and other functions. Includes 2 Large Premium Studios with 30+ people capacity, suitable for auditions and large rehearsals; 2 Medium Studios with people capacity of 20, suitable for casting, rehearsals and photoshoots, among other uses. Also houses a Yoga/Bodywork Studio, which holds up to 20 people for bodywork seminars or 30 people for sit-down presentations.

The Jerwood Space

171 Union Street, London SE1 0LN
tel 020-7654 0171 *fax* 020-7654 0172
email space@jerwoodspace.co.uk
website www.jerwoodspace.co.uk
Contact Richard Lee

Rehearsal space available for hire consisting of 5 large studios, 2 smaller studios and 2 meeting rooms. Open 9am-9pm weekdays and 10am-6pm on weekends. The spaces are accessible for wheelchair users. Rates vary – see website for current prices or email for more information.

London Studio Centre

42-50 York Way, London N1 9AB
tel 020-7837 7741
website www.london-studio-centre.co.uk

A full-performance training centre with a fully equipped body-conditioning studio that is open all day for use by students who wish to work under supervision. Also has a Studio Theatre used for the in-house production of plays and dance as well as for larger seminars and lectures, plus a wardrobe room where a large collection of ballet and theatre costumes collected over the years is supervised by a resident wardrobe mistress. There is also a scenery workshop and make-up studio fitted out as a theatre dressing room.

The Moving Arts Base

Syracusae, 134 Liverpool Road, Islington,
London N1 1LA
tel 020-7609 6969
email info@movingartsbase.co.uk
website www.studio10islington.co.uk
Bookings Michelle Collard

3 spacious sky-lit studios and 5 smaller rooms for hire.

The Others

6-8 Manor Road, Stoke Newington,
London N16 5DQ

Small live performance and rehearsal space.

Pineapple

7 Langley Street, Covent Garden, London WC2H 9JA
tel 020-7836 4004

Pineapple is London's most famous dance studio and has extensive rehearsal, audition, and casting space available. Regular customers include: Sony, Warner Bros, Walt Disney, Crystal Cruises, Lion King, Chicago, Polydor, EMI, BMG, and many many more. All studios have sprung floors, mirrors, barres, music systems and pianos. Chairs and tables can be provided on request. Privacy in all studios is easily arranged and the venue has showers, changing rooms, a rest area and a cafeteria.

Rambert Dance Company

94 Chiswick High Road, London W4 1SH
tel 020-8630 0601
website www.rambert.org.uk

Rambert Dance Company tours extensively throughout the UK and overseas, which means that its studios are often available for external hire for rehearsals, auditions, casting sessions, recordings or photoshoots. A choice of 3 studios is offered, all at affordable prices. The studios are situated at the Company's headquarters on Chiswick High Road, London (Stamford Brook, District Line) and all are equipped with TV, video, CD and cassette players, mirrored walls and ballet barres.

Red Rose Club

129 Seven Sisters Road, London N7 7QG
tel (07963) 618333
website www.redrosecomedy.co.uk

One of London's oldest Comedy Clubs, also available for hire.

The Script Factory (Rehearsal Rooms) – see page 6 for contact details.

The Soho Laundry

9 Dufours Place, London W1F 7SJ
tel 020-7734 8570

Location resources

The following companies provide a variety of location services, from holding extensive libraries of potential spaces to having the know-how to secure and manage locations for your shoot.

Amazing Space

74 Clerkenwell Road, London EC1M 5QA
tel 020-7251 6661 *fax* 020-7251 6808
email info@amazingspace.co.uk
website www.amazingspace.co.uk
General Manager Rebecca Beveridge *Office Manager* Olivia Badnell

Agency that has been providing locations to the film, television and commercials industry for over 11 years. Recent credits include: *Batman Begins*, *The Da Vinci Code*, *007 Die Another Day*, *The Constant Gardener*, *Spooks*, *Primeval*, and *Confessions of a Diary Secretary*.

Charnshaw Ltd

Dixcot 8, North Drive, London SW16 1RL
tel 020-8769 7144 *fax* 020-8769 4229
email juliet@dixcotlocations.com
website www.dixcotlocations.com

Established as a location in 1994, Dixcot Locations is now both a location in itself and a location agency. It offers high-level properties to the film and photographic industries, providing solutions for all location needs.

Compass Locations Ltd

19 All Saints Road, London W11 1HE
tel 020-7750 6912 *fax* 020-7792 8507
email charles@compasslocations.com
website www.compasslocations.com

An extensive catalogue of unusual, unique and exotic locations, available for photographic, film and commercial shoots, as well as for corporate and social events.

Dixcot Locations Ltd

8 North Drive, London SW16 1RL
tel 020-8769 7144 *fax* 020-8769 4229
email Juliet@dixcotlocations.com
website www.dixcotlocations.com
Director Juliet Bawden, *Assistant* Mia Stoker

A location company providing locations for both stills and film shoots. The company has a great variety of locations in the UK and abroad, and can do bespoke searches. Works in film, TV and commercials. Recent credits include: *The Bill*, *Rosemary and Thyme*, *The Clothes Show*, *Stop Treating Me Like A Kid*, *Sixty Six*, and *Jonathan Creek*.

Film It Locations

c/o Clinton Devon Estates, Rolle Estate Office, Oak Hill, East Budleigh, Budleigh Salterton, Devon EX9 7DP
tel (01395) 443881 *fax* (01395) 446126
email john.wilding@clintondevon.com
website www.filmitlocations.com

A large South West-based location service offering farmland, heathland, woodland, dramatic cliffs, rivers, houses, cottages or business parks, all accessed within nearly 25,000 acres of accessible and privately owned land.

jj Locations

Motordrive Location Co, 10 Harris Lane, Shenley, Radlett, Hertfordshire WD7 9EB
tel (01923) 853932 *fax* 0871-433 5801
email info@jjlocations.co.uk
website www.jjlocations.co.uk

A one-stop location company offering photographic and film locations as well as press and media venues. Company can provide cars, bikes, boats, planes and trains as props for shoots, and Winnebago location vehicles for hair/make-up/wardrobe/hospitality units.

Lavish Locations

Chiswick Town Hall, Heathfield Terrace, London W4 4JN
tel 020-8742 2992 *fax* 020-8742 2836
email info@lavishlocations.com
website www.lavishlocations.com

Established more than 20 years ago; in that time has grown to become one of the UK's largest and most respected location agencies for film, television and photographic productions in the industry.

Locality Ltd

Unit G2, Northside Studios, 16-29 Andrews Road, London E8 4QF
tel 020-7812 9144 *fax* 0870-128 2298
email info@localityunlimited.com
website www.localityunlimited.com
Managing Director Emma Plimmer

Locality has been providing locations for feature films, TV dramas, commercials, stills photography and events since 2001. The company is run by a team of location coordinators with first-hand experience of filming on location and an in-depth understanding of the practical and financial pressures involved.Locality's online location library lists hundreds of locations, mainly within the London area; properties also represented throughout the UK and abroad. All searches are free and confidential.

Recent TV credits include: *Primeval, Hustle, Spooks, The Bill, Waking the Dead, The Commander, Trial and Retribution, Miss Marple, Mitchell & Webb, Hogfather, The Amazing Mrs Pritchard, Silent Witness*, and *Little Britain*.

Recent film credits include: *The Golden Compass, Oxford Murders, Run Fat Boy Run, Harry Potter and the Order of the Phoenix, 28 Days Later*, and *Bullet Boy*.

Location-UK

Timbercroft, Ewell, Epsom, Surrey KT19 0DT
tel/fax 020-8393 2423
email info@locations-uk.com
website www.locations-uk.com

Large UK-based location finder.

The Location Partnership

82 Berwick Street, London W1F 8TP
tel 020-7734 0456 *fax* 020-7734 5411
email info@locationpartnership.com
website www.locationpartnership.com

Provides UK and worldwide film locations for film, television, photography and events. Has a large location library listing thousands of locations for film, TV, photography and events, as well as location scouts and location managers.

Location Works (UK) Ltd

42 Old Compton Street, London W1D 4TX
tel 020-7494 0888 *fax* 020-7287 2855
email info@locationworks.com
website www.locationworks.com

A large and busy location resource offering a one-stop service, including the UK's largest online locations library combined with a complete location scouting and management service.

Location X

74 Swaby Road, London SW18 3QZ
tel 020-8947 7597 *fax* 020-8946 2987
email info@locationx.net, roland@locationx.net
website www.locationx.net

A location library, scouting and management service for features, TV drama, commercials and stills. Provides locations and advice to production companies, agencies, photographers and event managers worldwide.

Movie Makers Guide

67 Ramuz Drive, Westcliff on Sea, Essex SS0 9JH
tel 0870-770 6240 *fax* (01702) 301385
email info@moviemakersguide.com
website www.moviemakersguide.com

North West Locations

Great Northern House, 275 Deansgate, Manchester M3 4EL
tel 0845-045 0608 *fax* 0845-045 0609
email info@northwestlocations.co.uk
website www.northwestlocations.co.uk

The premier film, TV, commercials and stills locations library for the North West of England, providing user-friendly locations for film and TV companies and photographers.

OIC Ltd

66 Charlotte Street, London W1T 4QE
tel 020-7419 1949 *fax* 020-7419 1950
email info@oic.co.uk
website www.oic.co.uk

Salt Film Ltd

5 Cornwall Court, Cleaver Street, London SE11 4DF
tel 020-7637 7885 *fax* 020-7637 7886
email mail@saltfilm.com
website www.saltfilm.com
Directors Ross Kirkman, Eugene Strange

Extensive library of private homes.

Snap Productions

Wimbourne House, 151-155 New North Road, London N1 6TA
tel 020-7684 7555 *mobile* (07909) 963963
fax 020-7684 7556
email alex@snap-pro.com
website www.snap-pro.co.uk
Location Library Manager Alex Pasley-Tyler

West Country Locations

Crosslands House, Ash Thomas, Tiverton, Devon EX16 4NU
tel (01884) 820888 *fax* (01884) 821328
email wcl@eclipse.co.uk
website www.westcountrylocations.co.uk

Experienced location finding and location management company in the South West of England. Run by Roger and Annie Elliott who, between them, have more than 30 years' film experience. Main services are location finding and location managing for shoots of all kinds, including features, stills, television films, commercials and promos – plus a large and extensive location library consisting of thousands of images of the South West. The company also offers general production services.

Yorkshire Locations

Commercial House, 57 Great George Street, Leeds, West Yorkshire LS1 3AJ
tel 0845-045 0608 *fax* 0845-045 0609
email info@yorkshirelocations.co.uk
website www.yorkshirelocations.co.uk
Location Library Manager Nick Jones

Film offices

These film offices and screen commissions are responsible for attracting film shoots to a particular town or region, and as such are an indispensible resource if you are planning to shoot in their area. Most offer free locations services and information as well as access to local crew and craft services. You should also check with the Screen Agency in the region where you plan to shoot, as most offer similar professional services – and in some cases funding support, if the production represents significant investment in the regional industry.

Bath Film Office

Abbey Chambers, Abbey Church Yard, Bath BA1 1LY
tel (01225) 477711 *mobile* (07770) 962878
fax (01225) 396442
email bath_filmoffice@bathnes.gov.uk
website www.visitbath.co.uk/film/
Head of Film Office Maggie Ainley

Offers information on locations, local crew and media facilities, as well as liason with local council departments and police. Also has local community contacts and information on crew-friendly hotels.

Edinburgh Film Focus

20 Forth Street, Edinburgh EH1 3LH
tel 0131-622 7337 *fax* 0131-622 7338
email info@edinfilm.com
website www.edinfilm.com
Film Focus Team Ros Davis, Rosie Ellison, Katie Crook

Edinburgh Film Focus is the local Film Commission for Edinburgh, the Lothians and the Scottish Borders. Offers information on location, help with permits and planning; also has an extensive crew database.

Glasgow Film Office

City Chambers, Glasgow G2 1DU
tel 0141-287 0424 *fax* 0141-287 0311
email info@glasgowfilm.com
website www.glasgowfilm.com

GFO offers council and community liason services, crew and cast data information, and has an extensive location database. Can also provide support to productions by offering an organised 'recce' for key personnel, including up to 2 nights' accommodation and the services of a professional location scout. Transport for this will also be provided.

Isle of Man Film Ltd – see page 57 for contact details.

In addition to funding incentives for shooting on the Isle of Man, IOMF also offers location, crew and services information.

Lanarkshire Screen Location

Dept of Planning & Environment, 4th Floor, Fleming House, 1 Tryst Road, Cumbernauld G67 1JW
tel (01236) 616559 *fax* (01236) 616283
email gibsonl@northlan.gov.uk

Location and planning advice and assistance.

Scottish Highlands & Islands Film Commission, Somisean Fiolm na Gaidhealtachd's nan Eilean Alba

Inverness Castle, Inverness IV2 3EG
tel (01463) 710221 *fax* (01463) 710848
email info@scotfilm.org

Location and planning advice and assistance.

South West Scotland Screen Commission

Gracefield Arts Centre, 28 Edinburgh Road, Dumfries DG1 1JQ
tel (01387) 263666 *fax* (01387) 263666
email screencom@dumgal.gov.uk

Location and planning advice and assistance.

Stirling Council Film Liaison

Department of Tourism and Rural Development, Viewforth, Stirling FK8 2ET
tel (01786) 442821 *fax* (01786) 443199
email willied@stirling.gov.uk

Location and planning advice and assistance.

TayScreen

DCA, 152 Nethergate, Dundee DD1 4DY
tel (01382) 432483 *fax* (01382) 432471
email info@tayscreen.com
website www.tayscreen.com

Screen Comission for Fife & Tayside for free help with locations, production and business development.

Wales Screen Commission

6G Parc Gwyddoniaeth, Cefn Llan, Aberystwyth, Ceredigion SY23 3AH
tel (01970) 627186/627831 *fax* (01970) 617942
email enquiry@walesscreencommission.co.uk
website www.walesscreencommission.co.uk

Wales Screen Commission has 4 regional offices across the country to help with location and planning.

Production

Introduction

Like all aspects of the filmmaking process, the shoot is demanding, stressful and absolutely crucial to the ultimate success or failure of the project. For the filmmaker, this is also the stage which requires militaristic advance planning, to ensure that you have time during the shoot to respond to the many crises and questions that will arise.

The Production section of this *Yearbook* is not a 'how to' guide to shooting your movie, but rather a collection of resources and helpful tips which should make planning your film shoot much easier. For newer filmmakers, Anita Overland's guide to physical production gives an overview of the process, with descriptions of the major duties for each production team member, information on what to expect from the shoot, and tips for maximising the experience. While the advice is based on Anita's experience of feature films, it should also be very relevant to filmmakers setting out to make a short film.

For more detailed technical information about production, there are numerous craft skills guides available. Steven Katz's *Film Directing Shot By Shot: Visualizing from Concept to Screen* comes highly recommended as a technical resource. *IFP/Los Angeles Independent Filmmaker's Manual* by indie producer Eden Wurmfeld and producer/teacher Nicole Laloggia gives a combination of practical, anecdotal and technical advice geared towards independent lower-budget filmmakers. For a more UK-specific guide, Chris Jones' and Genevieve Jolliffe's *Guerilla Filmmakers Handbook* is an excellent resource for the low-budget shoot, and includes a handy CD-ROM of useful production documents such as a sample call sheet, continuity sheet and production and locations checklists. Shooting People's website, **www.shootingpeople.org**, features numerous production resources, and the Shooting People digests are good places to seek advice from fellow filmmakers – or, when you are ready for your shoot, for crewing up.

In this section we also offer up filmmaking perspectives from three sets of filmmakers: the producer/director team of new low-budget indie *The Waiting Room*, Sarah Sulick and Roger Goldby; two-time documentary feature-maker, Stephen Kijak; and BAFTA and Oscar-winning writer/director Anthony Minghella.

Arguably the most important training or preparation you can have before your shoot will not come from a book or guide, but from experience. You might wonder: how many scenes can I shoot in a day? how should I organise my shooting schedule most efficiently? what are the best ways to communicate on set? There are no hard-and-fast rules for production, and gaining on-set experience in the early days of your career will be invaluable if you plan to direct or produce. Many established directors claim as one of the strangest things about their craft, the fact that they don't really know how other directors work because they haven't had the opportunity to watch their colleagues on set. If you are just starting out, find work – paid or volunteer – on as many productions as you can. The experience you gain will be endlessly useful in your future career.

To this end, while film courses can be expensive, if they offer hands-on practical training they are often a very good investment. You will get structured, supervised experience on set, and hopefully come away with a portfolio which can help you find work on another production or get funding for your next project. Refer to the Resources section of this *Yearbook* for a list of some of the UK's best film courses.

A producer's guide to physical production

Anita Overland

Production starts in pre-production

It's not possible to talk about physical production without first mentioning pre-production briefly. Well-planned pre-production is crucial in order to ensure a successful shoot. As the producer, you need to have absorbed all the requirements of the script, the director and each department. It takes meticulous amounts of planning and negotiation to then agree and finalise these requirements. The necessary detail can be overwhelming.

However, every minute of pre-production effort goes towards creating conditions to maximise the amount of time you have for shooting. The most important thing before the cameras roll is to understand what you need to shoot to get your story and to ensure that nothing delays your very expensive time on camera.

The production team

Before we look at what to expect on set, it is worth detailing the roles of the key people responsible for the smooth day-to-day running of the film shoot:

- **Executive producer**: this can be one of the financiers, or an experienced producer overseeing a project with a less experienced team.
- **Producer**: usually the person who initiates the project by optioning a book or script, or taking on a writer/director's original project. This person works throughout the filmmaking process – hiring a director and raising finance, and then overseeing the film to completion and delivery and release ... which can be many years' work.
- **Co-producer**: usually hired by the producer once finance is raised, to be the day-to-day producer on film if the main producer has a few projects in production at once or is not able to be 'hands on'.
- **Associate producer**: this could be a producer's assistant who is training to be a producer, or simply a title acknowledging someone's contribution to the film.
- **Line producer**: the person who breaks script down, schedules and budgets film, and then has to ensure that film stays on budget and schedule. Negotiates main deals. Oversees each department.
- **Production manager**: the line producer's right-hand person, s/he gets given a budget and negotiates deals accordingly. Deals are with crew, transport, equipment, etc. (smaller films would not necessarily have a production manager, and this would fall to the line producer or producer).
- **Production co-ordinator**: the right-hand person of the production manager, responsible for the flow of information to financiers, cast and crew. S/he ensures that everyone has up-to-date information (i.e. latest script, script changes, latest schedules, latest unit lists, any memos, info on any meetings).
- **Assistant co-ordinator/production secretary**: this person creates and maintains the cast, contact and unit lists for use throughout the shoot.
- **Production office runner**: photocopies, photocopies and photocopies ...

What to expect on a shoot

If you have put together the right team, the pre-production planning should pay off by giving the director more time to concentrate on directing the shoot, and you more time to manage the unforeseen problems and crises that will arise. This will take every ounce of your time, creativity and energy. During the shoot you are expected to ensure that all elements are in the right place at the right time and to the right budget. You can be asked to concentrate on anything from a stunt and special-effects sequence to a contact lens for an actor, so knowing who is doing what and when they are doing it makes the shoot run smoothly.

While every production is different, and you only learn the variations with experience, a typical day might run as follows:

05.30: leave home
06.15-07.00: breakfast call – talk to director/1st AD/any crew members about details for the day, any changes, pass on information, greet actors arriving for make-up/costume
07.00-12.30: shooting – you will move between set and production base:
on set: you will watch takes, perhaps give the director comments; cast or crew will approach you with issues or planning requirements or decisions needed from the director, which you will need to pass on
at the production base (which can be anything from a trailer to a step outside the location): you will go through details of the next day and the next week with the production team or assistant directors, sign cheques, go through costs with line producer/accountant
12.30-13.30: lunch and watch/discuss rushes with director; discuss schedule for next day, any changes, any problems
13.30-19.00: shooting – as above, wrap, make any other changes/arrangements for next day, discuss any comments on rushes or cost reports from financiers
19.45: home – but you may often get calls late into the night if there are any problems

You can imagine that after anything from three weeks to many months of this, you will be exhausted at the end of the process.

Giving your production shoot the best chance of success

There are a number of considerations which will help you to ensure that your shoot is run smoothly, and that everyone has the time and energy to perform their jobs as creatively as possible.

Schedule

The most pressure comes from trying to keep on schedule: even one day over schedule can cost between £40,000 and £250,000, depending on the scale of your production. It's the producer's responsibility to liaise with the financiers and to hire a good team to ensure that nothing goes wrong from an organisational point of view. Imagine that the director decides to have an actor in a scene that s/he is not scripted to be in. The producer on set must ensure that this is communicated to the relevant departments – production, ADS, costume, make-up – or it will have grave consequences on the schedule. It's a big no-no for any of those details to be responsible for holding up the shoot. Clear communication can ensure that many problems are avoided.

Flexibility

Scheduling is crucial; however, not everything on set can be controlled. Shoots are subject to many vagaries of chance that can impact on the schedule: changes in weather; a scene taking longer to shoot than expected; script changes; a location falling through. So the shoot becomes a constant adjustment. Cast and crew have to keep up with these changes as fluidly as possible. The producer has to re-evaluate the cost of these changes with the faithful support of the line producer and accountant (in the end, it often boils down to 'robbing Peter to pay Paul'!).

Budget

It is one of the responsibilities of the producer to ensure that the production stays within budget. At the same time, once production has begun, the director will often need things that will go beyond what you've budgeted for. If you are the producer, in such cases you must negotiate. A good relationship with the director is helpful, but in any case it's important to listen, consider the proposal and then find a compromise where you allow them to have what they need, with the agreement that they will work with you on giving up some other item to help balance costs. Any substantial movement of money will require you to persuade your financiers and completion guarantors that it is necessary.

Communication

As I said above, a good shoot relies on good communication, and as producer you are the conduit of vital information passing through each department – particularly with the director, who becomes less available during the shoot; therefore, you must use that time with him/her carefully. As things change, you need to ensure that everyone who needs to know is kept informed. If lines of communication break down, the shoot will not go well. If anything changes or happens, you need to go through a checklist of all the departments and decide who needs to be informed.

The chain of communication might run like this:

On set: 1st AD will make announcement to cast and crew

Off set: 1st AD will radio the 2nd AD if possible, or will ask 3rd AD to pass message to 2nd AD; depending on the nature of the occurrence, the 2nd AD will inform the producer and line producer/production manager and then inform individual departments. 2nd AD will also inform the production co-ordinator (usually at office) who will inform all the people affected who are not at the location

It's vitally important that you, the director, 1st AD, and your line producer have been clear and honest about what is expected of your team. You should have agreed the nature/hours of the shoot beforehand, and have agreed cast and crew deals accordingly. And it's important for you to then stick to what you have agreed, to keep the trust of your team.

People and politics

It's almost inevitable that half-way through a shoot, people will begin to get tired and start to complain – usually about the hours or financial issues. It's useful to always try to listen sympathetically. Even if you're unable to solve the complaint, at least they've been heard and their problem considered – even if the answer is 'No, you can't have more money!'

Stamina

Remember that the hours are long and tough, stamina is needed and, if you are away on location ,social stamina is required too!

Good food

In addition to good planning, good communication and flexibility, there is one other element which can seriously contribute to a smooth shoot: good food. The shoot will go well if cast and crew are happy. This means that the cast are looked after and respected (it doesn't have to mean expensive trailers, although this helps), and all crew treated fairly, respected and appreciated for their good work. Good food helps to communicate to a crew that you respect them and care about their on-set comfort and health, thus helping to maintain a happy set.

Avoiding common production pitfalls

• Don't overbudget on the cast.
• Don't wait until too late to make budget decisions – make them early and structure your shoot accordingly.
• Don't shoot a script that is too long for the shooting schedule you have created.
• Don't work long hours to try to squeeze in more than you have time for. Mistakes get made; problems are better dealt with when rested.

Words of advice

• Try to think of anything that might go wrong, and prepare for it.
• If things do go wrong (and they frequently do), try to fix them in a positive way.
• Keep calm at all times – it counts for a lot and stops other people panicking.
• Honesty is very important. Be straight with everyone; don't try and pull the wool over anyone's eyes.
• Set cast and crew deals that have parity with others. Be fair. Don't do side deals with one department.
• If there is a problem, don't be afraid to give the bad news. That said, if a financier is withdrawing and you are trying to fix the problem, you don't want to burden your director/cast/crew too much, as they need to concentrate on the shoot.
• Work with the same team if possible. Trust will build up and lines of communication become more efficient.
• Find a 1st AD with a good sense of humour.
• Try to make it fun: organise a few drinks/parties for your cast and crew.

Anita Overland has worked as a line producer for more than a decade on films such as *My Son the Fanatic*, Simon Magus and Michael Winterbottom's *Wonderland*, *The Claim*, and the BAFTA-winning *In This World*. She also line-produced Anthony Minghella's *Breaking and Entering*, and Jean-Marc Vallée's *The Young Victoria*. Most recently she both co-produced Winterbottom's *A Cock and Bull Story*, and line-produced his 2007 releaase, *A Mighty Heart*.

Production companies

If you are a newer filmmaker with what you feel is a great script, you may be tempted to send it to a producer or production company to assess interest as soon possible. There are a number of reasons to consider your strategy carefully, and many factors that will affect where and to whom you might send it.

The first and most obvious of these is that producers are incredibly busy and you can only expect them to read your script once. It needs to be 'ready' when you send it; they won't be interested in your much-improved second draft in six months' time if you haven't made a big impression with the first one. The same is true when you are sending work out to public production funds. You generally only get one shot.

The second reason is that very few companies in the UK will accept unsolicited work from independent filmmakers and screenwriters. Most will want submissions to come through recognised channels – an agent or a producer they are familiar with. This not only acts as a filtering system to avoid a deluge of work from first-time writers – work which is not yet ready (or not good enough) to comprise a viable project; disallowing open submissions also avoids potential legal problems that might arise if a screenwriter sends in an idea which is very similar to something the company is already developing. When that project comes to fruition, the screenwriter is likely to believe that the production company has 'stolen' their idea. Many production companies will simply throw away or delete unsolicited scripts and ideas which come to them.

While this can be frustrating for new filmmakers who feel that the industry is a closed shop, there are methods of working your way into the system. Make a short film and get it screened in festivals. Write more than one script before you even begin to think about getting an agent or contacting a producer. A portfolio of work will make you more appealing as a long-term prospect, and will certainly send out the message that you are a filmmaker who is intending to develop a professional career. Most filmmakers do attest to the fact that once you are 'on the radar' with an award or having screened in a credible festival, it becomes easier to get scripts read (if not made!) by people in the industry.

Having said that, in some cases sending out your script may be the right first step to take. In this section we do try to indicate where a company has made it clear that they welcome submissions directly from filmmakers. If you are an independent filmmaker with some experience and a good idea, it can sometimes still be worth a telephone call to a production company that claims not to accept unsolicited submissions – especially if you think they may be interested in your idea because of their previous work. If you are going to call, have your 'pitch' ready just in case, and remember that there is a fine line between a polite and a pushy enquiry. It may also be worth waiting until you have a pretence for the call – you want to invite the development producer to a screening of your digital shorts scheme short film, or you are having an extract read from your script at a Rocliffe night.

At the end of the day, production companies are usually looking for good new projects, so may ask you to send in a CV, or a showreel with a synopsis or treatment. If your project is ready, have a go and good luck!

Aardman Animations Ltd

Gas Ferry Road, Bristol BS1 6UN
tel 0117-984 8485 *fax* 0117-984 8486
email mail@aardman.com
website www.aardman.com

World-renowned company behind *Wallace and Gromit* and *Chicken Run*.

Absolutely Productions Ltd

Unit 19, 77 Beak Street, London W1F 9DB
tel 020-7644 5575
email www.absolutely.biz

Absolutely Productions is primarily a television production company which was formed in 1988 by a group of writer/performer/producers who wanted to produce their own material: Morwenna Banks, Jack Docherty, Moray Hunter, Pete Baikie, John Sparkes and Gordon Kennedy. Credits include: *Trigger Happy TV*, *Absolutely*, and *Stressed Eric.*

Acacia Productions Ltd

80 Weston Park, London N8 9TB
tel 020-8341 9392 *fax* 020-8341 4879
email projects@acaciaproductions.co.uk
website www.acaciaproductions.co.uk
Production Executive Nikki Nagasiri

Established in 1985 by Nikki Nagasiri and Edward Milner, Acacia primarily works in factual production – news feaures and documentaries for television. It is particularly interested in projects which focus on the environment, development and human rights. The company has also conducted video training in Nepal and Belize. Does not accept unsolicited project proposals.

Actaeon Films Ltd

50 Gracefield Gardens, London SW16 2ST
tel 020-8769 3339 *mobile* (07855) 859546
fax 0870-134 7980
email daniel@actaeonfilms.com
website www.actaeonfilms.com
Director Daniel Cormack

Actaeon Films Ltd was established in July 2004 by Daniel Cormack to produce feature-length theatrical motion pictures. Its focus is on films that use elements of established commercial genres in innovative and original ways to challenge and entertain audiences.

Addictive TV

The Old House, 39a North Road, London N7 9DP
tel 020-7700 0333
email mail@addictive.com
website www.addictive.com

London-based producers and DJs/audio-video artists who champion the art of the VJ through TV shows, DVD releases and performances, and with the Optronica festival at the *bfi* National Film Theatre in London.

Adventure Pictures

6 Blackbird Yard, Ravenscroft Street, London E2 7RP
tel 020-7613 2233 *fax* 020-7256 0842
email mail@adventurepictures.co.uk
website www.adventurepictures.co.uk

Sally Potter's production company. Credits include: *Yes*, *The Tango Lesson*, and *Orlando.*

After Image Ltd

47 Trinity Gardens, London SW9 8DR
tel 020-7737 7300
website www.afterimage.co.uk

After Image was founded by Jane Thorburn and Mark Lucas in 1979, to make innovative programmes for television and video distribution.

Alibi Productions

35 Long Acre, London WC2E 9JT
tel 020-7845 0400 *fax* 020-7379 7035
email rogerholmes@alibifilms.co.uk
website www.alibifilms.co.uk

All 3 Media

87-91 Newman Street, London W1T 3EY
tel 020-7907 0177 *fax* 020-7907 0199
email information@all3media.com
website www.all3media.com

Formed following the acquisition of Chrysalis Group's TV division in September 2003. Companies include: Company Pictures, Assembly TV, Bentley Productions and Cactus TV.

Amber Associates

5&9 Side, Newcastle-upon-Tyne NE1 3JE
tel 0191-232 2000
email amberside@btinternet.com
website www.amber-online.com

Amber was formed in 1968, originally to document the lives of Newcastle's working class and its culture through film and photography. The company produces all its own work, so is not open to submissions from outside producers. Award-winning work includes: *Seacoal* and *In Fading Light.*

AMC Pictures

tel (01753) 783900 *fax* (01753) 630651
email films@amcpictures.co.uk
website www.amcpictures.co.uk
Managing Director Alistair MacLean-Clark

AMC Pictures develops, finances and produces feature films and television productions for the UK and international markets. Managing Director MacLean-Clark has also launched and managed a number of tax-efficient film funds, including Random Harvest.

Anglia Television Ltd

Anglia House, Norwich NR1 3JG
tel (01603) 615151

website www.itvregions.com/anglia

Anglia broadcasts to more than 4 million viewers in the East of England, and is one of the best known and most successful companies of ITV.

Anglo American Pictures

Ealing Studios, Ealing Green, London W5 5EP
tel (07802) 666693
email info@anglo-ap.com
website www.angloamericanpictures.com

Production company of writer/director Chris Barfoot; has produced a number of short dramas which have been broadcast.

The Animation Station

Leisure and Tourism Department,
Cherwell District Council, Bodicote House,
Bodicote, Banbury, Oxon OX15 4AA
tel (01295) 221730 *fax* (01295) 270797
email animation.station@cherwell-dc.gov.uk
website www.animationstation.co.uk

The Animation Station is an art resource for young people in North Oxfordshire. Aimed at people aged between 9 and 25, it was set up to provide education in the art and practice of animation. Creative projects concentrate on production, exhibition and education, and target those sections of the community which have limited access through disability, cultural difference and rural location.

Apocalypso Productions

Fourth Floor, 61-63 Beak Street, London W1F 9SL

Independent production company started by producer Tanya Seghatchian. Credits include: *My Summer of Love* and the upcoming *The Restraint of Beasts.*

APT Films

APT Films, Ealing Studios, Ealing Green,
London W5 5EP
tel 020-8280 9125 *fax* 020-020 8280 9111
email admin@aptfilms.com
website www.aptfilms.com
Managing Director Jonny Persey, *Director* Paul Morrison, *Producers* Stewart le Marechal, Al Morrow

Enterprise dedicated to development and production of feature films for national and international audiences. Also produces short films. The company has a number of feature films in development.

Prefers not to receive unsolicited scripts, but specific enquiries should be addressed to the email address given above.

Recent credits include: *Deep Water, Wondrous Oblivion* and *Soloman & Gaenor.* Upcoming work includes: *Heavy Load* and *The Pied Piper of Hutzovina.*

Arcane Pictures

72 Wells Street, London W1T 3QG
tel 020-7636 4996 *fax* 020-7631 3969
email info@arcanepictures.com
website www.arcanepictures.com

Founded by George Duffield and Meg Thomson, Arcane Pictures aims to make intelligent, sexy, innovative and commercial films. Arcane focuses on forging long-term relationships with writers, directors and other creative talent. In addition to feature dramas and docs, the company has produced a number of short films. Credits include: *Live Free or Die*, and *Dot the i.*

Archer Street Ltd

66a Great Titchfield Street, London W1W 7QJ
tel 020-7612 1750 *fax* 020-7580 3061

Production company set up by independent producer, Andy Paterson, with director Anand Tucker and screenwriter Frank Cottrell Boyce. The company is known for making quality feature films. Credits include: *Girl With the Pearl Earring* and *Beyond the Sea.* The three creatives also made *Hilary and Jackie* together.

Avalon Television

4a Exmoor Street, London W10 6BD
tel 020-7598 8000 *fax* 020-7598 7281
email motionpictures@avalonuk.com
website www.avalonuk.com

Established in 2001, Avalon Motion Pictures is the most recent addition to The Avalon Group, and was set up to create film content. The Group also has divisions for PR, sales, television, promotions and management.

BBC Films Ltd

1 Mortimer Street, London W1T 3JA
tel 020-7765 0251 *fax* 020-7765 0278
website www.bbc.co.uk/bbcfilms
Head of BBC Films David Thompson

BBC Films is one of the leading co-producers of quality British independent filmmaking, and the only broadcaster in the UK which currently has a dedicated feature film production department. Co-produces approximately 8 films a year, and has a strong reputation for producing quality work. Recent credits include: *Matchpoint, Shooting Dogs,* and *The History Boys.*

BBC Films has a stated committment to finding and developing new talent, but does not directly accept unsolicited scripts. Unsolicited material may be submitted through the Writersroom (see page 6).

Bill Kenwright Films

BKL House, 106 Harrow Road, London W2 1RR
tel 020-7446 6200 *fax* 020-7446 6222
website www.kenwright.com

Bill Kenwright Ltd is the UK's largest independent theatre and film production company. Recent West End/Broadway productions include: *A Few Good Men* and *Festen*; films include *Die Mommie Die* and *The Purifiers*.

Black Coral Productions

2nd Floor, 241 High Street, London E17 7BH
tel 020-8520 2881 *fax* 020-8520 2358

Blue Dolphin Film & Video

40 Langham Street, London W1W 7AS
tel 020-7255 2494 *fax* 020-7580 7670
website www.bluedolphinfilms.com

Blue Dolphin is a distribution company which has been in business for 25 years; it also produce features. Invites proposals for feature film projects looking for gap finance and co-production opportunities. The projects should qualify as a British film and may be co-productions with Australia, Canada, New Zealand and all EC countries. Please send enquiries to Julian Ryan.

Blue Wand Productions Ltd

2nd Floor, 12 Weltje Road, London W6 9TG
tel 020-8741 2038 or (07885) 528743
fax 020-8741 2038
email lino@bluewand.co.uk
Managing Director Lino Omoboni *Executive Producer* Paola Omobomi

Established in 1990, the production company works exclusively in feature film production. Recent credits include: *Camelot*.

Box Film – see page 134.

Box TV

151 Wardour Street, London W1F 8WE
tel 020-7297 8040 *fax* 020-7297 8041
email info@box-tv.co.uk
website www.box-tv.co.uk

Founded in 2000 by award-winning producer Gub Neal, formerly Head of Drama at Channel 4 and Controller of Drama at Granada Television, Box produces film and television of the highest quality and vision for markets throughout the world. In its first 5 years, Box's core team has overseen more than £45m of production. Part of DCD Media (see page 307).

Braunarts

The Beehive, 226a Gipsy Road, London SE27 9RB
tel 020-8670 9917
website www.braunarts.com
Company Directors Terry Braun, Gabi Braun

Formerly known as Illuminations Interactive, Braunarts was set up to create interactive multimedia installations and CD-ROMs, and also to produce television programmes about the arts, science and new technologies for broadcasters in Britain and abroad.

BreakThru Films Ltd

2nd Floor, Highgate Business Centre,
33 Greenwood Place, London NW5 1LB
tel 020-7428 3963
website www.breakthrufilms.co.uk
Directors Alan Dewhurst, Hugh Welchman

Founded in 2002 to develop and produce narrative films, both live action and animation, and to provide related production and creative services such as co-production financing, and management, project planning, scheduling and budgeting for longform animation. BAFTA nominated for live action short film *The Most Beautiful Man in the World*.

Buxton Raven Productions

102 Clarence Road, London E5 8HB
tel 020-8986 0063
email info@buxtonraven.com
Producer Jette Bonnevie

Capitol Films – see page 310.

Carlton Television Productions

35-38 Portman Square, London W1H 0NU
tel 020-7486 6688 *fax* 020-7486 1132
Director of Programmes Steve Hewlett

Comprises Carlton Television Productions, Planet 24 and Action Time. Makes drama programmes for all UK major broadcasters (ITV, BBC, Channel 4, Channel 5 and Sky) and regional programmes for Carlton Central, Carlton London and Carlton Westcountry.

Carnival (Films and Theatre) Ltd

12 Raddington Road, London W10 5TG
tel 020-8968 0968 *fax* 020-8968 0155
email info@carnival-films.co.uk
website www.carnival-films.co.uk
Chairman Brian Eastman *Managing Director* Gareth Neame

One of the UK's leading independent drama producers, Carnival was founded by Brian Eastman in 1978, and has produced over 300 hours of drama for television, cinema and theatre, both in the UK and the US. Awards and nominations include: American Academy, Emmys, British Academy, Royal Television Society and TONY Awards. Carnival has been commissioned by all the major UK broadcasters, including the BBC, Channel 4, ITV Network and BSkyB, as well as US broadcasters such as NBC, HBO, TNT and the A&E Network. Credits include: *As If*; Agatha Christie's *Poirot*; and feature films such as the multi-award-winning *Shadowlands*. Does not accept unsolicited scripts, proposals or showreels.

Celador Films

39 Long Acre, London WC2E 9LG
tel 020-7845 6800 *fax* 020-7845 6980
website www.celador.co.uk
Managing Director Chris Coleson *Head of Development* Ivana MacKinnon

Celador Productions makes a wide range of programming, from factual and daytime TV to feature films. Celador Films' first foray into features was the hugely successful *Dirty Pretty Things*, and more recently, *The Descent*. A number of other projects are in development. Celador will only take submissions from agents, from talent already known to them, or from producers looking for co-producers.

Celador Productions – see page 134.

Charisma Films

507 Riverbank House, 1 Putney Bridge Approach, London SW6 3JD
tel 020-7610 6830 *fax* 020-7610 6836
email mail@charismafilms.net
website www.charismafilms.co.uk

Charisma has an extensive back catalogue of lesser-known Hollywood films; the company is also developing a number of newer projects. It does not accept unsolicited scripts; please send a synopsis first.

Cherry Red Films

Unit 17, 1st Floor, Elysium Gate West, 126-128 New Kings Road, London SW6 4LZ
email matt@cherryred.co.uk
website www.cherryred.co.uk
Contact Matt Bristow

Sister company to Cherry Red Records, an independent record label, Cherry Red Films is looking to expand its range of interesting music and related documentary films (previous releases include *Billy Childish Is Dead*, nominated for a British Independent Film Award). The company would like to hear from independent documentary filmmakers who have begun work on a music or related project ,and are seeking a partner to bring the film to fruition. Filmmakers should contact Matt Bristow with a brief synopsis of their film and details of its current status.

The Children's Film Unit

South Way, Leavesden, Herts WD25 7LZ
tel (01923) 354656
email Cfilmunit@aol.com
website www.btinternet.com/~cfu

An educational charity which trains young people from the ages of 10 to 16 in all aspects of filmmaking.

Classic Productions

tel (01932) 592016
email production@classic-media-group.com
website www.classicpictures.co.uk

Classic Productions is the video production arm of Classic Media Group, with in-house Editing, Sound, Graphics, Authoring, Production, and Marketing departments. Work is primarily commercial and corporate.

Collingwood O'Hare Entertainment and Convergence Productions

10-14 Crown Street, London W3 8SB
tel 020-8993 3666 *fax* 020-8993 9595
email info@crownstreet.co.uk
website www.collingwoodohare.com
Head of Development Helen Stroud

Company Pictures

Suffolk House, Whitfield Place, London W1T 5JU
tel 020-7380 3900 *fax* 020-7380 1166
email enquiries@companypictures.co.uk
website www.companypictures.co.uk
Managing Directors George Faber, Charlie Pattinson
Head of Film Robyn Slovo *Executive Producer (TV)* Suzan Harrison

Founded in 1998, Company has a strong reputation in film and TV production. Credits include: *P.O.W.*, *White Teeth*, *The Life and Death of Peter Sellers*, and *Morvern Callar*.

Does not accept unsolicited submissions; proposals should be submitted through agents.

Cowboy Films

34-35 Berwick Street, London W1F 8RP
tel 020-7758 4102 *fax* 020-7758 4108
email info@cowboyfilms.co.uk, charles@cowboyfilms.co.uk
website www.cowboyfilms.co.uk
Managing Director Charles Steel

Until recently, Cowboy Films represented a range of top-quality commercials and music video directors, and also worked on feature films such as *The Hole* and *Goodbye Charlie Bright*. Sister company Crossroads Films in the US has taken over the roster of music video and commercial projects, while Cowboy continues to work on features. Kevin Macdonald's *The Last King of Scotland* is the company's most recent project.

Dazed Film & TV

112-116 Old Street, London EC1V 9BG
tel 020-7549 6840 *fax* 020-7336 0966
email info.film&tv@dazedgroup.com
website www.dazedfilmtv.com
Company Director Laura Hastings-Smith

Production offshoot of Dazed & Confused, dedicated to producing intelligent, innovative and provocative documentary and drama. Has produced several short films and television works for Channel 4 and BBC, including Rankin's short film *Perfect*, and *The Love Doctor*.

Dirty Hands Productions

2nd Floor, 2-4 Noel Street, London W1F 8GN
tel 020-7287 7410

Established by Sir Alan Parker, the company has produced many of his films, including: *The Committments*, *Angela's Ashes*, and *Evita*.

Diverse Productions

6 Gorleston Street, London W14 8XS
tel 020-7603 4567 *fax* 020-7603 2148

email info@diverse.tv
website www.diverse.tv
Head of Development Mark Rossiter

Diverse is renowned for producing quality factual television programming, and has recently moved into producing docudrama.

DNA Films

First Floor, 15 Greek Street, London W1D 4DP
tel 020-7292 8700 *fax* 020-7292 8701
email info@dnafilms.com
website www.dnafilms.com

Co-chairmen Andrew Macdonald, Allon Reich

One of the most successful and influential production companies based in the UK, DNA was founded by Duncan Kenworthy and Andrew Macdonald before they, together with Allon Reich, set up DNA Films as a joint venture with Fox Searchlight (see page 137.). Extensive credits for DNA and DNA Films combined include: *Separate Lies*, *Notes on a Scandal*, *28 Days Later*, *Love Actually* and *The History Boys*.

Don Productions Ltd

26 Shacklewell Lane, London E8 2EZ
tel 020-7690 0108 *fax* 020-7690 4333
email info@donproductions.com
website www.donproductions.com
Director Donald Harding

Japanese/English bilingual TV and media production company based in London. Produces TV drama, documentaries, news and sports programmes. Clients include: Japan Broadcasting Corporation, Nippon Television and Channel 4. Recent work includes: *The Life of Charles Darwin*.

Done and Dusted

151 Wardour Street, London W1F 8WE

Part of DCD Media (see page 307.).

The Drama House

Coach Road Cottages, Little Saxham,
Bury St Edmunds, Suffolk IP29 5LE
tel (01284) 810521 *fax* (01284) 811425
email jack@dramahouse.co.uk
website www.dramahouse.co.uk
Chairman/Chief Executive Jack Emery

Produces drama and drama-documentaries for film and TV. Recent credits include: *Breaking the Code*, *Witness Against Hitler*, *Little White Lies* and *Suffer the Little Children*. Commissioned by major broadcasters including BBC and Channel 4. Hopes that high-profile work will encourage writers and other professionals to come to the Drama House.

Dramatis Personae

19 Regency Street, London SW1P 4BY
tel 020-7834 9300

Production company founded in 1983 by Maria Aitken and Nathan Silver working in theatre, film and television. No unsolicited submissions.

Ealing Studios – see page 137.

Ecosse Films

Brigade House, 8 Parsons Green, London SW6 4TN
tel 020-7371 0290 *fax* 020-7736 3436
email webmail@ecossefilms.com
website www.ecossefilms.com
Managing Director and Executive Producer Douglas Rae *Company Director and Executive Producer* Robert Bernstein *Film Development Producer* Matt Delargy

A leading film and television production company in the UK; productions have won several international awards including 2 Oscar nominations, a Golden Globe and 4 BAFTAs. Recent productions include: *Mrs Brown*, *Monarch of the Glen*, and *Wilderness*. Does not accept unsolicited submissions.

Elstree Film and Television Studios

Borehamwood, Hertfordshire WD6 1JG
tel 020-8953 0844 *fax* 020-8207 0860
email annahome@cftf.onyxnet.co.uk

Elstree is involved in the development and co-production of films for children and the family, both for the theatrical market and for television.

Endemol UK

Shepherd's Building Central, Charecroft Way,
London W14 0EE
tel 0870-333 1700 *fax* 0870-333 1800
email info@endemoluk.com
website www.endemoluk.com

One of the UK's largest independent producers of television content in the UK. Consists of companies, Brighter Pictures and Endemol UK Productions.

Eye Film and Television

Chamberlain House, 2 Dove Street, Norwich,
Norfolk NR2 1DE
tel (01603) 762551 *fax* (01603) 762420
email production@eyefilmandtv.co.uk
website www.eyefilmandtv.co.uk
Managing Director Charlie Gauvain

Independent producers of film and TV drama and documentaries. Also produces corporate, commercial, education and training material. Clients include: BBC, ITV1/Anglia, Channel 4, Five, and First Take Films. Recent credits include: *The Secret of Eel Island* and *POV*.

Feelgood Fiction Ltd

49 Goldhawk Road, London W12 8QP
tel 020-8746 2535 *fax* 020-8740 6177
email feelgood@feelgoodfiction.co.uk
Managing Director Philip Clarke *Drama Producer* Laurence Bowen

Producers of film and TV drama.

Film & General Productions Ltd

4 Bradbrook House, Studio Place, London SW1X 8EL
tel 020-7235 4495 *fax* 020-7245 9853

email cparsons@filmgen.co.uk
Directors Clive Parsons, Davina Belling

Founded in 1971, the company produces a wide range of feature films, television drama and children's drama. Work includes: *I am David, Tea with Mussolini, The Queen's Nose* and *Green-Eyed Monster.* Upcoming productions include: *Children of Glory.* Does not accept unsolicited submissions. Producers may send short synopsis by email to Clive Parsons, but the company only accepts showreels from agents.

Flashback Television Ltd

9-11 Bowling Green Lane, London EC1R 0BG
tel 020-7490 8996 *fax* 020-7490 5610
email mailbox@flashbacktv.co.uk
website www.flashbacktelevision.com
Managing Director & Executive Producer Taylor Downing *Creative Director & Executive Producer* David Edgar *Director of Production* Tim Ball

Founded in 1982. Produces factual entertainment programmes, which include documentaries, historical drama-documentaries, and full-length drama. Recent credits include: *Pacific: The Lost Evidence, Superhomes, Top Tens* and *Married to the Prime Minister*

Focus Films Ltd

The Rotunda Studios, rear of 116-118 Finchley Road, London NW3 5HT
tel 020-7435 9004 *fax* 020-7431 3562
email focus@focusfilms.co.uk
website www.focusfilms.co.uk
Director David Pupkewitz *Head of Production* Lucinda Van Rie

Indie production company founded by David Pupkewitz and Marsha Levin. Recent productions include: *51st State* with Robert Carlyle and Samuel L Jackson; *Book of Eve* with Claire Bloom and Julian Glover; and *Crimetime* with Stephen Baldwin and Pete Postlethwaite. Upcoming projects include: *Heaven and Earth* and *Chemical Wedding.*The company recently launched a separate investment division to finance development and production both of its own and of other companies' feature films (primarily $5 million to $25 million). The company is also in the process of establishing Chilla Productions, a new label for producing thrillers with budgets below $5 million. Focus Films has an international scope, with operations spanning both the European and US markets, and recently also the Asian market.

Does not accept unsolicited scripts or project proposals, but welcomes showreels from new directors. These should be addressed to Malcolm Kohll.

Mark Forstater Productions Ltd

27 Lonsdale Road, London NW6 6RA
tel 020-7624 1123 *fax* 020-7624 1124

Works in film and TV production.

Fox Searchlight Pictures

10201 W. Pico Blvd., Bldg. 38, 1st Fl., Los Angeles, CA 90035, USA
website www.fox.co.uk/searchlight
President Peter Rice

Established in 1994 as the independent arm of Twentieth Century Fox, Fox Searchlight Pictures is a filmmaker-oriented company which aims to create distinctive films helmed by world-class auteurs and exciting newcomers. The company has worked with filmmakers such as Deepa Metha, Danny Boyle, Alexandre Aja and Richard Linklater. Fox has a reputation for working closely with the British independent production sector, and has a joint venture with DNA Films (see page 136).

Fragile Films

Ealing Studios, Ealing Green, London W5 5EP
tel 020-8567 6655 *fax* 020-8758 8658
email info@fragilefilms.com
website www.fragilefilms.com

Fragile Films was set up in 1996 by Barnaby Thompson. It is part of a consortium that acquired Ealing Studios in 2000 to develop the famous old studios into a progressive multimedia digital studio, which brings the creative talents of writers, producers, directors, designers and actors under one roof.

Fragile Films/Ealing Studios does not accept unsolicited material from unrepresented writers, but will consider projects for co-development from third-party producers that fulfill certain criteria:

• the material should be intelligent and original, with clear commercial ambition and broad audience appeal (the company produces commercial feature films with budgets generally in excess of £4 million);
• the project should have a uniquely appealing talent element in either the writer, director or cast attached;
• at least 1 member of the creative team should have a proven track record.

To make an approach to the development department, submit a 1-2 page synopsis along with the credits of the team and any information regarding budget, co-financing, etc. to development@ealingstudios.com. All material is submitted on the understanding that it is possible Fragile Films/Ealing Studios may be developing similar material, and shall not be liable to you or any third party should this be the case. Fragile Films/ Ealing Studios will be in touch if they are interested.

Fremantle Media

1 Stephen Street, London W1T 1AL
tel 020-7691 6000 *fax* 020-7691 6100
website www.fremantlemedia.com

Leading producers of prime-time drama, serial drama, entertainment and factual entertainment, programming in around 43 territories. Runs production operations in more than 25 countries worldwide. Brands include: *Pop Idol, Grand Designs* and *Never Mind the Buzzcocks.*

Fulcrum TV

3rd Floor, Bramah House, 65-71 Bermondsey Street, London SE1 3XF
tel 020-7939 3160 *fax* 020-7430 2260
email info@fulcrumtv.com
website www.fulcrumtv.com

Well-regarded television production company.

Goldcrest Films International

65-66 Dean Street, London W1D 4PL
tel 020-7437 8696 *fax* 020-7437 4448
email mailbox@goldcrest-films.com
website www.goldcrestfilms.com
Director of Acquisitions & Development Seth Carmichael

Established in 1977, Goldcrest has since financed, produced and distributed a large number of commercially and artistically successful films and television programmes.The Goldcrest library has a significant number of acclaimed titles, including: *Chariots of Fire, Gandhi* and *The Killing Fields*; the company has won many prizes at international festivals, including 19 Academy Awards. Upcoming titles include: *Elvis and Annabelle* with Max Minghella, and award-winning documentary *39 Pounds of Love.*

Granada Media

The London Television Centre, Upper Ground, London SE1 9LT
website www.granadamedia.com/international

Granada Film was formerly the independent film production arm of Granada Media, which was founded in 1989 to produce major commercial feature films and smaller UK-based films. In 2002 it won the Golden Bear for Paul Greengrass' *Bloody Sunday*; later that year, the company was closed as a strand-alone company and brought in-house to become part of the drama department at Granada Media.

Green Umbrella

4 The Links, Old Woking Road, Old Woking, Surrey GU22 8BF
tel (01483) 726969 *fax* (01483) 721188
email jules@greenumbrella.co.uk
website www.greenumbrella.co.uk
Producers/Directors Steve Gammond, Mont Tombleson, Bruce Vigar *Managing Director* Jules Gammond

Founded in 1990. Works mainly in video and DVD production. Recent credits include: *The Story of Football, Britain in the 50s* and *Fight the Fat.*

Greenpoint Films

7 Denmark Street, London WC2H 8LZ
tel 020-7240 7066 *fax* 020-7240 7088
email info@greenpointfilms.co.uk
website www.greenpointfilms.co.uk

Producer of feature films for film and TV. Credits include: *Intimacy, Hideous Kinky* and *The Only Boy for Me.*

Greenwich Village Productions

Greenwich Village Productions, 14 Greenwich Church Street, London SE10 9BJ
tel 020-8853 5100 *fax* 020-8293 3001
email info@greenwichvillage.tv
website www.fictionfactory.co.uk/gvtv
Producer/Director John Taylor

An established producer of documentaries for the BBC World Service and BBC Radio 4, Greenwich Village Productions specialises in 'intelligent entertainment'. Recent credits include: *Adlestrop* and *Love & The Art of War.*

Harbour Pictures

11 Langton Street, London SW10 0JL
tel 020-7351 7070 *fax* 020-7352 3528
email info@harbourpictures.com
website www.harbourpictures.com

Harcourt Films

58 Camden Square, London NW1 9XE
tel 020-7267 0882
email jmarre@harcourtfilms.com
website www.harcourtfilms.com

Jeremy Marre's documentary production company primarily produces docs for international television.

Hat Trick Productions Ltd

10 Livonia Street, London W1F 8AF
tel 020-7434 2451 *fax* 020-7287 9791
email info@hattrick.com
website www.hattrick.com
Joint Managing Directors Denise O'Donoghue, Jimmy Mulville

Founded in 1986, Hat Trick Productions is one of the UK's most successful independent production companies working in situation and drama comedy series and light entertainment shows. Recent credits include: *The Kumars at No. 42, Worst Week of my Life, Have I Got News for You* and *Room 101.*

Heyday Films

5 Denmark Street, London WC2H 8LP
tel 020-7836 6333 *fax* 020-7836 6444
Founder & Managing Director David Heyman

British company established by Heyman in 1997, which has a first-look deal with Warner Bros. Best known for producing the Harry Potter films.

Hurricane Films Ltd

19 Hope Street, Liverpool L1 9BQ
tel 0151-707 9700 *fax* 0151-707 9149
email sol@hurricanefilms.co.uk
website www.hurricanefilms.net

Managing Director Solon Papadopoulos *Head of Development* Julie Currie

Founded in 2000, produces single films and documentary series from original ideas. Recent credits include: *Warship* (in association with Granada TV); *Comm-Raid on the Potemkin* (FilmFour); and *Wrecked* (BBC2).

Iambic Productions

89 Whiteladies Road, Clifton, Bristol BS8 2NT
tel 0117-923 7222 *fax* 0117-923 8343
email admin@iambic.tv
website www.iambicproductions.com

Independent television production company specialising in the fields of arts, music and entertainment. Part of DCD Media (see page 307).

Icon Entertainment International Ltd

Solar House, 915 High Road, North Finchley, London N12 8QJ
tel 020-8492 6300 *fax* 020-8492 6300
website www.iconmovies.co.uk
Head of Development (UK/Europe) Martha Coleman

International independent production, sales and distribution company. The international production arm was established in 1989 by Mel Gibson and his long-time business partner, Bruce Davey. They have had huge successes, including: *The Passion of Christ* and *What Women Want*. While the UK wing primarily operates as a distributor, the company does get involved in early stages on rare selected productions.

– see page 298.

Intermedia

Enterprise House, 59-65 Upper Ground, London SE1 9PQ
website www.intermediafilm.co.uk
Managing Director, UK Operations Gavin James *Head of UK Production & Development* Ollie Madden

Hugely successful international production and sales company with HQ in Germany. Credits include: *Adaptation*, *Iris* and *Nurse Betty*.

Intrepido

tel 020-8879 7100 *fax* 020-8879 7930
email mail@intrepido.co.uk
website www.intrepido.co.uk

An award-winning independent production and development copmpany which has focused on shorts.

Ipso Facto Films

London: 11-13 Broad Court, London WC2B 5PY *Newcastle*: 1 Pink Lane, Newcastle-upon-Tyne NE1 5DW
tel 020-7240 6166 *fax* 020-7240 6160
email info@ipsofactofilms.com
website www.ipsofactofilms.com
Managing Director Christine Alderson

Ipso Facto was established in 1993, and has since produced 10 features and more than 50 short films and documentaries for an international market. Welcomes submissions for film or TV in the form of a 1-page overview, which should include the following: title/pitch (1 paragraph capturing the essence of the story); writer (brief 2-line CV); and status (is it an idea still/first draft/ready to be made?). Send by email or by post with envelope or title clearly marked 'Project Submission'.

Kai Film & TV Productions

1 Ravenslea Road, London SW12 8SA
tel 020-8673 4550
email mwallington@btinternet.com

Small independent established in 1987. Welcomes script ideas and showreels from filmmakers on above contact email. Credits include: *Walking on Water*, *Casino World*, and *Big Hair* (upcoming).

Kaos Films

c/o Pinewood Studios, Pinewood Road, Iver Heath, Bucks SL0 0NH
email info@kaosfilms.co.uk
website www.kaosfilms.co.uk

Kaos Films is a film production company with a number of features in development and several short films in production. Also runs and manages the British Short Screenplay Competition in association with the National Film and Television School.

Kelpie Films

227 St Andrews Road, Glasgow G41 1PD
tel 0871-874 0328 *fax* 0871-874 0329
email yearbook@kelpiefilms.com
website www.kelpiefilms.com

Independent production company that produces a range of broadcast and corporate/commercial work, from computer-animated children's programmes to documentaries in the Middle East and low-budget feature films. Credits include: BAFTA-nominated animation, *Cannonman*; Grierson Award-winning documentary, *And So Goodbye*; and large-scale corporate work for global clients such as Shell and the UK Government.

Kismet Film Company

c/o The Works, 4 Great Portland Street, London W1W 8QJ
tel 020-7281 7121

Michele Camarda's feature film production company. Credits include: *The River King* and *Born Romantic*.

The Light House

email info@light-house.co.uk
website www.light-house.co.uk

– see page 338.

Lionsgate UK

(formerly Redbus Pictures)
Ariel House, 74a Charlotte Street, London W1T 4QJ

tel 020-7299 8800 *fax* 020-7299 8801
website www.lionsgatefilms.co.uk
Head of Development Emma Berkofsky

UK production and distribution outfit owned by Lionsgate. Credits include: *Bend it Like Beckham* and *Good Night and Good Luck*. Also see Emma Berkofsky's article on 'The Role of the Developer', on page 29.

Little Bird Co Ltd

9 Grafton Mews, London W1P 5LG
tel 020-7380 3980 *fax* 020-7380 3981
email info@littlebird.co.uk
Dublin Office 13 Merrion Square, Dublin 2, Republic of Ireland
tel (01) 613 1710
website www.littlebird.ie
Co-chairmen James Mitchell, Jonathan Cavendish
Producer Dixie Linder

Quality film and television production company. Credits include: *Bridget Jones – The Edge of Reason*, *Trauma* and *In My Father's Den*. Please note that Little Bird *does not* accept open submissions. Any material sent without prior written permission from Little Bird will be treated as non-confidential and non-proprietary.

LWT and United Productions

London TV Centre, Upper Ground, London SE1 9LT
tel 020-7620 1620
Controller of Drama Michele Buck

Founded in 1996. Producers of TV and film.

Material Entertainment

3rd Floor, 101-102 Jermyn Street, London SW1Y 6EE
fax 020-7839 3514
President Robert Jones

Established in 2005, Material is an ambitious production outfit owned and distributed worldwide by New Line Cinema and UK distributor Entertainment.

Maya Vision International Ltd

6 Kinghorn Street, London EC1A 7HW
tel 020-7796 4842 *fax* 020-7796 4580
email info@mayavisionint.com
website www.mayavisionint.com
Producer/Director Rebecca Dobbs *Producer* Sally Thomas *Writer* Michael Wood

Founded in 1982. Film and TV production company producing features, TV dramas and documentaries, and arts programmes. Recent credits include: *Alexander the Great, In Search of Shakespeare* and *Conquistadors* (BBC); *Caught Looking* (Channel 4); and *The World Turned Upside Down* (BBC2/Arts Council). Also manages the Short Film Completion Fund on behalf of the UK Film Council. See website for details of how to apply for funds.

Mentorn

43 Whitfield Street, London W1P 67G
tel 020-7258 6800 *fax* 020-7258 6888
email reception@mentorn.tv
website www.mentorn.tv

Producer of factual and entertainment TV.

Merchant Ivory Productions

46 Lexington Street, London W1F 0LP
tel 020-7437 1200 *fax* 020-7734 1579
email miplondon@merchantivory.co.uk
website www.merchantivory.com

Hugely successful collaboration between late director Ismail Merchant, screenwriter Ruth Prawer Jhabvala, and director James Ivory. Credits include: *A Room With a View, Howard's End* and *Maurice.*

The Mersey Television Company

Campus Manor, Childwall Abbey Road, Liverpool L16 0JP
tel 0151-722 9122 *fax* 0151-722 1969
email webteam@merseytv.com
website www.merseytv.com

Mirage Enterprises

Old Chapel Studios, 19 Fleet Road, London NW3 2QR
tel 020-7284 5588 *fax* 020-7284 5599

Sydney Pollack and Anthony Minghella's production company. Credits include: *Breaking and Entering, Cold Mountain* and *The Quiet American.*

Mirage Films Ltd

5 Wardour Mews, London W1F 8AL
tel 020-7734 3627 *fax* 020-7734 3735
email production@miragefilms.net
website www.miragefilms.net

Documentary and commercials production company.

Missing in Action Films Ltd

Flat 1, 2 Whitfield Street, London W1T 2RB
tel 020-7323 2895
email info@miafilms.co.uk
website www.miafilms.co.uk
Founder Mia Bays

An exciting up-and-coming production company, Missing In Action Films was founded by Mia Bays in 2003. The company has produced 2 short films and 1 feature documentary: *Six Shooter* (Martin McDonagh), winner of the Best Live Action Short at the Academy Awards 2006; *Ex Memoria* (Josh Appignanesi), nominated for Best Short at the British Independent Film Awards 2006; and its first (documentary) feature, *Scott Walker – 30 Century Man,* premiered at the BFI London Film Festival 2006 and screened at Berlin and South by Southwest 2007 film festivals. It was released in UK cinemas by Verve Pictures in April 2007. The company is also developing Neil Hunter and Natalie Sirett's *The Sycamores,* which stars Natalie Press and Peter Mullan; *The Man With Kaleidoscope Eyes*, with Joe Dante to direct; and *Within*, with Josh Appignanesi.

Mosaic Films Ltd
1A Flaxman Court, London W1A 0AU
tel (01594) 530708 *fax* (01594) 530094
email info@mosaicfilms.com
website www.mosaicfilms.com
Director Colin Luke

Mosaic Films was established in 1995. It has made a number of award-winning series and single films for BBC, Channel 4 and ITV in the UK and also for many continental broadcasters. In addition it makes corporates, music videos, and commercials.

Myriad Pictures
1520D Cloverfield Blvd, Santa Monica, CA 90404, USA
tel ++ 1 310 279 4000 *fax* ++ 1 310 279 4001
website www.myriadpictures.com
President/CEO Kirk Damico

With UK offices now closed, Myriad operates solely from its US offices. Credits include: *The Good Girl*, *Kinsey*, *Little Fish*, and *Trauma*.

New Line Cinema
Turner House, 16 Great Marlborough Street, London W1F 7HS
website www.newline.com
Development & Acquisitions (UK) Jack Arbuthnott

Also see page 140, for details of New Line and Entertainment-owned production outfit, Material Entertainment.

Newmarket Films
202 N. Canon Drive, Beverly Hills, CA 90210, USA
tel ++ 1 310 858 7472 *fax* ++ 1 310 858 7473
email info@newmarketcap.com
website www.newmarketfilms.com
Founders William Tyrer, Chris Ball

Founded in 1994, Newmarket has become one of the world's most influential indie producters. Credits include: *Memento*, *The Woodsman*, and *The Usual Suspects*. Does not accept unsolicited submissions.

Noel Gay
19 Denmark Street, London WC2H 8NA
tel 020-7836 3941
email info@noelgay.com
website www.noelgay.com

Initially a music-based agency and publisher, Noel Gay moved towards the growing television industry and has been one of the UK's premier entertainment agencies since the 1970s.

Nova Productions
62 Ascot Avenue, Cantley, Doncaster DN4 6HE
tel 0870-765 1021 *fax* 0870-169 2982
email info@novaonline.co.uk
website www.novaonline.co.uk

Oxford Film & Television
6 Erskine Road, London NW3 3AJ
tel 020-7483 3637 *fax* 020-7483 3567
email email@oftv.co.uk
website www.oftv.co.uk
Creative Director Nicolas Kent

An independent film and television production company which produces drama, docu-drama and documentaries on a wide variety of subjects for the BBC, Channel Four, ITV, PBS, Showtime, etc. The company has also produced 6 feature films, including the Oscar-winning *Restoration* and the Oscar- and BAFTA-nominated *Hilary and Jackie*.

Paladin Invision Ltd
8 Barb Mews, London W6 7PA
tel 020-7371 2123 *fax* 020-7371 2160
email pitv@pitv.com
website www.pitv.com
Directors William Cran, Clive Syddall

A multi-Emmy award-winning company producing factual programming including history, current affairs, religion, music and arts documentaries for the UK, the US and the international market. Credits include: *Nelson's Trafalgar* (C4), and *Hostile Waters* (HBO).

Passion Pictures
3rd/4th Floors, County House,
33-34 Rathbone Place, London W1T 1JN
tel 020-7323 9933
email info@passion-pictures.com
website www.passion-pictures.com
Managing Director Andrew Ruheman *Head of Film* John Battsek *Head of Development* Nicole Stott

Academy Award-winning production company working in a wide range of areas – from animated and live-action features and documentaries to acclaimed music promos and commercials. Credits include: *One Day in September*, and *Live Forever*.

Pathe Pictures
Kent House, 14-17 Market Place, London W1W 8AR
tel 020-7323 5151 *fax* 020-7631 3568
email pathe@pathe-uk.com
website www.pathepicturesinternational.co.uk

– see page 313 for Pathe International.

Penumbra Productions Ltd
80 Brondesbury Road, London NW6 6RX
tel 020-7328 4550 *fax* 020-7328 3844
email nazpenumbra@aol.com
Contact HO Nazareth

Founded in 1981. Independent film and TV producer making contemporary social-issue drama and documentaries. Also produces non-broadcast videos when commissioned.

Picture Palace Films Ltd
13 Egbert Street, London NW1 8LJ
tel 020-7586 8763 *fax* 020-7586 9048
email info@picturepalace.com
website www.picturepalace.com
Producer & Chief Executive Malcom Craddock

Founded in 1972. Works mainly in feature films and TV drama production. Recent credits include: *Sharpe's Challenge, Frances Tuesday* and *Extremely Dangerous* (all ITV); *Rebel Heart* (BBC); *A Life for a Life* (*The True Story of Stefan Kizko*); and the *Sharpe* series.

Planet 24 Productions

35-38 Portman Square, London W1H ONU
tel 020-7486 6268 *fax* 020-7612 0679
website www.planet24.com
Managing Director Ed Forsdick

Founded in 1992, Planet 24 is a wholly owned subsidiary of ITV. Its core activity is television development and production. Credits include: *The Big Breakfast* and *Little Friends.*

Priority Pictures

91 Berwick Street, London W1F 0NE
tel 020-7292 5081 *fax* 020-7292 8333
website www.prioritypictures.com
Partners Marion Pilowsky, Colin Leventhal

London-based company launched in 2004, which develops and produces feature films for an international audience. Credits include: *Nina's Heavenly Delights* and *The All Together.*

Sarah Radclyffe Productions

10-11 St Georges Mews, Primrose Hill, London NW1 8XE
tel 020-7483 3556 *fax* 020-7586 8063
email mail@srpltd.co.uk

Recorded Picture Company

24 Hanway Street, London W1T 1UH
tel 020-7636 2251
email rpc@recordedpicture.com
website www.recordedpicturecompany.com
Founder & Chairman Jeremy Thomas *Managing Director* Peter Watson *CEO* Stephan Mallmann *Head of Development* Hercules Belville

Founded in 1971 by Jeremy Thomas. Has supported the work of directors such as Richard Linklater, Stephen Frears and Bernardo Bertolucci, among many others. No unsolicited project proposals. Recent credits include: *Fast Food Nation*, *Sexy Beast*, and *Young Adam.*

Revolution Films

9a Dallington Street, London EC1V 0BQ
tel 020-7566 0700 *fax* 020-7566 0701
email email@revolution-films.com
website www.revolution-films.com
Co-founders Andrew Eaton (Producer), Michael Winterbottom (Director) *Head of Television* Kate Ogborn

Revolution Films was established by Michael Winterbottom and Andrew Eaton. Credits include: Winterbottom's *Wonderland*, *24 Hour Party People*, and *In This World.* Revolution also co-produced *Heartlands* and *Bright Young Things.* In 2006, it established a television division to be run by Kate Ogborn.

Ruby Films

26 Lloyd Baker Street, London WC1X 9AW
Director Alison Owen

London-based production company. Credits include: *Love + Hate*, *Sylvia*, *The Other Boleyn Girl*, *Brick Lane* and *The Bad Mother's Handbook.* Director Owen also recently produced *Proof* for Miramax.

September Films

22 Glenthorne Road, London W6 ONG
tel 020-8563 9393 *fax* 020-8741 7214
email september@septemberfilms.com
website www.septemberfilms.com
Chairman David Green *Director of Production* Elaine Day

September Films is a leading UK independent television and film production company with offices in London and Los Angeles. It was founded in 1992 by feature film director, David Green, who devised the groundbreaking Hollywood Women series that launched the company. Having produced over 1000 hours of primetime television during the last 13 years, September is an established specialist in factual entertainment, features, reality programming and entertainment formats.

Founded in 1992. Has offices in London and Hollywood and works mainly in TV production. Specialises in factual entertainment, reality programmes and entertainment formats. Also produces feature films and TV movies.

Sixteen Films

2nd Floor, 187 Wardour Street, London W2 5SH
tel 020-7734 0168 *fax* 020-7439 4196
email info@sixteenfilms.co.uk
website www.sixteenfilms.co.uk
Director Ken Loach *Producer* Rebecca O'Brien

Sixteen Films was set up by Ken Loach and Rebecca O'Brien following the dissolution of Parallax Pictures in Spring 2002. They are joined by Paul Laverty as Associate Director.

The company was set up by Ken Loach and Rebecca O'Brien following the dissolution of Parallax Pictures in 2002. Credits include: recent Cannes winner, *The Wind that Shakes the Barley*, *Sweet Sixteen*, and *Ae Fond Kiss.* Sixteen does not accept unsolicited project submissions.

Slate Films

20 Great Chapel Street, London W1F 8FW
tel 020-7734 1217 *fax* 020-7287 9622
email info@slatefilms.com
website www.slatefilms.com
Owners Andrea Calderwood, Vicki Patterson

Slate is an independent film and TV production company set up in 2000 by Andrea Calderwood and Vicki Patterson. Credits include: *Last King of Scotland*, *Once Upon a Time in the Midlands*, and *Hotel*.

Spellbound Productions Ltd

90 Cowdenbeath Path, Islington, London N1 0LG
tel 020-7713 8066 *fax* 020-7713 8066
email phspellbound@hotmail.com
Producer Paul Harris

Small independent production company specialising in feature films and drama for television. Current projects include: *Twist of Fate*, a romantic comedy in development with Columbia Pictures (LA); and *Chicane*, a NY crime thriller in development.

Stagescreen Productions

12 Upper St Martin's Lane, London WC2H 9JY
tel 020-7497 2510 *fax* 020-7497 2208
Director Jeffrey Taylor *Development Executive* John Segal

Founded in 1986, Stagescreen is a film and TV production company with offices in London and Los Angeles. Recent credits include: *What's Cooking*, directed by Gurinder Chadha (Lionsgate); *Alexander The Great* directed by Jalal Merhi (ProSeiben); and *Jekyll*, directed by Douglas Mackinnon and Matt Lipsey (BBC). Forthcoming work includes: *Young Cleopatra*.

TalkBack Productions

20-21 Newman Street, London W1T 1PG
tel 020-7861 8000 *fax* 020-7861 8001
website www.talkback.co.uk

Founded in 1981. Produces TV situation comedies and comedy dramas, features, and straight drama. Credits include: *Property Ladder*, *Jamie's Kitchen*, *Smack the Pony*, *The 11 O' Clock Show* and *Da Ali G Show*. TalkBack is part of the Fremantle Media Group (see page 137).

Tiger Aspect Productions

Drama address: 5 Soho Square, London W1V 5DE
tel 020-7434 0672 *fax* 020-7544 1665
email general@tigeraspect.co.uk
Comedy address: 7 Soho Street, London W1D 3DQ
tel 020-7434 0700 *fax* 020-7434 1798
website www.tigeraspect.co.uk
Head of Drama Greg Brenman

Founded in 1993. Produces TV drama, comedy and sitcoms with the aim of "investing in and working with the leading writers, performers and programme-makers to produce original, creative and successful programming". Credits include: *Teachers* (C4), *My Fragile Heart* (ITV), and *Playing the Field* (BBC1).

Tigerlily Films

Studio 5, 10-11 Archer Street, London W1D 7AZ
tel 020-7247 1107
email info@tigerlilyfilms.com
website www.tigerlilyfilms.com
Founders Natascha Dack, Nikki Parrot

Producers of independent feature film and documentary projects. Will not accept unsolicited materials.

TransAtlantic Films

Studio 1, 3 Brackenbury Road, London W6 0BE
tel 020-8735 0505 *fax* 020-8735 0605
email mail@transatlanticfilms.com
website www.transatlanticfilms.com

Formed in 1968 to produce films with a special emphasis on factual documentary.

Twenty Twenty Television

20 Kentish Town Road, London NW1 9NX
tel 020-7284 2020 *fax* 020-7284 1810
email mail@twentytwentytv.co.uk
website www.twentytwenty.tv
Managing Director Peter Casely-Hayford *Executive Producer* Claudia Milne *Head of Development* George Kay

Twenty Twenty Television is one of the UK's leading independent television production companies, making award-winning documentaries, hard-hitting current affairs, popular drama and attention-grabbing living history series. Its recent primetime children's shows are also bringing success in an exciting and challenging genre. *The Choir* won a 2007 BAFTA Award; the series *That'll Teach 'Em* won an Indie Award and was nominated for a British Academy Award. The *Lads Army* series gained the Royal Television Society primetime features award as well as a BAFTA nomination, and the international factual hit *Brat Camp* brought home an International Emmy from New York in November 2004.

Formed in 1982 by 'hands on' programme-makers, Twenty Twenty Television has always grown organically. Its industry-wide reputation for quality, intelligence and rigour was built in factual programmes. Twenty Twenty remains truly independent and is still run by creative and enthusiastic programme-makers. Its work has been broadcast by networks around the world including the BBC, CBBC, ITV, Channels 4 and Five in the UK, and ABC, The Discovery Channel, Turner Original Productions, Sundance Channel, CNN, The Arts and Entertainment Channel and WGBH in the USA.

Founded in 1982. Produces current affairs, documentaries, science and educational programmes, and reality TV. Began producing TV drama in 2000 and has been commissioned by the BBC and ITV networks. Credits include: *How to Beat Your Kid's Asthma*, *Lad's Army*, and *Second Sight*.

Video Enterprises

12 Barbers Wood Road, High Wycombe, Bucks HP12 4EP

tel (01494) 534144
email videoenterprises@ntlworld.com
website www.videoenterprises.co.uk
Director Maurice R Fleisher

Video Enterprises is a UK-based video production and crewing company specialising in Broadcast, Corporate, Industrial, Theatrical and Social Events programme-making.

Established in 1986 for corporate, industrial, advertising/promotion, training and events video production. Also produces artists' showreels and provides training in video production. Fully equipped for digital and High Definition production and post-production by experienced broadcast-trained personnel. For further details of the company's activities, visit the website.

Walsh Bros Ltd

24 Redding House, Harlinger Street,
King Henry's Wharf, London SE18 5SR
tel 020-8858 6870 *fax* 020-8858 6870
email info@walshbros.co.uk
website www.walshbros.co.uk
Director John Walsh *Casting Director* Maura Walsh
Producer David Walsh

John Walsh MA founded Walsh Bros Ltd with brother David after graduating from the London Film School. BAFTA-nominated productions range from television series and dramas for BBC and Channel 4, to feature film production. The BBC documentary series *Headhunting the Homeless* was short-listed for the Grierson Awards 2004. The 2005 series of Channel 4's *Don't Make Me Angry* was BAFTA nominated.

Warp X

email info@warpx.co.uk
website www.warpx.co.uk

– see page 75.

Working Title Films

76 Oxford Street, London W1N 9FD
tel 020-7307 3000 *fax* 020-7307 3003
email dan.shepherd@unistudios.com
website www.workingtitlefilms.com
Chairmen Tim Bevan, Eric Fellner *President* Liza Chasin *President UK Production* Debra Hayward

Recent films include *Atonement* (with James McAvoy, Keira Knightly, Romola Garai, Saoirse Ronan and Vanessa Redgrave) and *The Golden Age* (with Cate Blanchett and Geoffrey Rush, who reprise the roles they orginated in the award-winning *Elizabeth*, joined this time by Clive Owen).

One of the UK's most influential and international production companies, founded in 1982. Working Title has produced more than 70 films and won BAFTAs, Academy Awards, and prizes at Cannes and Berlin. Credits include: *Flight 93, Hot Fuzz, Pride and Prejudice, Notting Hill, Bridget Jones's Diary* and *Love Actually*; and novel adaptations *Captain Corelli's Mandolin* and *High Fidelity*.

The Works Production

(previously known as The Film Consortium)
4th Floor, Portland House, 4 Great Portland,
London W1W 8QJ
tel 020-7612 0030 *fax* 020-7612 0031
email info@theworkslimited.com
website www.theworkslimited.com

Sister production company to The Works (see page 314).

World Productions Ltd

Eagle House, 50 Marshall Street, London W1F 9BQ
tel 020-7734 3536 *fax* 020-7758 7000
email firstname@world-productions.com
website www.world-productions.com
Executive Producer Tony Garnett *Executive Producer/ Head of Development* Simon Heath *PA & Office Manager* Helen Saunders

Produces TV drama features, series and serials. Recent credits include: *Between the Lines, Ballykissangel* and *Love Again* – a film about Philip Larkin (BBC).

Zenith Productions Ltd

43-45 Dorset Street, London W1U 7NA
tel 020-7224 2440 *fax* 020-7224 3194
email general@zenith-entertainment.co.uk
website www.zenith.tv.co.uk
Managing Director Ivan Rendall *Casting Director* Matt Western *Head of Drama* Adrian Bate

Founded in 1984. Part of the Zenith group, which comprises Zenith North and Zenith Productions. Works mainly in producing a wide range of programmes for terrestrial, satellite and cable television and feature films for worldwide theatrical distribution.

Major studios

The global feature-film industry takes its lead from a handful of major studios based in Los Angeles, most of which are descendants of the original studios active in Hollywood's 'golden age'. All are production companies with some sales/distribution entity, and all have an aggressively commercial approach – although most now operate an additional 'diffusion' label alongside their main brand, to produce and release smaller-scale art-house product. Alongside the so-called 'majors', an increasing range of independents – often called 'mini-majors' – now flourish.

Buena Vista/Walt Disney Pictures

500 S. Buena Vista Street, Burbank, CA 91521, USA
tel ++ 1 818-560-1000

Dreamworks Pictures

100 Universal City Plaza, Bldg 5121, Universal City, CA 91608, USA
tel ++ 1 818-733-7000
website www.dreamworks.com

Created by Steven Spielberg, Jeffrey Katzenberg, and David Geffen as a new type of Hollywood studio and subsequently sold to Viacom. Now divided into Dreamworks Pictures and Dreamworks Animation, and responsible for giant global successes such as the *Shrek* franchise.

Lions Gate Pictures

4553 Glencoe Avenue, Suite 200, Marina Del Rey, CA 90292
tel ++ 1 310-314-2000
website www.lionsgate.com

Part of the Canadian-originated Lions Gate Entertainment group, Lions Gate Pictures is a producer/distributor which has traditionally focused on foreign-language and indie product. Major hits have included *Fahrenheit 9/11* and *Crash*. The company bought out Artisan Entertainment, responsible for *The Blair Witch Project*. A move into more commercial titles has produced *Bratz: The Movie, Saw IV* and *Hostel 2*.

Metro-Goldwyn-Mayer, Inc.

10250 Constellation Blvd., Los Angeles, CA 90067, USA
tel ++ 1 310-449-3000
website www.mgm.com

One of the most prominent of the old-style Hollywood studios operating since the silent era, MGM was aquired by Sony in 2005 and formed a distribution relationship with 20th Century Fox. Recent productions include the 2006 Bond feature *Casino Royale*, and *Rocky Balboa*.

Miramax Films

375 Greenwich Street, New York, NY 10013, USA
tel ++ 1 212-941-3800
website www.miramax.com

The first great independent production and distribution company, created by the Weinstein Brothers in 1979 to produce films that were considered financially unviable by the major studios. Sold to Disney in 1993, Miramax continued to be operated by the Weinsteins until they left to form their own company, taking with them the diffusion Miramax sub-brand 'Dimension Films'. Recent and forthcoming Miramax titles include: *Breaking and Entering, Brideshead Revisited,* and *Kill Bill.*

New Line Cinema Corporation

116 N. Robertson Blvd, 2nd Floor, Los Angeles, CA 90048, USA
tel ++ 1 310-854-5811
website www.newline.com

Originally an indie studio, and subsequently acquired by Time Warner, New Line Cinema has grown to take responsibility for a number of major franchises including the *Lord Of The Rings* trilogy. It began an early distribution relationship with John Waters, resulting in the company's involvement in the remake of *Hairspray*, alongside worldwide 'event' titles like *Snakes on A Plane*, and the *Rush Hour, Final Destination* and *Austin Powers* series. It retains a small independent sub-brand known as Picturehouse (formerly Fine Line), which it operates in partnership with HBO.

New Line International

website www.newline.com
President, New Line International Releasing, Inc.
Camela Galano

New Line Cinema is a fully integrated film company and one of the oldest and most successful independents. Develops and releases 12-15 films per year; as of spring 2005 the company has produced a small slate of modestly budgeted independent films through its collaboration with HBO, Picturehouse. New Line is part of the Time Warner Group. Titles include: *Hairspray, Lord of the Rings, The Wedding Crashers*, and *A History of Violence* (all New Line).

Paramount Pictures Corporation

5555 Melrose Ave, Los Angeles, CA 90038 USA
tel ++ 1 323-956-5000

website www.paramount.com

The oldest of all the Hollywood studios responsible for consistently producing blockbusters, including the all-time top grosser *Titanic.* Its complex history of takeovers and mergers has not interfered with its ability to produce high-budget/high-earning worldwide mainstream fare – from *Zoolander, Mission Impossible* and *Transformers* to *Lara Croft.*

Sony Pictures Entertainment

10202 W. Washington Blvd, Culver City, CA 90232 USA
tel ++ 1 310-244-4000
website www.sonypictures.com

Sony Pictures Entertainment (SPE) acquired Columbia Tristar in 1989. It has a specialist arm, Sony Pictures Classics, and acquired MGM as part of its group in 2005. Recent major titles have included: *The Da Vinci Code*, the *Spiderman* franchise and *Daddy Day Care.*

Twentieth Century Fox Film Corp.

10201 W. Pico Blvd., Los Angeles, CA 90035 USA
tel ++ 1 310-369-1000
website www.foxmovies.com

Created out of a merger between two of the original golden age Hollywood studios, 20th Century Fox is now a subsidiary of Rupert Murdoch's News Corporation. 20th Century Fox's recent international hits have included: *Die Hard 4, Simpsons The Movie* and *Fantastic Four: Rise of the Silver Surfer.*

Universal Pictures

100 Universal City Plaza, Universal City, CA 91608 USA
tel ++ 1 818-777-1000
website www.universalpictures.com

The second oldest of the original studios, Universal Pictures is owned by NBC Universal and operates as a producer and distributor wirth numerous off-shoots including its theme park, Universal Studios. Output varies from *Gladiator* and *Billy Elliot* to *The 40 Year old Virgin* and *American Pie.*

Warner Bros

4000 Warner Blvd., Burbank, CA 91522 USA
tel ++ 1 818-954-6000
website www.warnerbros.com

The third oldest of the great Hollywood studios and responsible for the first talking picture, Warner Bros. is a subsidiary of Time Warner. It has been behind the successful franchises *Harry Potter, Oceans 11/12/13*, and *The Terminator* as well as critical hits *Flags of Our Fathers, Zodiac* and *The Departed*. Warner Bros. also operates the Warner Independent label to produce and showcase smaller niche titles.

The Weinstein Company

345 Hudson Street 13th Floor, New York, NY 10014, USA
website www.weinsteinco.co

Founded by Harvey and Bob Weinstein in 2005 after they left Miramax Films, and incorporating the Dimension Films label (also previously owned by Miramax), which specialises in genre titles. Weinstein titles have included: *Derailed, Sicko* and *Factory Girl;* Dimension titles include: *Grindhouse, Scary Movie* and *Wolf Creek.*

Notes on filmmaking and collaboration

Anthony Minghella

Film is a trick. Bundles of still frames, collected at 24 frames per second and then projected onto a screen at the same rate, suggest a continuous movement. They conjure something like reality. The next part of the film-trick is that if we point the camera at different events and individuals – if we make shots of different sizes and duration and then join them together, *montage* – viewers will attempt to connect and relate the information in those shots. *A close-up of a woman's face. A baby crying in a cot. A dog barking on a pavement. An open window. A hand closing the window. The baby stops crying. The woman's face.* Join these shots together into what might be called a 'film sentence', and the audience interprets a narrative: a mother, seeing her baby disturbed by a dog barking on the street below, closes the window and calms her child. The fact that none of these shots, none of these events, can really be connected in time – unless multiple cameras are at work; the fact that none of the events need occur in the same week, the same city; that neither dog nor baby nor woman need to understand or commit to the connection – none of this can dilute the power of the sequence. As EM Forster asserted: "Only connect."

I have this mechanical mystery of film in my mind when I think about the wisdom of my partner – the distinguished director, actor and producer, Sydney Pollack. His mantra is, "Everything is technical." The first time I heard Sydney say this, I wanted to dispute it – to ask what was technical about the magic of cinema, its poetry, the wonder of a performance, the beauty of light, the intricacies of a spoken line. But, increasingly, I embrace his axiom, not least because it suggests firmly that work and rigour and method can improve a film; that every problem encountered during the odyssey of making a film can be solved. It might not be true, but it's a way of looking at it. I know that making a film is a marathon and not a sprint – not an activity for the faint-hearted. I know that, at best, filmmaking is a collective art authored by a director, if I might be allowed that ambiguity. And everything *is* technical. The film sentence I suggested above will not always work: there are rules of syntax in film, just as there are in prose. If the light is completely different in two shots, night and day, or if the colour palate is entirely unrelated, or if the woman's costume changes, the sequence will probably not work (although sometimes continuity is for cissies). If the woman is looking from left to right in her shot and the baby is looking from left to right in its shot, then no amount of emotion in their expressions will connect them.

These are largely simple errors to remedy. Other steps in the filmmaking process are less visible, and often more obliquely managed. Knowing how a co-production treaty might impact on a budget or a casting decision; knowing how to divide up the logistics of a production to create a sustainable schedule which accommodates and serves the competing interests of actors, contracts, locations, studios, weather, travel, lighting, and, most important, the story being told – this is as significant as any aesthetic intention the director might hold. Learning how to create the blueprint of the film, its screenplay, and understanding how it must serve as a map of a film and not as literature, is another elusive challenge. Learning how to *read* a screenplay is an even more elusive challenge.

Filmmaking finds analogies in many other activities: it's like conducting a military campaign; it's like working in a restaurant kitchen; it's like making a building; it's like performing in an orchestra. Many hands, many soldiers, many contributors, many things to go wrong; beautiful when correct and impossible to deconstruct. In success it's a pointless game to discover who did what, which ingredient crucially mattered. Similarly, one wrong ingredient, one missing beam, one false note, one false manoeuvre in what might be a four- or five-year project, and the whole undertaking can founder. This *Yearbook* can't provide the recipe for success, nor solve every problem in the making of a film. However, in a medium where everything just might be technical, it's good to have a bespoke technical guide, a reservoir of information. Navigating it will require you to acknowledge that your job begins with learning a profound respect for all those people who are not directors, whom you will lean on every day, and who will never get the credit.

A producer and director on why 'DIY' doesn't have to mean 'low fi'

Making a super-low-budget drama feature constitutes a myriad of challenges. With barely £500,000 in place, first-time producer **Sarah Sulick** and TV director **Roger Goldby** set off with a strong script, an excellent cast and crew and the unshakeable will to make their film, and have delivered an outstanding debut in *The Waiting Room*, which had a Gala premiere at the 2007 Edinburgh International Film Festival. Here they share their experiences of development, the producer/director relationship and making a low-budget feature that will more than hold its own against other quality indie dramas.

Given that you both came into this feature as first-timers, what made each of you convinced that the other would be able to pull off their role?

Sarah Sulick: We met when I was working at Scorpio Films in development, and Roger became attached to another project I was on. I wasn't wary of him but I didn't know his work. He has a great sense of humour and doesn't take himself too seriously, which isn't to say he isn't serious about the work – he is. But as we got to know each other we started to have lots of laughs, which is a help during development as it can be a painful and slow process. We also seemed to be able to talk about writing and scripts in a way that was somehow in tune with each other. In deciding to make *The Waiting Room* as our first feature, I think we both took a leap of faith. We believed in each other and hoped we could pull it off. I really responded to the script and was amazed that he could be so perceptive and on-the-mark about relationships, especially from a woman's point of view. The script spoke to me as a wife, mother, basically as a human being, and I felt that he could transfer all of that to the screen.

Roger Goldby: We met through producer Stephen Evans, who attached me to direct *Stupid Cupid*, a script based on a book by Arrabella Wier, and I think we were both a little wary of each other at the start of that project! I did a rewrite on *The Waiting Room* and then Sarah and I started to work on it together in earnest. To my relief, I realised that we were on exactly the same wavelength about it and the way we both like to work. Sarah is very clever *and* very positive. While we don't always agree on which films we like, somehow we just clicked on our ideas and views on scripts. I began to see that we had the makings of a really good working relationship. As a writer in the first instance, it is so important to have someone I can trust. Sarah is brutally honest – she can't lie; however, she is also wonderfully positive, so one constantly feels very encouraged.

How much did you rigidly stick to your own defined job roles prep, production and post?

RG: Well ... I'm a control freak! I guess that our roles were both defined *and* fluid. When it came to crewing and other logistical work, I just got on with it; I had done it before and knew who I wanted. With setting up the company Bright Pictures, setting up the EIS [Enterprise Investment Scheme, the government scheme that allows certain tax reliefs for investors] and other financial and business duties like that, I took an interest, but Sarah did most of that work. Creatively we worked together on the script and cast and I would consult her opinion on style, locations, etc. On the floor in production, I just got on with it, and Sarah would be around some of the time on set, but otherwise sorting things out off set. We get on very well, and so bar the normal little scraps everyone has, it all went like a dream. In the edit, her notes were great too.

Basically, making the film was a wonderful experience from start to finish. I had a chance to make the film for a higher budget a few years ago, and it all fell through; now I am glad it did, because I would not have made as good a film. That serendipity started when Sarah came on board. I needed a producer exactly like her; creative – that goes without saying – but also someone really hungry to make the film, who believed with me that we could not only make it, but make it well for little money. That's the thing: anyone can make a low-budget film, but we wanted to make a great one that competes with the rest, and I think we have. We kept each other going, which is what you need.

SS: I think that our roles were a bit more fluid than in conventionally made films, especially at the outset because Roger was involved in setting up our company. Once we started crewing and casting, I gave my creative input and was in on the meetings but there was no doubt that he was the director and running the show. He also had a team of Heads of Department that he wanted to work with and I trusted his judgement. With one HoD, we took a real risk and I did push for that because I thought it was the more interesting choice, and ultimately he agreed. I remember that just before we started shooting I saw Whit Stillman, and he said: "Don't go to the set – just let him get on with it." I was like, "Whaddya mean? I want to be there every second." In the end I was there most of the time but not *all* of the time.

Also, a newer producer who had just made two very successful films back-to-back had said to me, "Make sure you have a good relationship with the director, because on set everyone's looking to him. If he rates you then you'll really have a say," which I took to heart. On set Roger would bounce things off me occasionally but he was completely confident and in his element. It's been said before, and it's true that the crucial periods for the producer are in prep and in post, and I think particularly I was quite useful in post.

Did you have areas of conflict, and if so how did you deal with that?

RG: I'm sure we did, I tend to go on a bit! We did, but what I think is so important in any creative relationship like this is that you are allowed to get cross, because you are safe in the knowledge that you are both on the same side and team, so it's always resolved. And that is how we work. Both of us, I like to think, are capable of listening and of realising when we might be wrong, and able to admit that and get on, because ultimately all we want to do is make the best thing possible, and we need to do that as a team.

SS: Yes we definitely had our moments. I can be a bit of a hot-head and sometimes need to shout just to let off steam, but I think Roger understood that. Funnily enough he is more controlling and detail-oriented than I am, which is a reversal on the whole 'mad artist'/ 'anal business person' model. I'm organised but more relaxed, so I'd be saying "chill out, it'll all come together" while he was freaking and nagging.

How hands-on was Sarah as a 'creative producer'? How much script editing did you do?

SS: I was hands-on but the script was quite developed by the time I came on board, so it was a dream in a way because I didn't have to go through all the agony of development.

Roger had been working on the script for about five years, so it was very nearly there. That said, I did give notes and we went through a short but intensive development period together. The great thing about it was that, at that point, we knew that we were definitely making the film, which was exhilarating. One key change we made was the title – it seems like a minor thing but actually it made a huge difference in terms of our perception of the whole project.

What were the best qualities you saw in each other, and how confident were each of you as development progressed that you were actually trying to make the same film?

SS: This is going to sound awful, but I have to say I was so relieved to see that he could really direct! I had seen and appreciated Roger's television work and his shorts, but was still operating mainly on hope and belief until we started rolling. Also he worked tirelessly and was incredibly focused. He's wonderful with actors and I'm so impressed by what he pulled off (... OK, I'm sounding like a luvvie now!). In terms of making 'the same film' – based on the script itself and the films we had both referenced to each other, I felt reasonably confident that we wanted the same type of thing. We certainly knew what we *didn't* want.

RG: I was always very confident, not in an arrogant way, but we always knew we had a good script. I had spent a considerable time honing it, Sarah had then given some invaluable input, so we were very confident. And it was really that confidence that kept us going.

Did you tend to have the same views on casting?

RG: Yes (at the risk of sounding nauseatingly agreeable!). I tend to work actors hard in a reading, as it gives them and you the best opportunity to get it right. Often there are many ways to play a character and you need to spend time with actors to work that out. So by the time we needed to make a decision, it was pretty clear.

SS: We both agreed that we weren't going to waste time trying to send it to Gwyneth, or whoever – which would have been pointless – and that we would simply get the best actors we could who were available for that time. Once we started having readings, it all fell into place because we felt similarly about who worked and who didn't in the roles. And we were thrilled about who we got. *[Cast includes Anne-Marie Duff, Ralf Little, Rupert Graves, Phyllida Law and Frank Finlay.]*

The film was made on a very low budget of under £500K. What would have been different had you had more money to spend?

RG: As I said, a few years ago it nearly got made for a *normal* low budget (i.e. a couple of million), but it all fell through. Neither of us had the appetite to try and raise conventional finance, we could have spent years doing it and never got it and gone mad doing it. It just wasn't one of those scripts that was going to get that finance (though *what* is?), and to be honest, there is something very liberating about doing it on your own ... as long as you don't make a heap of shit, which we thankfully haven't! It meant we could do it our own way, no hassle or fuss or interference. I pulled together the most wonderful crew of people whom I had worked with and trusted completely. We were all there, cast and crew, for one reason: the script. Everyone worked brilliantly hard to get it done. And honestly, no, I would not have done too much differently if we'd had more money. The style of shooting (no dolly, no fuss) suited the film *and* the budget just right. It just would have been nice to pay people more, properly. But we shot five-day weeks, stuck to schedule, and got it done.

SS: I had reached a point where I was determined to make a film, and I knew it wasn't going to happen in the conventional way – i.e. if they happen to like your concept, Pathe and/or whoever give you the money but dictate casting and everything else and take all the rights. *The Waiting Room* was always going to be a tough sell because it's not about dwarves or zombies and doesn't have an obvious 'hook'. I had tracked lots of similarly 'difficult' low-budget and digital films at Sundance and elsewhere when I worked in acquisitions, so I was intrigued by that model of filmmaking. Also there is this American indie tradition of making your first film however the hell you can – and hey, I'm American! It all came together for me when I took this Arista seminar on low-budget filmmaking, and got completely fired up about just going ahead and doing it despite everybody telling you it won't work. Roger was as determined as I was, so we buoyed each other up. Not having lots of money was a drag, but also very freeing in a way. I knew we were going to make something special, either in spite of, or because of the constraints the budget imposed. I'd love to do the next film with more dosh. It'd be nice to pay people a decent wage, but everyone did get paid!

You created a company to make the film – did you talk about a company 'brand' for the type of films you want to make? And how will you work differently on your next film, *Stupid Cupid*?

RG: We did think about it, but yes, firstly we just wanted to make this one. However, we do work very well and we do now have a first draft of another script. Yes, there will be more. We share the same views on what we want to see: strong, character-based, true but not miserablist drama. How will we work differently on the next one? Golly, I don't really know, raise more money?!

SS: When we first set up the company we didn't really know where it was all heading beyond *The Waiting Room*, but the kind of relationship we now have is invaluable and we definitely want to make more films together. It'll be interesting to see what happens now – certainly the next film will be easier in one sense because we have developed a shorthand between ourselves. I think that overall, we'll be a little bit less uptight and worried about everything because we've managed to make a really good film together – not that I'm biased or anything!

Read more about *The Waiting Room* at **www.thewaitingroomfilm.com**.

Case study of two independent documentaries

Director/Producer **Stephen Kijak** gives a personal account of the contrasting stages of development, financing and distribution on two feature documentary projects.

I'm an American filmmaker with two feature documentaries to my credit, both of which were made with significant foreign partnership and collaboration (the second of which was a fantastic collaboration with a UK-based producer). I got hooked on the whole notion of the foreign co-production very early on, and the experience of working abroad has proved creatively very satisfying. I start here because the *means* by which my two films were made was very much a product of *why* they were made and vice versa. I'm going to compare and contrast the two projects, focusing on the origin of the idea and the financing of the films, in the hope that I may offer up some practicalities that arose out of the experiences, which might be of use to other filmmakers working on a documentary.

Origin of the ideas

Cinemania, a portrait of five of the most manic-obsessive film buffs in New York City.

My first feature, the narrative *Never Met Picasso*, sank without a trace. Broke, without a deal in sight, struggling to find work and the next project, I met a very interesting character: a guy named Jack. Jack spent his days running around New York City watching four or five movies a day. Jewish, dangerously intellectual, prone to violent outbursts and perverse romantic delusions involving Rita Hayworth's black-and-white lips, he was the perfect character – a real NY eccentric that Woody Allen would be hard-pressed to invent. And he was a total exhibitionist. If you meet someone like this, turn your camera on immediately; it is a gift from documentary heaven, if such a place exists.

I spent a week following Jack around and had the good fortune to be commissioned to do so by a friend who worked for IFC (The Independent Film Channel) producing a show called *Split Screen*. The brief was to make an eight-minute portrait. Zero budget of course, but a great opportunity. Following Jack around pulled me into a world of extreme and bizarre cinephilia beyond my wildest dreams, with a whole cast of characters that eventually found their way into what became the feature doc *Cinemania*. That's how it started: great access to a vibrant character who pulled me into a unique world populated with other fantastic characters. It was a great opportunity for human portraiture that also reflected the environment that bred them – New York City – and the medium that bound them together: cinema. And no one else had ever done it … well, except for one person … but more on that later.

Scott Walker – 30 Century Man, a portrait of one of the most influential and enigmatic figures in rock history.

After spending two years producing and another two years distributing and promoting a film about other people's obsessions, I turned to an obsession of my own: Scott Walker.

Virtually unknown in the USA, Scott Walker is the American-born existential crooner who found unparalleled fame in the UK in the late 60s as one-third of The Walker Brothers – then as an increasingly idiosyncratic solo star, only to morph, decades later, into a shadowy recluse, the Samuel Beckett of rock, releasing dense, dark, ear-challenging music. An enigma, an untouchable icon. And, to my knowledge in June 2001, someone who had never before been the subject of a film.

This one could fall into the 'be careful what you wish for' category. Unlike *Cinemania*, which practically fell into my lap, this was going to be tricky. The idea is one thing but the holy grail, *access*, is another. This could have gone one of two ways: a straight-up commission to do a standard-issue TV portrait which, it turns out, the elusive Mr Walker has resisted in the past; or a more cinematic feature doc, privately funded and made independently outside the system on a shoestring, lots of good faith, and one or two near-nervous breakdowns. Guess which path I stumbled down?

Timing, of course, was everything. I was something of the obsessive fan-boy for years, and always toyed with the idea of making a film about Scott Walker, but when I read that he was about to step into the studio to begin work on a new album I leapt into action. Now, having come out the other end of this experience with a film that I am very happy with, I will say that in a perfect world a proper broadcast partner/commission scenario would have most advisable. It would have been great to have had a strong financial partner on board early, who could have travelled with us to various pitch/co-production markets like IDFA, HotDocs, etc. as we cobbled the financing together, but that was not to be the case. Scott Walker, in the grand scheme of things, is a very cult artist and in the UK, where he has frustrated many a commissioning editor's desires to turn the cameras on him, he was seen as a high-risk subject. But I walked the plank regardless.

Access to Scott Walker was hard-earned. Faxes, phone calls, carefully worded pitches, treatments – I researched things that he liked: bands, artists, designers, filmmakers; slowly I built a team that reflected a sensitivity to his world view, tastes and interests in the hope of creating a comfort-zone that he would feel inclined to venture into. A lot of time was spent just meeting his managers and discussing ideas with them, letting them get to know me on a personal level. It was a two-year long process of trust-building, and with that, eventually, came the access that I was seeking. Part of the conception of the project was in a way to follow in his footsteps, do the ex-pat thing, steep myself in British culture, take it all on and work in sympathy with my subject.

It was also important that I was the only one doing it. Access is one thing, but exclusive access is another. And despite the fact that no one would come on board to finance the film, I had a solid team and some great VIPs lined up to talk about their admiration for 'the Great Scott' (David Bowie, Radiohead, Brian Eno – interviews that were almost as difficult to set up as getting access to Scott) and a subject who is nearly impossible to get to. It was like a wildlife photographer getting an appointment with the Loch Ness Monster. I had the access, I couldn't back off now.

Financing

Cinemania

What transformed my eight-minute portrait of a movie-mad New Yorker into a feature-length doc was luck and timing. It was also a case of recognising a great opportunity. While

I was filming Jack one day at the Anthology Film Archive in the East Village, I met a German filmmaker who was filming me filming him. Angela Christlieb, experimental German filmmaker/editor studying at NY's The New School, was in the middle of making her own film about New York's "cinemaniacs" as she had dubbed them. I wished her well, finished my eight minutes and thought nothing more about it ... until she called me a year later. She had brought her trailer back to Berlin where she met a producer who made low-budget docs for German TV. They pitched it to a German broadcaster, got a commission to make the film and she was promptly sent back to New York with a new camera, a few boxes of DV tapes, and a commission to produce a feature film – something she had never really done before. Not knowing if I was out there doing the same thing, she got in touch with me. Her desire to check out the competition (which I wasn't, having walked away from the cult of the cinemaniacs after a few weeks of shooting), turned into an offer to collaborate, to expand and blend our shared knowledge, access, and resources. What made it work creatively was a shared knowledge, two different cultural perspectives that created a very good creative tension and cohesion. Resources on both sides of the Atlantic made the film possible.

An essay on German TV and state funds could fill this book. Suffice it to say, a relationship with a German-based producer is a great thing to have. It's always worth thinking about international co-producers. You can meet them anywhere – film festivals, markets ... go to where the documentary community gathers, IDFA, Sheffield, BritDocs (see further listings in the Festivals section of this book on page 266). What I was able to bring to the table was a relationship with a US-based sales company, the now defunct Wellspring (not our fault, I swear!). In a stroke of luck and good timing, one of their international sales managers was my next-door neighbour, and I turned a social opportunity into the beginning of a business relationship when cinemaniac Jack came to a party at my house and they got to meet. When she saw our promo DVD, she brought the film to the attention of the rest of the company. I formally pitched her colleagues at the No Borders' Co-Production Market in NYC and eventually they committed 25 per cent of the budget against world broadcast and North American DVD rights, thus allowing our German producer to get the four German funds he had pitched to agree to provide the rest. All the while we were out there shooting non-stop with whatever cash our producer was able to send our way. It is very often the case that you will have the film in the can and practically finished before you have raised the entire budget. Many doc-makers share this experience; it's always a case of pushing every aspect – the creative and the financial – up hill at the same time.

Scott Walker – 30 Century Man

This was different, and more difficult. Following a world premiere at the London Film Festival, an international premiere at the Berlin Film Festival in 2007 and many more international film fests (including SXSW, Hong Kong, Tribeca and HotDocs at the time of writing), the film was still painfully in debit!

Higher-profile due to the famous faces attached, yet higher-risk; we have had to 'push it up hill' with all of our efforts. The key factor in getting this film made was networking, networking, networking – which basically involved me talking about it non-stop to anyone who would listen for years on end. I spoke with the usual suspects like broadcasters on both sides of the Atlantic, but also to producers, distributors, and anyone with a lead on private equity (something we seem to do a bit better here in the US). It's not an ideal way to finance a film, but it did give us an incredible amount of creative freedom.

The team was everything. This was going to be a long, hard haul and I needed a producing partner with whom I could work closely for several years, through many lows and some occasional highs. I needed someone whose experience was complimentary to mine, who could be passionate about the subject but also practical. I had met Mia Bays, former marketing and distribution manager for The Film Consortium, on one of my many pitch trips through the UK. We struck up a friendship and eventually, when she formed her own production company, Missing in Action Films (see page 140), it seemed a logical next step for us to work together. Mia didn't have a fund of her own, but she had a great network in the UK and a short but impressive track-record as a producer (she would go on to win an Oscar for producing the short film *Six Shooter*). We also got on really well. I mention it again because without a good, strong personal/professional bond, we would never have got the film made. It's like dating. Sometimes it just comes down to chemistry.

The actual financing, as I said, came about through non-stop blabbing about the film. While Mia was able to interest both a UK-based sales agent and distributor in the film, we still didn't have offers to finance. I was talking up the film at a film festival party in New York and caught the ear of an actor with a little money to burn – one who, as luck would have it, had actually heard of Scott Walker. He became our seed-money. He put up $25,000 of his own money and kickstarted the project. With that money we shot for three months and cut an impressive ten-minute trailer. The networking continued. We pitched it to everyone and anyone. Still, it seemed too risky or people were more interested in seeing it when it was finished so they could consider it as an acquisition.

Undeterred, I was at the Provincetown Film Festival in Massachusetts when a friend told me of a woman he had met the previous night who actually asked if anyone knew of a documentary that needed money. I kid you not. A private individual expressing interest in financing documentaries. You can meet 20 of these people a night at Cannes and other such places; there are a lot of people blowing hot air about the money they have to invest in films. I listen to as many of them as possible, and let my gut determine who is worth perusing. This one turned out to be a knight in shining armour. It seems like luck and timing, but without chasing up this longest of long shots we would never have scored our production financing. And without a solid team in place, including a great producer, a professional demo DVD, a solid treatment and business proposal, and a clear understanding of the market for a film of this sort, we would not have been able to close the deal.

This private individual took a risk jumping into the financing of it, but at every step of the way we were able to show the fruits of our labour and of our investor's cash, involving them as much as we could in the process. This included inviting our key backer to be an observer when we participated in the HotDocs Toronto Pitch Forum.

Having private equity in the project allowed us to get the film in the can and completely edited with 100 per cent creative control intact – which of course is useless if you don't parlay that into film festival screenings, sales and distribution. We were way out on a limb financially (music and archival footage costs a LOT of money, by the way), but by now we had an international sales agent, Moviehouse Entertainment, talking about the film to international buyers. We had also been exploring our own personal network of contacts at home and abroad, from potentially sympathetic broadcasters to other Scott Walker fans in high places. The networking never stops. You are laying the foundation for potential future sales.

Exhibition

Cinemania

This went on to play more than 50 international film festivals. A film about people who are crazy about film is a shoe-in for the film festival circuit. It sold well to broadcasters internationally and has become a bit of a cult item on DVD. US theatrical distribution, without coming on strong at a major festival in the states, was harder to come by. We got more mojo internationally (Locarno, Rotterdam, Edinburgh) but did win the Hamptons Film Festival. I ended up self-distributing the film with two 35mm prints, 2 Digibetas and a $5000 loan from a friend's production company. It was a great learning experience; I booked it in about 35 cities eventually. Yet it's one I would never, ever want to repeat. Believe it or not, the release did not lose money. I think I made about $300 when all was said and done. This one was clearly not a moneymaking opportunity – but it was an opportunity. From a failed first-feature to international exposure at major festivals – it was the foundation on which I built my current network of contacts.

30 Century Man

Scott came out of the gate a bit stronger. With literally only a few hours separating the final layback to the Digibeta master and the world premiere, it was all about momentum. We had a wonderful 'home-turf' premiere at the London Film Festival (home turf for an ex-pat filmmaker making a film about an ex-pat musician, that is) and were then invited to the 2007 Berlin International Film Festival with a US premiere at South by Southwest (SXSW).

Our festival strategy was informed by the film. Berlin has a major film market – the European Film Market – attached, and the major buyers for the territories where Scott Walker has a fan base were all there. SXSW is a film and music festival – the sort of event where a film like ours can get more of a buzz and stand out from the pack, as opposed to at a fest like Sundance, where the response would most likely have been, "Scott who ...?"

Again, continuous networking within the filmmaking community will eventually put you in contact with the programmers of film festivals, personal connections that are essential to develop and nurture, as you may eventually discover that one of them becomes a champion of your work.

Many major feature films come out of a festival like Berlin with lots of deals, but we've found the docs take a bit longer. The word-of-mouth needs to spread, the trades need to review it, and lots of buyers will want to wait and see how it's playing out in different territories, which is why it helps to be selective and strategic with how you plan your festival run. From SXSW we did two other major doc festivals, Thessaloniki in Greece and HotDocs in Toronto. Both have markets attached so there is a strong industry awareness about what happens there.

In the UK, we already had a relationship with a distributor (Verve Pictures) and felt it was important to get the home territory locked and loaded before we hit the festival circuit. By the time this book comes out, the film will have played theatrically on ten-to-twelve prints around the UK. We were lucky in that our subject has fans all over the UK, including the folks who book a lot of the different cinema chains.

Every step of the way, it's important to find sympathetic allies, specific-interest target groups who will get behind your film and help you find the right home for it. You also must understand the limitations of your own work. I had limited expectations for the film's theatrical life outside of the UK, yet we have been surprised that following very strong reactions at festivals, we made a string of 'all-rights' deals in some of the major territories (US, France, Spain, Australia, etc.) The theatrical runs are likely to be limited/specialised, but this helps lay the groundwork for DVD sales. All the companies seem to be smaller boutique-style distributors with a small but dedicated staff and a very respectable catalogue both indies, foreign and documentary fare.

Most of these deals were closed at the 2007 Cannes Market, a whole year after our sales agents started talking it up there, building momentum and word-of-mouth with buyers throughout the year at the American Film Market, then Berlin and closing in on the deals at Cannes. All the while, I was traveling around and working the film on the festival circuit, keeping our website updated with press, building a strong network of fans on myspace, and working with a publicist to insure we got the word out to the press – multiple levels of buzz that helps to keep the momentum going, both in the consciousness of your audiences around the world, and with the buyers.

General observations

Having now laid out a map of our gameplans on both films, I should also add that it does help to have made a good film – and I think we did a pretty good job on this one. But the creative development of the project went hand-in-hand with a continuing strategy for how the film would be financed and distributed and continues long after the first premiere screening.

What these two case studies hopefully show is that luck and timing are nothing without a solid personal and professional network, the tenacity to know what to do with what you have, and a determination to see it through. The film itself must also be built to last, to be unique as a subject and unique in the marketplace.

There are as many ways to get a film made as there are films out there.

Summary advice

1. Chose your subject carefully. Unless you're in a director-for-hire situation, a doc can take over your life for three, four, five years … you had better be certain from the get-go that you have exclusive access to the subject, it is unique, you have a specific POV/angle/ story to tell, and you have a sense of the audience for the film.

2. Let the subject guide you. Sometimes, the means by which your film will get made are reflected in the subject itself.

3. Network constantly. There is a fine line between persistence and just being a pest, but a lot of doc makers, by necessity, must also be their own producers. You'll be well served in the future if you start to understand the *business* of documentary making as well as the art.

4. Build a great team. Filmmaking is a collaborative art. Be open to the creativity and influence of your collaborators (producers, DoPs, editors) and you will make a better film.

5. Have patience. From development to distribution, things may not always happen as quickly as you would like, and you may not reap the rewards right away. A a doc can be a slow-burner with its own particular lifespan; go with the flow.

6. Take risks. Luck and timing should always be backed up by knowledge and hard work – but sometimes it is the leap of faith that turns the idea into a reality.

A graduate of Boston University's College of Communication, **Stephen Kijak** is a NY-based filmmaker who received universal acclaim for his first documentary, *Cinemania* – a portrait of five of New York's most obsessive film buffs. A favourite at over 50 international film festivals, the film was released theatrically in the US, UK and Germany and is now widely available on DVD in the US and Europe. Kijak also co-produced Louisa Achille's debut doc *The Naked Feminist*; his first feature film, *Never Met Picasso*, starred Margot Kidder, Alexis Arquette, and Don McKellar (and featured a haunting score by Kristin Hersh). Kijak's second documentary feature, *Scott Walker – 30 Century Man* premiered at the London Film Festival and was invited to Berlin International Film Festival. It is currently touring international film festivals and is being released in territories around the world. He has also directed episodes of the popular reality-TV series, *Queer Eye for the Straight Guy* for Bravo/NBC.

Professional bodies/unions

Advertising Producers' Association (APA)

26 Noel Street, London W1F 89Y
tel 020-7434 2651 *fax* 020-7434 9002
email info@a-p-a.net
website www.a-p-a.net

APA is the trade body that protects the interests of production companies, post-production and VFX and editing companies which make commercials.

Amicus

35 King Street, Covent Garden, London WC2E 8JG
tel 0800-587 1222
website www.amicustheunion.org

Amicus is the largest manufacturing union in the United Kingdom, with over a million members in the public and private sectors. Also represents Electrical Engineers.

AMPS (Association of Motion Picture Sounds)

28 Knox Street, London W1H 1FS
tel 020-7723 6727 *fax* 020-7723 6727
email admin@amps.net
website www.amps.net

Founded in 1989 to establish a forum for sound crafts in the film and television industries to exchange information, solve common problems and keep abreast of changing technology. Recently, aims have widened to promote and encourage the science, technology and creative application of all aspects of sound recording and reproduction for motion pictures, television and other media, and to promote recognition of the contribution of those engaged in these crafts. AMPS publishes a quarterly journal as well as various technical booklets; a Membership Booklet is available for production companies who are looking for skilled sound craftspeople.

A minimum of 6 years' experience is required for Full Membership, but AMPS also offers a range of other memberships for newer professionals. Fees range from £20 to £50 per year.

APRS – The Professional Recording Association

PO Box 22, Totnes TQ9 7YZ
tel (01803) 868600
website www.aprs.co.uk

Trade association for the recording and audio/post-production industries. Activities include industry accreditation of courses, legislative initiatives, and provision of a database for people looking for studios or post-production facilities.

BECTU (Broadcasting Entertainment Cinematograph and Theatre Union)

373-377 Clapham Road, London SW9 9BT
tel 020-7346 0900 *fax* 020-7346 0925
email info@bectu.org.uk
website www.bectu.org.uk
General Secretary Gerry Morrissey

BECTU is the trade union for workers in the film industry who work 'behind the camera' (i.e. in technical, craft, design and sound); it also represents 'extras'. BECTU offers collective and individual represenation, legal advice, contract rates advice and, where appropriate, legal representation. Seeks to ensure that workers receive a proper rate of pay and have sensible working conditions; also campaigns with Government for the future of the British film industry. Offers a range of courses – some vocational, some to do with trade union representation, and many in co-operation with Skillset.

All professionals working, or seeking to work, in these fields are eligible for membership. Membership is £10 per month for first year and 1% of earnings thereafter (dispensation available for low-paid individuals).

BKSTS – The Moving Image Society

Suite 104, G Block, Pinewood Studios, Iver Heath, Buckinghamshire SL0 0NH
tel (01753) 656656 *fax* (01753) 657016
email wendy@bksts.com
website www.bksts.com

BKSTS was established in 1931, and supports those people actively involved in the film and television industries through a range of seminars, courses and publications. The Society regularly publishes *Image Technology* as well as the quarterly *Cinema Technology*; also produces an acclaimed series of technical wall charts with information on film stocks and camera formats, as well as a projectionist's manual.

Full Membership is for creative and technical professionals; Associate Membership is open to those with an interest in the industry; and Student Membership is for full-time students who intend to pursue a career in the moving image industry. Membership fees range from £22 to £88.

British Academy of Composers and Songwriters

2nd Floor, British Music House, 26 Berners Street, London W1T 3LR
tel 020-7636 2929 *fax* 020-636 2212
email info@britishacademy.com
website www.britishacademy.com

The Academy represents the interests of composers and songwriters across all genres, providing advice on professional and artistic matters.

British Design & Art Direction (D&AD)

9 Graphite Square, Vauxhall Walk, London SE11 5EE
tel 020-7840 1111 *fax* 020-7840 0840
website www.dandad.org

D&AD is a charitable association whose purpose is to promote good standards of design and advertising.

British Film Designers Guild

Flat G, 344 Finchley Road, London NW3 7AJ
tel 020-7794 0017
email enquiries@filmdesigners.co.uk
website www.filmdesigners.co.uk

The Guild exists to promote better design in British film. Membership includes production designers, art directors, set decorators, costume designers, storyboard illustrators, special effects designers and scenic artists of all kinds. The Guild's site includes a database of members with a list of credits.

British Institute of Professional Photography

Fox Talbot House, 2 Amwell End, Ware, Herts SG12 9HN
tel (01920) 464011 *fax* (01920) 487056
website www.bipp.com

Exists to promote high standards in professional photography. The site has the world's largest search engine for qualified professional photographers, which allows the user to search by specialism and location.

British Interactive Multimedia Association Ltd

Briarlea House, Southend Road, Billericay CM11 2PR
tel (01277) 658107 *fax* 0870-051 7842
email info@bima.co.uk
website www.bima.co.uk

Trade association representing the interests of the interactive media industries. Hosts the BIMA Awards ('the BIMAs') for excellence in new media.

British Society of Cinematographers (BSC)

PO Box 2587, Gerrards Cross, Bucks SL9 7WZ
tel (01753) 888052 *fax* (01753) 891486
email bscine@btconnect.com
website www.bscine.com
Secretary/Treasurer Frances Russell

Formed in 1949, BSC is an educational, cultural and professional organisation which promotes high standards in photographic and digital cinematography. Membership is by invitation.

Equity

Guild House, Upper St Martin's Lane, London WC2H 9EG
tel 020-7379 6000 *fax* 020-7379 7001
email info@equity.org.uk
website www.equity.org.uk

Formed as an actors and performers union, Equity is now the only trade union to represent all people working in the entertainment industries. Film, Television, Radio & Audiovisual Helpline: 020-7670 0247.

Federation of Entertainment Unions (FEU)

1 Highfield, Twyford, Nr Winchester, Hants SO21 1QR
tel (01962) 713134 *fax* (01962) 713134
email harris.s@btconnect.com

A confederation of all the TUC-affilated unions in the media and entertainment industries.

Film Artistes' Association (FAA)

373-377 Clapham Road, London SW9 9BT
tel 020-7436 090 *fax* 020-7436 0901
email info@bectu.org.uk
website www.bectu.org.uk

FAA represents extras, doubles, and stand-ins.

Film Unit Drivers Guild

136 The Crossways, Heston, Middlesex TW5 0JR
tel 020-8569 5001 *fax* 020-8569 6001
email info@filmdriversguild.co.uk
website www.filmdriversguild.co.uk

Guild of British Camera Technicians

c/o Panavision Building, Metropolitan Centre, Bristol Road, Greenford, Middlesex UB5 8GD
tel 020-8813 1999 *fax* 020-8813 2111
email admin@gbct.org
website www.gbct.org

Membership of professional TV and film technicians, with more than 500 members. Formed in 1978 as a 'voice' and forum for camera technicians, GBCT is dedicated to upholding standards in the film and television industries, while seeking progress through innovation.

GBCT gives production companies access to professional crew with skills recognised throughout the industry, and also runs the GAS Diary Service to keep working technicians up to date on enquiries made by production teams.

Membership applicants need to provide references from 4 current members to join. £50 for first year and £150 per year thereafter. Provides training through the NFTS.

Guild of British Film Editors

72 Penbroke Road, London W8 6NX
tel 020-7602 8319 *fax* 020-7602 8319
email secretarygbfe@btopenworld.com
website www.filmeditorsguild.com

Guild of Television Cameramen

1 Churchill Road, Whitchurch, Tavistock, Devon PL19 9BU
tel (01822) 614405 *fax* (01822) 615785
website www.gtc.org.uk

Guild of Vision Makers

147 Ship Lane, Farnborough, Hampshire GU14 8BJ
tel (01252) 514953 *fax* (01252) 656756
email peter.turl@dtn.ntl.com
website www.guildofvisionmixers.org.uk

Music Video Producers' Association (MVPA)

26 Noel Street, London W1V 3RD
tel 020-7434 2651 *fax* 020-7434 9002
email info@mvpa.co.uk
website www.mvpa.co.uk

Musicians' Union (MU)

60-62 Clapham Road, London SW9 0JJ
tel 020-7582 5566 *fax* 020-582 9805
email pt1@musiciansunion.org.uk
website www.musiciansunion.org.uk

Producers' Alliance for Film and Television (PACT) – see Producers Alliance for Cinema and Television (PACT).

The Production Guild of Great Britain

Pinewood Studios, Pinewood Road, Iver Heath, Bucks SL0 0NH
tel (01753) 651767 *fax* (01753) 652803
email patrick@productionguild.com
website www.productionguild.com

The Guild works on behalf of its members to improve members' employment opportunities across all available incoming and domestic feature film and television drama production, and to advise on legal, financial and commercial developments.

Among its services, the Guild provides:

• current and relevant information on all members' availability for work for incoming, UK and other feature film and television production via its website, email and fax notifications;
• the most current and relevant information on feature film and television drama projects in development and pre-production, to support members' opportunities for employment.

Membership is conditional upon the application being accepting by a committee, but anyone working in the film and television industries is free to apply. Costs are as follows: Application fee (returnable) £100; Full membership £250; Overseas membership £100; Retired £50; and Supplementary (includes application fee) £50.

Production Managers Association (PMA)

Ealing Studios, Ealing Green, London W5 5EP
tel 020-8758 8699 *fax* 020-8758 8658
email pma@pma.org.uk
website www.pma.org.uk
Manager Caroline Fleming

A professional body of production managers and line producers who work across the film, television, corporate and multimedia sectors, with the aim of enabling members to assist one another by sharing experience and professional advice. Members have a number of additional benefits which are detailed on the website. Also provides the wider industry with a list of recommended production co-ordinators (see website) and a list of available production managers.

Applicants must have at least 3 years' experience as a production manager, plus 6 broadcast credits (or equivalent in feature films, commercials or corporate sector). Fee is currently £188 per year (including VAT).

Society of Cable Telecommunication Engineers (SCTE)

Fulton House Business Centre, Fulton Road, Wembley Park, Middlesex HA9 0TF
tel 020-8902 8998 *fax* 020-8903 8719
email office@scte.org.uk
website www.scte.org.uk

Society of Television Lighting Directors

Longwall, Crayburne, Betsham, Kent DA13 9PB
tel (01474) 833997
website www.stld.org.uk

UK Post & Services Ltd

47 Beak Street, London W1F 9SE
tel 020-7734 6060
email info@ukpost.org.uk
website www.ukpost.org.uk
CEO Gaynor Davenport

Trade association that represents and promotes the commercial interests of companies providing post services to the broadcast and feature film industry. The sector includes companies and individuals involved in visual, audio and physical effects; animation; picture and sound editing services; computer generated images; interactive media; equipment hire and outside broadcast and studios. UK Post & Services acts as the strategic lobbying group with government agencies, and provides support and a voice for its members.

Crew

The United Kingdom is widely regarded as having the some of the best film technicians and technical craftspeople in the world. One look at the heavyweight subscription film and television contact resource *The Knowledge* (**www.theknowledgeonline.co.uk**) will reveal just how many experienced film and television professionals there are working in the UK – literally thousands in every field.

In this section, we have provided selected listings for the people who are among the best in their field in three of the major film production departments. Where applicable, you will be expected to make enquiries via an agent. It should go without saying that they will want all enquiries to be serious and for paid work; these are the most in-demand professionals in the UK. You should make your first email as succint as possible; it's not advisable to send attachments by email, as many companies will delete unexpected emails which have documents attached. Agents will appreciate brief details about the project, along with information on fees for their client, shoot dates and the film's key personnel. They will then request further information as needed.

If you are a new filmmaker making a low-budget or super-low-budget film, then your best bet is to try to team up with people who are at the same stage in their career, and for whom the experience and the chance to add to their own showreel is important.

Talk to your regional Screen Agency. Most of them will have listings of local crew and may be able to put you in touch with experienced people who are willing to work with promising new talent. Also try online filmmakers' network Shooting People (**www.shootingpeople.org**),which puts filmmakers in touch with one other. The company has more than 25,000 members working across all aspects of production: they communicate with each other via daily email bulletins to share knowledge and make contact for possible collaboration. UKscreen (**www.ukscreen.com**) also offers a valuable free database with listings for cast, crew and technicians. Individuals upload their own professional details, so while it's not selective, it is constantly growing and currently has more than 30,000 contacts.

DOPS

The DOP is responsible for working with the production designer and director to help achieve the visual style of the film. S/he chooses the camera and lighting equipment to help to get the desired look, and will manage the team of lighting and camera crew on the shoot. As such, the DOP will often have preferred teams of people with whom they work regularly.

Alan Almond BSC

c/o PFD, Drury House, 34-43, Russell Street, London WC2B 5HA
tel 020-7344 1000 *fax* 020-7836 9543
email streacher@pfd.co.uk
website www.pfd.co.uk

Agent Louisa Thompson at PFD

Contact via agent and send script with enquiries. Credits include: *Gabriel & Me*, *Kevin & Perry*, and *Guest House Paradiso*.

Alex Barber

c/o PFD, Drury House, 34-43, Russell Street, London WC2B 5HA
tel 020-7344 1000 *fax* 020-7836 9543
email streacher@pfd.co.uk
website www.pfd.co.uk

Agent Louisa Thompson at PFD

Contact via agent. Credits include: *Cashback* (short), *Swept Away*, and *Mean Machine*.

Adrian Biddle BSC
tel (01932) 821401
email mobiddle@madasafish.com

Credits include: *Laws of Attraction*, and *Bridget Jones: The Edge of Reason*.

Jonathan Bloom
c/o The Dench Arnold Agency, 10 Newburgh Street, London W1F 7RN
Agent's tel 020-7437 4551 *fax* 020-7439 1355
email contact@dencharnold.com
Agent Michelle Arnold at The Dench Arnold Agency

Credits include: *Daddy's Girl*, *Speak Like a Child*, and *Last King of Scotland* (2nd Unit).

Nigel Bluck
Agent's tel 020-7287 4450
email info@sandramarsh.com, smarshmgmt@earthlink.net
website www.sandramarsh.com, www.nigelbluck.com

Credits include: *The Lord of the Rings*, and *Heavenly Creatures*.

Sean Bobbitt
c/o Casarotto Marsh Ltd, National House, 60-66 Wardour Street, London W1V 4ND
tel 020-7287 4450 *fax* 020-7287 5644
email casarottomarsh@casarotto.co.uk
website www.casarotto.co.uk

Agents Sarah Pritchard (film), Emma Trouson (TV) at Casarotto Marsh Ltd

Credits include: *The Long Firm*, *Wonderland*, and *Cargo*.

Balazs Bolygo
c/o McKinney Macartney Management, The Barley Mow Centre, 10 Barley Mow Passage, London W4 4PH
tel 020-8995 4747 *fax* 020-8995 2414
email bodo@badi.freeserve.co.uk

Contact via agent. Please send script or synopsis with enquiries. Credits include: *Family Man*, *Life on Mars* (TV), *Boy Meets Girl*, and *It's All Gone Pete Tong*.

Henry Braham
c/o Casarotto Marsh Ltd, Waverley House, 7–12 Noel Street, London W1F 8GQ
tel 020-7287 4450 *fax* 020-7287 5644
email casarottomarsh@casarotto.co.uk
website www.casarotto.co.uk

Agents Sarah Pritchard (film), Emma Trouson (TV) at Casarotto Marsh Ltd

Credits include: *Nanny McPhee*, *Shackelton*, and *Fly Boys*.

Natasha Braier
c/o Casarotto Marsh Ltd, Waverley House, 7–12 Noel Street, London W1F 8GQ
tel 020-7287 4450 *fax* 020-7287 5644
email casarottomarsh@casarotto.co.uk
website www.casarotto.co.uk

Agents Sarah Pritchard (film), Emma Trouson (TV), Lucie LLewellyn (commercials) at Casarotto Marsh Ltd

Credits include: *Holiday*, and *Breaking Out*.

Trevor Brooker
tel (01202) 291410 *mobile* (07771) 691643
fax (01202) 291410
email cinematog@yahoo.com

Credits include: *Razorfish*, *The Borrowers*, and *Gulliver's Travels*.

Bill Broomfield
tel (01865) 351670
email bill@billbroomfield.com
website www.billbroomfield.com

Credits include: *Dalziel & Pascoe*, and *Teachers*.

Charlotte Bruus Christensen
c/o PFD, Drury House, 34-43, Russell Street, London WC2B 5HA
tel 020-7344 1000 *fax* 020-7836 9543
email sllaguno@pfd.co.uk
website www.pfd.co.uk

Agent Linda Mamy at PFD

Contact via agent. Speaks Danish, German and Norwegian; award-winner for short film, *Between Us*. Credits include: *Callanish*, and *One Minute Silence*.

Ben Butler
c/o McKinney Macartney Management, The Barley Mow Centre, 10 Barley Mow Passage, London W4 4PH
tel 020-8995 4747 *fax* 020-8995 2414
email mail@mckinneymacartney.com

Contact via agent. Credits include: *The Call* (short), and *Goldfish* (short).

Simon Chaudoir
c/o PFD, Drury House, 34-43 Russell Street, London WC2B 5HA
tel 020-7344 1000 *fax* 020-7836 9543
email sllaguno@pfd.co.uk
website www.pfd.co.uk

Agent Linda Mamy at PFD

Contact via agent. Credits include: *Alien Autopsy*, *Spooks 3*, and *Goodbye Cruel World* (short).

Christopher Clayton
tel 0113-230 1300
email cca@clayt.demon.co.uk

Credits include: *Absolutely Fabulous*, and *Father Ted*.

Daniel Cohen
PFD, Drury House, 34-43 Russell Street, London WC2B 5HA

tel 020-7344 1000 *fax* 020-7836 9543
email streacher@pfd.co.uk
website www.pfd.co.uk

Agent Louisa Thompson at PFD

Contact via agent. Credits include: *This is England*, *Longford* (HBO), and *Festival.*

Andy Collins BSC

tel (01208) 871106 *fax* (01208) 873843
email ajc.bsc@virgin.net

Credits include: *Brassed Off*, and *Thunderpants.*

Mick Coulter BSC

c/o McKinney Macartney Management,
The Barley Mow Centre, 10 Barley Mow Passage,
London W4 4PH
tel 020-8995 4747 *fax* 020-8995 2414
email mail@mckinneymacartney.com

Contact via agent. Credits include: *Love Actually*, *Mansfield Park*, and *Killing Me Softly.*

Vincent G Cox

tel 020-7724 5720 *mobile* (07714) 462400
email debimage@compuserve.com
website www.unitalfilms.com

Credits include: *Hotel Rwanda*, and *Beserkers.*

Denis Crossnan

c/o McKinney Macartney Management,
The Barley Mow Centre, 10 Barley Mow Passage,
London W4 4PH
tel 020-8995 4747 *fax* 020-8995 2414
email mail@mckinneymacartney.com

Contact via agent. Credits include: *Agent Cody Banks*, *Me Without You*, and *The Hole.*

Oliver Curtis BSC

ICM London, Oxford House, 76 Oxford Street,
London W1D 1BS
tel 020-7636 6565 *fax* 020-7323 0101
email suegreenleaves@icmlondon.co.uk
website www.olivercurtis.co.uk

Agent Sue Greenleaves at ICM London

Contact via agent; please send script with enquiries. Credits include: *Uncle Adolf*; *The Wedding Date*; commercials for Guinness, Wella, Rimmel, HSBC, Escada, and Ghost perfume.

John Daly

Agent's tel 020-7636 6565
email johndalybsc@btopenworld.com
Agent International Creative Management

Credits include: *Johnny English*, and *Life 'n' Lyrics.*

Benoit Delhomme

c/o Casarotto Marsh Ltd, Waverley House,
7–12 Noel Street, London W1F 8GQ
tel 020-7287 4450 *fax* 020-7287 5644
email casarottomarsh@casarotto.co.uk
website www.casarotto.co.uk

Agent Sarah Pritchard (film) at Casarotto Marsh Ltd

Credits include: *The Proposition*, and *Scent of Green Papaya.*

Jon Driscoll

c/o Creative Media Management, 3b Walpole Court,
Ealing Studios, London W5 5ED
tel 020-8584 5363 *fax* 020-8566 5554
email enquiries@creativemediamanagement.com
website www.creativemediamanagement.com

Graduate of NFTS (MA in Film and Television). Credits include: *Family Futures* (doc); *The Pulse of Tala* (dance promo for Talvin Singh); and *Acts of Kindness* (35mm short film).

Andrew Dunn BSC

PFD, Drury House, 34-43 Russell Street,
London WC2B 5HA
tel 020-7344 1000 *fax* 020-7836 9543
email streacher@pfd.co.uk
website www.pfd.co.uk

Agent Louisa Thompson at PFD

Contact via agent. Credits include: *Mrs Henderson*, *History Boys*, and *Miss Potter.*

Patrick Duval

tel 020-7241 0683 *mobile* (07973) 233293
email patduval@blueyonder.co.uk

Credits include: *Distant Voices*, and *Still Lives.*

Mike Eley

c/o Casarotto Marsh Ltd, National House,
60-66 Wardour Street, London W1V 4ND
tel 020-7287 4450 *fax* 020-7287 5644
email casarottomarsh@casarotto.co.uk
website www.casarotto.co.uk

Agents Sarah Pritchard (film), Emma Trouson (TV) at Casarotto Marsh Ltd

Credits include: *Touching the Void*, *He Knew He Was Right*, and *No Man's Land.*

Frederic Fabre

tel 020-7871 9695
email fredfabre1@aol.com

Credits include: *A Picture of Britain*; *George Eliot: A Scandalous Life* (BAFTA winner 2002).

Mary Farbrother

tel 020-8969 0247 *mobile* (07802) 753123
email mary@farbrother.com

Credits include: *The Darkest Light*, and *Spooks.*

John Fenner BSC

c/o Dinedor Management, 81 Oxford Street,
London W1D 2EU

Agent's tel 020-7851 3575 *tel* 020-8883 3492
mobile (07767) 870412
email info@dinedor.com, john.fenner@gmail.com
website www.dinedormanagement.co.uk
Agent Andrew Downer, Dinedor Management

Credits include: *Jack and the Beanstalk*, and *Borrowers*.

Gavin Finney BSC

c/o McKinney Macartney Management,
The Barley Mow Centre, 10 Barley Mow Passage,
London W4 4PH
tel 020-8995 4747 *fax* 020-8995 2414
email mail@mckinneymacartney.com

Contact via agent. Credits include: *Keeping Mum*, and *The Hogfather*.

Gerry Floyd

c/o The Dench Arnold Agency, 10 Newburgh Street,
London W1F 7RN
Agent's tel 020-7437 4551 *tel* 020-7607 7129
fax 020-7439 1355
email contact@dencharnold.com,
flogerry@globalnet.co.uk
Agent Michelle Arnold at The Dench Arnold Agency

Credits include: *Tomorrow La Scala!*.

Martin Fuhrer

c/o ICM London, Oxford House, 76 Oxford Street,
London W1D 1BS
Agent's tel 020-7636 6565 *fax* 020-7323 0101
email mfdop@aol.com

Credits include: *Perfume*, and *The Gathering*.

Sue Gibson

c/o McKinney Macartney Management,
The Barley Mow Centre, 10 Barley Mow Passage,
London W4 4PH
tel 020-8995 4747 *fax* 020-8995 2414
email mail@mckinneymacartney.com

Contact via agent. Credits include: *Mrs Caldicot's Cabbage War*, and *Alien vs. Predator* (2nd Unit Director).

Brendan Galvin

c/o PFD, Drury House, 34-43 Russell Street,
London WC2B 5HA
tel 020-7344 1000 *fax* 020-7836 9543
email sllaguno@pfd.co.uk
website www.pfd.co.uk

Agent Linda Mamy at PFD

Contact via agent. Credits include: *Blood and Chocolate*, *The Flight of the Phoenix*, and *Thunderbirds*.

Len Gowing

tel (01925) 232919 *mobile* (07973) 210090
email len@lengowing.co.uk
website www.lengowing.co.uk

Credits include: *Revenger's Tragedy*, and *Silent Witness*.

Jess Hall

c/o ICM London, Oxford House, 76 Oxford Street,
London W1D 1BS
Agent's tel 020-7636 6565 *fax* 020-7323 0101
email jesshall@bigfoot.com

Credits include: *Stander*, *Hot Fuzz*, and *Son of Rambo*.

Jakob Ihre

c/o The Dench Arnold Agency, 10 Newburgh Street,
London W1F 7RN
Agent's tel 020-7437 4551 *fax* 020-7439 1355
email contact@dencharnold.com
Agent Michelle Arnold at The Dench Arnold Agency

Credits include: *The Virgin of Liverpool*, and *Reprise*.

Tony Imi

Screen Talent Agency tel 020-7628 5180
tel 020-8224 0603 *fax* 020-8224 0603
email tony.imi@ntlworld.com

Credits include: *Blackwater Lightship*, and *Rancid Aluminium*.

Baz Irvine

c/o Casarotto Marsh Ltd, Waverley House,
7–12 Noel Street, London W1F 8GQ
tel 020-7287 4450 *fax* 020-7287 5644
email casarottomarsh@casarotto.co.uk
website www.casarotto.co.uk

Agents Sarah Pritchard (film), Emma Trouson (TV), Lucie LLewellyn (commercials) at Casarotto Marsh Ltd

Credits include: *Little Man*, *Six Shooter* (Oscar-winning short), and *Spooks*.

David Johnson BSC

c/o The Dench Arnold Agency, 10 Newburgh Street,
London W1F 7RN
Agent's tel 020-7437 4551 *fax* 020-7439 1355
email contact@dencharnold.com
Agent Michelle Arnold at The Dench Arnold Agency

Credits include: *Alien vs. Predator*, *On a Clear Day*, *An Ideal Husband*, and *Resident Evil*.

David Katznelson

c/o Casarotto Marsh Ltd, Waverley House,
7–12 Noel Street, London W1F 8GQ
tel 020-7287 4450 *fax* 020-7287 5644
email casarottomarsh@casarotto.co.uk
website www.casarotto.co.uk

Agents Sarah Pritchard (film), Emma Trouson (TV), Lucie Llewellyn (commercials) at Casarotto Marsh Ltd

Credits include: *Pleasureland*, *Margaret*, and *This Little Life*.

Nina Kellgren BSC

c/o McKinney Macartney Management,
The Barley Mow Centre, 10 Barley Mow Passage,
London W4 4PH

tel 020-8995 4747 *fax* 020-8995 2414
email mail@mckinneymacartney.com

Contact via agent. Credits include: *Pepys* (TV), *Wondrous Oblivion*, and *The Echo* (TV).

Rob Kitzmann

mobile (07092) 081201
fax 0870-922 3936
email mail@robkitzmann.com
website www.robkitzmann.com

Credits include: *The League of Gentlemen's Apocalypse*, and *Green Wing.*

Nic Knowland BSC

c/o The Dench Arnold Agency, 10 Newburgh Street, London W1F 7RN
Agent's tel 020-7437 4551 *fax* 020-7439 1355
email contact@dencharnold.com
Agent Michelle Arnold at The Dench Arnold Agency

Credits include: *The Piano Tuner of Earthquakes*, and *Simon Magus.*

Alwin Kuchler BSC

c/o PFD, Drury House, 34-43 Russell Street, London WC2B 5HA
tel 020-7344 1000 *fax* 020-7836 9543
email sllaguno@pfd.co.uk
website www.pfd.co.uk

Agent Linda Mamy at PFD

Contact via agent. Credits include: *Proof*, *The Deal*, *Sunshine*, and *Code 46.*

Stefan Lange

tel (01544) 370300 *mobile* (07973) 506792
email stefan.lange@virgin.net

Credits include: *Die Another Day*, *Alexander*, and *Tomb Raider.*

Vernon Layton BSC

c/o McKinney Macartney Management, The Barley Mow Centre, 10 Barley Mow Passage, London W4 4PH
tel 020-8995 4747 *fax* 020-8995 2414
email layton@freebie.net, mail@mckinneymacartney.com

Contact via agent. Credits include: *Seed of Chucky*, *Blackball*, and *I Still Know What You Did Last Summer.*

Bryan Loftus BSC

c/o Dinedor Management, 81 Oxford Street, London W1D 2EU
Agent's tel 020-7851 3575 *fax* 020-7851 3576
email info@dinedor.com
website www.dinedormanagement.co.uk
Agent Andrew Downer, Dinedor Management

Credits include: *Company of Wolves.*

Sam McCurdy

c/o Dinedor Management, 81 Oxford Street, London W1D 2EU
Agent's tel 020-7851 3575 *fax* 020-781 3576
email info@dinedor.com
website www.dinedormanagement.co.uk
Agent Andrew Downer, Dinedor Management

Credits include: *The Descent*, and *Dog Soldiers.*

Seamus McGarvey

c/o Casarotto Marsh Ltd, Waverley House, 7–12 Noel Street, London W1F 8GQ
tel 020-7287 4450 *fax* 020-7287 5644
email casarottomarsh@casarotto.co.uk
website www.casarotto.co.uk

Agents Sarah Pritchard (film), Emma Trouson (TV), Lucie Llewellyn (commercials) at Casarotto Marsh Ltd

Credits include: *The Hours*, *Charlotte's Web*, *Along Came Polly*, *Atonement*, *World Trade Center*, *High Fidelity*, *The War Zone*, and *Enigma.*

Phil Meheux BSC

c/o McKinney Macartney Management, The Barley Mow Centre, 10 Barley Mow Passage, London W4 4PH
tel 020-8995 4747 *fax* 020-8995 2414
email mail@mckinneymacartney.com

Contact via agent. Credits include: *Around the World in 80 Days*, *Casino Royale*, and *The Legend of Zorro.*

Chris Menges

c/o Casarotto Marsh Ltd, Waverley House, 7–12 Noel Street, London W1F 8GQ
tel 020-7287 4450 *fax* 020-7287 5644
email casarottomarsh@casarotto.co.uk
website www.casarotto.co.uk

Agents Sarah Pritchard (film), Emma Trouson (TV) at Casarotto Marsh Ltd

Credits include: *North Country*, *Dirty Pretty Things*, and *Notes on a Scandal.*

Peter Middleton BSC

c/o PFD, Drury House, 34-43 Russell Street, London WC2B 5HA
tel 020-7344 1000 *fax* 020-7836 9543
email petmidbsc@btinternet.com, sllaguno@pfd.co.uk
website www.pfd.co.uk

Agent Linda Mamy at PFD

Credits include: *Foyle's War*, and *New Tricks.*

Alec Mills BSC

c/o Creative Media Management, 3b Walpole Court, Ealing Studios, London W5 5ED
tel 020-8584 5363 *fax* 020-8566 5554
email am@suzymills.co.uk, enquiries@creativemediamanagement.com
website www.creativemediamanagement.com

Credits include: *Pointmen*, and *Christopher Columbus – The Discovery.*

Zubin Mistry

c/o ICM London, Oxford House, 76 Oxford Street, London W1D 1BS
Agent's tel 020-7636 6565 *fax* 020-7323 0101
email zubinmistry@btinternet.com
website www.zubinmistry.com

Credits include: *Leo*, and *Killing Joe*.

Nic Morris BSC

tel (01747) 812400 *mobile* (07860) 515154
email dop@nicmorris.com
website www.nicmorris.com

Credits include: *Minotaur*, *Spooks*, and *Long Time Dead*.

Shaun O'Dell

ICM London, Oxford House, 76 Oxford Street, London W1D 1BS
Agent's tel 020-7636 6565 *fax* 020-7323 0101
email shaunodell@hotmail.com

Credits include: *Doom*, and *The Hitchhiker's Guide to the Galaxy*.

Gyula Pados

c/o The Dench Arnold Agency, 10 Newburgh Street, London W1F 7RN
Agent's tel 020-7437 4551 *fax* 020-7439 1355
email contact@dencharnold.com
Agent Michelle Arnold at The Dench Arnold Agency

Credits include: *Basic Instinct 2*, *The Heart of Me*, and *Fateless*.

Tony Pierce-Roberts BSC

c/o McKinney Macartney Management, The Barley Mow Centre, 10 Barley Mow Passage, London W4 4PH
tel 020-8995 4747 *fax* 020-8995 2414
email mail@mckinneymacartney.com

Contact via agent. Credits include: *Underworld*, *Delovely*, and *Separate Lives*.

Chris Plevin

tel (01895) 457100 or (01494) 783393
email cplevin@cix.co.uk

Credits include: *Alfie*, *Ladies in Lavender*, and *Charlotte Gray*.

Simon Richards

c/o PFD, Drury House, 34-43 Russell Street, London WC2B 5HA
tel 020-7344 1000 *fax* 020-7836 9543
email sllaguno@pfd.co.uk
website www.pfd.co.uk

Agent Linda Mamy at PFD

Contact via agent. Credits include: *Flyboys* (2nd Unit), *Breather* (35mm short film), and *Carla*.

Nanu Segal

c/o The Dench Arnold Agency, 10 Newburgh Street, London W1F 7RN
Agent's tel 020-7437 4551 *tel* 020-8964 8483
fax 020-7439 1355
email contact@dencharnold.com
Agent Michelle Arnold at The Dench Arnold Agency

Credits include: *The Most Beautiful Man in the World*, *Song of Songs*, and *Ex Memoria*.

Eduardo Serra

c/o PFD, Drury House, 34-43 Russell Street, London WC2B 5HA
tel 020-7344 1000 *fax* 020-7836 9543
email sllaguno@pfd.co.uk
website www.pfd.co.uk

Agent Linda Mamy at PFD

Contact via agent. Credits include: *Blood Diamond*, *Beyond the Sea*, *Girl with a Pearl Earring*, and *The Flower of Evil*.

Antony Shearn

78 Elsham Road, London W14 8HH
tel 020-7371 2327 *mobile* (07973) 261396
email antonyshearn@aol.com
website www.bigtonemegaproductions.com

Credits include: *Mirrormask*, *Lullabelle*, *Neon*, and *The Week Before* (all short films).

Tony Slater-Ling

c/o PFD, Drury House, 34-43 Russell Street, London WC2B 5HA
tel 020-7344 1000 *fax* 020-7836 9543
email sllaguno@pfd.co.uk
website www.pfd.co.uk

Agent Linda Mamy at PFD

Contact via agent. Credits include: *Yasmin*, *Spooks 5*, and *Shameless III*.

Witold Stok

c/o McKinney Macartney Management, The Barley Mow Centre, 10 Barley Mow Passage, London W4 4PH
tel 020-8995 4747 *fax* 020-8995 2414
email mail@mckinneymacartney.com

Contact via agent. Please send script with enquiries. Credits include: *Gladiatress*, *Among Giants*, and *The Match*.

Ivan Strasburg

c/o The Dench Arnold Agency, 10 Newburgh Street, London W1F 7RN
Agent's tel 020-7437 4551 *tel* 020-8964 8483
fax 020-7439 1355
email contact@dencharnold.com, ivanstras@btopenworld.com
Agent Michelle Arnold at The Dench Arnold Agency

Credits include: *Bloody Sunday*, *Shooting Dogs*, and *The Hades Factor*.

Katie Swain

c/o McKinney Macartney Management, The Barley Mow Centre, 10 Barley Mow Passage, London W4 4PH

tel 020-8995 4747 *fax* 020-8995 2414
email mail@mckinneymacartney.com, katie@katieswain.com
website www.mckinneymacartney.com, www.katieswain.com

Contact via agent for work enquiries. Credits include: *Killing Hitler*, *Little Britain*, *Rescue Me*, and *Lock Stock & Two Smoking Barrels* (TV).

Wojciech Szepel

c/o Casarotto Marsh Ltd, Waverley House, 7-12 Noel Street, London W1F 8GQ
tel 020-7287 4450 *fax* 020-7287 5644
email casarottomarsh@casarotto.co.uk
website www.casarotto.co.uk

Agents Sarah Pritchard (film), Emma Trouson (TV), Lucie Llewellyn (commercials) at Casarotto Marsh Ltd

Credits include: *Kiss of Life*, *Skin Deep*, *Apfelbaumhaus*, *Herrn Kukas Emfelungen*, *Recovery* (TV), *Kissing Tickling and Being Bored*, *Mein Erstes Wunder* (engl. *My First Miracle*), *Haensel und Gretel*, *Warszawa* (engl. *Warsaw*), *Whatever Love Means* (TV).

Fraser Taggart

tel 0118-940 1723 *fax* 0118-940 1723
email name.tag@virgin.net

Credits include: *Troy* (2nd Unit), and *Unleashed* (2nd Unit).

Tom Townend

c/o Dinedor Management, 81 Oxford Street, London W1D 2EU
Agent's tel 020-7851 3575 *fax* 020-781 3576
email info@dinedor.com
website www.dinedormanagement.co.uk
Agent Andrew Downer, Dinedor Management

Credits include: *28 Days Later*, *Proof*, and *Pride and Prejudice* (all 2nd Unit).

Brian Tufano BSC

c/o McKinney Macartney Management, The Barley Mow Centre, 10 Barley Mow Passage, London W4 4PH
tel 020-8995 4747 *fax* 020-8995 2414
email mail@mckinneymacartney.com

Contact via agent. Credits include: *Kidulthood*, *I Could Never Be Your Woman*, and *Once Upon a Time in the Midlands*.

James Welland

c/o Casarotto Marsh Ltd, Waverley House, 7–12 Noel Street, London W1F 8GQ
tel 020-7287 4450 *fax* 020-7287 5644
email casarottomarsh@casarotto.co.uk
website www.casarotto,co.uk www.jameswelland.com

Agents Sarah Pritchard (film), Emma Trouson (TV), Lucie Llewellyn (commercials) at Casarotto Marsh Ltd

Credits include: *Beautiful Creatures*, and *Palais Royal!*.

Ian Wilson BSC

c/o McKinney Macartney Management, The Barley Mow Centre, 10 Barley Mow Passage, London W4 4PH
tel 020-8995 4747 *fax* 020-8995 2414
email mail@mckinneymacartney.com, folkcottagecs.com

Credits include: *Blind Flight*, *Emma*, and *The Crying Game*.

Marcel Zyskind

c/o PFD, Drury House, 34-43 Russell Street, London WC2B 5HA
tel 020-7344 1000 *fax* 020-7836 9543
email sllaguno@pfd.co.uk
website www.pfd.co.uk

Agent Linda Mamy at PFD

Contact via agent. Credits include: *Mister Lonley*, *Nine Songs*, and *Code 46*.

1ST ADS

While the 1st Assistant Director is the Director's right hand on set, they generally concentrate on the more logistical elements of the shoot, in order to free the Director up for creative concerns. On most feature productions, a 1st AD is responsible for scheduling; once on set, they are usually are expected to keep the production moving and on time. Becuase they often have to 'crack the whip' to meet tight scheduling demands, finding a 1st AD with a sense of humour, people skills and lots of patience will help to make the shoot run smoothly.

Tony Aherne

tel 029-2071 0770
(Gems Diary Service) *mobile* (07973) 217687
email tony_aherne@hotmail.com

Credits include: *King Arthur*, and *Intermission*.

Claire Alderton

mobile (07812) 596878
email mail@clairealderton.com

Credits include: *Mockingbird* (short film), *Starlight Express 3D*, and *Ocean's Eleven* (2nd Unit).

ARRI Crew

3 Highbridge, Oxford Road, Uxbridge, Middlesex UB8 1LX

tel (01895) 457100 *fax* (01895) 457101
email info@arrimedia.com
website www.arricrew.com

Diary service which represents freelance technicians and crew within the film and TV industry. Also see ARRI Media.

Roger Arscott

tel (01235) 848087 *mobile* (07973) 653863
email bigrog@onetel.com

Credits include: *Lost For Words*, *Murder in Mind*, and *Liam* (Locations Manager).

Howard Arundel

tel 020-8399 2155 *mobile* (07836) 575027
fax 020-8399 2155
email howie.a@virgin.net

Credits include: *Monarch of the Glen*, *Jude*, and *Solomon & Gaenor*.

Daf Arwyn-Jones

tel 029-2049 4862 *mobile* (07850) 993885
email daf@roathmill.com
website www.roathmill.com

Credits include: *The Story of Tracy Beaker* (CBBC), and *High Hopes* (BBC).

John Bennett

tel (01332) 831952 *mobile* (07974) 751758
fax (01332) 831952
email jbenno@ukonline.co.uk, benno@ukonline.co.uk

Credits include: *Hotel Babylon*, *The Street*, and *Auf Weidersehen, Pet*.

Peter Bennett

tel (01932) 886714 *mobile* (07715) 034537
email p-b-jnr@dirconco.uk

Credits include: *Mummy Returns*, *Alexander*, and *Back in Business*.

William Booker

Agent's tel (01753) 646677
email sue@execmanagement.co.uk
Agent Exec Management

Credits include: *Lives of the Saints*, and *Johnny English* (2nd Unit).

Edward Brett

c/o Sara Putt Associates, Room 923, The Old House, Shepperton Studios, Studios Road, Shepperton, Middlesex TW17 0QD
Agent's tel (01932) 571044 *mobile* (07860) 443895
fax (01932) 571109
email edwardbrett@aol.com

Credits include: *A Christmas Carol*, *Alien vs. Predator*, and *The Lost Prince*.

Alex Bridcut

tel 029-2071 0770
(Gems Diary Service) *mobile* (07778) 787449
email alex.bridcut@virgin.net

Credits include: *London*, and *The Inspector Lynley Mysteries*.

Giles Butler

tel 020-8994 1332 *mobile* (07973) 528220
email gilesbutler101@hotmail.com

Credits include: *Madcows*, *Gormenghast* (2nd), and *Tunnel of Love*.

Grantly Butters

tel (01630) 656873 *mobile* (07976) 295232
fax (01630) 653539
email grantlybutters@hotmail.com

Credits include: *Waking the Dead*, and *The Family Man*.

Rob Cannon

Agent's tel (01753) 646677
email sue@execmanagement.co.uk
Agent Exec Management

Contact via agent. Credits include: *Hibernation* (award-winning short), and *Ghosts*.

Matt Carter

email matt.carter@boltblue.com

Contact via email. Works in television and film. Credits include: *Holby City*, and *Eastenders*.

Marco Ciglia

c/o Creative Media Management, 3b Walpole Court, Ealing Studios, London W5 5ED
tel 020-8584 5363 *fax* 020-8566 5554
email marco.ciglia@ntlworld.com, enquiries@creativemediamanagement.com
website www.creativemediamanagement.com

Credits include: *Highlander V: The Source*, *The Last Drop*, and *Cashback* (American Academy award-nominated short film).

Joanna Crow

tel 020-7503 3612 *mobile* (07966) 235683
email joannacrow@yahoo.com

Credits include: *Life on Mars*, *Dirty Filthy Love*, and *The Descent*.

Paul Dale

tel 029-2071 0770
(Gems Diary Service) *mobile* (07971) 263846
email paul.dale01@tesco.net

Credits include: *Blackbeard*, and *Shameless*.

David Daniels

c/o Caroline Cornish Management Ltd, 12 Shinfield Street, London W12 0HN
Agent's tel 020-8743 7337 *mobile* (07973) 732202
fax 020-8743 7887
email info@carolinecornish.co.uk, dd.daniels@virgin.net

website www.carolinecornish.co.uk

Credits include: *Agent Cody Banks II*, *Ella Enchanted*, and *The Heart of Me.*

Kristian Dench

tel (01923) 351968 *mobile* (07956) 640793
email kristiandench@aol.com

Credits include: *Footballers' Wives*, and *Bad Girls.*

Melanie Dicks

c/o McKinney Macartney Management,
The Barley Mow Centre, 10 Barley Mow Passage,
London W4 4PH
tel 020-8995 4747 *fax* 020-8995 2414
email mail@mckinneymacartney.com,
meldicks@aol.com

Contact via agent. Credits include: *Imagine Me & You*, *Severence*, and *Mike Bassett: England Manager.*

John Dodds

tel 020-8940 6670 *mobile* (07801) 441010
Agent: Bookends tel (01727) 841177
email john.dodds8@btinternet.com

Credits include: *Merchant of Venice*, *Red Mercury*, and *Ghost Boat* .

Peter F Errington

tel 020-8979 0572 *mobile* (07050) 030112
email avidx@screaming.net

Credits include: *Nine Dead Gay Guys*, *The Bill*, and *Family Affairs.*

George Every

tel (01491) 574825 *mobile* (07766) 632619
email george_every@hotmail.com

Credits include: *The Last King of Scotland*, *Seed of Chucky*, *The White Countess*, and *Dragnet.*

Jonathan Farmer

tel 0141-423 4591 *mobile* (07802) 406812
fax 0141-423 6819
email jonathan_farmer@yahoo.co.uk

Credits include: *Afterlife*, and *Festival.*

Mark Fenn

c/o Sara Putt Associates, Room 923, The Old House, Shepperton Studios, Studios Road, Shepperton, Middlesex TW17 0QD
Agent's tel (01932) 571044 *fax* (01932) 571109
email info@sara-putt.co.uk
website www.sara-putt.co.uk

Credits include: *Morvern Callar Carol*, *The Lawless Heart*, and *Gangster No. 1.*

Marcia Gay

c/o Creative Media Management, 3b Walpole Court, Ealing Studios, London W5 5ED
tel 020-8584 5363 *fax* 020-8566 5554
email enquiries@creativemediamanagement.com
website www.creativemediamanagement.com

Credits include: *Sky Captain and The World of Tomorrow*, *Silence Becomes You*, and *Esther Khan.*

Nick Gorman

Agent's tel (01753) 646677 *mobile* (07787) 975334
email nick.gorman@virgin.net
Agent Exec Management

Credits include: *Casualty*, and *Waking the Dead.*

Tommy Gormley

c/o ICM London, Oxford House, 76 Oxford Street, London W1D 1BS
Agent's tel 020-7636 6565 *mobile* (07778) 527866
fax 020-7323 0101
website tommy.gormley@virgin.net

Credits include: *Mission Impossible III*, *Phantom of the Opera*, and *Thunderbirds.*

Lee Grumett

c/o ICM London, Oxford House, 76 Oxford Street, London W1D 1BS
Agent's tel 020-7636 6565 *mobile* (07768) 372510
email leegrumett@mac.com
Agent Kate Chilcott at ICM

Contact via mobile and send scripts via email. Credits include: *Magic Flute* (2nd Unit), *Fingersmith*, and *Spooks.*

Martin Harrison

mobile (07931) 596758
email harrison.mw@virgin.net

Credits include: *Finding Neverland*, *On a Clear Day*, and *Notes on a Scandal.*

Nick Heckstall-Smith

tel 020-8743 7337 *fax* 020-8743 7887
email carolinecornish@btconnect.com
Agent Caroline Cornish

Contact via agent. Credits include: *Stormbreaker*, and *Around the World in 80 Days.*

Guy Heeley

mobile (07973) 309032
email purplguy@globalnet.co.uk

Credits include: *Pride & Prejudice*, *Keeping Mum*, *Starter for Ten*, and *Alien Autopsy.*

Ben Howarth

Agent's tel (01753) 646677
email sue@execmanagement.co.uk,
ben-h@dircon.co.uk
Agent Exec Management

Credits include: *Young Hannibal: Behind the Mask*, and *Chromophobia.*

Nic Juene

tel (01308) 459891 *mobile* (07958) 967574
email nicjeune@anna.demon.co.uk

Credits include: *The Baker*, *Boudica*, and *Tomorrow La Scala!.*

Bill Kirk

c/o Creative Media Management, 3b Walpole Court, Ealing Studios, London W5 5ED
tel 020-8584 5363 *fax* 020-8566 5554
email Williamkirk@skynet.be, enquiries@creativemediamanagement.com
website www.creativemediamanagement.com

Fluent written and spoken French. Credits include: *Dear Wendy*, and *Heidi*.

Tracy Lane Chapman

tel 0161-747 8615 *mobile* (07855) 456055
fax 0161-747 8615
email tracychapman@ntlworld.com

Credits include: *Where The Heart Is*, and *Waterloo Road*.

Cliff Lanning

tel 020-8343 3277 *mobile* (07802) 877442
email clifflan1@aol.com

Credits include: *Batman Begins*, *Mummy Returns*, *Harry Potter and the Order of the Phoenix*, and *Alfie*.

Terry Madden

tel (01923) 774510 *mobile* (07831) 681282
fax (01923) 774510
email Terryadmadden@aol.com

Credits include: *X-Men 3*, *Troy* (2nd Unit), and *Tomb Raider*.

Simon Moseley

c/o McKinney Macartney Management, The Barley Mow Centre, 10 Barley Mow Passage, London W4 4PH
Agent's tel 020-8995 4747 *tel* 020-7431 7669
fax 020-8995-2414
email mail@mckinneymacartney.com
website www.mckinneymacartney.com

Contact via agent. Credits include: *Last Orders*, *Blow Dry*, and *Cheeky*.

Kiaran Murray-Smith

c/o Caroline Cornish Management Ltd, 12 Shinfield Street, London W12 0HN
Agent's tel 020-8743 7337 *tel* 020-8580 0693
fax 020-8743 7887
email info@carolinecornish.co.uk, kiaranms@hotmail.com
website www.carolinecornish.co.uk

Credits include: *Jam*, and *French and Saunders' Xmas Special*.

Chris Newman

Agent's tel (01753) 646677
email sue@execmanagement.co.uk, chrisnewman8@btopenworld.com
Agent Exec Management

Credits include: *Matchpoint*, *About a Boy*, and *Goal!*.

Steve Newton

tel (01483) 812011
(The Production Switchboard Diary Services) *tel* 020-8671 8113 *mobile* (07989) 570769
email pointblank@clara.co.uk

Credits include: *My Summer of Love*, *Cashback*, and *Silence Becomes You*.

Alexander Oakley

tel 020-8977 5337 *mobile* (07976) 242982
fax 020-8977 5337
email alexander.oakley@virgin.net

Contact via phone or email; please send details of script. Credits include: *Children Of Men* (2nd Unit), *Alexander*, *Wimbledon*, and *Love & Other Disasters*.

Matthew Penry-Davey

c/o ICM London, Oxford House, 76 Oxford Street, London W1D 1BS
Agent's tel 020-7636 6565 *mobile* (07956) 312348
email matthew@penrydavey.freeserve.co.uk

Credits include: *10,000 B.C.*, *Trauma*, and *Love and Other Disasters*.

Kieron A Phipps

Agent's tel (01753) 646677 *tel* (01442) 865178
email sue@execmanagement.co.uk, kieron.phipps@talk21.com
Agent Exec Management

Credits include: *Everything is Illuminated*, *Enduring Love* (2nd Unit), and *The Lion in Winter*.

Jack Ravenscroft

c/o ICM London, Oxford House, 76 Oxford Street, London W1D 1BS
Agent's tel 020-7636 6565 *tel* (01727) 845761
email jmrave@btinternet.com

Contact via agent. Credits include: *The Descent*, *Straightheads*, and *The Long Firm*.

Stuart Renfrew

Agent's tel (01753) 646677 *tel* 020-7402 2788
email sue@execmanagement.co.uk, stuartad@hotmail.com
Agent Exec Management

Contact via agent. Credits include: *The Queen*, *Mrs Henderson Presents*, and *The Blue Train Mystery*.

Josh Robertson

c/o McKinney Macartney Management, The Barley Mow Centre, 10 Barley Mow Passage, London W4 4PH
Agent's tel 020-8995 4747 *tel* 020-7627 2925
fax 020-8995 2414
email mail@mckinneymacartney.com, josh@debosh.com
website www.mckinneymacartney.com

Contact via agent. Credits include: *The Magic Flute*, *Kinky Boots*, *Vera Drake*, and *De-Lovely*.

Richard Styles
tel 020-8735 0495 *mobile* (07768) 151636
email richardstyles@onetel.net.com

Credits include: *The Constant Gardener, The Walker, Gosford Park*, and *28 Days Later.*

Gareth Tandy
Agent's tel (01753) 646677
(01753) 651767 (The Production Guild Diary Services)
email sue@execmanagement.co.uk, tandygazza@aol.com
Agent Exec Management

Contact via agent. Credits include: *Nanny McPhee*, and *Charlie and the Chocolate Factory* (2nd Unit).

Tom Dunbar
mobile (07976) 614487
tel (01753) 646677
email tom@tomdunbar.co.uk
website www.tomdunbar.co.uk

Agent Exec Management

Credits include: *Gypo, Joy Division, Resident Evil*, and various commercials.

Guy Travers
c/o Creative Media Management, 3b Walpole Court, Ealing Studios, London W5 5ED
tel 020-8584 5363 *fax* 020-8566 5554
email enquiries@creativemediamanagement.com
website www.creativemediamanagement.com

Credits include: *Being Julia, Stander*, and *A Knight's Tale.*

Barry Wasserman
tel 020-7485 8579 *mobile* (07776) 254343
fax 020-7916 9745
email bazwaz77@hotmail.com

Credits include: *The Borrowers*, Jim Henson's *The Storyteller*, and *Hard Candy.*

SOUND PROFESSIONALS

The following sound professionals are some of the UK's most experienced and respected. A production sound mixer is the person responsible for all sound recorded during a production. This might involve choosing the microphones, managing a sound crew (such as boom operator), and mixing live effects and dialogue on set.

Ronald Bailey
tel 020-7348 1910 or 020-7267 6323
mobile (07956) 378679
email ronaldnbailey@excite.com

Sound mixer/recordist. Credits include: *The Last Sign, Bridget Jones's Diary* (2nd Unit), and *Kiss of Life.*

Fraser Barber
c/o McKinney Macartney Management, The Barley Mow Centre, 10 Barley Mow Passage, London W4 4PH
Agent's tel 020-8995 4747 *fax* 020-8995-2414
email mail@mckinneymacartney.com, fraser@widescreensound.com
website www.mckinneymacartney.com
Agents Flic McKinney, Kim Macartney, Brigid Holland, Matthew Rose at McKinney Macartney

Sound mixer. Contact via agent. Credits include: *Mike Bassett: England Manager, A Previous Engagement*, and *Silent Witness* (TV).

Simon Bishop
c/o Sara Putt Associates, Room 923, The Old House, Shepperton Studios, Studios Road, Shepperton, Middlesex TW17 0QD
Agent's tel (01932) 571044 *mobile* (07836) 345092
fax (01932) 571109
email sb@simonbishop.com
website www.simonbishop.com

Sound mixer/recordist. Credits include: *Star Wars – Revenge of the Sith, Chopratown* (TV), and *Bent.*

John Brady
Diary Service tel 020-8876 8553 (Audiosend)
tel 020-8943 3897 *mobile* (07973) 223320
email johnbrady9@hotmail.com

Credits include: *Mean Machine*, and *Tomb Raider II.*

Peter Brill
tel 0141-357 0617 *mobile* (07971) 780572
email peter_brill@beeb.net

Sound mixer/recordist. Credits include: *Dear Frankie, On a Clear Day*, and *Festival.*

Simon Clark
c/o Sara Putt Associates, Room 923, The Old House, Shepperton Studios, Studios Road, Shepperton, Middlesex TW17 0QD
Agent's tel (01932) 571044 *mobile* (07785) 228588
fax (01932) 571109
email simonclarkaudio@beeb.net

Sound recordist/mixer. Credits include: *Best*, and *Waking the Dead.*

Clive Copeland
Agent's tel (01753) 646677 *fax* (01753) 646770
email sue@execmanagement.co.uk
website www.execmanagement.co.uk
Agent Exec Management

Production sound mixer. Credits include: *Piccadilly Jim*, and *A Waste of Shame.*

David Crozier
tel (01753) 642338 *mobile* (07850) 206303
fax (01753) 644622
email crozier@globalnet.co.uk

Sound mixer. Credits include: *Harry Potter and the Goblet of Fire, Sky Captain and the World of Tomorrow, Finding Neverland*, and *The Hours*.

Malcolm Davies
Agent's tel (07973) 159320 *fax* 0161-622 0166
email malcolm@manxmoviesound.com
website www.manxmoviesound.com
Agent The Annis Agency

Production sound mixer. Credits include: *16 Years of Alcohol, Ted & Alice*, and *Pour Le Plaisir*.

Tony Dawe
c/o Sara Putt Associates, Room 923, The Old House, Shepperton Studios, Studios Road, Shepperton, Middlesex TW17 0QD
Agent's tel (01932) 571044 *mobile* (07831) 312903
fax (01932) 571109
email tonydawe@aol.com

Sound mixer. Credits include: *Charlie and the Chocolate Factory, Troy*, and *The Good Night*.

Mick Duffield
Diary Service tel 020-7348 1910 (Digital Garage)
tel 020-7281 0077 *mobile* (07885) 274016
email micksound@blueyonder.co.uk
website www.mdsound.co.uk

Sound recordist. Credits include: *Touching the Void*, and *Cut Sleeve Boys*.

Tim Fraser
c/o ICM London, Oxford House, 76 Oxford Street, London W1D 1BS
Agent's tel 020-7636 6565 *mobile* (07836) 630148
fax 020-7323 0101
email timfraser@btinternet.com
Agent International Creative Management

Sound mixer. Contact via agent. Credits include: *Vera Drake, Sunshine*, and *Fingersmith* (TV).

Jim Greenhorn
c/o ICM London, Oxford House, 76 Oxford Street, London W1D 1BS
Agent's tel 020-7636 6565 *fax* 020-7323 0101
email jim.greenhorn@lineone.net
Agent International Creative Management

Sound mixer/recordist. Contact via agent. Credits include: *Breaking and Entering, Amazing Grace, Notes on a Scandal*, and *Stage Beauty*.

Danny Hambrook
tel 020-8692 2578 *mobile* (07966) 427028
fax 020-8692 2578
email dannyhambrook@hotmail.com

Sound mixer/recordist/supervising sound editor. Credits include: *Venus, The Mother, Enduring Love*, and *Pride & Prejudice*.

John Hayes
Diary Service tel 020-8876 8553 (Audiosend)
mobile (07768) 747617
fax 020-8876 9381
email soundman@talk21.com

Production sound mixer/recordist. Credits include: *Bend It Like Beckham, Bride and Prejudice, The Libertine*, and *Broken Thread*.

Simon Hayes
Agent's tel 020-7636 6565
Diary Service tel 020-8876 8553 (Audiosend)
mobile (07973) 671053
fax 020-7323 0101
email soundman@talk21.com
Agent International Creative Management

Sound mixer/recordist. Credits include: Bridget Jones: *The Edge of Reason, Nanny McPhee*, and *Sixty Six*.

Malcolm Hirst
26 Farley Court, Allsop Place, London NW1 5LG
mobile (07778) 183202
Diary Service tel 020-7348 1910 (Digital Garage)
email Malcolmhirst@aol.com

Sound recordist. Credits include: BBC1's *Judge John Deed*.

Mark Holding
c/o McKinney Macartney Management, The Barley Mow Centre, 10 Barley Mow Passage, London W4 4PH
Agent's tel 020-8995 4747 *fax* 020-8995-2414
email mail@mckinneymacartney.com
website www.mckinneymacartney.com
Agents Flic McKinney, Kim Macartney, Brigid Holland, Matthew Rose at McKinney Macartney

Sound mixer. Contact via agent. Credits include: *The Hitchhiker's Guide to the Galaxy, Chromophobia*, and *Stormbreaker*.

Neil Kingsbury
tel (01923) 825250 *mobile* (07973) 635443
fax (01923) 825250
email neilkingsbury@btinternet.com

Sound recordist/mixer. Credits include: *The Da Vinci Code, Troy*, and *Charlie and the Chocolate Factory* (2nd Unit).

Emma Meadon
mobile (07779) 244886
email emmalmeaden@yahoo.co.uk

Sound recordist/boom operator/playback. Contact via mobile or diary service (**www.zoo-diaries.com**). Also speaks fluent French and can work on French-language productions here or abroad.

Credits include: *Fear of ... Trilogy*, *Oona and I* (both as sound recordist); *Titty Titty Bang Bang* (as boom op); and *Charlie and the Chocolate Factory* (as playback).

Chris Munro

Agent's tel (01753) 646677 *mobile* (07956) 548717
email sue@execmanagement.co.uk, chrismunno@btinternet.com
website www.editstation.com
Agent Exec Management

Production sound mixer. Credits include: *Van Helsing*, *Casino Royale*, and *Flight 93*.

Ian Munro

Agent's tel (01753) 646677 *mobile* (07973) 218279
email sue@execmanagement.co.uk, fosterfilm@tiscali.co.uk
Agent Exec Management

Production sound mixer. Credits include: *Die Another Day*, *Cold Mountain*, and *The Phantom of the Opera* (2nd Unit).

Simon Okin

c/o McKinney Macartney Management,
The Barley Mow Centre, 10 Barley Mow Passage,
London W4 4PH
Agent's tel 020-8995 4747 *mobile* (07710) 078577
fax 020-8995 2414
email mail@mckinneymacartney.com, simon@smokinokin.fsnet.co.uk
website www.mckinneymacartney.com
Agents Flic McKinney, Kim Macartney, Brigid Holland, Matthew Rose at McKinney Macartney

Sound mixer. Contact via agent. Credits include: *Five Children and It*, *The Seed of Chucky*, and *Beowolf and Grendel*.

Ian Richardson

Diary Service tel 029-2071 0770
(Gems) *tel* 029 2022 1938 *mobile* (07973) 263784
fax 029-2031 8346
email ian@filmsound.co.uk
website www.filmsound.co.uk

Sound recordist. Speaks French. Credits include: *Dr Who*, *A Way of Life*, *The I Inside*, and *Tomorrow La Scala!*.

John J Rodda

Diary Services tel 020-8883 1616 (Prince Stone)
tel (01844) 353985 *mobile* (07785) 504606
fax 0870-0523365
email jr@jrsound.com
website www.jrsound.com

Production sound mixer/recordist. Speaks French. Credits include: *28 Days Later*, *Shackleton*, and *King Arthur*.

Ivan Sharrock

tel 020-7267 3170 or *tel* 020-7284 4306
mobile (07768) 627856
fax 020-7284 4250
email ivansharrock@raspberry-ss.com

Sound mixer/recordist. Credits include: *Closer*, *Cold Mountain*, *The Da Vinci Code*, and *The Blood Diamond*.

Brian Simmons

Agent's tel (01753) 646677 *mobile* (07710) 237065
email sue@execmanagement.co.uk, soundcan@clara.co.uk
Agent Exec Management

Production sound mixer. Credits include: *Star Wars – Revenge of the Sith* (additional shooting), *Tea With Mussolini*, and *Braveheart* (won BAFTA sound award).

David Stephenson

c/o ICM London, Oxford House, 76 Oxford Street, London W1D 1BS
Agent's tel 020-7636 6565 *mobile* (07885) 639332
Agent's fax 020-7323 0101 *fax* (01276) 857757
email dasmix@aol.com

Sound mixer. Contact via agent. Credits include: *Kingdom of Heaven*, *Munich*, *Love Actually*, and *V is for Vendetta*.

Nick Thermes

tel ++33 4 67 26 70 55 *fax* ++33 6 86 61 76 99
email nick@soundmixer.biz
website www.soundmixer.biz

Sound recordist. Speaks French and has bases both in the UK and in France. Credits include: *The Descent*, *Dog Soldiers*, and *Tales from France*.

Becky Thomson

tel (01475) 670105 *mobile* (07710) 762607
email beckythomson@email.com
website www.beckythomson.com

Sound recordist. Credits include: *Afterlife*, and *A Woman in Winter*.

Ian Voight

c/o McKinney Macartney Management,
The Barley Mow Centre, 10 Barley Mow Passage,
London W4 4PH
tel 020-8995 4747 *fax* 020-8995 2414
email mail@mckinneymacartney.com

Production sound mixer. Please make contact via agent; send script with enquiries. Credits include: *The Omen 666*, *Flyboys*, and *Greyfriars Bobby*.

Bruce Wills

c/o ICM London, Oxford House, 76 Oxford Street, London W1D 1BS
Agent's tel 020-7636 6565 *fax* 020-7323 0101
email bruce.wills@virgin.net

Sound recordist. Credits include: *Kinky Boots*, *Canterbury Tales* (TV), and *Perfect Day* (TV).

Stuart Wilson

c/o ICM London, Oxford House, 76 Oxford Street, London W1D 1BS
Agent's tel 020-7636 6565 *mobile* (07771) 533816
fax 020-7323 0101
email mail@stuartwilson.com
website www.stuartwilson.com
Agent Sue Greenleaves at ICM

Production sound mixer. Contact via agent. Credits include: *The Constant Gardener, Marie Antoinette, Cock and Bull Story, The Dreamers, In This World,* and *The Road to Guantanamo.*

ART DIRECTORS/PRODUCTION DESIGNERS

This section includes the heads of the art department who work with the director to determine the overall look of the film and also oversee the craftspeople who make up the art department, from costume designers to set builders.

Andrew Ackland-Snow

email andrew.acklandsnow@bt.openworld.com

Art Director with extensive credits including *Harry Potter 1-5, Titanic, The World Is Not Enough, Notting Hill,* and *The Avengers.*

Charmian Adams

email charmian.adams@virgin.net

Charmian works predominantly as a Supervising Art Director, but also designs lower budget projects such as *The Inquisition (*dr: Betsann Morris Evans). She has worked on many projects including *Proof* (dr: John Madden), *Hilary and Jackie* (dr: Anand Tucker), *The Hound of the Baskervilles* (dr: David Attwood) and *State of Play,* a 6 part drama for the BBC.

Dave Allday

email dvaday@aol.com

Art Director whose credits inlude *Amazing Grace, Charlie and the Chocolate Factory, Thunderbirds, Charlotte Gray, Lara Croft: Tomb Raider, The Lost Empire, Gladiator.*

Melanie Allen

PFD, Drury House, 34-43 Russell Street, London WC2B 5HA
tel 020-7344 1000

Production designer whose feature credits include *Grow Your Own* and *Bullet Boy* aswell as TV productions includng *In The Line Of Beauty* and *All About George.*

Allset Ltd.

Caroline Amies

C/O Casarotto, Waverley House, 7–12 Noel Street, London W1F 8GQ

Production Designer, Caroline Amies, won the BBC RTS award for best Production Design for *Gormenghast.*

Eddy Andres

email eddy.andres@btopenworld.com

Draughtsman and production buyer with credits including *The Wind in the Willows.*

Dave Arrowsmith

3b Walpole Court, Ealing Studios, London W5 5ED
tel 020-8584 5363
email enquiries@creativemediamanagement.com

TV and film prodcution designer with credits including *Monarch of the Glen, Losing It* and *Titanic Town.*

Anna Asp

Jille Azis

Creative Media Managament, 3b Walpole Court, Ealing Studios, London W5 5ED
020-8584 5363
email enquiries@creativemediamanagement.com

Set Decorator whose credits include *Rendition, Sixty Six* and *The Good Shepherd.*

John Beard

ICM, 4-6 Soho Square, London W1D 3PZ
tel 020-07636 6565

Production designer whose credits include *Thunderbirds, K-Pax* and *Enigma.*

Sophie Becher

c/o Casaroto Marsh, Waverley House, 7-12 Noel Street, London W1F 8GQ
tel 020-7287 4450

Prodction designer with credits including *Run Fat Boy Run* (dir David Schwimmer), *To Kill A King* (dir Mike Barker) and *Alfie* (dir Charles Shyer).

Gavin Bocquet

email gbocq@aol.com

Experienced production designer with credits including the *Star Wars* trilogy, *Indiana Jones Chronicles* and *XXX.*

Simon Bowles

tel (07774) 852 777
email mail@simonbowles.com
website www.simonbowles.com

Production designer with credits including *The Descent, Lara Croft,* and *Straightheads.*

Tom Bowyer

c/o The Dench Arnold Agency, 10 Newburgh Street, London W1F 7RN
tel 020-7437 4551 *fax* 020-7439 1355

email contact@dencharnold.com

Production designer with film and TV credits including *The Dinner Party, The Amazing Mrs Pritchard, Cracker, The Last Resort* and *Out Of Control.*

Stephen J. Bream

tel (01727) 843990 *mobile* (07811) 345048
email stevebream519@hotmail.com

Assistant Art Director with credits including *Laws of Attraction, Reign of Fire* and *Around the World in 80 Days.*

Richard Bridgland

c/o Drury House, 34-43 Russell Street,
London WC2B 5HA
tel 020-7344 1000 *fax* 020-7836 9539
website www.pfd.co.uk

Production Designer with credits including *Tsunami: The Aftermath, Alien Versus Pradator* and *League Of Gentlemen's Apocalypse.*

Brigitte Broch

c/o Waverley House, 7–12 Noel Street,
London W1F 8GQ

Tom Brown

Creative Media Management, 3b Walpole Court,
Ealing Studios, London W5
tel 020-8584 5363

Credits include: *Kevin and Perry Go Large, I Want Candy* and *The Parole Officer.*

Jon Bunker

email artifx@aol.com

Credits include: *I'll Sleep When I'm Dead, Marigold* and *The Hive.*

Tony Burrough

Oxford House, 76 Oxford Street, London, W1D 1BS
tel 020-7636 6565

Credits include: *Chromophobia, Ladder 49* and *Hotel Rwanda.*

Tom Burton

The Dench Arnold Agency, 10 Newburgh Street,
London W1F 7RN
tel 020-7437 4551

Credits include: *Velvet Goldmine, Churchill The Hollywood Years* and numerous commercials.

Maurice Cain

12 Shinfield Street, London W12 0HN
Agent's tel 020-8743 7337 *tel* 020 8580 0693
fax 020-8743 7887
email info@carolinecornish.co.uk,
kiaranms@hotmail.com
website www.carolinecornish.co.uk

Credits include: *Between Two Rivers* and *Foyles War.*

Stephen Campbell

email escala23@blueyonder.co.uk

Credits include: *Dockers* and *Robin Hood.*

Jason Carlin

email jason@kinego.com

Credits include: *Fat Friends, Yasmin* and *Feather Boy.*

Michael Carlin

c/o Casarotto Marsh Ltd, Waverley House,
7–12 Noel Street, London W1F 8GQ
tel 020-7287 4450 *fax* 020-7287 5644
email casarottomarsh@casarotto.co.uk
website www.casarotto.co.uk

Credits include: *The Last King of Scotland, Crime & Punishment*

Alan J. Cassie

email ajc@btopenworld.com

Credits include: *Hitchhikers Guide to the Galaxy, Muppet Treasure Island, Patriot Games.*

Ray Chan

tel 020 8767 7505 *mobile* 07973 132034
fax 020 8767 7505
email raymondochan@aol.com

Credits include: *Alien vs Predator, Flyboys, The Children of Men*

Martin Childs

email martin.childs@btinternet.com

Titles: *Calendar Girls, Lady in the Water, Quills*

Jim Clay

c/o Casarotto Marsh Ltd, Waverley House,
7–12 Noel Street, London W1F 8GQ
tel 020-7287 4450 *fax* 020-7287 5644
email casarottomarsh@casarotto.co.uk
website www.casarotto.co.uk

Credits include: *Children of Men, Matchpoint*

Joel Collins

email joelcollins@blueyonder.co.uk

Credits include: *The Calcium Kid, Goal! 2, Hitchhikers Guide to the Galaxy*

Tom Conroy

email tomasconroy@yahoo.com

Credits include: *Breakfast on Pluto, East is East, Intermission*

Carlos Conti

c/o Casarotto Marsh Ltd, Waverley House,
7–12 Noel Street, London W1F 8GQ
tel 020-7287 4450 *fax* 020-7287 5644
email casarottomarsh@casarotto.co.uk
website www.casarotto.co.uk

Credits include: *Motorcycle Diaries, The Golden Door*

Stuart Craig
email stuart.craig@mac.com

Credits include: *Harry Potter and the Philosopher's Stone, Notting Hill, The English Patient*

Emma de Polnay
email emma.depolnay@virgin.net

Laurence Dorman
c/o McKinney Macartney Management,
The Barley Mow Centre, 10 Barley Mow Passage,
London W4 4PH
tel 020-8995 4747 *fax* 020-8995 2414
email mail@mckinneymacartney.com

Credits include: *Asylum, Goal, Young Adam*

Nicholas Ellis
tel 020-8892 0334 *mobile* (07831) 668397
fax 020-8891 6909
email nick@nellis.demon.co.uk

Credits include: *Bend It Like Beckham, Bride and Prejudice, Killing Joe*

Philip Elton
tel 020-8959 2359 *mobile* (07710) 458493
fax 020-8959 2359
email phile333@aol.com

Credits include: *Bourne Supremacy, Event Horizon, Flyboys*

Ricky Eyres
mobile (07980) 606424
email reyres@aol.com

Credits include: *Farscape, Saving Private Ryan, Stormbreaker*

John Fenner
tel (01628) 523000 *mobile* (07850) 641889
fax (01628) 523000
email john@fenner.wanadoo.co.uk

Credits include: *Stormbreaker, Phantom of the Opera, The Talented Mr Ripley, Tomb Raider II*

Richard Field
tel (01728) 663347 *mobile* (07767) 684825
fax (01728) 664094
email richardafield33@yahoo.co.uk

Credits include: *Imagine Me & You, Wah-Wah*

Paul Ghirardani
tel 020-7624 4230 *mobile* (07713) 074702
email paul.ghirardani@virgin.net

Credits include: *Being Julia, Gathering Storm, Mrs Henderson Presents*

Sarah Greenwood
c/o ICM, Oxford House, 76 Oxford Street, London, W1D 1BS
tel 020-7636 6565

Credits include: *Pride & Prejudice, Starter for Ten, This Year's Love*

Tony Halton
tel (01400) 230099 *fax* (07831) 113936
email tony.halton@virgin.net

Credits include: *I'll Sleep When I'm Dead, Spy Game, Wimbledon*

Luana Hanson
c/o Casarotto Marsh, Waverley House,
7–12 Noel Street, London W1F 8GQ

Credits include: *Life 'n' Lyrics, Nathan Barley, Saltwater*

Guy Hendrix Dyas
email info@guyhendrixdyas.com
website www.guyhendrixdyas.com

Credits include: *Elizabeth: The Golden Age, Superman Returns, The Brothers Grimm*

John Henson
c/o Casarotto Marsh Ltd, Waverley House,
7–12 Noel Street, London W1F 8GQ
tel 020-7287 4450 *fax* 020-7287 5644
email casarottomarsh@casarotto.co.uk
website www.casarotto.co.uk

Credits include: *Brothers of the Head, Wind in the Willows*

Richard Holland
c/o Screen Talent Agency, 58 Speed House, Barbican, London EC2Y 8AT
email screentalentagency@yahoo.com

Credits include: *Agent Cody Banks - II, End of Days, The Santa Clause 3*

Rebecca Holmes
email rebeccahindle@uk2.net

Credits include: *Dirty Pretty Things, Friends and Crocodiles, Gideon's Daughter*

Marc Homes
mobile (07850) 726851
email mh003g9907@blueyonder.co.uk

Credits include: *Alfie, Sahara, V for Vendetta*

Grenville Horner
c/o Casarotto Marsh Ltd, Waverley House,
7–12 Noel Street, London W1F 8GQ
tel 020-7287 4450 *fax* 020-7287 5644
email casarottomarsh@casarotto.co.uk
website www.casarotto.co.uk

Credits include: *Alien Autopsy, Jane Eyre*

Michael Howells
c/o Casarotto Marsh Ltd, Waverley House,
7–12 Noel Street, London W1F 8GQ

tel 020-7287 4450 *fax* 020-7287 5644
email casarottomarsh@casarotto.co.uk
website www.casarotto.co.uk

Credits include: *Bright Young Things, Nanny Mcphee, Sixty Six*

Paul Inglis

mobile (07966) 275014
email paulinglis@mac.com

Credits include: *Basic Instinct 2: Risk Addiction, Bridget Jones: The Edge of Reason, The Children of Men*

John-Paul Kelly

email jpk@johnpaulkelly.com
website www.johnpaulkelly.com

Credits include: *Cock & Bull Story, Lassie, Venus*

Jennifer Kernke

(07956) 506411
email jkernke@macunlimited.net

Credits include: *Dear Frankie, In My Father's Den, Institute Benjamenta*

Neil Lamont

tel 020-8674 2924 *mobile* (07850) 451991
fax 020-8674 2926
email nrlamont@btopenworld.com

Credits include: *Enemy at the Gates, Harry Potter and the Order of the Phoenix, The World Is Not Enough*

James Lewis

tel (01753) 862240 *fax* (07710) 410755
email mail@jameslewisdesign.com
website www.jameslewisdesign.com

Credits include: *Alexander, Charlie and the Chocolate Factory*

Hugo Luczyc-Wyhowski

email h.wyhowski@btinternet.com

Credits include: *Dirty Pretty Things, Mrs Henderson Presents, The Martian Child*

Giles Masters

tel (01932) 867513 *mobile* (07710) 762483
email gilesmast@aol.com

Credits include: *The Da Vinci Code, The Mummy, Van Helsing*

Andrew McAlpine

email andrewmca@compuserve.com

Credits include: *Aeon Flux, Clockers, The Piano*

Amanda McArthur

tel 020-8960 3448 *mobile* (07831) 88941
fax 020-8960 3448
email Mcarthur6@hotmail.com

Credits include: *Crush, Piccadilly Jim, Susie Gold*

Stephen Morahan

mobile (07944) 606112
email steve@filmdesign.co.uk

Credits include: *Batman Begins, Sunshine, Thunderbirds*

Andrew Munro

Dench Arnold Agency, 10 Newburgh Street, London W1F 7RN
tel 020 7437 4551 *mobile* (07831) 833328

Credits: *Breakfast on Pluto, Gormenghast, Mansfield Park*

Alice Normington

Dench Arnold Agency, 10 Newburgh Street, London W1F 7RN
tel 020 7437 4551

Credits include: *Hilary and Jackie, Miranda, Proof*

Kevin Phipps

tel/fax (01932) 730003
mobile (07885) 478647
email kevinmphipps@aol.com

Credits include: *Blood & Chocolate, Charlie and the Chocolate Factory, V for Vendetta*

Kave Quinn

c/o Casarotto Marsh Ltd, Waverley House, 7–12 Noel Street, London W1F 8GQ
tel 020-7287 4450 *fax* 020-7287 5644
email casarottomarsh@casarotto.co.uk
website www.casarotto.co.uk

Credits include: *Restraint of Beasts, Layer Cake, Trainspotting*

Mark Raggett

tel 020-8960 7306 *mobile* (07889) 441225
fax 020-8964 2335
email markragget@aol.com

Credits include: *Calendar Girls, Closer, Shakespeare In Love*

Crispian Sallis

Creative Media Management, 3b Walpole Court, Ealing Studios, London W5 5ED
tel 020-8584 5363

Credits include: *Colour Me Kubrick, Keeping Mum, Trauma*

John Stevenson

c/o Casarotto Marsh Ltd, Waverley House, 7–12 Noel Street, London W1F 8GQ
tel 020-7287 4450 *fax* 020-7287 5644
email casarottomarsh@casarotto.co.uk
website www.casarotto.co.uk

Credits include: *My Summer of Love, Tomorrow La Scala!*

Eve Stewart

ICM, 4-6 Soho Square, London, W1D 3PZ
tel 020-7432 0800

Credits include: *De Lovely, Revolver, Vera Drake.*

Mark Tanner

email mail@yellowinc.co.uk

Production designer and art director whose credits include *Paranoid, Waking Ned* and *The Clandestine Marriage.*

Andy Thomson

tel/fax (01436) 678007
mobile (07712) 674205
email thomsonandy@mac.com

Credits include: *Hitchhikers' Guide to the Galaxy, The Brothers Grimm, The Golden Age*

Malcolm Thornton

ICM, 4-6 Soho Square, London, W1D 3PZ
tel 020-7432 0800
email thomsonandy@mac.com

Credits include: *Fingersmith, The Long Firm, Derailed*

Karen Wakefield

tel/fax 020-7978 1389
mobile (07831) 669889
email wakefield@mywebspace.co.uk

Credits include: *Munich, Shaun of the Dead, What a Girl Wants*

Justin Warburton-Brown

tel 020-7326 4930 *mobile* (07973) 854665
email jbrown9483@aol.com

Credits include: *Alien vs Predator, Love Actually, Reign of Fire*

Peter Wenham

tel 020-8940 5650 *mobile* (07860) 480293
email peterwenham@hotmail.com

Credits include: *Agent Cody Banks II, Blood Diamonds, The Bourne Supremacy*

Lynne Whiteread

Dench Arnold Agency, 10 Newburgh Street, London W1F 7RN
tel 020 7437 4551

Credits include: *Second Generation, Stella Does Tricks, The Lawless Heart*

Fleur Whitlock

tel/fax 020-8948 0016
fax (07831) 415780
email fleur_whitlock@yahoo.co.uk

Credits include: *Heidi, The Libertine, The Return of Sherlock Holmes*

Charles Wood

c/o Casarotto Marsh Ltd, Waverley House, 7–12 Noel Street, London W1F 8GQ
tel 020-7287 4450 *fax* 020-7287 5644
email casarottomarsh@casarotto.co.uk
website www.casarotto.co.uk

Credits include: *Amazing Grace, The Italian Job*

Production hire

EQUIPMENT

Acorn Film & Video
13 Fitzwilliam St, Belfast, Co Antrim BT9 6AW
tel 028-9024 0977 *fax* 028-9022 2309
email info@acorntv.com
website www.acorntv.com
Managing Director Roger Fitzpatrick

One of the longest-running facilities houses in Northern Ireland, specialising in crewing and post-production. Only HD provider in the Northern Ireland.

Aerial Camera Systems
Innovation House, Douglas Drive, Godalming, Surrey, Middlesex GU7 1JX
tel (01483) 426767 *fax* (01483) 413900
email info@aerialcamerasystems.com
website www.aerialcamerasystems.com
Managing Director & Finance Director Philip Beckett

Established in 1979 to provide aerial cinematographic equipment to the film and television industries. Equipment includes helicopters, cranes and remotes.

AFL Television Facilities
Unit 5, 181a Verulam Road, St Albans AL3 4DR
tel (01727) 844117 *fax* (01727) 847649
email facilities@afltv.com
website www.afltv.com

Established in 1986, AFL provides a range of video, audio and lighting and associated crew services primarily to broadcast and corporate clients.

Aimimage Camera Company
Unit 5, St Pancras Commercial Centre, 63 Pratt Street, London NW1 0BY
tel 020-7482 4340 *fax* 020-7267 3972
website www.aimimage.com

Aimimage has a full range of camera (film and video) facilities and technical expertise for hire. The company also runs The Camden Studio, which is a fully soundproofed, air-conditioned stage with green room, make-up and production offices, and a crewing service which works across all genres.

Alpha Grip
The Matte Stage, Pinewood Studios, Iver Heath, Iver, Buckinghamshire SL0 0NH
tel (01753) 656886 *fax* (01753) 656950
email eugene@alphagrip.co.uk
website www.alphagrip.co.uk

A new company with the latest grip and crane technology. Specialises in providing all gripping needs.

ARRI Lighting Rental
4 Highbridge, Oxford Road, Uxbridge, Middlesex UB8 1LX
tel (01895) 457200 *fax* (01895) 457201
email sales@arrirental.com
website www.arri.com

Equipment includes: daylight, tungsten and fluorescent; stands, clamps and accessories; flags; nets, butterflies; lighting controls and dimmers; cable & distribution; consumables and expendables; trucks and generators.

ARRI Media
3 Highbridge, Oxford Rd, Uxbridge, Middlesex UB8 1LX
tel (01895) 457100 *fax* (01895) 457101
email info@arrimedia.com
website www.arrimedia.com www.arricrew.com

Major camera and grip equipment rental facility established in 1991. Has an extensive range of equipment for hire, including 35mm, 16mm, HD, digital video, grip and cranes, as well as providing consumables and a digital transfer service. ARRI Media also runs a diary service, ARRI Crew, which represents freelance technicians and crew within the film and TV industries. Can deliver to location.

Associated Press Television News
The Interchange, Oval Road, Camden Lock, London NW1 7NU
tel 020-7482 7400 *fax* 020-7413 8311
email aptninfo@ap.org
website www.aptn.com

Audiohire
The Old Dairy, 133-137 Kilburn Lane, London W10 4AN
tel 020-8960 4466 *fax* 020-8964 0343
email admin@audiohire.co.uk
website www.audiohire.co.uk

All audio equipment rental for live music, and equipment for band performances.

Awfully Nice Video Company Limited
30 Long Lane, Ickenham, London UB10 8TA
tel (07000) 345678 *fax* (07000) 345679
email nicevideo@aol.com
website www.awfullynicevideo.com

Established in 1987. Provides wet and dry hire of lighting and camera equipment, as well as production services. Credits include: a range of commercials for British Airways, Littlewoods and Vidal Sassoon, as well as broadcast productions for BBC and ITV.

Axis Glasgow
64-68 Brand St, Glasgow, Lanarkshire G51 1DW
tel 0141-427 9944 *fax* 0141-427 1199

email glasgow@axisfilms.co.uk
website www.axisfilms.co.uk
Manager Mark Thomas

Film and tape production equipment rental – from 35mm to Hi-Def and Mini DV. Also has facilities for HD editing. Axis can recommend freelance technicians for running equipment.

Axis Leeds

Suite 7.3, Joseph's Well Building, Hanover Walk, Leeds, West Yorkshire LS3 1AB
tel 0113-380 4862 *fax* 0113-380 4863
email leeds@axisfilms.co.uk
website www.axisfilms.co.uk
Leeds Office Manager Amartage Barn

Offices in London and Glasgow. Film and tape production equipment rental – from 35mm to Hi-Def and Mini DV. Axis can also recommend freelance technicians for running equipment.

Beat About The Bush

Unit 23, Enterprise Way, Triangle Business Centre, Salter St, London NW10 6UG
tel 020-8960 2087 *fax* 020-8969 2281
email info@beataboutthebush.com
website www.beataboutthebush.com

Specialists in musical instruments and equipment from vintage to modern day for hire.

Bristol Batteries Ltd

3 Dove Lane, Off Newfoundland Rd, Bristol BS2 9HP
tel 0117-955 0536 *fax* 0117-935 1791
email sales@bristolbatteries.com
website www.bristolbatteries.com

Specialist in battery supply of all types.

Broadcast RF Ltd

Unit 16, Acorn Industrial Park, Crayford Road, Dartford DA1 4AL
tel (01322) 520202 *fax* (01322) 520204
email hire@broadcastrf.com
website www.broadcastrf.com
Sales Manager Chris Brandrick

Established in 1998. Europe's leading source of digital and analogue RF systems, microwave links and radio cameras for hire to the film and television industries. Can also provide technical engineers for projects. Will deliver to location.

Camera Revolution Ltd

Building 37d, Shepperton Studios, Studios Rd, Shepperton, Middlesex TW17 0QD
tel (01932) 592322 *fax* (01932) 592202
email mail@camerarevolution.com
website www.camerarevolution.com

For the last 12 years, Camera Revolution has specialised in remote camera applications for features and commercials. Also supplies mini 35mm cameras and VistaVision cameras for VFX. Systems include: Libra stabilised remote, mega remote, Mancam camera systems and Flying wire systems – the company can provide specialist technicians to operate all of these. Credits include: the Harry Potter and Bond series.

Central Rental Ltd

Basement, 28 Newman Street, London W1T 1PR
tel 020-7631 4455 *fax* 020-7631 3400
email hire@centralrental.co.uk
website www.centralrental.co.uk

Cinebuild

Studio House, Rita Road, Vauxhall, London SW8 1JU
tel 020-7582 8750 *fax* 020-7793 0467
email cinebuild@btclick.com
website www.cinebuild.com

Provides lighting and effects.

The Cruet Company

11 Ferrier Street, London SW18 1SN
tel 020-8874 2121 *fax* 020-8874 9850
email info@cruet.com
website w www.cruet.com

Cruet have a good selection of digital cameras and kit with dry or wet hire.

Edric Audio-Visual Hire

34-36 Oak End Way, Gerrards Cross, Bucks SL9 8BR
tel (01753) 481 400 *fax* (01753) 887 163
website www.edric-av.co.uk

Projectors, conference AV hire and production.

Elstree Light and Power

Millennium Studios, Elstree Way, Borehamwood, Herts WD6 1SF
tel 020-8236 1300 *fax* 020-8236 1333
email elp@elstree-online.co.uk
website www.elstree-online.co.uk

Eye Film and Television

Chamberlain House, 2 Dove Street, Norwich NR2 1DE
tel (01603) 762 551 *fax* (01603) 762 420
email production@eyefilmandtv.co.uk
website www.eyefilmandtv.co.uk

Faction Films

26 Shacklewell Lane, London E8 2EZ
tel 020-7690 4446 *fax* 020-76904447
email faction@factionfilms.co.uk
website www.factionfilms.co.uk

Two AVID suites for dry or wet hire.

FinePoint Broadcast

Hill House, Furze Hill, Kingswood, Surrey KT20 6EZ
tel 0800-970 2020 *fax* 0800-970 2030
email hire@finepoint.co.uk
website www.finepoint.co.uk

Specialist in the dry hire of broadcast television equipment.

Fish Eye Productions

Unit 5, Vanguard Trading Estate, Britannia Road, Chesterfield S40 2TZ
tel (01246) 216016 *fax* (01246) 563785
email steve@fep.co.uk
website www.fep.co.uk

Specialises in Light and Motion underwater video, digital stills and lighting equipment.

Four Corners

121 Roman Road, Bethnal Green, London E2 OQN
tel 020-8981 6111 *fax* 020 8983 7866
email info@fourcornersfilm.co.uk
website www.fourcornersfilm.co.uk

Great location for hiring film cameras. They have Arri Super 16mm and 16mm, and Bolexes plus flat bed editing equipment as well as sound and lighting equipment.

Fuel Film & Television Ltd

30 Kingsfield Road, Oxhey, Watford WD19 4PS
tel (01923) 233956 *fax* (01923) 224289
email allen@fuelfilm.com
website www.fuelfilm.com
Owner Allen Della-Valle

A one-stop hire company with 16mm and video kits for hire in a package that includes camera, lights, sound, grips and transportation at reasonable rates. Can also provide crew at an additional cost.

FX Rentals Ltd

38-40 Telford Way, London W3 7XS
tel 020-8746 2121 *fax* 020-8746 4100
email nickharris@fxgroup.net
website www.fxgroup.net

Established in 1992. Offers a range of audio equipment, PA, instruments, studio and AV gear, backline, recorders, microphones, video and location equipment – all available 24 hours a day. Supplies to both film and television. Can deliver to all locations. Also available for hire: ProtoolsHD; Pyramix; Vcube; RadarV; Lexicon; TC; Cedar. 24-hour technical support available. Clients: the LOTR trilogy; the Harry Potter films; *Charlie and the Chocolate Factory*.

GB Audio

Unit D, 51 Brunswick Rd, Edinburgh EH7 5PD
tel 0131-661 0022
email hire@gbaudio.co.uk
website www.gbaudio.co.uk

Established in 1983 for sound equipment sales and rental, and sound system design. Hire equipment includes audio, recording, PA systems, radio mics, intercom and recording media. Can also provide sound operators and technicians.

Gearhouse Broadcast Ltd

Unit 12 Imperial Park, Imperial Way, Watford, Hertfordshire WD24 4PP
tel 0845-8200 0000 *fax* (01923) 691499
email uk@gearhousebroadcast.com
website www.gearhousebroadcast.com

Gearhouse Broadcast is a leading international broadcast services company with offices located in the UK, Australia and the USA. Provides a comprehensive range of broadcast solutions including Broadcast Sales, Broadcast Rental, Project Solutions, Outside Broadcast Solutions and Systems Integration.

Glasgow Media Access Centre (GMAC)

3rd Floor, 34 Albion Street, Glasgow G1 1LH
tel 0141-553 2620 *fax* 0141-553 2660
website www.g-mac.co.uk

Scotland's longest-running open-access facility for young filmmakers, providing training, information and facilities hire as well as running 2 short film production initiatives (see page 74 for further details of funding schemes). Offers hire of film and video equipment to members at income-related prices. Facilities and equipment include lights, sound recording equipment, post-production editing facilities, projectors, film and digital video cameras and studio space.

Hammerhead Television Facilities Ltd.

Unit 19, Liongate Enterprise Park, 80 Morden Road, Surrey CR4 4DA
tel 020-8646 5511 *fax* 020-8646 6163
website www.hammerheadtv.com

Carries one of the largest ranges of broadcast video cameras in the UK. The company provides kit hire (video only) and can also supply crew. Offices are in London, Manchester, Edinburgh and Glasgow; also operates on a nationwide basis, offering hire and 24-hour, 7-days-a-week technical support and back-up to clients.

Hammerhead TV – Edinburgh

9 Merchiston Mews, Edinburgh EH10 4PE
tel 0131-229 5000 *fax* 0131-229 2831
email scotland@hammerheadtv.com
website www.hammerheadtv.com

– see entry under Hammerhead Television Facilities Ltd.

Holloway Film TV

68-70 Wardour Street, London W1V 3HP
tel 020-7494 0777 *fax* 020-7494 0309
website www.hollowayfilm.co.uk

Offers DVD/CD encoding, authoring and duplication; also conversion services and AVID facilities.

Kitroom Monkey Ltd

Ealing Film Studios, Ealing Green, London W5 5EP
tel 0845-166 2597
email mail@kitroommonkey.co.uk
website www.kitroommonkey.co.uk

Established in 2000, Kitroom Monkey offers documentary kits to freelance cameramen and production companies primarily for broadcast productions. Hires HD, Digibeta, Dvcam, DV, Minicam, lights, grips and sound equipment; also provides self-shooting DV operators, camera and sound technicians.

The company offers training in camera, sound and lighting.

Lee Film & TV Hire

Unit 32 Sheraton Business Centre,
20 Wadsworth Road, Perivale, London UB6 7JB
tel 020-8998 9977 *fax* 020-8998 2781
email info@leefilmhire.co.uk
website www.leefilmhire.co.uk

Lee Lighting Ltd

Wycombe Road, Wembley, Middlesex HA0 1QD
tel 020-8900 2900 *fax* 020-8902 5500
email info@lee.co.uk
website www.lee.co.uk

Lee has more than 40 years of experience providing lighting hire and service to the film industry. Facilities include a sound stage with production offices, and on-set catering.

Skarda International Communications

(The Miniature Camera Company)
7 Portland Mews, D'Arblay Street, London W1F 8JQ
tel 020-7734 7776 *fax* 020-7734 1360
email sales@skarda.net
website www.skarda.net

Skarda provides radio communications, sound recording and DV camera equipment to the film and TV industries. Also hires minature cameras and underwater kit housing systems.

Panavision

Metropolitan Centre, Bristol Road, Greenford, Middlesex UB6 8UQ
tel 020-8839 7333 *fax* 020-8578 1536
email enquiries@panavision.co.uk
website www.panavision.co.uk
Managing Director Mark Fussedonn

All camera quipment, tracks and cranes. Offices in London, Manchester and Ireland.

Panavision Manchester

Unit 3, Littlers Point, The Village, Trafford Park, Manchester M17 1LT
tel 0161-872 4766 *fax* 0161-872 6637
email mike.heaney@panavision.co.uk
website www.panavision.co.uk

ProVision

96 Kirkstall Road, Leeds LS3 1HD
tel 0113-222 8222 *fax* 0113-222 8110
email provision@granadamedia.com
website www.provisionequipment.tv

Supplies camera, lighting, grip and sound equipment to the film and TV industries. Kit list includes 16mm and many video formats.

Purple Crew

The Pie Factory, 101 Broadway, Salford Quays, Manchester M50 2EQ
tel 0161-380 0075
email ferdia@purplecrew.com OR kay.crewdson@purplecrew.com
website www.purplecrew.com
Crew and Equipment Co-ordinator Kay Crewdson

Established in 1998, Purplecrew primarily provides professional and reliable camera crews and equipment rental for film and television. Based in Manchester, but can supply for all of the UK. Equipment includes: all popular video plus HDCAM, 16mm and 35mm plus an extensive range of lights. Can also provide sound and electrical crew.

Richmond Film Services

The Old School, Park Lane, Richmond, Surrey TW9 2RA
tel 020-8940 6077 *fax* 020-8948 8326
email bookings@richmondfilmservices.co.uk
website www.richmondfilmservices.co.uk
Technical Director Nigel Woodford

Established for more than 30 years, RFS supplies sound equipment on hire to the film, television, recording and radio industries. Large range of sound equipment, from amps and speakers to effects, samplers, mics and recording devices, both analogue and digital.

Sheffield Independent Film

5 Brown Street, Sheffield S1 2BS
tel 0114-272 0304 *fax* 0114-279 5225
email admin.sif@workstation.org.uk
website www.sheffieldindependentfilm.co.uk

Services include workspace, studios, post-production facilities and equipment hire.

Wall to Wall Communications

Danbury Lodge, 14 Danbury Mews, Wallington, Surrey SM6 0BY
tel 020-8647 4758 *fax* 020-8669 1338
email hire@walltowallcomms.co.uk
website www.walltowallcomms.co.uk

Sales, service and hire of 2-way radio communications systems and walkie-talkies, and associated props. Also provides answerphone, fax, copiers, etc.

The Warehouse Sound Services

23 Water Street, Leith, Edinburgh EH6 6SU
tel 0131-555 6900 *fax* 0131-555 6901
website www.warehousesound.co.uk

Established more than 25 years ago, providing a full range of sound and communication equipment and technical personnel (sound supervisors, sound mixers, sound assistants). Location delivery available.

Widescreen Ltd

The Garth, Barnet Lane, Elstree, Borehamwood, Hertfordshire WD6 3HJ
tel 020-8953 5190 *fax* 020-8236 0553
email info@widescreen.uk.com
website www.widescreen.uk.com

Supplies crews and epuipment for the broadcast industry.

STUDIOS AND LOCATIONS

Black Island Studios

Alliance Road, London W3 0RA
tel 020-8956 5600 *fax* 020-8956 5604
email info@islandstudios.net
website www.islandstudios.net

Central London's largest film and television studio complex with 6 stages, including drive-in access, cycs, motion control rigs, lighting facilities and on-site catering.

Capital Studios

13 Wandsworth Plain, London SW18 1ET
tel 020-8877 1234 *fax* 020-8877 0234
website www.capitalstudios.com

An independent facilites house that has been servicing broadcasters and independent television for more than 20 years.

Classic T Stage

Classic Media Group, Shepperton Film Studios, Studios Road, Shepperton TW17 0QD
tel (01932) 592016
email T-stage@classic-media-group.com
website www.classicpictures.co.uk

Classic T Stage is Classic Media Group's film stage and recording studios based at Shepperton Studios, and offering high quality, fully equipped multi-camera and sound recording stage under one roof. Hire is available for complete facilities and equipment, or as stage only. Sound, production and post-production services are also available.

Dukes Island Studios

Dukes Road, Western Avenue, London W3 OSL
tel 020-8956 5600 *fax* 020-8956 5604
email info@islandstudios.net
website www.islandstudios.net

A West London-based studio complex offering 3 stages, all with excellent facilities including drive-in access, cycs, motion control rigs, lighting facilities and on-site catering.

Ealing Studios

Ealing Studios, Ealing Green, London W5 5EP
tel 020-8567 6655 *fax* 020-8758 8658
email john.abbott@ealingstudios.com
website www.ealingstudios.com

These famous old studios were purchased in 2000 and have been redeveloped into state-of-the-art-digital facilities with 6 stages, offices and support and catering facilities. Part-owner Fragile Films is based at the studios (see page 137).

Edinburgh Film & TV Studios

Nine Mile Burn, Penicuik EH26 9LT
tel (01968) 672131 *fax* (01968) 672685

Greenford Studios

Metropolitan Centre, Bristol Road, Greenford, Middlesex UB6 8UQ
tel 020-8839 7333 *fax* 020-8578 1536
email enquiries@panavision.co.uk
website www.panavision.co.uk

Greenford Studios is a 4-stage complex situated on the same estate as Panavision London and Panavision Grips Greenford – less than 10 miles from London's West End (also see page 184). All stages have lighting, production offices, construction and catering.

The Hospital

24 Endell Street, London WC2H 9HQ
tel 020-7170 9110 *fax* 020-7170 9101
email studio@thehospital.com
website www.thehospital.dreamhost.com//studio

Studio facilities based in central London, occupying 2 floors of The Hospital's enormous home. Facilities are multi-camera, high definition and with chroma key blue drapes set up for high-end television and event production.

Pinewood Shepperton Group

Pinewood Road, Iver Heath, Bucks SL0 0NH
tel (01753) 656844 *fax* (01753) 651700
email info@pinewoodshepperton.com
website www.pinewoodshepperton.com

Pinewood Shepperton's facilities are used for major national and international film production, filmed television, studio television recording, the filming of commercials and post-production sound services. The group consists of Pinewood Studios, Shepperton Studios and Teddington Studios. Sites have 41 stages, including 6 digital TV studios, audio post facilities, preview theatres, backlots, gardens and woodland for outdoor shooting, one of Europe's largest exterior water tanks, a new dedicated underwater stage, and full production support services at all sites.

Twickenham Film Studios

The Barons, St Margaret's, Twickenham, Middlesex TW1 2AW
tel 020-8607 8888 *fax* 020-8607 8889
email caroline@twickenhamstudios.com
website www.twickenhamstudios.com

Comprehensive film and television production and post-production facilities, including shooting stages, sound stages, recording stages, dubbing theatres and ADR recording/effects theatre.

PROPS AND COSTUMES

Academy Costumes Ltd

50 Rushworth Street, London SE1 0RB
tel 020-7620 0771 *fax* 020-7928 6287
email info@academycostumes.com
website www.academycostumes.com

Established in 1984 by Adrian Gwillym. Covers all aspects of costume realisation, from design, cutting and making, to rental from its stock of 20th-century vintage clothing, costume and accessories.

Allprops Ltd

Unit 2/3, Acton Central Estate, 2a Rosemont Rd, Acton, London W3 9LR
tel 020-8993 1625 *fax* 020-8993 7570
email allprops1@btconnect.com
Director Peter Benson

Established in 1984, to hire a variety of small props to the film and TV industries. Contact by phone or email for details.

Angels The Costumiers

1 Garrick Road, London NW9 6AA
tel 020-8202 2244 *fax* 020-8202 1820
email angels@angels.uk.com
website www.angels.uk.com

Founded in 1840, Angels is the largest costumiers in the world. Its costume collection covers all periods from prehistoric to modern; the company also makes costumes with full attention to historical accuracy.

BBC Costume & Wigs

Victoria Road, London W3 6WL
tel 020-8576 1761 *fax* 020-8993 7040
email costume@bbc.co.uk, wigs@bbc.co.uk
website www.bbcresources.com/costumewig

Provides consultancy services and hire of costumes and wigs to film and TV companies (both BBC and non-BBC clients). Has a stock of more than a million costumes, wigs and hair pieces relevant to different periods of time, styles, fashions, ages and characters. Can also assist with construction and/or styling of costumes and wigs, and offer consultation and advice as well as links to freelance designers appropriate to a project's budget and style.

Recent credits include: *Munich*, *Charlie and the Chocolate Factory*, *Pride and Prejudice*.

Costume Studio Ltd

Montgomery House, 159-161 Balls Pond Rd, Islington, London N1 4BG
tel 020-7275 9614 *fax* 020-7923 9065
email costume.studio@btconnect.com
website www.costumestudios.co.uk

Hire, design and manufacture of costumes of all periods. Can also provide stylists and dressers.

The Devils Horsemen

The Wychwood Stud, Salden, Mursley, Milton Keynes, Buckinghamshire MK17 0HX
tel (01296) 720854 *fax* (01296) 720855
email info@thedevilshorsemen.com
website www.thedevilshorsemen.com

Equity stunt arranger and horse master for film and television. Credits include: *Batman Begins*, *Black Beauty*, *Elizabeth I*, and *The Da Vinci Code*.

Dressing Up Box

PO Box 360, Bristol BS34 8ZD
tel 0870-207 1423 *fax* (01454) 854451
email kev@dressingupbox.com
website www.dressingupbox.com

Flints Theatrical Chandlers

Queens Row, London SE17 2PX
tel 020-7703 9786 *fax* 020-7708 4189
email sales@flints.co.uk
website www.flints.co.uk
Director Alasdair Flint

Established 25 years ago to supply the film, TV, opera and theatre industries with backstage hardware. Can supply rigging, hardware, fixings, paint, texture, propmakers' materials (for sale), staging, weights and braces. Order online or request 190-page catalogue.

Graham Sweet Studios

5 Dock Chambers, Bute Street, Cardiff CF10 5AG
tel 029-2052 2510 *fax* 029-2052 2459
email sales@grahamsweet.com
website www.grahamsweet.com

Produces technical and machine-cut custom polystyrene shapes, which can be used for set design.

House of Haynes Fancy Dress Hire

1st Floor, 32 Oldham Street, Northern Quarter, Manchester M1 1JN
tel 0161-237 3775
email houseofhaynes@supanet.com
website www.houseofhaynes.co.uk

Thousands of costumes, wigs, teeth and accessories.

Jim Laws Lighting

West End Lodge, Wrentham, Beccles, Suffolk NR34 7NH
tel (01502) 675264 *fax* (01502) 675565
email jimlawslighting@btconnect.com

Established in 1986. Provides period entertainment lighting and small backstage props. Consultants on historical theatre settings, with particular speciality in backstage production lighting for period TV, film and theatre. Can provide riggers and dressers. Also provides lectures on lighting history.

Credits include: *Mrs Henderson Presents*, *Topsy Turvy*, and *Tipping the Velvet*, *Death Defying Acts*.

Lesters TV & Film Services

Land End Road, Sands, High Wycombe,
Buckinghamshire HP12 4HG
tel (01494) 448689 *fax* (01494) 527552
email info@lesterstvandfilm.com
website www.lesterstvandfilm.com

Provides transport of film sets, props and associated equipment anywhere within the UK, with labour force. Has comprehensive range of plant, machinery and transport for moving earth, landscaping and set construction; can also provide props.

Credits include: the Harry Potter films; *Shackleton*.

Lewis & Kaye (Hire) Ltd

3b Brassie Avenue, London W3 7DE
tel 020-8749 2121 *fax* 020-8749 9455
email props@lewisandkaye.eclipse.co.uk
website www.lewisandkaye.co.uk

Established in 1949. Specialists in silver and silver plate, glass and crystal (large stocks of complete dinner services), pewter, china and realistic copies of historic pieces, jewellery, bronzes and art. Props covering all periods.

Credits include: *Titanic*, *Pride & Prejudice*, and *Monarch of the Glen*.

Living Props Ltd

Sevenhills Road, Iver Heath, Iver,
Buckinghamshire SL0 0PA
tel (01895) 835100 *fax* (01895) 835757
email karen@livingprops.co.uk
website www.livingprops.co.uk

Hires plants, trees, shrubs, etc. for film, TV and events.

Mediscene Ltd

9 Croffets, Tadworth, Surrey KT20 5TX
tel (07973) 385654 *fax* (07977) 112152
email info@mediscene.co.uk
website www.mediscene.co.uk

Offers equipment hire for medical scenes in film and on TV, as well as on-set medical expertise.

Prop a Scene

Unit 256, 14 Tottenham Court Road,
London W1T 1JY
email info@propascene.com
website www.propascene.com

The website is a brilliant resource, providing a database of UK prop suppliers to the film and TV industries and a location database.

Prop Solutions

91a Acton Lane, Harlesden, London NW10 8UT
tel 020-8965 5152
email info@propsolutions.co.uk
website www.propsolutions.co.uk

Sources props, furininture and dressings for film and TV. The company can find exactly what you are looking for, and offers a delivery service. The website has a useful gallery.

The Prop Store of London

Great House Farm, Chenies, Rickmansworth,
Hertfordshire WD3 6EP
tel (01494) 766485 *fax* (01494) 766487
email info@propstore.co.uk
website www.propstore.co.uk

Primarily a consumer site, which stocks film and TV props for collectors.

Studio & TV Hire

3 Ariel Way, Wood Lane, White City,
London W12 7SL
tel 020-8740 3443 *fax* 020-8740 9662
website www.stvhire.com

STV has been in the business for more than 50 years, and stocks around 500,000 props from 1880 to present-day, available for hire for film, TV and theatre. The website includes a gallery of sample props.

Weird & Wonderful Prop Hire Ltd

Weird Ranch, PO Box 371, Potters Bar,
Hertfordshire EN6 3YT
tel (01707) 659 840 *fax* (01707) 661 599
email info@weirdandwonderful.com
website www.weirdandwonderful.com

Has a vast stock of unusual props for film and TV production, and model-making studios for bespoke prop creation. Excellent website allows user to browse collection by category.

STUNTS AND SPECIAL EFFECTS

124 Facilities

124 Horseferry Road, London SW1P 2TX
tel 020-7306 8040 *fax* 020-7306 8041
email 124facilities@channel4.co.uk
website www.124.co.uk

Part of the Channel 4 group; facilities include offline and online linear and non-linear editing equipment.

Any Effects

B2 Ockham Park Barns, Ockham, Woking,
Surrey GU23 6NG
tel (01483) 223222 *fax* (01483) 223233
email ben@anyeffects.com
website www.anyeffects.com

Provides physical special effects for the film, television and commercials industries, from rain crane and pyrotechnics to snow and shatterglass.

Asylum

20 Thornsett Road, Wandsworth, London SW18 4EF
tel 020-8871 2988 *fax* 020-8874 8186
email info@asylumsfx.com
website www.asylumsfx.com

Established for 20 years, Asylum has a reputation for world-class model making, animatronics and special effects for the film, commercials, music video and television industries.

Bickers Action

Ivy Farm Works, High Street, Coddenham, Ipswich, Suffolk IP6 9QX
tel (01449) 761300 *fax* (01449) 760614
email paulbickers@bickers.co.uk
website www.bickers.co.uk

Produces mechanical stunts for film and TV, and hires action props. Credits include: *Saving Private Ryan*, *Sleepy Hollow*, and *The World is not Enough*.

Bizarre Props

55 Moss Lane, Lydiate, Liverpool L31 4DB
tel 0151-520 1116
email info@bizarreprops.com
website www.bizarreprops.com

Bizarre has a range of props suitable for horror, fantasy and sci-fi productions; also runs a model-making service.

Display Electronics

29-35 Osborne Road, Thornton Heath, Surrey CR7 8PD
tel 020-8653 3333 *fax* 020-8653 8888
email admin@electroprops.co.uk
website www.electroprops.co.uk

Electronic prop hire with a wide variety of period and contemporary electronic props, such as military electronic items, fully working and practical credit card ATM machines, CCTV and security service machines, etc.

Enterprises Unlimited

Unit 10, Glen Industrial Estate, Essendine, Stamford, Lincolnshire PE9 4LE
tel (01780) 752166 *fax* (01780) 752167
email harry@snowboy.co.uk
website www.snowboy.co.uk

Physical special effects for the film and TV industries, including snow, rain, wind, smoke, pyrotechnics and fire effects.

Credits include: *Bridget Jones's Diary*, and *24 Hour Party People*.

Steve Griffin

mobile (07860) 711009
email info@stevegriffin.co.uk
website www.stevegriffin.co.uk

Hugely experienced stunt co-ordinator. Credits include: *Alfie*, *The Hitchhicker's Guide to the Galaxy*, and *Decameron*.

Hybrid Enterprises Ltd

41 Stock Road, Billericay, Essex CM12 0AR
tel 0113-217 1300 *fax* (01277) 654862
email studio@hybridfx.com
website www.hybridfx.com

Specialises in make-up design and prosthetic creation.

Image FX Ltd

Pinewood Studios, Pinewood Road, Iver, Buckinghamshire SL0 0NH
tel (01753) 656598 *fax* (01753) 630394
email keenbs@aol.com

Supplier of animatronics. Credits include: *Dog Soldiers*, and *Candyman*.

The London Stunt School

Old School Building, Sudbury Primary School, Watford Road, Wembley, Middlesex HA0 3EY
tel 020-8385 0884 *fax* 020-8385 1588
email info@londonstuntschool.com
website www.londonstuntschool.com
Head Coach & Director Alasdair Monteith

Established in 1997. Provides training for people entering into the stunt business; also supplies action extras for film, TV and theatre. Provides shoot stunt co-ordinators and performers, as well as safety equipment such as mats, pipe rams, weapons, body pads and fire safety equipment. Offers stunt training courses across a range of skills.

Makeup & SFX Company

55 Moss Lane, Lydiate, Liverpool L31 4DB
tel 0151-520 1116
email bryan@makeup-sfx.co.uk
website www.makeup-sfx.co.uk

Provides make-up, prosthetics, animatronics, model-making services and mechanical effects. Can also provide teaching workshops.

Millennium FX Ltd

Unit 9, Spring Field Road, Chesham, Buckinghamshire HP5 1PW
tel (01494) 775576 *fax* (01494) 775526
email info@millenniumfx.co.uk
website www.millenniumfx.co.uk

FX company working in animatronics, prosthetics, and special FX make-up for film and televsion. Also holds short courses in prosthetic creation and make-up as Neil Gorton Prosthetics Studio.

Credits include: *Dr Who*, and *Little Britain*.

Neil Corbould Special Effects Ltd

Pinewood Studios, Pinewood Road, Iver Heath, Iver, Buckinghamshire SL0 0NH
tel (01753) 656415 *fax* (01753) 656147
email ncorbould@aol.com
website www.neilcorbouldsfx.co.uk

Provides a full range of special effects to both the film and television industries, including animatronics, pyrotechnics, mechanical and electronic. Can also supply equipment and technicians. Credits include: *Superman Returns*, *Kingdom of Heaven*, *The Day After Tomorrow*, *King Arthur*, *Gladiator*, and *Saving Private Ryan*.

Screen Stunt Supplies Ltd

Stonepits Manor, Marringdean Road, Billinghurst, West Sussex RH14 9HE
tel (07000) 478868
email info@stuntsupplies.co.uk
website www.stuntsupplies.co.uk

Provides services covering all stunt needs for the film and TV industries, from equipment such as fire suits, air bag and trampolines to personnel. All equipment carries personal liability.

Special Effects GB Ltd

Shepperton Studios, Shepperton, Middlesex TW17 0QD
tel (01932) 592416 *fax* (01932) 592415
email sfxnealchamp@hotmail.com
website www.sfxgb.co.uk

Based at Shepperton Studios, Special Effects GB aims to supply special effects to meet any film and TV needs. Effects include large-scale pyrotechnic effects, models, soft props and gadgets to large-scale rain, snow and atmospheric effects, and stunts. Hires skilled technicians who can create any special effect required.

Special Effects (UK) Ltd

Pinewood Studios, Iver Heath, Buckingham, Buckinghamshire MK18 0NH
tel (01753) 650658 *fax* (01753) 650659
email info@specialeffectsuk.com
website www.specialeffectsuk.com

Special effects company based in Pinewood. Can provide most special-effects services: electronic models, pyrotechnics, animatronics, etc. Hire equipment includes smoke, rain, snow and wind machines, and water pumps.

The Stunt Company

78 Chandos Street, White Cross, Hereford, Herefordshire HR4 0EX
tel (07831) 571127
email tom@stunt.co.uk

Labs and stock

Bucks Laboratories Ltd

714 Banbury Avenue, Slough, Berks SL1 4LR
tel (01753) 501500 *fax* (01753) 691762
email mail@bucks.co.uk
website www.bucks.co.uk

Offers a range of services, from negative processing to bulk orders or film and trailer prints.

Deluxe Laboratories Ltd

North Orbital Road, Denham, Uxbridge, Middlesex UB9 5HQ
tel (01895) 823 323 *fax* (01895) 823 446
email Terry.lansbury@bydeluxe.com
website www.bydeluxe.com
Manager Terry Lansbury

Film and Photo Ltd

13 Colville Road, South Acton Industrial Estate, London W3 8BL
tel 020-8992 0037 *fax* 020-8993 2409
email info@film-photo.co.uk
website www.film-photo.co.uk

Film Lab North

96 Kirkstall Road, Leeds LS3 1HD
tel 0113-222 8333 *fax* 0113-222 8110
email hnd@filmlabnorth.co.uk
website www.filmlabnorth.tv
Operations Manager Howard Dawson

Sky Photographic Services Ltd

Ramilies House, Ramilies Street, London W1F 7AZ
tel 020-7434 2266 *fax* 020-7434 0828
website www.sky-photographic.co.uk

Soho Images

8-14 Meard Street, London W1V 3HR
tel 020-7437 0831 *fax* 020-7734 9471
email paul.jones@sohoimages.com
website www.sohoimages.com
Managing Director Paul Jones

Full-service film laboratory and digital post-production facility for the whole post process, from 24-hour film processing through to digital post. Lab is Kodak-endorsed and offers a complete range of Standard 35mm, Super 35mm, Standard 16mm and Super 16mm processing and printing.

Extensive post-production facilities include telecine and sound sync, edit suites, computerised negative cutting, digital post-production on Standard-Definition and High-Definition formats, Spirit DataCine, URSA Gold, and Avid Symphony Universal with 24P.

Technicolour Film Services

Bath Road, West Drayton, Middlesex UB7 0DB
tel 020-8759 5432 *fax* 020-8759 6270
website www.technicolor.com

Services include: 16mm/35mm processing, 35mm & 16mm B&W picture and sound negative processing, 70/35mm contact & optical printing, ENR processing, skip bleach processing, restoration services, optical sound transfers, standard & HD dailies, standard & HD mastering, DVD compression and authoring, audio mixing, sound restoration and audio laybacks, video online editing, mastering & duplication, 3D graphics and subtitling creation.

Todd-AO UK

13 Hawley Crescent, London NW1 8NP
tel 020-7284 7900 *fax* 020-7284 1018
email schedules@todd-ao.co.uk
website www.todd-ao.co.uk

Market leaders in 16mm processing. The company's team works 6 nights per week to deliver processed film by 9am. Lab processes super 8mm, 16mm & 35mm colour negative for telecine transfer & sound sync. Also provides a digital streaming service for rushes.

Post-production

Introduction to post-production

Larry Sider

"We'll save it in post!" is a favourite mantra of all filmmakers during the stress and confusion of shooting. Unable to take the time or money to solve a problem at that moment, they know there will be another chance – another time working with new people in a different location, when problems can be worked out calmly and creatively.

It is indeed valid to consider post-production as a time for solving all of the scriptwriting and shooting problems that have so far proved insuperable. But to treat the post-production stage of your film as nothing more than a time for remedial work is to short-change your production. 'Post' is a time for creativity; for taking the time to blend all of your material – the images, dialogue, atmospheres, sound effects, music, special visual effects – to carefully orchestrate these in a process that has been likened to cooking or even alchemy.

As with so many creative endeavours, the last stages of the process depend on the first. Cooking a dish or baking a cake relies on having a good recipe, choosing the best ingredients, following procedures accurately, and adding appropriate amounts of intuition and inspiration at the correct moment. The same is true of filmmaking. The development of your original idea, pre-production and shooting all influence post-production. Many of the departments involved in those stages also have a hand in post.

The main components of post-production are: picture editing, sound editing, sound mixing, music composition and recording, special visual effects, picture grading and printing,. These involve 'sub-components' like ADR and Foley recording, designing and filming titles and credit sequences, and preparing deliverables and foreign versions. While most of these can be considered stand-alone procedures, your film will benefit enormously if the artists and craftspeople working in post communicate with each other and with those working on the earlier stages of the film.

Picture editing

On most features, the editor is preparing the first – or editor's – cut during the shoot. This allows him/her to check continuity within scenes; to alert the director to any mistakes that can be corrected by re-shooting; to look for technical problems with camera or sound; and generally to get a sense of whether or not scenes are working.

Following the shoot, the edit will continue for an amount of time that is largely dependent on the film's budget, the amount of film shot, and the complexity of special effects, visual effects and CGI (computer-generated imagery) work. A low-budget film may have five or six weeks after the shoot to finish, or 'lock-off', the picture edit; for a high-budget feature it may be anything up to six months or a year. During this time the edit will go through a number of stages, each one further developing the film's narrative, pace and emotional arc. At each stage the director, editor, producer(s), funders and other members of the post-production team – such as Supervising Sound Editor, Composer, Special Effects or Visual Effects Supervisor and Post-Production Supervisor – may view the film.

Ideally, the film reaches a stage where the picture is finished or locked, when no further changes are made. However, digital technology, the increased reliance on audience research, and the amount of CGI work on high-end features means that the picture is often being edited and revised during the sound edit and into the sound mix.

CGI/visual effects is a perfect example of how planning and consultation in pre-production will affect post, with consequences for the film's budget. While CGI can be used for remedial work on images – removing film scratches, reframing, settling camera shake or taking out the distant trail of a passing jet in a period scene – it can also be used to create visual effects either too complicated or too expensive to achieve on location. Creating fantastic backdrops, impossible camera angles or shots too dangerous for ordinary actors has been the stock and trade of special effects since the advent of cinema. Now it can be done digitally rather than with paint, glass and the photo-chemical process. A special-effects specialist can advise you during the development or pre-production stages whether a particular effect can best be achieved through CGI – with possible savings in time and money – rather than physically during the shoot.

The final process is colour-grading the images and then making prints of the film. Grading involves correcting the colour and contrast for individual shots: essentially, this is the final stage of the cinematographic process, which will balance the colour to give an overall look to the film, enhancing its emotional tone. It involves the combined contributions of the director, cinematographer, editor and grader (or colourist).

Next comes the printing. The traditional process requires the original camera negative to be cut or 'conformed' to the final Avid edit by means of the EDL (Edit Decision List). The conformed negative is then printed onto positive stock. The Digital Intermediate (DI) process, however, is becoming more popular as an alternative to the conformed negative route. DI is the process whereby the entire post-production pipeline uses digital disk-based material, rather than the original negative, and copy prints or video tape. The rushes are telecined onto disk (either from negative, video or High Definition material), digitally graded, digitally edited and the visual effects, CGI and audio added digitally. The basic theory is that by keeping everything in the digital domain, there is less room for technical error and more flexibility for making changes to the material – both of which are essential considerations in post-production. The final stage of DI involves making a graded telecine, which is then scanned and transferred to negative. This is becoming the accepted method of making film prints for distribution for projects originating on video, as well as a money-saving way of making prints from film negative. Again, the point is to see how each method can benefit your project both in terms of quality and cost. Ask yourself, "Where will my film be projected? What quality do I need? How much can I spend?" Whatever you decide, it is advisable to firm up your post-production route in the planning and budgeting stages – in consultation with the cinematographer (and special effects supervisor, if applicable) because it will influence decisions on how you shoot and edit.

Sound

For many filmmakers, sound is the last part of post-production. It is not a concern until the end of editing, after the picture is finished, and can be considered largely a technical necessity – involving remedial work to mistakes in the dialogue (recording faults and performance) while brightening the overall sound of the film's world, giving it more detail and richness. This can be highly creative, highly technical, or a combination of both. I will discuss this in detail, but first will go through the various elements of sound post-production.

The number of people involved in 'sound post' can range from one to several dozen, again depending on the length and complexity of the film and the amount of money available to create the soundtrack. (On features, sound usually accounts for about 3 per cent of the budget.) Most features will employ a supervising sound editor, who in turn will create a team of dialogue editors, ADR editors, FX and atmos editors, Foley editors and sound designers.

The most basic part of the sound edit is taking the sound that has been used in the picture edit and preparing it for the sound mix. The sound is transferred from the picture editing workstation (Avid, Final Cut Pro or similar) onto the sound editing workstation (Pro Tools, Nuendo or similar). The sound used by the picture editor will comprise dialogue and any other sound recorded on location, music and some FX. The very least that must be done is to separate this onto separate tracks for mixing. But the beginning of the sound edit also involves an assessment of which dialogue and sounds need to be replaced, added or augmented.

Dialogue and ADR (Automatic Dialogue Replacement)

If the location recordings of dialogue are technically unacceptable, then the actors will be brought back into a studio to re-record their lines. Perhaps levels of background traffic make the lines unintelligible; the actor's personal neck microphone scratched against his coat, obscuring some words; or, in the case of a film with special effects, equipment on set such as wind or rain machines create unwanted background noise. The dialogue editor will decide if alternative sound-takes can be edited-in to solve these problems. If not, the actor will go into a studio and, while looking at himself on screen, will say the lines synchronously with his filmed performance. This is ADR – Automatic Dialogue Replacement – and can be done for individual words, lines, whole scenes or, in some cases, whole films. Hollywood films traditionally have a very high proportion of ADR, creating very clear, dramatic dialogue. ADR can also be used to add lines that were not scripted or to improve a performance. The re-recorded lines are then blended with the other dialogue and sound elements during the mix.

ADR quickly becomes an expensive process. You will need to pay for a recording studio at an hourly rate, the actor's fee and travel expenses, an ADR editor and sound editing equipment. One way of planning ahead is to include in the actor's contract a certain number of days for ADR as part of their fee.

Your film may involve an international star who, when needed to record ADR, is on location with another film somewhere else in the world. In that case, you will need to fly to them and find a recording studio near their location. Another solution is to record the ADR down a telephone line from one sound studio (where the actor is) to a studio (where you are editing). This is a costly method and is usually beyond the means of most low- or medium-budget films.

Foleys

This is one of the more fascinating aspects of sound post-production. Devised by Jack Foley in Hollywood in the 1930s, it involves one or more Foley 'artists' looking at the film in a recording studio and performing the movements of the actors on screen while being recorded. In its simplest form it comprises the recording of footsteps for each character, along with their body movements and clothes' rustles. If you ever have the chance to watch a Foley session, you will see someone staring intently at the projected image while making exaggerated movements with their arms and legs, or matching the actor's gait by performing footsteps on a plank of wood (for floorboards), a paving stone or a little pile of leaves and grass for a stroll in the park. Foley is really a generic term referring to any sound created in this way in the studio. The Foley artist will also do the movement of any props (pouring drinks, cutlery, doors, windows) and will also attempt to do more complicated sounds such as helicopters, large animals, crashing furniture or battle scenes.

There are three reasons to go through this arcane procedure. First, location sound recording often will not pick up these details with sufficient volume to be heard through dialogue, atmospheres and music. In order to enhance the actor's physical presence on screen, and to build up the feeling of reality (an actor without accompanying footsteps can become somewhat 'ghostly'), these small sounds are added judiciously in the mix. Second, for scenes where all the sound is replaced, each aspect of the soundtrack must be added artificially. In a scene involving a crowd of people walking, horses galloping by, guns being fired, rain pouring down and birds swooping in and out of frame, all of the sound elements – in this instance, the footsteps on wet pavement, horses' hooves, gunshots, rain falling on puddles and wing flaps – must be added for each character and every movement. And third, any film for which the producer hopes to achieve a foreign sale must have an M&E (music and effects) track prepared. Essentially, this is a film's soundtrack without the dialogue. It gives a foreign distributor all the music and sound needed to create the full soundtrack when mixed with foreign dubbed dialogue. The M&E can include large amounts of location sound but is often completely produced with Foleys and other sound FX. The M&E will be part of any co-production or distribution contract.

In addition to Foleys, the sound editor will add particular sound effects needed to enhance or amplify the image. Anything from gunshots to car squeals to dog barks come under this category. The last part of the sound edit includes atmospheres – the sound of places. This may be as minimal as the 'buzz' of a quiet room (every room has different acoustics, so there are an infinite number of variations on this) or as dense and nuanced as a market in Calcutta.

Sound design/sound designer

This is a problematic term, the meaning of which can change between people and productions. It was originally coined as a title to describe a sound supervisor who attended to the technical and creative details of the soundtrack, from pre-production through the shoot and post, ending with the mix – much the same way the Director of Photography is responsible for everything to do with lighting and camera. Walter Murch was first to be credited in this way on *Apocalypse Now*. The job, however, has never taken hold in a big way; most prefer the term Supervising Sound Editor (though, to some, this is a more administrative job).

Some sound editors consider a sound designer as someone who literally designs any sound that is not natural. So, the person who creates the sounds of prehistoric monsters or intergalactic spaceships would be credited as such. Skip Lievsay, Supervising Sound Editor on all the Coen Brothers' films, describes his team as having a Dialogue Editor, FX Editor, Foley Editor and a Sound Designer, when necessary, to create non-natural sounds on a synthesiser, sampler, etc. But the term has become more common on smaller films, shorts and animation where the sound editor often has an enhanced role. Personally, I prefer the term sound editor in those cases.

As I have mentioned, sound can be treated as a technical necessity involving mostly remedial processes. But sound can also alter the emotion, the feel and even the meaning of a film. David Lynch has said that for him, "sound can provide 50 per cent, 70 per cent, sometimes 100 per cent of the meaning of a scene". There are film school exercises that show how sound can completely change an audience's interpretation of the images on screen. Therefore, for some directors, leaving sound until after the picture is edited is not a satisfactory way to work. They prefer to work on the sound alongside the picture, with either the picture editor working with the soundtrack or the sound editor providing material for the picture editor to integrate into the cut. As location sound is often relatively 'flat' (consisting of the hermetic feel of a soundproof studio or the limited acoustic of dialogue recorded on neck microphones), the addition of a mere atmos track can dramatically shift the feel of a scene. In short, sound can change your perception of the image.

Music

Music is arguably the single most persuasive element in any film, subtly – but forcefully – swaying the audience's feelings and perception of the story. And your decisions as to the style of music and how you acquire it reflect the style of your film and how you work as a filmmaker. Once again, we come to an aspect of filmmaking that connects the kind of film you want to make, creative responsibility and money.

The most common practice for composing for film involves the use of temp (temporary) tracks during editing, which are then replaced by the composer, who writes the full track based on the style and placement of the temp tracks. Either the picture editor or a music editor works with the director to find pre-recorded music that achieves the desired effect and emotion. Though temp tracks can be literally any kind of music, more and more they are taken from other film scores, often in the same genre as the film being edited. Late in the edit, the composer will be brought in to create a score based on the edited temp track. This is efficient in terms of time and money (the production does not have to pay for rights to dozens of pre-recorded tracks, and the composer works for a specified amount of time), but the composer has the unenviable task of writing a score that may have to sound like Beethoven, Miles Davis, Hans Zimmer or Coldplay – whoever has been used on the temp tracks – while not really sounding like any of them. The most famous use of temp tracks is in Stanley Kubrick's *2001: A Space Odyssey*. The film's unique score, featuring music by Strauss, Khachaturian and Ligeti, is actually the temp tracks, chosen in preference to original music written by composer Alex North.

Even when temp tracks are not used, some composers prefer to come in late in the edit. Their feeling is that the director will change his mind so often, and the edit will go through so many alterations, that they should wait until the overall structure is decided upon. But you then have a situation whereby the picture edit tells one story and a composer's score – *possibly* – another. Why spend a year or 18 months creating a very particular film during scriptwriting, rehearsals, shooting and editing, only to have it changed – in a fundamental way – by the music?

My feeling is that music should be part of the whole filmmaking process, and fully integrated during editing. One way to do this is for the composer to write his or her initial sketches to the script: after all, everyone else in the crew and cast works to the script, so why shouldn't the composer? These early musical ideas begin a dialogue between composer and director and can be a useful influence for the acting and camera style. Most importantly, the composer's preliminary work will become temp tracks in the cutting room to be edited, moved and manipulated, and then reworked, elaborated and refined by the composer him or herself. It is much easier for a composer to rework their own compositions than temp tracks (which may comprise the entire history of written music). In this method the choice and placement of music is integrated within the editing process rather than added at the end.

Of course, not all films require an original score. Some use pre-recorded commercial music to exploit popular songs, achieve period or geographical accuracy, or create an emotional feel personal to the director (for example, Martin Scorsese's audacious combinations of 60s and 70s rock music with opera and popular Italian tracks in *Goodfellas* and *Casino*). The overriding concern when using pre-recorded commercial tracks is the payment of licensing rights. Every piece of recorded music is protected, or copyrighted, in four ways: composition, publishing, performance and recording. Clearing music copyright for film is a complicated business involving several different parties, and is beyond the scope of this article to explain in detail. In light of the debate about downloading MP3 files, music copyright may have become a contentious issue for some. Film productions, however, cannot take the risk of being sued for not clearing music. To find out more, contact the Performing Right Society (PRS) or the Mechanical-Copyright Protection Society (MCPS).

Copyright clearance and music research are specialised and time-consuming tasks, which – depending on the size of your production – might be best left to a music supervisor. They not only help to set a creative tone for the music (in collaboration with the director and producer), but also look after legal and delivery requirements related to the track. Whether you use a composer or pre-recorded music, if music plays a large role in your film then you might need a music supervisor with the following key areas of responsibility:

- choosing and arranging the copyright clearance (permissions) for use of commercially recorded music;
- choosing a composer for an original score;
- organising the score recording sessions;
- assisting the composer in choosing the rest of his/her team;
- overseeing the temp scoring process as it proceeds through test screenings, ensuring that all music elements are consistent with any physical and legal delivery requirements;
- controlling the music budget;
- preparing materials for playback (if any), and supervising actual playback on set.

Few directors know about music, and few composers understand filmmaking. Music is so abstract, so ineffable, that ordinary language is often not adequate for the composer and director to communicate effectively. A music supervisor can help bridge this gap. Communicating through the music itself by making it part of the filmmaking process, the music supervisor, director, composer and editor can – as a creative team – allow the right music to find its place in relation to the picture (and vice versa), bringing out feelings that complement and resonate with the edited story.

The post-production supervisor

What I have described is a series of complicated, interrelated processes often taking place simultaneously in a relatively short amount of time. Coordinating the needs of CGI production with the picture edit, organising the sound design alongside the scoring, arranging

ADR sessions with actors scattered around the world, and all the time keeping an eye on costs and the final delivery date is a delicate balancing act – both in terms of personalities and resources. On small productions this maze of activity will be overseen by the producer or production manager, but on larger films a post-production supervisor will be employed. The post-production supervisor has specialist knowledge in the image and sound procedures outlined above. S/he is also responsible for the deliverables – the detailed list of prints, soundtracks, elements of sound and image and documentation that are part of any production contract.

Filmmaking is a series of linked procedures, each one affected by the one before and impacting on the one next down the line. Looking over the number of technical procedures and creative decisions that occur during post, one could view it almost as a second shoot ... except, rather than working from the script, you are now working from the shot film. Like the preparation of food or the production of a garment, first there is the enormous effort to create the raw materials, and then an equally laborious process to fabricate those materials into the final product.

Larry Sider is Director of the School of Sound symposium and was previousy Head of Post-Production at the National Film and Television School (UK). He is a film editor and sound designer who has worked in documentary, animation and fiction. Most recently, he was Supervising Sound Editor for the Quay Brothers' *The Piano Tuner of Earthquakes* and Dave McKean's *Mirrormask*. Past projects include Patrick Keiller's *London* and *Robinson in Space* and *Street of Crocodiles* and *Institute Benjamenta* by the Quays. He has taught at numerous schools including the Royal College of Art, IFS (Köln), European Film College (Ebeltoft), California Institute of the Arts, Surrey Institute of Art and Design, Maurits Binger Institute and Bournemouth Media School. He is co-editor of *Soundscape: The School of Sound Lectures 1998-2001* and *The Soundtrack Journal.*

Editing

Film editor **Tony Lawson** shares his thoughts on a career that has seen him work with some of the industry's top directors over nearly four decades and more than 30 feature films.

At what stage do you start to work on a film?

The point at which I get involved in a film varies with each production. For example, in my association with Neil Jordan I'm often consulted at the script stage – not so much for comments on the writing or planning, but more as a sounding-board for ideas. On other productions it can be as little as a few days before the shoot. I've found that in the early stage of pre-production an editor's contribution is only useful if a relationship with the director already exists.

Can you describe your editing process?

I'm not used to putting into words that which I do by instinct. Most of what I've learnt about editing has been from my own experience or from analysing the work of others, so I'll try to give an idea of the editing process by describing how I work.

I've come to understand that a film editor is first and foremost a storyteller. I look for the most appropriate and efficient way to reveal a story, to link the ideas in order that they lead naturally from one to another. For me, the editing process begins at the dailies' screening. This first sight of the raw material at my disposal is very important; it's where the script changes from an idea to a reality. It's also the last time I'll ever see the material with fresh eyes so, in an effort to remember my thoughts and impressions, I make early notes about performance and structure. When I come to edit a scene I view again the relevant material and make further detailed notes.

Having considered the purpose of the scene within the film, I'll make my first pass at the edit as quickly as possible – sometimes ignoring obvious errors such as continuity, just to confirm that the direction I've chosen is the correct one. I'll continue to work with the scene until I am happy with the dramatic structure and the way I believe it will function within the film. At this point, unless it's part of a larger montage, I'll put the scene aside and only reconsider it again when the whole film is together.

Once the filming and first cut are complete, the real work begins. The first screening of the film is another important moment, and I try to clear away as much of the learned knowledge of the film as possible, putting myself in the place of a first-time viewer. In close collaboration with the director, my task now shifts from looking at details to considering the whole piece. During the fine-cutting period I find that I rely as much on my emotional as my rational response; it's very important to be able to understand and interpret those feelings in a way that's useful to the process. Questions about pace and the flow of ideas become important; this is a time where shifts in emphasis and construction can change the mood and direction of the film. I have to remain alert to new ideas, to recognise when things work and how to correct things that don't.

An editor's conundrum is how to make scenes flow and change in a way that seems obvious yet unexpected; how to surprise the audience and yet also give them what they want, to fulfill their expectations.

How much of the sound edit do you do yourself? And at what stage do you start working on this?

The use of sound in films is very important, and is a discipline in itself – a full-time job. Therefore I encourage the early involvement of a sound designer. I believe that film works best when visuals and sound are complimenting each other and adding to the storytelling. During the editing process I'm constantly thinking about how sound can change the perceived pace or mood of a scene, even on a practical level. The sound of an explosion, for example, is much longer than you imagine it to be. Consequently I use a lot of temporary tracks, both sound effects and music, because I know that the dramatic intentions will be made clear and the viewing experience enhanced.

What editing equipment do you use now?

The system I use most often is Lightworks Touch.

From *Straw Dogs* to *Breakfast on Pluto*, you have seen enormous changes in your field's technology. How have these changes affected you creatively?

Although technology has brought enormous changes to the way in which films are edited, it's only the machinery that's changed, not the desire to tell a story in the most effective way. In almost all film disciplines there have been technical innovations over the years that have affected the way films look: the zoom lens had a very marked influence on the films of the 1970s, for example. But they're only tricks if they don't help to tell the story.

For editors, the decisions or choices are the same as they always were. The ideas are what's important, not the equipment. However, non-linear editing systems have dramatically increased the ease with which it is possible to access any shot or scene and to evaluate changes to the structure of a film.

There's also an interesting and unexpected bonus in working with a new technology or medium: the search to find a way through the unfamiliar brings into consciousness what I normally do by instinct – namely, why cut here? Why not somewhere else? I've always been excited by the possibilities of film, and rediscovering the language through new technology confirms that excitement.

What makes an edit work? How do you know when you've got it right?

There are times when I wish I knew what makes an edit work. I think that on a basic level, any edit has to tell or advance the story. You'll know when it's right because the effect will become obvious. Having said that, in my experience there is no right or wrong edit. There are many ways to cut a scene, and all can tell a story; the choice is which story you wish to tell.

What is your favourite scene that you have edited?

I don't have a 'favourite scene' that I've edited. There are a lot of scenes that have given me pleasure for a variety of reasons, and not all to do with the editing. However, one that comes to mind is the tense family party scene from *The Butcher Boy*. The family is in disarray and drunk; they're desperately trying to enjoy themselves, but the tensions are too great and it all ends badly. I enjoy the way the scene moves towards its inevitable end, and how the second part is driven by a voice-over that wipes out the sound of the ensuing argument, taking our thoughts in a different direction. The editing of the voice-over section caused me problems until I realised that it wasn't necessary to hear the production sound; the visuals alone were telling that part of the story.

Do you think test screenings are helpful in determining how the edit is working?

Films live in a world somewhere between art and commerce. Filmmakers are stuck with the desire to make something personal and yet popular – a fine balance of seeming opposites. In ideal circumstances, test screenings can be a useful tool for fine-tuning a film. They can tell you about comprehension, both in terms of dialogue intelligibility and audience understanding of the story; they can point to problems with pacing; they can show whether suspense or comedy are working to the advantage of the film. A whole list of issues can be thrown into light. With the sensible interpretation of an audience response, test screenings can be an aid to the creative process. However, they can also be overused to the point where a film loses its individuality in an effort to please everyone.

What makes the relationship between the editor and the director a successful one?

Ideally the relationship between editor and director should be honest and open. An honest response to the film isn't always welcome and you may have to choose your words carefully, always remembering that criticism has to be constructive to be useful.

With the edit in mind, what advice would you give to a new filmmaker before their first shoot?

A new filmmaker is never going to be short on advice. The only advice I would give is to listen carefully, take only what seems appropriate, and trust your instinct.

Tony Lawson's first job was as a 'gofer' in a small documentary film company, doing everything from making tea to coiling sound cables. He moved to another company where he gained a whole range of experience, working mostly on sponsored documentaries and TV programmes – his interest gradually moving towards editing, until he became a full-time assistant editor. After a few years he moved to feature films, still as an assistant working in picture and sound. His editing career proper started when he was working on *Straw Dogs*: the editor left the project due to differences of opinion with the director, and Tony was asked to take over the incomplete tasks. He has been editing ever since – working for directors such as Stanley Kubrick, Nicolas Roeg, Sam Peckinpah, Dusan Makavejev and Neil Jordan.

Editors

Tariq Anwar
PFD, Drury House, 34-43 Russell Street, London WC2B 5HA
Agent's tel 020-7344 1000 *fax* 020-7836 9543
email sllaguno@pfd.co.uk
website www.pfd.co.uk
Agent Linda Mamy at PFD

Contact via agent. Credits include: *Stage Beauty*, and *Alien Love Triangle*.

Marguerite Arnold
c/o PFD, Drury House, 34-43 Russell Street, London WC2B 5HA
tel 020-7344 1000 *fax* 020-7836 9543
email sllaguno@pfd.co.uk
website www.pfd.co.uk

Agent Linda Mamy at PFD

Contact via agent; please send script with enquiries. Credits include: *Snow Cake*, *Trauma*, and *Calcium Kid*.

Tim Arrowsmith
Diary Services tel 020-7287 6110 (TOVS Ltd)
tel (01590) 626207 *fax* (01590) 672720
email tim@arrow24.freeserve.co.uk

Credits include: *The Woodlanders*, and *South Bank Show*.

Nick Arthurs
c/o Creative Media Management, 3b Walpole Court, Ealing Studios, London W5 5ED
tel 020-8584 5363 *fax* 020-8566 5554
email enquiries@creativemediamanagement.com
website www.creativemediamanagement.com

Credits include: *Love and Other Disasters*, *White Noise*, and *Othello* (BAFTA-winning TV film).

Mick Audsley
c/o Casarotto Marsh Ltd, Waverley House, 7–12 Noel Street, London W1F 8GQ
tel 020-7287 4450 *fax* 020-7287 5644
email casarottomarsh@casarotto.co.uk
website www.casarotto.co.uk
Agents Sarah Pritchard (film), Emma Trouson (TV) at Casarotto Marsh Ltd

Credits include: *Proof*, *Mona Lisa Smile*, and *Dirty Pretty Things*.

Sean Barton
c/o McKinney Macartney Management, The Barley Mow Centre, 10 Barley Mow Passage, London W4 4PH
tel 020-8995 4747 *fax* 020-8995 2414
email mail@mckinneymacartney.com

Contact via agent. Credits include: *Seed of Chucky*, and *Chaos*.

Nigel Bate
Diary Service tel (01932) 571044 *tel* 023-8045 5240
email nigel.bate@lineone.net

Credits include: *The Bill*, and *Down to Earth – Series IV*.

Guy Bensley
c/o McKinney Macartney Management, The Barley Mow Centre, 10 Barley Mow Passage, London W4 4PH
tel 020-8995 4747 *fax* 020-8995 2414
email mail@mckinneymacartney.com

Contact via agent. Credits include: *Fade to Black*, *Sex Lives of the Potato Men*, and *The Importance of Being Earnest*.

Peter Beston
tel 020-7630 6303 (CCA Management), 020-7267 6399 *mobile* (07879) 478427
email redcat@dircon.co.uk

Credits include: *The Oyster Farmer*, and *Once Upon A Time in the Midlands*.

David Blackmore
c/o Casarotto Marsh Ltd, Waverley House, 7–12 Noel Street, London W1F 8GQ
tel 020-7287 4450 *fax* 020-7287 5644
email casarottomarsh@casarotto.co.uk
website www.casarotto.co.uk
Agent Emma Trouson at Casarotto Marsh Ltd

Credits include: *Class of '76*, and *Stranded*.

Caroline Bleakley
tel 020-8579 1256 *mobile* (07788) 660958
email home@cbleakley.freeserve.co.uk

Credits include: *Hearts & Bones*, *Monarch of the Glen*, and *Sea of Souls*.

Christopher Blunden
c/o PFD, Drury House, 34-43 Russell Street, London WC2B 5HA
tel 020-7344 1000 *fax* 020-7836 9543
email sllaguno@pfd.co.uk
website www.pfd.co.uk
Agent Linda Mamy at PFD

Contact via agent; please send script with enquiries. Credits include: *Nine Dead Gay Guys*, *Blackball*, and *Flyboys*.

Victoria Boydell
c/o Casarotto Marsh Ltd, Waverley House, 7–12 Noel Street, London W1F 8GQ

tel 020-7287 4450 *fax* 020-7287 5644
email casarottomarsh@casarotto.co.uk
website www.casarotto.co.uk
Agents Sarah Pritchard (film), Emma Trouson (TV) at Casarotto Marsh Ltd

Credits include: *Kidulthood*, *The Visitor*, and *Hustle*.

Michael Bradsell

tel 020-8992 4266 *mobile* (07711) 941643
email kaberna@freeuk.com

Credits include: *Henry V*, *Wilde*, *Martha – Meet Frank*, and *Daniel & Lawrence*.

Chris Brainwood

mobile (07050) 234045
email brainwood@onetel.com

Primarily television. Credits include: *Ramsay's Kitchen Nightmares*, and *War at the Door*.

Martin Brinkler

c/o PFD, Drury House, 34-43 Russell Street, London WC2B 5HA
tel 020-7344 1000 *fax* 020-7836 9543
email sllaguno@pfd.co.uk
website www.pfd.co.uk
Agent Linda Mamy at PFD

Contact via agent. Credits include: *Sparkle*, and *The Long Weekend*.

Doug Bryson

tel 020-8852 8934 *mobile* (07957) 230674
email dougbryson@zoom.co.uk
website www.dougbryson.co.uk

Credits include: *No Going Back*, and *Horizon*.

Kate Buckland

tel 020-8571 6952 *mobile* (07710) 768642
email kate.filmeditor@talk21.com

Credits include: *Hidden City*, *Cleopatra*, and *Thomas The Tank Engine*.

Lois Bygrave

mobile (07818) 064613
email lois_bygrave@excite.com

Credits: regularly edits *Holby City* and *No Angels* (TV); also *Woman X* (short film), *Number One*, *Longing*, *Number Two*, and *Regret*.

Leo Carlyon

tel 020-7274 0170 *mobile* (07860) 479962
email leocarlyon@hotmail.com

Credits include: *Gods in the Sky*, *Made For Each Other*, and *The Salon* (TV).

David Charap

c/o PFD, Drury House, 34-43 Russell Street, London WC2B 5HA
tel 020-7344 1000 *fax* 020-7836 9543
email streacher@pfd.co.uk
website www.pfd.co.uk
Agent Louisa Thompson at PFD

Contact via agent; please send script with enquiries. Credits include: *My Summer of Love*, *Wrong Side Up*, and *Kiss of Life*.

Reva Childs

mobile (07939) 546490
email revachilds@gmail.com
website www.revachilds.net

Credits include: *Walking on Water*, *Boom*, *My Mother India*, and *Who Do You Think You Are?: Meera Syal*.

Jim Clark

c/o PFD, Drury House, 34-43 Russell Street, London WC2B 5HA
tel 020-7344 1000 *fax* 020-7836 9543
email streacher@pfd.co.uk
website www.pfd.co.uk
Agent Louisa Thompson at PFD

Contact via agent; please send script with enquiries. Credits include: *Vera Drake*, *Pobby & Dingham*, and *The Decameron*.

Fiona Colbeck

tel (01932) 571044 (Sara Putt Associates)
tel 020-7690 8639 *mobile* (07785) 757001
email fionacolbeck@hotmail.com

Credits include: *Shameless*, *Gladiatress*, and *Clocking Off*.

Mark Day

c/o ICM London, Oxford House, 76 Oxford Street, London W1D 1BS
Agent's tel 020-7636 6565 *tel* 020-7870 0932
email mark@markdayediting.freeserve.co.uk
Agent Chris Smith at ICM

Contact via agent. Credits include: *Harry Potter and the Order of the Phoenix*, *Sex Traffic* (BAFTA & RTS winner), and *State of Play* (BAFTA winner).

Sascha Dhillon

tel 020-8455 6329 *mobile* (07941) 355411
email saschadhillon@hotmail.com

Credits include: *The History Boys* (1st Assistant Editor), *Mike Bassett – England Manager* (Associate Editor), and *Five Children & It* (Visual Effects Editor).

Pia Di Ciaula

c/o ICM London, Oxford House, 76 Oxford Street, London W1D 1BS
Agent's tel 020-7636 6565

Contact via agent. Credits include: *Silk*, *Tara Road*, *Pure*, and *Hideous Kinky*.

Bill Diver

c/o Jessica Carney Associates, 4th Floor, 23 Golden Square, London W1F 9JP

Agent's tel 020-7434 4143 *mobile* (07905) 181041
fax 020-7434 4175
email bill.diver@blueyonder.co.uk

Credits include: *Twenty Four Seven*, *This Little Life*, and *Miranda*.

Humphrey Dixon

c/o Jessica Carney Associates, 4th Floor, 23 Golden Square, London W1F 9JP
Agent's tel 020-7434 4143 *mobile* (07939) 143908
fax 020-7434 4175
email humphrey.dixon@btopenworld.com
Agent Jessica Carney Associates

Credits include: *Wimbledon*, *Enemy at the Gates*, and *My House in Umbria*.

Clare Douglas

c/o McKinney Macartney Management, The Barley Mow Centre, 10 Barley Mow Passage, London W4 4PH
tel 020-8995 4747 *fax* 020-8995 2414
email mail@mckinneymacartney.com

Contact via agent. Credits include: *Flight 93*, *Way of Life*, and *Bloody Sunday*.

Luke Dunkley

c/o PFD, Drury House, 34-43 Russell Street, London WC2B 5HA
tel 020-7344 1000 *fax* 020-7836 9543
email streacher@pfd.co.uk
website www.pfd.co.uk
Agent Louisa Thompson at PFD

Contact via agent; please send script with enquiries. Credits include: *Dog Eat Dog*, and *Ashes and Sand*.

Michael Ellis

14 Floral Street, London WC2
Agent' tel 020-7632 5292 *tel* 020-7435 6463
email technicians@berlinassociates.com, mike.e@dial.pipex.com
Agent Berlin Associates

Credits include: *Five Children and It*, *Brassed Off*, and *The Last Drop*.

Kate Evans

c/o ICM London, Oxford House, 76 Oxford Street, London W1D 1BS
Agent's tel 020-7636 6565
email kateevans@boltblue.com

Contact via agent. Credits include: *Creep*, *Girl With The Pearl Earring*, and *Wilderness*.

Mary Finlay

c/o PFD, Drury House, 34-43 Russell Street, London WC2B 5HA
tel 020-7344 1000 *fax* 020-7836 9543
email streacher@pfd.co.uk, oblivion@ftech.co.uk
website www.pfd.co.uk
Agent Louisa Thompson at PFD

Contact via agent; please send script with enquiries. Credits include: *Grand Theft Parsons*, and *Nina's Heavenly Delights*.

David Freeman

c/o PFD, Drury House, 34-43 Russell Street, London WC2B 5HA
tel 020-7344 1000 020-7836 9543
email sllaguno@pfd.co.uk
website www.pfd.co.uk
Agent Linda Mamy at PFD

Contact via agent. Credits include: *Piccadilly Jim*, and *Wondrous Oblivion*.

David Gamble ACE

c/o PFD, Drury House, 34-43 Russell Street, London WC2B 5HA
tel 020-7344 1000 *fax* 020-7836 9543
email sllaguno@pfd.co.uk
website www.pfd.co.uk
Agent Linda Mamy at PFD

Contact via agent. Credits include: *Shop Girl*, *Lucky Break*, and *My Son the Fanatic*.

Paul Garrick

c/o Jessica Carney Associates, 4th Floor, 23 Golden Square, London W1F 9JP
Agent's tel 020-7434 4143 *fax* 020-7434 4173
email info@jcarneyassociates.co.uk

Works in television. Prefers a script with enquiries. Please send via agent, as above. Credits include: *Poirot: After the Funeral*, and *William and Mary*.

Stuart Gazzard

c/o The Dench Arnold Agency, 10 Newburgh Street, London W1F 7RN
Agent's tel 020-7437 4551 *tel* 020-8682 9373
fax 020-7439 1355
email contact@dencharnold.com, stuartgazzard@hotmail.com
Agent The Dench Arnold Agency

Contact via agent. Credits include: *The Business*, *Football Factory*, and *It's All Gone Pete Tong*.

David Gibson

c/o Creative Media Management, 3b Walpole Court, Ealing Studios, London W5 5ED
tel 020-8584 5363 *fax* 020-8566 5554
email davidgibson@gmx.de, enquiries@creativemediamanagement.com
website www.creativemediamanagement.com

Credits include: *The Forest*, *Gregory's Two Girls*, and *On the Road With Kiarostami*.

Chris Gill

c/o ICM London, Oxford House, 76 Oxford Street, London W1D 1BS
Agent's tel 020-7636 6565 *mobile* (07973) 297113
email editgill@ntlworld.com

Credits include: *Sunshine*, *The Lives of Saints*, *28 Days Later*, and *Crime and Punishment*.

Tracy Granger

c/o Creative Media Management, 3b Walpole Court, Ealing Studios, London W5 5ED
tel 020-8584 5363 *fax* 020-8566 5554
email pooka77@mac.com, enquiries@creativemediamanagement.com
website www.creativemediamanagement.com

UK/US dual nationality. Credits include: *Chromophobia*, *Boys Don't Cry*, and *Gas Food Lodging*.

Colin Green

c/o Casarotto Marsh Ltd, Waverley House, 7–12 Noel Street, London W1F 8GQ
tel 020-7287 4450 *fax* 020-7287 5644
email casarottomarsh@casarotto.co.uk
website www.casarotto.co.uk
Agents Sarah Pritchard (film), Emma Trouson (TV) at Casarotto Marsh Ltd

Credits include: *Five Children and It*, and *Merli*.

Jon Harris

c/o ICM, 76 Oxford Street, London WIN 0AX
Agent's tel 020-7870 0932 *fax* 020-7323 0101

Credits include: *Snatch*, *Layer Cake*, and *The Banker* (BAFTA-winning short film).

Emma Hickox ACE

c/o PFD, Drury House, 34-43 Russell Street, London WC2B 5HA
tel 020-7344 1000 *fax* 020-7836 9543
email sllaguno@pfd.co.uk
website www.pfd.co.uk
Agent Linda Mamy at PFD

Contact via agent. Credits include: *Blood & Chocolate*, and *Cheaper By the Dozen*.

Masahiro Hirakubo

c/o PFD, Drury House, 34-43 Russell Street, London WC2B 5HA
tel 020-7344 1000 *fax* 020-7836 9543
email sllaguno@pfd.co.uk
website www.pfd.co.uk
Agent Linda Mamy at PFD

Contact via agent. Credits include: *Bullet Boy*, and *Ella Enchanted*.

Niven Howie

c/o McKinney Macartney Management, The Barley Mow Centre, 10 Barley Mow Passage, London W4 4PH
tel 020-8995 4747 *fax* 020-8995 2414
email mail@mckinneymacartney.com

Contact via agent. Credits include: *Goal! II*, *The Hitchhiker's Guide to the Galaxy*, and *The Godsend*.

Martin Hunter

c/o The Dench Arnold Agency, 10 Newburgh Street, London W1F 7RN
Agent's tel 020-7437 4551 *fax* 020-7439 1355
email contact@dencharnold.com
Agent The Dench Arnold Agency

Credits include: *Full Metal Jacket*, *The Chronicles of Riddick*, *Event Horizon*, and *Underworld*.

Annie Kocur

Agent' tel 020-7244 1159
Agent Amanda MacAllister

Credits include: *Rose and Maloney* (Series 2 – TV), *Anita and Me* (film), and *A Thing Called Love* (TV).

Simon Laurie

Diary Service tel 020-7494 4922 (TOVS Ltd)
mobile (07710) 358178
fax 020-7482 2911
email simonlaurie@edits.fsnet.co.uk

Credits include: *The Piano Tuner of Earthquakes*, and *The Sandman* (TV).

Tony Lawson

c/o Casarotto Marsh Ltd, Waverley House, 7–12 Noel Street, London W1F 8GQ
tel 020-7287 4450 *fax* 020-7287 5644
email casarottomarsh@casarotto.co.uk
website www.casarotto.co.uk
Agent Sarah Pritchard (film) at Casarotto Marsh Ltd

Credits include: *Breakfast on Pluto*, *The Good Thief*, and *The Butcher Boy*.

Beverley Mills

c/o McKinney Macartney Management, The Barley Mow Centre, 10 Barley Mow Passage, London W4 4PH
tel 020-8995 4747 *fax* 020-8995 2414
email mail@mckinneymacartney.com

Contact via agent. Credits include: *Shameless*, and *Outlaws*.

Nick Moore

c/o PFD, Drury House, 34-43 Russell Street, London WC2B 5HA
tel 020-7344 1000 *fax* 020-7836 9543
email streacher@pfd.co.uk
website www.pfd.co.uk
Agent Louisa Thompson at PFD

Contact via agent; please send script with enquiries. Credits include: *Love Actually*, *About a Boy*, and *Freedomland*.

Patrick John Moore

c/o The Dench Arnold Agency, 10 Newburgh Street, London W1F 7RN
Agent's tel 020-7437 4551 *mobile* (07940) 929823
fax 020-7439 1355
email contact@dencharnold.com, patrick.moore7@ntlworld.com
Agent The Dench Arnold Agency

Contact via agent. Credits include: *Human Traffic*, and *Goodbye Charlie Bright.*

Bryan Oates

mobile (07747) 611130
email oateseditor@hotmail.com

Credits include: *Fingersmith* (TV), and *Song for a Raggy Boy.*

St John O'Rorke

c/o Casarotto Marsh Ltd, Waverley House,
7–12 Noel Street, London W1F 8GQ
tel 020-7287 4450 *fax* 020-7287 5644
email casarottomarsh@casarotto.co.uk
website www.casarotto.co.uk
Agents Sarah Pritchard (film), Emma Trouson (TV) at Casarotto Marsh Ltd

Credits include: *Tomorrow La Scala, The Hamburg Cell*, and *Four Last Songs.*

Frances Parker

c/o Casarotto Marsh Ltd, Waverley House,
7–12 Noel Street, London W1F 8GQ
tel 020-7287 4450 *fax* 020-7287 5644
email casarottomarsh@casarotto.co.uk
website www.casarotto.co.uk
Agents Sarah Pritchard (film), Emma Trouson (TV) at Casarotto Marsh Ltd

Credits include: *Inside I'm Dancing*, and *Band of Brothers.*

Xavier Russell

c/o Jessica Carney Associates, 4th Floor,
23 Golden Square, London W1F 9JP
Agent's tel 020-7434 4143 *fax* 020-7434 4173
email info@jcarneyassociates.co.uk
Agent Jessica Carney Associates

Contact via agent. Credits include: *The Kindness of Strangers, Secret Smile*, and *The Rotters' Club* (all TV).

Yannis Sakaridis

tel 020-7625 1164 *mobile* (07855) 798232
fax 020-7372 3515
email irisfilms@btconnect.com

Credits include: *The Purifiers, The Freediver*, and *A Woman in Winter.*

John Scott

c/o Casarotto Marsh Ltd, National House,
60-66 Wardour Street, London W1V 4ND
tel 020-7287 4450 *fax* 020-7287 5644
email casarottomarsh@casarotto.uk.com
website www.casarotto.uk.com
Agents Sarah Pritchard (film), Emma Trouson (TV) at Casarotto Marsh Ltd

Credits include: *The Quiet American, Rabbit Proof Fence*, and *Sexy Beast.*

Ian Seymour

c/o Dinedor Management, 81 Oxford Street,
London W1D 2EU
Agent's tel 020-7851 3575 *fax* 020-781 3576
email info@dinedor.com
website www.dinedormanagement.co.uk
Agent Andrew Downer, Dinedor Management

Credits include: *Donnie Brasco, The Proposition*, and *Ned Kelly.*

Anne Sopel

c/o Casarotto Marsh Ltd, Waverley House,
7–12 Noel Street, London W1F 8GQ
tel 020-7287 4450 *fax* 020-7287 5644
email casarottomarsh@casarotto.co.uk
website www.casarotto.co.uk
Agents Sarah Pritchard (film), Emma Trouson (TV) at Casarotto Marsh Ltd

Credits include: *Guy X*, and *Canterbury Tales.*

Alan Strachan

c/o Creative Media Management, 3b Walpole Court,
Ealing Studios, London W5 5ED
tel 020-8584 5363 *fax* 020-8566 5554
email strawnie1@aol.com,
enquiries@creativemediamanagement.com
website www.creativemediamanagement.com

Credits include: *The Baker, Withnail and I*, and *Saving Grace.*

Neil Thompson

c/o PFD, Drury House, 34-43 Russell Street,
London WC2B 5HA
tel 020-7344 1000 *fax* 020-7836 9543
email sllaguno@pfd.co.uk
website www.pfd.co.uk
Agent Linda Mamy at PFD

Contact via agent. Credits include: *Bad Girls*, and *Silent Witness* (both TV).

Paul Tothill

c/o Casarotto Marsh Ltd, Waverley House,
7–12 Noel Street, London W1F 8GQ
tel 020-7287 4450 *fax* 020-7287 5644
email casarottomarsh@casarotto.co.uk
website www.casarotto.co.uk
Agents Sarah Pritchard (film), Emma Trouson (TV) at Casarotto Marsh Ltd

Credits include: *The Long Firm, Pride and Prejudice*, and *Boudica.*

Jamie Trevill

c/o Creative Media Management, 3b Walpole Court,
Ealing Studios, London W5 5ED
tel 020-8584 5363 *fax* 020-8566 5554
email jamie@trevill.com,
enquiries@creativemediamanagement.com
website www.creativemediamanagement.com

Credits include: *Oyster Farmer, Conspiracy of Silence*, and *The Tichborne Claimant.*

Trevor Waite

c/o PFD, Drury House, 34-43 Russell Street,
London WC2B 5HA

tel 020-7344 1000 *fax* 020-7836 9543
email sllaguno@pfd.co.uk
website www.pfd.co.uk
Agent Linda Mamy at PFD

Contact via agent. Credits include: *Driving Lessons*, and *Beyond the Sea*.

Cliff West

4 Chapel Road, London W13 9AE
tel 020-8810 1584
email cliff.west@talk21.com

Primarily works on TV arts docs and drama. Credits include: *UFOs: The Secret Evidence*, *Gone to the Dogs* (short film), and *Zero Hour*.

Justine Wright

c/o PFD, Drury House, 34-43 Russell Street, London WC2B 5HA
tel 020-7344 1000 *fax* 020-7836 9543
email streacher@pfd.co.uk
website www.pfd.co.uk
Agent Louisa Thompson at PFD

Contact via agent; please send script with enquiries. Credits include: *Late Night Shopping*, *Touching the Void*, and *One Day in September*.

Lucia Zucchetti

c/o Casarotto Marsh Ltd, Waverley House, 7–12 Noel Street, London W1F 8GQ
tel 020-7287 4450 *fax* 020-7287 5644
email info@casarotto.co.uk
website www.casarotto.co.uk
Agents Sarah Pritchard (film) at Casarotto Marsh Ltd

Credits include: *Morvern Callar*, *The Merchant of Venice*, *Mrs Henderson Presents*, and *The Queen*. BAFTA nominee for Best Editing 2007, and American Cinema Editors Best Drama Editing nominee 2007.

Composers' agents

Cool Music Media

1A Fishers Lane, Chiswick, London W4 1RX
tel 020-8995 7766 *fax* 020-8987 8996
email enquiries@coolmusicltd.com
website www.coolmusicltd.com

Represents composers for film and TV.

Eaton Music Ltd

Eaton House, 39 Lower Richmond Road, Putney, London SW15 1ET
tel 020-8788 4557 *fax* 020-8780 9711
email info@eatonmusic.com
website www.eatonmusic.com
Director Mandy Oates

Founded in 1975. Mainly represents film and TV composers including George Fenton and David Mackey. Potential clients should submit material by post or email.

Faber Music Media

Film & TV Department, 3 Queen Square, London WC1N 3AU
tel 020-7833 7924
email information@fabermusic.com

Represents composers for film and TV.

HotHouseMusic

Greenland Place, 115-123 Bayham Street, London NW1 0AG
tel 020-7446 744 *fax* 020-7446 7448
email info@hot-house-music.com
website www.hot-house-music.com

HotHouse is a music supervisors and score coordination group which also represents composers. Between them, the all-women team have credits on many big feature productions. Credits include: (Music Supervision) *Children of Men, The Queen, The Constant Gardner*; (Score Coordination) *Blood Diamond, Flushed Away, The Da Vinci Code.* Composers include: Hans Zimmer, Simon Boswell, James Brett, Christopher Gunning.

SMA Talent

SMA Talent Ltd, The Cottage, Church Street, Fressingfield, Suffolk IP21 5PA
tel (01379) 586734 *fax* (01379) 586131
email carolynne@smatalent.com
website www.smatalent.com
Agents Carolynne Wyper, Olav Wyper, Iain Rousham

Represents a number of composers and music producers. Clients include: John Altman (*Little Voice, Titanic, The Roman Spring of Mrs Stone*); Tim Atack (*Much Ado About Nothing, Elephant Juice, Among Giants*); Alan Parker (*Fallen Angel, Walking With Cavemen, Rhodes*); and Paul Leonard-Morgan (*Spooks, Galapagos, Silent Witness*).

Composers

John Altman
c/o SMA Talent Ltd
tel (01379) 586734 *fax* (01379) 586131
email carolynne@smatalent.com
website www.smatalent.com

Credits include: *Hear My Song*, *Mr Harvey Lights a Candle*, and *Shall We Dance*.

Tim Atack
c/o SMA Talent Ltd
Agent's tel (01379) 586734 *fax* (01379) 586131
email carolynne@smatalent.com
website www.smatalent.com

Credits include: *Among Giants*, and *Much Ado About Nothing*.

Christopher Barnett
tel/fax 020-8931 0738
mobile (07976) 647146
email mail@christopherbarnett.com
website www.christopherbarnett.com

Credits include: *Last Summer*, and *Tristram Shandy: A Cock & Bull Story*.

Garry Bell
tel 020-8994 8301 *fax* 020-8994 2449
email garry@gbell.demon.co.uk

Credits include: *Beautiful People*.

Simon Boswell
c/o HotHouse Music, Greenland Place,
115-123 Bayham Street, London NW1 0AG
tel 020-7446 7446 *fax* 020-7446 7448
email info@hot-house-music.com
website www.hot-house-music.com

Credits include: *Shallow Grave*, *Hackers*, *The War Zone*, and *Free Jimmy*.

James Brett
c/o HotHouse Music, Greenland Place,
115-123 Bayham Street, London NW1 0AG
tel 020-7446 7446 *fax* 020-7446 7448
email info@hot-house-music.com
website www.hot-house-music.com

Credits include: *The Island*, *Mrs Harris*, and *Four Last Songs*.

David Buckley
mobile (07957) 258914
email info@davidbuckleymusic.co.uk
website www.davidbuckleymusic.co.uk

Credits include: *Shrek 3* (additional music), *Flushed Away* (additional music), and *Boudica* (score).

Edmund Butt
c/o Cool Music Ltd, 1A Fishers Lane, Chiswick, London W4 1RX
Agent's tel 020-8995 7766 *fax* 020-8987 8996
email enquiries@coolmusicltd.com
website www.coolmusicltd.com

Credits include: *The Dark*, and *True North*.

Avshalom Caspi
mobile (07747) 801634
email contact@avshalomcaspi.com
Editor www.avshalomcaspi.com

Credits include: *Brick Lane*, *Macbeth*, and *You Don't Know Your're Born*.

Mark Desvaux
email mark@trlmusic.com

Credits include: *Dirt*, *Ugly Betty* and performance with The Urban Myth Club.

Andrew Dickson
PFD, Drury House, 34-43 Russell Street, London WC2B 5HA
tel 020-7344 1000

Credits include: *Vera Drake*, *All Or Nothing*, and *Secrets and Lies*.

Anne Dudley
c/o HotHouse Music, Greenland Place,
115-123 Bayham Street, London NW1 0AG
tel 020-7446 7446 *fax* 020-7446 7448
email info@hot-house-music.com
website www.hot-house-music.com

Credits include: *Pushing Tin*, *Perfect Creature*, and *The Full Monty*.

Paul Englishby
c/o HotHouse Music, Greenland Place,
115-123 Bayham Street, London NW1 0AG
tel 020-7446 7446 *fax* 020-7446 7448
email info@hot-house-music.com
website www.hot-house-music.com

Credits include: *Death of the Revolution* (short), *Ten Minutes Older: The Trumpet*, and *Goal 2* (as Orchestrator/Arranger).

Guy Farley
c/o Cool Music Ltd, 1A Fishers Lane, Chiswick, London W4 1RX
Agent's tel 020-8995 7766 *fax* 020-8987 8996
email enquiries@coolmusicltd.com
website www.coolmusicltd.com

Credits include: *Cashback*, *The Flock*, and *Land of the Blind*.

Magnus Fiennes

c/o Cool Music Ltd, 1A Fishers Lane, Chiswick, London W4 1RX
Agent's tel 020-8995 7766 *fax* 020-8987 8996
email enquiries@coolmusicltd.com
website www.coolmusicltd.com

Credits include: *Chromophobia*, *The Reckoning*, and *Hustle* (TV).

Simon Fisher Turner

Faber Music Limited, 3 Queen Square, London WC1N 3AU
tel 020-7833 7900
email information@fabermusic.com

Credits include: *Caravaggio*, *I'll Sleep When I'm Dead*, *Sweeney Todd*, and *The Romantics*.

Michael Gibbs

c/o PFD, Drury House, 34-43 Russell Street, London WC2B 5HA
tel 020-7344 1036 *fax* 020-7836 9543
email llewis@pfd.co.uk
website www.pfd.co.uk

Agent Charles Walker at PFD

Contact via agent. Credits include: *Purely Belter*, and *Being Human*.

Christopher Gunning

c/o HotHouse Music, Greenland Place, 115-123 Bayham Street, London NW1 0AG
tel 020-7446 7446 *fax* 020-7446 7448
email info@hot-house-music.com
website www.hot-house-music.com

Credits include: *La Vie En Rose*, and *Poirot*.

Richard Hartley

c/o PFD, Drury House, 34-43 Russell Street, London WC2B 5HA
tel 020-7344 1036 *fax* 020-7836 9543
email llewis@pfd.co.uk
website www.pfd.co.uk

Contact via agent. Credits include: *The Life and Death of Peter Sellers*, and *The Lion in Winter*.

Alex Heffes

mobile (07775) 635836
email info@alexheffes.com
website www.alexheffes.com

Credits include: *Last King of Scotland*, and *Touching the Void*.

Nigel Hess

tel (01895) 835749 *fax* (01895) 834264
email nigel@myramusic.co.uk
website www.myramusic.co.uk

Credits include: *Ladies in Lavender*, and *Ballykissangel*.

Steve Isles

DNA Music Ltd tel 020-8800 2276 *fax* 020-8800 4840
email amanda@dna-music.com
website www.dna-music.com

Credits include: *Joe Strummer: The Future is Uncertain*, and *Nina's Heavenly Delights*.

Adrian Johnston

Faber Music Limited, 3 Queen Square, London WC1N 3AU
tel 020-7833 7900
email information@fabermusic.com

Credits include: *Becoming Jane*, *Sparkle*, and *Kinky Boots*.

Simon Lacey

Faber Music Limited, 3 Queen Square, London WC1N 3AU
tel 020-7833 7900
email information@fabermusic.com

Credits include: *British Film Forever*, and *Good*.

Rob Lane

c/o Cool Music Ltd, 1A Fishers Lane, Chiswick, London W4 1RX
Agent's tel 020-8995 7766 *fax* 020-8987 8996
email enquiries@coolmusicltd.com
website www.coolmusicltd.com

Credits include: *Mrs Ratcliffe's Revolution*, *Lives of the Saints*, and *Aileen: The Life and Death of a Serial Killer*.

Adam Lewis

mobile (07967) 741623
email borag.productions@tiscali.co.uk

Credits include: *Void*, and *Kidulthood*.

John Lunn

c/o Cool Music Ltd, 1A Fishers Lane, Chiswick, London W4 1RX
Agent's tel 020-8995 7766 *fax* 020-8987 8996
email enquiries@coolmusicltd.com
website www.coolmusicltd.com

Credits include: *Once Upon a Time in the Midlands*, and *Wisdom of Crocodiles*.

Nathan McRee

DNA Music Ltd tel 020-8800 2276 *fax* 020-8800 4840
email amanda@dna-music.com
website www.dna-music.com

Acclaimed composer for computer games. Credits include: *Tomb Raider I, II, III* (games).

Guy Michelmore

DNA Music Ltd tel 020-8800 2276 *fax* 020-8800 4840
email amanda@dna-music.com
website www.dna-music.com

Credits include: *Frozen*, and *The Invincible Iron Man*.

Richard G Mitchell

c/o HotHouse Music, Greenland Place, 115-123 Bayham Street, London NW1 0AG
tel 020-7446 7446 *fax* 020-7446 7448
email info@hot-house-music.com
website www.hot-house-music.com

Credits include: *To Kill A King, Grand Theft Parsons*, and *A Good Woman.*

Charlie Mole

c/o Cool Music Ltd, 1A Fishers Lane, Chiswick, London W4 1RX
Agent's tel 020-8995 7766 *fax* 020-8987 8996
email enquiries@coolmusicltd.com
website www.coolmusicltd.com

Credits include: *The Importance of Being Earnest, Guy X*, and *Fade to Black.*

Julian Nott

c/o Cool Music Ltd, 1A Fishers Lane, Chiswick, London W4 1RX
Agent's tel 020-8995 7766 *fax* 020-8987 8996
email enquiries@coolmusicltd.com
website www.coolmusicltd.com

Credits include: *Wallace and Gromit: Curse of the Wererabbit, New Year's Day*, and *Christmas Carol – The Movie.*

Barrington Pheloung

DNA Music Ltd tel 020-8800 2276 *fax* 020-8800 4840
email amanda@dna-music.com
website www.dna-music.com

Credits include: *Hilary and Jackie*, and *Shopgirl.*

Andrew Phillips

c/o PFD, Drury House, 34-43 Russell Street, London WC2B 5HA
tel 020-7344 1036 *fax* 020-7836 9543
email llewis@pfd.co.uk
website www.pfd.co.uk

Agent Charles Walker at PFD

Contact via agent. Credits include: *Landlords, Animals*, and *Pinochet in Suburbia* (all doc and docu-drama).

Michael Price

c/o HotHouse Music, Greenland Place, 115-123 Bayham Street, London NW1 0AG
tel 020-7446 7446 *fax* 020-7446 7448
email info@hot-house-music.com
website www.hot-house-music.com

Credits include: *Children of Men* (original source music), and *Hot Fuzz* (additional music).

Kevin Sargent

c/o Cool Music Ltd, 1A Fishers Lane, Chiswick, London W4 1RX
Agent's tel 020-8995 7766 *fax* 020-8987 8996
email enquiries@coolmusicltd.com
website www.coolmusicltd.com

Credits include: *Crush, The Upside of Anger*, and *Fakers.*

Nitin Sawhney

c/o Cool Music Ltd, 1A Fishers Lane, Chiswick, London W4 1RX
Agent's tel 020-8995 7766 *fax* 020-8987 8996
email enquiries@coolmusicltd.com
website www.coolmusicltd.com

Credits include: *The Namesake, Pure*, and *Anita and Me.*

Dominik Scherrer

c/o Cool Music Ltd, 1A Fishers Lane, Chiswick, London W4 1RX
Agent's tel 020-8995 7766 *fax* 020-8987 8996
email enquiries@coolmusicltd.com
website www.coolmusicltd.com

Credits include: *Scenes of a Sexual Nature, The Nine Lives of Thomas Katz*, and *The Honeytrap.*

Ilona Sekacz

c/o PFD, Drury House, 34-43 Russell Street, London WC2B 5HA
tel 020-7344 1036 *fax* 020-7836 9543
email llewis@pfd.co.uk
website www.pfd.co.uk

Agent Charles Walker at PFD

Contact via agent. Credits include: *The Only Boy for Me, Wonderous Oblivion*, and *Antonia's Line.*

Mark Thomas

c/o Cool Music Ltd, 1A Fishers Lane, Chiswick, London W4 1RX
Agent's tel 020-8995 7766 *fax* 020-8987 8996
email enquiries@coolmusicltd.com
website www.coolmusicltd.com

Credits include: *The Magic Roundabout, Agent Cody Banks II*, and *Dog Soldiers.*

Colin Towns

c/o Cool Music Ltd, 1A Fishers Lane, Chiswick, London W4 1RX
Agent's tel 020-8995 7766 *fax* 020-8987 8996
email enquiries@coolmusicltd.com
website www.coolmusicltd.com

Credits include: *Double Zero, Red Mercury, Guest House Paradiso*, and *Vampire's Kiss.*

Stephen Warbeck

c/o PFD, Drury House, 34-43 Russell Street, London WC2B 5HA
tel 020-7344 1000 *fax* 020-7836 9543
email sllaguno@pfd.co.uk
website www.pfd.co.uk

Agent Linda Mamy at PFD

Contact via agent. Credits include: *Proof, Flawless*, and *Billy Elliot.*

Hans Zimmer

c/o HotHouse Music, Greenland Place,
115-123 Bayham Street, London NW1 0AG
tel 020-7446 7446 *fax* 020-7446 7448
email info@hot-house-music.com
website www.hot-house-music.com

Credits include: *Shark Tale*, *Pearl Harbour*, and *Gladiator*.

Notes from a music supervisor

Liz Gallacher is the UK's most successful music supervisor, with 40 film credits in less than a decade. In this interview she clarifies her role and shares her experiences.

Can you describe the role of music supervisor?

I assist the director in achieving the musical vision of the film, through researching and selecting tracks, as well as co-ordinating with the composer to achieve a unique original score.

At what stage do you normally get involved with a project?

It varies – but usually in the pre-production stage.

Can you give an example of a common challenge in your job?

Often – and especially on UK films – filmmakers come to you with very fixed ideas of which tracks they would like to have in the film, only to discover that these are impossible to license within the film's budget. In such instances I work at identifying *why* they want those particular tracks, and then search long and hard for alternatives. This can be a big challenge.

What has been the hardest sound track you have put together, and why?

Probably *Life 'n' Lyrics*, a UK hip-hop film I've just finished working on. We used a huge amount of music, and because hip hop can be a very difficult genre in relation to music clearances, it was a tricky job.

... and which was your favourite?

One Day in September and *24 Hour Party People*.

What advice would you give to a filmmaker when putting together their sound track?

I think it is important only to use music where it is needed. Also try and have a music budget for both source music and score – and make sure you allow enough time to be creative in negotiating the music rights. Many artists don't own the rights to their music, so writing to them directly doesn't necessarily help.

Do you have an all-time favourite sound track?

This is a tough one to answer, as there are so many. I do have a particular fondness for *Pretty in Pink*; it was the first film I saw in the 80s that made me want to be a music supervisor ... even through I didn't know then that such a job existed!

Liz Gallacher has established herself as the one of the most experienced and creatively diverse music supervisors in film and television today. Her work on projects such as *The Full Monty* (winner of a Brit Award for Best Soundtrack) and *Resident Evil* (Grammy nomination for Best Metal Performance) has garnered praise from producers, directors and the press. *24 Hour Party People* was shortlisted for Film Music at the 2003 NME Awards. Liz's film credits also include: the Oscar Award-winning documentary *One Day in September*, Golden Globe winner *The Gathering Storm*, and feature films such as *Where The Truth Lies, Layer Cake, Being Julia, Calendar Girls* and *Bend It Like Beckham*. She has worked with such acclaimed directors as Atom Egoyan, Simon West, Michael Winterbottom, Marc Evans, Gurinda Chadha and Istvan Szabo. In 2007 Liz joined Cutting Edge, a music supervision and publishing company, as Director of Music Supervision.

Music publishers

Air-Edel Associates Ltd

18 Rodmarton Street, London W1U 8BJ
tel 020-7486 6466 *fax* 020-7224 0344
email air-edel@air-edel.co.uk
website www.air-edel.co.uk
Business Manager Mark Lo

Established over 35 years ago, Air-Edel is a leading music company representing composers, arrangers, music editors and music supervisors worldwide. The company has offices based in LA and central London (including recording studios with picture sync facilities). Air-Edel offers full music supervision and production services for feature film, television and commercial projects, and works closely with the composer, director, producer, musicians and artists handling all aspects of music production – from the initial creative briefing to budgeting, booking of all musicians and recording studios, copyright clearance and negotiation of contracts, to final production of the music. It also acts as an agent. The group's activities include a specialist publishing company, AE Copyrights, whose role includes administering both catalogue and individual works on behalf of composers working in the area of specially commissioned music for feature film, TV, radio, theatre, ballet and commercials.

Associated Music International Ltd

Studio House, 34 Salisbury Street, London NW8 8QE
tel 020-7402 9111 *fax* 020-7723 3064
email eliot@amimedia.co.uk
website www.amimedia.co.uk
Managing Director Eliot M Cohen

Based in central London, Associated Music International Ltd (AMI) is the new name for what was the Red Bus Group of Companies. It is run by the original founder, Eliot Cohen, who started Red Bus in 1970. AMI has a long and varied experience of the entertainment industry; the group's activities are divided into several sectors, covering: Music Publishing, Music Licensing, Music Recording (with 2 fully automated studios at the London offices), Video and TV production, and Video and TV sales. AMI is a fast and efficient music consultancy service to clear recordings and compositions, producing original music from a team of talented and experienced writers, or specially commissioning writers from a database to best suit the creative and commercial needs of clients.

BMG Music Programming

The Fulham Centre, 20 Fulham Broadway, London SW6 1AH
tel 020-7835 5200
email intl.coregeneral@bmg.com
website www.bmgmusicsearch.com
Executive VP Andrew Jenkins

Music publisher with hundreds of thousands of titles from Coldplay, Robbie Williams and Nelly to Ravel and Puccini, designed to help clients find the right music for each project.

Carlin Music Corporation

Iron Bridge House, 3 Bridge Approach, Chalk Farm, London NW1 8BD
tel 020-7734 3251 *fax* 020-7439 2391
email info@carlinmusic.com
website www.carlinmusic.com
CEO David Japp *A&R Manager* Simon Abbott

A major music catalogue founded in 1966. Covers all genres. Clients have included: Elvis Presley, The Kinks, Phil Spector and Aretha Franklin. Potential clients should submit no more than 3 songs on CD. Please do not chase.

Chrysalis Music Ltd

The Chrysalis Building, 13 Bramley Road, London W10 6SP
tel 020-7221 2213 *fax* 020-7465 6178
email info@chrysalis.com
website www.chrysalis.com
Managing Director Alison Donald

Independent music publisher founded in the 1960s.

Cutting Edge Group

36 King's Street, London WC2E 8JS
Managing Director Phil Hope

A music supervising and publishing company that provides music to the UK film business. It can provide film and TV producers with a unique range of services from music supervision, music search, clearance and music publishing to development finance and music budget gap finance.

Edel Publishing

12 Oval Road, London NW1 7DH
tel 020-7482 9700 *fax* 020-7482 4846
email phil_hope@edel.com
website www.edel.com
Managing Director Phil Hope

One of Europe's leading independent music companies specialising in several aspects of the industry. Markets artists and products of all music genres to a worldwide audience through a network of partners and subsidiaries.

EMI Music Publishing Ltd

127 Charing Cross Road, London WC2H 0QY
tel 020-7434 2131 *fax* 020-7434 3531

email firstinitiallastname@emimusicpub.com
website www.emimusicpub.com
Managing Director Guy Moot

Major publishing company with roster including material by Justin Timberlake, Pink, Mutya, Jamiroquai and The Libertines.

Music Sales Film & TV

14-15 Berners Street, London W1T 3LJ
tel 020-7612 7545 *fax* 020-7836 4874
email media@musicsales.co.uk
website www.musicsales.com/filmandtv
Head of Media John Boughtwood

Northstar Music Publishing

PO Box 868, Cambridge CB21 4SJ
tel (01787) 278256 *fax* (01787) 279069
email info@northstarmusic.co.uk
website www.northstarmusic.co.uk
Managing Director Grahame Maclean

Established in 1996. Aims to provide clients worldwide with music in all styles of the highest possible quality. Recent clients include: Universal, Warner, and Sony BMG. Also supplies film and television music. Potential clients should make contact via email or post.

Post and special FX houses

Abbey Road Studios
3 Abbey Road, St John's Wood, London NW8 9AY
tel 020-7266 7000 *fax* 020-7266 7250
email bookings@abbeyroad.com
website www.abbeyroad.co.uk
Studio Manager Colette Barber

Abbey Road opened in 1931, becoming famous for its large orchestral recording sessions. Hosts technically advanced recording and mixing, stereo and surround mastering and remastering, interactive design and a digital video service. Contains 3 studio spaces.

Absolute Post
8 Poland Street, London W1F 8PX
tel 020-7851 6700 *fax* 020-7851 6767
email sally@absolutepost.co.uk
website www.absolutepost.co.uk
Owner David Smith

Established in 2004. Specialises in providing high-end visual effects.

AFM Lighting Ltd
Waxlow Road, London NW10 7NU
tel 020-8233 7000 *fax* 020-8233 7001
email info@afmlighting.com
website www.afmlighting.com

Provides equipment and crew for a full spectrum of film and television production needs.

AHC Productions
Newburg Street, London W1F 7RB
tel 020-7734 9792 *fax* 020-7434 4339
email bryn@ahc.tv
website www.ahc.tv
Managing Director Andrew Cummings

AHC Post is a small post-production facility located in the heart of Soho. It was founded 5 years ago and is now a multi-resolution facility with experienced and talented staff. Equipment/services include: Quantel eQ system for HD editing; colour grading; effects and deliverables; Quantel Edit box for SD; and HD shooting packages, including the Sony HDW-F900 Cinealta camera with a variety of HD lenses.

AHC's creative team can operate a range of effects programmes, including: 3D Studio Max; Combustion; MatchMover; and Mokey. The company is also able to provide camera operators and technicians who specialise in HD. Offers services in 3D graphics, HD/SD conversions, DVD authoring and deliverables.

Credits include: HD mastering on *The Proposition*; online and grade for *Comic Relief Featuring Peter Kay*; and special features for *Phantom of the Opera* (DVD).

Air Studios
Lyndhurst Hall, Lyndhurst Road, Hampstead, London NW3 5NG
tel 020-7794 0060 *fax* 020-7794 8518
email alison@airstudios.com
website www.airstudios.com

One of London's premier audio post studios, which can provide for all post-production sound needs – from rushes through to final mix. Services and facilities include: mixing, sound design, tracklay, ADR, Foley, network FX library and production offices.

Angel Recording Studios
311 Upper Street, London N1 2TU
tel 020-7354 2525 *fax* 020-7226 9624
email info@angelstudios.co.uk
website www.angelstudios.co.uk

Angel Studios is a state-of-the-art recording and mixing complex with 3 studios and up-to-the-minute equipment.

Ani Sounds Ltd
Ealing Studios, Ealing Green, Ealing, London W5 5EP
tel 020-8758 8550 *fax* 020-8758 8658
website www.anisounds.com

Ani Sounds is an editing facility for drama and doc programmes, with stereo and 5.1 surround sound design for film, and facilities for voice-over, post synching, ADR and Foley. Equipment includes: Final Cut Pro and Avid Digidesign ProTools.

Anvil Post Production Ltd
Denham Studios, North Orbital Road, Denham, Uxbridge, Middlesex UB9 5HL
tel (01895) 833 522 *fax* (01895) 835 006
website www.anvil-post.com

Anvil is a full-service post-production facility with 3 mixing studios, ADR and Foley stage, and full transfer facilties to and from any digital or analogue format. Parent company is Technicolor Creative Services, which operates 24 hours per day, 7 days a week with a full range of post services.

Aquarium Studios
122 Wardour Street, London W1F 0TX
tel 020-7734 1611 *fax* 020-7494 1962
email info@aquariumstudios.co.uk
website www.aquariumstudios.co.uk

ArenaP3
74 Newman Street, London W1T 3EL
tel 020-7436 4360 *fax* 020-7436 3989
email edit@arenap3.tv
website www.arenap3.tv

Services include: Nitris HD telecine; ProTools audio editing; Avid Offline; DVD Authoring Avid Unity VO booths; Avid Symphony 2D & 3D graphics; digital tape online; encoding and grading; online review and approval; ACSR-certified support; and duplication & standards conversion.

Arion Facilities

Global House, Denham Media Park,
North Orbital Road, Denham, Uxbridge,
Middlesex UB9 5HL
tel (01895) 834484 *fax* (01895) 833085
email sales@arion.co.uk
website www.arion.co.uk

Offers a range of post-production, mastering and duplication services: telecine suites; Avid suites; serial component digital editing; video tape mastering; duplication of video, DVD and CD; and encoding of DVD.

Ascent Media

13 Hawley Crescent, London NW1 8NP
tel 020-7284 7900 *fax* 020-7284 1018
email mark.beard@ascentmedia.co.uk
website www.ascentmedia.co.uk

Provides a full range of post-production services for the broadcast television industry.

Ascent Media Services

Film House, 142 Wardour Street, London W1F 8DD
tel 020-7878 0000 *fax* 020-7878 7800
email paul.kind@ascentmedia.co.uk
website www.ascentmedia.co.uk

Ascent Media Services Wardour Street is a major supplier to international content distributors working in standard-def, high-def, 2K and 4K. Provides duplication, standards conversion, distribution and digital content management for major studios, international broadcasters and production companies. Also offers restoration services and audio mastering and sound restoration, as well as feature-film mastering for worldwide distribution.

Aztec Facilities

7 Charlotte Mews, London W1T 4ED
tel 020-7580 1591 *fax* 020-7580 1270
email askus@aztec.cd
website www.aztec.cd
Director Sam Fraser

Established in 1989. Post services include: standards conversion, dubbing, encoding, DVD authoring & duplication, and library service. Provides worldwide and national delivery. Clients include: HBO, Film 2006, and Marks & Spencer.

Barcud

Cibyn, Caernarfon, Gwynedd LL55 2BD
tel (01286) 684300 *fax* (01286) 684379
email enq@barcud-derwen.co.uk
website www.barcud-derwin.co.uk

Barcud is a television facilities company providing digital outside broadcast units, 2 purpose-built studios, and full post-production facilities and PSC units.

blue

58 Old Compton Street, London W1D 4UF
tel 020-7437 2626 *fax* 020-7439 2477
website www.bluepp.co.uk

Post-production facility serving mainly the television and commercial markets. Facilities include: linear and non-linear editing in both standard and high-def; film and tape grading; sound, design and effects; and 11 Avid systems.

BUFVC

77 Wells Street, London W1T 3QJ
tel 020-7393 1500 *fax* 020-7393 1555
email ask@bufvc.ac.uk
website www.bufvc.ac.uk

Supports and promotes screen-based learning in all disciplines. The website has useful tools such as a researchers' guide, publications, DVDs and CD-ROMs.

Capital FX

2nd Floor, 20 Dering Street, London W1S 1AJ
tel 020-7493 9998 *fax* 020-7493 9997
email liz.clarke@capitalfx.co.uk
website www.capital-fx.co.uk

Cinecontact

27 Newman Street, London W1T 1AR
tel 020-7323 1690 *fax* 020-7323 1215
email info@cinecontact.co.uk
website www.cinecontact.co.uk

Independent post-production facilities company that has been in the West End for 20 years. Offers 9 offline editing suites for hire – Avid Media Composer, Avid Xpress Pro with Mojo, all Mac-based systems. Technical support is available, as are in-house editors. Can also offer dry hire.

Cinesite (Europe) Ltd

Medius House, 2 Sheraton Street, London W1F 8FH
tel 020-7973 4000 *fax* 020-7973 4040
email info@cinesite.co.uk
website www.cinesite.com

Kodak-owned company providing high-end digital effects and compositing to the film industry. Credits include: *V is for Vendetta*, and *Charlie and the Chocolate Factory*.

De Lane Lea Ltd

75 Dean Street, London W1D 3PU
tel 020-7432 3800 *fax* 020-7432 3838
email info@delanelea.com
website www.delanelea.com

Caters for a full scope of current mixing formats, from television to digital cinema, with fully automated consoles. Each edit suite can be equipped to cater for client's needs.

Deluxe Digital Studios

7-11 Lexington Street, London W1F 9AF
tel 020-7437 4402 *fax* 020-7437 4402
email simon.valley@bydeluxe.com
website www.bydeluxe.com

Denman Productions

60 Mallard Place, Strawberry Vale, Twickenham TW1 4SR
tel 020-8891 3461 *fax* 020-8891 6413
email info@denman.co.uk
website www.denman.co.uk

Produces digital imagery for film, TV and advertising industries.

Derwen

74-78 Park Road, Whitchurch, Cardiff CF14 7BR
tel 029-2061 1515 *fax* 029-2052 1226
email enq@barcudderwen.com
website www.barcudderwen.com

TV post-production facilities house based in Cardiff, with 18 full-time editors working on Discreet Smoke HD, Smoke (SD), Digital linear on-line suite, 2 Avid Symphony, and 11 Avid Media Composer suites.

Digital Audio Technology

Studio 33, Shepperton Studios, Studios Road, Shepperton, Middlesex TW17 0QD
tel (01923) 593454 *fax* (01923) 593613
email ian@digitalaudiotech.com
website www.digitalaudiotech.com

DAT sales, rentals and studio facilities.

Dolby Laboratories

Wootton Bassett, Wiltshire SN4 8QJ
tel (01793) 842100 *fax* (01793) 842101
email info@dolby.co.uk
website www.dolby.com

Services include: digital mastering and distribution; theatre presentation inspections; and lab quality-control during print manufacture.

Dubbs

25-26 Poland Street, London W1F 8QN
tel 020-7629 0055 *fax* 020-7287 8796
email info@dubbs.co.uk
website www.dubbs.co.uk

Elite Television

248 Meanwood Road, West Yorkshire, Leeds LS7 2HZ
tel 0113-262 3342 *fax* 0113-262 3798
email info@elitetv.co.uk
website www.elitetv.co.uk

Services/facilities include: Smoke HD/SD editing; audio post with ProTools & AudioVision; Avid online & offline; computerised Video Rostrum camera system; VTR machine room; studio sound stage with cyc & cove + blue/green chroma drapes & ready-rigged cyc lighting; DVD encoding, authoring & duplication; 3D Studio Max graphics & Combustion.

Film Work Group Studios

Top Floor, Chelsea Reach, 79-89 Lots Road, London SW10 0RN
tel 020-7352 0538 *fax* 020-7351 6479

Framestore CFC

9 Noel Street, London W1F 8GH
tel 020-7208 2600 *fax* 020-7208 2626
email info@framestore-cfc.com
website www.framestore-cfc.com

Well-respected and award-winning international post-production facility, which specialises in CG animation and digital visual effects.

Frontline Television Services

35 Bedforbury, Covent Garden, London WC2N 4DU
tel 020-7836 0411 *fax* 020-7379 5210
website www.frontline-tv.co.uk

Glassworks London Limited

33-34 Great Pulteney Street, London W1F 9NP
tel 020-7434 1182 *fax* 020-7434 1183
email romilly@glassworks.co.uk
website www.glassworks.co.uk
Managing Director Romilly Endacott

Glassworks provides digital animation and effects expertise for the production of creative visual content. Acclaimed work includes the award-winning promo for Bjork, and commercials for Aero and Sprite.

Goldcrest Post Production Facilities Ltd

1 Lexington Street, 36-44 Brewer Street, London W1F 9LX
tel 020-7439 7972 *fax* 020-7437 5402
email info@goldcrestpost.co.uk
website www.goldcrestpost.co.uk

One of London's premier post-production houses. Facilities include: 5 newly refitted digital mixing theatres; 60 editing rooms/production offices; 60-seat presentation theatre and bar; 7 luxury self-catering apartments; motion capture/voice-over booth; Foley recording theatres; ADR recording theatres; sound design; and Avid/Lightworks editing systems.

Feature credits include: *Batman Begins*, *The Brothers Grimm*, *The Lion, The Witch and The Wardrobe*, and *Flight 93*.

Herbert Media

Bond Street, Coventry CV1 4AH
tel 024-7683 2310
email info@theherbert.org
website www.theherbert.org

A community arts resource, which includes an art gallery and museum, creative media studios, and an arts information centre. Studios include: 2 x edit suites (Mac based – Final Cut & Avid); recording studio; DVC Pro 50 & DV camera kits; lighting & audio kit; and New Media production suites. Also offers training and community project support.

Humphries Video Services

Unit 2, The Willow Business Centre,
17 Willow Lane, Mitcham, Surrey CR4 4BNX
tel 020-8648 6111 *fax* 020-8648 5261
email sales@hvs.co.uk
website www.hvs.co.uk

In addition to video editing facilities, Humphries also has new media facilities ranging from CD and DVD encoding, authoring and low-volume burning to high-volume replication.

Terry Jones Post Productions Ltd

Goldcrest International, 65-66 Dean Street,
London W1D 4PL
tel 020-7434 1173 *fax* 020-7494 1893
email terryjonespost@btconnect.com
website www.terryjonespostproductions.co.uk

Kinetic Pictures at Light House Media Centre

The Chubb Buildings, Fryer Street,
Wolverhampton WV1 1HT
tel (01902) 716044 *fax* (01902) 717143
email info@light-house.co.uk
website www.light-house.co.uk

Based at the Light House, Kinetic has been producing high-quality promotional training and corporate videos since 1996. The company offers experienced production staff and crew, up-to-date filming and editing technology, graphic design and 3D animation. Duplication is available on a variety of formats, including DVD, VHS and DV, and can incorporate graphic design to produce a media package of high standard.

The Machine Room

54-58 Wardour Street, London W1D 4JQ
tel 020-7734 3433 *fax* 020-7287 3773
email info@themachineroom.co.uk
website www.themachineroom.co.uk

Mersey Film and Video (MFV)

13 Hope Street, Liverpool L1 9BQ
tel 0151-708 5259 *fax* 0151-707 8595
email info@mersey-film-video.co.uk
website www.mersey-film-video.co.uk

Mersey dry-hires video camera, lighting and grip equipment and Avid post-production equipment. Also offers a range of creative production and post services.

Met Film & TV

126 Bolingbroke Grove, Clapham,
London SW11 1DA
tel 020-7738 2727
website www.mftv.co.uk
Contact Julie Montagu

Met Film & TV supplies a full range of competitive post services for film, broadcast, commercials and corporate clients. As part of the Arts Alliance Media group, Met has particular expertise in all aspects of digital film post-production. With locations in Clapham and Ealing Studios, facilities include several HD/SD offline suites, 3 SD and 1 HD online suites, as well as a 2000 sq. ft. stage, plus a real-time, uncompressed 2K or HD colour grading system plus voiceover and audio suites.

The Mill

40/41 Great Marlborough Street, London W1F 7JQ
tel 020-7287 4041 *fax* 020-7287 8393
email mproducers@the-mill.com
website www.the-mill.com

Internationally acclaimed visual effects company, with offices in London, New York and Los Angeles. The Mill specialises in CG, digital effects, digital grading and telecine, with many high-profile credits in the film, commercials and music promo industries. Film credits include: *The Wilderness*, *Gladiator* and *Black Hawk Down*.

Molinare

34 Fouberts Place, London W1F 7PX
tel 020-7478 7000 *fax* 020-7478 7199
email bookings@molinare.co.uk
website www.molinare.co.uk

MiliFilm is a department of Molinare, which provides full film and digital post services. Services for 16mm, super 16mm, 35mm and super 35mm take the film from telecine through to release prints, and for digital video, from grading and FX processes through to the final print.

The Moving Picture Company

127 Wardour Street, London W1F 0NL
tel 020-7434 3100 *fax* 020-7437 3951
email mailbox@moving-picture.com
website www.moving-picture.com

One of the UK's major post facilities. Creates high-end digital visual effects and computer animation for the advertising, music, television and feature film industries. Post-production capabilities and facilities include: telecine, compositing, visual effects, digital intermediate, tape-to-film transfer, motion capture, and HD post. Specialist creative staff include: VFX supervisors (2D & 3D), computer animators and compositors.

Recent clients/projects include: Adidas – 'Gimme the Ball' (Fredrik Bond); Stella Artois – 'Ice Skating Priests' (Jonathan Glazer); *Kingdom of Heaven* (Ridley Scott); and *Batman Begins* (Christopher Nolan).

Oasis Television

6-7 Great Pulteney Street, London W1F 9NA
tel 020-7434 4133 *fax* 020-7494 2843

email bookings@oasistv.co.uk
website www.oasistv.co.uk

Oxford Film and Video Makers (OFVM)

Centre for Film and Digital Media,
54 Catherine Street, Oxford OX4 3AH
tel (01865) 792732
email office@ofvm.org
website www.ofvm.org

A community-based production initiative with post-production facilities and courses in post, from editing to using digital sound software and animation. Also see page 221.

The Pierce Rooms

Pierce House, London Apollo Complex,
Queen Caroline Street, London W6 9QU
tel 020-8563 1234 *fax* 020-8563 1337
website www.pierce-entertainment.com

High-end music recording studios in Soho.

Rushes

66 Old Compton Street, London W1D 4UH
tel 020-7437 8676 *fax* 020-7851 6392
email joce@rushes.co.uk
website www. rushes.co.uk
Managing Director Joce Capper

One of the world's leading post-production facilities, Rushes is synonymous with creative excellence and expertise. Its creative teams boast the best talent in town working with the best technology available, including world-class Telecine and 3D/CGI departments, and a comprehensive Motion Control Studio. Also runs Rushes Soho Shorts Film Festival.

Salon Ltd

12 Swainson Road, London W3 7XB
tel 020-8746 7611 *fax* 020-8746 7613
email hire@salonrentals.com
website www.salonrentals.com

Offers Avid, Lightworks and Apple non-linear editing systems for hire, plus a full range of VTRs and also a fleet of linear editing equipment. Editing suites are available; can also offer ACSR technicians.

TVMS (TV Media)

420 Sauchiehall Street, Glasgow G2 3JD
tel 0141-331 1993 *fax* 0141-332 9040
email mail@tvms.wanadoo.co.uk
Director Peter McNeill

Rental of Sony DSR 500 DvCam with wide-angle lens, as well as production facilities and services of editors for Avid and Final Cut Pro high-def.

Videosonics Cinema Sounds

68a Delancey Street, London NW1 7RY
tel 020-7209 0209 *fax* 020-7419 4470
email info@videosonics.com
website www.videosonics.com

Videosonics specialises in sound for film and television, covering all aspects of the audio post-production process. The company has 3 sites – 2 in Camden and 1 in Central London.

VTR Ltd

64 Dean Street, London W1V 5HG
tel 020-7437 0026 *fax* 020-7439 9427
email info@vtr.co.uk
website www.vtr.co.uk

Windmill Lane

4 Windmill Lane, Dublin 2, Ireland
tel ++353 1 671 3444 *fax* ++353 1 671 8413
email nfo@windmilllane.com
website www.windmilllane.com

Post-production facility with a number of on- and offline Avid suites for both Mac and PC; telecine; and special effects capabilities.

Courses

01zero-one

c/o Westminster Kingsway College, Soho Centre, Peter Street, London W1F 0HS
tel 020-7025 1985
email info@01zero-one.co.uk
website www.01zero-one.co.uk

Creative learning lab in Soho which uses state-of-the-art facilities and software for Professional Film, Broadcast, Internet Convergence and Post Production Courses in the heart of Soho. 01zero-one has state-of-the-art, TV studio, Mac Suites and kit. It runs courses in partnership with BBC Training and Skillset. Courses include: Final Cut Pro, Avid, Internet Broadcasting, HDV camera, Shake and Vjing.

Alchemea

The Windsor Centre, Windsor Street, Islington, London N1 8QG
tel 020-7704 4035 *fax* 020-7704 2056
email info@alchemea.com
website www.alchemea.com

A leading college of sound engineering, music production and post-production training. Offers a Diploma course, certificate and range of evening and weekend courses in post-production skills and software education. Fees vary depending on course.

BBC Training and Development

Wood Norton, Evesham, Worcs WR11 4YB
tel 0870-122 0216 *fax* 0870-122 0145
email training@bbc.co.uk
website www.bbctraining.com

BBC Training and Devlopment offers a number of courses, which are primarily aimed at professionals who work in the media industry.

Bournemouth University – see page 23 for contact details.

Bournemouth offers an MA in Post-Production for composers, editors and sound designers.

Cintel International

Watton Road, Ware, Herts SG12 0AE
tel (01920) 463939 *fax* (01920) 484722
email training@cintel.co.uk
website www.cintel.co.uk

Cintel offers a week-long full-time course for telecine operators and colourists.

University of East London

Visual Arts, Digital Arts & Visual Communications, Docklands Campus, 4-6 University Way, London E16 2RD
tel 020-8223 3000
website www.uel.ac.uk

Escape Studios

Shepherds West, Rockley Road, London W14 0DA
tel 020-7348 1920 *fax* 020-7348 1921
email info@escapestudios.co.uk
website www.escapestudios.co.uk

First Post London – see page 162 for contact details.

A new entrants' trainee programme for the post-production industry. Launched by Skillset and UK Post's Post-Production Training Committee, the programme helps employers provide structured development for junior employees. It is a modular scheme covering technical, commercial and customer skills.

Intermedia Film & Video (Nottingham) Ltd

19 Heathcote Street, Nottingham NG1 3AF
tel 0115-955 6909 *fax* 0115-955 9956
email enquiries@intermedia-notts.demon.co.uk
website www.intermedianotts.co.uk

Intermedia is a production support, training and facilities company based in the centre of Nottingham.

London College of Communication – see page 24 for contact details.

Offers a part-time 10-day course on post-production for film and video.

Metro Broadcasting

53 Great Suffolk Street, London SE1 0DB
tel 020-7202 2000 *fax* 020-7202 2001
email info@metrobroadcast.com
website www.metrobroadcast.com

Metro New Media

35 Kingsland Road, Shoreditch, London E2 8AA
tel 020-7729 9992 *fax* 020-7739 7742
email training@metronewmedia.com
website www.metronewmedia.com

National Film and Television School – see page 354 for contact details.

Offers a Diploma in Digital Post-Production, and an MA in Sound Post-Production. Short Courses @ NFTS also runs a range of part-time short post-production courses.

Northern Media School – see entry under page 354 for contact details.

Northern Media School's MA in Film and Media Production allows students to choose a post-production specialism.

Oxford Film and Video Makers

Centre for Film & Digital Media, 54 Catherine Street, Oxford OX4 3AH
tel (01865) 792731
email office@ofvm.org
website www.ofvm.org
Course Manager Richard Duriez

Offers a range of training in weekend courses on many aspects of post-production, from editing to using digital sound software and animation. Also offers courses from beginner to intermediate levels in film and video production, and in screenwriting. Some courses are accreditated and many are run during evenings and weekends as well. Each summer, OFVM runs a Summer Screen programme for young people, with training and free events.

Ravensbourne College of Design and Communication

Walden Road, Chislehurst, Kent BR7 5SN
tel 020-8289 4900 *fax* 020 8325 8320
email info@rave.ac.uk
website www.ravensbourne.ac.uk

Ravensbourne offers a full-time BA in Broadcasting Post-Production.

The Recording Workshop

Unit 10, Buspace Studios, Conlan Street, London W10 5AP
tel 020-8968 8222 *fax* 020-7460 3164
email info@therecordingworkshop.co.uk
website www.trwuk.com

VET Training

Lux Building, 2-4 Hoxton Square, London N1 6US
tel 020-7505 4700 *fax* 020-7505 4800
email training@vet.co.uk
website www.vet.co.uk
Training Manager Urte Sonnenberg

Training providers in multimedia, digital and post-production technology, with regular short courses covering a wide variety of post-production skills including: Video Technology; HD Camera Operation; DVD Authoring; and Final Cut Pro Editing. Also offers extensive series of Avid-certified courses. Course booking forms, dates and fees are available from the website. Bursaries are also available.

University West of England

Media Centre, Bower Ashton, Bristol BS3 2JT
tel 0117-328 4775 *fax* 0117-328 4743
website www.uwe.ac.uk

Publicity
How film productions can use well-planned PR throughout the movie lifecycle

Charles McDonald demystifies the process, with an A-Z of film PR ...

And God Created Woman – setting the scene

Just as filmmaking is an art and not a science (despite the efforts of big blockbusters to sledgehammer their way into the purses of the worldwide cinema-going public), so is the supporting craft of film PR. It may seem as though I am laying down the rules of the game in this introduction, but I am actually spicing the accepted practices with various preferred methodologies of my own, to suggest one particular way to pursue this craft. It is not necessarily the only way, but – given some exceptions – it seems to work for us.

Hiring a PR company to handle all the aspects of publicity from announcement onwards is definitely the preferred approach, if a film's budget allows. It's hard enough for you as a filmmaker to write your script and get it made without having to become a PR expert too. So much of effective PR relies on knowing what information to release and to whom. Films compete for attention with so many other types of information, entertainment and art; your window of opportunity to get press attention is actually quite narrow, so timing is essential. Ideally, if you do hire PR, it's preferable to do it well before the cameras roll. This will help to start developing a strategy for raising interest in the film that anticipates its international distribution roll-out.

As a filmmaker reading this, you will want to think about this section on Publicity as it relates to your film. What are the newsworthy elements of your project? The list is potentially endless. It could be a theme, your cast, based on a real-life incident, the setting ... are you filming on an unusual site? Even the costumes could be newsworthy. If you read newspapers and the film press, then you have a better understanding of what types of stories they are interested in and you will better know how to present your film. Marketing shouldn't *drive* the content of your film, but you can find a story in anything.

Of course, some films could almost be said to have been dreamed up to milk publicity, such as the one that heads this paragraph, where Svengali director Roger Vadim's marketing of Brigitte Bardot seems to determine the content of the film. PR and movie became inseparable. However, those are still the exceptions, even in Cannes ...

Absolute Beginners – make the most of the announcement

The first chance you have to create a buzz about any film is by announcing the creative team and the acting talent who will be combining to make the project fly. Ideally, this should take place at one given time to foster the impression of a unified, coherent whole – but we all know that the film world often doesn't allow such luxuries. If the announcements have to be piecemeal, then a steady drip-feed of exciting names attaching themselves to the project can accomplish the same result.

Even one big name can sometimes do the trick. For instance, the news in 1986 that David Bowie was to appear in and write the music for *Absolute Beginners* was naturally received with great enthusiasm. Ironically, the same film also offers a cautionary tale on this type of PR approach. The enormous media interest in the film generated in the production phase may very well have contributed to the film's failure at the box office. The hype was so extraordinary that it was almost impossible for the film to live up to those inflated expectations.

One of Our Aircraft is Missing – the importance of unit publicity

Unit publicity often tends to get forgotten in the blaze of advertising, marketing and PR that surrounds the launch of a movie – yet it is a crucial part of the mix. The most important job during production is to ensure that your basic materials are in place: good stills, an EPK (electronic press kit – see below), and the written materials. The last thing you want to do is realise that you don't have the right materials to promote your film later down the line.

Depending on the PR value of your story, and on your actors, you may also get requests from journalists who want interviews during the shoot. It's obviously important to balance your need for publicity with the sensitivities of the shoot. Asking actors to conduct lengthy interviews on set is a little unfair, I feel. Shooting out of sequence demands a pretty serious level of concentration for an actor, and if that concentration is compromised by a media interview, then the eventual quality of the performance and film could be jeopardised. In addition to which, I wonder to what extent a film's eventual audience remembers the carefully placed location report in the *Daily Telegraph* (or wherever), 12 months earlier? Having said that, these location reports can be valuable in building awareness within the industry – among distributors, exhibitors, other press, etc. – in the trade publications, so I'd never say 'never'. It's all about balance, so prioritise wisely.

If you are planning to announce your film during production, you should carefully consider how you position it. In the case of Tim Roth's powerful directorial debut *The War Zone* and Roger Michell's *The Mother*, we decided to not even announce the film to the media during production. This avoided the danger of either film being inaccurately labelled before its completion. Once a film is described in a particular way by the media, it is notoriously hard to shift that description.

The Man Who Shot Liberty Valance – hire a killer photographer

In the general run of things, our job is to register the idea of the film in the collective unconscious, so that when the pre-launch publicity begins, it seems as though it were an organic development of a creative work, rather than a surprise (however welcome it may be).

So, assuming that we've joined the team in the early stages, the immediate thing we do is make sure that there is a first-rate stills photographer attached to the project. Striking images are very important in embedding the idea of the movie in the consciousness of the film-going public; far more so than articles. Film is a visual medium, after all.

The fact is, often when reading a magazine or newspaper, your attention is first drawn to an image rather than to a block of copy or even a provocative headline. It may not always be true that a picture beats a thousand words – but often, it is. An iconic image makes a film resonate in the public consciousness. One only has to look at the pictures of the films of Quentin Tarantino or Pedro Almodóvar for examples. The stills photographer may be our choice, or s/he may be a pet photographer of the director, star or producer – whoever is chosen, you must make sure that s/he delivers the goods.

In our experience, directors do not always quite get the idea that the first thing most of their potential audience will see of their work is a still. From that image, your audience will make a conscious or unconscious decision as to whether they are interested in learning more about the film, and eventually whether they will pay to see the film.

The Front Page – the electronic press kit

The press kit is designed to give journalists and editors of all media a comprehensive background to the film, incorporating full cast and crew lists, biographies, interviews, synopses, and (if necessary) background information. It does not impinge on the advertising campaigns, although it does support them fully.

The electronic version (the EPK) was initially designed and created to give the electronic media access to cast and crew interviews, B roll taken during the shoot, and filmed features on interesting aspects of the film – special effects or make-up, historical research, locations, etc. Historically, the EPK was a source of some frustration for producers – an apparently unnecessary add-on to their already stretched budget. Now, however, they are an integral part of the delivery, and on a film's DVD release, the added extras (primarily EPK material) are reviewed as much as the film itself. It's so important in publicity terms, that we've asked Colin Burrows from Special Treats to write an article about it, which you will find on page 242.

Death in Venice, Funeral in Berlin or *That Riviera Touch* – festivals and awards

I've only got one thing to say about festivals – go to them. Even if your film doesn't win an award (although that would be outstanding, of course) you will still learn a great deal as well as meeting likely buyers and influencers who can help your project succeed.

Part of your PR campaign is also designed to secure distribution, usually in your home territory (if not agreed already) and then overseas. Festivals and markets are key opportunities to unleash your PR campaign on potential buyers.

Sunset Boulevard – line up the filmmakers to walk alongside you

When an international campaign is planned, it makes sense to ensure well in advance that the acting talent is booked-in to support the film. It should go without saying that your actors will help you to get editorial publicity. Although usually the preserve of star actors, in certain cases the director or other core filmmakers can also be used to striking effect. The cult of the *auteur* is alive and well, particularly in continental Europe.

We find it useful, when planning an international campaign, to decide which territories we would like key talent to visit in advance of the requests coming in. Invariably, it is the smaller territories who ask first – and often most persuasively. If a director accepts several trips to these less significant territories, his or her enthusiasm for interviews may well have waned before the essential trips to the major countries.

No Orchids for Miss Blandish – identify the core audiences

One of the vital tasks that we have to fulfil is work out the key types of people who are likely to go to see the movie, and make sure the publicity campaign is directed squarely at them. We need to know how to reach them and understand what captures their attention.

To use an example, you might be making a period drama which you feel will appeal to an older audience, and which you are shooting in a National Trust property. It may sound unnecessary to you while you are shooting, or seem like a pain to release a photograph, but it just might plant a seed with this core audience. And if the truth be told, this older audience takes a little longer to be convinced about a film. This is one of the problems with modern distribution plans, where everything is geared towards that opening weekend. If it doesn't work on that brutal opening weekend, then you are in trouble theatrically. Your PR campaign needs try to get to the core audience well before the reviews come out on the opening weekend.

Of course, focusing on your main audience shouldn't mean that you don't try to dream up clever ways of reaching other film-goers – just not at the expense of your core target. Tom Grieveson of Metrodome's press and marketing campaign for *Donnie Darko* was a brilliant example of tapping into a number of varied potential audiences.

When we were working on Ian McKellen's *Richard III* (this was 1996, the pre-Gandalf era, when he was merely known as a great classical theatre actor), we did our best to make the film appear as attractive as we could to mainstream audiences. This was indeed the intention of Richard Loncraine and McKellen in setting the action in some neo-fascistic state, albeit with 30s overtones. It is probable that in emphasising the action elements of the film – tanks, explosions, black uniforms, etc – the modern strand of publicity may have put off some of the core Shakespeare lovers (a slightly older crowd), and only bemused the multiplexers. The moral to draw from this is: we ignore our core audiences at our peril.

My Name Is Nobody – don't destroy your credibility

Some people say that, in publicity terms, you can never do too much. I'm sure that may be so in some fields of PR, but as far as film publicity goes, I disagree. It really can be the case that you can over-hype a movie and push it down people's throats so much that they react against it. To me, the essence of film PR is that we have to create enough awareness about its existence but still let the audience feel that they're discovering the film for themselves. This is a very fine line to have to judge, of course, but a welcome and stimulating challenge of course.

How The West Was Won – plan your international strategy

There is usually a creative agency that is hired specifically to work on the poster and press advertising campaign – their people will be responsible for dreaming up the taglines. We do have an opportunity to comment and may have a say in the eventual outcome, but there is still a distinction between that sort of advertising copy and the free editorial copy which we are aiming to place.

So the international strategy you dream up must be designed to bolster, rather than deflect from, the main strands of the advertising campaigns. This is sometimes easier said than done – especially when so many countries and territories have such different outlooks and needs.

A Zed And Two Noughts – conclusions

If you are a new filmmaker, I understand that PR won't be your first priority. It'll be enough to just think about raising finance, getting your cast together, finding locations. Yet the bottom line is that if you are making a feature, there are two crucial things you will need to do:

1. Create an awareness in the trade papers. This is the least that you should do; it will help you to get distributors and sell the film, and it will plant a seed with national and regional press as well.

2. Get your basic press materials in place, because you can't go back and recreate them later. By this I mean the EPK and photography. It's so essential; I have said it here already and we will bang it home in this section: basic good publicity stills can make or break a film. Look through the colour supplements this weekend: it will be an image that gets your attention. An image will say: 'it shocks me', 'it intrigues me', 'it horrifies me', 'it's sexy' ... then you will read about the film.

In conclusion: is film PR a good life? In short, yes – although it's by no means an easy one. I've met some great directors, cinematographers, art directors, film editors, musicians, actresses and actors, along with many other inspiring creative talents, and visited some wonderful places and taken part in many lively festivals. But it is long hours, hard work, and if you think the big money in films filters down to the publicity machines, forget it. But then you'll know that it's not about the money, if you are reading this as a new filmmaker or producer!

Charles McDonald co-founded McDonald & Rutter in 1994. In 2006, M&R merged with Premier PR, becoming the CEO of the newly formed company. Premier PR (including McDonald & Rutter) covers PR for film, theatre, television, brands, events media management and personal representation. Over the years, Charles has worked on many high-profile and successful campaigns, including *Bend It Like Beckham*, which saw a small film crash through the barrier to become an international hit; French hit film *Amelie*; and *Downfall*, which was nominated for numerous awards and had a level of publicity and praise not usually given to foreign films in the UK. In his work Charles has built long-term client relationships with filmmakers like Jim Jarmusch, Lars von Trier, Lukas Moodysson, Michael Winterbottom, Peter Greenaway, Terence Davies, Ken Loach, Pawel Pawlikowski, Lynne Ramsay, François Ozon, Roger Michell and Wim Wenders.

PR COMPANIES

The companies listed in this section offer a wide range of corporate and consumer publicity and marketing services to the film, broadcast and theatre industries. We have indicated where a company specialises in film PR.

The Associates

Monticello House, 45 Russell Square,
London WC1B 4JP
tel 020–7907 4770 *fax* 020-7907 4771
email info@the-associates.co.uk
website www.the-associates.co.uk
Executive Director Lisa Richards

PR company that specialises in press for DVD and video releases. Handles the home-entertainment press campaigns for companies such as Metrodome, Arrow Films and Anchor Bay.

Avalon Public Relations

4a Exmoor Street, London W10 6BD
tel 020-7598 7222 *fax* 020-7598 7223
email edt@avalonuk.com
website www.avalonuk.com

Established in 1997, Avalon PR offers a range of PR and marketing services: unit and broadcast publicity; product, media and theatrical launches; corporate and personal publicity; strategic release planning; and creative services for local, regional and national arts and entertainment events.

The Big Group

91 Princedale Road, London W11 4NS
tel 020-7229 8827 *fax* 020-7243 1462
email info@biggroup.co.uk
website www.biggroup.co.uk

Blue Dolphin PR and Marketing

40 Langham Street, London W1W 7AS
tel 020-7255 2494 *fax* 020-7580 7670
email info@bluedolphinpr.com
website www.bluedolphinpr.com

This PR company is an offshoot of Blue Dolphin Film & Video, which offers arts and entertainment publicity for feature films in its theatrical release, DVD and video releases, and also for TV programmes and music PR. Established in the mid-1980s, clients have included: BMG, Island Records, MGM, Universal Pictures, Warner Brothers, and BBC Worldwide.

The Braben Company

18b Pindock Mews, London W9 2PY
tel 020-7289 1616 *fax* 020-7289 1166
email enquiries@braben.co.uk
website www.braben.co.uk

Launched in 1994 by the former marketing director of Capital Radio, this PR company has specialist divisions in Broadcast, Publishing and Entertainment. Recent campaigns have included: *Nefertiti Uncovered* for Discovery, and the DVD releases of *Thirteen* for Universal and *Indiana Jones* for Paramount.

Byron Advertising, Marketing and PR

Byron House, Wallingford Road, Uxbridge,
Middlesex UB8 2RW
tel (01895) 252131 *fax* (01895) 252137
email enquiries@byron.co.uk
website www.b-different.com

Max Clifford Associates

Moss House, 15-16 Brooks Mews, Mayfair,
London W1K 4DS
tel 020-7408 2350 *fax* 020-7409 2294
email max@maxclifford.com
website www.maxclifford.com

Major entertainment and media PR company.

DDA Public Relations Ltd

192-198 Vauxhall Bridge Road, London SW1V 1DX
tel 020-7932 9800 *fax* 020-7932 4950
email info@ddapr.com
website www.ddapr.com

Specialist international film PR company established in 1970, DDA represents all aspects of the film industry. With offices in London, Los Angeles, and Sydney as well as affiliates and associates in most other parts of the world, it aims to offer a global reach for film and television producers and distributors. Performs a wide range of media relations, publicity and marketing tasks – either international or targeted to specific markets. Services include: strategic PR planning, unit publicity, UK theatrical release publicity, and festival publicity and event management.

Emfoundation

The Old Truman Brewery, 91-95 Brick Lane,
London E1 6QN
tel 020-7247 4171 *fax* 020-7247 4170
email info@emfoundation.com
website www.emfoundation.co.uk
Publicist Keeley Naylor

Established in 1998, Emfoundation is a specialist film PR company which covers unit/production publicity, distribution and DVD publicity as well as offering premiere and event management and corporate publicity. Titles range from independent labels to major studio releases. Campaigns cover all media and are national and regional (all cities).

Frank PR

3rd Floor, Centro 4, 20-23 Mandela Street,
London NW1 0DU
tel 020-7693 6999 *fax* 020-7693 6998
email contactus@frankpr.it
website www.frankpr.it

Creative general media PR and marketing company.

Freud Communications

19-21 Mortimer Street, London W1T 3DX
tel 020-7580 2626 *fax* 020-7637 2626
email info@freud.com
website www.freud.com

Specialises in film and broadcast, and offers strategic planning and marketing for clients cuch as the BAFTA Awards, SKY and a number of distribution and production companies.

HPS-PR Ltd

Park House, Desborough Park Road,
High Wycombe, Bucks HP12 3DJ
tel (01628) 894700
email letstalk@hpsgroup.co.uk
website www.hpsgroup.co.uk

Broad-ranging PR, advertising and marketing consultancy firm.

Sue Hyman Associates

St Martin's House, 59 St Martin's Lane,
London WC2N 4JS
tel 020-7379 8420 *fax* 020-7379 4944
email sue.hyman@btinternet.com
website www.suehyman.com
Director Sue Hyman

Publicity company whose clients include a number of West End musicals; plays include *Festen* as well as Kristin Scott Thomas and Bob Hoskins in *As You Desire Me*. Royal Galas include the John Betjeman Centenary; also David Suchet in *The Last Confession* and *Nicholas Nickleby* in the West End and Canada.

McDonald and Rutter (M&R) – see page 229.

Media Communications Ltd

Research House, Fraser Road, Perivale,
Middlesex UB6 7AQ
tel 020-8998 1517 *fax* 020-8566 8290
email chinapa.aguh@mediacomms.co.uk

Media Communications primarily covers PR for the release of home-entertainment titles.

The PR Contact

Assessoria em Artes Ltd, Rua Visconde de Piraja,
N 434 Casa 5 – Ipanema, Rio de Janeiro – RJ,
CEP: 22410-022, Brazil
tel ++ 55 21 3201 1072
email pressoffice@theprcontact.com
website www.theprcontact.com
Directors Phil Symes, Ronaldo Mourao

International film PR company based in Brazil but with much work in the UK. The company primarily handles unit publicity, festival publicity and individual film campaigns at international film festivals.

Premier PR

91 Berwick Street, London W1F 0NE
tel 020-7292 8330 *fax* 020-7734 2024
email enquiries@premierpr.com
website www.premierpr

Premier manages the media activity of clients in film, TV, home entertainment, theatre and events. The company's roster of corporate clients includes BBC Films and Hanway Films. Premier has also worked on film press and media campaigns for *The Queen*, all 3 *Shrek* films, *Notes on a Scandal* and *Babel*, covering premieres, festivals and theatrical release respectively. Handles press and media activity from announcement to unit publicity, through theatrical release.

Also see Charles McDonald's article on page 223.

Rogers & Cowan

5th Floor, Cardinal Place, 80 Victoria Street,
London SW1E 5JL
tel 020-3048 0480
email inquiries@rogersandcowan.com
website www.rogersandcowan.com
Account Director, Film Emma McCorkell

International PR company specialising in film publicity.

Peter Thompson Associates

12 Bourchier Street, London W1D 4HZ
tel 020-7439 1210
email info@ptassociates.co.uk

Verve Public Relations

(formerly CJP Public Relations)
Park House, 8 Grove Ash, Mount Farm,
Milton Keynes MK1 1BZ
tel (01908) 275271
website www.vervepr.co.uk

Verve was established in 1993 and handles all kinds of publicity, including brand launches, event management and consumer PR. Corporate film and media clients have included: Working Title Films, Sky Movies, UIP, and Film Four.

Sarah Wilby Creative Publicity

45a Rathbone Street, London W1T 1NW
tel 020-7580 0222 *fax* 020-7580 0333

email sarah@swcp.co.uk

PR company specialising in UK and international film publicity. Recent campaigns include: *Little Miss Sunshine.*

TRADE MAGAZINES

These publications carry business and creative news and analysis for the film, broadcast and new media industries.

Broadcast

EMAP Media, 33–39 Bowling Green Lane,
London EC1R 0DA
tel 020-7505 8014 *fax* 020-7505 8050
website www.broadcastnow.co.uk
Editor Lisa Campbell

Weekly trade magazine covering TV and radio industries.

Cinema Business

Quadrant House, 250 Kennington Lane,
London SE11 5RD
tel 0845-270 7871
email mark.moran@landor.co.uk
website cinemabusiness.co.uk

Monthly magazine for people who show, distribute and market films. Includes industry news, analysis and theatrical release information.

Creative Review

50 Poland Street, London W1F 7AX UK
tel 020-7970 4000
email patrick.burgoyne@centaur.co.uk
website www.creativereview.co.uk
Editor Patrick Burgoyne

Monthly magazine for visual communication industries, including design and new media.

The Hollywood Reporter

London Office: 50-51 Bedford Row,
London WC1R 4LR
tel 020-7420 6004
website www.hollywoodreporter.com
Editor Cynthia Littleton

Major industry news source with emphasis on US industry and world industries as they interact with the US. Established in the 1930s. Now has significant online presence.

Home Entertainment Week

3rd Floor, Jordon House, 47 Brunswick PLace,
London N1 6EB
website www.heweek.co.uk
Editor Peter Dodd

In Camera

Kodak House, Entertainment Imaging, PO Box 9B,
Thames Ditton, Surrey KT7 0BR

indieWIRE

indieWIRE LLC, 320 7th Avenue, #297, Brooklyn,
NY 11215, USA
tel ++ 1 212 675 3908
email office@indiewire.com (for editorial contact and press releases)
website www.indiewire.com
Editor Brian Brooks

Influential online daily publication launched in 1996 and covering the world of independent moviemaking and film festivals.

International Connection

Brave New World International Ltd,
Orchardton House, Auchencairn, Galloway DG7 1QL
tel 0845-130 6249 *fax* 0845-658 8329
email maker@bnw.demon.co.uk
website www.britishfilm.tv
Editor Susan Foster

Quarterly print publication, which includes reviews, news and industry analysis. Also publishes consumer film site, Movie Club News.

Media Week

Haymarket Publishing Ltd, 174 Hammersmith Road,
London W6 7JP
tel 020-8267 8026
email mweeked@mediaweek.co.uk
Editor Philip Smith

News and analysis of the UK advertising media and marketing industry. Illustrations: full colour and b&w. Founded 1985.

The PACT Magazine

Monthly members' magazine about UK film and television business issues, published by the Producers' Alliance for Film and Television. See page 96.

Press Gazette

Press Gazette Ltd, 10 Old Bailey, London EC4M 7NG
tel 020-7038 1055 *fax* 020-7038 1155
email ianr@pressgazette.co.uk
website www.pressgazette.co.uk
Editor Ian Reeves

News and features of interest to journalists and others working in the media. Founded 1965.

Screen Digest

Lyme House Studios, 38 Georgiana Street,
London NW1 0EB
tel 020-7424 2820 *fax* 020-7424 2838
email fay.hamilton@screendigest.com,
dan.stevenson@screendigest.com
website www.screengigest.com
Editor David Fisher

Key source of business intelligence, data, research and

analysis on global audiovisual media. Screen Digest is a research company that provides a range of syndicated research services with a database of global audiovisual market research information. It also publishes a monthly research briefing. Magazine covers: television, broadband, home entertainment (DVD & video), interactive (games consoles, mobile and TV), and cinema.

Screen International

EMAP Media, 33–39 Bowling Green Lane, London EC1R 0DA
tel 020-7505 8000 *fax* 020-7505 8117
email screeninternational@hotmail.com
website www.screendaily.com
Editor Michael Gubbins

UK-published, weekly magazine with international news, reviews and features on film business around the world.

Screentrade Magazine

PO Box 144, Orpington, Kent BR6 6LZ
tel/fax (01689) 833117
email leslie@screentrademagazine.co.uk
PO Box 24, Spring Lake, MI 49456 (Pamala Stanton)
website www.screentrademagazine.co.uk
Editor Philip Turner

Founded 2000; the business magazine for the UK, European and North American Film Exhibition Industry, having also recently moved into Russian and Indian territory and, shortly, China. *Screentrade* is the only truly international magazine to represent all aspects of Cinema Exhibition & Film Distribution; and, recently engaging US exhibitors as columnists, has turned attention to independent filmmaking to help filmmakers better connect with theatre owners.

The Stage

(incorporating Television Today)
Stage House, 47 Bermondsey Street, London SE1 3XT
tel 020-7403 1818 *fax* 020-7357 9287
email editor@thestage.co.uk
website www.thestage.co.uk
Editor Brian Attwood

Weekly magazine which has articles on of interest to the broadcast and stage professions. Founded 1880.

Stage Screen & Radio

BECTU, 373-377 Clapham Road, London SW9 9B
tel 020-7346 0900 *fax* 020-7346 0962
email janice@stagescreenandradio.org.uk
website www.bectu.org.uk
Editor Janice Turner, Rebecca Wingate-Saul

Magazine published for members of BECTU trade union, and covering industry matters affecting writers, editors and all other grades in film. Published 10 times per year with Dec/Jan and July/Aug released jointly. Magazine editors welcome press releases about industry business issues, rather than consumer ones.

Television

Media House, Azalea Drive, Swanley, Kent BR8 8HH
tel (01322) 660070 *fax* (01322) 616376
Editor Boris Sedacca

Monthly magazine which covers the technical aspects of domestic TV and video equipment, such as servicing, long-distance TV, constructional projects, satellite TV, video recording, teletext and viewdata, test equipment, monitors. Founded 1950.

Televisual

48 Charlotte Street, London W1T 2NS
tel 020-3008 5779
email tim.dams@centaur.co.uk
Editor Tim Dams

Monthly magazine for the production community, covering broadcast and film. Coverage includes: analysis, interviews, features and unique industry surveys.

Variety

84 Theobalds Road, London WC1X 8RR
tel 020-7611 4580 *fax* 020-7611 4591
email news@variety.com
website www.variety.com
Vice President, Editor-in-Chief Peter Bart, *Editor* Timothy M Gray, *Executive Editor – News* Michael Speier, *Executive Editor – Features* Steven Gaydos, *Chief Film Critic* Todd McCarthy

Weekly trade magazine for all media industries, with emphasis on film coverage. Excellent website is accessed by subscription but has searchable archive of all film reviews and news coverage.

FILM PRESS

Not all of the publications in this section are specialist film magazines, but the following cover theatrical and/or home-entertainment film releases. Many also include serious writing about films and filmmaking – particularly the dedicated film publications listed throughout the section.

Arena

EMAP East, Endeavour House,
189 Shaftesbury Avenue, London WC2H 8JG
tel 020-7437 9011
email arenamag@emap.com
Editor Giles Hattersley
Monthly £3.60

Intelligent men's magazine, which features a small number of theatrical and DVD releases monthly.

Attitude

Remnant Media, Northern Shell Tower,
City Harbour, London E14 9GL
tel 020-7308 5090 *fax* 020-7308 5384
email attitude@nasnet.co.uk
website www.attitude.co.uk
Editor Adam Mattera

Men's style magazine aimed primarily, but not exclusively, at gay men; includes 6-7 film reviews monthly on intelligent commercial, independent and arthouse films.

Bella

H Bauer Publishing, Academic House,
24–28 Oval Road, London NW1 7DT
tel 020-7241 8000 *fax* 020-7241 8056

General-interest weekly magazine for women. Film coverage is limited to celeb interest and some reviews.

The Big Issue

1–5 Wandsworth Road, London SW8 2LN
tel 020-7526 3200
website www.bigissue.com
Editor-in-Chief John Bird

Weekly magazine featuring film reviews and interviews. Covers a range of film styles.

Cashiers du Cinema

website www.cahiersducinema.com

Legendary monthly French publication for cineastes, filmmakers, film historians and serious fans. Now publishes an English translation.

Cineaste

243 Fifth Avenue, Suite #706, New York, NY 10016, USA
tel ++ 1 212 366-5720
email cineaste@cineaste.com
website www.cineaste.com
Editor Cynthia Lucia, Richard Porton

Long-running quarterly magazine on the art and politics of cinema, with an emphasis on independent and world filmmakers. Also see website for writing submission guidelines.

Cinema Minima

email mail@cinemaminima.com
website www.cinemaminima.com

Daily online news digest for people who make films. Based in LA, news and the readership are international; the service has been running since 1999. Coverage includes: moviemaking, digital tools, editing, intellectual property rights, story, sound, acting, and distribution and festival news.

Dazed and Confused

112-116 Old Street, London EC1V 9BG
tel 020-7336 0766 *fax* 020-7336 0966
email rod@confused.co.uk, cath@anothermag.com
website www.confused.co.uk
Editor Rod Stanley *Film Editor* Cath Clarke

Monthly style magazine with some feature and review coverage of interesting independent films, and actors. The magazine also occasionally features interviews with actors and filmmakers.

Diva

Millivres Prowler Ltd, Spectrum House,
32-34 Gordon House Road, London NW5 1LP
tel 020-7424 7400 *fax* 020-7424 7401
email edit@divamag.co.uk
website www.divamag.co.uk
Editor Jane Czyzselska

Monthly style magazine which covers art and culture from a lesbian perspective. Feature 4-6 theatrical releases and 1 DVD release monthly. Covers mainly arthouse, G&L and independent releases.

Empire

Mappin House, 4 Winsley Street, London W1W 8HF
tel 020-7182 8781 *fax* 020-7182 8703
website www.empireonline.com
Editor Mark Dinning

Specialist monthly film magazine aimed at serious film fans, covering all releases; also includes interviews and features. Website features additional content.

FHM (For Him Magazine)

EMAP Élan Network, Mappin House,
4 Winsley Street, London W1W 8HF
tel 020-7182 8028 *fax* 020-7182 8021
website www.fhm.com
Editor Anthony Naguera

Monthly men's magazine with some film coverage – DVD, theatrical, interviews.

Film Comment

70 Lincoln Center Plaza, New York, NY 10023, USA
tel ++ 1 212 875 5610
email editor@filmlinc.com
website www.filmlinc.com
Editor Gavin Smith

Series film buffs' magazine published bimonthly by the Film Society of Lincoln Center. Covers arthouse, international and American indie cinema.

Film Ireland

Filmbase, Curved Street, Temple Bar, Dublin 2, Republic of Ireland
tel ++353 1 6711303 *fax* ++353 1 6796717
email editor@filmbase.ie
website www.filmireland.net
Editor Lir Mac Cárthaigh

Aims to be an open and pluralist forum for the

exchange of ideas and news on filmmaking and cinema, both Irish and international. Special reports, interviews and reviews; acts as a unique archival mirror of film activity in Ireland. Founded 1987.

Film Quarterly

University of California Press, Journals, 2000 Center Street, Suite 303, Berkeley, CA 94704-1223, USA
email journals@ucpress.edu
website www.filmquarterly.org
Editor Rob White

Quarterly film publication from University of Californa Press with serious scholarship on cinema and television, along with in-depth discussion of film business issues, serious film reviews and interviews.

Film Review

Visual Imagination Ltd, 9 Blades Court, Deodar Road, London SW15 2NU
tel 020-8875 1520 *fax* 020-8875 1588
website www.visimag.com
Editor Grant Kempster

Intelligent monthly film magazine which includes reviews for all theatrical and DVD releases as well as interviews and features.

Filmmaker Magazine

104 West 29th Street, 12th Floor, New York, NY 10001, USA
tel ++ 1 212 563 0211 *fax* ++ 1 212 563 1933
email scott@filmmakermagazine.com
website www.filmmakermagazine.com
Editor Scott Macaulay

Monthly US magazine for independent filmmakers. Includes interviews with filmmakers, reviews, and useful information about the industry.

Filmwaves

email filmwaves@filmwaves.co.uk
website www.filmwaves.co.uk
Editor Marco Zigiotti

Filmwaves is a non-profit quarterly publication dedicated to the art and culture of filmmaking. Magazine provides film cultural analysis and technical dialogue for filmmakers.

Gay Times – GT

Spectrum House, 32–34 Gordon House Road, London NW5 1LP
tel 020-7424 7400 *fax* 020-7424 7401
email edit@gaytimes.co.uk
website www.gaytimes.co.uk
Editor Joseph Galliano

Monthly magazine for gay men which reviews around 8 films/DVDs a month and runs related features. The Film/DVD editor is Andrew Copestake.

Glamour

The Condé Nast Publications Ltd, Vogue House, Hanover Square, London W15 1JU
tel 020-7499 9080 *fax* 020-7493 1345
email features@glamourmagazine.co.uk
website www.glamourmagazine.com
Editor Jo Elvin

Women's lifestyle magazine with some film coverage – celebrity features and film reviews.

GQ

Condé Nast Publications, Vogue House, Hanover Square, London W1S 1JU
tel 020-7499 9080 *fax* 020-7495 1679
website www.gq-magazine.co.uk
Editor Dylan Jones

Monthly men's style magazine with several film reviews each month and occasional film-related interviews.

Heat

Emap plc, Endeavour House, 189 Shaftesbury Avenue, London WC2H 8JG
tel 020-7859 8657 *fax* 020-7859 8670
email heat@emap.com
Editor Mark Frith
Film Editor Charles Gant
Weekly £1.65

Features and news on celebrities. Founded 1999.

Weekly film reviews covering theatrical releases and DVDs.

Hotdog

Jordan House, 47 Brunswick Place, London N1 6EB
tel 020-7608 6500
website www.hotdog-magazine.co.uk
Editor Xavier Robleda

In-depth film news, features and reviews for serious film fans with a sense of humour.

i-D Magazine

124 Tabernacle Street, London EC2A 4SA
tel 020-7490 9710 *fax* 020-7251 2225
email editor@i-dmagazine.co.uk
website www.i-dmagazine.com
Editor Glen Waldron

Fashion-orientated monthly with smart film coverage and interviews; tends to focus primarily on arthouse and independent releases.

Jump Cut

email jhess@igc.org
website www.ejumpcut.org
Editor John Hess

Launched in 1974, *Jump Cut* is a politically and intellectually engaged American film journal with an online site that includes much good content.

The List

14 High Street, Edinburgh EH1 1TE
tel 0131-550 3050 *fax* 0131-557 8500
email editor@list.co.uk
Editor Claire Prentice

Bi-weekly entertainment guide for Glasgow and Edinburgh; covers theatrical releases and includes film-related interviews and features.

Loaded

IPC Ignite, The Blue Fin Building,
110 Southwark Street, London SE1 0SU
tel 020-3148 5000 *fax* 020-3148 8107
website www.loaded.co.uk
Editor Martin Daubney

Monthly men's magazine with limited film coverage.

Marie Claire

European Magazines Ltd, 7th Floor,
The Blue Fin Building, 110 Southwark Street,
London SE1 0LU
tel 020-3148 7513
email marieclaire@ipcmedia.com
Editor Marie O'Riordan

Monthly womens' life and style magazine, which reviews several new films each month and includes celebrity interviews.

Maxim

Dennis Publishing Ltd, 30 Cleveland Street,
London W1T 4JD
tel 020-7907 6410 *fax* 020-7907 6439
email editorial.maxim@dennis.co.uk
website www.maxim-magazine.co.uk
Editor Derek Harbinson

Glossy men's monthly with capsule reviews of DVD and theatrical releases. Mostly mainstream blockbusters, but some cult and Asia extreme.

Radio Times

BBC Worldwide Ltd, 80 Wood Lane,
London W12 0TT
tel 020-8433 3400 *fax* 020-8433 3160
email radio.times@bbc.co.uk
website www.radiotimes.com
Editor Gill Hudson
Film Editor Andrew Collins

Articles that preview the week's TV and radio programmes, including film reviews. Website has an extensive searchable database of film reviews, including current theatrical releases.

Red

Hachette Filipacchi UK Ltd, 64 North Row,
London W1K 7LL
tel 020-7150 7000 *fax* 020-7150 7685
website www.redmagazine.co.uk

Smart monthly women's magazine aimed at an audience aged 25-45 years. Includes occasional features and some film reviews.

Sight and Sound

BFI, 21 Stephen Street, London W1T 1LN
tel 020-7255 1444 *fax* 020-7436 2327
website www.bfi.org.uk/sightandsound
Editor Nick James

Monthly specialist film magazine published by the BFI. Features topical and critical articles on world cinema of all genres and styles, reviews of all theatrical and DVD/video releases, and film book reviews with some television coverage. Aimed at serious film fans, academics and professionals.

Time Out

Time Out Group Ltd, Universal House,
251 Tottenham Court Road, London W1T 7AB
tel 020-7813 3000 *fax* 020-7813 6001
website www.timeout.com

Film Editor Tom Charity

Weekly London listings magazine covering all theatrical releases and festival screenings. Website includes additional content and searchable reviews database.

Total Film

Future Publishing, 2 Balcombe Street,
London NW1 6NW
tel 020-7042 4000 *fax* 020-7317 0275
email totalfilm@futurenet.co.uk
website www.futurenet.com
Editor Nev Pierce

Monthly movie magazine established in 1997. Film coverage includes reviews of all the new theatrical and home-entertainment releases, interviews, competitions and previews. Also publishes daily updates on the website. Send preview/screening invitations to Reviews Editor, Andy Lowe.

Uncut

IPC Media, 25th Floor, King's Reach Tower,
Stamford Street, London SE1 9LS
tel 020-7261 6992 *fax* 020-7261 5573
website www.uncut.co.uk
Editor Allan Jones *Deputy Editor* Paul Lester

Monthly music and movie magazine with features, interviews and reviews. Website includes much of magazine content.

Vanity Fair

The Condé Nast Publications Ltd, Vogue House,
Hanover Square, London W1S 1JU
tel 020-7499 9080 *fax* 020-7493 1962
website www.vanityfair.co.uk
Editor-in-Chief Graydon Carter

Monthly magazine covering media, glamour and politics for a savvy audience. Media coverage is primarily smart major mainstream or politically significant.

Vertigo

4th Floor, 26 Shacklewell Lane, London E8 2EZ
tel 020-7690 0124
email vertigo@vertigomagazine.co.uk
website www.vertigomagazine.co.uk
Co-editors Holly Aylett, Gareth Evans

Excellent quarterly magazine for serious film fans, cinema students, educators and other film professionals. The magazine champions innovation and diversity in cinema, and supports a culture of independent film.

Vogue

Vogue House, Hanover Square, London W1S 1JU
tel 020-7499 9080 *fax* 020-7408 0559
website www.vogue.co.uk
Editor Alexandra Shulman

Fashion and beauty magazine with some film coverage.

Notes from a picture editor

In this interview, **Debi Berry** gives tips on how to use your stills to get coverage in the film press.

What is the role of the picture editor within the film press?

For a magazine like *Empire*, the picture editor is in charge of sourcing all the images for the magazine. This includes pictures to run with reviews and features. Ultimately, the picture chosen will draw the reader in to the article, so selecting the best and strongest pictures is really important.

So, stills help to determine the amount of publicity a film is likely to get?

The better the imagery, the more pages we are likely to offer a film. We often have to cut pages and even reviews because we do not have sufficiently strong (if any) art to run with it. The earlier the stills can be made available, the better, too – this gives the film a better chance of coverage; it can be put into previews, so not limited to time-of-release coverage.

Do you think filmmakers generally understand how important stills are when they are on set?

Sometimes; it really depends how much they look at film press. I'm often shocked by the lack of awareness and also the lack of picture quality. With the move to digital, some stills really aren't up to the grade they should be for media print.

What do you look for in a photograph?

Something striking and intriguing; something that makes you want to learn more about the film. Also good quality – and the more exclusive, the better.

Are there common mistakes that film stills photographers make?

Shots that don't bring in enough of the world around the actor. A head shot or a portrait dosen't tell as much of a story as a character interacting with another, or with their surroundings. Also, the first shot released should be as exciting as possible. It gets us – and ultimately the reader – excited about the film.

What qualities does an image need, to be considered for a magazine cover?

For the cover of *Empire*, it really needs to be a special, not a still. The image has to be pin-sharp and have eye contact: the more dynamic the shot, the more likely it will get used.

Any tips you would give to filmmakers planning their stills photography?

Take as many pictures as possible. Think of slowly releasing the material early, letting people see what you have a good couple of months before release (even if they are lower images) so that editorial can plan pages around it.

Debi Berry is Picture Editor at *Empire* magazine.

Creative film photography for publicity

Getty Images' **Matthew Somorjay** explores the idea that a little imagination with film photography can go a long way in getting additional publicity for your film.

Can you define what it is that makes a good film still?

The photographer has to take a discerning approach to each and every film that they are involved in, to reflect the tone and mood of the project. Peter Mountain is a great contemporary exponent of this through his stills photography, and it is reflected in the eclectic range of the movies he has worked on – *The Beach*, *Spider*, *28 Days Later*, *Code 346*, *Love Actually*, and *Charlie and the Chocolate Factory*.

Film stills as required reproduce what is being filmed on set, but there is a case for the photographer to be given greater freedom and encouraged to produce more stand-alone iconic imagery that would really reflect the true spirit of the film … think Eve Arnold's images taken on set for *The Misfits*. However, more often than not there are restrictions imposed on the talent and set areas which prevent and discourage greater creativity and strikingly unique imagery.

How might a filmmaker think about creatively exploiting the promotional opportunities offered by stills and related film photography, and what might a film stills library be able to offer?

There is certainly good potential and scope for a collaborative relationship between photographer, film marketing departments and PR companies. There are a number of ways in which this can manifest itself.

As a photo agency, we can work closely with publicists on what we call 'spec' shoots. At these, we will produce a portrait session of the talent in a studio or on location. A day's shoot will provide eight to ten looks, which can be split up. Liaising with the publicist, we can place these across a wide range of editorial publications. So, for example, actress Sienna Miller was photographed by Lorenzo Agius; there were eight different looks created over the course of the day, and the photography was placed to coincide with the release of her film, *Casanova*. Publications such as *Empire*, *Times Magazine* and *The Telegraph Magazine* ran images from this shoot.

Likewise, a film company can commission a photographer to shoot individual cast members in character, or as they are, for a worldwide editorial campaign to raise the profile of their film. These shoots are in addition to existing stills material, but generally speaking such 'specials' secure much better placements – such as magazine covers and spreads across a broad range of editorial titles. A very successful assignment was a shoot done of Tom Cruise for the film *Collateral*, which got many editorial leads worldwide. Photographer Mitch Jenkins has just completed a highly visible campaign for Channel 5, for the launch of their dramas *CSI*, *House*, and *Prison Break*.

The collaborative process can also begin during the production of a film. Polly Borland was on set for the duration of the making of *The Proposition* in Western Australia, and produced a wide range of startling portraits of the cast in character. This folio of images has been successfully placed in *The Telegraph Magazine*, *Empire*, *Total Film*, and various publications in Australia, etc. As an agency we can work on these shoots from initial concepts, in pre-/post-production, and where appropriate in the editorial placement of the final imagery.

What advice you would give to filmmakers planning their photography?

I understand that on many occasions, budgetary constraints mean that the kind of photography we're discussing cannot necessarily be afforded – or is left to the last minute. A poorly executed campaign is the result. So where possible, marketing concepts should be entertained as early as possible.

Photography can play a significant role in the promotion and marketing of a film. A well-conceived and well-produced concept for a high-end photographic shoot is a very sound marketing tool; it will give a film the kind of potency that is not necessarily attained with a batch of stills that are made readily available to every picture desk. Opening any magazine and being presented with a great set of quality images will excite the reader and raise their anticipation of seeing the film. We as consumers are inundated with visual imagery, so to make any kind of impact the benchmark for photography relating to a film has to be high if it is going to achieve a reaction, stay in our mind's eye, and get us to go and see the film.

Matthew Somorjay is Celebrity Assignments Editor at Getty Images, and is responsible for the syndication of portrait photography for Exclusive, a new division within Getty Images.

National newspapers UK and Ireland

Daily Express
Northern & Shell Building, 10 Lower Thames Street, London EC4R 6EN
tel 0871-434 1010
email news-desk@express.co.uk
website www.express.co.uk
Editor Peter Hill
Supplements **Daily Express Saturday**

Daily Mail
Northcliffe House, 2 Derry Street, London W8 5TT
tel 020-7938 6000 *fax* 020-7937 3251
email managingeditor@dailymail.co.uk
website www.dailymail.co.uk
Editor Paul Dacre
Features Editor Jim Gillespie
Showbiz Editor Richard Simpson

Daily Record
1 Central Quay, Glasgow G3 8DA
tel 0141-309 3000 *fax* 0141-309 3340
email reporters@dailyrecord.co.uk
London office 1 Canada Square, Canary Wharf, London E14 5AP
tel 020-7293 3000
website www.record-mail.co.uk/rm
Editor Bruce Waddell
Features Editor Melanie Harvey

The Daily Telegraph
1 Canada Square, Canary Wharf, London E14 5DT
tel 020-7931 2000 *fax* 020-7513 2506
email dtnews@telegraph.co.uk
website www.telegraph.co.uk
Editor John Bryant
Arts Editor Sarah Crompton
Features Editor Liz Hunt

Financial Times
1 Southwark Bridge, London SE1 9HL
tel 020-7873 3000 *fax* 020-7873 3076
email news.desk@ft.com
website www.ft.com
Editor Lionel Barber
Arts Editor Jan Dalley

The Guardian
119 Farringdon Road, London EC1R 3ER
tel 020-7278 2332 *fax* 020-7837 2114
email national@guardian.co.uk
164 Deansgate, Manchester M60 2RR
tel 0161-832 7200 *fax* 0161-832 5351
website www.guardian.co.uk, commentisfree.com
Editor Alan Rusbridger
Arts Editor Melissa Denes
Features Editor Katharine Viner
Film & Music Editor Michael Hann
The Guide Editor Malik Meer
Media Editor Matt Wells
Film Editor Andrew Pulver
Weekend Merope Mills
Guardian Unlimited Editor-in-Chief Emily Bell

The Herald
Newsquest Ltd, 200 Renfield Street, Glasgow G2 3QB
tel 0141-302 7000 *fax* 0141-302 7171
email news@theherald.co.uk
London office 30 Cannon Street, London EC4M 6YJ
tel 020-7618 3421
website www.theherald.co.uk
Editor Charles McGhee
Arts Editor Keith Bruce

The Independent
Independent House, 191 Marsh Wall, London E14 9RS
tel 020-7005 2000 *fax* 020-7005 2999
email newseditor@independent.co.uk
website www.independent.co.uk
Editor-in-Chief Simon Kelner
Arts Editor David Lister
Features Editor Adam Leigh
Media Editor Ian Burrell

Independent on Sunday
Independent House, 191 Marsh Wall, London E14 9RS
tel 020-7005 2000 *fax* 020-7005 2999
email sundaynews@independent.co.uk
website www.independent.co.uk
Editor Tristan Davies, *Editor-at-Large* Janet Street-Porter
Arts Editor, ABC Ian Irvine

Irish Independent
Independent House, 90 Middle Abbey Street, Dublin 1, Republic of Ireland
tel (01) 7055333 *fax* (01) 8720304/8731787
website www.independent.ie
Editor Gerard O'Regan

The Irish Times
The Irish Times Building, PO Box 74, 24–28 Tara Street, Dublin 2, Republic of Ireland

tel (01) 6758000 *fax* (01) 6758035
email editor@irish-times.ie
website www.ireland.com
Editor Geraldine Kennedy
Arts Editor Deirdre Falvey
Features Editor Hugh Linehan

Mail on Sunday

Northcliffe House, 2 Derry Street, London W8 5TS
tel 020-7938 6000 *fax* 020-7937 3829
email news@mailonsunday.co.uk
website www.mailonsunday.co.uk
Editor Peter Wright
Features Editor Sian James

News of the World

1 Virginia Street, London E98 1NW
tel 020-7782 4000 *fax* 020-7583 9504
email newsdesk@notw.co.uk
website www.newsoftheworld.co.uk
Editor Colin Myler

The Observer

3–7 Herbal Hill, London EC1R 5EJ
tel 020-7278 2332 *fax* 020-7837 7817
website www.observer.co.uk
Editor Roger Alton
Film & Music Editor Akin Ojomu
Review Editor Jane Ferguson
7 Days Editor Rob Yates

Scotland on Sunday

108 Holyrood Road, Edinburgh EH8 8AS
tel 0131-620 8620 *fax* 0131-620 8491
email newssos@scotlandonsunday.com
website www.scotlandonsunday.co.uk
Editor Les Snowdon

The Scotsman

Barclay House, 108 Holyrood Road,
Edinburgh EH8 8AS
tel 0131-620 8620
email newsdesk@scotsman.com
website www.scotsman.com
Editor Mike Gilson
Arts Editor Andrew Eaton
Features Editor Jacqueline Hunter

The Sun

News Group Newspapers Ltd, 1 Virginia Street,
London E1 9XP
tel 020-7782 4000 *fax* 020-7782 4095
email news@the-sun.co.uk
website www.the-sun.co.uk
Editor Rebekah Wade
Features Editor Ben Jackson
Showbiz Editor Dominic Mohan

Sunday Express

Northern & Shell Building, 10 Lower Thames Street,
London EC4R 6EN
tel (0871) 434 1010 *fax* (0871) 434 7300
email news.desk@express.co.uk
website www.express.co.uk
Editor Martin Townsend
Features Editor Giulia Rhodes

Sunday Herald

200 Renfield Street, Glasgow G2 3QB
tel 0141-302 7800 *fax* 0141-302 7815
email news@sundayherald.com
website www.sundayherald.com
Editor Richard Walker
Features Editor Susan Flockhart
Magazine Editor Jane Wright

Sunday Independent

27–32 Talbot Street, Dublin 1, Republic of Ireland
tel (01) 7055333 *fax* (01) 7055779
website www.independent.ie
Editor Aengus Fanning

Sunday Mail

1 Central Quay, Glasgow G3 8DA
tel 0141-309 3000 *fax* 0141-309 3582
email mailbox@sundaymail.co.uk
London office 1 Canada Square, Canary Wharf,
London E14 5AP
website www.sundaymail.com
Editor Allan Rennie
Showbiz Editor Billy Sloan

Sunday Mirror

1 Canada Square, Canary Wharf, London E14 5AP
tel 020-7293 3000 *fax* 020-7293 3939
email news@sundaymirror.co.uk
website www.sundaymirror.co.uk
Editor Tina Weaver

Sunday Telegraph

111 Buckingham Palace Road, London SW1W 0DT
tel 020-7931 2000
email stnews@telegraph.co.uk
website www.telegraph.co.uk
Editor Patience Wheatcroft
Seven Editor Ross Jones (Acting Editor)

The Sunday Times

1 Pennington Street, London E98 1ST
tel 020-7782 5000 *fax* 020-7782 5731
email newsdesk@sunday-times.co.uk
website www.timesonline.co.uk
Editor John Witherow
Culture Editor Helen Hawkins
Magazine Editor Robin Morgan

The Sunday Times Scotland

Times Newspapers Ltd, 124 Portman Street, Kinning Park, Glasgow G41 1EJ
tel 0141-420 5100 *fax* 0141-420 5262
website www.timesonline.co.uk
Editor Carlos Alba
Sun £1.60

The Times

1 Pennington Street, London E98 1TT
tel 020-7782 5000 *fax* 020-7488 3242
website www.timesonline.co.uk
Editor Robert Thomson
Arts and Entertainment Editor Alex O'Connell
Features Editor Michael Harvey

Wales on Sunday

Thomson House, Havelock Street, Cardiff CF10 1XR
tel 029-2058 3583 *fax* 029-2058 3725
website www.icwales.co.uk
Editor Tim Gordon

Creating an effective electronic press kit (EPK)

Colin Burrows

"What's the point of an EPK?" That angry question has echoed around many a film set, as a stumbling cameraman trips up the director on the way back to his or her monitor. So let's have a quick look at some of the reasons why you need one.

First of all – what is an Electronic Press Kit? The clue is in the cumbersome title. An EPK is a collection of materials for TV broadcast use: literally, a kit from which TV programmes can construct their own material on your film.

Behind-the-scenes footage and interviews are shot on set and in post-production, then edited into a collection of soundbites from the key cast and crew – usually director and producer(s) – together with a short assembly of the best of the behind-the-scenes material (commonly referred to as B Roll). Then, having been approved by those who have that right, the tape, which varies in length from half an hour to a full hour of material, is duplicated and distributed to TV stations around the world by the local distributors. Like filmmaking itself, the end product can grow out of all recognition, but that's the essence of it.

Why do you need an EPK?

In many cases, an EPK will be part of your delivery requirements for a distributor. If you look through the small print of your contract, you'll find that you are obliged to hand one over with the other delivery items. Hopefully, though, by the time you have finished reading this you will want to have an EPK done out of conviction, rather than obligation.

Does anyone actually use an EPK?

The fact that Special Treats is still in business after more than 20 years of producing EPKs perhaps attests to that. Without an EPK, you are severely reducing your chances of reaching the key outlets for your film. You are working in a visual medium; you need another such to give full rein to representing your work.

My company also produces press junkets (a completely different but complementary angle of TV publicity). At each one, the question asked most frequently by journalists (well all right, perhaps second to "Have you got a goodie bag for me?") is, "Have you got a copy of the EPK?" Film show producers (and I have been one myself) will say that if they don't have EPK footage, they can't expand the interviews they get at junkets ... and if they don't have junket interviews, the EPK is the only chance they have of including a film in their show.

There are at least three or four interesting films released each week. If you are the one without an EPK, you'll be the one to suffer in terms of coverage.

What else does an EPK do for you?

It keeps your set clear

You want to have TV coverage, and any publicist has endless enquiries from TV stations about doing a set-visit. But such visits are intrusive and often annoying; a news crew that has never been on set before can cause you more problems than an outbreak of scrofula in your principal cast. They will get in the way, film when they are not supposed to, upset your cast, and unsettle your crew. If you have an EPK crew at work, then your publicist can fob off all but the most important with some B Roll they have shot.

It documents your filmmaking – how *you* want it to be documented

Unless you want to make *Lost in La Mancha II*, the EPK crew should be filming when *you* feel it is appropriate, and not when *they* do. Film sets are pressure cookers of emotion and stress – no-one ever has enough time to do their jobs, and having someone pointing a camera at you or dipping a boom mic into your private conversations will not help you achieve a Zen-like state of calm. All our crews have heard me say this many times: we are paid to know when not to film, as well as to know when to film.

Having said that, if you have a good EPK production company working for you, they don't have to be slavishly watching you for a sign to cut. A good crew will have worked this out already and will be actively working with you to get the best coverage possible. In other words, they are part of your crew. Talk to them. Brief them as you would any other department and you will get more from them. Ignore them, and the only way they can find out what you don't want is by doing it and incurring your wrath.

Other advantages

The EPK is the front line of your publicity campaign. When your actors sit down to do their EPK interview, what they are asked and how they reply will form the template of all future publicity. EPK interviews will be transcribed and used in the production notes; journalists at the time of release will form their views on what the film is about from this. Never lose sight of the fact that journalists are generally as unoriginal as any other group of professionals – and this is particularly true of film journalists. I know of many TV interviewers at press junkets who will simply ask questions to get the same four or five answers they have already seen on the EPK.

The corollary of this is – make sure you get an EPK company that has editorial experience. There are EPK producers with a background in publicity, and EPK producers with a handycam who are interested in movie-making, but neither necessarily offers the best training for what will interest an audience.

What is shot for your EPK should, when used correctly, serve a multitude of other masters too. There is the non-broadcast use – part of the teaser reel for the AFM, behind-the-scenes footage on a promotional VHS in a car show room, on a give-away DVD with the Saturday edition of *The Times* – the list as long as your publicity and promotions teams' imagination. Not least, if your ambition runs in that direction, it is the EPK crew's footage of the director at work that runs in the Academy Awards show when they read out "the nominees for best director are …"

And then there is web use. This gets talked about a lot more than it is acted upon, but when co-ordinated correctly can be a whole new use of the EPK material, and a completely different audience for the footage. There are differences in approach when editing material for the Internet than for broadcast, but these are relatively minor and have only limited impact on how you shoot the footage in the first place. It is easier to adapt broadcast footage for the web than the other way round, so make your EPK crew work for you while they are on set.

Longer-form programming

So the EPK itself is only a starting point. What we've outlined so far all relates to the basic EPK. In addition to the uses we have already discussed, the footage has other important work to do in terms of longer-form programming. This takes three basic forms:

- An EPK featurette
- A 'making of' special
- DVD bonus material

There is a whole additional article to be written on this, but let's touch on some key principles here. It is better to think of your DVD content first and then work backwards towards your EPK footage. EPK content is by its nature more straightforward editorially – you need to introduce the film, its themes, style and cast, making it all seem a must-see movie. Unless you are going on to produce a 'making of', that's pretty much it.

An EPK featurette (usually 4-7 minutes long, although that is entirely arbitrary) is, in effect, an extended trailer. It will showcase the film and maybe highlight one or two key aspects of the production (big stunts, interesting location, curious casting, etc). Its editorial use will range from being run in full on some programmes to being used in excerpts on others. It is particularly helpful for non-English-language territories, to save them having to make their own material from scratch in a different language (it will be produced in mixed and split-track versions, so local stations can re-edit and revoice them where required). It is also useful as a positioning tool for non-broadcast journalists. A canny publicity department will include a featurette on the CD-Rom of the press materials as a statement of the main editorial elements in the film.

The 'making of' special – usually half an hour in duration – is an extension of the featurette's basic principles. It will need planning in advance and diligence on the part of the EPK producers to make that sure there is enough material to make something other than a basic, platitudinous 30 minutes of television. Most 'making ofs' follow this pattern, and a programme on the genuine making of a film is all the more refreshing as a result when it is broadcast.

This is why it is usually better to think of the DVD content first. It is in the DVD programming that you can really get into detail about how a film is made. If you have the right material for your DVD, you can then extrapolate your EPK needs from that. Although it is sometimes desirable to have competely new and exclusive material on your DVD, a carefully planned shoot can yield both EPK and DVD material without conflict.

So what should you be doing about your next EPK?

1. Listen to what your publicity company is saying. They will be working with EPK producers every week, and will have a firm idea of who is good and who isn't. Talk to other producers – just as you would about other key hirings.

2. Get yourself a company that likes movies and enjoys what it does. *Not* a company that sees EPKs as a stepping stone to making their own films, or to producing their own documentary series.

3. Grit your teeth and spend the money. Just when your film is going into production, money is at its tightest and an EPK can look like a good thing to save on. A kid with a DV camera is not an EPK: at best, it is a supplement to your EPK coverage; at worst, is is an active hindrance. Of the 30 or so films that we are currently working on, at least three have been brought to us by sheepish producers who need us to fix the problems this option has

brought. That doesn't mean it is always a disaster – on a couple of our current films it is working very nicely as we have sat down and briefed the cameraman.

4. Listen to what your EPK producers are telling you. Although you are very keen to have your big production day covered when you have the largest numbers of extras hired or the biggest number of horses and carriages booked, that is not always the best day for EPK coverage. Behind-the-scenes coverage can make sets and locations look smaller if they are not filmed correctly. There may be other days that reflect your film more advantageously.

5. Make sure that your crew value and assist the EPK crew. An unwilling 1st AD will cost you money by reducing the amount of coverage the crew gets on set or the time they have with actors for interview. A good AD will add immeasurably to the range of their work.

Above all, see the EPK team as the bridge to your audience rather than the barrier to your film-making.

Colin Burrows is Managing Director of The Special Treats Production Company Ltd. Colin and his partner in the company, David Castell, founded Special Treats Productions more than 20 years ago as a part-time operation to run in conjunction with their activities as journalists. David was then the film critic of the *Sunday Telegraph* and the film critic of Capital Radio; Colin was a producer at Radio One. The pair has worked on many of the key European films of the last two decades, from *Four Weddings and a Funeral* to the lastest James Bond film, *Casino Royale*; from the smallest productions, like *Vera Drake*, to the largest, like *Saving Private Ryan*. The company has about 12 full-time staff, a group of 30 or so key freelances, and affliations in most of the European countries, Australia, Canada, South Africa, Morocco and the US.

Screening rooms

In addition to these screening rooms, which are used primarily for test and press screenings, most cinemas listed in our exhibition section are also open for private hire.

Artificial Eye

tel 020-7240 5353 *fax* 020-7240 5355
website www.artificial-eye.com

Renoir and the Chelsea in London can be booked through simon.pye@curzoncinemas.com (also see Curzon listing on page 246).

Formats: 35mm, 16mm, DVD, MiniDV, Beta SP or Digibeta, digital projection

BBFC Preview Theatre

3 Soho Square, London W1D 3HD
tel 020-7440 1590 *fax* 020-7287 0141
email projection@bbfc.co.uk
website www.bbfc.co.uk

1 screen: 33 seats

British Film Institute (Viewing Theatres)

21 Stephen Street, London W1P 2LN
tel 020-7957 8976 *fax* 020-7957 4832
email roger.young@bfi.org.uk
Hire Manager Roger Young

Venue has disabled access and also a hospitality room for use with screen hire.

2 screens: both 36 seats

Formats: 35mm, 16mm (can also screen 16mm and 35mm sep mag), VHS, SVHS, BETA SP, Digibeta, DVD

BUFVC

77 Wells Street, London W1T 3QJ
tel 020-7393 1500 *fax* 020-7393 1555
email services@bufvc.ac.uk
Deputy Director Geoff O'Brien

1 screen: 30 seats

Formats: DVD, VHS, 16mm

Rates: £70 + VAT/hour

Century Preview Theatres

c/o Fox, 31-32 Soho Square, London W1V 6AP
tel 020-7753 7135 *fax* 020-7753 7138
email projection@fox.com
Projection Manager Nick Ross

2 screens: 72, 37 seats

Format: 35mm. 16mm, DVD, Digibeta, Beta SP (PAL or NTSC), VHS, SHVS

Rates: Range from £130-£180/hour, depending on which screen and whether hire is day or evening

Chapter Cinema

tel (01222) 311050 *fax* (01222) 313431

– see page 336.

Charlotte Street Screening Rooms

15-17 Charlotte Street, London W1T 1RJ
tel 020-7806 2000 *fax* 020-7806 2002
email charlotte@firmdale.com
website www.firmdale.com

1 screen: 67 seats

Formats: 35mm, DVD, Beta SP, Multi-standard Nicam VHS, Epson EMP8000 SXGA LCD projector

Rates: £200 per hour

Covent Garden Screening Rooms

10 Monmouth Street, London WC2H 9HB
tel 020-7806 1000 *fax* 020-7806 1100
email covent@firmdale.com
website www.firmdale.com

1 screen: 53 seats

Formats: 35mm, Beta SP, Multi-standard Nicam VHS, Epson EMP8000 SXGA LCD projector

Rates: £180 per hour

Curzon Soho/Curzon Mayfair

tel 020-7292 1695/6
email privatehires@curzoncinemas.com
website www.curzoncinemas.com

Curzon has 2 cinemas in the West End, which are excellent for larger previews and events. Both have spaces for post- or pre-event hospitality.

Curzon Mayfair: 2 screens (311, 83 seats); both screens can project 35mm and most video formats.

Curzon Soho: 3 screens (249, 133, 120 seats); all screens have 35mm and can screen most video formats, with Screens 1 and 3 having 2K HD projection. For 16mm projection, please enquire for details.

De Lane Lea

tel 020-7432 3800 *fax* 020-7432 3838

– see page 216.

Eon Productions Ltd

Eon House, 138 Piccadilly, London W1J 7NR
tel 020-7493 7953 *fax* 020-7408 1236
email reception@eon.co.uk
Hire Manager Ray Aguilar

Filmhouse – see page 337.

Framestore CFC

tel 020-7344 8000 *fax* 020-7344 8001
email previewtheatre@framestore-cfc.com
website www.framestore-cfc.com

1 screen: 64 seats

Formats: most, including 35mm

The Hospital Screening Rooms

24 Endell Street, London WC2H 9HQ
tel 020-7170 9110 *fax* 020-7170 9102
email joeb@thehospital.co.uk
website www.thehospital.co.uk/studio

1 screen: 30 seats

Formats: most; enquire for details

ICA

The Mall, London SW1Y 5AH
tel 020-7766 1413 *fax* 020-7306 0122
email donnah@ica.org.uk
website www.ica.org.uk
Hires Manager Donna Hay

Also see page 338.

2 screens: 185, 45 seats

Formats: all format DSN, 35mm, 16mm, Dolby Digital EX and HD capability in Cinema 1 only; also Dolby Digital SR, 16mm in cinema 2 only; both screens Digibeta and Beta SP both pal and ntsc. 2 x spacious rooms available for private functions.

Imperial War Museum Film and Video Archive

Imperial War Museum, All Saints Annex,
Austal Street, London SE11 4SJ
tel 020-7416 5293 *fax* 020-7416 5229
email mlee@iwm.org.uk, thaggith@iwm.org.uk
website www.iwm.org.uk
Hire Dr Toby Haggith, Mr Matthew Lee

1 screen: 25 seats

Formats: 35mm, 16mm, most video formats in PAL only

King's Lynn Arts Centre – see page 338.

Picture Production Company

tel 020-7439 4944 *fax* 020-7434 9140

1 screen: 25 seats

The Rex Cinema and Bar

21 Rupert Street, London W1V 7FE
tel 020-7287 0102 *fax* 020-7478 1501
email info@rexbar.co.uk
website www.rexbar.co.uk

1 screen: 75 seats

Formats: 35mm, most video

RSA

8 John Adam Street, London WC2N 6EZ
tel 020-7839 5049 *fax* 020-7321 0271
email matthew.johnson@rsa.org.uk
website www.rsa.org.uk

2 screens: The Great Room (200); Durham Street Auditorium (70)

Formats: VHS, SVHS and DVD in both and BETA SP in The Great Room

The Vault is also available for parties. Call Monica Turner to book a space, and for prices.

Soho Hotel Screening Rooms

4 Richmond Mews, London W1D 3DH
tel 020-7559 3000 *fax* 020-7559 3003
email events@firmdale.com, soho@firmdale
website www.firmdale.com

2 screens: 45, 100 seats

Formats: 35mm, DVD, Beta SP, Multi-standard Nicam VHS, Epson EMP8000 SXGA LCD projector, 2K HD projection

Rates: £250 per hour + VAT; D Cinema £350 per hour + VAT

Soho Images

8-14 Meard Street, London W1F 0EQ
tel 020-7437 0831 *fax* 020-7734 9471
email emma.devonshire@sohoimages.com
website www.sohoimages.com

In addition to the screening formats listed below, also has a fully digital preview theatre for viewing works-in-progress, projected in highest quality from editing facilities.

1 screen: 36 seats

Formats: Digi Beta/Beta SP, Dolby Digital, DVD and Video, 35mm

Soho Screening Rooms

(formerly Mr Young's)
14 D'Arblay Street, London W1F 8DY
tel 020-7437 1771 *fax* 020-7734 4520
email agnes@sohoscreeningrooms.co.uk
website www.sohoscreeningrooms.co.uk
Accounts Administrator Agnes Pifeteau

Preview screening theatre in the heart of Soho. Screens can be hired for private press and preview screenings or conference activities.

3 screens: 44, 41 and 25 seats

Formats: 35mm, Beta SP, Digibeta, HD and DVD

Rates: Range between £110-£140 per hour before 6pm, and £145-£175 per hour after 6pm

Sony Pictures Screening Room

Europe House, 25 Golden Square, London W1F 9LU
tel 020-7533 1006 *fax* 020-7533 1531
email gordon_ireland@spe.sony.com

1 screen: 80 seats

The Screening Room at MPC

The Moving Picture Company, 127 Wardour Street, London W1V 0NL
tel 020-7494 7879 *fax* 020-7287 9698
email screening@moving-picture.com
Hires Paul or Mark

1 screen: 74 seats

Formats: all

Rates: £230 + VAT per hour before 5pm, and £270 + VAT per hour after 5pm

Twickenham Film Studios – see page 185 for contact details.

UIP International Theatre

45 Beadon Road, Hammersmith, London W6 0EG
tel 020-8563 4144 *fax* 020-8741 2532
website greg_grey@uip.com

1 screen: 43 seats

Formats: 35mm, most video, DVD

Warner Bros

98 Theobald's Road, London WC1X 8WB
tel 020-7984 5272 *fax* 020-7984 5253
email pablo.nascimento@warnerbros.com

2 screens: 65, 13 seats

Watershed

1 Canons Road, Harbourside, Bristol BS1 5TX
tel 0117-927 6444 *fax* 0117-921 3958
email info@watershed.co.uk
website www.watershed.co.uk
Head of Programme Mark Cosgrove

Media Centre which programmes arthouse and independent cinema and offers a number of media courses and events. Hosts Brief Encounters short film festival.

3 screens: 200, 100, 50 seats

Formats: 35mm, 16mm, Beta SP, DVD, VHS, SVHS, slide projection and data projections

For bookings, contact Robert Walker or Karen Welboum at events@watershed.co.uk.

Wired Preview Theatre

76-78 Charlotte Street, London W1T 4QW
tel 020-7580 0171 *fax* 020-7580 0175
email theatre@wired.uk.com
website www.wired.uk.com

1 screen: 30 seats

Formats: 35, DVD, Video

Companies that make trailers and posters

The Creative Partnership

13 Bateman Street, London W1D 3AF
tel 020-7439 7762 *fax* 020-7437 1467
website www.thecreativepartnership.co.uk
Head of Production Sarah Fforde

Award-winning agency that creates film advertising materials for the UK, US and international markets, from offices in London and Los Angeles. Caters for all stages of development, production and release through to home entertainment with posters, trailers, web design, sales materials, positioning advice, etc. Projects include: *King Kong*, *Nanny Mcphee*, and *Pride & Prejudice*.

Empire Design

29 Queen Anne Street, London W1G 9HU
tel 020-7436 2202
website www.empiredesign.com

A specialist boutique film design company with offices in London and New York. Recent poster designs include: *Casino Royale* and *The Queen*; trailers include *Sunshine* and *The Bourne Ultimatum*.

Kennedy Monk Ltd

Second Floor, 38-40 Eastcastle Street, London W1W 8DT
tel 020-7636 9142
email info@kennedymonk.com
website www.kennedymonk.com

Design company specialising in creating poster and outdoor campaigns, specialist packaging and additional marketing materials for the film industry. Work includes: a bus campaign for *Shrek*, and posters for *Capote* and *Devil's Rejects*.

Momentum Productions

Century House, 351 Richmond Road, Twickenham TW1 2ER
tel 020-8843 8300 *fax* 020-8538 9568
email production@momentum.co.uk
website www.momentum.co.uk

Production company that creates TV and radio commercials, trailers, promos, EPKs and online marketing material.

Omni Productions

Location House, Dove Lane, Bristol BS2 9HP
tel 0117-941 5820
website www.omniproductions.co.uk
Director Richard Penfold

Offers a wide range of design and production services, including: brand-aware website design; graphic design; film and video production; design for events and exhibitions; and CD-Rom/DVD design. Recent productions include: award-winning dramas for the Criminal Justice Board; promos for The DfES; and multimedia work for Microsoft. No unsolicited requests.

Special Treats Productions

96-98 Camden High Street, London NW1 0LT
tel 020-7387 4838 *fax* 020-7529 8969
email thosenicepeople@specialtreats.co.uk
website www.specialtreats.co.uk

Special Treats creates EPKs, video news releases and DVD programming; also offers full-service production of press junkets. Work includes: *Vera Drake*, *Die Another Day*, and *Shaun of the Dead*.

Also see Colin Burrows' article on page 242.

Stylorouge

57-60 Charlotte Road, London EC2A 3QT
tel 020-7729 1005 *fax* 020-7729 1005
email rob@stylorouge.co.uk
website www.stylorouge.co.uk
Creative Director Rob O'Connor

Established in 1981. Specialises in all creative media for the music industry. Main areas of interest include: promo clips, TV commercials, documentary/EPKs, and screen graphics. The company also offers services such as film and TV production, design and art direction, web design, and print/TV/online marketing.

Stylorouge has worked on poster campaigns for films such as *Trainspotting* and *Another Country*; on pop promos/TVCs for The Corrs, Madonna, Sony BMG, EMI, Universal; and on documentaries/live concerts for artists such as Kula Shaker, David Gilmour, and The Corrs.

Tomato

Top Floor, 14 Baltic Street East, London EC1Y 0UJ
tel 020-7490 2599
email info@tomato.co.uk
website www.tomato.co.uk

Tomato is a design collective that specialises in moving image design, graphic and architectural design.

Tomorrow London Ltd

Studio 5, 222 Kingsland Road, London E2 8DG
tel 020-7739 0911
email contact@tomorrowlondon.com
website www.tomorrowlondon.com

Design agency that works across media (on arts books, film and video, magazine, web, event production and DVD/CD creation).

Photographers

David Bache
mobile (07790) 018315
fax 020-8876 0115
email bache.photography@virgin.net

Alex Bailey
mobile (07774) 117395
email alexbaileyphoto@aol.com
website www.alexbailey.com

Credits include: *Tomb Raider*, and *Bridget Jones's Diary*.

Jaap Buitendijk
mobile (07790) 909561
fax 0131-477 1102
email jaap@jaapphoto.com
website www.jaapphoto.com

Credits include: *Gladiator*, *Girl with a Pearl Earring*, and *Alexander*.

Stuart Chorley
tel 020-8883 0483 *mobile* (07956) 283164
email stuart@stuartchorley.com
website www.stuartchorley.com

Credits include: *Creep*.

Clive Coote
tel 020-8868 1169

Credits include: *Closer*, *Finding Neverland*, and *The Hours*.

Karl Grant
tel 020-7247 4750 (Eminent Management & Production) *fax* 020-7247 4712
email colin@eminentmanagement.co.uk
website www.karlgrant.co.uk

Primarily very high-quality fashion shoots.

Keith Hamshere
tel (01442) 863035 *fax* (01442) 863347
email khamshere@yahoo.com

Credits include: *Star Wars: Episode III*, *Man on Fire*, and *Die Another Day*.

John Keedwell
email know@echelonfilms.co.uk

Marysia Lachowicz
tel 020-8314 1516 *mobile* (07803) 606165
email info@marysia.co.uk
website www.marysia.co.uk

Credits include: *Bollywood Queen*, and *Love, Honour and Obey*.

Jay Maidment
tel 020-8943 4620 *mobile* (07771) 711804
email jmaidphoto@aol.com
website www.jaymaidment.com

Credits include: *Beyond the Sea*, and *Die Another Day*.

Stephen Morley
tel (01798) 861400 *fax* (01798) 861400
email steve@stephenstills.demon.co.uk

Credits include: *Fingersmith*, and *School for Seduction*.

Clare Muller
Clare Muller Photography, 45 Kelly Street, London NW1 8PG
tel 020-7691 8791 *mobile* (07887)510702
email cmuller@blueyonder.co.uk

Stills photographer Clare Muller has worked on set on feature films, docs, commercials, promos, and has specialised in music videos photographing artists ranging from Frankie Goes to Hollywood to Cliff Richard, The Stranglers, Charlotte Church, Madness, Will Young, Dido, and The Buzzcocks.

Dean Rogers
mobile (07710) 472485
email dean@deanrogers.co.uk
website www.deanrogers.co.uk

Credits include: *Dead Man's Shoes*, *Once Upon A Time In The Midlands*, and *A Room for Romeo Brass*.

Will Sweet
mobile (07769) 736775
email wills@solutions-inc.co.uk

Mark Tillie
tel 020-8968 9031 *mobile* (07941) 491163
email studio@marktillie.com
website www.marktillie.com

Credits include: *Wings of the Dove*, and *Gosford Park*.

Nick Wall
tel 020-8444 7470 *mobile* (07778) 290818
fax 020-8883 6243
email nick@nickwall.com
website www.nickwall.com

Credits include: *Sexy Beast*, and *In My Father's Den*.

Lucy Williams
mobile (07968) 097219
fax (07968) 408406
email lucywilliams@mac.com
website www.lucywilliamsphotography.co.uk

Credits include: *Me Without You*, and *Bend It Like Beckham*.

David Wootton

2 East Farm Studio, Nordelph, Downham Market, Norfolk PE38 0bG
tel (01366) 324346 *mobile* (07703) 542804
email dw@dw-photography.co.uk
website www.dw-photography.co.uk
Director David Wootton

Photographer varying from commercial clients who require images to promote their business and or products, to action and adventure photography for numerous publishers. Also specialises in aerial photography and is an assigned BBC stills photographer.

Festivals and markets
Introduction

Sandra Hebron

In any given week of the year, somewhere in the world there will be at least one film festival taking place.

The longest-standing festivals began their lives in the 1930s and 40s, but during the intervening years the international festival calendar has expanded dramatically, such that there are hundreds (if not more) events internationally which claim to be fully fledged festivals. Alongside these are a host of film markets. This plethora of events can offer an exciting but seemingly bewildering choice to filmmakers. What are the benefits to you, the filmmaker, of having a film screened in one or more festivals, and how should you choose which one(s) to take part in?

Why put your film in a festival?

There are several fairly obvious reasons for trying for a festival place for your film. As Asif Kapadia reiterates in his article in this section of the *Yearbook*, all are linked to the fact that if you've managed to navigate the arduous process of making a film, then you are presumably keen to get it out there and seen by as many people as possible. A festival will often be the first link in the chain of bringing your film to audiences, and launching the film in a festival can bring any or all of the following benefits:

- The film could find a sales agent or a distributor.
- You or the film could win an award.
- The festival screenings will generate a buzz around you and help raise your profile; this in turn could help you find support for future projects.
- A festival can be a great place to network and meet like-minded individuals, who can either directly help your career, or more indirectly become firm friends or part of a wider raft of people offering support, insight and understanding.
- Screening in a festival exposes the film to other festival programmers, and invitations to other festivals will often follow.

First steps: what kind of festival is right for your film?

First of all, there is an important distinction to be made between festivals and markets. Markets are essentially trade fairs attended by sales agents, whose job it is to represent and sell films – either by screening finished works to buyers, or by pitching proposed projects to them (a process known as pre-sales). The buyers are usually from companies looking to acquire films for theatrical distribution through cinema exhibition and ancillary markets such as video and DVD, or in some instances for a range of TV outlets, or both. There are generally no public screenings attached to markets, and members of the press are also often excluded, so that any screenings are purely for buyers and sellers. Unless your film already has a sales agent attached, or unless the market has some kind of production pitching event (or scheme which selects and invites filmmakers to attend), a market tends to be of limited use to the average filmmaker. And like most trade fairs, it is arguably not likely to be much fun.

While a market is essentially business-oriented, a festival will usually claim some kind of cultural purpose, and to predicated on screening films to public audiences. Good festivals have informed and knowledgeable programmers or curators with an understanding of how to position and present films. Many larger festivals also have a market which runs alongside the public screenings programme (Cannes, Berlin) or at the very least an industry office which organises screenings for buyers and sellers (Toronto, Venice, Sundance, London). These festivals ensure that your film is likely to be seen by film professionals as well as by audiences. Additionally, such festivals tend to have sizeable numbers of critics and reviewers attending, all of whom will be looking for interesting films and filmmakers to write about or feature. The relative importance of a festival in the international hierarchy of festivals will determine whether the film industry and press attendance is mostly national or international.

Festivals themselves break down into several types, both generalist and more specialist, and it goes without saying that it is important to think carefully about which kind of festival is best for your film. Some festivals are affiliated to the international film producers' body, FIAPF (see entry on page 95), which regulates the terms and conditions under which films can be screened. FIAPF has a slightly mystifying categorisation of festivals which splits them into 'A grade' competitive festivals, 'B' festivals and so on. These strict categorisations are likely to be less useful to filmmakers than a working knowledge of the linked, somewhat more informal, but nevertheless well-embedded international league table of which festivals are most important. Of course, the notion of important is relative to what you are trying to achieve. If your ambition is to get your 12-minute experimental short film programmed in the Whitney biennale, you are likely to be looking for a different kind of festival than if you really want to secure a three-picture deal with Miramax.

While festivals do win or lose favour depending on a host of circumstances, most industry insiders (at least within the UK) would see the premiere league of international festivals as including the following: Cannes, Berlin, Venice, Sundance, Toronto. There is then a second tier of festivals which would include: San Sebastian (general competition plus a strong emphasis on Spanish-language film), Locarno (competitive, specialising in 'young cinema' and film- and videomakers of the future), Telluride (non-competitive, with an emphasis on quality US indie film), London (non-competitive, but with awards for first and second features, documentaries and short films), and Rotterdam (competitive, specialising in emerging and expanded cinema). Others such as Pusan, Karlovy Vary, Deauville, Melbourne and Edinburgh each have their champions. It is worth remembering that many festivals which are not formally categorised as competitive do give a range of awards, sometimes with a cash element; also that non-competitive and audience-centred festivals such as Toronto and London can provide significant and rewarding platforms for new films.

Alongside the generalist festivals, there is a host of more specialised festivals around the world which deal with almost every possible form or genre of film or moving image: shorts; animation; documentaries; underground and avant-garde work; comedy; thrillers; digital work; lesbian, gay and transgender cinema; work by or for specific ethnic groups; campaigning films … the list is almost endless, including several festivals which specialise in showing films about extreme sports. If you have made a film that could be regarded as having niche appeal, it could be worth considering approaching the relevant festivals first, as these can often offer an informed context for the film's presentation, and for first-time filmmakers can be a relatively relaxed entry into the festival world. The bigger and/or better-established specialist festivals (for instance, Amsterdam's documentary festival, or Claremont Ferrand and Oberhausen's short film festivals) have strong international reputations and are likely to attract key industry figures with an interest in that particular type of film. A recent example would be Jonathan Caouette's film *Tarnation*, which initially screened in New York's cutting-edge Mix festival, picked up Gus Van Sant and John Cameron Mitchell as executive producers, and then went on to be selected for Sundance and Cannes, with a slew of international sales and festival awards to follow.

Each festival – and each festival location – has its own idiosyncrasies and characteristics, and there are already a number of published guides available which give a snapshot of a large number of festivals around the world. It is also worth seeking out festival reviews in publications such as *Sight and Sound* and *Film Comment*, which, in addition to reviewing individual films, can also give a useful indication of the overall flavour of a festival – as do the myriad excellent online sites such as Senses of Cinema and Indiewire. Best of all, ask around for other filmmakers' first-hand experiences.

How to get your film into a festival

Films find their way into festivals either because someone who works on the festival has tracked or heard about the film, and asks to see it; or because a filmmaker or film company has entered the film through an open submission process. Calls for entries are often made via film magazines such as *Filmmaker*, and via websites such as **filmfestivals.com**. Many festivals are now also using a online submission service called 'withoutabox' (**withoutabox.com**), which is free for filmmakers. The service allows you to complete a single application, which can be sent electronically to all participating film festivals as their deadlines arise. The site also allows you to upload press materials about your film, which the festivals can access.

While it is so obvious as to be almost insulting to say it, it is important to follow the guidelines for how to enter your film. Send whatever is asked for (or if this isn't possible, call and discuss with the festival organisers). Don't send anything which isn't asked for – programmers are unlikely at this stage to be swayed by your glossy marketing materials or full press notes, and will just want to make their own minds up as to whether a particular film is right for their festival. Make sure you know what the deadlines are, and meet them. Most festivals screen a tiny percentage of the films they view, and it is important not to slip up in the early stages.

Many festivals make a charge to filmmakers for submitting their films, to cover the administration costs of dealing with the thousands of applications they are likely to receive. This is all the more reason to select carefully which festivals to target. It is also a fact of life that for most festivals, the proportion of films selected which are from unknown filmmakers who come through the open submission schemes is relatively low. Although all festivals that take films through open submission will have a procedure for entering (and you should adhere to this), it may well be worthwhile to make direct contact with the relevant programmer before you submit. They can advise whether or not the film is likely to be of interest to them; assuming that it is, they are more likely to view it themselves when it arrives, rather than send it out to a pre-selection committee (in much the same way that many companies deal with unsolicited scripts, so many festivals will send unsolicited films out to relatively junior programmers who will then flag up the titles which they think should be considered seriously). However, one call to a programmer or the festival administrator can be a good idea; multiple calls rarely are. Festival staff are invariably busy, but even the most patient will grow weary of endless questions at the submission stage, which could just make a difference when it comes to the crunch about whether to invite a film or not.

When a festival asks to see your film, or when you submit it, it is reasonable to ask when a decision is likely to be made. Don't hound the festival staff before this date. If your film is selected, be gracious. If your film is turned down, be equally gracious. You never know when you might want to submit to the same festival again. You can ask for feedback, and many festivals may also be willing to advise if they think there are other festivals to which your film may be better suited. A word of caution: it is probably a good idea to wait until well after the programmers have finalised their selection before asking for this kind of feedback, otherwise they simply may not have time to give it.

Once your film is selected

Having your film presented provides a great opportunity, and you will want to make the most of your participation in the festival. There are a number of questions that you will need to consider. How will the festival be promoting your film, and what kind of marketing support do they offer? Will they be able to assist you in getting key people to your screening by providing tickets or other services? Do they have an industry office, and if so, what resources does it have which you can draw on, such as contact databases or networking opportunities? Will the festival invite you to attend, and if you are travelling from outside the city or country, what will they contribute towards your travel and accommodation costs?

If the festival is not able to invite you, or only able to partially fund your trip, it is undoubtedly worthwhile trying to beg, steal or borrow in order to attend. Investigate the possibility of any bursaries or grants which might be available. In the UK, try approaching the British Council, the UK Film Council and/or your regional screen agency. There is much to gain by being present with the film, particularly in the early stages of your career. However much festivals are able to promote and publicise your film, they will be dealing with a large number of titles, whereas you will obviously be able to bring focused attention and legwork to raising your film's profile. And it goes without saying that press and media coverage is more likely to be generated if you are physically at the festival to speak to journalists. The opportunity to meet fellow filmmakers and other industry figures will prove invaluable: even the most far-flung or seemingly low-profile festival can throw up interesting contacts, and the experience of presenting your film to an audience, and hearing their responses to it (whether these are illuminating, uplifting or humbling), can be an important part of your development as a filmmaker.

On a practical level, try to find out in advance who will be attending the festival as delegates, so that you can invite the relevant ones to your screenings. If the festival hasn't provided you with an itinerary, ask what is expected of you in terms of presenting your film and any other activities you might be involved in, such as workshops or discussions. When you arrive at the festival, make contact with the festival staff as soon as practicable. If you want to get the most out of your visit, ask about informal opportunities to meet other people at receptions, parties, etc. However, be polite; don't hassle for party tickets which are not forthcoming, and don't turn up at events which you have been told you are not invited to. Remember that the festival staff will want you to have a great experience of being at their festival, but they may not be able to meet all your requests. Being assertive is reasonable; being tiresomely pushy is not, and will do little to further your professional reputation.

It's as well to remember that festivals didn't get their name for nothing. As far as the 'festive' element goes, one filmmaker described her experience of the circuit as "sex, drugs and rock'n'roll in every country in the world", and it can be this if you so desire. But it is probably advisable to be reasonably discreet about at least two of the three aforementioned – festivals are well connected with each other, and festival gossip travels. You may not want to arrive in Toronto with stories of your behaviour in Melbourne preceding you ... Conversely, do remember that everyone has moments when they find being at a festival hard work – it can be a peculiarly lonely and depressing experience to feel that everyone else knows each other and that they are all having a ball, while you are feeling nervous and ill at ease. Again, a good festival will have staff or volunteers who will be happy to rescue you, but only if they know you want them to.

After the festival

Assuming that you have attended the festival, hopefully you will have come away having found it rewarding to present your film, and having made some new friends and business contacts. You will want to follow up on these, and also drop an email to the festival team to thank them. They are likely to have dealt with hundreds of filmmakers during the festival, and the ones they will remember are the very rude ones, and the considerate, appreciative ones. So saying thank you is not just a lovely gesture, it may also reap benefits the next time you want to get your film into a festival.

Sandra Hebron is Artistic Director, BFI Film Festivals, responsible for *The Times* BFI London Film Festival and the London Lesbian and Gay Film Festival – two of Europe's leading public film festivals. She began her working life in academia, researching in the fields of sociology and cultural studies. She has worked in independent film exhibition for more than 15 years, and was Cinemas Director at Manchester's Cornerhouse before joining the bfi Festivals Department in 1997. She has made several short films, regularly writes and broadcasts about cinema, and is currently Chair of Lux, the London-based organisation specialising in distributing and promoting artists' films and videos.

UK film festivals

Bath Film Festival

7 Terrace Walk, Bath BA1 1LN
tel (01225) 401149 *fax* (01225) 401149
email info@bathfilmfestival.org
website www.bathfilmfestival.org
Co-ordinator Chris Baker

Audience festival held in October/November over 18 days, and screening approximately 50 titles in a range of new films and upcoming releases.

fees: none
deadline: August (tbc)

Bite the Mango

National Museum of Photography,
Film & Television, Pictureville, Bradford BD1 1NQ
tel (01274) 203311 *fax* (01274) 394540
email BTM@nmsi.ac.uk
website www.nmpft.org.uk/btm/2006
Festival Director Addy Rutter

Bite the Mango screens world cinema with an emphasis on Asia and Africa. Held for a week in September.

Bradford Film Festival

National Museum of Photography,
Film & Television, Pictureville, Bradford BD1 1NQ
tel (01274) 203320 *fax* (01274) 394540
email tony.earnshaw@nmsi.ac.uk
website www.bradfordfilmfestival.ac.uk
Artistic Director Tony Earnshaw

Held in March and established in 1995, Bradford Film Festival screens a range of new features and short films, and also programmes talks and events aimed at industry delegates. Offers the 'Shine' award for Best New Short Film (selection by jury of industry professionals).

fees: none
deadline: January

Britdoc

PO Box 60415, London E2 6WQ
tel 020-7366 5650 *fax* 020-7366 5652
email jackie@britdoc.org
website www.britdoc.org
Festival Director Beadi Finzi *Festival Programmer* Maxyne Franklin *Festival Manager* Jackie Dickinson

Launched in July 2006 at Keble College Oxford, BRITDOC is the essential annual meeting of every key player in British feature documentary production. Comprising 3 days of intensive networking, pitching and screenings, this is a documentary 'thinktank' – a place to debate the art and business of documentary. Brings together international industry leaders to make deals on British documentaries, to spread its core message that documentaries can change the world.

Cambridge Film Festival

Arts Picture House, 38-39 St Andrews Street,
Cambridge BS2 3AR
tel (01223) 504444
email cff@picturehouses.co.uk
website www.cambridgefilmfestival.org.uk

An 11-day film event held each July, with a growing reputation for screening new, quality international features and short films with many UK premieres and a number of talks and events aimed at filmmakers and the industry. The festival is produced by City Screen (see page 341), the company which owns the chain of Picturehouse cinemas around the UK. For submission guidelines, refer to the website.

Cardiff Screen Festival

10 Mount Stuart SW, Cardiff CF10 5EE
tel 029-20 333 324 *fax* 029-20 333 320
email sarah@sgrin.co.uk
website www.cardiffscreenfestival.co.uk

Cardiff Screen Festival will be in its 20th year in 2008, and is devoted to celebrating Welsh screen talent. The event culminates in the presentation of the prestigious DM Davies Short Film Award, which stakes a claim to being the largest prize for a short film competition in Europe (cash and in-kind prizes of up to £20,000).

eligibility: film must be less than 2 years old and must either be from a Welsh filmmaker, a resident of Wales, or someone who attended a Welsh college or university. DM Davies short films must be made in Wales

fees: none
deadline: see website

Celtic Film and Television Festival

249 West George Street, Glasgow G2 4QE
tel 0141-302 1737
email mail@celticfilm.co.uk
website www.celticfilm.co.uk

An annual international event, held each spring. Celebrates and promotes the cultures and languages of the Celtic countries and regions.

Chichester Film Festival

Chichester Cinema, New Park Road, Chichester,
West Sussex PO19 1XN
tel (01243) 784881 *fax* (01243) 790235
email info@chichestercinema.org
website www.chichestercinema.org

2-week audience festival screening approximately 70 new works each August.

Cinemagic – World Screen Festival for Young People

3rd Floor, Fountain House, 17-21 Donegall Place, Belfast BT1 5AB
tel 028-9031 1900 *fax* 028-9031 9709
email info@cinemagic.org.uk
website www.cinemagic.org.uk
Festival Programmer Chris Shaw

Cinemagic is held each November/December, and showcases new moving-image work for young people. It aims to educate through the use of film and television. Films are selected with the input of young viewers; prizes are awarded for the best short and feature for teenagers and for children. Winners of the short film prizes receive £500; winners of the feature prizes receive £1000.

eligibility: films must be less than 2 years old and must be appropriate for a young audience
fees: none
deadline: August

Discovering Latin America Film Festival

5 Holme Court, 158 Twickenham Road, Isleworth TW7 7DL
email gustavo@discoveringlatinamerica.org
website www.discoveringlatinamerica.com/dlaff
Festival Director Jorge Garayo

Audience festival devoted to showcasing new works from Latin American filmmakers. Held each November in London.

Edinburgh International Film Festival

Filmhouse, 88 Lothian Road, Edinburgh EH3 9BZ
tel 0131-228 4051 *fax* 0131-229 5501
email info@edfilmfest.org.uk
website www.edfilmfest.org.uk
Artistic Director Hannah McGill, *Managing Director* Ginnie Atkinson, *Programme Producer* Nicola Kettlewood

One of the UK's 2 premier international film fests (along with London). Established in 1947 and traditionally held each August, EIFF will be moving to June for its 2008 fest. EIFF's programme is a broad selection of strong New World and European work with a clear committment to new discoveries and emerging filmmakers. The festival also has a strong focus on new British film, and often world premieres new works from UK filmmakers.

Awards include: Michael Powell Best British Feature; Standard Life Audience Award; New Directors Award; Best British Short Film; European Short Film; McLaren Award for British Animation; and Saltire Award for Best Short Documentary. Active industry services include: delegate centre with videoteque, and industry office with advice; delegates have special industry events and screenings of all programmed films.

eligibilty: all films must be UK premieres and produced within last 18 months
fees: none
deadlines: please check website for 2008 dates

Encounters Short Film Festival

Watershed, 1 Canons Road, Harbourside, Bristol BS1 5TX
tel 0117-929 9188 *fax* 0117-929 9988
email info@encounters-festival.org.uk
website www.encounters-festival.org.uk
Managing Director Sue Lion

Encounters Short Film Festival (encompassing Animated Encounters and Brief Encounters) takes place annually in November in Bristol. Key focus of the event is on emerging talent and innovation. The Festival is one of the more important on the international short film calendar; it aims to provide a dynamic event of appeal to professional, student and general audiences, including: competition and guest programmes; animation workshops; industry forums; masterclasses and meet-the-filmmaker sessions; and a selection of networking and social events.

As a service to buyers and programmers attending the festival, Encounters offers The HP Digital Viewing Library to allow delegates to view film entries on demand.

eligibility: short films of up to 30 minutes (including animation, documentary, drama and experimental film)
fees: none
deadline: May

Festival of Fantastic Films

95 Meadowgate Road, Salford, Manchester M6 8EN
email gil@glaneyoung.freeserve.co.uk
website www.fantastic-films.com

Weekend-long fan festival and conference held in Manchester each September. Also runs an amateur film competition during the festival.

FILMSTOCK International Film Festival

24 Guildford Street, Luton LU1 2NR
tel (01582) 402200 *fax* (01582) 423347
email contact@filmstock.co.uk
website www.filmstock.co.uk
Directors Justin Doherty, Neil Fox

Independent film festival established in 2000 and held in early November each year. Awards a prize for short films (no cash). Recently screened titles include: *Thank You For Smoking*, *Cars*, and *The Wind That Shakes The Barley*.

fees: various (festival directors recommend that filmmakers call or email before sending their film)

Foyle Film Festival

The Nerve Centre, 7-8 Magazine Street, Derry BT48 6HJ
tel 028-71 276 432 *fax* 028-71 371 738
email s.kelpie@nerve-centre.org.uk
website www.foylefilmfestival.com
Director Sauna Kelpie

Established in 1988 and held in November each year. Screens a wide mix of feature films and shorts; has awards for Best Irish and Best International Short, Best Animation, Best Documentary and Best Film.

eligibility: open
fees: £5
deadline: September

Frightfest

c/o Ian Rattray Films, 10 Wiltshire Gardens, Twickenham, Middlesex, London TW2 6ND
tel 020-8296 0555 *fax* 020-8296 0556
email info-frightfest@blueyonder.co.uk
website www.frightfest.co.uk

Frightfest is devoted to horror and fantasy film. Held each year on the August Bank Holiday in London's Leicester Square. Recent titles screened: *Dead Meat, Wolf Creek*, and *Hellboy*.

eligibility: no unsolicted submissions, but filmmakers who want their work screened should see the website for further details about how to make contact

Human Rights Watch International Film Festival

2-12 Pentonville Road, London N1 9HF
tel 020-7713 1995 *fax* 020-7713 1800
email events@hrw.org
website www.hrw.org/london
Director Bruni Burres

Held each March, the London edition of this International Festival programmes fiction, documentary and animation with a human rights theme. This is primarily an audience festival, with the aim of raising awareness of international human rights issues. There are no awards given in London. Recent titles include: *Fog of War, Born into the Brothels*, and *Sometimes in April*.

eligibility no open submissions
– see page 273.

Italian Film Festival

82 Nicholson Street, Edinburgh EH8 9EW
tel 0131-668 2232 *fax* 0131-668 2777
email cinema@italcult.org.uk
website www.italianfilmfestival.org.uk

This festival is a touring programme of new Italian work; travels to 6 cities each autumn.

KinoFilm: Manchester International Short Film Festival

42 Edge Street, Manchester M4 1HN
tel 0161-288 2494 *fax* 0161-281 1374
email info@kinofilm.org.uk
website www.kinofilm.org.uk
Festival Director John Wojowski

Kinofilm has expanded its short film festival to include features under the banner of 'Transitions' for those filmmakers who have recently made the successful transition from short film to feature. The primary aim of the Kinofilm Shorts festival is to build support for short filmmakers and raise awareness of short film production; the new features strand of the Festival aims to provide a valuable platform for the exhibition of first and second features by directors who have made that transition.

Leeds International Film Festival

Leeds Film, Town Hall, The Headrow, Leeds LS1 3AD
tel 0113-247 8389 *fax* 0113-247 8397
email filmfestival@leeds.gov.uk
website www.leedsfilm.com
Head of Leeds Film Chris Fell

Held over 10 days in November. Awards include: The Golden Owl Award (Best Debut Feature); Louis Le Prince Award (Best International Fiction Short); World Animation Award (Best Animated Short); Yorkshire Film Award (Best Short made in the Yorkshire Region); Silver Melies (Best European Fantasy Feature); and Audience Award for Best Feature.

fees: none
deadlines: Aug/Sept

The Times *bfi* London Film Festival

bfi South Bank, London SE1 8XT
tel 020-7815 1322 *fax* 020-7633 0786
email sarah.lutton@bfi.org.uk
website www.lff.org.uk
Artistic Director Sandra Hebron *Festival Producer* Helen de Witt *Festival Programme and Guest Co-ordinator* Sarah Lutton

One of the key film events in the British industry calendar, and the largest in the UK; screens approximately 180 feature films and 100 shorts titles. With audiences of well over 100,000, the festival is also increasingly important as a UK launch for new work. Held in October each year, the LFF celebrated its 50th anniversary in 2006. One of the British Film Institute's core annual activities, with a remit to screen the best of world cinema.

LFF is a non-competitive festival but gives awards for emerging talent, including the *bfi* Sutherland Trophy, a FIPRESCI prize, a documentary feature award and the Turner Classic Shorts Award. Sections include: Galas/Special Screenings; Films on the Square; New British Cinema; French Revolutions; Cinema Europa; World Cinema; Experimenta; Treasures from the Archive; and Short Cuts and Animation.

The festival is well regarded by filmmakers as being particularly supportive and welcoming, and also for being receptive to experimental works.

eligibility: all international films must be UK premieres; British features and short films can have screened in EIFF
fees: none
deadline: July

London Lesbian and Gay Film Festival

BFI South Bank, London SE1 8XT
tel 020-7815 1323 *fax* 020-7633 0786
email anna.dunwoodie@bfi.org.uk
website www.llgff.org.uk
Contact: Anna Dunwoodie

LLGFF is Europe's premier L&G film festival, and one of the oldest and most important on this specialist international circuit. The festival is based at the *bfi* Southbank (formerly The National Film Theatre) each April, and screens a range of new features and short films over 2 weeks.

eligibility: films must not have been broadcast or released on DVD or video in the UK, and must be of interest to gay, lesbian, bisexual and transgender audiences
fees: none
deadlines: December

Media Guardian Edinburgh International Television Festival (MGEITF)

117 Farringdon Road, London EC1R 3BX
tel 020-7278 9515 *fax* 020-7278 9495
website www.mgeitf.co.uk

Key annual event for professionals working in the UK television industry. It brings together all of the key players for the August Bank Holiday, for conference sessions, speeches and events on important topical and cultural issues in TV broadcast.

onedotzero

Unit 212c, Curtain House, 134-146 Curtain Road, London EC2A 3AR
fax 020-7729 0057
email info@onedotzero.com
website www.onedotzero.com

onedotzero is the UK's pioneering festival of digital cinema, which celebrated its 11th year in 2007. Held at the Institute of Contemporary Arts, onedotzero screens a wide range of digital works – from short films and features to pop promos, commercials and moving-image visuals; also stages talks, workshops and club events. The company runs a DVD label which releases new groundbreaking digital works.

Raindance Film Festival

81 Berwick Street, London W1F 8TW
tel 020-7287 3833 *fax* 020-7439 2243
email info@raindance.co.uk
website www.raindance.co.uk/festival
Producer Jesse Vile

Running for 2 weeks in October, Raindance is committed to screening innovative independent cinema from the UK and around the world. Weighted heavily towards new talent, the festival offers more than 100 features (many of which are directorial debuts), 20 shorts programmes and a wide range of events, workshops, parties and the British Independent Film Awards.

fees: €20 for a short and €70 for a feature
deadline: June

– see page 359.

Sand-Swansea Animation Days

Swansea Institute, Mount Pleasant, Swansea SA1 6ED
tel (01792) 481194 *fax* (01792) 481122
email sand@sihe.ac.uk
website www.sand.org.uk
Director Felicity Blastland

Held over a weekend in November. International computer graphics event with animation screenings, conference sessions on games, films, CGI and post-production techniques. Industry guests are offered conference participation, and networking and recruiting opportunities.

Screenwriters' Festival – see page 6.

Sheffield International Documentary Festival

The Workstation, 15 Paternoster Row, Sheffield S1 2BX
tel 0114-276 5141 *fax* 0114-272 1849
email info@sidf.co.uk
website www.sidf.co.uk
Festival Director Heather Croall

Held late October/early November. The festival screens a wide-ranging programme of documentaries from all over the world, and offers a number of industry networking opportunities and access to commissioners.

fees: none
deadline: June

Viva! Spanish Film Festival

Cornerhouse, 70 Oxford Street, Manchester M1 5NH
tel 0161-228 7621
website www.vivafilmfestival.com

Audience festival which celebrates the best in new Spanish and Latin American cinema. Held in March at Manchester's Cornerhouse.

Wildscreen

PO Box 366, Bristol BS99 2HD
tel 0117-328 5950 *fax* 0117-328 5955
email info@wildscreen.org.uk
website www.wildscreen.org

Held in October, biennially, in even years. Focuses on wildlife and environmental films to celebrate biodiversity and promote conservation. The festival is mainly for industry and not for the public; promotional benefits of inclusion in the programme include a listing in the Delegate Directory, and availability for viewing in the video library.

fees: to enter a film for 1 category/award costs £100; each additional category £40 (an exception is made for the Newcomer category, which costs £35 to enter)

deadline: March

WOW! Wales One World Film Festival

Taliesin Arts Centre, University of Wales Swansea, Swansea
tel (01239) 615066 *fax* (01239) 615066
email sa3657@eclipse.co.uk
website www.wowfilmfestival.org
Director David Gillam

Audience festival consisting of a small and selective programme of quality feature films from the continents of Africa, Asia, and Latin America. Tours to venues in Wales throughout March and April.

A filmmakers' festival survival guide

Asif Kapadia

Making a movie is tough – writing the script, getting the finance, finding the equipment, putting together the cast and the crew, not to mention the pain and trials of the shoot and the post-production. These stages take a long time and cost a lot of money. Once you've finished the film, the last thing you want is to have it sit on the shelf. You want your film to be seen by an audience on the big screen.

Film festivals are one of the purest elements of the filmmaking process. Audiences the world over turn up in snow and rain and pay money to see movies by filmmakers they don't know, starring people they have never heard of, telling tales that are often far from their own personal experiences.

If you don't have a big-budget commercial film, with big star names and backed by a studio or a distribution company willing to spend a lot of money to promote your movie, then you don't have many options. It's even more difficult if you have made an indie, European or arthouse film. So having your film screened by an international film festival is one of the key ways to get your work onto the big screen before an audience, with the aim of creating a buzz around your film and making a name for yourself as an interesting filmmaker within the UK and internationally.

If the film does well, it might get invited to other festivals, and maybe win some awards – all of which helps to create publicity, which makes audiences, producers and financiers want to see your film. Hopefully some of these producers and financiers will want to work with you in the future. Festivals just might make it a little easier to get your next movie together.

Festival strategies

It is important to think hard about where you first screen your film, because this may affect where you get reviewed and what kind of impact your film makes on an international stage. You need a lot of luck, and need to be in the right place at the right time to get into the key 'A list' festivals that Sandra mentions in the introduction: Cannes, Venice, Berlin, Toronto, Clermont Ferrand. These festivals have the pick of world cinema; you are literally fighting against the most well-known and talented filmmakers in the world for a few key slots in competition, so you need to be realistic. Yet festivals always want to discover a new talent, so there is always a chance of your film being selected. You will never know unless you apply.

The bigger festivals also want premieres, so be aware that if you screen your film at a small festival, it may ruin your chance to screen it somewhere grander. Or you could just forget to mention it on the form …

It is sometimes possible to show a film abroad and still get it shown at key festivals in the UK, like Edinburgh and London. If however there is a particular festival you have your heart set on, find out what its regulations are.

You also need to keep track of the deadlines for the festivals, bearing in mind that it is not unusual to show your film to the selection committee of an 'A list' festival before you have even finished it. So you need to be aware of the festival calendar when in post-production, so that you don't miss the deadlines – or else you may have to wait a year to approach the festival again.

If your film is not accepted by one of the bigger festivals, it's not the end of the world – but it is the start of the really hard work. Filling in application forms and sending out tapes and DVDs is a full-time job and can prove costly (again, as Sandra mentioned, some of the festivals charge a fee to enter, particularly the US ones). You may have to keep sending the film out and not lose heart in your work in order to find the festival that understands it. I would also advise you not to narrow your options to UK festivals. It is easy to forget just how many prestigious festivals there are around the world, and how much screening in these can open other doors for you and your film.

I've found the British Council's Films Division to be an invaluable resource. It has a list of festivals it considers important, and organises screenings of features for the festival selectors, so it is a good idea to keep the team informed about the progress of your movie. The Division also selects some short films to represent, and for these it sends tapes and DVDs to key short film festivals. If your work is selected, it handles the print costs and can assist with air fares so that you can attend. This can save you a lot, as the postage costs when sending your films out can really add up.

Once your film is shown at a key festival, the momentum can build quickly. This was certainly true for *The Sheep Thief*: suddenly the film was off and running with a life of its own. Selectors from other festivals will see your movie and may invite the film to theirs; it is possible to spend a year travelling with a film if it does well. All you have to do is try to organise getting the prints from one festival to the next … easier said than done, sometimes.

On the road with your film

I travelled a lot with my shorts and my first feature. For me it was fascinating to travel the world to the festivals that showed an interest in my work. It gave me the chance to see my film with different international audiences, and do the Q&As to see for myself how the films worked – or didn't – within different cultures.

That said, if you are working on a new project you will have to make choices. Do you go to every festival that invites you, or stay home to work on the new stuff? Of course, when you are invited to a festival, you never know if it will be the last one that wants to show the movie, so it is dangerous to try to be too clever about it! I preferred not to hedge my bets. If I was able to attend, I went along and never regretted it (the other thing is, if you do turn up, I think it helps your chances of winning something!).

Sometimes the most memorable experiences come from the smaller, friendlier festivals, in a place you have never heard of, or never wanted to go to. Conversely, the bigger festivals in major cities can be lonely and stressful and you might find yourself wandering around, having trouble getting into events or screenings and never meeting the same person twice. During a trip to the Tromso film festival in the north of Norway I saw the Northern Lights and took a dog sledge ride across the tundra. The experience was so amazing that it triggered something in me and my co-writer, and I wrote a screenplay set in the landscape – a movie we hope to shoot later this year.

Once you are there, how do you make the most of the experience? There are different types of festivals: some are all about the films and the filmmakers; others are all about business. Often you are only invited for a few days, so you have to try to cram in as much as you can while there. I really don't think being at a festival should be all about trying to sell yourself; sometimes it's fun to just watch movies. It was always exciting for me to be blown away by a film that I would never get the chance to see in the UK.

Going to the parties and dinners is obviously part of the fun. I loved spending time with other directors from around the world, watching lots of movies, swapping stories and learning about their style and techniques. It is a great way to make friends. There is always something to learn from the experience, and travelling to film festivals with your film is one of the perks of being a filmmaker – a real joy at the end of the long and challenging process.

Other festivals – Cannes, for example – are all about doing deals. If you are a filmmaker, rather than a programmer, here the film screenings almost seem to go on the background. You find yourself pitching an idea for a film in the strangest places, collecting the business cards of producers, financiers, journalists, and selectors from other festivals who show an interest in your film. It's always worth following up these meetings once you get home. I first met my producer, Bertrand Faivre, at the Brest Short Film Festival in France when I was there with my short, *The Sheep Thief*. A year or two later I met him in the bar of the Edinburgh Festival and pitched him my idea for *The Warrior*. Three years later, the film premiered there.

It's a good idea to take a package of material with you when you go to a festival – DVDs, production stills, press packs, posters and postcards. Try to get the festival to pin your posters up, showing the times and dates of the screenings. You want your screenings to be full, to create a buzz for your movie. Good production stills from the shoot are key – they will hopefully get printed in the festival brochure. When there are hundreds of films at a festival, a really strong image will always help the audience choose your film.

If you are invited to attend a festival as its guest, you will generally be spoilt rotten. Your travel will probably be paid for (if not, the British Council can sometimes assist, as Sandra has mentioned) and you will be put up for a few days. You should expect there to be a couple of screenings of your film; you will be asked to present the film before it begins, and take part in a Question & Answer session with the audience at the end. So you have to lose the shyness! You will have to get used to standing with a microphone in front of an audience, discussing your work and intentions, and often speaking via an interpreter. There is a good chance that you may end up doing local press or the odd TV interview. You will also probably be given a festival pass that will enable you to get into most screenings – so see as many as possible. And then there are the parties … these usually happen on most nights, so it is worth getting to know the festival organisers to find out the places to go. They can get you in if there is a particularly hot ticket.

You should expect to fly home totally shattered and absolutely energised to go out and make another movie.

Asif Kapadia's *The Return* was released in the UK in early 2007. His debut feature, *The Warrior*, was released in the UK in 2002 and won two BAFTA awards, together with a host of other prizes including the *Evening Standard* British Film Award for the Most Promising Newcomer. Asif's student film from the Royal College of Art, *The Sheep Thief* – a 25-minute drama shot in India – won numerous awards around the world and is available on the Cinema 16 DVD collection of short films. Asif has also directed documentary films for the BBC and was a director of documentaries for Carlton Television on Shift. He continues to direct commercials.

Key international film festivals

AFI Fest: American Film Institute Los Angeles International Film Festival

American Film Institute, 2021 N Western Avenue, Los Angeles, CA 90027-1657, USA
tel ++ 1 323 856 7600 *fax* ++ 1 323 467 4578
email afifest@AFI.com
website www.AFI.com/AFIFEST
Director, Festivals Christian Gaines

Established in 1987; runs in partnership with AFM each November (see page 285). The festival and market have an increasingly international industry turnout, and enjoy substantial support from the commercial and independent film communities in LA. AFI Fest has international competitions of features, documentaries and shorts, and audience awards in the same categories.

eligibility: US premieres are given priority, and films which have previously screened in LA are not eligible

fees: $55 Early Deadline or $65 Final Deadline / Shorts $35 Early Deadline or $45 Final Deadline

deadline: July

American Black Film Festival

c/o Film Life, PO Box 688, New York, NY 10012, USA
fax 00 212 966 2497
email abbf@thefilmlife.com
website www.abff.com

The festival's mission is to create the most prestigious platform in the world for showcasing pan-African films. Offers a range of prizes for Best Feature, Best Short, Best Animation and Best World Film, among others.

fees: $40 per film

deadline: April

International Documentary Film Festival, Amsterdam (IDFA)

Kleine-Gartmanplantsoen 10, 1017 RR Amsterdam, The Netherlands
tel ++ 31 20 6273329 *fax* ++ 31 20 6385388
email info@idfa.nl
website www.idfa.nl
Festival Director Ally Derks

One of the more important documentary festivals on the annual calendar, the event is held each November and attracts audiences of more than 60,000. A market – Docs for Sale – also runs alongside it. Offers a forum for filmmakers to present works-in-progress for potential funders and buyers.

Awards include: VPRO Joris Ivens Award; a Special Jury Award; a Silver Wolf; a Fipresci prize for Best Film; and an Audience award. Many of these have cash prizes attached.

eligibility: competitions require World, European or International premieres; all other sections require the film never to have been braodcast or screened in the Netherlands

fees: none

Anima – Brussels Animation Film Festival

Folioscope asbl, Avenue de Stalingrad 52, B – 1000 Bruxelles, Belgique
tel ++ 32 2 534 41 25 *fax* ++ 32 2 534 22 79
email info@folioscope.be
website folioscope.awn.com

Animation festival held in March. Prizes are given for the best short films in international, student and children's film categories, and there are audience awards for feature film.

Animafest – World Festival of Animated Films

Koncertna Direkcija Zagreb, Kneza Mislava 18, 100 00 Zagreb, Croatia
tel ++3851 450 1191 *fax* ++3851 450 1193
email animafest@animafest.hr
website www.animafest.hr

Held in June in even-numbered years, with focus on short animation (under 30 mins). In odd-numbered years, Animafest is held in October for animated features. Awards include cash prizes.

fees: none

deadlines: January for short films and June for features

Annecy International Animated Film Festival

c/o Conservatoire d'Art et d'Histoire, 18 ave. du Tresum, BP 399 74013 Annecy, France
tel ++ 33 4 5010 0900 *fax* ++ 33 4 5010 0970
email info@annecy.org
website www.annecy.org
Managing Director Tiziana Loschi

Established in 1960, the International Animated Film Festival is held each June in Annecy, France. Screens animated films of any length, and offers many awards including Grand Prix and Jury awards for short animated films and Grand Prix for features and for a TV film. Also awards work by student filmmakers.

eligibility: films must be less than 18 months old

fees: none

deadline: January

Art Film Festival – Trencianske Teplice

Bajkalská 25/a 825 02 Bratislava 26 Slovak Republic
tel 00 421 2 487 000 42 *fax* 00 421 2 487 000 43

email artfilm@artfilm.sk
website www.artfilm.sk
Artistic Director Peter Hledik

Established in 1993 to encourage interest in art films which innovate in form and visual content. Held in June; submission guidelines available on the website.

Asian American International Film Festival

Asian CineVision, 133 W 19th Street, Suite 300, New York, NY 10011, USA
tel 00 212 989 1422 *fax* 00 212 727 3584
email info@asiancinevision.org
website www.asiancinevision.org
Festival Director Diana Lee

Hosted by non-profit organisation Asian CineVision, the festival is committed to showcasing the best new work from Asian and Asian American filmmakers. Held in Manhattan in August, and Long Island in July. Awards include: Emerging Filmmaker Award (to first-/second-time feature filmmaker); Excellence in Short Filmmaking; Best Music Video Award; Youth Vision Award; and a Screenwriting competition. The first 2 have cash prizes pending funding.

fees: $10-$30
deadline: February

Aspen Shortsfest

110 E Hallam St, Suite 102 Aspen, CO 81612, USA
tel ++1 970 925 6882 *fax* ++ 1 970 925 1967
email trigney@aspenfilm.org
website www.aspenfilm.org
Executive Director Laura Thielen

Celebrating 16 years in 2007, this short film festival aims to stay small and specialist, screening a selective programme of short films each April. It has a reputation for creating a very different atmosphere from many fests, with much intimate interaction between filmmaker, audience and the industry who attend. Films screening at the festival compete for over $20,000 in prizes, which are given for the best films in a number of genre categories.

fees: $35-$55 depending on when the film is submitted
deadline: November

Atlantic Film Festival

5600 Sackville Street, Suite 220, Halifax, Nova Scotia, Canada B3J 1L2
tel ++ 1 902 422 3456 *fax* ++ 1 902 422 4006
email festival@atlanticfilm.com
website www.atlanticfilm.com

Celebrates its 27th anniversary in 2007; held in September each year. Awards include: Best Atlantic Short Film ($5000 in services): Outstanding Writer's Award; and Rex Tasker Award for Best Documentary ($1000 cash).

fees: CA$25 for early entry, or CA$30 for late entry
deadline: June

Auckland International Film Festival

The New Zealand Film Festival Trust, PO Box 9544, Marion Square, Wellington, New Zealand
tel ++ 64 4 385 0162 *fax* ++ 64 4 801 7304
email festival@nzff.co.nz
website www.enzedff.co.nz

Non-competitive festival held in July and as part of a wider association of New Zealand film festivals. Contact details above also apply to Wellington and to a number of other smaller local fests in the country; submissions for all of these are centralised with one application process.

eligibility: films must be New Zealand premieres
fees: none
deadline: March

Bangkok Film Festival

1600 New Phetchaburi Road, 17th Fl, Makkasan, Ratchathewai, Bangkok 10400, Thailand
tel ++ 66 2250 5500 *fax* ++ 66 2250 0019
email info@bangkokfilm.org
website www.bangkokfilm.org
Director of Programming Jennifer Stark

BFF is a new film festival established to support and reflect the emergence of Thai film on an international stage. Held in February and presents a range of Golden Kinnaree Awards in major categories (Film, Director, Short, etc.). Runs concurrently with the Bangkok Film Market. Refer to the website for submission deadlines.

L'Alternativa – Festival of Independent Cinema Barcelona

Centre de Cultura Contemporanea Montalegre 5, 080 01 Barcelona, Spain
tel ++ 34 306 41 00
email alternativa@cccb.org
website www.alternativa.cccb.org
Programmer Tess Renaudo

Held in November and screens primarily independent, *auteur* and experimental work. Fest awards are given for Best Short, Feature, Animation and Documentary.

fees: none
deadline: July

Belgrade International Film Festival

Majke Jevrosime 20, Belgrade, Yugoslavia 11000
tel ++ 381 11 334 6837 *fax* ++ 381 11 334 6946
email info@fest.org.yu
website www.fest.org.yu
Programmer Miroljub Vuckovic

Held at the end of February; screens documentaries and features to a largely public audience.

fees: none
deadline: December

Berlinale – Berlin International Film Festival

Potsdamer Strasse 5, D-10785 Berlin, Germany
tel ++ 49 30 259 20 0 *fax* ++ 49 30 259 20 299

email info@berlinale.de
website www.berlinale.de
Festival Director Dieter Kosslick

Established in 1951, the Berlinale is one of the major 'A List' international film festivals, and is held each February. With the European Film Market (see page 285), it attracts more than 16,000 film professionals, including 3600 journalists, from approximately 80 countries each year. Competitive sections include: Main Competition (major world premieres intended for a broad audience); Panaroma (new works by well-known *auteurs* or new discoveries, with an emphasis on personal perspectives); and Forum (experimental or daring works).

Also hosts a Kinderfilmfest, which features films for children and young people, and awards a special prize for the best new gay or lesbian film (Teddy Award). Every year the Berlinale presents about 60 short films across all of the sections.

eligibility: films must be world premieres outside of their country of origin
fees: none
deadline: published each autumn

Bilbao International Festival of Documentary & Short Films

Colón de Larrátegui 37-4, Apdo. 579, 48009 Bilbao, Spain
tel ++ 34 94 424 86 98 *fax* ++ 34 94 424 56 24
email info@zinebi.com
website www.zinebi.com
Director Ernesto del Rio

Held at the end of November and has a number of major awards, most of which have cash prizes.

eligibility: films must be under 45 minutes' duration
fees: none
deadline: September

Brussels International Festival of Fantastic Films

Rue de la Comtesse de Flandre 8, B-1020 Brussels, Belgium
tel ++ 32 2 201 17 13 *fax* ++ 32 2 201 14 69
website www.bifff.org/en
President Georges Delmo

Festival of fantasy, sci-fi and thriller films held each March.

fees: none
deadline: December

Cairo International Film Festival

17 Kasr El Nil Street, Cairo, Egypt
tel ++ 202 3923962 *fax* ++ 202 3938979
email info@cairofilmfest.com
website www.cairofilmfest.com

Cannes Film Festival

Festival Du Cannes, 3 rue Amelie, F-75007 Paris, France
tel ++ 33 1 53 59 61 00 *fax* ++ 33 1 53 59 61 10
email festival@festival-cannes.fr
website www.festival-cannes.fr
President Gilles Jacob *Artistic Director* Thierry Frémaux *Artistic Director, Critics' Week* Olivier Pere *Artistic Director, Directors' Fortnight* Olivier Pere

Arguably the world's most prestigious film festival, Cannes is held in May each year. With the market (see page 285), it attracts the world film industry for 2 weeks of screenings and meetings. The festival's organisation can be bewildering to many newcomers; it is divided into sections, which operate like mini-festivals in their own right with separate programming teams, awards and submission rules and criteria. Below is an overview of the main festival sections:

Official Selection

Competition is the main competitive section for major new features and shorts. Each year the best feature and short in this section are awarded the Palme d'Or, and the feature which shows the most original vision is awarded the Grand Prix, with other prizes being given for performance and direction. The jury also awards a Special Jury Prize to another standout film.

Un Certain Regard is for films which express a 'personal vision', and which are innovative in form. First-time films can compete for Caméra d'Or in this section.

Special Screenings include out-of-competition films which may not be eligible or appropriate for Competition. These screenings often feature new works from returning directors.

Cinefondation is set up to highlight the work of new emerging filmmakers and student filmmakers.

Deadlines for the Official Selection are in March, and all films must be international premieres

Non-Official Selection

Directors' Fortnight (La Quinzaine des Réalisateurs) is organised by the Directors' Guild in France and includes films which "express the diversity and personal visions" of filmmakers.

Critics' Week (La Semaine Internationale de la Critique) includes a selective group of 7 features and 7 short films which are first or second features. The programme aims to identify and highlight up-and-coming talent. Also organises special screenings outside of the main selection for the section. Prizes include Grand Prix, the Short Film Award and the Young Critic's Award.

Deadlines for Non-Official Selections are in April, and all films must be international premieres

Cape Town International Film Festival

FAO: Ms Tshepiso Sello, Sithengi, SABC Building, 209 Beach Road, Sea Point, Cape Town, 8001, South Africa

tel ++ 27 21 430 8160 *fax* ++ 27 21 430 8186
email info@sithengi.co.za
website www.sithengi.co.za

Cartagena International Film and Television Festival

Calle San Juan de Dios,
Baluarte de San Francisco Javier, Cartagena,
Columbia, AA 1834
tel ++ 575 6601037 *fax* ++ 575 6600970
email info@festicinecartagena.com
website www.festicinecartagena.com

Chicago International Film Festival

30 East Adams, Suite 800, Chicago, Illinois 60603,
USA
tel ++ 1 312 683 0121 *fax* ++ 1 312 683 0122
email info@chicagofilmfestival.com
website www.chicagofilmfestival.com

Competitive festival held in October, with a New Director's Award and Gold and Silver 'Hugos' given to winning films.

eligibility: must be Chicago premieres and not have aired on US television

fees: $35-$100

deadlines: post-marked in July

Chicago Underground Film Festival

c/o IFP/Chicago, 1104 S Wabash Suite 405,
Chicago IL 60605
email info@cuff.org
website www.cuff.org

This August fest aims to screen experimental and underground short films and features which are radically different in form and content from the independent mainstream.

fees: $30-$35

deadlines: May; festival prefers for filmmakers to submit films via **www.withoutabox.com**

Cinekid

Korte Leidesedwarsstraat 12, 1017 RC Amsterdam,
The Netherlands
tel ++ 31 20 531 78 90 *fax* ++ 31 20 531 78 99
email info@cinekid.nl
website www.cinekid.nl

An annual film, television and new media festival for children held in October; celebrated its 21st anniversary in 2007.

fees: none

Cinema du Reel – International Documentary Film Festival

25, rue du Renard, 75197 Paris Cedex 04, France
tel ++ 33 1 44 78 44 21 *fax* ++ 33 1 44 78 12 24
email cinereel@bpi.fr
website www.bpi.fr
Festival Director Marie-Pierre Duhamel-Müller

Held each March, this documentary festival prioritises creative and artistic expression in documentary over commercial interest. Programmers look for shorts and features which express a clear point of view. Prizes include Grand Prix Award worth €8000 and Short Film Prize worth €2500.

eligibility: competition films must be French premieres

fees: none

deadline: November 30

Clermont-Ferrand Short Film Festival

La Jetee, 6 place Michel-de-l'Hospital,
63058 Clermont-Ferrand Cedex 1, France
tel ++ 33 473 91 65 73 *fax* ++ 33 473 92 11 93
email info@clermont-filmfest.com
website www.clermont-filmfest.com
Festival Director Roger Gonin

With Oberhausen, and increasingly the Worldwide Short Film Festival, Clermont-Ferrand is widely regarded as one of the most important short film events on the industry calendar. Held in February, the festival also runs a short film market and attracts many buyers and exhibitors. Awards include: Grand Prix (€4000); a Special Jury Prize (€4000); and an Audience Prize (€4000).

eligibility: any film of up to 40 minutes, which is less than 2 years old, on 35mm, DigiBeta or Beta SP

fees: none

deadline: October

Cleveland International Film Festival

Cleveland Film Society, 2510 Market Avenue,
Cleveland, OH 44113-3434, USA
tel ++ 1 216 623 3456 *fax* ++ 1 216 623 0103
email cfs@clevelandfilm.org
website www.clevelandfilm.org

Columbus International Film and Video Festival

Film Council of Greater Columbus,
1430 South High Street, Columbus, Ohio 43207, USA
tel ++ 614 444 7460
email info@chrisawards.org
website www.chrisawards.org

Copenhagen Gay & Lesbian Film Festival

Gothersgade 175, 2 sal – 1123 Copenhagen, Denmark
tel ++ 45 3393 0766
email kontakt@cglff.dk
website www.cglff.dk

Cork International Film Festival

Emmet House, Emmet Place, Cork, Ireland
tel 353 21 427 1711 *fax* 353 21 427 5945
email info@corkfilmfest.org
website www.corkfilmfest.org
Director Mick Hannigan

Held in October each year; established in 1956. The festival includes a competition for short films of

under 30 minutes, with a range of awards including best Irish, international and gay and lesbian short films.
fees: none
deadline: June

Créteil – Festival International de Films de Femmes

Maison des Arts, Place Salvador Allende, 940 00 Créteil, France
tel ++ 33 1 49 803 858 *fax* ++ 33 1 49 804 10
email iris@filmsdefemmes.com
website www.filmsdefemmes.com
Director Jackie Buet

Held each year in March; screens films of all lengths and genres which are made by women. Offers industry delegates meeting places and access to market.
fees: none
deadline: November

Cuba – International Festival of New Latin American Cinema

Festival Internacional del Nuevo Cine, Latinoamericano ICAIC, Calle 2, no.411 e/17y19, Vedado, CP 10400 La Habana, Cuba
tel ++ 5 37 55 2841 *fax* ++ 5 37 33 4273
email festival@icaic.inf.cu
website www.habanafilmfestival.com
Festival Director Ivan Giroud

December festival which screens the best in new work from Latin America.

Denver International Film Festival

Denver Film Society, 1725 Blake Street, Denver, CO 80202, USA
tel ++ 1 303 595 3456 *fax* ++ 1 303 595 0956
website www.denverfilm.org
Director Ron Henderson *Program Director* Brit Withey

Held for 10 days in November, DIFF presents 3 juried awards: Emerging Filmmakers Award; the Maysles Brothers Award for Best Documentary Film; and the Krzysztof Kieslowski Award for Best Feature Film. Additional awards include: the John Cassavetes Award for outstanding contributions in independent film; the Stan Brakhage Vision Award for cutting-edge experimental work; and the Mayor's Lifetime Achievement Award for extraordinary contributions to world cinema.
fees: $20-$60 depending on when film is submitted
deadline: August

Dinard Film Festival of British Film

Festival du Film Britannique de Dinard, 2 Boulevard Feart, 358 00 Dinard, France
tel ++33 2 99 88 19 04 *fax* ++ 33 2 99 46 67 15
email fest.film.britan@ville-dinard.fr
website www.festivaldufilm-dinard.com

French-audience festival devoted to British film.

Dublin Lesbian and Gay Film Festival

c/o Nexus, Tower One, Fumbally Court, Fumbally Lane, Dublin, Ireland 8
tel ++ 353 1 4158414 *fax* ++ 353 1 4730597
email dlgff@ireland.com
website www.gcn.ie/dlgff

Edinburgh International Film Festival – see page 259.

Encounters South Africa International Documentary Festival

PO Box 2228, Cape Town 8000, South Africa
tel ++ 27 21 465 46 86 *fax* ++ 27 21 461 69 64
email distribution@encounters.co.za
website www.encounters.co.za

Fantasporto – Oporto International Film Festival

Rua Anibal Cunha, 84 – sala 1.6, 4050-048 Porto, Portugal
tel ++ 351 2 2207 6050 *fax* ++ 351 2 2207 6059
email info@fantasporto.online.pt
website www.fantasporto.com

Festival devoted to fantasy, horror and science fiction; held in February each year.
eligibility: fantasy films of any length
fees: none
deadline: December

Feminale – International Womens' Film Festival

Maybachstr, 111, D-50670 Cologne, Germany
tel ++ 49 2211 300 225 *fax* ++ 49 2211 300 281
email info@feminale.de
website www.feminale.de

FESPACO – Panafrican Film Festival of Ouagadougou

01 BP 2505, Ouagadougou 01, Burkina Faso
tel ++ 226 50 39 87 01 *fax* ++ 226 50 39 87 05
email sg@fespaco.bf
website www.fespaco.bf

This pan-African film event is the largest film festival in Africa; it is held every other year. Screens new shorts and features from around the continent, and attracts a large international audience of journalists and programmers.

Festival dei Popoli

Borgo Pinti 82 rosso, 501 21 Firenze, Italy
tel ++ 39 055 244 778 *fax* ++ 39 055 241 364
email festivaldeipopoli@festivaldeipopoli.191.it
website www.festivaldeipopoli.org

Festival du Nouveau Cinema (MONTREAL)

3805 Saint-Laurent Blvd, Office 304, Montreal, Quebec, Canada, H2W 1X9

tel ++ 1 514 282 0004 *fax* ++ 1 514 282 6664
email ngirard@nouveaucinema.ca
website www.nouveaucinema.ca
Acting Director Nicolas Girard

The Festival du Nouveau Cinéma is committed to highlighting and contributing to the development of new trends in cinema and new media. It is a showcase for new, original works, particularly in the fields of independent cinema and digital creation. Established in 1971, this week-long festival is held mid-October. Gives a number of awards each year.

fees: US$25 for films submitted from outside Canada

Festival International du Film d'Amiens

MCA Place Leon Gontier, 80000 Amiens, France
tel ++ 33 3 22 71 35 70 *fax* ++33 3 22 92 53 04
email contact@filmfestamiens.org
website www.filmfestamiens.org

The aim of the festival is to promote films contributing to the expression of the identity of people of ethnic minorities (within France), and to the understanding of different ethnic cultures. Held each November; has a relationship with FESPACO.

eligibility: any French premiere which is less than 18 months old
fees: none
deadline: July

Festival International du Film Policier

Le Public Systeme Cinema, 40 rue Anatole, 92594 Levallois-Perret Cedex, France
tel ++ 33 1 41 34 20 00 *fax* ++ 33 1 41 34 20 77
email emitacinema@le-public-systeme.fr
website www.festival.cognac.fr

Crime festival held each April. See website for submission details.

Festival of American Cinema – Festival du Cinéma Américain

Festival du Cinéma Américain, 14800 Deauville, France
tel ++ 33 2 31 14 40 00 *fax* ++ 33 2 31 88 78 88
email accueil@deauville.org
website www.festival-deauville.com

Audience festival which screens new American short and feature films.

Festival of the Dhow Countries

ZIFF, PO Box 3032, Zanzibar, Tanzania
tel 00 255 4 747 411499 *fax* 00 255 4 747 419955
email ziff@ziff.or.tz
website www.ziff.or.tz

Flanders International Film Festival – Ghent

Leeuwstraat 40b, B-9000 Ghent, Belgium
tel ++ 32 9 242 8060 *fax* ++ 32 9 221 9074
email wim.dewitte@filmfestival.be
website www.filmfestival.be
www.worldsoundtrackawards.com
Executive Programmer Wim de Witte

Held annually in October. Programming emphasises the link between music and film (although is not exclusively themed); includes an award each year for Best Music, as well as a number of other, more traditional festival awards. 35th edition 7-18 October 2008, 36th edition 6-17 October 2009.

fees: none
deadline: 1st August

FlickerFest International Short Film Festival

Bondi Pavillion, PO BOX 7416, Sydney, Australia, NSW 2026
tel ++ 61 2 9365 6888
email info@flickerfest.com.au
website www.flickerfest.com.au

This January festival is in its 15th year, and screens short films of all genres. Consists of a main competitive programme, a short documentary competition, an Australian competition, and a number of additional programmes and forums out of competition. Awards include: Best Film, with a prize of $2000AUD; Best Animation, for $1250AUD; and Best Documentary, for $1000AUD.

eligibility: films of up to 30 minutes which are Sydney premieres
fees: $35AUD
deadline: September

Fort Lauderdale International Film Festival

1314 East Olas Blvd #007, Fort Lauderdale, FL 33301, USA
tel 1 954 760 9898 *fax* 1 954 760 9099
email info@fliff.com
website www.FlIFF.com

Competitive fest held annually in mid-October.

fees: $40 per feature; $30 per short (student films $25)

Fribourg International Film Festival

Fribourg International Film Festival, Case postale 550, CH – 1701 Fribourg, Switzerland
tel + 41 26 347 42 00 *fax* + 41 26 347 42 01
email info@fiff.ch
website www.fiff.ch

Gerardmer Fantasy Film Festival

29 avenue du 19 Novembre, BP 105, 884 03 Gerardmer, France
tel ++ 329 60 98 21 *fax* ++ 329 60 98 14
email info@gerardmer-fantasticart.com
website www.gerardmer-fantasticart.com

Giffoni Film Festival

c/o Cittadella del Cineam, 84095 Giffoni Valle Piana, Italy

tel ++39 089 8023 001 *fax* ++39 089 8023 210
email intl2.relationship@giffoniff.it
website www.giffoniff.it
Director Claudio Gubitosi

An internationally respected film festival designed to promote and enable cinema for young people; includes a jury made up of 6-19 year olds.

Going Underground International Short Film festival

Tempelhofer Ufer 1a, 109 61 Berlin, Germany
tel ++ 49 (0)30 2529 1322 *fax* ++ 49 (0)30 2529 1322
email festival@interfilm.de
website www.interfilm.de

International short film festival founded in 2001 and held each November. Films must be narrative and no longer than 30 minutes. 3 awards have cash prizes of between €1000 and €3000.

fees: none
deadline: August

Göteborg Film Festival

Olof Palmes plats, 413 04 Göteborg, Sweden
tel ++ 46 31 339 3000 *fax* ++ 46 31 41 0053
email info@filmfestival.org
website www.filmfestival.org
Artistic Director Jannike Ahlund

Held in January; includes Europe's most important showcase of Nordic film during the Nordic Event in the second half of the festival.

fees: see website
deadline: November

Haifa International Film Festival

142 Hanassi Avenue, Haifa 34633, Israel
tel ++ 972 4 835 3523 *fax* ++ 972 4 838 4327
email film@haifaff.co.il
website www.haifaff.co.il
Editor Festival Coordinator Amalia Rosen

The Haifa IFF, Israel's leading cinematic event, is held in late September at Mount Carmel, overlooking the Mediterranean Sea, and brings together an ever-growing audience of 70,000 spectators along with hundreds of Israeli and foreign professionals from the film industry. Dozens of journalists from Israel and abroad cover the event. The festival premieres 150 new films each year and has 2 international competitions: Golden Anchor Competition for Mediterranean Cinema and the Fipresci New Directors, and an Israeli Film Competition. It also stages tributes, masterclasses, guests and more. In 2008 the Festival celebrates its 24th edition.

Hamburg International Short Film Festival

KurzFilmAgentur, Hamburg e.V., Filmhaus, Friedensallee 7, D-22765 Hamburg, Germany
tel ++ 49 40 39106323 *fax* ++ 49 40 39106220
email festival@shortfilm.com
website www.shortfilm.com
Art Director Jürgen Kittel

Held in early June; programmes international short films of all genres and a children's short film strand. Awards include: prizes for best 'no budget' and international films. Festival also includes a market and special screenings for distributors.

eligibility: all films of up to 25 minutes
fees: none
deadline: February

Hamburg Film Festival

Filmfest Hamburg GmbH, Steintorweg 4, D-20099 Hamburg, Germany
tel ++ 49 40 399 19 00 14 *fax* ++ 49 40 399 19 00 10
email programm@filmfesthamburg.de
website www.filmfesthamburg.de

Established in 1992, Hamburg Film Festival is held annually in September/October and gives several prizes each year, including the Douglas Sirk Award presented to a personality or a company that has made outstanding contributions to film culture and the film industry.

fees: none
deadline: August

Hawaii International Film Festival

680 Iwilei Road, Suite 100, Honolulu, Hawaii 96817 USA
tel ++ 1 808 528 3456 *fax* ++ 1 808 536 2707
email info@hiff.org
website www.hiff.org
Executive Director Chuck Boller

Established in 1981, the Hawaii International Film Festival (HIFF) takes place in April and is dedicated to the advancement of understanding and cultural exchange among the peoples of Asia, the Pacific and North America through the medium of film.

Hong Kong International Film Festival

7/F, United Chinese Bank Building, 31-37 Des Voeux Road, Central, Hong Kong
tel ++ 852 2970 3300 *fax* ++ 852 2970 3011
email info@hkiff.org.hk
website www.hkiff.org.hk

One of Asia's biggest platforms for launching new films; established in 1977. Screens more than 200 new works each year and is held in March. See the website for submission details.

Hot Docs Canadian International Documentary Festival

110 Spadina Ave, Suite 333, Toronto ON M5V 2K4, Canada
tel ++ 1 416-203-2155 *fax* ++ 1 416-203-0446
website www.hotdocs.ca
Executive Director Chris McDonald

North America's largest documentary film festival; screens in April/May each year.

eligibility: documentaries of any length
fees: $35
deadline: December

Houston International Film Festival (WorldFest)

9494SW Freeway, Suite 200, Houston, Texas 77074, USA
tel ++ 1 713 965 9955 *fax* ++1 713 965 9960
email mail@worldfest.org
website www.worldfest.org

Huesca Film Festival

Avda. Parque, 1-2, 22002 Huesca, Spain
tel ++ 34 974212582 *fax* ++ 34 974210065
email info@huesca-filmfestival.com
website www.huesca-filmfestival.com

Spanish festival held each June, which showcases the best in new short films and documentaries. Numerous prizes include the International Short Film Contest, for which the main prizewinner gets €9000 and automatic shortlisting for the Academy Awards. Also has a European Documentary Competition for which the winner receives €6000.

eligibility: films must be less than 1 year old and must be submitted on 35mm or 16mm at no longer than 30 minutes for the short film contest, and on 16mm, 35mm, DVD or Digibeta at no longer than 50 minutes for the Documentary Contest
fees: none
deadline: March

Human Rights Watch International Film Festival

350 Fifth Ave, 34th Floor, New York, NY 10018, USA
tel ++ 1 212 216 1264 *fax* ++ 1 212 736 1300
email burresb@hrw.org, biaggij@hrw.org
website www.hrw.org/iff
Director Ms Bruni Burres

International festival held in June in NYC, which screens work that raises human rights issues. Also see page 260. While the London festival doesn't accept open submissions, the NY edition does: filmmakers should contact the festival directly with a short description of the film and a biography of the filmmaker. The festival will be in touch for more details or a screening tape if interested.

International Film Festival for Young People

Alvarez Garaya 2, 6a planta, PO Box 76, 3201 Gijon, Spain
tel ++ 34 985 182 940 *fax* ++ 34 985 182 944
email info@gijonfilmfestival.com
website www.gijonfilmfestival.com

International Mystery Festival – Noir In Festival

Via Tirso 90, 00198 Rome, Italy
tel ++ 39-6 8848030 *fax* ++ 39-06 884 0450
email noirfest@noirfest.com
website www.noirfest.com

International Short Film Festival interfilm Berlin

interfilm Berlin Management GmbH, Internationales Kurzfilmfestival und Kurzfilmverleih, Tempelhofer Ufer 1a, 10961 Berlin
tel +49 (0)30 25 29 13 22 *fax* +49 (0)30 693 29 59
email interfilm@interfilm.de
Festival Directors & CEO Heinz Hermanns, Alexander Stein

The International Short Film Festival 'interfilm' takes place in November and is a meeting place for the international short film and video scenes. More than 400 short films and videos are shown during the 6-day festival, with an estimated 100 films nominated to compete in the international competition. An international jury awards the 'interfilm Short Awards' in the following categories: International Competition; International Films for Children; International Films Against Violence and Intolerance; German Short Films. A total of €40,000 is awarded in cash and prizes.

Includes seminars, parties and the 'eject-night', where the audience chooses the weirdest and most wonderful film at 'The Long Night of the Unexpected'. Accredited guests are welcome to view any of the festival entries at the film market.

Festival organisers Interfilm, alongside Berliner Fenster, also present 'Going Underground' – the 7th International Short Film Festival in the Berlin Subway (February 2008). This event screens 'Ultra Shorts' in Berlin's underground trains: on more than 4000 monitors in Berlin subways, 1.6 million passengers turn into an underground movie audience for a week, and can vote for their favourite of the 14 films. The 3 winning filmmakers receive prizes of €1000-3000.

International Istanbul Film Festival

Istanbul Foundation for Culture & Arts, Istiklal Caddesi Luvr Apt. No 146, Beyoglu 34435 Istanbul, Turkey
tel ++ 90 212 334 0723 *fax* ++ 90 212 334 0702
email film.fest@iksv.org
website www.iksv.org

Jerusalem Film Festival

The Jerusalem Cinemateque, 11 Hebron Road, PO Box 8561, Jerusalem 91083, Israel
tel ++ 972 2 565 4333 *fax* ++ 972 2 565 4334
email festival@jer-cin.org.il
website www.jff.org.il

Held each July, the festival is in its 23rd year; screens a mix of new international features and short films with a focus on Israeli cinema. See the website for submission guidelines.

Karlovy Vary International Film Festival

Panska 1, 110 00 Praha 1, Czech Republic
tel ++ 420 221 411 011 *fax* ++ 420 221 411 033

email festival@kviff.com
website www.kviff.com
Artistic Director Eva Zaoralova

This competitive festival is held each June and is a stop-over for industry professionals interested in films from Eastern Europe. Films screening in the main competition must not have screened in any other international competition. Awards include a Grand Prix (Crystal Globe) worth US$20,000. The fest also presents a number of other awards which recognise achievement in documentary film. Many industry insiders praise its hospitality and beautiful location.

eligibility: films in competition should be World, International or European premieres and not older than 18 months

fees: none

deadline: April

International Film Festival of Kerala

Kerala State Chalachitra Academy, Mani Bhavan, Sasthamangalam, Thiruvananthapuram 695 010, India
tel ++ 91 471 231 0323 *fax* ++ 91 471 231 0322
email chitram@md3.vsnl.net.in
website www.keralafilm.com

This December festival presents a selection of the best of World Cinema, with a strong emphasis on films from Asia. The competition is devoted to films from Asian, African and Latin American countries; the fest has an award for the Best Debut filmmaker from these countries.

eligibility: films from outside India must have had their first theatrical screening after 1st September in the year prior to the festival; all competition films must be produced in a country from the continents listed above, and must have never played in a competitive Indian festival prior to Kerala

fees: none

deadline: September

Krakow Film Festival

ul.Morawskiego 5, room 434, 30-102 Krakow, Poland
tel ++ 48 12 294 69 45 *fax* ++ 48 12 294 69 45
website www.cff.pl
Director Janusz Nowak

Held at the end of May/early June. Established in 1961 the festival screens documentaries of up to 60 minutes, plus short fiction, animation and experimental films of the same duration. It makes several awards with cash prizes and stages a film market with conference events and a video library. The 47th edition of the Festival ran in 2007, and was accompanied by the 2nd Krakow Film Market Pitching Dragon Forum, including a new competitive section presenting long documentaries.

fees: none

deadline: January

Leipzig International Festival for Documentary and Animated Film

DOK Filmwochen GmbH, Grosse Fleischergasse 11, 041 09 Leipzig, Germany
tel ++ 49 341 308640 *fax* ++ 49 341 308 6415
email info@dok-leizig.de
website www.dok-leipzig.de
Festival Director Claas Danielsen

Annual festival held at the end of October and screening documentary and animated films. Awards include: Golden and Silver Doves for Best Long Documentary Film; Best Short Documentary Film; and Best Animated Film. Industry activities include screenings and access to video library, as well as pitching sessions for new projects.

eligibility: films must not have been screened in Germany, and must be no older than 12 months

fees: no submission fees

deadline: end of July

Locarno International Film Festival

Via Ciseri, CH-6600 Locarno, Switzerland
tel ++ 41 91 756 21 21 *fax* ++ 41 91 756 21 49
email info@pardo.ch
website www.jahia.pardo.ch
President Marco Solar *Festival Director* Irene Bignardi

A competitive festival held each August, with a reputation for a commitment to *auteur* cinema and eclectic individual works. Attracts many international journalists and has a strong European industry presence. Awards include: a Golden Leopard worth 90,000SF for the best film in the International Competition; a Special Jury Prize worth 30,000SF; and Silver Leopards for the second-best film and the best first or second features, both worth 30,000SF. The fest also awards a Leopards of Tomorrow prize to the best short film.

eligibility: films must be completed within the 12 months prior to the festival; competition films must be world premieres (excluding the country of origin), and other sections should be European premieres (eligibility is determined partly by length: the main competition is for films over 60 minutes, while Leopards of Tomorrow is open to films of up to 20 minutes)

fees: none

deadline: May

London Film Festival – see page 260.

Festival de Cine Espanol de Malaga

C/ Cárcer, no 6, 29012 Malaga, Spain
tel ++ 952 22 82 42 *fax* ++ 952 22 77 60
email info@festivaldemalaga.com
website www.festivaldemalaga.com

Malta Golden Knight International Amateur Film & Video Festival

Malta Amateur Cine Circle, PO Box 450, Marsa GPO CMR 01 Malta
tel ++ 356 21446617
email asn1939@hotmail.com
website www.global.net.mt/macc
Festival Secretary Alfred Stagno Navarra

The festival is divided into 3 classes: Class A for productions by individuals, groups or clubs made for pleasure with no commercial rationale; Class B for films made by film school and university students; and Class C Open, for any productions that do not qualify for the first 2 categories and are on the semi-professional side.

eligibility: entries must not have indications of previous awards, and should not be projects made primarily for commercial purposes
fees: none
deadline: 30 September

Mannheim-Heidelberg International Film Festival

Collini-Center, Galerie, 681 61 Mannheim, Germany
tel ++ 49 621 1029 43 *fax* ++ 49 621 2915 64
email ifmh@mannheim-filmfestival.com
website www.mannheim-filmfestival.com
Director Dr Michael Koetz

Held in October; includes a focus on new directors. Awards a number of prizes, including including the MAIN Award of Mannheim-Heidelberg, and the Rainer Werner Fassbinder Prize for the best unconventionally narrated feature. The festival also includes an Arthouse Market for buyers and programmers to view new innovative non-mainstream, independent and experimental work, as well as the MANNHEIM MEETINGS, an international coproduction and distribution market for producers, world sales and distributors.

fees: none
deadline: refer to website

Festival Internacional de Cine de Mar del Plata

Hipolito Irigoyen 1255- 3er Piso,
(C1085ABO) Ciudad de Buenos Aires, Argentina
tel ++ 5411 4383 5115
email mfm@mardelplatafilmfest.com
website www.mardelplatafilmfest.com

Melbourne Intrenational Film Festival

PO Box 2206, Fitzroy Mail Centre, Melbourne, Australia, Vic 3065
tel ++ 61 3 9417 2011 *fax* ++ 61 3 9417 3804
email miff@melbournefilmfestival.com.au
website www.melbournefilmfestival.com.au
Programmer Nick Feik

Australia's largest and most significant film festival, screening more than 380 films. It is held annually for 2 weeks in July/August, and screens new work from around the world in all genres. Also hosts the country's major short film competition, which includes prizes of more than $35,000 across different categories. See the website for submission and fee details.

Miami International Film Festival

Film Society of Miami, Miami Dade College,
300 NE 2nd Ave, Miami, FL 33132-2204, USA
tel ++ 1 305 237 3456 *fax* ++ 1 305 237 7344
email info@miamifilmfestival.com
website www.miamifilmfestival.com
Director Nicole Guillemet

Held each March. Programmes new World and Ibero-American cinema. Competition includes prizes for Best Dramatic Feature in World and Ibero-American strands, and for Best Documentary Feature. Hosts an industry event – Encuentros – during the fest to help bring projects from Spain and Latin America to the US. See the website for submission guidelines.

deadline: August – October

Midnight Sun Film Festival

Kansanopistontie 5, FI-99600 Sodankyla, Finland
tel ++ 358 16 614 525 *fax* ++ 358 16 614 522
email office©msfilmfestival.fi
website www.msfilmfestival.fi

A non-competitive festival held in June, which primarily invites titles from other festivals (rather than encouraging open submissions). Selection prioritises fictional 35mm feature films and a few of the best short and documentary films of the year. Videos are shown only in special cases.

eligibility: see above
fees: none
deadline: April

Mix: New York Lesbian and Gay Experimental Film Festival

79 Pine Street, PMB 132, New York, NY 10005, USA
tel ++ 1 212 742 8880
email info@mixnyc.org
website www.mixnyc.org
Director Ioannis Mookas

Well-regarded festival which screens experimental work of interest to a gay and lesbian audience. Held in November, with satellite festivals around the world.

eligibility: films with gay, lesbian, bisexual and transgender subject matter, or from gay filmmakers
fees: range from $10 to $35 depending on when the film is submitted
deadline: May

Festival de Television de Monte Carlo

4 Boulevard du Jardin Exotique, Monte Carlo, Monaco, MC 98000
tel ++377 93 10 40 60 *fax* ++377 93 50 70 14
email info@tvfestival.com
website www.tvfestival.com

Montreal World Film Festival (Festival des Films du Monde)

1432 Rue de Bleury Street, Montreal, Quebec, Canada, H3A 2J1
tel ++ 415 848 3883 *fax* ++ 415 848 3886
email info@ffm-montreal.org
website ffm-montreal.org

Held at the end of August, this competitive international film festival is recognised by FIAPF. While many awards are for North American and Canadian filmmakers, the festival does have World and First Film Competitions, which each award a main prize. Audiences are asked to vote on a best film from each continent. Also hosts an international film market.

eligibility: films must be less than 12 months old and must not have been released commercially outside of origin country, or screened in any competitive festival; priority is given to world premieres

fees: CA$25 for shorts; CA$50 for features

deadline: late June

Moscow International Film Festival

Interfest, 10/1 Khoklhovsky pereulok, 109028 Moscow, Russia

tel ++ 7 095 917 2486 *fax* ++ 7 095 916 0107

email info@miff.ru

website www.miff.ru

Munich Film Festival

Internationale Müenchner Filmwochen, Sonnenstrasse 21, 803 31 Munich, Germany

tel ++ 49 89 3819040 *fax* ++ 49 89 3819 0427

email info@filmfest-muenchen.de

website www.filmfest-muenchen.de

Festival Director Andreas Stroehl

Held in mid June; programmes a broad range of new features, with particular emphasis on New German, French and American Independent Cinema.

fees: none

deadline: mid-April

Netherlands Film Festival

Netherlands Film Festival/Stichting Nederlands Film Festival, PO Box 1581, 3500 BN Utrecht, The Netherlands

tel ++ 31 30 2303800 *fax* ++ 31 30 2303801

email info@filmfestival.nl

website www.filmfestival.nl

International Film Festival of India – Goa

Siri Fort Auditorium Complex, August Kranti Marg, Khel Gaon, New Delhi, India, 110049

tel ++ 91 11 2649 9356 *fax* ++ 91 11 2649 9357

email ddiffi.dff@nic.in

website www.iffi.nic.in

Director/Programmer Srinivasa Santhanam

Held in November and programmes feature films only. Includes a competition for African, Asian and Latin American directors.

fees: none

deadline: September

New York Film Festival

Film Society of Lincoln Centre, 70 Lincoln Centre Plaza, New York, NY 10023-6595, USA

tel ++ 1 212 875 5610

email festival@filmlinc.com

website www.filmlinc.com

Festival held at the Lincon Center each Sept/Oct, screening a select group of 28 feature films and 12 short films each year. There are no categories and no prizes awarded; the fest has a main section and a special section, 'Views from the Avant-Garde' (which premieres non-narrative, experimental film and video). Filmmakers may not submit to both the main festival and the Avant-Garde section.

eligibility: films must have screening print in 16mm or 35mm, and must be NYC premieres

fees: none

deadline: July

Nordic Film Days Lübeck

Schildstr 12, 235 39 Lübeck, Germany

tel ++ 49 451 122 4109 *fax* ++ 49 451 122 1799

website www.filmtage.luebeck.de

Held over 4 days each November. Presents work from filmmakers in the North and North East of Europe. Countries represented include: Denmark, Estonia, Finland, Iceland, Latvia, Lithuania, Norway and Sweden.

Norwegian International Film Festival (Haugesund)

PO Box 145, 5501 Haugesund, Norway

tel ++ 47 52 7433 70 *fax* ++ 47 5274 3371

email info@filmfestivalen.no

website www.filmfestivalen.no

Director Gunnar Johan Lovvik

Held each August; screens new features.

fees: none

deadline: June

Oberhausen International Short Film Festival

Grillostrasse 34, 460 45 Oberhausen, Germany

tel ++ 49 208 825 2652 *fax* ++ 49 208 825 5413

email info@kurzfilmtage.de

website www.kurzfilmtage.de

One of the world's most important short film festivals and short film markets, held each year in early May. The festival screens short films of all genres, including music videos. Looks for short films which offer something new and original, regardless of genre, production quality and budget. Programmers are looking for films which engage with questions of social reality, cultural difference and/or aesthetic innovation.

Oberhausen's 4 competitions are: International, German, Children's/Youth, and Music Video; across these the festival awards 17 prizes worth a combined €40,000.

Industry services include a video library with approximately 6000 new short films, market screenings, and daily panel discussions about issues relevant to short formats.

eligibility: films must be less than 2 years old and less than 35 minutes' duration

fees: none

deadline: January

Odense International Film Festival

Norregade 36-38, DK-5100 Odense C, Denmark
tel ++ 45 6613 1372 *fax* ++ 45 6591 0144
email off.ksf@odense.dk
website www.filmfestival.dk

Oslo International Film Festival

Dronningensgt. 16, N-0152 Oslo, Norway
tel ++ 47 22 200 766 *fax* ++ 47 22 201 803
email info@oslofilmfestival.com
website www.oslofilmfestival.com

Held over 11 days in November; screens the best in new features and short films from around the world. See the website for submission details.

Ottawa International Student Animation Festival

2 Daly Avenue, Suite 120, Ottawa, Ontario, Canada, ON K1N 6E2
tel ++ 613 232-8769 *fax* ++ 613 232 6315
email info@animationfestival.ca
website www.ottawa.awn.com

Palm Springs International Festival of Short Films

1700 E Tahquitz Canyon Way, #3 Palm Springs, CA 92262, USA
tel ++ 1 760 322 2930 *fax* ++ 1 760 322 4087
email info@psfilmfest.org
website www.psfilmfest.org

One of 2 fests organised by the Palm Springs Film Society (along with Palm Springs International Film Festival), Shortsfest is held in August each year and includes a competition and a short film market. The festival screens more than 300 films each year, with over 20 awards given and prizes worth $70,000 in cash and services.

eligibility: no films completed prior to January of the year preceding the fest; all films must be less than 40 minutes' duration; films must not have been broadcast or been made available on cable, satellite or the Internet prior to the fest

fees: range from $30 to $60 depending on date submitted and whether filmmaker is a student

deadlines: April – June

Pesaro Film Festival

Via Villafranca 20, 001 85 Rome, Italy
tel ++ 39 06 456643 *fax* ++ 39 06 491163
email info@pesarofilmfest.it
website www.pesarofilmfest.it
General Manager Pedro Armocida

Held at the end of June; focuses on independent cinema from around the world.

fees: none

deadline: May

Pordenone Silent Film Festival (Le Giornate del Cinema Muto)

c/o La Cineteca del Friuli, Via G. Bini 50, Palazzo Gurisatti, 330 13 Gemona, Italy
tel ++ 39 0432 982208 *fax* ++ 39 0432 970542
email info.gcm@cinetecadelfriuli.org
website www.cinetecadelfriuli.org/gcm

Specialist festival screening silent film only; held over 7 days in October.

Portland International Film Festival

Northwest Film Centre, 1219 SW Park Avenue, Portland, OR 97205, USA
tel ++ 1 503 221 1156 *fax* ++ 1 503 294 0874
email info@nwfilm.org
website www.nwfilm.org

Prix Europa

RBB Berlin, D-14046 Berlin, Germany
tel ++ 49 30 97 993 1 09 10
fax ++ 49 30 97 993 1 09 19
email office@prix-europa.de
website www.prix-europa.de

Festival aims to screen the best European television, radio and Internet productions over a week in October. Prizes are intended to promote the quality of new work that is being made in Europe.

fees: none

deadline: July

Pusan International Film Festival

Annex 2-1, 1393 Woo 1-Dong Yachting Center, Haeundae-Gu, Busan, Korea
tel ++ 82 51 747 3010 *fax* ++ 82 51 747 3012
email program@piff.org
website www.piff.org

After just a decade, Pusan has established itself as arguably the most important international film event in East Asia. Programming emphasises young talented directors. Awards are given to best new Asian film, an international short, and a documentary (also see Asian Film Market).

eligibility: Korean premieres; priority given to world and international premiere screenings

fees: none

deadline: July

RESFEST

601 West 26th Street, 11th Floor, New York, NY 10001, USA
tel ++ 1 212 320 3750 *fax* ++ 1 212 320 3709
website www.resfest.com

Acclaimed film festival; tours to cities all over the world. The fest aims to explore the interplay between film, art, music and design. Each year it showcases the year's best shorts, features, music videos and animation in an environment that combines screenings, live music events, parties, panel discussions and technology demonstrations.

eligibility: entries may be any length, any genre and shot on any format, with the main selection criterion being innovation

fees: $25 for early deadline; $30 for final deadline

deadline: May – June

Rio de Janeiro Film Festival – Festival do Rio BR

Rua Voluntarios da Patria 53/4th Floor,
22270-000 Botafogo, Rio de Janeiro, Brazil
tel ++ 55 21 2579 0352 *fax* ++ 55 21 2539 3580
email films@festivaldorio.com.br
website www.festivaldorio.com.br
Festival Director Ilda Santiago

Held in September each year, screening the best new international features and short films. Has a strong reputation for providing great hospitality to filmmakers and providing a South American launch for new work.

eligibility: films must be Brazilian premieres

fees: none

deadline: June

Rose d'Or Festival

PO Box 265, CH-3000 Bern 13, Switzerland
tel ++ 41 31 318 3737 *fax* ++ 41 31 318 3736
email info@rosedor.com
website www.rosedor.com

Rotterdam International Film Festival

PO Box 21696, 3001 AR Rotterdam, The Netherlands
tel ++ 31 10 8909090 *fax* ++ 31 10 8909091
email tiger@filmfestivalrotterdam.com
website www.filmfestivalrotterdam.com

Held at the end of January each year, the festival is committed to programming independent, innovative and experimental cinema and visual arts. Has an unusual take on awards; instead of the big films competing for prizes, Rotterdam spotlights new talent by giving 3 Tiger Awards to Best First or Second Feature, with prizes of €10,000 for each and a TV broadcast in The Netherlands. Also awards a Tiger Cub to the Best Short Film.

Runs the Hubert Bals Fund, which supports films and filmmakers from developing countries. This fund has provided financial support to more than 350 projects thus far; roughly 60% of these have been produced.

An important European film market also runs alongside the festival (see page 286).

eligibility: films must be less than 1 year old; Tiger Award submissions should be from filmmakers making their first or second feature (all films should be premieres outside of their own country)

fees: none

deadline: November

San Francisco International Film Festival

30 Mesa Street, Suite 100, The Presidio,
San Francisco, CA 94129, USA
tel ++ 1 415 561 5000 *fax* ++ 1 415 561 5099
email frontdesk@sffs.org
website www.sffs.org/festival

San Francisco International Lesbian and Gay Film Festival

Frameline, 145 Ninth Street # 300, San Francisco, CA 94103, USA
tel ++ 1 415 703 8650 *fax* ++ 1 415 861 1404
email info@frameline.org
website www.frameline.org/festival

One of the oldest, and definitely the largest, of specialist festivals screening work by and for gay, lesbian, bisexual and transgender audiences. Widely regarded as the 'Cannes' of the L&G festival circuit, San Francisco attracts many international programmers, and screenings at this festival usually result in further invitations to smaller festivals. Also awards cash jury prizes totalling US$20,000.

eligibility: content must be appropriate

fees: $20

deadlines: December (early), January (late)

San Sebastian International Film Festival (Donostia)

PO Box 397, 20080 Donostia-San Sebastian, Spain
tel ++ 34 943 481212 *fax* ++ 34 943 481218
email ssiff@sansebastianfestival.com
website www.sansebastianfestival.com

San Sebastian is a highly regarded competitive festival held each September and now in its 54th year. The festival's Official Selection has awards in categories of Best Film, Special Jury Prize, and several for individual craft achievement. Also offers a number of other awards for films screening outside of the Official Selection.

eligibility: competition films must be less than 12 months old, screened on 35mm, and must not have screened in another competitive international festival either prior to or during San Sebastian

fees: none

deadline: late July

Sao Paulo International Film Festival – Mostra BR de Cinema

Rua Antonio Carlos, 288 2nd floor,
CEP 01309-010 São Paulo – SP Brazil
tel ++ 55 11 3141 0413 *fax* ++ 55 11 3266 7066
email info@mostra.org
website www.mostra.org
Director Leon Cakoff

Sao Paulo is held over 15 days at the end of October/beginning of November each year. Last year, it screened 360 features and 52 shorts. Each year, a New Filmmaker Award goes to the best work from a filmmaker who is presenting their first or second feature.

eligibility: films must be Brazilian premieres and must have been made no later than January 2 years prior to the fest (approximately 18 months old)

fees: none

deadline: August

Sarajevo Film Festival

Sarajevo Film Festival, Zelenih beretki 12/I, 71000 Sarajevo, Bosnia and Herzegovina
tel ++ 387 33 209-411
email info-sff@sff.ba
website www.sff.ba

Annual international film festival which takes place in August, with the specific goal of supporting and promoting regional cinematography and authors. Due to this regional focus, the festival is recognised by FIAPF as a Competitive Specialised Festival.

Seattle International Film Festival

400 9th Ave N, Seattle, WA 98109, USA
tel 00 206 464 5830 *fax* 00 206 264 7919
email info@seattlefilm.org
website www.seattlefilm.com
Managing Director Deborah Person *Artistic Director* Carl Spence

Takes place in June each year.

Shanghai International Film Festival

11/F STV Mansions, 298 Wei Hai Road, Shanghai 200041, China
tel ++ 86 216 253 7115 *fax* ++ 86 216 255 2000
email siff@public4.sta.net.cn
website www.siff.com

Singapore International Film Festival

45A Keong Saik Road, Singapore, 89149
tel ++ 65 67387567 *fax* ++ 65 67387578
email filmfest@pacific.net.sg
website www.filmfest.org.sg
Festival Director Philip Cheah

Held in April each year; established in 1987. Gives several awards including Best Asian Feature, Best Director and a Special Jury Prize.

fees: none

deadline: January

Slamdance

5634 Melrose Ave, Los Angeles, California 90038, USA
tel ++ 1 323 466 1786 *fax* ++ 1 323 466 1784
email mail@slamdance.com
website www.slamdance.com
President/Co-founder Peter Baxter *Director of Programming* Sarah Diamond

Festival which runs concurrently with Sundance (see Sundance Film Festival on page 280) in January, and which focuses on first-time features and all short films. While not a 'competitive' fest, Slamdance awards Grand Jury, Audience and Specialty prizes. Also has an Industry Day at which meetings are arranged between visiting industry and fest filmmakers.

fees: $25 shorts, $45 features for early deadlines, and $45/$60 for 2nd deadline

deadline: August (early)/October (late)

South by Southwest (SXSW)

Box 4999, Austin, TX 78765
tel ++ 1 512 467 7979 *fax* ++ 1 512 451 0754
email film@sxsw.com
website www.sxsw.com

Emphasises all aspects of the art and business of independent filmmaking. The festival has gained international acclaim for the quality of its programming, which has a special focus on emerging talents; these bask in being included in the company of the cinematic greats, whose work is regularly presented. Runs in March each year.

Southern African Film & Television Market

SABC Building, 209 Beach Road, Sea Point, Cape Town, South Africa
tel ++ 27 21 430 8160 *fax* ++ 27 21 430 8186
email info@sithengi.co.za
website www.sithengi.co.za

Split International Festival of New Film

PO Box 244, HR-21000 Split, Croatia
tel ++ 385 21 539 600 *fax* ++ 385 21 539 700
email split.filmfest@st.htnet.hr
website www.splitfilmfestival.hr

St Barth Film Festival and 'Cinema Caraibe'

tel ++ 590 590 27 80 11 *fax* ++ 590 590 29 74 70
email staff@stbarthff.org
website www.stbarthff.org
Directors Ellen Lampert-Gréaux, Joshua Harrison

A 12-year-old festival that screens films covering many aspects of the Caribbean experience: films focusing on music, culture, history, political oppression and social dramas. Takes place during the last week of April annually, and is run by the non-profit association CINE SAINT BARTH.

St Petersburg Film Festival

10 Kamennoostrovsky Ave, 197101 St Petersburg, Russia
tel ++ 7 812 237 0304 *fax* ++ 7 812 237 0304
email info@filmfest.ru
website www.filmfest.ru

Takes place in June; Russia's largest non-competitive festival of recent outstanding works of International and Russian cinema, licensed under UNESCO. The event strives to act as a link between film and audience, and is a wonderful opportunity for film directors and producers to showcase their pictures in one of the world's largest cultural centres. Screens more than 100 films from around the world to audiences in excess of 40,000. A number of awards are made, including an Audience Award and one for Best Experimental film.

Stockholm International Film Festival

PO Box 3136, 103 62 Stockholm, Sweden
tel ++ 46 8 6775000 *fax* ++ 46 8 200590
email info@stockholmfilmfestival.se
website www.stockholmfilmfestival.se
Festival Director Git Scheynius

Audience festival and meeting place for Scandanavian industries held each November. Offers a screening a library with much new Swedish work and meeting services for visiting delegates.

fees: none
deadline: September

Sundance Film Festival

PO Box 684429, Park City, UT 84060, USA
tel ++1 435 658 3456 *fax* ++1 435 6583457
website www.sundance.org
Director of Programming John Cooper

Sundance is the USA's most important launch event for new independent cinema, with most of the industry in attendance. The festival is divided into the following sections:

- **Premiere** This section is out of competition and showcases the diversity of world cinema with a selective programme of World and US premieres by established directors.
- **Independent Feature Film Competition** Showcases the best new independently produced American docs and fiction features, with a Grand Jury Prize awarded to both and a Screenwriting Award going to the film with the best screenplay. This section also gives an Audience Award.
- **American Spectrum** An out-of-competition showcase of independent American narrative and documentary feature films. Films in this section are also eligible for the Audience Award.
- **World Cinema Competition (Dramatic)** A new competitive section for new features from international filmmakers and innovative filmmakers. Has an official juried award and a World Cinema Audience Award winner, with a Latin American filmmaker winning an additional juried award.
- **World Cinema Competition (Documentaries)** New competitive section for world documentaries, with a Jury Award.
- **Short Film Competition** A final competitive section of American and international short films. The best film in this section receives a Special Jury Award.
- **Frontier** Non-competitive showcase of experimental work (visual art, feature, short, documentary) by American and international artists.
- **Park City at Midnight** This is a late-night showcase of American and international feature films, which might be risky, provocative, outrageous. Some festival-goers regard this as a section which celebrates the 'B Movie'.

eligibility: features must be over 70 minutes, and short films under 70 minutes; doc features should be over 50 minutes and doc shorts under 50 mins. No films may have been broadcast on television. Feature films in any category may not have been broadcast on the Internet. Short films may have been broadcast on the Internet. US films must be World premieres and International films should be US (preferrably North American) premieres. No feature should have screened in more than 2 festivals

fees: from $25 to $70, depending on date submitted and the type of film

deadlines: range from August to late September

Sydney Film Festival

PO BOX 96, Strawberry Hills, Sydney, Australia, NSW 2012
tel ++ 61 2 9280 0511 *fax* ++ 61 2 9280 1520
email info@sydneyfilmfestival.org
website www.sydneyfilmfestival.org

Taipei Golden Horse Film Festival

3F, 37 Kaifeng St Sec 1, Taipei 100, Taiwan
tel ++ 886 2 2388 3880 *fax* ++ 886 2 2370 1616
email festival@goldenhorse.org.tw
website www.goldenhorse.org.tw

Golden Horse is a competitive festival held in November and established in 1962, with active aims of encouraging and showcasing regional and Tawainese cinema. There are 21 permanent Golden Horse Awards, including Best Picture, Best Short Film, Best Documentary and Best Animation. See the website for more details on fees and eligibility.

deadline: August

Tampere Film Festival

Box 305, FIN-33101 Tampere, Finland
tel ++ 358 3 223 56 81 *fax* ++ 358 3 223 0121
email office@tamperefilmfestival.fi
website www.tamperefilmfestival.fi
Festival Director Jukka-Pekka Laakso

Important competitive short film festival held in March. Accreditated industry guests get access to a film library with all submitted short films. Awards include: Grand Prix worth €5000; Category Prizes in drama, doc and experimental worth €1500 each; and a Special Prix of the Jury worth €1500.

eligibilty: films must be completed after January in the year prior to the festival, and must be under 30 minutes' duration

fees: none
deadline: December

Taormina International Film Festival

Corso Umberto 19, 98039 Taormina, Italy
tel ++ 39 06 5833 3145 *fax* ++ 39 06 5833 3164

email info@taoarte.it
website www.taorminafilmfest.it/2004/

Tehran International ShortFilm Festival

Iranian Young Cinema Society, 17 Ghandi Sq, Shariati Ave, 15569 Tehran, Iran
tel ++ 98 21 851 1241 *fax* ++ 98 21 851 1242
email info@shortfilmfest-ir.com
website www.shortfilmfest-ir.com

Telluride Film Festival

Telluride Film Festival, G395379 State Street, Portsmouth, USA, NH 03801
tel ++ 1 603 433 9202 *fax* ++ 1 603 433 9206
email Mail@telluridefilmfestival.org
website www.telluridefilmfestival.org

Thessaloniki International Film Festival

9 Alexandras Avenue, 114 73 Athens, Greece
tel ++ 30 210 87 06 000 *fax* ++ 30 210 64 48 143
email info@filmfestival.gr
website www.filmfestival.gr

Thessaloniki is a popular event on the festival calendar, held in late November each year. The International Competition is reserved for first and second films by directors from all over the world. The prizes, awarded by a 7-member international jury, include: the Golden Alexander for Best Film (€36,700 cash prize); the Special Jury Award – Silver Alexander (€22,000 cash prize); and awards for Best Direction, Best Screenplay, Best Actor, Best Actress and Artistic Achievement.

eligibility: films must be made within the 18 months prior to the fest, and must be Greek premieres; for the competition, films must be first or second features

fees: none

deadline: September

Festival of 3 Continents (Festival des Trois Continents)

19a, Passage Pommeraye, BP 43302, 440 33 Nantes Cedex 1, France
tel ++ 33 2 40 69 74 14 *fax* ++ 33 2 40 73 55 22
email festival@3continents.com
website www.3continents.com
General Manager Marion Guillaume

Held late November. Programmes drama and documentary from Asia, Africa and South America.

fees: none

deadline: October

Tokyo International Film Festival

5F, Tsukiji YASUDA BLDG. 2-15-14 Tsukiji, Chuouku, Tokyo 104-0045, Japan
tel ++ 81 3 3524 1081 *fax* ++ 81 3 3524 1087
email info@tiff-jp.net
website www.tiff-jp.net

Tokyo Video Festival

c/o Victor Co of Japan Ltd, 1-7-1 Shinbashi, Victor Bldg, Minato-ku, Tokyo, Japan, 105-0004
fax ++ 81 3 3289 2819
website www.jvc.co.jp

Toronto International Film Festival

2 Carlton Street, Suite 1600, Toronto, Ontario, Canada M5B IJ3
email tiffg@torfilmfest.ca
website www.e.bell.ca/filmfest
Festival Director Piers Handling

Toronto is arguably the most important non-competitive festival in the world, with an enormous programme of 300 films from over 50 countries. It is a key meeting place for the North American industry, and is increasingly important to international sellers. Sections include: Gala (high-profile world or North American premieres); Discovery (up-and-coming talent); Contemporary World Cinema (best of world); Real to Reel (significant, cutting-edge docs); Special Presentations (high-profile films from renowned filmmakers); Masters (established International heavyweight filmmakers); Wavelengths (avant-garde); Director's Spotlight (new directors); and Midnight Madness (weird, cult, eccentric titles).

eligibility: priority given to premieres; screening copy should be 16mm or 35mm, and film should be made in the 18 months prior to the festival

fees: CA$65

deadline: June

Tough Eye International Turku Animated Film Festival

Linnankatu 54, 210 00 Turku, Finland
tel ++ 10 5535 258 *fax* ++ 10 5535 273
email info@tough-eye.com
website www.tough-eye.com

Tribeca Film Festival

tel ++ 1 212 941 2400
email festival@tribecafilmfestival.org
website www.tribecafilmfestival.org

Held in Spring each year (usually in April), the Tribeca Film Festival was founded in 2002 by Robert De Niro, Jane Rosenthal and Craig Hatkoff as a response to the attacks on the World Trade Center, and conceived to foster the economic and cultural revitalisation of Lower Manhattan through film, music and culture. The festival has quickly become one of the most important on the US film festival calendar, and has a growing reputation among filmmakers as a good festival for US industry networking. See the website for submission details and fees.

TriggerStreet

website www.triggerstreet.com

Online site which allows filmmakers to upload short films or screenplays; these can be viewed and reviewed by peers and the industry. Hosts online festivals with judges like Danny DeVito and Cameron Crowe.

Troia International Film Festival

Av. Luisa Todi, Av. Luisa Todi, 65, 2900-461 Setubal, Portugal
tel ++ 351 265 525 908 *fax* ++ 351 265 525 681
email geral@festroia.pt
website www.festroia.pt
Director Fernanda Silva

Held in June; specialises in screening films from countries which produce fewer than 30 films per year.

Torino Film Festival (Cinema Giovani)

Via Monte di Pieta 1-10121 Torino, Italy
tel ++ 39 011 5623309 *fax* ++ 39 011 5629796
email info@torinofilmfest.org
website www.torinofilmfest.org

Held in November each year, the festival is committed to screening works by new directors. Awards for international filmmakers include: a Grand Prize (worth €20,500); a Special Jury Prize; and a Prize for Best Director. There are also a number of special awards for Italian films. Films must be Italian premieres; works entered into competition at one of the principal festivals (Cannes, Berlin, etc.) are ineligible. There is no submission fee for entry and deadlines are in September.

Turin Gay and Lesbian Film Festival (Festival Internazionale di Film con Tematiche Omosessuali)

C.so Principe Oddone, 3 10144, Turin, Italy
tel ++ 39 011 534 888 *fax* ++ 39 011 535 796
email info@tglff.com
website www.turinglfilmfestival.com

Festival programming films of interest to a gay and lesbian audience; held each April. Considered by many filmmakers screening on the G&L circuit to be one of the best for hospitality.

deadline: December

US International Film & Video Festival

713 S Pacific Coast Highway, Suite A,
Redondon Beach, CA 90277-4233, USA
tel ++ 1 310 540 0959 *fax* ++ 1 310 316 8905
email filmfestinfo@filmfestawards.com
website www.filmfestawards.com

Uppsala International Short Film Festival

PO Box 1746, 751 47 Uppsala, Sweden
tel ++ 46 18 12 0025 *fax* ++ 46 18 12 1350
email info@shortfilmfestival.com
website www.shortfilmfestival.com
Festival Director Niclas Gillberg

Well-regarded short film festival established in 1982, and held each October in Sweden. Fest awards several prizes: International Grand Prize and 2 Special Prizes; a National Prize; and an award for Best Children's Film. Industry guests recieve free accreditation and may use the videoteque, which includes all submitted films.

fees: none
deadline: June

International Film Festival of Uruguay

Lorenzo Carnelli 1311, Montevideo, Uruguay, 11200
tel ++ 598 2 419 8516 *fax* ++ 598 2 419 4572
email cinemuy@chasque.net
website www.cinemateca.org.uk
Director Manuel MartInez Carril

Held at the end of March. Offers a number of awards for Best Feature, Best Short Film, Best Documentary, Best Experimental and/or Animated Feature, and a Special Jury Prize for Artistic Quality.

fees: none, but entrant must cover cost of shipping screening prints
deadline: January

Valladolid International Film Festival

Teatro Calderon, Calle Leopoldo Cano, s/n 4th fl, PO Box 646, 47003 Valladolid, Spain
tel ++ 34 983 42 64 60 *fax* ++ 34 983 42 64 61
website www.seminci.com
Festival Director Fernando Lara

Valladolid is one of the oldest film fests in Europe, and celebrated 60 years in 2006. The competitive festival is held in October and screens more than 200 features and short films from around the world. Extensive prizes have generous cash awards; they include Golden and Silver Spike for first- and second-best features (€35,000 and €17,500 respectively), and a Golden and Silver Spike for short film (€9000 and a second prize of €4500).

eligibility: films must be Spanish premieres
fees: none
deadline: June

Vancouver International Film Festival

1181 Seymour Street, Vancouver BC,
Canada V6B 3M7
tel ++ 1 604 685 0260 *fax* ++ 1 604 688 8221
email viff@viff.org
website www.viff.org

Held in the first 2 weeks in October; programmes 300 films from more than 50 countries.

eligibility: only accepts international entries of feature and medium-length films (over 30 minutes); films entered must not have been screened commercially, or broadcast, in the Greater Vancouver area
fees: CA$20-$40
deadline: June

Venice International Film Festival

Ca' Giustinian, San Marco 1364 – 30124 Venice, Italy
tel ++ 39 041 5218711 *fax* ++ 39 041 5227539
email cinema@labiennale.org
website www.labiennale.org
Festival Artistic Director Marco Muller

Venice is the world's oldest film festival and is widely considered one of the most important of the major competitive fests (along with Cannes and Berlin). The festival is broken into the following sections:

- **Competition (Venezia)** This international section includes features and short films on 35mm or 70mm. Films must have not screened publicly outside country of origin, and short films should be under 10 minutes. Prizes include a Golden Lion for Best Film, a Special Jury Prize and a Director's Award.
- **Out of Competition** Includes important work by already-established directors.
- **Orizzonti** This includes unusual and innovative films that represent the breadth of contemporary cinema. Films need to be 35mm and world premieres.
- **International Critics' Week (SIC Settimana Internazionale della Critica)** These screenings are outside of the competition and are selected by the National Association of Italian Film Critics.
- **Corto-Cortissimo** A competitive section for short non-animation films (maximum 30 minutes). Jury awards a Silver Lion and 2 Special Mentions.
- **Directors' Selection** A small selection of 10-12 films independently programmed by a commission nominated by the Italian Association of Filmmakers (ANAC), and by the Association of Independent Directors and Producers (API).

eligibility: see above
fees: €50 for features
deadline: June

Viennale – Vienna International Film Festival

Siebensterngasse 2, A-1070 Vienna, Austria
tel ++ 43 1 526 5947 *fax* ++ 43 1 523 4172
email office@viennale.at
website www.viennale.at
Director Hans Hurch

Held annually in October, Viennale is Austria's most important film event. The festival screens new international work of all genres, but gives special attention to documentary, short film and experimental works. Of its 3 awards, The Standard Readers' Prize is awarded to a film that does not yet have an Austrian distributor but is highly recommended for release in Austrian theatres. If the prizewinning film finds an Austrian distributor, the Austrian daily *Der Standard* will support the distributor with free advertising space.

fees: none
deadline: August

VIPER – International Festival for Film, Video and New Media

St Alban-Rheinweg 64, CH-4052 Basel, Switzerland
tel 00 41 61 283 27 00 *fax* 00 41 61 283 27 05
email information@viper.ch
website www.viper.ch

Visions du Reel – Nyon International Documentary Film Festival

18, rue Juste-Olivier, 1260 Nyon, Switzerland
tel ++ 41 22 365 44 55 *fax* ++ 41 22 365 44 50
email docnyon@visionsdureel.ch
website www.visionsdureel.ch
Festival Director Jean Perret

This well-respected festival showcases the variety of documentary filmmaking from around the world. Visions du Réel is a competitive festival, with awards including : International Competition, Best Feature Documentary and Best Short Film. There is also an International Competition for young filmmakers, and several new sections: Reprocessing Reality (video art flirting with docs), Fictions du Réel (films tackling borders between fiction/docs) and A l'Ecoute du Réel (listening to the sounds of reality).

withoutabox

website www.withoutabox.com

This website simplifies the process of film festival submissions for both the filmmaker and the festival. Filmmakers can complete 1 application form, which can be sent to participating festivals online; submission fees can also be paid online. The site allows filmmakers to upload press materials, which the the festival can access, and also notifies filmmakers of upcoming festival deadlines. These standard services are all free for filmmakers.

World Wide Video Festival

Keizersgracht 462, 1016 GE Amsterdam, The Netherlands
tel ++ 31 20 421 38 15 *fax* ++ 31 20 421 38 28
email tomvanvliet@wwvf.nl
website www.wwvf.nl

Worldwide Short Film Festival

2489 Bayview Ave. Toronto, ON M2L 1A8 Canada
tel ++ 1 416 445 1446 *fax* ++ 1 416 445 9481
email shortfilm@cdnfilmcentre.com
website www.worldwideshortfilmfest.com

This up-and-coming short film festival is held in June each year. It is fast becoming a meeting place for buyers and sellers with a strong North American presence, as it is North America's largest short-film market. Awards are largely for Canadian films in the festival, but Sony gives a DV camcorder to the best film in live action, documentary and experimental categories. There are also a number of audience awards and a screenplay award.

fees: $15 per film
deadline: February

Yamagata International Documentary Film Festival

ID Kawadacho Bldg, 3 fl., 7-6 Kawadacho, Shinjuku-Ku, Tokyo, Japan 162-0054

tel ++ 81 3 5362 0672 *fax* ++ 81 3 5362 0670
email mail@tokyo.yidiff.jp
website www.yidff.jp

Biannual documentary festival. Sections include: an international competition; and a focus on Asian documentary filmmaking. New submission guidelines will be posted on the website.

Zimbabwe International Film Festival

2 Canterbury Road, Kensington, Harare
tel ++ 263 4 730361 *fax* ++ 263 4 734884
email zimfilmfest@zol.co.zw
website www.ziff.co.zw
Trust Director Nakai Matema, *Festival Coordinato:* Isabel Manuel

Competitive festival held in August/September. 12 prizes are: Best Documentary, Short Film, Picture, Animated Film, Actor, Actress, Screenplay, Audience Choice Award, Calabash Award for Best Zimbabwean Production, and Zimbabwe Film Service Award. Fest also holds an African Co-productions forum. Open submissions. No fee.

Key international markets

American Film Market (AFM)

10850 Wilshire Boulevard, 9th Floor, Los Angeles, CA 90024-4311, USA
tel ++ 1 310 446 1000 *fax* ++ 1 310 446 1600
email AFM@ifta-online.org
website www.ifta-online.org/afm

Founded in 1981, the American Film Market (AFM) has grown steadily to become a premiere global marketplace. Independent cinema's decision-makers and trendsetters all gather under one roof to screen films and close production and distribution deals. The market hosts more than 8000 participants from over 70 countries. Produced by the Independent Film & Television Alliance (**www.ifta-online.org**).

Asian Film Market – see page 277 for contacts.

Runs as part of the Pusan International Film Festival and includes a co-production market where Asian filmmakers can find potential co-producers, buyers and partners, as well as a television market with buyers from the Asian broadcast sectors well represented.

Bangkok Film Market – see page 267.

BFM is a new film market in its fourth year; aims to provide a meeting place for the Asian film industries, and help position Thai cinema within an international industry.

Marché du Film at Cannes Film Festival

3 rue Amélie, 75007 Paris, France
tel ++ 33 1 53 59 61 30 *fax* ++ 33 1 53 59 61 50
email marketinfo@festival-cannes.fr
website www.marchedufilm.com
Director Jerome Paillard

One of the most important film markets in the annual film calendar, run during Cannes Film Festival in May. Costs range from €395 to €1600 for exhibitors wishing to show their films. Buyer registration costs €299 and gives access to market screenings and database. Also hosts The Producers' Network to allow producers to present works-in-progress and meet with potential partners.

Docs for Sale – see page 266.

European Film Market at Berlin International Film Festival

Potsdamer Straße 5, D-10785 Berlin
tel ++ 49 30 259 20 666 *fax* ++ 49 30 259 20 619
email market@berlinale.de
website www.berlinale.de
Market Director Beki Probst

Connected to the Berlinale; one of the key trade events for the international film industry. The event includes more than 1000 screenings; 30% of the films in the Berlinale also have market screenings. EFM also offers a Co-Production Market for producers with new projects who are looking for co-producers and potential investors.

Filmart – Hong Kong Film Market

Head Office: Hong Kong Trade Development Council, 38/F, Office Tower, Convention Plaza, 1 Harbour Road, Wanchai, Hong Kong
tel ++ 852 1830 668 *fax* ++ 852 2824 0249
email film@tdc.org.hk
website www.hkfilmart.com/hkfilmart

Multimedia trade fair for producers, exhibitors and buyers held each March.

Independent Feature Project Market

104 West 29th Street, 12th Floor, New York, NY 10001-5310, USA
tel ++ 1 212 465 8200 ++ 212 465 8525
email marketreg@ifp.org
website www.ifp.org

IFP Market was launched in 1979 to connect truly independent filmmakers to the wider film industry. The IFP Market is a week-long showcase, held each autumn in New York, for new features, works-in-progress, shorts, and scripts. The Market allows independent filmmakers to present new film and television work-in-development directly to the film industry; in turn the film industry has a unique forum to discover new talent and see films before they screen at festivals. There are 3 distinct sections: Emerging Narrative, Spotlight on Documentaries, and No Borders International Co- Production Market.

MIPCOM

UK Office: Reed Midem, Walmar House, 296 Regent Street, London W1B 3AB
tel 020-7528 0086 *fax* 020-7895 0949
email peter.rhodes@reedmidem.com
website www.mipcom.com
Managing Director Peter Rhodes (Reed Midem)

MIPCOM is an international trade event produced by Reed Midem for co-producing, buying, selling, financing and distributing entertainment content across all platforms (video/DVD, broadcast TV, VOD, mobile, broadband, interactive TV, etc.). The conference is hosted in October in Cannes at the Palais des Festivals. Reed Midem also organises more specialist conferences, MIPTV and MIPDOC, in April.

MIPDOC – see page 285.

A 2-day trade conference for documentary content providers and buyers.

MIPTV – see page 285.

A trade show for content producers in television.

Montreal International Film Market

1432 de Bleury Street, Montreal, Quebec, Canada, H3A 2J1
tel ++ 1 415 848 3883 *fax* ++ 1 415 848 3886
email accreditations@ffm-montreal.org, info@ffm-montreal.org
website ffm-montreal.org

Part of Montreal World Film Festival (see page 275) at the end of each August. Includes a production exchange programme to foster co-productions, as well as conferences and symposiums.

CineMart at Rotterdam International Film Festival

Karel Doormanstraat 278-B, 3012 GP Rotterdam, The Netherlands
tel ++ 31 10 890 90 90 *fax* ++ 31 10 890 90 91
email cinemart@filmfestivalrotterdam.com
website www.filmfestivalrotterdam.com

CineMart is held as part of the Rotterdam International Film Festival and is in its 24th year. It was the first platform of its kind to offer filmmakers the opportunity to launch their ideas to the international film industry, and make the right connections to get projects financed. Every year, the CineMart invites a select number of directors/producers to present their film projects to potential co-producers, bankers, funds, sales agents, distributors, TV stations and other potential financiers and information sources. 1:1 meetings are set up before the market to take place between filmmakers and potential partners.

Awards

British Academy of Film and Television (BAFTA)

195 Piccadilly, London W1J 9LN
tel 020-7734 0022 *fax* 020-7734 1009
email info@bafta.org
website www.bafta.org

One of the principal functions of the British Academy of Film & Television Arts is to identify and reward excellence in the artforms of the moving image. It achieves this objective by bestowing awards on those practitioners who have excelled in their chosen field of expertise.

In 1947, BAFTA granted 3 awards; today, more than 100 are given annually in the fields of film, television and video games. The 5 annual awards ceremonies in London are as follows: The Orange British Academy Film Awards; The British Academy Video Games Awards; The British Academy Television Awards; The British Academy Television Craft Awards; and The 10th British Academy Children's Film & Television Awards.

The Orange British Academy Film Awards are held each year in the month before the Oscars, and reward achievements in all areas of film craft and for the best in feature, documentary, British, short and aminated categories.

Major winners in 2007: *The Queen* (Best Film); *The Last King Of Scotland* (Alexander Korda Award); Andrea Arnold, *Red Road* (Carl Foreman Award); Paul Greengrass, *United 93* (Best Director); Michael Arndt, *Little Miss Sunshine* (Best Screenplay); Asitha Ameresekere, *Do Not Erase* (Best Short); Ian Gouldstone, *Guy 101* (Animated Short).

British Independent Film Awards

81 Berwick Street, London W1F 8TW
tel 020-7287 3833 *fax* 020-7439 2243
email info@bifa.org.uk
website www.bifa.org.uk
Producer Johanna von Fischer *Head of Film Submission* Deena Manley

Created in 1998, The British Independent Film Awards set out to celebrate merit and achievement in independently funded British filmmaking, to honour new talent, and to promote British films and filmmaking to a wider public. A film is eleigible if it was released theatrically or if it screened for a paying audience at a British-based festival. The film must have at least 51% of its funding from British sources, and must not be solely funded from a single studio.

Recent major awards: *This is England* (Best Film); Kevin Macdonald, *The Last King of Scotland* (Best Director); Peter Morgan, *The Queen* (Best Screenplay); Menhaj Huda, *Kidulthood* (Best Debut Director); and *Cubs* (Best Short Film).

Critics' Circle Film Awards

c/o 32 Eburne Road, London N7 6AU
tel 020-7263 3523
email marianne.gray@virgin.net
website www.criticscircle.org.uk
Chairman Marianne Gray

Critics' Circle is made up of 380 critics who work in the arts. The film section of the organisation holds its own awards ceremony each February. All films released theatrically in the UK between Feb 8th and Feb 7th of the previous year are eligible. Awards are decided by a members' vote.

Major awards in 2007: *Volver* (Best Foreign Film); *United 93* (Film of the Year); Paul Greengrass (Director of the Year); and *The Queen* (Best British Film).

DepicT!

Watershed, 1 Canon's Road, Bristol BS1 5TX
email maddy@watershed.co.uk
website www.depict.org

DepicT! is Watershed's unique filmmaking competition; part of Encounters Film Festival, which challenges filmmakers from across the globe to come up with a compelling, imaginative idea and distill it into 90 seconds of originality. In addition to being in the running for the top prize of £2000 and gaining valuable industry exposure through Encounters Short Film Festival, each filmmaker shortlisted for the DepicT! Award receives a free Network Delegate pass with all the trimmings, as well as a free place to the Encounters Film School and entry to the DepicT! Showcase and the Encounters Award Ceremony.

Recent winners include: Animation: *Flighty*, directed by Leigh Hodgkinson (UK); and Live Action: *And the Red Man Went Green*, directed by Ruth Meehan (Ireland). 2006 DepicT! Audience Award (voted by the public, with shortlisted films posted on **www.depict.org** from early October): *Flighty*, directed by Leigh Hodgkinson (UK).

European Film Academy Awards

European Film Academy, Kurfürstendamm 225, 107 19 Berlin, Germany

tel ++ 49 30 887 167 0 *fax* ++ 49 30 887 167 77
email efa@europeanfilmacademy.org
website www.europeanfilmacademy.org

EFA's awards ceremony is held in December and is for European feature films intended for theatrical release. Awards are voted for by the 1800 members of the Academy and go to all major categories: Film, Director, Actor, Actress, Cinematographer, Screenwriter, Composer, etc. Also to Best Discovery, Short Film and Documentary. The short film award Prix UIP has a donated prize of €10,000. Producers may submit directly to the Academy in June, with the short film nominations coming from the prizewinners at affiliated film festivals. Previous winners have included: *The Lives Of Others, Habla con Ella, Head-on, Goodbye Lenin*, Michael Haneke, and Charlotte Rampling.

Golden Globe Awards

c/o The Hollywood Foreign Press Association, 646 N Robertson Blvd, West Hollywood, CA 90069, USA
tel ++ 1 310 657-1731 *fax* ++ 1 310 657-5576
email info@hfpa.org
website www.hfpa.org
President HFPA Philip Berk

The Golden Globes are the awards given each year by the Hollywood Foreign Press Association, founded more than 60 years ago by a group of Los Angeles-based journalists working for overseas publications. The Golden Globe awards have enabled the non-profit organisation to donate more than $5.5 million in the past 11 years to entertainment-related charities, and to funding scholarships and other programmes for future film and television professionals.

Held before the American Academy Awards each year, the film awards are widely seen as indicators of which films will win an Academy Award. Awards are given for film and television.

Major 2007 winners: *Babel* (Best Motion Picture – Drama); *Dreamgirls* (Best Motion Picture – Comedy or Musical); Martin Scorsese for *The Departed* (Best Director); Peter Morgan for *The Queen* (Best Screenplay); Helen Mirren for *The Queen* (Best Actress – Drama); Forest Whitaker for *The Last King of Scotland* (Best Actor – Drama); *Walk the Line* (Best Musical or Comedy).

Oscars – American Academy of Motion Picture Arts and Sciences Awards

c/o Academy Foundation, 8949 Wilshire Boulevard, Beverly Hills, California 90211, USA
tel ++1 310 247 3000
website www.oscars.org

– see page 343 for more information on the Academy of Motion Picture Arts and Sciences.

Each year, the Academy holds the film world's most prestigious awards ceremony, the 'Oscars', to reward outstanding achievement in cinema. Awards are decided by a vote from Academy members. Any film which is less than 2 years old, and which was released theatrically in the USA, is eligible. Short films must have screened at one of the Academy's designated films festivals, where it must have won the 'Best Of' award.

Major awards for 2007: *The Departed* (Best Picture); Martin Scorsese (Achievement in Directing); *Little Miss Sunshine* (Original Screenplay); *The Lives of Others* (Best Foreign Language Film); *An Inconvenient Truth* (Best Documentary); and *West Bank Story* (Best Short Film).

Pocket Shorts – see page 74.

Screen Nation Film and Television Awards

Screen Nation, PO Box 43831, London NW6 5WE
mobile (07904) 125727
email screennation@yahoo.co.uk
website www.screennation.co.uk
Founder & CEO Charles Thompson

Awards for television and film achievement by filmmakers of African heritage working in the US and UK industries. Awards are given for professional recognition to actors and to those working behind the camera (e.g. director, writer, producer), and are judged by juries and public voting. Ceremony is usually held in the second week of September. Recent winners include: *Hotel Rwanda*, and *Ray*.

The Reel Talent Awards

c/o The Hospital, 24 Endell Street, London WC2H 9HQ
tel 020-7170 9100 *fax* 020-7170 9101
email info@reeltalentawards.co.uk
website www.reeltalent.co.uk

A relatively new but increasingly prestigious award offered to 3 short film scripts annually. The awards are administered by The Hospital (see page 347), involve a title sponsor (Smirnoff Experience in 2006, Audi Channel in 2007), and run with support from The Script Factory (see page 6) and production company, Intrepido (see page 139). A comprehensive development opportunity, the Reel Talent Awards offer 3 producer/writer/director teams the chance to turn a screenplay into an award-winning film with a £10,000 prize, a development week, and numerous other in-kind benefits. Previous winners include: Luke Morris & Toby MacDonald for *Heavy Metal Drummer*, and Tinge Krishnan & Sasha Guttenstein for *First*.

Turner Classic Movies Short Film Competition

Turner House, 16 Great Marlborough Street, London W1F 7HS
website www.tcmonline.co.uk

Since its launch in 1999, TCM Classic Shorts has arguably become the important short film awards in the UK, with prize money totalling £10,000. The awards ceremony is held as part of the London Film Festival each October; the short films are always judged by some of the biggest names across the film industry. The films are subsequently screened on Turner Classic Movies.

Many past winners and finalists have gone on to achieve BAFTA success: Brian Percival's *About a Girl* won the Best Short, with nominations coming for Harry Wootliff (*Nits*), Alicia Duffy (*The Most Beautiful Man in the World*), Gerald McMorrow (*Thespian X*) and Toby MacDonald (*Je T'aime John Wayne*).

Distribution and exhibition
Delivering a film to its audience

Mark Batey

Every filmmaking journey ends with the audience. It's well-nigh impossible to attract anyone to see a film in which they have no interest. So how are people persuaded to part with £5 or more for a cinema ticket? Why do they choose to go and see a particular film?

In the UK, the average number of cinema visits per person is about three a year, although a quarter of the population goes at least once a month. The cinema offers the first opportunity to see a new film – it's an immersive, shared experience; an occasion. Most people go to the cinema knowing in advance what they want to see – the individual film is usually the main motivation behind the visit.

Films are made to be seen by paying audiences, and it's only when they are screened to an audience that the full potential of the filmmakers' work is realised. But public knowledge of, and interest in, new releases does not just happen by accident. Like any other product, films must be brought to market in a planned way that is right for the individual title. Bridging the gap between the filmmakers who create the work, the cinemas where it is shown, and the paying public audience is the film distributor. It is the distributor who plans and executes the launch of each new film on behalf of its producers, and draws an audience to the cinemas where it's showing.

Distribution is a commercial business and, as we shall see, an intensely competitive one. The aim is always to make a profit on the release so that funds may be generated for further productions – a virtuous circle. In most cases, films do not make a profit from their cinema run alone, although more go on to do so after release on other platforms, such as DVD, pay-per-view and television. This article explores in generic terms how the process of distribution – of delivering an audience film by film, week by week – works.

The key decisions that the distribution company must take regarding each film it is handling are when to open it, and how to release it – how to launch and hopefully sustain it in cinemas. But first, distributors must have a licence to release the film in the first place. UK distributors may acquire their releases from various sources: a flow of product from a parent studio; a production company or studio with whom the distributor has negotiated an output deal; or a third-party sales agent acting on the producer's behalf. A title may be acquired at any stage before, during or even after a film is made. Sometimes a distributor becomes a partner in a film project, advising on its playability, advancing an agreed proportion of its development and production costs, and later launching it in cinemas. Like most countries, the UK has a number of 'major' distributors affiliated to the multinational studios, and several 'independent' (unaffiliated) distributors who tend to handle films made outside the studios or niche titles. Any distributor, whatever its ownership, may compete to pick up a film with available rights.

When considering acquiring a new title, distributors will look for something fresh, distinctive or outstanding – a 'hook' to persuade people that this film has an extraordinary story which must be told. Who is the film for? Is it intended for the most frequent cinemagoing population of teenagers, students and young adults (broadly, 15 to 34 year-olds)? Is it for the family market, or does it have appeal for older adults? Does it skew significantly towards a male or female audience?

It's preferable for filmmakers to have a distribution deal in place before shooting starts. Indeed, for larger-budget films, it's normally essential. Sometimes a distribution deal can be viable on the basis of a hot script or the anticipated cast or director. There are no fixed formulae in film financing; every case is affected by variables such as the film property itself, the script, cast and market conditions.

More than 400 feature films are released in UK cinemas every year, typically eight or nine every week. The marketplace moves unforgivingly fast and has a rapid churn. A film that has been in development and production for two or three years may end up having played in cinemas for little more than two or three weeks.

Distributors gauge the likely audience. Understanding who the target audience is – their age, sex, lifestyles, media consumption – naturally informs subsequent decisions on how and where the film is promoted. While never losing sight of the core target, the distributor's challenge is to attract as broad a demographic spread as possible, to help the film 'break out' or 'cross over'. The greater a film's box-office takings, the more likely it is to be attracting infrequent cinemagoers and repeat visits.

Launching any film is expensive and risky. Audiences have a wealth of other entertainment options, in and out of the home, and their tastes are notoriously unpredictable. Nobody can be absolutely certain what makes a hit, or when and where it might happen, as cinemagoers discover particular films they like or dislike when they open. Just because one romantic comedy or action adventure has played successfully does not automatically mean that the next such release will do likewise. Pre-release test screenings are sometimes held to explore audience reactions and help the distributor to be more confident of the box-office prospects.

When weighing up the most appropriate release date and strategy, distributors give careful consideration to the competition their films will face in the marketplace. What other titles are likely to be on release at the same time and during the following few weeks, especially those aimed at a similar audience? Are the most appropriate screens for this film likely to be available? Are any cast members available for publicity or to attend a premiere? Will the film lead the reviews of the week's new releases? Has it already opened in the US or elsewhere and, if so, how did it perform?

Different films are released in different ways. A big film, probably with international stars and a leading director, aimed at a mass audience, may receive a 'saturation' release on say 800 to 1200 screens UK-wide. This is between a quarter and a third of all the cinema screens in the country. Occasionally, a new release is 'platformed' in just one location before rolling out more widely. Most films go out on fewer than 200 prints. The expansion of digital cinema in the UK is giving rise to new opportunities for niche-audience 'specialised' films, which may be released on significantly more digital copies that cost less than celluloid prints. Distributors pay all the release costs associated with bringing the film to market, such as media advertising, publicity, trailers and the prints themselves.

In recent years, UK distributors have spent £250 to £300 million a year on releasing films, including prints and advertising. Distributors' income is a share of the box-office takings generated by their releases. Though it varies film by film, week by week, over the course of a year the UK distributors' share tends to average out at around one-third of the total (gross) box-office receipts. This income has to pay off the film release costs, cover the company overheads and ideally leave a surplus that is remitted back to the producers.

On many titles, the distributor's marketing effort kicks off many months before the film is released and sometimes long before production is completed. The marketing aim is to build visibility and awareness, convincing the audience that this is a must-see film with desire peaking as it opens. So, brilliant, passionate, innovative marketing is as vital as brilliant, passionate, innovative filmmaking. Distributors strive to make their films stand out from the crowd but their advertising and publicity must reach and inspire the target audience as cost-effectively as possible. A combination of word of mouth and further promotion will give the film 'legs' during its theatrical run, which can last any period but nowadays rarely exceeds eight weeks. Often, close to half of the entire year's box-office takings are generated by just the top 20 blockbusters.

From an assessment of a film's target audience and box-office potential, distributors estimate what to spend on the release. The level of investment and projected return can be re-assessed each week, according to actual market performance. A film's marketability (ways to promote it to audiences) is not necessarily the same as its playability (how it performs in the market place). Within the agreed release budget, individual elements are allocated a proportion, such as designing/printing the posters, media advertising, duplicating and delivering the film prints and trailers, publicity costs such as press packs, preview screenings, possibly a premiere and travel and accommodation for any visiting talent.

Blockbusters with top stars need heavy marketing spends to back up their wide releases. UK media costs are high – terrestrial television advertising may be prohibitively expensive for most films given their likely returns, but distributors increasingly run trailers on websites and use digital TV channels for 'narrowcasting' to niche audiences. As with any advertiser, a wide array of media and promotional options is available to film distributors. A poster with a striking, memorable image is designed and replicated in the advertisements in newspapers, magazines, outdoor poster sites or bus panels. Probably the single most cost-effective film marketing tool is the trailer, which plays on the big screen to a captive audience of current cinemagoers.

As broadband Internet usage continues to expand, the web becomes an ever more important communications channel. Snippets of film information may be released online to seed interest among fans, and production diaries may be published to build anticipation further. Most films have an official website that includes ticket purchasing links, while chat-room communities may exchange reviews and opinions instantly and constantly around the world, perhaps even before a film has opened locally.

Publicists working in the distributor's marketing department, or perhaps at an external PR agency, ensure that the film is presented to journalists and critics, and that images and production notes are approved and available for use. The film must be certified by the British Board of Film Classification and of course its certificate has an important bearing on who can be admitted to see it in cinemas. Distributors are always concerned that the given certificate allows all of the natural audience for whom the film was intended to have the opportunity to see it at its best, in the cinema.

Premieres are perceived as glamorous and exclusive but in fact they are expensive and painstaking to organise. Their purpose is to secure extra media coverage of a film's launch, while reflecting its 'event' stature. Around 50 premieres are staged in London's West End each year. Sometimes distributors opt to launch films, particularly independent works of a certain quality, at a suitable international festival such as Cannes, Venice, Berlin, Toronto, Sundance, the American Film Market (AFM) or MIFED, the annual market in Milan. The eyes of the film world and the media are focused on these principal festivals, which can serve as high-profile showcases for premieres, junkets and global coverage. Trade papers publish daily editions for industry members and journalists, further helping to build the 'buzz' on hot properties.

Distributors present their forthcoming titles to exhibitors (the cinema operators) and discuss release dates and advertising plans with them. Like any retailers, exhibitors must be persuaded to 'stock the product' – to play a new film – and the distributor's sales team negotiates a licence agreement bilaterally and confidentially with each individual exhibitor interested in playing it. Under English law, the maximum booking period for a new release is two weeks, after which the distributor and exhibitor may decide that the film will continue to play one week at a time, so long as it is drawing a significant audience. Distributors arrange for a print to be despatched to cinemas playing the film a few days before its public release date. The 35mm prints are joined together and looped on to the film projectors, while digital copies are loaded into the projection room server and played out via state-of-the-art digital projectors.

A film can only be launched once – no second chances! – and the first weekend in cinemas is crucial to its further progress. It's not uncommon for a film to take one-third of its entire box-office in its opening weekend frame. Almost two-thirds of cinema visits take place during Friday to Sunday; Monday is normally the least busy weekday. On Mondays, once the weekend box-office takings are collated, the distributor's sales team discusses with each exhibitor the holding-over of current releases for a further week from Friday, taking into account the new openers and any previews that may be scheduled for the coming weekend, all of which are competing for the available screens and for public attention.

Distributors take advantage of digital subtitles and audio description systems to make their releases increasingly accessible to cinemagoers with sensory impairments. They also contribute to the study of film and media in schools by commissioning study packs themed to appropriate releases, normally from an industry body named Film Education. Distribution is a team effort that involves working persuasively and effectively with many other parties.

Happily, audiences worldwide possess an insatiable desire for quality filmed entertainment. With box-office receipts amounting to more than £800 million a year, the UK is the third most valuable cinema market in the world, after the US/Canada and Japan. But cinema revenues constitute a minority of the total that a film can earn – substantial revenues can also be derived from the subsequent release platforms. Today, the global entertainment business (all platforms) has annual revenues of around $70 billion, with a healthy compound annual growth forecast of 6 per cent. But the cinema remains the first window of opportunity, influencing a film's value and prospects in other platforms, and effective distribution is a prerequisite for success.

Mark Batey is Chief Executive of the Film Distributors' Association (FDA), the long-standing trade body that works on behalf of UK theatrical film distributors. With a strong membership whose releases account for around 95 per cent of UK cinema admissions, FDA offers a portfolio of services and activities to assist and support the distribution sector, the media and the wider cinema industry. For further information on UK film distribution and lots of other news and data, visit FDA's website, **www.launchingfilms.com**.

UK distribution companies

Amber Films

5 Side, Newcastle-Upon-Tyne NE1 3JE
tel 0191-232 2000 *fax* 0191-230 3217
website www.amber-online.com

Making films since 1968, Amber has a back catalogue of over 40 documentaries, dramas and feature films. As well as releasing new films, the filmmaking collective is making its back catalogue available in DVD format in addition to VHS and theatrically, and is now introducing downloads.

Anchor Bay Entertainment

38 Broadhurst Avenue, Edgware, London HA8 8TS
tel 020-8958 8512 *fax* 020-8958 5112
website www.anchorbay.co.uk

Books through Miracle Communications.

Arrow Film Distributors

18 Watford Road, Radlett, Herts WD7 8LE
tel (01923) 858306 *fax* (01923) 850673
website www.arrowfilms.co.uk

A Film Distribution company based in Hertfordshire and holding the UK rights to many World Cinema, Classic, Horror and Adult titles on DVD and VHS. With over 160 titles in its catalogue, Arrow Films has 95% of its business in the home entertainment sector/DVD Market; also releases films theatrically from time to time.

Artificial Eye

14 King Street, London WC2E 8HN
tel 020-7240 5353
email info@artificial-eye.com
website www.artificial-eye.com

Independent distributor of quality arthouse, european and world cinema. Titles include: *Time to Leave*, *Hidden*, and *The Beat That My Heart Skipped*.

Axiom Films

2nd Floor, (above The Gate Cinema),
87 Notting Hill Gate, London W11 3JZ
tel 020-7243 3111 *fax* 020-7243 3152
email mail@axiomfilms.co.uk
website www.axiomfilms.co.uk

With an expanding portfolio of diverse and award-winning theatrical films to their name, most Axiom titles have been made in co-production with established producers worldwide. Each film has premiered in official selection at one of the major international film festivals (Berlin, Cannes, Venice, Locarno, Toronto, San Sebastian).

bfi National Archive

21 Stephen Street, London W1T 1LN
tel 020-7255 1444
website www.bfi.org.uk

A selection of over 275,000 titles in the national archive collection, including feature films, short films, documentaries and television material are available to view. Many feature films, such as *Night of the Hunter* and *Breakfast at Tiffany's*, have been re-released theatrically by the *bfi*.

The *bfi* produces free catalogues which list thousands of the titles held; most of these catalogues are online. Over 10,000 titles are available on 35mm, 16mm and VHS (PAL format) for theatrical, non-theatrical and group screening purposes, plus material available on DVD and Beta SP.

Blue Dolphin Films

40 Langham Street, London W1N 5RG
tel 020-7255 2494 *fax* 020-7580 7670
email info@bluedolphinfilms.com
website www.bluedolphinfilms.com
Managing Director Joseph D'Morais

Established in 1980; distributes 6-10 films per year for theatrical and home video markets in UK. Also handles the MGM/UA library theatrically in the UK, together with own catalogue. Welcomes tape submissions but no scripts. Titles include: *West Side Story*, and *One Love*.

Brian Jackson Films

39/41 Hanover Steps, St George's Fields,
Albion Street, London W2 2YG
tel 020-7402 7543 *fax* 020-7262 5736

Specialist disributor of classic children's films.

Buena Vista International (UK)

3 Queen Caroline Street, London W6 9PE
tel 020-8222 1000
website www.thefilmfactory.co.uk

Releases high-quality specialised and commercial film theatrically and for home entertainment. Titles include: *Pirates of the Carribean 2*, *Venus*, and *Déjà Vu*.

Cinefile Ltd

12 Sunbury Place, Edinburgh EH4 3BY
tel 0131-225 6191 *fax* 0131-225 6971
email info@cinefile.co.uk
website www.cinefile.co.uk

World cinema on DVD and for theatrical release.

Cinefile World

12 Sunbury Place, Edinburgh EH4 3BY
tel 0131-225 6191 *fax* 0131-225 6971
email info@cinefile.co.uk
website www.cinefile.co.uk

Small distributor of French films. Titles include: *Russian Dolls*, and *The Bridesmaid.*

Circuit Distribution

63 Hartingdon Road, Brighton BN2 3LJ
tel (07771) 857 652

Small specialist distributor.

Contemporary Films

24 Southwood Lawn Road, London N6 5SF
tel 020-8340 5715 *fax* 020-8348 1238
email inquiries@contemporaryfilms.com
website www.contemporaryfilms.com

A film distribution library and documentary archive based in London, supplying footage to programme-makers, films to cinemas and TV, and videos and DVDs to the general public.

Contender Entertainment

48 Margaret Street, London W1W 8SE
tel 020-7907 3759
website www.contender.ltd.uk

Contender Entertainment Group is the biggest independent distributor of DVD and video in the UK. Has a number of brands which release different genres, such as TV, Kult, Kids and special interest (e.g. Asian Cinema labels, Hong Kong Legends and Premier Asia). The company also releases a small number of films theatrically each year. Titles include: *Ju-On: The Grudge 2*, *The Warrior King* (theatrical), *Life on Mars*, *Bullet in the Head*, and *Will and Grace* (all home entertainment).

ContentFilm

19 Heddon Street, London W1B 4BG
tel 020-7851 6500 *fax* 020-7851 6505
email london@contentfilm.com
website www.contentfilm.com

ContentFilm has an exclusive video and DVD output deal with Universal Pictures.

Distant Horizon

28 Vernon Drive, Stanmore, Middlesex HA7 2BT
tel 020-8861 5500 *fax* 020-8861 4411
email london@distant-horizon.com
website www.distant-horizon.com

Docspace

63 Hartingdon Road, Brighton BN2 3LJ
tel (07771) 857652

Small specialist distributor.

Dogwoof Pictures

2nd Floor, 1A Neal's Yard, Covent Garden, London WC2H 9DP
website www.dogwoofpictures.com
Managing Director Andy Whittaker

New British theatrical distributor with home entertainment arm representing the best of international independent film.

Entertainment Film Distributors

Eagle House, 108-110 Jermyn Street, London SW1Y 6HB
tel 020-7930 7744 *fax* 020-7930 9399
Managing Directors Trevor Green, Nigel Green

UK's major independent distribution company, which has a long-standing relationship with New Line Cinema in the US. The company recently launched a production venture in partnership with New Line (see page 140). Titles include: *The Departed*, *Brokeback Mountain*, *Lord of the Rings* Trilogy, *Final Destination 3*, and *Texas Chainsaw Massacre: The Beginning*.

Eros International

Unit 26, 23 Sovereign Park, Britannia Way, London NW10 7PR
tel 020-8963 8704 *fax* 020-8963 8414
website www.erosentertainment.com

Major specialists in Bollywood cinema.

Film and Video Umbrella

50 Bermondsey Street, London SE1 3UD
tel 020-7407 7755 *fax* 020-7407 7766
website www.fvumbrella.com

Artist film, video and new media specialists.

Filmbank Distributors

Warner House, 98 Theobalds Road, London WC1X 8WB
tel 020-7984 5959 *fax* 020-7984 5951
website www.filmbank.co.uk

A joint venture between Warner Bros and Sony Pictures, Filmbank is one of the leading non-theatrical film distributors (outside North America), representing most of the major Hollywood and independent film studios in the area of film licensing outside the cinema and home.

Gala Film Distributors

26 Danbury Street, London N1 8JU
tel 020-7226 5085 *fax* 020-7226 5897

One of the UK's oldest distributors, started by industry veteran the late Kenneth Rive; Gala Films is a small specialist in foreign-language arthouse cinema.

Goldcrest Films International

65-66 Dean Street, London W1D 4PL
tel 020-7437 8696 *fax* 020-7437 4448

Predominantly a post-production facility, Goldcrest Films also exclusively distributes Goldcrest titles.

Hammer Film Productions

92 New Cavendish Street, London W1M 7FA
tel 020-7637 2322 *fax* 020-7323 2307
website www.hammerfilms.com

Best known for its gothic horror productions in the 50s and 60s, when it was the most innovative producer in the horror genre and enjoyed global box-office success – making the Hammer brand synonymous with horror. Has a vast back catalogue largely available on DVD and VHS, including the classic movie series of *Dracula, Frankenstein*, and *Quatermass.*

Handmade Films

(formerly Equator Films)
6 Heddon Street, London W1B 4BT
tel 020-7025 7400 *fax* 020-7930 9399
website www.equatorfilms.co.uk

A UK-based international film distributor which licenses rights for all forms of television (terrestrial/pay/cable/video on demand) in addition to DVD and VHS rights for the home entertainment market. Equator has 3 film libraries and over 100 titles representing quality contemporary film entertainment.

Hollywood Classics

Linton House, 39-51 Highgate Road,
London NW5 1RS
tel 020-7424 7280 *fax* 020-7428 8936
website www.hollywoodclassics.com

Vast back-catalogue of a range of classics, including those produced by major studios from Fox and MGM to Warner Bros.

ICA Projects

12 Carlton House Terrace, London SW1Y 5AH
tel 020-7766 1416 *fax* 020-7306 0122
email sara@ica.org.uk
website www.ica.org.uk
Projects Manager Sara Squire

Releases approximately 8-10 specialised and arthouse films per year. Screening invitations and tapes may be send to Sara Squires or Mark Adams. Recent titles include: *Osama, Turtles Can Fly*, and *In This World.*

Icon Film Distribution

Solar House, 915 High Road, North Finchley,
London N12 8QJ
tel 020-8492 6300 *fax* 020-8492 6300
website www.iconmovies.co.uk
Head of Acquisitions Alex Hamilton

UK wing of international production, sales and distribution company. Picks up films for release in UK and also releases Icon's own films. Also see page 139. Titles include: *Matchpoint, The Night Listener*, and *Down in the Valley*.

Imperial War Museum Film Archive

Imperial War Museum, Lambeth Road,
London SE1 6HZ
tel 020-7416 5291/2 *fax* 020-7416 5299
website www.iwmcollections.org.uk/qryFilm.asp

A large archive of film and video detailing war and wartime daily life up to the present day.

Independent Cinema Office

3rd Floor Kenilworth House, 79-80 Margaret Street,
London W1W 8TA
tel 020-7636 7120 *fax* 020-7636 7121
email info@independentcinemaoffice.org.uk
website www.independentcinemaoffice.org.uk
Director Catharine Des Forges

ICO is a national organisation which aims to support the development of independent cinema exhibition in the UK. Its key activities are: offering film programming advice and booking services for culturally significant films into a number of independent cinemas across the UK; handling touring packages of films; and taking into limited distribution, films which may not otherwise be released in the UK. ICO does not pay advances, and takes films on for cultural, rather than commercial, reasons. Handles about 4-5 releases per year. Also advises on programming short films into client cinemas. Screening invitations and tapes may be sent to Catharine Des Forges or Simon Ward. Releases include: *Yasmin, Soy Cuba*, and *Born into Brothels.*

K5 International

18 Sherwoods Road, Watford WD19 4AZ
tel (01923) 333597
email info@k5international.com
website www.k5international.com

Lionsgate UK

(formerly Redbus Pictures)
Ariel House, 74a Charlotte Street, London W1T 4QJ
tel 020-7299 8800 *fax* 020-7299 8801
website www.lionsgatefilms.co.uk
Managing Director of Theatrical Distribution
Christopher Bailey

UK production and distribution company releasing theatrically and for home entertainment. Titles include: *Bend It Like Beckham, Good Night and Good Luck*, and *Hard Candy*.

Also see page 139.

Lumina Films

3rd floor, 1A Adpar Street, London W2 1DE
tel 020-7535 6714 *fax* 020-7563 7283
email sales@lumina-films.com
website www.lumina-films.com

International company that sells features, docs and TV series.

Lux

18 Shacklewell Lane, London E8 2EZ
tel 020-7503 3980 *fax* 020-7503 1606
website www.luxonline.org.uk

Leading distributor of artists' film, video and new media work.

Merchant Ivory

46 Lexington Street, London W1F 0LP
tel 020-7437 1200 *fax* 020-7734 1579

website www.merchantivory.com

Large back catalogue of films ranging from *Shakespeare Wallah*, to *A Room with a View* and the poignant Oscar-winning *Howards End*, produced by Merchant Ivory.

Metrodome Distribution

33 Charlotte Street, London W1T 1RR
tel 020-7153 4421 *fax* 020-7409 1935
website www.metrodomegroup.com
Managing Director Peter Urie

Established in 1997, Metrodome releases 8-12 films theatrically each year. Acquires primarily independent and arthouse. Recent titles include: *Dear Wendy*, *Mad Hot Ballroom*, and *Assasination of Richard Nixon*. Screening invitations and scripts should be sent to Kate Falconer or Peter Urie.

Millivres Multimedia

Unit M, Spectrum House,
32-34 Gordon House Road, London NW5 1LP
tel 020-7424 7426 *fax* 020-7424 7401
website www.millivresmultimedia.co.uk

Lesbian and gay cinema specialist distributor.

Miramax Films

43 Queen Caroline Street, London W6 9PE
tel 020-8222 1501 *fax* 020-8222 1534
email lucas.webb@miramax.com
website www.miramax.com
Manager, Production & Acquisitions Lucas Webb

UK arm of North American distributor. No unsolicited tapes or scripts, but screening invitations may be sent to Lucas Webb.

Momentum Pictures

184-192 Drummond Street, London NW1 3HP
tel 020-7391 6900 *fax* 020-7383 0404
website www.momentumpictures.co.uk
Managing Director Xavier Marchand *Head of Theatrical Distribution* Sam Nichols

Established in 2000 and owned by Canadian production, sales and distribution outfit Alliance Atlantis, Momentum releases approximately 20 films per year theatrically, as well as many home entertainment titles. Titles include: *Tsotsi*, *Downfall*, *Lost in Translation*, and *Broken Flowers*.

onedotzero – see page 261.

The pioneering digital festival also runs a distribution label and releases acclaimed collections of shortfilm DVDs.

Optimum Releasing

22 Newman Street, London W1T 1PH
tel 020-7637 5403 *fax* 020-7637 5408
email info@optimumreleasing.com
website www.optimumreleasing.com
Managing Director Will Clarke

Highly regarded independent distributor releasing *auteur*, international arthouse, horror, animation and documentary for the theatrical and home entertainment markets. Welcomes script submissions or screening invitations from producers. Titles include: *Howl's Moving Castle*, *9 Songs*, and *Last Days*.

Palm Pictures

8 Kensington Park Road, London W11 3BU
tel 020-7229 3000 *fax* 020-7229 0897
website www.palmpictures.co.uk

Paramount

12 Golden Square, London W1A 2JL
email info@paramountpictures.co.uk
website www.paramountpictures.co.uk

Park Circus Films

Woodside House, 20-23 Woodside Place,
Glasgow G3 7QF
tel 0141-332 2175
website www.parkcircus.com

Park Circus is the UK's leading distributor of classic and back catalogue films for theatrical exhibition. The company currently represents over 7000 titles from Buena Vista International (UK), Granada International, MGM/UA and other film collections. Beyond its UK activities, Park Circus also has a significant presence in international territories, where it distributes titles both theatrically and non-theatrically.

Pathé Distribution

14-17 Kenthouse, Market Place, London W1W 8AR
tel 020-7323 5151 *fax* 020-7631 3568
website www.pathe.co.uk
Head of Acquisitions Berenice Fugard

Theatrical and home entertainment distributor releasing approximately 20 titles per year. Titles include own productions and third-party films acquired for UK release. Titles include: *Volver*, *Severance*, and *Crash*.

Peccadillo Pictures

Unit 117, Panther House, 38 Mount Pleasant,
London WC1X 0AN
tel 020-7837 1118 *fax* 020-7837 3049
email info@peccadillopictures.com
website peccadillopictures.com
MD Tom Abell *Director Aquisitions* Kahloon Loke

Peccadillo Pictures is an independent film distribution outlet based in London. Specialises in arthouse cinemas and gay and lesbian themed films.

Revelation Films

Revelation Films Ltd, The Barn House,
38 Meadow Way, Eastcote, Middlesex HA4 8SY
tel 020-8866 7145
website www.revfilms.co.uk

Large home entertainment supplier with documentary and fiction films, comedy, television programmes and animation.

Revolver Entertainment

PO Box 31643, London
tel 020-7243 4300 *fax* 020-7243 4302
email info@revolvergroup.com
website www.revolvergroup.com

Revolver is a large independent distributor which releases a wide variety of films for home entertainment each year, and a number of titles for theatrical release. Also releases selected books. To contact the company about submission details, email acquisitions@revolvergroup.com. Titles include: *Destricted*, *Tideland*, and *Grizzly Man.*

Shooting People Films

8 Hoxton Square, London N1 6NG
email penny@shootingpeople.org
website www.shootingpeoplefilms.co.uk, www.bestvbest.com
Head of Label Penny Nagle

Shooting People Films is a new distribution label set up in December 2005 to release "films they want to tell their friends about". The company aims to be a filmmaker's label and is an offshoot of filmmakers' organisation, Shooting People. Titles include: Oscar-shortlisted *Unknown White Male* by Rupert Murray; *KZ* by Rex Bloomstein; *The Gigolos* by Richard Bracewell; and an annual DVD series, *Best v Best*, which brings together the year's major award-winning short films.

Short Circuit Films

The Workstation, 15 Paternoster Row, Sheffield S1 2BX
tel 0114-221 0569 *fax* 0114-249 2293
website www.shortcircuitfilms.com

Short-film sales agent, consultancy and distributor.

Soda Pictures

11-13 Broad Court, London WC2B 5PY
tel 020-7240 6060 *fax* 020-7240 6160
email info@sodapictures.com
website www.sodapictures.com
Managing Directors Edward Fletcher, Eve Gabereau

Independent distributor which handles quality arthouse and world cinema titles for cinema and DVD. Titles include: *Head-On, Heading South, C.R.A.Z.Y.* and *Into Great Silence.*

Sony Pictures Releasing

Europe House, 25 Golden Square, London W1F 9LU
tel 020-7533 1111 *fax* 020-7533 1105
website www.sonypictures.co.uk
Managing Director Peter Taylor

Company handles UK distribution for Sony Pictures Entertainment. Titles include *Spider-Man, The Da Vinci Code* and *Casino Royale.*

Squirrel Films/Sands Films Distribution

119 Rotherhithe Street, London SE16 4NF
tel 020-7231 2209 *fax* 020-7231 2119
website www.sandsfilms.co.uk

Production company which also distributes family films for children.

Swipe Films

79 Wardour Street, London W1D 6QB
tel 020-7851 8602
website www.swipefilms.com

An award-winning film production, sales and distribution company. Titles include: *Grand Theft Parsons;* the Golden Globe-winning Afghan movie, *Osama*; double Sundance winner, *Down to the Bone;* and Peter Bogdanovich's *The Cat's Meow* – among many others.

Tartan Films Distribution

72-74 Dean Street, London W1D 3SG
tel 020-7494 1400 *fax* 020-7439 1922
email info@tartanvideo.com
website www.tartanvideo.com
Managing Director Laura de Casto

Arthouse, indie and world cinema distributor releasing approximately 40 films per year. Scripts and screening invitations should be sent to the attention of Laura de Casto. Titles include: *Lady Vengeance*, *The Proposition*, and *Battle in Heaven.*

TLA Releasing

234 Market Street, Philadelphia, PA 19106, USA
tel ++ 1 215 733 0608 (ext. 210)
fax ++ 1 215 733 0637
email contact@tlareleasing.co.uk
website www.tlareleasing.co.uk

US indie and gay distributor based in Philadelphia; recently began to release titles in the UK. Primarily home entertainment, but with some theatrical titles. Titles include: *Ellie Parker*, and *Yossi & Jagger*.

Transmedia Pictures

Caparo House, 3rd Floor, 103 Baker Street, London W1U 6LN
tel (07000) 434567 *fax* 020-8207 6600
email simon.caplan@transmediareleasing.com
website www.transmediapictures.com
CEO Simon Caplan

Transmedia was established in 2004 by Simon Caplan, a qualified Accountant and International Tax Adviser who had advised clients in the media over a 25-year period. Transmedia has no defined aquisition policy, save only that its films should be well-made and as varied as possible in genre. The company will only buy films where all rights are available (theatrical, DVD, and satellite and terrestrial TV).

Twentieth Century Fox

20th Century House, 31-32 Soho Square, London W1A 2JL

tel 020-7437 7766
website www.fox.co.uk
Managing Director Ian George

UK distribution arm of the US studio. Titles inclue: *The Omen*, and *Little Miss Sunshine.*

United International Pictures (UIP)

45 Beadon Road, Hammersmith, London W6 0EG
tel 020-8741 9041 *fax* 020-8748 8990
website www.uip.com
Chairman & CEO Stewart Till *President & Chief Operating Officer* Andrew Cripps

Europe's largest distributor jointly owned by Paramount and Universal, and established in 1981. While UIP currently operates in 35 countries, from 2007 Universal and Paramount will divide up the duties of self-distributing in 15 of those countries, including the UK which will see Paramount take over distribution duties. UIP will continue to distribute in the other 20 countries. Titles include: *Nacho Libre, Flight 93*, and *Miami Vice.*

Vertigo Films

The Big Room Studios, 77 Fortess Road, London NW5 1AG
email mail@vertigofilms.com
website www.vertigofilms.com

A vertically integrated UK Development, Finance, Production and Distribution media company founded in July 2002. In 2003 Vertigo produced *It's All Gone Pete Tong* and co-released the film with Redbus Film Distribution. It subsequently produced *The Business* – Nick Love's follow-up to *The Football Factory* – and *Outlaw*. In 2005 Vertigo Films released *A Good Woman* starring Scarlett Johansson and Helen Hunt; *Clean*, starring Nick Nolte and Maggie Cheung; and *Pusher 2*, which was nominated for 11 Danish Oscars. In 2007 its slate increased further, with releases including: Neil Hunter and Tom Hunsinger's *Sparkle*, and the documentary *In the Shadow of the Moon.*

Verve Pictures Limited

3rd Floor, Kennilworth House,
79/80 Margaret Street, London W1W 8TA
tel 020-7436 8001 *fax* 020-7436 8002
email julia@vervepics.com, colin@vervepics.com
website www.vervepics.com
Managing Directors Colin Burch, Julia Short

One of the UK's newer independent UK specialist distributors; has particular interest in British and independent films. Titles include: *Code 46, Red Road, Favela Rising*, and *30 Century Man.*

Warner Bros

98 Theobalds Road, London WC1X 8WB
tel 020-7984 5200 *fax* 020-7984 5201
website www.warnerbros.co.uk

A major distributor of mainstream commercial features and selected smaller independent titles.

The Works UK

4th Floor, Portland House, 4 Great Portland Street, London W1W 8QJ
tel 020-7612 0090 *fax* 020-7612 0091
website www.theworksmediagroup.com

Part of The Works sales and media group. Has an increasingly substantial UK distribution catalogue.

Yash Raj Films International

Wembley Point, 1 Harrow Road, Wembley HA9 6DE
tel (08707) 397345 *fax* (08707) 397346
website www.yashrajfilms.com

Production company which also distributes; concentrates on Bollywood film.

Marketing a cult film

Tom Grievson, former Marketing Manager at Metrodome and now with the marketing team at Warner Bros, talks about the marketing campaign that turned *Donnie Darko* into an instant cult classic *and* a commercial success.

Donnie Darko became a huge hit for Metrodome, despite the fact that it didn't do very well on its initial theatrical release in the USA. Can you tell us a little bit about when you released it, and what your distribution expectations were?

The US release was about two weeks after 9/11 – which probably didn't help! Metrodome released *Donnie Darko* on 25th October, approximately a year after the film was released in America. Ben Roberts (Metrodome's former Head of Acquisitions) saw the film at one of the big international film festivals, at the point when it had already gone around to quite a few of the other distributors. No-one else had wanted it – I think there had been a lack of understanding about exactly what to do with it, and it seemed to be too much of a challenge.

We weren't really sure exactly what we could do with it until we did a standard screening to press and exhibitors. The exhibitors' screening went down particularly well. The DVD had also come out in America and there was a buzz about it which did help get people excited about the film here. Then we employed EM Foundation to do the publicity and organised a giant screening in the IMAX cinema on 5th August. The IMAX is a 500-seater and we filled it with press, friends, and any contacts we had in the art world, media world and so on – we just thought it was an incredible place to watch it. For that screening we produced a paper mask – exactly 500 of them – so that everyone who came to the screening walked away with a mask. On the back it just said **donniedarko.com** and the release date.

Who was your target audience for the film? How much was that set here, and how much inspired or influenced by the type of people who had picked up on the film in America?

We didn't really look at America at all – we decided that what they had done wasn't right for the film here so we wanted to do something completely different. With our approach – and it's an approach that we take to our marketing on every film – we watch the film and work out the different audience groups that we think are going to be interested. When it plays and instantly cries out 'cult', there are a lot of different networks we can tap into.

The film had Drew Barrymore in it and a really great 80s soundtrack at a time when 80s music was suddenly getting more popular again, so we wanted to tap into that. We created partnerships with bars in East London, and with Warp Records, which is a very cool record label, to begin to get a buzz. We used Warp particularly to tap into the music audience, because we thought this particular audience would be open to good quality cinema. And then we broke it down into subjects that are in the film. For example: in the film, Donnie says, "Destruction is creation," and from this idea – that you may be destroying something, but by doing it you're creating something else – I thought about friends I have who are into graffiti. I showed it to them and one particular graffiti artist went mental for it; he watched it five times in two days. When he came back and told me that, I knew that we had something that was going to be special for a certain audience. I watched it myself four or five times during the first two weeks I had it, just trying to absorb it more and more, and each time I sensed more potential audiences.

The 'Goth' audience suddenly seemed like a big one – the darkness of the film seemed perfect for them. When we did a screening at Cambridge Film Festival back in July (actually, this was the very first public screening we had for the film), I introduced it so I could look out and see who was there. I noticed a pocket of about eight Goths, so I came back to that and started to explore the Goth angle, alongside 'people into technology', 'people into music' and so on. I went off and did my own little informal research and found that everyone was blown away by it.

We split the marketing campaign up. There was an 'above the line' campaign, which was the traditional P&A spend with a poster. For the poster, we looked at several different options but the one we used – the rabbit mask – was such an iconic image. Obviously we're always after the most iconic image for the poster and that seemed to be such a great 'logo'. We did a tube campaign, quite extensive advertising in the media, and a radio campaign on XFM – all the things you would do on a release of that size. We went out on 55 prints, which was one of our biggest releases at that time.

With your non-traditional marketing, was it all down to you to build other relationships to get the message out?

Yes – it was all about tapping in to people who already knew about the film and then following up leads to help spread the word. So much of it came from the August IMAX screening which we'd packed with people we knew from different worlds. They all came back saying, "You should do this, and look at this ...", all of which created all these different opportunities,. Then it was a matter of putting them together. The one thing we made sure of was that there were four key things to hang everything on across the whole campaign: the rabbit; the 28 Days/6 hours/14 minutes/12 seconds; the release date; and the name of the film. We always had at least two of those elements in everything we did, whether it was above or below the line. So the stickers had the countdown and the words *Donnie Darko*; other things had the name and the rabbit. They seemed such strong elements, particularly the countdown which gave a sense of tension – of countdown towards something, which seemed ideal.

A lot of what we did just evolved organically. We knew what we were going to do above the line, but below the line our activity just kept on increasing. Every week it seemed that new opportunities jumped up. It's definitely all about the passion, and personally I was just so into the film that it took over my life for six months! Below the line is all about building relationships and coming up with different ideas. Because the film is so different and many people had never seen a film like this before, we wanted the campaign to reflect that – get across that sense that this was something completely new. Then when we started getting 5-star reviews from *Total Film* and *Empire* – also a good indication that we were on to something the press would support. Everything was falling into place; we knew it had the potential to be really big.

Our main concern became that we needed to get to the different audience groups and 'speak to them in their own language'. So we sponsored Goth clubs across the country and on the back of their flyers we had *Donnie Darko* and the rabbit – just very subliminal. We produced 10,000 pin badges of the rabbit. I remember having a battle with my boss at the time about whether that would be a good thing to do, but they spread like wildfire – two weeks before we released the film they were on eBay for £10, which was crazy! The postcards we made were on eBay the week we released – for £5, which was thrilling.

Tell us about the graffiti art campaign ...

We did a screening in Central London. Through my contact in the graffiti world we made contact with lots of different artists all around London – some of the most respected artists in the country. We invited them all to a screening and then went out for drinks and just talked to them about the ideas in the film. Everyone had different ideas about what the film was about, and on the back of that we decided to do an exhibition where each artist had 6 hours, 42 minutes and 12 seconds to produce a canvas with a piece of work that they felt represented the film.

The great thing was that we met in this warehouse in East London one night – I had £100 petty cash to buy food and beers – and we just met and hung out the whole night. We started at 9pm and went on for the 6 hours, etc. So we had 14 pieces of work by the most respected graffiti artists in the country ready for a month-long exhibition which launched two days before we released the film. We held the exhibition in a bar – I had invited the owners to the screening – and called the exhibition *They Made Me Do It* (referencing a bit of graffiti in the film). We had subtle *Donnie Darko* imagery in the promo; 20,000 flyers, which we produced and distributed around London clubs, bars, record shops and through the artists and their friends as well. We got so much press out of it, as the exhibition generated another whole element of publicity, which you'd never normally get for a film.

The director loved it! We did a traditional premiere which was themed as an 80s Halloween party and then the next night, one night before we released, we did another cool party at the art exhibition with all these East London DJs ... it went on until 3am. We got Frank's mask shipped over by the director and had it in a big box hanging over the bar, and I managed to source a countdown clock from a sports channel with days, hours, minutes, seconds on it – it was set at 28 days from the night the artists did the work – and the exhibition came down when the 28 days had run down. So it broke the film out in to a whole different set of audiences, all curious to know what it was about.

Interestingly enough, a year and a half later they did a *Kill Bill* exhibition at the same venue – and then after that, a *Sin City* thing there too. We were only the second art exhibition they did in the bar ever, and it was only opened a month before – so there were a lot of fortunate opportunities which fell into our laps.

The exhibition also led to a street campaign. One of the artists hand-painted two posters with the rabbit head. We had them put onto 1000 labels – giant labels on a photocopier – and started putting them up in September in all kinds of high-visibility places. We got one of the other artists to do a big mural on a wall on the way to the Notting Hill carnival – just the name, the countdown and so on – and no-one knew what it was at that point (August bank holiday) ... but the artist and I walked the carnival giving out stickers which no-one understood. It was us being ambassadors for the film – it even appeared on carnival news footage with *Donnie Darko* on the wall behind. It started generating a little buzz. It all built organically from that groundwork, three months before release.

What about the relationship with Warp?

A friend working at Warp produced little stickers, and put one on to everything they mailed out. They didn't charge us for it, but it went out to the Warp market – people who were really into their music – and spread through those networks. The image just seemed to be everywhere: it was spray-painted on pavements, it just went on and on. It's not something we spent a lot of money on – the whole exhibition including the flyer had a budget of £1000.

We convinced Radio 1 to give us Film of the Month, which had never gone to an independent film before. That helped the film cross into a more mainstream audience. They were always playing 'Mad World' and funny thing is, we had been to loads of record companies to try to persuade them to release Gary Jules' version of the song, but no-one wanted to do it – then two years later it was released and went to Number 1, selling 600,000 singles.

By the time you were making your release plans, were you aware of how big the film was becoming?

Yeah – by that time there was a cult thing happening in America, the DVD was out and they were doing midnight screenings and so on. We could feel the anticipation and excitement. Everyone seemed to be talking about it – *Sleazenation Magazine* put Frank (the rabbit) on a little bar on the cover with the line '*Donnie Darko* – Movie of the year'. It was a desperately cool mag at the time, and this was in September, so two months pre-release. It had just worked, screening the film early to the right groups. We had no budget for a TV campaign; while we had a reasonably decent above-the-line budget of £200,000, it was still nowhere near what a mainstream film or even a bigger indie film would normally spend. Below the line in this case was all about time.

The final box-office was £6 million, plus we sold a million DVDs. It was easily our biggest ever, more so because of the life it has had on DVD. Interestingly we were the only territory in the world to have a successful theatrical opening of the film. It's had a good cult DVD life elsewhere, but not theatrical. But Richard (the director) tells us we were the only ones who did below the line to the extent we did. And that's the way marketing is going; you can't rely on above the line anymore. There's so much 'noise' you have to compete with, so you need to be talking to audiences in their own language to make a difference. I think this was one of the first film campaigns that did it successfully.

We do it on every film now. We make sure we draw up a list of different groups and figure out how to reach them. Obviously we do it through press to a certain extent – but not everyone reads, and certainly not everyone who goes to the cinema reads – so you have to try to get your awareness elsewhere. More recently with *Mad Hot Ballroom* we had posters, flyers, stickers up in every dance hall in the country and we've done screening programmes to hit every dance teacher. It all helps to generate the buzz and open up your film to a potential new audience.

With *Donnie* we were lucky; we had a cool film with a cool name. That said, when we first started the campaign, people were like, "*Donnie Brasco*?"

Tom Grievson is the former Marketing Manager for theatrical releases at Metrodome Distribution, which has released such titles as *Pretty Persuasion*, *Tell Them Who You Are*, *Monster*, and *Lilya 4-Ever*. He is now part of the Marketing team at Warner Bros.

UK sales companies

AV Pictures Ltd

Caparo House, 2nd Floor, 103 Baker Street,
London W1U 6LN
tel 020-7467 5012 *fax* 020-7224 5149
email info@avpictures.co.uk
website www.avpictures.co.uk
Managing Director Vic Bateman

Beyond Films – see page 310.

bfi Archival Footage Sales

21 Stephen Street, London W1T 1LN
tel 020-7957 4842
email footage.films@bfi.org.uk
website www.bfi.org.uk/afs

Archival Footage Sales allows television producers and filmmakers to use the *bfi* National Archive, possibly the largest collection of film and television in the world. Many unique and rarely seen collections can be licensed directly to clients by the *bfi*, usually from digibeta sub-masters.

Blue Star Movies

185 Gray's Inn Road, London WC1X 8UE
tel 020-7812 0700 *fax* 020-7812 0650
email sales@bluestarmovies.com
website www.bluestarmovies.com

An international film production and finance business with offices in London and Rome. Credits for executive production, production, finance and sales include: Michael Radford's *The Merchant Of Venice* (Al Pacino, Jeremy Irons and Joseph Fiennes); John Duigan's *Head In The Clouds* (Charlize Theron, Penelope Cruz and Stewart Townsend); and *Irresistible* (Susan Sarandon, Sam Neill and Emily Blunt).

British Film Institute Film Sales

21 Stephen Street, London W1T 1LN
tel 020-7957 8909 *fax* 020-7436 4014
email salesfilms@bfi.org.uk
website www.bfi.org.uk

British Film Institute's sales arm; sells classic and culturally significant feature films, shorts and documentaries. Revivals, archival and significant but "little seen" titles are of particular interest. New films are acquired relatively rarely; no tapes or screening invitations are accepted. Titles include: *Pink Narcissus, Sympathy for the Devil*, and *The Night of Truth* (*La Nuit de La Verite*).

British Home Entertainment

5 Broadwater Road, Walton-on-Thames,
Surrey KT12 5DB
tel (01932) 228832 *fax* (01932) 247759
email cw@britishhomeentertainment.co.uk
website www.britishhomeentertainment.co.uk
Director Clive Williamson

Releases British classics on video and DVD. Titles include: *Othello, The Mikado, Uncle Vanya, The Soldier's Tale*, and *King and Country*.

Canal + Image

Pinewood Studios, Pinewood Road, Iver,
Bucks SL0 0NH
tel (01753) 631111 *fax* (01753) 655813

Capitol Films – see page 310.

Carnaby International

New London House, Drury Lane,
London WC2B 5QR
tel 020-7074 1273
email info@carnabyentertainment.com
website www.carnabyinternational.com

Celsius

4th Floor, Portland House, 4 Great Portland Street,
London W1W 8QJ
tel 020-7612 0040 *fax* 020-7612 0031
email info@celsiusentertainment.com
website www.celsiusentertainment.com

Having previously traded as Entco Ltd, Celsius was re-launched in November 2004 at the American Film Market. The company has put together a number of productions via a combination of pre-sales and relationships with banks and investors that specialise in media financing; currently represents projects with budgets ranging from \$10m to \$55m, and directors such as Penelope Spheeris (*Wayne's World*) and Chuck Russell (*The Mask, The Scorpion King*).

Celsius is a private company, wholly owned and managed by Thierry Wase-Bailey. A veteran of international film sales and distribution, Thierry was previously the Managing Director and Head of Sales at HanWay Films, which he co-founded in 1999 with producer Jeremy Thomas.

Credits include: *Paris, Je T'aime Tara Road*, and *River Queen*.

Centre Film Sales

46 Crispin Street, London E1 6HQ
tel 020-8566 2388 *fax* 020-8566 2388
email eleahy@centrefilmsales.com
website www.centremediasales.com

Channel Four International

124 Horseferry Road, London SW1 2TX
tel 020-7396 4444 *fax* 020-7306 8363
website www.c4i.tv

Columbia TriStar International Television
tel 020-7533 1000 *fax* 020-7533 1246

ContentFilm International
tel 020-7851 6500 *fax* 020-7851 6505
– see page 297.

Coolabi
(Formerly Alibi Films International)
48 Broadley Terrace, London NW1 6LG
tel 020-7258 7080
email info@coolabi.com
website www.coolabi.com

Company primarily specialising in animation and children's programming.

Cumulus Distribution
Sanctuary House, 45-53 Sinclair Road, London W14 0NS
tel 020-7300 6624 *fax* 020-7300 6529
website www.cumulusdistribution.com

Dazzle Films – see page 315.

DCD Media
(Formerly Digital Classics)
31 Eastcastle Street, London W1W 8DL
tel 020-7636 1400 *fax* 020-7299 8190
email nb@digitalclassics.co.uk
website www.digitalclassics.co.uk

UK-based group specialising in production, distribution, and sales of TV programming. Comprises 5 operating companies: Iambic Productions, Box TV, Done and Dusted, NBDtv, and Digital Classics DVD.

Distant Horizon
28 Vernon Drive, Stanmore, Middlesex HA7 2BT
tel 020-8861 5500 *fax* 020-8861 4411
email london@distant-horizon.com
website www.distant-horizon.com

DLT Entertainment UK Ltd
10 Bedford Square, London WC1B 3RA
tel 020-7631 1184 *fax* 020-7636 4571
email info@dltentertainment.com
website www.dltentertainment.com

Documedia International Films Ltd
19 Widegate Street, London E1 7HP
tel 020-7325 6200 *fax* 020-7625 7887

Dreamachine
24 Hanway Street, London W1T 1UH
tel 020-7290 0750 *fax* 020-7290 0751
email info@dreamachinefilms.com
website www.dreamachinefilms.com

Created by a merger of HanWay Films and Celluloid Dreams in 2007. Has offices in London, Paris and Toronto. See Celluloid Dreams on page Celluloid Dreams and HanWay Films on page 312.

Endemol UK – see page 136.

Entertainment Rights
Colet Court, 100 Hammersmith Road, London W6 7JP
tel 020-8762 6200 *fax* 020-8762 6299
email info@entertainmentrights.com
website www.entertainmentrights.com

Freemantle International Distribution
1 Stephen Street, London W1T 1AL
tel 020-7691 6000 *fax* 020-7691 6060
email fidsales@fremantlemedia.com
website www.fremantlemedia.com

Goldcrest Films International
65-66 Dean Street, London W1D 4PL
tel 020-7437 8696 *fax* 020-7437 4448
website www.goldcrestfilms.com

London-based sales company established in 1977 with highly regarded post-production wings in London and New York. No unsolicited scripts accepted, but screening tapes may be sent to Acquisitions & Development Coordinator, Wayne Godfrey.

Granada International
48 Leicester Square, London WC2H 7F
tel 020-7491 1441 *fax* 020-7493 7677
website www.granadamedia.com/international
Managing Director Nadine Nohl

One of the largest commercial television distributors in Europe. Catalogue ranges from own Granada productions to Hollywood TV movies, and work from independent producers. Also represents classic British films. Producers should contact Louise Stagg in sales. Titles include: *Dr Zhivago*, *Miracle of the Heart*, and *Brief Encounter*.

HanWay Films – see page 312.

High Point
25 Elizabeth Mews, London NW3 4UH
tel 020-7586 3686 *fax* 020-7586 3117
email piers@highpointfilms.co.uk
website www.highpointfilms.co.uk
Head of Feature Film Acquisitions Piers Nightengale

International sales company and television distributor established in 1990. Specialises in thriller, horror, drama and *auteur* films. Recent acquisitions include: *The Front Line*, *Moon on the Snow*, *Z00 Rangers in Africa*, and *Vinci*. Screening invitations and tapes should be sent to Piers Nightengale.

Hollywood Classics
Linton House, 39/51 Highgate Road, London NW5 1RS

tel 020-7424 7280 *fax* 020-7428 8936
email info@hollywoodclassics.com
website www.hollywoodclassics.com

IAC Film

22 Elysium Gate, 125-128 New Kings Road, London SW6 4LZ
tel 020-7610 8160 *fax* 020-7610 8161

Icon Entertainment International – see page 139.

In-Motion Pictures

5 Percy Street, London W1T 1DG
tel 020-7467 6880 *fax* 020-7467 6890
email enquiries@in-motionpictures.com
website www.in-motionpictures.com

Indigo

116 Great Portland Street, London W1W 6PJ
tel 020-7612 1700 *fax* 020-7612 1705
email info@indigofilm.com
website www.indigofilm.com
Managing Director David Lawley

Established in 1998 as independent distributor and co-producer of films, drama series, documentaries, entertainment series and children's programming for the international market. Primarily exploits TV, home video and non-theatrical rights worldwide, but is extending to include Internet, mobile phone and new media. New producers should send scripts and screening tapes to Chairman, Paul Shields. Titles include: *The Collingwood Story*, *Best*, and *The Jealous God*.

Lakeshore Entertainment – see page 312.

London Films

71 South Audley Street, London W1Y 5FF
tel 020-7499 7800 *fax* 020-7499 7994
website www.londonfilms.com

MovieHouse Entertainment

9 Grafton Mews, London W1T 5HZ
email info@moviehouseent.com
website www.moviehouseent.com

Independent film sales company. Titles include: *Scott Walker – 30 Century Man*, and *Credo*.

NBD TV

151 Wardour Street, London W1F 8WE
tel 020-7297 8021 *fax* 020-7297 8022
email distribution@nbdtv.com
website www.distribution@nbdtv.com

One of the largest contemporary and classical music programming libraries in the world; reps producers and rights owners from the UK and US, including: Warner Vision International, Elvis Presley Enterprises, Paul McCartney's MPL, Experience Hendrix, Apple Corps Ltd, Amnesty International, American Movie Classics, and Showtime Networks Ind. Part of DCD Media (see page 307).

Odyssey Entertainment

10A James Street, London WC2E 8BT
tel 020-7520 5610 *fax* 020-7520 5611
email sales@odyssey-entertainment.co.uk
website www.odyssey-entertainment.co.uk

Paramount Television

49 Charles Street, London W1J 5EW
tel 020-7318 6400 *fax* 020-7491 2086

Park Entertainment

4th Floor, 50-51 Conduit Street, London W1S 2YT
tel 020-7434 4176 *fax* 020-7434 4179
email sales@parkentertainment.com
website www.parkentertainment.com

Established in 1987, Park is a worldwide distributor and sales agent for independently produced television and film content. Titles include: *Goose*, *Niagra Motel*, and *The Purifiers*.

Pathe International – see page 313.

Photoplay Productions

21 Princess Road, London NW1 8JR
tel 020-7722 2500 *fax* 020-7722 6662
email photoplay@compuserve.com
Director Kevin Brownlow

Photoplay makes film history documentaries and restores silent films. Titles include: *Buster Keaton – So Funny It Hurts*, and *Cecile B De Mille – American Epic*.

Portman Film and Television

21-25 St Anne's Court, London W1F 0BJ
tel 020-7494 8024 *fax* 020-7494 8046
email sales@portmanfilm.com
website www.portmanfilm.com
Chief Executive Jeremy Fox

Represents and develops rights and content for television programming.

S4C International

50 Lambourne Crescent, Llanishen, Cardiff CF4 5DU
tel 029-20 741 440 *fax* 029-20 754 444
email international@s4c.co.uk
website www.s4ci.com

Screen Projex

13 Manette Street, London W1D 4AW
tel 020-7287 1170 *fax* 020-7287 1123
email info@screenprojex.com
website www.screenprojex.com

Titles include: *Club Le Monde*, and *Strong Language*.

Screen Ventures

49 Goodge Street, London W1T 1TE
tel 020-7580 7448 *fax* 020-7631 1265

email info@screenventures.com
website www.screenventures.com
Managing Director Christopher Mould

Screen Ventures is a production and international sales company which has worked primarily in broadcast for all of the major channels. Specialises in drama and doc series, with an emphasis on music. Filmmakers are welcome to send proposals, scripts, tapes and/or showreels to the Managing Director. Titles include: *Bob Marley: The Director's Cut*, and *The Church of St Coltrane.*

Shorts International

25 Beak Street, London W1F 9RT
tel 020-7734 2277 *fax* 020-7734 2242
email simon@shortsinternational.com
website www.shortsinternational.com

Short film sales and distribution company.

SMG

3 Waterhouse Square, 138-142 Holborn, London EC1N 2NY
tel 020-7882 7000 *fax* 020-7882 1020
website www.smg.plc.uk

Southern Star

12 Raddington Road, London W10 5TG
tel 020-8968 2424 *fax* 020-8968 0177
email sales@sstar.co.uk
website www.southernstargroup.com

Sullivan Entertainment

Suites 30-32, Savant House,
63-65 Camden High Street, London NW1 7JL
tel 020-7383 5192 *fax* 020-7383 0627
email info@sullivan-ent.co.uk
website www.sullivan-ent.co.uk

Summit Entertainment

77 Dean Street, London W1D 3SH
tel 020-7494 1725 *fax* 020-7494 1724
website www.summit-ent.com

UK office of US sales company. Titles include: *Mr & Mrs Smith*, *Down in the Valley*, and *Resident Evil.*

Target Entertainment

Drury House, 34-43 Russell Street,
London WC2B 5HA
tel 020-7344 1950 *fax* 020-7344 1951
website www.target-entertainment.com

Twentieth Century Fox Television

31-32 Soho Square, London W1V 6AP
tel 020-7437 7766 *fax* 020-7439 1806

Universal Pictures International

Prospect House, 80-110 New Oxford Street,
London WC1A 1HB
tel 020-7079 6000 *fax* 020-7079 6500

Vine International Pictures

VIP House, Greenacres, New Road Hill, Downe,
Orpington, Kent BR6 7JA
tel (01689) 954123 *fax* (01689) 850990
email info@vine-international.co.uk
website www.vine-international.co.uk

Warner Bros International Television

98 Theobalds Road, London WC1X 8WB
tel 020-7494 3710 *fax* 020-7287 9086

Television distribution/production arm of Time Warner's entertainment company, Warner Bros Entertainment.

The Works International – see page 314.

Key international sales companies

2929 Entertainment

2425 Olympic Blvd, Ste 6040W, Santa Monica, CA 90404, USA
tel ++ 1 310 309 5701 *fax* ++ 1 310 309 5716
website www.2929entertainment.com
Co-founder/CEO Todd Wagner *Co-founder* Mark Cuban

2929 is a vertically integrated company with production, distribution and exhibition holdings. It recently experimented with Stephen Soderbergh on *Bubble*, which had a simultaneous release in theatres, on television and on home video. Owns 2929 Productions, which makes films for $10-$30 million, and HDNet Films for lower-budget films shot on high definition.

To submit an idea or screenplay to 2929, contact Couper Samuelson at csamuelson@2929productions.com; to submit to HDNet Films, contact hdinquiries@hdnetfilms.com. Do not send materials before making an enquiry by email.

Titles include: *Good Night and Good Luck*, *Bubble*, *Enron: The Smartest Guys in the Room*, and *The Jacket*.

Bavaria Film International

Bavariafilmplatz 8, DE-82031 Geiselgasteig
tel ++49 89 64 99 26 87 *fax* ++49 89 64 99 37 20
email thorsten.schaumann@bavaria-film.de
website www.bavaria-film-international.de
Head of Bavaria Film International Thorsten Schaumann

Bavaria Film co-produces and sells German and a range of international arthouse titles for a world audience. The International Feature Films label features films that were co-produced with international partners, shot in a language other than German and/or shot in other countries. Titles include: *Lost Embrace*, *The Man Without a Past*, *Shake it All About*, and *The Legends of Rita*.

Beyond Films

41-42 Berners Street, London W1T 3NB
tel 020-7323 3377 *fax* 020-7580 6479
website www.beyond.com.au

Australian sales company. Credits include: *A Good Woman*.

Beyond International

Sydney Office: 109 Reserve Road, Artarmon, NSW 2064, Australia
tel ++61 2 9437 2000 *fax* ++ 61 2 9437 2132
London Office: 41-42 Berners Street, London W1T 3NB
tel 020-7323 3377 *fax* 020-7580 6479
website www.beyond.com.au
Head of Sales & Acquisitions Hilary Davis

Beyond Films is the largest film sales company based in Australia, established in 1990. The company has a catalogue of more than 100 feature films, either exec produced or acquired. Titles include: *No One Gets Off In This Town*, and *The Dead Wait*.

Big Film Shorts

100 S. Sunrise Way #289, Palm Springs, CA 92262
tel ++ 1 760 219 6269
email info@bigfilmshorts.com
website www.bigfilmshorts.com

Short film sales agent.

Capitol Films

23 Queensdale Place, London W11 4SQ
tel 020-7471 6000 *fax* 020-7471 6012
email films@capitolfilms.com
website www.capitolfilms.com
Managing Directors Jane Barclay, Hannah Leader, Nick Hill

Founded in May 1989 by Sharon Harel and Jane Barclay, Capitol Films has become one of Europe's most important international film production, financing and sales companies. Titles include: *Alpha Dog*, *Ghost World*, *Gosford Park*, and *Stormbreaker*.

Celluloid Dreams

2 rue Turgot, FR-75009 Paris, France
tel ++33 1 49 70 03 70 *fax* ++33 1 49 70 03 71
email info@celluloid-dreams.com
website www.celluloid-dreams.com
President Hengameh Panahi *Acquisiitions and Sales* Charlotte Mickie

Celluloid Dreams has one of the most impressive track records in the world with arthouse, independent and Asian cinema. The company has a strong commitment to director-led projects, and has helped develop and establish both Francois Ozon and Takeshi Kitano. Titles include: *Me, You and Everyone We Know*, *Swimming Pool*, *Election* (Johnnie To), and *Lemming*.

Constantin Film

Feilitzschstrasse 6, D-80802 Munich, Germany
tel ++49 89 44 44 60 0 *fax* ++49 89 44 44 60 666
email zentrale@constantin-film.de
website www.constantin-film.de

The Coproduction Office

Mommenstrasse 27, DE-10629 Berlin, Germany
tel ++49 30 3277 7879 *fax* ++49 30 3232 091

email info@thecopro.de
website www.thecopro.de
Founder Philippe Bober

A production and international sales company working with a select number of arthouse feature films. The group was founded in 1987 by Philippe Bober, and has offices in Paris and Berlin. Has a reputation for selecting strong individual works from edgy and exciting new filmmakers. Titles include: *Nói Albínói*, *Songs From the Second Floor*, and *Japón*.

Dreamachine – see page 307.

EuropaCorp

137 rue du Faubourg Saint-Honoré, 75008 Paris, France
tel ++33 1 53 83 03 03 *fax* ++33 1 53 83 03 04
email info@europacorp.com
website www.europacorp.com
Director of International Sales Grégoire Melin

Primarily co-produces and sells French feature films, with certain exceptions. Titles include: *Danny the Dog*, *Love and Other Disasters*, and *Quand J'etais Chanteur*.

Filmax

81-87 Miguel Hernandez,
Dist Eco l'Hospitalet – l'Hospitalet de Llobregat, ES-08908 Barcelona, Spain
tel ++ 34 (0)933 368 555 *fax* ++34 (0)932 630 824
email a.nava@filmax.com
website www.filmaxinternational.com
Chairman Julio Fernández *CEO* Carlos Fernández *MD International Production* Antonia Navas *Head of International Division* Vicente Canales *MD Marketing* Rafael Cabrera

Spanish-owned and run company; makes and sells international titles. The company works as a full-service studio and is organised into 5 areas: production, distribution, multimedia, exhibition and communication. Titles include: *The Machinist*, *The Backwoods*, *Transsiberian*, and *The Abandoned*.

FilmExport Group

Via del Pianeta Urano, 60-00144 Rome, Italy
tel ++39 06 5220 7432 *fax* ++39 06 5227 8416
email info@filmexport.com
website www.filmexport.com
President Roberto di Girolamo

Founded in 1970; more than 600 international film and television titles, including a huge library of Italian films. Screening invitations may be sent to the President.

Films Distribution

20 rue Saint-Augustin, 75002 Paris, France
tel ++33 1 53 10 33 99 *fax* ++33 1 53 10 33 98
email info@filmsdistribution.com
website www.filmsdistribution.com
CEO Nicolas Brigaud-Robert *Head of Acquisitions* Sébastien Beffa

Films Distribution was set up in 1997 by Nicolas Brigaud-Robert and François Yon. Since then, the company has made a name for itself working exclusively with feature films, which it sells to international distributors and broadcasters. Films Distribution has a library of approximately 200 titles for worldwide sales (and 800 in total); it adds 15-20 new titles to its international sales slate each year. Primarily French-language titles. Titles include: *Flanders*, *C.R.A.Z.Y.*, and *Trilogy*.

First Look International

First Look Media, 8000 Sunset Blvd, East Penthouse, Hollywood, CA 90046, USA
tel ++ 1 323 337 1000
email filmsales@firstlookmedia.com
website www.flp.com, www.firstlookmedia.com
President, First Look Media Ruth Vitale *Executive VP of Worldwide Sales* Ken DuBow

The international sales wing of First Look Media; orginally known as Overseas Filmgroup. Titles include: *Smiley Face*, *A Guide to Recognising Your Saints*, and *The Mayor of Sunset Strip*.

Focus Features

65 Bleeker Street, 3rd Floor, New York, NY 10012, USA
tel ++1 212 539 4000 *fax* ++1 212 539 4099
website www.focusfeatures.com
Co-presidents James Schamus, David Linde *CEO* Andrew Karper *President of Focus Features International* Alison Thompson

Focus is a worldwide production, finance and distribution company committed to making innovative international cinema. It was founded by David Linde and James Schamus, who were behind former indie production and sales giant, Good Machine. The company also has another label, Rogue Pictures, which was set up to produce and distribute edgy suspense, action and thriller, and comedy with mainstream potential. Focus is owned by Universal. Focus titles include: *Brick*, *Lost in Translation*, and *Brokeback Mountain*; Rogue titles include: *The Return*, *Hot Fuzz*, and Jet Li's *Fearless*.

Fortissimo Film Sales

Main Office: Veemarkt 77-79, NL-1019, Amsterdam, Netherlands
tel ++ 31 20 627 32 15 *fax* ++ 31 20 626 11 55
email info@fortissimo.nl
website www.fortissimofilms.com
Co-Chairmen Wouter Barendrecht, Michael J Werner (based in Hong Kong office) *Vice President – Development & Acquisitions* Ashley Luke (based in Sydney office)

An international organisation which has an excellent reputation for producing and distributing a range of unique, innovative and often award-winning features from independent filmmakers from all over the world. Company is also well known for its investment in quality East Asian cinema, and has long supported the work of directors such as Wong Kar Wai and Oxide and Danny Pang.

Catalogue includes more than 250 films from around the globe; approximately 12-15 films per year are added to the line-up as both acquisitions and co-productions.

Titles include: *Super Size Me*, *Capturing the Friedmanns*, *2046*, and *In the Mood for Love*.

Gaumont International

30 avenue Charles-de-Gaulle,
F-92200 Neuilly-sur-Seine, France
tel ++ 33 1 46 43 20 00 *fax* ++ 33 1 46 43 21 68
website www.gaumont.com
Head of Sales Loic Trocme

One of the main European production companies; founded in 1895. Gaumont has a vast film library, which includes the works of directors such as Luc Besson, Jean-Marie Poiré, Mathieu Kassovitz, Federico Fellini and Francis Veber. Titles include: *The Science of Sleep*, *The Fifth Element*, and *The Closet*.

Golden Harvest Ltd

The Peninsula Office Tower, 18 Middle Road,
Tsimshatsui, Kowloon, Hong Kong
tel ++ 852 2352 8222 *fax* ++ 852 2353 5989
email info@goldenharvest.com
website www.goldenharvest.com

One of Asia's major players across all sectors of the industry – production, distribution, exhibition and financing. Titles include: *Fist of Fury*, and *Police Story*.

Golden Network Asia Ltd

Unit 2003, Futura Plaza,
111-113 How Ming St Kwun Tong, Kowloon,
Hong Kong
tel ++ 852 2751 1886 *fax* ++ 852 2750 4852
email info@goldnetasia.com

Successful East Asian production and sales company. Titles include: *Ong Bak*, *Nothing to Lose*, and *Hollywood Hong Kong*.

HanWay Films

25 Hanway Street, London W1T 1UH
tel 020-7290 0750 *fax* 020-7290 0751
email info@hanwayfilms.com
website www.hanwayfilms.com
CEO Tim Haslam

Sister company to Recorded Picture Company. Established in 1999; sells international rights on many big titles. Also owns rights to RPC back catalogue. No scripts or project proposals accepted, but screening invitations may be sent to Matthew Baker. Titles include: *Matchpoint*, *Brothers of the Head*, *Rabbit Proof Fence*, *Fast Food Nation*, and *Glastonbury*.

Intramovies

via E. Manfredi 15, 00197 Rome, Italy
tel ++ 39 680 76157 *fax* ++ 39 608 76156
email j.nuyts@intramovies.com
website www.intramovies.com

Kinowelt International

Karl-tauchnitz Strasse 10, Leipzig 04107, Germany
tel ++ 49 341 355 96 410 *fax* ++ 49 341 355 96 419
email filmverlag@kinowelt.de
website www.kinowelt-international.de
Head of World Sales Stelios Ziannis

Lakeshore Entertainment

14 Garrick Street, London W1F 9UN
tel 020-7539 8360 *fax* 020-7539 8362
email info@lakeshoreentertainment.com
website www.lakeshoreentertainment.com

UK offices of major US sales agent. Titles include: *The Last Kiss*, *Underworld*, and *Million Dollar Baby*.

Lionsgate Entertainment

Los Angeles: Lionsgate International,
2700 Colorado Ave, Santa Monica, CA 90404, USA
tel ++1 310 449 9200 *fax* ++ 1 310 255 3870
New York: 157 Chambers Street, 11th Floor, New York, NY 10007, USA
tel ++ 1 212 577 2400 *fax* ++ 1 212 962 2872
website www.lionsgate.com

Lionsgate is one of the premier independent international producers and distributors of films, television and home entertainment content. Titles include: *Lord of War*, *Saw*, and *Fahrenheit 9/11*.

Media Luna Entertainment

Hochstadenstr. 1-3, D-50674 Cologne, Germany
tel ++ 49 221 8014980 *fax* ++ 49 221 8014 9821
email info@medialuna-entertainment.de
website www.medialuna-entertainment.de

MK2

55 rue Traversière, FR-75012 Paris, France
tel ++ 33 1 44 67 30 00 *fax* ++33 1 43 07 29 63
email florence.stern@mk2.com
website www.mk2.com
Head International Sales Florence Stern

Established in 1974, MK2 was the first fully integrated independent company in France, with production, distribution and sales. The company has an extensive catalogue of arthouse, classic and animated feature films, which have won numerous awards (including 3 Golden Palms). Catalogue includes: works by Chaplin, Truffaut, Lynch, Altman, Wenders, Kieslowski, Resnais, Haneke, Chabrol, Bresson and Kiarostami.

Nordisk Film

Mosedalvej 14, DK-2500 Valby
tel ++ 45 36 18 82 00 *fax* ++ 45 36 18 93 00

email inga.jespersen@nordiskfilm.com
Editor www.sales.nordiskfilm.com
Managing Director Michael Ritto *International Sales* Kenneth Wiberg

Nordisk is involved in the production, distribution and international sales of its films. Titles include: *Aftermath*, and *Reconstruction*.

Pathe International (UK)

Kent House, 14-17 Market Place, London W1W 8AR
tel 020-7323 5151 *fax* 020-7631 3568
email international.sales@pathe-uk.com
website www.pathepicturesinternational.co.uk
Head of Sales Mike Runagall

One of the UK's most established international sales outfits. Company has a reputation for handling quality arthouse/commercial crossover films. Titles include: *The Queen*, *The Descent* and *The Wind That Shakes the Barley*.

Pony Canyon International

2-5-10 Toranomon, Minato-ku,
Tokyo 105-8487 JAPAN
tel ++ 81 35521 8048 *fax* ++ 81 3 5521 8122
email intl@ponycanyon.co.jp
website www.ponycanyon.co.jp
General Manager, Production & Acquisition Shinji Sakoda

Japanese film and television sales company.

Pyramide International

5, rue du Chevalier de Saint George, 75008 Paris, France
tel ++33 1 42 96 02 20 *fax* ++33 1 40 20 05 51
email pricher@pyramidefilms.com
website www.pyramidefilms.com
Managing Director Eric Lagesse

Founded in 1989; a well-respected international sales agent which actively focuses on *auteur* films, with films from newer directors of world cinema such as Diego Lerman, Wang Xiao-Shuai, Baltasar Kormakur and more established names such as Catherine Breillat and Olivier Assayas. Titles include: *Beijing Bicycle*, and *Meanwhile*.

Roissy Films

58 rue Pierre Charron, 75008 Paris, France
tel ++ 33 1 5353 5050 *fax* ++ 33 1 4289 2693
email a-rayroles@roissyfilms.com
website www.roissyfilms.com
Head of International Sales Beatrice Roig

Roissy Films co-produces and sells about 10 new feature films per year. Its back catalogue includes some of the top French films of the last 30 years. Titles include: *Eros*, and *Friends Forever*.

SND Films

PO Box 15703, 1001 NE Amsterdam,
The Netherlands
tel ++31 20 404 07 07 *fax* ++31 20 404 07 08
email info@sndfilms.com
website www.sndfilms.com

Short film and documentary sales company with a strong catalogue, including many Sundance short film favourites.

Sogepaq

Leganitos 47,7, 28013 Madrid, Spain
email sogepaqint@sogecable.com
website www.sogecine-sogepaq.com

Sogecable produces and distributes films through Sogecine and Sogepaq. Sogepaq is responsible for the acquisition, management and sale of film rights for international distribution and television; it has a catalogue of more than 400 titles. These are primarly Spanish films, but the company acquires international rights for films outside Spain. Titles include: *The Sea Inside*, and *Princesses*.

Sonet Film

Tappvägen 24, SE-16102 Bromma, Sweden
tel ++ 46 8 555 248 31 *fax* ++ 46 8 98 68 63
email ann-mari@sonetfilm.se
website www.sonetfilm.se

Sonet Film was founded in 1984 and is today one of the leading production, distribution and sales companies in Scandinavia.

Sony Pictures Classics

550 Madison Avenue, 8th Floor, New York,
NY 10022, USA
tel ++ 1 212 833 8833

Summit Entertainment – see page 309.

TF1 International

9 rue Maurice Mallet, Immeuble Central Park,
92130 Issy-les-Moulineaux, France
tel ++ 33 1 41 41 17 63 *fax* ++ 33 1 41 41 17 69
email neschbach@tf1.fr
website www.tf1international.com
Sales & Acquisitions Director Nicolas Eschbach

Created in 1995, TF1 International is the worldwide distribution and acquisition arm of the TF1 Group – one of the leading media groups in France. Titles include: *Ignorant Fairies*, *8 1/2 Women*, and *Sade*.

Trust Film Sales

Filmbyen 12, DK-2650 Hvidovre, Denmark
tel ++ 45 36 868-788 *fax* ++ 45 36 774-448
email trust@trust-film.dk
website www.trust-film.dk
CEO Annakarin Wolfsberg *Senoir Sales Executive* Rikke Ennis

Trust Film Sales handles worldwide distribution rights for Nordic and international feature films. The company was founded as an independent branch of the Danish production company Zentropa in 1997;

also works as a sales agent for producers from around the world. Represents approximately 20 feature films each year. The main sales wing focuses primarily on high-quality arthouse titles. Titles include: *Dogville*, *Container*, and *Red Road*.

Wild Bunch

Paris office: 99 rue de la Verrerie, 75004 Paris, France
tel ++33 1 53 01 50 20 *fax* ++33 1 53 01 50 49
London office: 231 Portobello Road, London W11 1LT
tel 020-7792 9791 *fax* 020-7792 9871
website www.wildbunch.biz
Head of International Sales Vincent Maraval

Wild Bunch is dedicated to the nurture and development of radical and innovative projects worldwide. The company has a reputation for supporting bold films, which may be provocative or controversial. Titles include: *The Brown Bunny*, *Howl's Moving Castle*, *Baise Moi*, *Raising Victor Vargas*, and *Bully*.

The Works International

Portland House, 4 Great Portland Street, London W1W 8QJ
tel 020-7612 1080 *fax* 020-7612 1084
website www.theworkslimited.com
Head of The Works International Joy Wong

The Works was established in 1986 and is now one of the most respected and successful sales companies in Europe. Formerly known as The Sales Co, The Works is a sister company to The Works Production (previously The Film Consortium). Recent successes include: *Bend it Like Beckham*, *In the World*, *Whale Rider*, *My Summer of Love* and *Sweet Sixteen*. The Works does not accept unsolicited scripts or project proposals, but screening tapes and invitations may be sent to Joy Wong.

Short film sales

These are the leading sales and distribution companies which specialise in short films.

Big Film Shorts
100 S. Sunrise Way #289, Palm Springs, CA 92262
tel ++ 1 760 219 6269
email email info@bigfilmshorts.com
website website www.bigfilmshorts.com

Dazzle Films
388 Old Street, London EC1V 9LT
tel 020-7739 7716
email studio@dazzlefilms.co.uk
website www.dazzlefilms.co.uk
Founder Dawn Sharpless

International short film distributor and sales company based in the UK.

Future Shorts
34-35 Berwick Street, London W1F 8RP
*tel*020-7734 3883
email email info@futureshorts.com
website website www.futureshorts.com

KurzFilmAgentur Hamburg
Friedensallee 7, D-22765 Hamburg, Germany
tel ++49 40 39 10 63 19 *fax* ++49 40 39 10 63 20
email sales@shortfilm.com
website www.kurzfilmagentur.de

Short film sales agent.

Lux – **see page 298.** **Distributor of artist film and video including short works.**

Microcinema International
1636 Bush Street, Suite 2, San Francisco, CA 94109, USA
tel ++ 1 415 447 9750 *fax* ++ 1 509 351 1530
email info@microcinema.com
website www.microcinema.com

Short film sales.

onedotzero – **see page 261.** **Distributor of digital works including short form media.**

Shooting People Films
website www.bestvbest.com

– **see page 300.****Shooting People's distribution arm releases annual collections of the best short films from around the world, in a series entitled *Best v Best*.**

Shorts International
London Office: 25 Beak Street, London, W1F 9RT
tel 020-7734 2277 *fax* 020-7734 2242
email simon@shortsinternational.com
website www.shortsinternational.com

Short film sales company with one of world's largest catalogues of award-winning shorts, some of which are sold through Apple's iTunes. The company also creates regular podcasts, which are distributed through iTunes and give news on the short film industry.

SND Films – **see page 313.**

Home entertainment/DVD distribution in the UK

Abbey Home Media

435-437 Edgware Road, London W2 1TH
tel 020-7563 3910 *fax* 020-7563 3911
website www.abbeyhomemedia.com
Managing Director, Acquisitions & Programme Development, Anne Miles

Abbey Home Media Group is one of the UK's leading creators and distributors of pre-school children's programming for broadcast, audio, video, DVD and publishing channels. The company believes that children respond best when their senses are stimulated by words, pictures and sounds that are magical, colourful, and fun. Abbey's award-winning title range delivers this promise to a wide international audience, including young babies, toddlers, pre-schoolers and older children.

Anchor Bay UK

6 Heddon Street, London W1B 4BT
tel 020-7025 7400 *fax* 020-7025 7406
email info@anchorbay.co.uk
website www.anchorbay.co.uk

Anchor Bay Entertainment UK is well established in the home entertainment market and releases many classic and cult titles each year. Titles include: *Tintin*, *Evil Dead*, and *Wings of Desire*.

Arrow Film Distributors

Orchard Villas, Porters Park Drive, Radlett, Herts WD7 9DS
tel (01923) 858306 *fax* (01923) 859673
email info@arrowfilms.co.uk
website www.arrowfilms.co.uk
Company Director Alex Agra

Distributor primarily in home entertainment market with some theatrical. Releases 3-4 films per month; back catalogue includes a range of world, horror, classic and adult. Arrow is interested in producing its own slate, and welcomes script submissions or enquiries to Company Director Alex Agra. Titles include: *Russ Meyer Collection*, *Dawn of the Dead*, and *Cinema Paradiso*.

Cherry Red Films

website www.cherryred.co.uk

– see page 135 for further details and a call for production proposals.

Cherry Red Films releases music-related DVDs; titles include: *Billy Childish is Dead*, *Robyn Hitchcock & The Egyptians*, and *Gotta Let This Hen Out*.

Classic Media Group

tel (01932) 592016
email info@classic-media-group.com
website www.classicpictures.co.uk

Releases a number of music and special-interest DVD titles, including: *The Drifters Greatest Hits Live*, and *The Other Side of Rick Wakeman* – released through the company's brand, Classic Direct.

Clear Vision

Mega Mail, PO Box 148, Enfield EN3 4NR
tel 020-8292 4875
email info@clearvision.co.uk
website www.clearvision.co.uk

Small DVD distributor with specialist titles.

Contender Entertainment Group

120 New Cavendish Street, London W1W 6XX
tel 020-7907 3773 *fax* 020-7907 3777
website www.contendergroup.com
Contact Arabella Jupp

CEG has expertise in home video distribution, TV production and distribution, licensing and merchandising; has recently moved into the online arena. The company specialises in a number of genres, which include film, children's, TV and general/factual entertainment. With a TV division to develop its own IPs, and with the Licensing & Merchandising arm, the company is well placed to manage represented brands, as well as its own, in all sectors of the UK consumer market.

Entertainment in Video

Eagle House, 108-110 Jermyn Street, London SW1Y 6HB
tel 020-7930 7766

Large London-based home video/DVD label.

Eros International

Unit 23, Sovereign Park, Coronation Road, London NW10 7PA
website www.erosentertainment.com

Distributor with theatrical and home entertainment arms specialising in Bollywood titles.

Firefly Entertainment Limited

First Floor, 110 Harley Street, London W1G 7JG
tel 020-7034 3410 *fax* 020-7034 3419
email info@fireflyentertainment.co.uk
website www.fireflyentertainment.co.uk

MD Gareth Watson, *Commercial Director* Neil Allen, *Financial Director* Ray Edward

Firefly Entertainment was created in 2003 with the ambition of lighting up the DVD and Video Industry in the UK – holding true to the values of an Independent distributor by utilising its considerable knowledge and maintaining an open mind. Its management has 25 years of combined experience in the video industry; the company currently has over 300 titles on its roster and is constantly looking to add to this tally by capitalising on its expertise in developing new products and licences across all genres. Firefly Entertainment's core business has traditionally focused on distribution into mainstream retail, but is now exploring many non-traditional avenues.

Fremantle Media Home Entertainment

1 Stephen Street, London W1T 1AL
tel 020-7691 6729 *fax* 020-7691 6079
email videodvd@fremantlemedia.com
website www.fremantlehomeentertainment.com
International Marketing Manager Charlotte Richards

Releases international arthouse, horror, documentary and drama for home entertainment. Producers may send screening invitations and/or tapes to Brad Blain or Charlotte Richards. Titles include: *Punk:Attitude*, *Faster Pussycat Kill Kill*, and *Fellini's Casanova*.

Granada Ventures

tel 020-7389 8555
email granadaventures@itvplc.com
website www.granadaventures.co.uk

Granada Ventures is the merchandising, licensing and publishing division of ITV plc. Established in October 2003 following the merger of Granada and Carlton, the company's remit is to drive secondary revenue streams for the corporation by moving brands beyond broadcast.

The company currently licenses almost 1000 products and 3000 DVD titles across 200 household-name television, film and sports brands. This includes licensing the rights to must-have brands of the future such as Pocoyo and Numberjacks, as well as hugely successful established brands such as *I'm A Celebrity ... Get Me Out Of Here!* and *Classic Thunderbirds*. With comedy entertainment brands such as *Little Britain* and *Catherine Tate*, a strong sporting offer that includes Arsenal and Liverpool football clubs, and the highly successful *World Poker Tour*, Granada Ventures has a strong and varied portfolio. The company is committed to the expansion of its core offerings across its 5 key sectors of DVD, music, books, mobile and merchandise.

Green Umbrella Sport & Leisure

Basement Suite, 3 Nottingham Court,
Covent Garden, London WC2H 9AY
tel 020-7379 7246 *fax* 020-7836 0937
website www.greenumbrellashop.co.uk

Green Umbrella is one of Europe's leading independent producers and distributors of sports and special-interest programmes and books. Founded in 1990, the Surrey-based company has a catalogue of more than 1000 DVD titles across a variety of genres, from football, golf and rugby to health, history and motoring; also publishes sports and special-interest books for distribution around the world. Latterly, the company has moved into entertainment product, including the distribution of feature films and music CDs from its new offices in London's Covent Garden.

guerilla films

35 Thornbury Road, Isleworth TW7 4LQ
tel 020-8758 1716 *fax* 020-8758 9364
email info@guerilla-films.com
website www.guerilla-films.com
MD David Wilkinson

guerilla films limited was founded in 1995 by filmmaker David Nicholas Wilkinson, having previously used the name guerilla films during the 1980s for the more edgy productions he made whilst running Britannia Entertainment. The company was originally set up primarily as a production company before moving into distribution, concentrating solely on distributing British and Irish films within the UK and Ireland. Its films have screened in all the leading UK chains – UGC, Cineworld, Odeon, UCI and VUE – as well as in numerous independent cinemas. guerrilla DVDs are, or have been, available in all the high street outlets as well as online. The company is happy to consider any completed film looking for UK distribution, especially British or Irish ones.

Manga Entertainment

website www.manga.co.uk

An entertainment company specialising in the production, marketing and distribution of Japanese animation for theatrical, television, Internet, DVD and home video release worldwide (ex-Asia). The company is headquartered in Chicago with offices in Los Angeles, London and Tokyo.

MGM Home Entertainment (Europe) Ltd

5 Kew Road, Richmond, London TW9 2PR
website www.MGM.com/dvd

Metro-Goldwyn-Mayer Inc is an independent, privately held motion picture, television, home video, and theatrical production and distribution company. The company owns the world's largest library of modern films, comprising approximately 4000 titles, and over 10,400 episodes of television programming. Its film library has received 208 Academy Awards, one of the largest award winning collections in the world, and includes numerous successful film franchises, including James Bond, Pink Panther and Rocky.

Millivres Multimedia

Spectrum House, Unit M,
32-34 Gordon House Road, London NW5 1LP
tel 020-7424 7400 *fax* 020-7424 7401
website www.millivresmultimedia.co.uk
MD Kim Watson

Formed in February 1998, as a wholly owned subsidiary of the Millivres Prowler Group. Millivres Multimedia has established itself as the UK's leading distributor of independent cinema with a "sexuality" theme. Most of its titles are based on the complexities of relationships between families, friends and lovers. Hence the core portfolio is made up of world cinema, accessible to UK mainstream and "queer" cinema-goers alike.

Millivres Multimedia is a natural source of ground-breaking world independent cinema for the UK, and has distributed more than 60 titles to the UK in this time – including 14 cinematic releases and video, DVD and TV rights sales. Previous titles include: *Head On*, *Trick*, *Relax … It's Just Sex*, *Pourquoi Pas Moi?*, *Chutney Popcorn*, *Better Than Chocolate*, *Finding North*, *Goldfish Memory*, and *A.K.A.*

Miramax Films

43 Queen Caroline Street, London W6 9PE
tel 020-8222 1501 *fax* 020-8222 1534
email lucas.webb@miramax.com
website www.miramax.com
Manager, Production and Acquisitions Lucas Webb

Nova Productions

62 Ascot Avenue, Cantley, Doncaster DN3 6HE
tel 0870-879 0079
email info@novaonline.co.uk
website www.novaonline.co.uk

Nova Productions is one of the North of England's fastest growing digital video multimedia production companies. Video productions range from music promos to special-interest documentaries released on DVD; from multi-camera Outside Broadcasts of special events, like Remembrance Sunday, to training and promotional DVDs for companies, education providers and councils.

Odyssey Video

4 Canonbury Place, London N1
tel 020-7704 6355

Orbit Media Ltd

PO Box 48273, London W2 4ZJ
email info@orbitmedia.co.uk
website www.orbitmedia.co.uk

Specialises in classic films supplied on DVD and VHS. Has an extensive collection of classic Sherlock Holmes titles, including DVD and VHS box sets from the 1930s, 1940s and 1950s.

Paramount Home Entertainment

180 Oxford Street, London W1N 0DS
website www.paramount.com/paramount

Major DVD label attached to Paramount Pictures.

Quantum Leap

1A Great Northern Stree, Huntingdon PE29 7HJ
tel (01480) 450006 *fax* (01480) 456686
email kimlyon@qleap.co.uk
website www.qleap.co.uk
Director Kim Lyon

Predominantly releases documentary and films related to the arts. Releases 30 titles worldwide on DVD each year. Does not accept unsolicited ideas for projects or scripts, but does welcome tape submissions and screening invitations. Separate arm releases erotic films (**www.eroticfanstasies.com**).

Screen Edge

St. Anne's House, 329 Clifdon Drive South,
Lytham St Annes, Lancashire FY8 1LP
website www.screenedge.com

Releases movies, DVDs, photos, music and books. Dedicated to bringing the work of talented and unknown film directors and artists into the public eye.

Tartan Video

28 Poland Street, London W1F 8QW
tel 020-7292 2570
website www.tartanvideo.com

For over 20 years, Tartan Video has been working alongside Tartan's theatrical arm to release the very best of cinema from all over the world on DVD and video. Also manages Tartan's Asia Extreme and Tartan Terror labels.

TLA Releasing UK

tel 020-7287 0605
website www.tlareleasing.co.uk
UK Press Liaison Mike Hird

A leading voice in gay and international cinema distribution. Launched in 2001 in Philadelphia, TLA Releasing was established as a result of the overwhelming popularity of **tlavideo.com**, an online retail site catering to film-lovers of all tastes. Today, it is a major source for DVD shopping, browsing and information. The new London-based branch of TLA Releasing, like its North American counterpart, is dedicated to spotlighting quality gay, lesbian and international cinema throughout the UK and Ireland.

Universal Pictures Video

1 Sussex Place, Hammersmith, London W6 9XS
website www.universalpicturesvideo.co.uk

Warner Home Video

Warner House, 98 Theobald's Road,
London WC1X 8WB
website www2.warnerbros.com

With distribution in more than 90 territories, WHV has the largest distribution infrastructure in the global marketplace. It has access to the largest film library of any studio, and was instrumental in the development of DVD technology.

Warner Vision

35-38 Portman Square, London W1H 6LR
tel 020-7938 5500
website www.warnervision.co.uk

WVI, which was established as Warner Music Vision in 1990, expanded, together with a name change, in 1995 to include non-music programming. Music video releases, including classical titles from WMI's classical music divisions, continue to be issued on the original Warner Music Vision label.

Yah Raj Films

Wembley Point, 1 Harrow Road, Wembley, Middlesex HA9 6DE
tel 0870-739 7345 *fax* 0870-739 7346
email ukoffice@yashrajfilms.com
website www.yashrajfilms.com
Contact Avtar Panesar

Spearheaded by Yash Chopra, a leading light of the Indian entertainment industry for the last 5 decades. YRF started out as a filmmaking company in 1970; over the last 3 decades it has grown from strength to strength, and today has to its credit India's most enviable film catalogue – some films of which have been the highest grossers in the entertainment business. YRF has expanded to distribution of films all over the world – its own as well as films made by other well-known Indian names. It has also widened its horizons into Home Entertainment by marketing and distributing DVDs and VCDs of classic Indian films all over the world through its offices in UK, USA, UAE and India.

New models of distribution

Penny Nagle

In 2006, the UK triumphed at the Cannes Film Festival, with Ken Loach's *The Wind That Shakes The Barley* taking the Palme D'Or, and Andrea Arnold's *Red Road* taking a Special Jury prize – at a time when it was easier to go and see *Mission Impossible III* than anything by either of these directors, both of whom are undoubtedly classified as 'specialised' by great British film institutions. As Ken Loach himself said at the press conference, "In Britain we have a really rich film culture which rarely gets onto cinema screens. Our writers, dramatists and visual culture are much stronger than people think. We are limited by what the Americans want us to do. We need film distributors and especially exhibitors (cinemas) to put our films on the screen. We need to be seen as part of European and world cinema, not as an extension of America." Loach's pleas came in response to UK cinemas having programmed *The Wind That Shakes The Barley* into just 30 of its 3000 screens prior to the win.

So, why the lack of support for one of our venerable directors by the British film industry (let's include everyone in the distribution sweep this time – exhibitors, distributors, media, retail)? Why is Ken Loach not the toast of every film critic and journalist in Britain (so much *not* so that George Monbiot had to write in his defense in the *Guardian* on June 6th 2006, lambasting journalists for critiquing a film and filmmaker without even having seen his film)? Why is Andrea Arnold not feted here as, say, is Claire Denis is in France? Just what is it about British film distribution that makes our filmmakers so unhappy?

To answer these questions we need to look at how traditional film distribution has worked up until now, and then to extrapolate this to see to how new models of distribution might work. Skip the next section if you are already familiar with copyright and a basic distribution model.

The layers of (copy)right which exist in any film are testament to the number of distribution platforms that exist. So, for example there are:

• **Theatric rights** – right to screen the film within theatres and public places (cinemas). Traditionally this was from big 35mm film prints, which were quite delicate, wore out easily, and cost an awful lot to make and then transport.
• **Rental video rights** – right to rent a video to the public before the public can buy.
• **DVD/Video Rights** – right to sell a copy of the film (and any extras) to the public.

Then there are the newer platforms/rights, which are still contentiously defined:

• **Video On Demand** – a tricky new-ish kind of right which could be part of TV Broadcast rights, or now part of the new Internet and mobile rights, depending on who you are (BskyB, MSN, Channel 4 …).
• **Broadcast Rights** – these comprise a vast array of existing and potential rights, including the right to broadcast pay per view, free to air, from or to mobile handsets– and arguably now include a separate but related strand of rights ...
• **Internet and mobile rights** – is it a broadcast to a mobile handset, or is it delivery of a file? Nobody knows – it all depends on how you define it, and what shakes down between the big players over the next few years.

In addition there are secondary rights such as merchandise, book rights, right to remake as TV Mini Series, right to release the soundtrack, and any number of other copyrights that exist in any work.

You must be now starting to understand just how difficult it can be to cut the layer cake of rights so that you don't end up with all icing and no filling.

For aeons, the first few of these layered copyrights (theatric, rental video, video retail) has each demanded an exclusive 'release' window on any subsequent rights. This means that back in the 80s, you would go to watch *Grease* or *The Jazz Singer* (my personal favourites as an eight-year-old) and not rent the video for six months afterwards. Then, maybe a year after its cinematic screening, you might be able to buy the video, totaling an 18-month lifecycle from theatre screen to retail store. Cinemas argued that they invested all that money in equipping screens with expensive projectors, Dolby sound, and popcorn, and it was so cumbersome and expensive to have a 35mm print in each screen that it was virtually impossible to show anything else. They just had to be rewarded with some kind of exclusive time period in which to recoup their costs. Presumably this worked quite well for distributors too, because everyone seemed satisfied with a simple analogue world with distinct platforms and exclusive windows for quite some time. This model allowed a film to build a word-of-mouth campaign around itself, meaning that smaller distributors could manage a theatrical release with just a few prints.

However, digital technology interrupted the happy equilibrium of this analogue world. Very recently, digital projectors have been installed in many cinemas (particularly aided by the UK Film Council's new Digital Screen Network – see page 328 – with 250 screens installed), which in theory pushes down expenses for exhibitors and distributors alike (far fewer 35mm prints taking up all that space and expense in production and transport). Those traditional windows of exclusivity have collapsed; there are often only three months between theatric and DVD releases, and rental video now seems to be simultaneous with rental DVD. TV broadcast often falls a couple of months later. Film is also available online and on your mobile phone (bandwidth and connectivity permitting), with a couple of minutes of encoding.

Platforms, windows of exclusivity and copyrights are shifting and blurring, and a new picture is emerging, in which the following feature:

• the lifting of some copyright restrictions by select artists and creators, to allow for the greater flow of information and creativity, particularly via the Internet (Creative Commons);

• the substitution of retail-based per unit models with subscription or rental models (mentioned further below);

• the shift of control from the official gatekeepers (Hollywood Studios, film distributors, established film directors) to an audience of filmmakers familiar with basic editing and filming (so, Jar Jar Binks is edited out of *The Phantom Menace* by countless geeky *Star Wars* fans);

• the layering and carve-up of rights – commercial filmmakers getting savvy about how to maximise control, and therefore income, from their intellectual property rights.

Perhaps the best examples of just how far things have changed are Steven Soderbergh's *Bubble,* and Michael Winterbottom's *The Road to Guantanamo* – both of which were released simultaneously in cinema, on TV, via Video On Demand (VOD) and on DVD. By all accounts and reported figures, the *Mission Impossible* franchise is hardly quaking in its boots. However, that's not the point. In both cases filmmakers and distributors were keen to maximise their control and marketing campaign, rather than having to spread their marketing investment over several months. While this is not entirely revolutionary – Nik Powell and Stephen Woolley were doing this with their release of *Evil Dead* in the late 80s (for more, see later) – it *is* changing the way we audiences and filmmakers look at film again, this time through the prism of 21st digital technology.

So, what are the new models of distribution? Where is it all going to go?

The Internet: blanket licences, peer to peer (P2P)

Christmas is a fine time to slip legislation past those who have already booked their flights to Barbados. On December 20th 2005, the French government had just suspended the passage of its draconian anti-piracy bill (drafted word for word by the mighty giants of Vivendi Universal and French publishers), following a last-minute proposed amendment by a (conservative) coalition MP to include an 'optional blanket licence agreement'. The amendment proposed a 7-12 euro monthly subscription, which allows users in France unlimited access to film, music and other copyright material. And yes, they do propose paying the artists (they are obliged to under EU Copyright Directive), although just how has yet to be worked out.

This is a neat introduction to Cory Doctorow, award-winning science fiction writer and outgoing European spokesperson for the Electronic Frontier Foundation (which really does seem to be 'defending freedom in the digital world', as it claims on its website at **www.eff.org**). Cory Doctorow believes that the best way to bolster creative spirit, grapple with interruptive technology that makes life quicker, cheaper and easier, and ensure some kind of remuneration for artists is for artists/copyright-owners to issue a blanket licence that could be collected by ISPs or paid directly by the public. Income is divvied up pro-rata among creative contributors (although anyone who's worked in the music industry, and specifically with black box income, knows just how difficult this can be). One potential problem is that this might not support the smaller and independent creators, whose work is less well known and who have lobby groups less powerful than the likes of Vivendi, or the Hollywood studios.

Using the music industry in the US as an example, Doctorow points out that it's simply nuts. If the Recording Industry Association of America (RIAA) were forced to pursue individual instead of class actions against offending file sharers, one in 50 US lawsuits would be the US music industry taking legal action against P2P (peer to peer) users. Ultimately the courts would not sanction this kind of abuse of process, bringing together defendants who have never met or communicated with each other prior to litigation. This is a waste of everyone's time and money (except the lawyers') because P2P is here to stay. It makes films and music more accessible, faster, and cheaper for end consumers.

A collective licence would give us the right to share files, however acquired. It wouldn't give others the right to download them, unless they too had paid for it. It would work great for P2P, which is a network operating much like the neural brain network, where discrete nodes pass information along to each other – rather than, say, the heart, which pumps blood in one direction to different parts of the body.

As a P2P user, if you're accused of infringing, you can show your licence to absolve yourself (or ISPs will pay all their users' fees in order to get the commercial advantage of being able to advertise that they are a source whereby all the music can be had in with the price of your DSL line). Enforcement against non-licence-takers can be pursued under the current system. Going back to Doctorow's music industry example: if only half of only the

American file-sharing population were to opt-in to a $5 per month file-sharing license fee, it would double the music-industry's profit. It's pure, evergreen profit: no breakage, distribution fees, or network charges. And presumably this model can be reworked to apply to films too.

DVD: rental, retail, Video On Demand – saving the independent filmmaker?

For a while, back in the early noughties, DVD was the fastest-selling format of all time. In rental, retail or promotional it was the hot ticket. Retail alone, its sales increased 75 per cent between 2002 and 2003, and 40 per cent between 2003 and 2004. It's only now that the curve has turned, flattening out year on year 2004/5 at an estimated £2.5 billion retail market in the UK. Yes, that's £2.5 billion, which is three times the size of the £800 million UK cinema attendance market in 2005, and more than four times the size of the £450 million UK rental DVD market for the same period. So pretty substantial – which is presumably why former Internet whizz kid Ernesto Schmitt (Peoplesound) launched Silverscreen. Silverscreen was retail store dedicated to film entertainment and special interest DVD. Note key words 'dedicated' and 'specialist', which tell a story of frustrated film buyers shopping in high street music stores, searching through badly categorised sections for films priced out of the reach of most pockets.

Silverscreen was part of a retail DVD trend which offered 'price value' in three ways to its main consumer market (25 to 45 year-olds): the value of home viewing (nobody else coughing, no babysitter fee, no deadline); ownership for an average of £7 (all those DVD extras and no late return penalties); and collectors' value ("see my 'character' displayed on my shelves").

In theory, TIVO and Sky+ boxes should be a threat to retail DVD, but Schmitt reports that research suggests otherwise. While it seems that during a first year of recording programmes via one of these new methods, a consumer's DVD retail consumption falls by 20 per cent, early indicators are that they resume their normal DVD spending patterns. This must have been a relief to Silverscreen, with its nationwide stores opening on an almost daily basis. Sadly, Silverscreen is no more.

Schmitt suggested that Video On Demand (VOD) might more of an eventual threat to retail DVD. Yet given the three value indicators of retail DVD outlined above, he felt that retail still had distinct advantages, as VOD fails to address the collectors' value – and to a certain extent the ownership value offered by retail DVD. He also estimated that broadband limitations would restrict commercial roll-out of VOD for some time yet, particularly as more consumers turn to high-definition formats to show on their 50-inch digital TV screens (each high-definition file is 25 Gig, as opposed to standard DVD which is 4 Gig). For now at least, Schmitt argues that consumers see VOD as a replacement for rental but not retail DVD.

Still, with regards to VOD's future, there is no denying that the big Internet players are in for the long game. Internet giants Google and Yahoo! are expected to unveil aggressive moves to offer video download services, both advertiser-funded and via subscription. BSkyB and Microsoft will be developing a service offering VOD downloads via the latter's Windows Media Centre software. Intriguingly, though, it is indie DVD rental service, LOVEFiLM (see page 328) that has launched the first consumer VOD service in the UK, retailing films at £2.99 per download – deliberately priced to match the local video store.

At 40 minutes to download, it's probably quicker than a roundtrip for most. Their system, Digital Rights Management, uses a Microsoft package to allow the user to retain a copy on their hard disc for seven days.

The interesting thing for you as filmmakers is that LOVEFiLM is also scoring quite highly with short films, which download more quickly. And it's entirely feasible that in the very near future, VOD providers will be offering a VOD service to new young undistributed filmmakers who, in return for attending VOD offices to monitor encoding plus a small fee, will be able to make their film available online for download by anybody in the world (subject either to payment or to password access – so you can actually tell whether Sundance Film Festival has viewed your film or not). Of course, this is already happening on free sites like MySpace, but there could be revenue in it for the future. Definitely a space to watch, for filmmakers ...

There are also those filmmakers who have managed to get their film directly to the consumer through sale of a DVD via their own websites, such as Ashvin Kumar with his Oscar-nominated short film *Little Terrorist*. As a general rule, if you have the infrastructure to start doing this, then indeed it is a wonderful thing – much like a band building up a fanbase through touring its local pubs and clubs. But sooner or later you're going to need help, because very few people who make films really like doing the distribution part – the skillset required is totally different from that needed to make one. Besides, you probably want to make more films, rather than pack DVDs and do deals with local newspapers for special offers!

Beyond DVD, VOD, more platforms and formats: personal portable entertainment

Sony Playstation tells me that the company has moved "beyond gaming". I am seated on a red foam chair in the basement of Playstation HQ in Golden Square. Stephane Hareau, PSP Senior Brand Manager Europe, Africa, Middle East, Australia & NZ Sony Computer Entertainment Europe (that's the full title Sony likes to have quoted) says that the new PSP is "personal portable entertainment"; it is a new platform, and UMD (the dinky 2-inch discs that go inside) are the new format. PSP is about film, it's about music, it's about entertainment. Certainly Sony is committed to supporting the new platform and format (stung perhaps by accusations of a repeat of Minidisc, which consumers bought in the 90s and then couldn't buy any music for). Their 2005 Christmas marketing push meant that 800,000 PSPs were sold in the 19 weeks to mid-January 2006. 50 Cent also sold 30,000 units of his latest musical offering as UMD. It all bodes well for a stylish iconic product, sleek and black, and 20cm of fun that appeals to the 24 to 35 year-old male as well as the 18 to 24 demographic (as Sony admits, its skew is 80 per cent male purchasers; given that the 12 to 18 gaming group makes up only 15 per cent of the population, there is reason enough to move beyond gaming).

At the moment, feature films and product can only be played or viewed from the UMD. But in July of 2007, Sony announced a deal with BSkyB that will see users able to download movies and football to watch on the devices. It's a service that will be available to users by January 2008. They can already do this with short films and music videos. Hareau wants to demonstrate this to me, so takes me outside to the Golden Square street, beyond Playstation HQ's large glass doors. It's freezing. Inside the (warm) Playstation lobby are lots of gaming pods, and one little ball for the PSP. This small sphere is a mini-server with wireless access; it allows Hareau to download a new game, in Japanese, to play as we stand outside. We gaze forlornly at the animated fluorescent animals jumping around his PSP screen, speaking squeaky Japanese. Clicking away, he says, "Imagine that this is your film trailer, and it's behind a poster in the cinema. Someone walks by with a Sony Playstation in their pocket; it will download automatically to the PSP." He's right. The PSP could be what brings gadget blokes to independent film. The picture quality is amazing. There is something peculiarly appealing about having a whole entertainment centre in your pocket.

Other players in this field include iRiver (Apple's portable video device), Epson, and Archos – none of which quite yet have the punch of the PSP.

There are no new models – just people responding quite predictably to new technology like the Internet

Many in the film industry believe that there are no new models for distribution – just new technologies (like the Internet, or UMD, or DVD), which cause consumers to behave quite predictably.

Stephen Woolley may well be one of these people. He has just directed his first feature, *Stoned*, produced numerous films (*Absolute Beginners*, *The Crying Game*), and spent ten years as a distributor at Palace Pictures with Nik Powell (Palace was responsible for releasing cult 80s gems like *Diva*, *Erasurehead*, *Evil Dead*, and *Paris Texas*). Prior to that Woolley also owned and programmed the Scala cinema in King's Cross, which programmed an average of 80 films per month. As a professional in the industry, he has experienced every sector.

Woolley argues that there are fundamentals in film which do not change. We may think that we are living in a brave new world of alternative distribution models, but already there has been a simultaneous theatric and video release: over 20 years ago *Evil Dead* was released in cinemas and on video, largely because exhibitors didn't believe that video could threaten cinemagoing.

Woolley maintains that repertory cinemas and arthouse films will always rely on press coverage and critical review for their success. And, he says, the Internet is simply another way of reaching a niche community, a film audience who will generate the buzz.

Woolley's former partner, Nik Powell, seems to share similar views. He is currently the Head of the National Film and Television School, training a new generation of filmmakers, and feels that nothing and everything has changed since his day of producing *Mona Lisa*, *The Crying Game*, and *Fever Pitch*, and distributing with Palace Pictures. Films are made by people for people. There is nothing new in that, and there are certain fundamental principles to follow in order to successfully distribute a film. He sent these to me, written on a napkin via Cath Le Couteur of Shooting People (see below). Here they are, as I received them:

- **Press and critics** – treat 'em right! Nik would have cars take important journalists to private screenings; he would personally call them afterwards, and engage in debate with them if they didn't like the film. He says it is essential to treat them with respect.
- **Media buyers** – any distributor should always talk to the people who buy ads, and whose job it is to know about new platforms, new formats and ways of getting in front of your audience.
- **Right audiences in the right cinemas** – it seems obvious, but choose the right cinemas for your audience (and the principle extends to any other platform). The wrong cinema

just won't be attended by your audience. The same goes for different distribution platforms: DVD and VOD, are all just ways of allowing an audience to see your film. So finding an arts VOD channel (like LOVEFiLM ... ?) is the prime way of getting an arts audience to view an arts film. Likewise, releasing an arts movie on a non-art platform (see my comment about above PSP) may not be the best idea.

• **Connections** – exploit 'em all!

I did insist on meeting Nik – notes on a napkin being a bit rock & roll for me. As I sat with him in Soho House on a cold evening in early January, I realised that ours was simply one of three meetings that night, each one with a different film person. His whole career has been premised on knowing who to call, and when.

But in the flesh, I got the impression that Powell's film world has changed. Back then, Powell only had to call a few major broadsheet journalists to ensure coverage. Now, with the Net and multichannel environment, there is a proliferation of influential online journalists, from Kulturescape to the Collective, all of whom need servicing; all of whom have their own agenda and niche audience. There are more filmmakers than ever before. Thanks to a digital revolution, anyone can buy a camera and film their friends. The Internet allows these same people to post their videos online, and (provided there is enough bandwidth and they know how to encode) to act as their own distributors. So things have changed ... but not the fundamentals.

Which takes us to Shooting People's very own founder, Cath Le Couteur (see page 351). Le Couteur feels that the consumer could be the ultimate 'super distributor'. She uses the cult online website, Weed (**www.weedshare.com**) to demonstrate that very very soon, independent filmmakers will be building their own networks, enabling them to share things they love, like film clips, great songs, and hard-won event information, with their friends. On Weed, you can buy files and then share the ones you like, receiving a commission when someone else buys the file because of your introduction. In other words an individual acts as superdistributor for their own and their friends' films, passing online recommendations, film clips, even actual features and being rewarded (somehow) by the owner of the film to do so. Le Couteur feels that the film industry should not learn the hard way (as the music industry has had to) in terms of getting to grips with digital technologies and copyright issues.

This is the way people have been behaving in the real world for aeons, mirrored online. And is why we – collectively, Shooting People and me – want to get back to the sense that this is how the best information is passed and respected among communities, whether in the real or virtual world.

Penny Nagle started life in the music industry as an IP lawyer, and migrated across to film and new media as a producer and distributor when she realised that lawyers get paid to implement other people's ideas – not their own. She developed the distribution of alternative content into digital cinema in the UK, with artists such as Stereophonics, Kylie, U2, Led Zeppelin and Robbie Williams, through her company, igig.tv. She has set up a joint venture, Shooting People Films, with the UK's largest online film community, Shooting People. Penny's favourite films are *Medea* and *Some Like It Hot*, though Fatih Akin's *Head On* is a close recent contender.

Alternative distribution markets for film and video content

This section includes companies operating across a variety of new distribution channels, from mobile phones and online viewing to downloads which can be watched on TV sets. Many filmmakers, especially those with a short film completed, now upload their work so that audiences can view it online. Of course there are many benefits to submitting your film to one of the user upload sites. Perhaps it's an older short film which has finished its festival run, and you want to make it more readily available? Or it might be your no-budget feature for which you don't have distribution, or a sales agent working on your behalf. The online and VOD landscape is changing on a daily basis, and companies like Revver and CinemaNow are finding ways of getting revenue back to filmmakers. However, it goes without saying that whether you have a short or a feature, you should consider your strategy carefully. Making your film available online *will* have an effect on other exhibition possibilities – be that screening in festivals or selling your film to a DVD distributor. Choose the site carefully and be sure to go through the submission guidelines with a 'fine tooth-comb'. Be very wary of uploading anything without fully understanding the website's submission regulations: many sites demand an irrevocable, non-exclusive royalty-free licence. By submitting your film, you are often contractually agreeing to their conditions.

Atom Films

225 Bush Street, Ste 1200, San Francisco, CA 94104, USA
tel ++1 415 503 2400 *fax* ++1 415 503 2401
email info@atomfilms.com
website www.atomfilms.com
Acquisitions Karla Milosevich

International distributor and sales company for short films of less than 30 minutes, and any genre. Tapes and screening announcements may be sent for the attention of the Acquisitions team.

BitTorrent

201 Mission Street, Suite 900, San Francisco, CA 94105, USA
email bizdev@bittorrent.com
website www.bittorrent.com

BitTorrent is file-sharing software which allows users to download bits of a large file (such as a feature film) from many sources, thereby making it faster and more reliable. While the software has widely been used by sites for pirate or illegal distribution of new feature films, BitTorrent itself has partnerships with studios to deliver back-catalogue movies through its VOD service online. Site currently has pay and free movie downloads.

Blink

The Old Caretakers House, JL Brierley Mill, Quay Street, Huddersfield, West Yorkshire HD1 6QT
tel (01484) 301805
email lisa@blinkmedia.org
website www.blinkmedia.org

Blink designs large-scale mobile-phone media projects, including the UK's first SMS poetry initiative with *The Guardian* in 2000 and City Poems, a transnational media project in Leeds and Antwerp. The company uses SMS, Bluetooth or RFID in designing projects for creative expression. Commissions award-winning short film for both cinema and mobile phones which enable filmmakers to explore a new platform and consider the impact of mobile technology on the future of film and distribution (see the entry for their Pcoket Shorts initiative on page 74). Blink also programmes and delivers We Love Technology – a showcase event which promotes Yorkshire as a hub of creative technology.

Brightcove

Brightcove, Inc, One Cambridge Center, Cambridge, MA 02142, USA
tel + 1 617 500 4947 *fax* + 1 617 395 8352
website www.brightcove.com

Brightcove offers a new model in Internet TV service by allowing content owners – both independent producers and major broadcast networks — to reach audiences directly through the Internet. The company helps content providers to publish their own channels, helps to sell the ads that generate revenue, and also links up with web publishers to place the syndicated video programming.

CinemaNow

c/o Acquisitions Department, 4553 Glencoe Avenue, Suite 200, Marina Del Rey, CA 90292, USA
email acquisitions@cinemanow.com
website www.cinemanow.com
CEO Curt Mavis

One of the first sites to offer a 'download to own' movie service. The site has Hollywood movies and TV shows, which are available on a download-to-own basis (electronic sell-through) and can be viewed on up to 3 devices. Also has a more standard VOD rental service allowing the customer 24 hours to view the film once they start watching it.

Filmmakers wishing to submit content to the site for consideration may send a VHS or DVD screener to the address above. Please include full contact information (screeners will not be returned). The Acquisitions department will try to respond within 2 weeks.

Current TV

118 King Street, San Francisco, CA 94107, USA
tel ++1 415 995 8200 ++ 1 415 995 8201
email info@current.tv
website www.current.tv

Digital channel in US and UK which screens short factual work on current events, news, music, politics. Viewers may submit own work and the channel also commissions pieces.

Digital Screen Network

email def.administrator@ukfilmcouncil.org.uk
website www.ukfilmcouncil.org.uk

The UK Film Council's initiative to broaden the range of what is available on UK cinema screens. It is a 'virtual network' of 240 screens, located in 200 cinemas spread around the UK. Every full-time licensed cinema was eligible to apply to have a state-of-the-art digital projector and play-out machines installed; in return for the UK Film Council's financial contribution towards the equipment, network cinemas will devote a set percentage of playing time to specialised programming. Full details of the scheme can be found on the UK Film Council's website, including a comprehensive explanation of what is considered 'specialised' cinema for the purpose of this scheme.

– see page 52.

FilmFlex

email hello@filmflexmovies.com
website www.filmflexmovies.co.uk

Virgin Media's on demand film service with over 500 titles to download.

Future Shorts

34-35 Berwick Street, London W1F 8RP
tel 020-7734 3883
email info@futureshorts.com
website www.futureshorts.com

Organisation which hosts monthly short film event screenings in clubs and cinemas in the UK and across Europe.

Independent Film Channel Media Lab

website www.medialab.ifc.com

Launched in September 1994, the Independent Film Channel (IFC) presents independent films through its American TV channel. Also hosts an online user-upload site, Media Lab, which allows filmmakers to share their short films with users and other filmmakers who can rate and discuss them. Also see page 76.

IndieFlix

911 East Pike Street, Suite 310, Seattle, WA 98122, USA
tel ++1 206 323 3549 *fax* ++1 206 860 8406
email info@indieflix.com
website www.indieflix.com

New US-based online distributor that helps filmmakers sell their films directly to the viewer. Viewers select titles through an online catalogue, with films ranging in price from $2.95 to $9.95. Selected films are then burned onto a customised DVD and mailed directly to the customer. Filmmakers receive one-third off the top of the sales price.

LOVEFiLM

Head Office, 9-11 North End Road,
London W14 8ST
email marketing@lovefilm.com, pr@lovefilm.com
website www.lovefilm.com
CEO Simon Calver

After a 2006 merger with competitor ScreenSelect, LOVEFiLM is now the biggest online rental outlet and online distributor in Europe. Customers can either rent DVDs, which are delivered through the post, or download titles through a VOD service. Library includes more than 70,000 titles and the company has shown a strong interest in delivering short films as well, with shorts available for 50p a download through VOD.

LOVEFiLM is also developing a LOVEFiLM PRO service through which trailers, films and EPKs can be delivered from a producer to a potential buyer or to a cinema.

movieflix.com

Code 7 Entertainment, Inc, PO Box 480764,
Los Angeles, CA 90048, USA
tel ++ 1 323 939 6260 *fax* ++ 1 323 939 6472
website www.movieflix.com

Movie site with a large selection of DIY and B Movie titles. Filmmakers may submit films via website.

Movielink

website www.movielink.com

A joint project of MGM Studios, Paramount Pictures, Sony Pictures Entertainment, Universal Studios and

Warner Bros Studios, Movielink allows US-based users to download first-run studio movies as well as classics from these studios' back catalogues. Not yet available to users outside the USA.

Nintendo DS

website wwww.nintendo.com/systemsds

Nintendo's hand-held gaming console, which can be used to download video content.

Sony PSP

website www.sonypspinfo.com

This is a format to watch in the next few years. Users can convert movie files to view on Sony PSP players, using the Pocket Video MakerTM PSP Edition. In July 2007, Sony launched a partnership with BSkyB in a deal that enables British users of the PSP games console to download films and TV programmes.

Exhibition

FILM PROGRAMMING FOR CINEMAS

Jason Wood – film programmer for City Screen, the UK's largest independent chain of cinemas – explains the relationship between distributors and exhibitors.

I've been a cinema programmer for eight years, joining City Screen Limited after previously working in the film industry as a documentary filmmaker, a distributor, and the editor of a film website. Outside of City Screen I've also been involved in curating specialist seasons, including an extensive Mexican cinema season at the *bfi* Southbank (formerly NFT) and a recent Road Movies event at the Riverside Studios in Hammersmith. Of all the various roles I've performed (and I still have fingers in a few film pies through my writing and a small production company), programming is the one for which I retain the greatest drive and passion.

In terms of providing an insight into the activities of the film programmer and an overview of the machinations of specialised exhibition in the UK, it is worth beginning with a précis of City Screen and Picturehouse cinemas. At some point every distributor, filmmaker and producer will come to us to show their wares, so an understanding of who we are and how we work may prove beneficial for those of you reading this who may either wish to pursue a career in programming – and be warned, it's not the most financially lucrative vocation – or who have a film that you would like to see played in one of our venues.

City Screen was formed in 1989 to challenge the multiplex model and to provide cinemas in city-centre locations that serve their local communities. Independent (or 'arthouse') films have always been core to the company, but each cinema is programmed in response to its local audience, and most have some mainstream blockbusters in the mix. The company's first cinema was the Phoenix in Oxford, bought as a going concern when the previous owners retired. In 1992 the company opened its first custom-built cinema, Clapham Picturehouse, and since then we've grown steadily through a mixture of new builds and acquisitions, particularly in university cities such as Oxford, Cambridge, London, Brighton and York. In addition to running our own venues we also offer a bespoke film booking service; our range of customers includes owner-operator cinemas, council-run venues and charitable trusts. These programming contracts include Curzon (Chelsea, Soho, Mayfair, Renoir, Richmond), The Everyman, The Electric, The Phoenix East Finchley, Tyneside Newcastle, The Rex Berkhampstead, and The Dukes Lancaster, and have cemented our pole position in the UK's independent exhibitor sector.

Each Picturehouse cinema is programmed in response to its local audience, and in many cases this defines the type of films that we play. For example, results have proved that our site in London's Stratford East is less likely to sustain an audience for specialised titles, whereas in Brighton the audience have proved our faith in the independent. Indeed, central to the company philosophy is maintaining the individuality of each cinema. Our cinemas are also marked by being a central and much-loved feature of their local communities, with the buildings easily distinguished by their unique style, ranging from historic venues like The Belmont, Aberdeen with extravagant facades and ornate interiors to contemporary award-winning, state-of-the-art venues like the FACT Centre, Liverpool.

City Screen frequently works alongside organisations such as Future Shorts, the British Film Institute and the Independent Cinema Office to encourage the work of new talent, and is dedicated to supporting a dynamic film culture, working closely with directors, producers and distributors to help the broadest possible range of films reach the widest possible audience. To do this, we provide printed programmes and electronic communications which inform, educate and encourage planned entertainment to our large membership and email database. We also run other active membership schemes involving diverse groups such as young mothers, teenagers and the elderly, and generate and partner on educational work and courses which develop an appreciation and understanding of film. A year-round programme of events, festivals and Q&A screenings aims to grow the film-going audience and brings filmmakers into contact with the general public.

Setting release dates to optimise a film's potential

We take a very active part in how and when a distributor releases a film in the UK. We are able to do this because of our cultural and commercial position within the marketplace. The major studios – Sony, Warners, Fox, BVI, Universal and Paramount – all from time to time release 'independent' pictures, invariably produced through their boutique US divisions, and will also work with us in harmony on titles such as *Little Miss Sunshine*, *All the Real Girls*, *The Science of Sleep* and *Hallam Foe*. However, these releases are not at the core of their business and they have less time to dedicate to them. They will consult us on a release date for the UK, the consultation revolving primarily around when the screens that we programme are free, but they may be restricted by the fact that many of the decisions are pending what happens regarding US distribution. In many instances – though not all – these films will not have been acquired exclusively for the UK but are part of the expansive US release slate that is passed on to the UK sales team to release. The tradition of the Studios working with 'independent' or *auteur* talent has persisted throughout the history of film, gaining prominence in the advent of the success of *Easy Rider* in 1969. In this respect the landscape has not changed that much.

The independent distributors in the UK are invariably able to operate with more freedom, and it is with these 'indies' that our main consultation takes place. The prominent companies dealing with specialised product in the UK include Artificial Eye (foreign-language, *auteur* titles), ICA Projects (documentaries, cinema from the Far East and Iran), Icon (Mel Gibson pics and crossover titles such as *La vie en rose*), Metrodome (quality arthouse pictures that have made a splash at festivals such as Water), Optimum (currently the largest and most successful of the indies, particularly after *Pan's Labyrinth*), Pathé (French and long-time distributor of *Almodovar* through its production arm), Revolver (right across the board from docs to *Jindabyne* and *Tell No One*), Soda (who scored a huge hit with *Into Great Silence*) and Verve (a prime investor in UK breakthrough filmmakers such as Amma Asante, Saul Dibb and Andrea Arnold). These companies, and there are many others (too many in fact), acquire films at script, post-production and at completed stage – most often at international festivals such as Cannes, Berlin and Venice. Often our opinion on a title may be sought, as was recently the case with *The Lives of Others*.

Generally, discussions between a film's distributor and an exhibitor are lengthy. Firstly, after the film has been viewed, a release date has to be decided upon. This is done by studying the EDI calendar, an industry document produced on a weekly basis that reveals what distributor is releasing what film and on which date. Factors that may influence the release date, excluding release in other territories, include:

- absence of similar title (ideally two foreign-language films would not be released on the same date);
- availability of core audience (i.e. a film appealing to students will go in term time);
- study of date from previous year, when a similar title has performed successfully;
- analysis of whether the film will benefit from recent screening exposure at one of the major UK festivals;
- availability of talent to support the marketing and press.

Once a date is mutually agreed – the film's producer and, though invariably less so, its filmmaker may be consulted on this – the EDI calendar will be informed and the really hard part begins: preparing the film for release (production of prints, BBFC certification, etc.), and marketing the film through posters, trailers, print and online promotions and through our own aforementioned channels of communication, to ensure that audiences will actually come and see it. It is important here to add that, as programmers, the question of whether a title will appeal to the sites we are responsible for is paramount. This calls for objectivity and the withdrawing of our own personal tastes from the equation.

Challenges in releasing specialised films in the UK

One of the biggest problems facing exhibitors and distributors in the UK is a vast increase in the number of available titles. A few years ago there would have been perhaps three films released each week, and maybe only two specialised titles a month. Now, on any given week there can be up to ten films released; three or four a week may be specialised. There simply aren't the screens to support this amount of product.

Previously, there would be a handful of companies in the UK looking to acquire 'niche' product; now they are legion. Added to this is the fact that although the majority of our discussions are between the distributor and UK rights holder of a particular title, we are now increasingly being approached directly by filmmakers and producers. We receive between five and ten unsolicited screeners per week, the vast majority of which are films by British filmmakers that have failed to find distribution. If the quality peeks through – as it did recently on *The Gigolos* – we will try and find screen space, despite obvious concerns about a lack of resources to market to an audience, and a lack of track record in actually getting the film on screen.

Another problem facing the UK exhibition sector is the steady increase in trading terms. In many instances, pre-agreed terms exist between the cinema exhibitor and the distributor. These terms, which may vary not only from cinema to cinema, but also from screen to screen depending on seating capacity, stipulate how much of the box office the distributor will receive for a title on release after a seven-day exhibition period. A certain percentage is guaranteed, but the distributor has the chance to exceed this percentage if the film is particularly successful. On this model, the distributor's share can reach as much as 50 per cent of the film's take.

However, distributors are constantly negotiating increased terms or uplifts. These often take the form of a flat percentage, regardless of the film's success or otherwise. This means that UK exhibitors have to commit in advance to paying as much as 60 per cent for the first week of a film, with terms decreasing by 5 per cent during each of the film's successive release weeks before levelling out to another, but lower, flat percentage, most often after the first three weeks. These terms can be crippling and put extra onus on the sale of concessions to ensure that exhibitors remain profitable. Though mainly consigned to blockbuster titles, where a flat 60 per cent is regularly demanded, this is also beginning to spread to independent releases, where minimums are becoming commonplace. The trading model is slightly different for repertory titles and those that are no longer first run; here a percentage of 25 per cent is usually agreed, accompanied by a minimum guarantee (which can vary from £60 to £120), to ensure that print transport costs are covered.

Judging a film's box-office potential

In addition to whether or not we feel a film may be suitable for a particular cinema's local audience, and dependent on whether or not we have screen space available to play it (unlike the multiplexes, the number of screens at our sites varies between one and three – or five at the Ritzy), there are other factors that come into play when we decide which films to programme. To judge a film's potential, we would consider:

- overseas box-office performance and critical response;
- word of mouth;
- marketing spend and quality of the campaign;
- concurrencies/number of prints;
- whether the film has UK Film Council financial support;
- access to talent for Q&As;
- the track record of director/writer/actor;
- awards;
- analysis of cinema's history with similar types of films;
- and, as many films open in London's West End first (which will account for something like 70 per cent of a film's box office), we'd often consider the opening box office in London before committing our regional sites.

The final factor above is also important in judging for how long we may screen the film in our regional sites. If the London results and critical reaction is good, it will play for seven days on maximum performances per day. If the London figures are weak, the duration of the booking will be reduced and performance times adjusted accordingly. This is all part of contract negotiatons with a distributor, the vast majority of which take place on a Monday – the holdover day in the industry when, following an anaylsis of the weekend's box-office figures, timings and titles for the coming Friday are agreed between the exhibitor and the distributor. These timings and titles will then be circulated to local press agencies. In general terms, the day of word-of-mouth 'hits' gradually gathering steam are slowly disappearing; the contemporary economic landscape dictates that if the opening three-day figures are poor, then the film will not generally play for longer than a week.

Exhibition variety and the Digital Screen Network

This is where the brave new digital world is seen as offering solutions. Perhaps the main function of the UK Film Council's Digital Screen Network (DSN) is to improve access to specialised film across the UK. In return for the UK Film Council's financial contribution towards digital equipment, network cinemas (over 200 of them, with more than 240 screens) are expected to devote a set percentage of playing time to specialised programming.

Although London's West End and some other metropolitan areas offer a genuine variety of films, the choice for many audiences outside these areas remains limited. One of the principal reasons for this restriction has to do with the delivery medium. As with all films, distribution of specialised product is currently via 35mm celluloid prints. Such prints are expensive to produce and are a major cost consideration for a distributor when they plan a specialised film's release. Furthermore, exhibitors are often inhibited in their ability to build an audience for specialised film because of this restriction on prints. 35mm cinema, therefore, does not encourage the wider distribution and exhibition of specialised product. Digital technology offers a potential solution to this economic constraint, as the cost of producing digital copies can offer significant cost savings on striking 35mm prints. The Digital Screen Network will facilitate enough of a 'critical mass' in terms of exhibition outlets to ensure that specialised product can reach a much wider audience. But the jury is out as to whether the audience numbers for arthouse and independent film will retain the attention of the multiplex operators who dominate more than 70 per cent of the marketplace.

One of the key advantages that digital technology theoretically affords is increased programming flexibility. Exhibitors (in partnership with distributors) will be able to respond more effectively to the appetites of their audience, because the usual need to return the print or move it on to another cinema will no longer exist. After a digital film's initial run, it can be left stored on the cinema server so that it can be screened again – either replicating earlier success (the film may have had to 'finish' due to other booking commitments), or enjoying new screening times that may match the film to the audience most likely to see it. For example, older audiences flocked at matinee screening times to see *Into Great Silence* and *Casablanca* when re-issued (again here, digital policy has a positive impact on restorations and the preservation of classics). Having the films on the cinema servers allowed us to simply keep showing these titles for periods of up to seven or eight weeks by requesting an open-ended key from the distributor when the film was initially booked.

It is hoped that this will also translate to films that may not have met with huge audiences on initial release. Despite 5-star reviews, films such as *Keane*, *Old Joy* and British titles *Red Road* and *London To Brighton* did not get the large audiences they deserved. Storing the films on our server should allow us to bring the films back in repertory or 'Did you Miss?' slots. This policy may go some way to giving the films and filmmakers in question increased exposure, but will also perform the function – and this can be extended to the screening of archive classic titles such as *Los Olvidados* and *Distant Voices, Still Lives* – of educating future generations of filmgoers as to the wider world of film culture.

However, a current failing of the digital medium is that it seems to still stack the odds in favour of the larger distributors, who are simply using the mechanism to release blockbusters in even greater numbers. Of even greater concern is their general reluctance to contemplate losing shows from their high-profile titles, which may be digital or playing in the largest screen at Picturehouse cinemas – invariably our digital screen – for specialised digital screenings or events. Another wonder of digital is that it genuinely has the potential to re-think what we can exhibit, leading to satellite link-up Q&A events with directors such as Danny Boyle, Quentin Tarantino and Ken Loach, and newer initiatives such as live performances from the Metropolitan Opera. Should we eradicate the aforementioned obstacles and the prohibitive terms demanded by some distributors for one-off digital screenings, then the digital future could be really very bright indeed.

Jason Wood is a senior programmer at Picturehouse Cinemas, the UK's leading independent exhibitor with a unique circuit specialising in screening arthouse, foreign-language and quality mainstream films. Alongside his work as a film programmer, Wood is also a film writer whose publications include *100 American Independent Films* (2004), *Nick Broomfield: Documenting Icons* (2005), *The Faber Book of Mexican Cinema* (2006), *Talking Movies: Contemporary World Filmmakers in Interview* (2007), and *100 Road Movies*. His writing has also appeared in *Enthusiasm*, *Vertigo*, *Time Out*, *Sight & Sound* and *The Guardian*.

NOTES FROM A CULTURAL EXHIBITOR

Mark Cosgrove

What differentiates an independent cinema like Watershed Media Centre from a high-street multiplex?

The fundamental distinction is that we treat cinema as a cultural artefact and not primarily a commercial one. We want to engage in the breadth and depth of possibilities of cinema, open up debate and expose audiences to the range and variety of cinema culture.

What qualities do you look for when you select the programme?

Over the years, and particularly most recently, I have believed that audiences want to engage in debate and discussion about this complex world we live in. Film is a brilliant way into those discussions and discovering more about the world. I look for cinema which can engage audiences in that way. It doesn't mean it all has to be earnest and dry; pPleasure and enjoyment are important as well.

What role does press play in the success or failure of an independent film in the UK? Can an indie film overcome bad, or indifferent, coverage?

The press has an important role, and I think the critical debate is getting better. The traditonal press is responding to the plurality of voices offered by the Internet and podcasting, so it is becoming more open and flexible in its repsonses. However, some smaller films do get lost and it is important to work on other methods to make sure they get out to an audience.

What are the challenges of running an independent/arts cinema in the UK right now?

Well – mostly, we have lots of ideas and never enough finance to deliver them. It's also true that cinema is viewed as a commercial rather than a cultural activity, so funding is a challenge.

How different will the exhibition sector in the UK look in ten years time? People have been prophesising its death for the last two decades, but it seems to be resistant ...

The key thing about exhibition is still the social element – the communal sharing of a cinematic experience. I think there is something special that people value about that. I'm an optimist ... Digital is making people specialist consumers, and independent cinemas are ideally placed to cater for those specialisms. Digital projection offers more flexibility and potential, which is great. It has the chance of radicalising the exhibition sector by offering more variety. In ten years time there will be more independents and therefore a more dynamic UK film culture.

Mark Cosgrove is Head of Programme at Watershed Media Centre in Bristol.

INDEPENDENT CINEMAS

The Aldeburgh Cinema
51 High Street, Aldeburgh, Suffolk IP15 5AU
tel (01728) 452996 *fax* (01728) 454026
email web@aldeburghcinema.co.uk
website www.aldeburghcinema.co.uk

Part of the UK Film Council Digital Screen Network.
1 Screen: 252

Arnofini
Arnolfini, 16 Narrow Quay, Bristol BS1 4QA
tel 0117-917 2320 *fax* 0117-917 2303
website www.arnolfini.org.uk
Film Coordinator Paul Pargas

Arts centre and gallery which shows arthouse, artist film and video, short films and independent cinema. Programmed jointly by Paul Pargas and Soda Pictures. Short films may be sent to Film Coordinator for consideration.
1 Screen: 231
Formats: 35mm, 16mm and digital formats

Barn Theatre
Dartington Hall, Dartington Totnes, Devon TQ9 6DE
tel (01803) 847072 *fax* (01803) 847087
email colin@dartingtonarts.org.uk
website www.dartingtonarts.org.uk
Programmer Colin Orr

Screens primarily arthouse and independent; also short films regularly as regional showcases and as part of festivals – contact Programmer to submit short films. Part of Digital Screen Network. No private hires.
1 Screen: 185 seats
Formats: all formats once Digital Screen Network is active

Brewery Arts Centre
Kendal Brewery Cinema, 122A Highgate, Kendal, Cumbria LA9 4HE
tel (01539) 722833 *fax* (01539) 730257
email tim.young@breweryarts.co.uk
website www.breweryarts.co.uk
Cinema Manager Tim Young

The cinemas of Kendal Arts Centre are South Lakelands' leading independent commercial and arts exhibitor. Cinema occasionally programmes short film material – primarily in touring packages. Short films may be sent to Tim Young for consideration. Part of the Digital Screen Network.
3 Screens: 250, 189, 115
Formats: all

Broadway Media Centre
Broad Street, Nottingham NG1 3AL
tel 0115-952 6600 (administration) *fax* 0115-952 6622
email info@broadway.org.uk
website www.broadway.org.uk

Arts, world and quality mainstream programming.
2 Screens: 337, 130

The Capitol Horsham
North Street, Horsham RH12 1RG
tel (01403) 750220 (box office)
tel (01403) 756095 (administration)
fax (01403) 756092
email contact@thecapitolhorsham.com
website www.thecapitolhorsham.com
2 Screens: 177, 89 (and Theatre, 423)

Chapter
Market Road, Canton, Cardiff CF5 1QE
tel 029-2031 1050 (Administration)
tel 029-2030 4400 (Box Office)
email enquiry@chapter.org
website www.chapter.org

Vibrant Media Centre with 3 theatres, 2 cinemas, a gallery, studios, 2 bars, a cafe, and 60 cultural workspaces.

Cinema 3
University of Kent, Canterbury CT2 7NB
tel (01227) 823491 *fax* (01227) 827444
email cinema3@kent.ac.uk
website www.gulbenkiantheatre.co.uk
Cinema Manager and Film Programmer David Joyce

Cinema 3 is located in University of Kent's Gulbenkian Theatre. They screen a range of arthouse, independent and second-run titles.
1 Screen: 290
Formats: 35mm, DVD, video

Clapham Picturehouse
76 Venn Street, London SW4 0AT
tel 0871-704 2055 *fax* 020-7498 0490
email clapham@picturehouses.co.uk
website www.picturehouses.co.uk

Programmed by: City Screen
The 4 auditoria accommodate 198, 152, 133 and 115 people, screening an eclectic programming mix of arthouse and quality mainstream films. The venue also includes an art exhibition area, fortnightly film quiz, Saturday Morning Kids Club, Thursday Parents and Babies Club and Sunday repertory double bills.

The Cube
4 Princess Row, Kingsdown, Bristol BS2 8NQ
email cubeadmin@microplex.cubecinema.com
website www.microplex.cubecinema.com
Film Programmer Liam Kirby

The Cube is a Microplex Cinema and venue in Central Bristol, run by voluntary artists/workers/ enthusiasts. It presents cinema, music (acoustic, electric and half-amped), and a host of other events in a vibrant programme, including: "Burlesque in full 3D, discussions, secret and overt community groups, the full-on ARTS, and 'Live Social Cinema' - that's cocktails served in front of flickering 35mm, ushers that tear tickets and smile, ice-creams, live scores to new movies, music and visuals, talks on how to build your own house, and BYO films". Also available for private hire.

1 Screen: 105

Formats: 35mm, 16,mm Super 8, Video and Digital

Curzon Chelsea

206 Kings Road, London SW3 5XP
tel (08708) 506 926
website www.curzoncinemas.com

Programmed by: City Screen

Chelsea cinema has one impressive screen of 713 seats, a fully licensed bar, and is situated in one of the most fashionable locations in London.

Curzon Mayfair

38 Curzon Street, London W1J 7TY
tel 0870-756 4621
website www.curzoncinemas.com

Programmed by: City Screen

Renowned for staging glamorous film premieres and other gala events, using Screen 1 with 319 seats – including 2 royal boxes. Screen 2 is an intimate 83-seater room. Both bar and auditoria are fully licensed.

Curzon Soho

99 Shaftesbury Avenue, London W1D 5DY
tel 0870-756 4620
website www.curzoncinemas.com

Programmed by: City Screen

Curzon Soho has 3 floors with reception areas and 3 auditoria of 249, 133 and 120 seats. The bar and auditoria are fully licensed.

David Lean Cinema – Croydon Clocktower

Croydon Clockltower – David Lean Cinema
tel 020-8253 1037 *fax* 020-8253 1032
email jonathan.kennedy@croydon.gov.uk
website www.croydon.gov.uk/clocktower
*Arts Programme Manage*r Jonathan Kennedy

Named after Croydon-born filmmaker David Lean. Primarily screens arthouse, second run, documentary, independent, children and family films. Has semi-regular short film screenings. Tapes and screening invitations may be sent to Arts Programme Manager. Also programmed by City Screen.

1 Screen: 68

Formats: all, and part of Digital Screen Network

Everyman Cinema Club

Holly Bush Vale, Hampstead Village,
Hampstead NW3 6TX
tel 020-7435-1600
email danielb@everymancinema.com
website www.everymancinema.com

Beautiful independent cinema in North London which programmes quality international titles and has a loyal local audience.

2 Screens

Formats: 35mm, DVD, Digibeta, TV; can connect to laptop for powerpoint slides. Everyman is part of the Digital Screen Network

Private hires may contact Daniel.

FACT (Foundation for Art and Creative Technology)

88 Wood Street, Liverpool L1 4DQ
tel 0151-707 4450
email info@fact.co.uk
website www.fact.co.uk

The FACT Centre has 2 gallery spaces which present newly commissioned work by internationally significant artists working in film, video and new media. There are also presentations of work highlighting new developments in video and new media art, alongside key historical works. A Picturehouse within FACT hosts the very best cinema from around the world in its 3 state-of-the-art screens. The Box presents film and video programmes as well as acting as a transmission studio for FACT's online TV channel and hosting regular sound and music events. The Media Lounge is a curated space for online projects and is where you can catch new artists' projects on DVD.

Filmhouse

88 Lothian Road, Edinburgh EH3 9BZ
tel 0131-228 6382 *fax* 0131-229 6482
email admin@filmhousecinema.com
website www.filmhousecinema.com
Programmer Rod White *Manager* James McKenzie
Hires Jenny Leask

One of the most respected independent cinemas in the UK; screens a range of arthouse, indie, international and festival work and hosts the Edinburgh Film Festival each August. Cinema One screens the latest international releases and presents special events with guests talking about their work in different branches of the film industry. Cinemas Two and Three include a wider range of material from the history of world cinema and from 16mm to video and digital video work.

3 Screens: 280, 97, 72

Formats: all, part of Digital Screen Network

Forum Cinema

Lings Forum Leisure Centre, Wellingborough Road, Northampton NN3 8JR
tel (01604) 837300 *fax* (01604) 786393
email forumcinema@northampton.gov.uk
website www.forumcinema.org.uk
Film Programmer Angela Reed

Independent and arthouse cinema with 1 screen. Occasionally screens short films, which are in touring package; these are primarily programmed through the Independent Cinema Office.

Gate Picturehouse

87 Notting Hill Gate, London,W11 3JZ
tel 0871-704 2058 *fax* 020-7792 2684
email gate@picturehouses.co.uk
website www.picturehouses.co.uk

Programmed by: City Screen

The Gate has a digital sound system and a variety of projection formats.

Genesis Cinema

93-95 Mile End Road, London E1 4UJ
tel 020-7780 2000
email info@genesis-cinema.co.uk
website www.genesis-cinema.co.uk

A local independent with 5 auditoria with seating capacity ranging from 100-566 seats. The cinema is equipped with DTS Surround Sound.

Greenwich Picturehouse

180 Greenwich High Road, Greenwich, London SE10 8NN
tel 0871-704 2059
email greenwich@picturehouses.co.uk
website www.picturehouses.co.uk

Programmed by: City Screen

The Greenwich Picturehouse opened in September 2005 as a luxury 4-screen cinema with a panoramic first-floor bar and a basement Screening Room that offers a mix of films, music and comedy events. The main auditoria accommodate 174, 129, 115 and 74 people.

Hull Screen

University of Lincoln, George Street, Hull HU1 3BW
email www.hullcc.gov.uk
House Manager Mark Ogden

Hull Screen cinema can be found in the University of Lincoln building. Cinema hosts a short films festival in October.

ICA Cinema

The Mall, London SW1Y 5AH
tel 020-7930 3647
website www.ica.org.uk
Director of Cinema Mark Adams *Programmer* David Cox *Co-ordinator* Tejinder Jouhal

The Institute of Contemporary Arts programmes unique and culturally significant arthouse, documentary and world cinema titles, as well as hosting festivals and special screenings. Specialises in independent, art and experimental film, work by new filmmakers, British and international documentary, shorts, music film and video and digital work. Selects shorts via established shorts initiatives such as Halloween and Uncut, and welcomes filmmakers submitting their work. ICA has 2 screens with 35mm, 16mm (C2 only), Digi/Beta SP, NTSC or PAL, Mini DV, DVD, and is part of the Digital Screen Network.

King's Lynn Arts Centre

Tuesday Market Place, Kings Lynn, Norfolk PE30 1JW
tel (01553) 765565 *fax* (01553) 762141

Light House Media Centre

The Chubb Buildings, Fryer Street, Wolverhampton WV1 1HT
tel (01902) 716044 *fax* (01902) 717143
email info@light-house.co.uk
website www.light-house.co.uk
Film Programmer Emma Bangham

Independent arthouse cinema and media centre in Wolverhampton with 2 cinema auditoria, a media training centre, art gallery, media reference library, and conference and production facilities. Runs a programme of screenings, training courses, exhibitions, festivals, events and media projects (also see page 218). Short films may be sent for consideration to the Programmer.

2 Screens: 242, 67

Formats: 35 mm, 16 mm, DVD, Beta SP. Also part of Digital Screen Network

Macrobert

University of Stirling, Stirling FK9 4LA
tel (01786) 4666666 *fax* (01786) 466600
email macrobert-arts@stir.ac.uk
website www.macrobert.org
Programmer Amy McCallum

Arts centre which programmes a range of both commercial and independent cinema. Short films may be sent to the programmer for consideration. Private hire enquiries should contact programmer.

2 Screens: 468, 135

Formats: 35mm, Beta SP, and is part of the Digital Screen Network

Metro Derby

Green Lane, Derby DE1 1SA
tel (01332) 340170 (Office)
tel (01332) 347765 (Bookings) *fax* (01332) 205499
email metro.cinema@virgin.net
website www.metrocinema.org.uk
Director Andrew McIntyre

Independent cinema which screens primarily arthouse and indie. Has a yearly short film competition and screens short films regularly as part of one-off special events and screenings. Films may be sent to Director by post.

1 Screen: 126

National Film Theatre

Belvedere Road, South Bank, Waterloo, London SE1 8XT

tel 020-7928 3535 (Switchboard)
tel 020-7928 3232 (Box Office)
website www.bfi.org.uk/whatson/southbank
Director, National Centre for the Moving Image Eddie Berg, *NFT Programmer* Geoff Andrew

Run by the British Film Institute, the *bfi* Southbank (formerly the National Film Theatre) is the oldest cinemateque in the world and a highly respected arts cinema. Hosts the London Film Festival each October and the London Lesbian and Gay Film Festival in April; also screens a changing programme of world, arthouse and selected first-run titles, as well as hosting regular retrospectives, events and talks. Hire enquiries should ring 020-7815 1308. The 2007 redevelopment of the *bfi*'s South Bank site into a National Centre for the Moving Image has included improvements to NFT 1, 2 and 3; a brand new informal walk-in studio cinema; contemporary films, television, talks and educational events; a gallery space; a study area; and a Filmstore.

Also see page 345.

3 Screens: 450, 162, 134 plus Studio, Gallery and Mediatheque

Formats: all

National Media Museum

National Media Museum, Bradford BD1 1NQ
tel (01274) 203345 *fax* (01274) 203387
email bill.lawrence@national mediamuseum.org.uk
website www.nationalmediamuseum.org.uk/FilmAndIMAX

Includes the Pictureville and Cubby Broccoli cinemas which screen primarily independent, arthouse and world cinema. Pictureville hosts Bradford Animation Festival, Bradford Film Festival and and Bite the Mango Film Festival and the Fantastic Films Weekend. The venue prides itself in projecting films as they are meant to be seen, in a range of historical and modern formats from Cinerama 3-strip to digital. Information on the films screened, and many others, can be found in its online database. A further large-screen IMAX cinema offers a daily programme of exciting large-format films in 2-D and 3-D.

3 Screens: 300, 100 and 275

Formats: IMAX, 70mm, 35mm, 16mm, BETA plus DVD

For bookings: contact ben.eagle@nationalmediamuseum.org.uk.

Pavilion Cinema Galashiels

Market Street, Galashiels TD1 3AF
tel (01896) 752767
email info@pavilioncinema.co.uk
website www.pavilioncinema.co.uk
Programmer Eddie Poole

Independent cinema which screens primarily studio and commercial. Part of Digital Screen Network.

4 Screens: 300, 172, 147, 56

Phoenix Arts

21 Upper Brown Street, Leicester LE1 5TE
tel 0116-224 7700 (Administration)
website www.pheonix.org.uk
Head of Cinema Alan Smith

Plymouth Arts Centre

38 Looe Street, Plymouth PL4 0EB
tel (01752) 206114 *fax* (01752) 206118
email anna@plymouthac.org.uk
website www.plymouthac.org.uk
Programmer Anna Navas

Programmes primarily independent, foreign-language, arthouse and crossover work. Hire enquiries should contact Anna Navas or Andy Jex. Filmmakers may also submit short films for screening consideration directly to the programmer. Part of the Digital Screen Network.

1 Screen: 86

Formats: 35mm, 16mm, DVD and VHS

Prince Charles Cinema

7 Leicester Place, Leicester Square, London W1
tel 020-7437 7003
website www.princecharlescinema.com
General Manager Gregory Lynn

Long-running rep and second-run cinema off Leicester Square. The venue often hosts independent previews and premieres, and is the home cinema of Frightfest.

1 Screen: 474

Formats: 35mm and most video and DVD formats

Renoir Cinema

The Brunswick, London WC1N 1AW
tel (08708) 506 927
website www.curzoncinemas.com

Renoir Cinema is located in the newly reopened and rejuvenated Brunswick Centre in the heart of Bloomsbury in Central London. Both screens hold 251 seats, and there is a fully licensed bar.

Richmond Filmhouse

Water Lane, Richmond TW9 1TJ
tel (08708) 506 928
website www.curzoncinemas.com

Programmed by: City Screen

Richmond Filmhouse is newly decorated with beautiful polished marble. A 1-screen 144-seat cinema with a licensed bar.

Rio

Kingsland High Street, London E8 2PB
tel 020-7254 6677
email mail@riocinema.org.uk
website www.riocinema.ndirect.co.uk

The Rio is a local cinema with a strong tradition of screening independent and arthouse film. For private hires, please call Gemma on 020-7241 9419.

1 Screen: 402

Ritzy Picturehouse

Brixton Oval, Coldharbour Lane, London SW2 1JG
tel 0871-704 2065

email ritzy@picturehouses.co.uk
website www.picturehouses.co.uk

Programmed by: City Screen

The 5 auditoria accommodate 352, 179, 118, 108 and 84 people.

Screen on Baker Street

96-98 Baker Street, London W1U 6TJ
tel 020-7935 2772
website www.screencinemas.co.uk/bakerstreet

Programmed by: Mainline

2 Screens: Screen 1 has 85 seating capacity; Screen 2 has 77 seating capacity. Venue has 35m Projection and Dolby Stereo Sound

Screen on the Green

83 Upper Street, Islington, London N1 0NP
tel 020-7226 3520
website www.screencinemas.co.uk/green

Programmed by: Mainline

Single screen with 300 seating Capacity. The venue has 35m Projection, 16m Projection and a new digital sound system.

Screen on the Hill

203 Haverstock Hill, London NW3 4QG
tel 020-7435 3366
website www.screencinemas.co.uk/hill

Programmed by: Mainline

Single screen with 254 seating capacity. The venue has 35m Projection, VHS Video, DVD, BETA SP, DIGI BETA, MINI DISC, and Dolby DTS Sound.

Showroom

The Workstation, Paternoster Row, Sheffield S1 2BX
tel 0114-275 7727 (box office) *tel* 0114-276 3534 (admin) *fax* 0114-249 3204
email info@showroom.org.uk
website www.showroom.org.uk
Chief Executive Ian Wild, *Programmer* Andrew McIntyre

Quality independent cinema screening the best in world cinema, independent and quality mainstream. Hosts Showcomotion Young People's Film Festival. Also presents Digital Space, a showcase for creative digital work, and is part of Digital Screen Network. Films may be sent to Programmer Andrew McIntyre andrew.mcintyre@showroom.org.uk, Kathy Loizou for Showcomotion kathy@showroom.org.uk and Jamie Wyld for Digital Space jamie.wyld@showroom.org.uk

4 Screens: 282, 178, 110, 83

Formats: 35mm, 16mm, HD Digital (DSN), all video formats by appointment

For bookings: info@showroom.org.uk

Stamford Arts Centre

27 St Mary's Street, Stamford, Lincs PE9 2DL
tel (01780) 763203
(Box Office) *tel* (01780) 480846 (Administration)
fax (01780) 766690
website www.stamfordartscentre.com
Arts Centre Manager David Popple

Stoke on Trent Theatre

College Road, Stoke on Trent ST4 2DH
tel (01782) 411188

1 Screen: 212

Stratford East Picturehouse

Salway Road, London E15 1BX
tel 0871-704 2066
email stratfordeast@picturehouses.co.uk
website www.picturehouses.co.uk

Programmed by: City Screen

4 auditoria with fixed raked seating accommodate 260, 242, 215 and 151 people.

Strode Theatre

Strode College, Church Road, Street, Somerset BA16 OAB
tel (01458) 446529 *fax* (01458) 446529
email info@strodetheatre.co.uk
website www.strodetheatre.co.uk
Programmed by: Independent Cinema Office

Part-time cinema combined with theatre and educational programmes. Screens primarily arthouse and some mainstream. Short films occassionally programmed by IOC.

1 Screen: 379

Formats: 35mm (can hire in others)

For bookings contact Liz Leyshon at info@strodetheatre.co.uk.

The Screen Oxted

7 Station Road West, Oxted RH8 9EE
tel (01883) 722 288
website www.screencinemas.co.uk/oxted

Programmed by: Mainline

Single screen with 440 seating capacity. The venue has 35m Projection and Dolby DTS Sound.

The Screen Reigate

Bancroft Road, Reigate, Surrey RH2 7RP
tel (01737) 223213
website www.screencinemas.co.uk/reigate

Programmed by: Mainline

2 screens: Screen 1 has 139 seating capacity; Screen 2 has 142 seating capacity. The venue has 35m Projection and Dolby Stereo.

The Screen Walton

85-89 High Street, Walton on Thames KT12 1DN
tel (01932) 252825
website www.screencinemas.co.uk/walton

Programmed by: Mainline

2 screens: Screen 1 has 200 seating capacity; Screen 2 has 140 seating capacity. The venue has 35m Projection and Dolby Stereo.

The Screen Winchester

Southgate Street, Winchester SO23 9EG
tel (01962) 877 007
website www.screencinemas.co.uk/winchester

Programmed by: Mainline

2 screens: Screen 1 has 214 seating capacity; Screen 2 has 170 seating capacity. The venue has 35m Projection, 16m Projection, Dolby Stereo and VHS Video, plus a Small Stage in Screen 1.

Tyneside Cinema

Old Town hall, West Street, Gateshead, NE8 1HE (until mid-2008), then 10 Pilgrim Street, Newcastle upon Tyne NE1 6QG
tel 0191-232 8289 *fax* 0191-221 0535
email boxoffice@tynecine.org
website www.tynecine.org
Programmed by: City Screen/Tyneside Cinema

Arthouse, independent and quality mainstream programming as well as film events and special seasons. Hosts Northern Lights Film Festival and AV Festival. UNdergoing major refurbishment during 2007.

Until 2008, 1 Screen: 148, then **3 Screens:** 268, 101, 30

Formats: 35mm, DVD, VHS, Digibeta, part of Digital Screen Network

For bookings contact Joss Spires at joss@tynecine.org.

Watershed

1 Canons Road, Harbourside, Bristol BS1 5TX
tel 0117-927 6444 *fax* 0117-921 3958
email info@watershed.co.uk
website www.watershed.co.uk
Head of Programme Mark Cosgrove

Media Centre in the heart of Bristol programmes arthouse and independent cinema daily, and offers a number of media courses and events in its gallery space and cinemas. Also hosts Encounters short film and animation festival (see page 259).

3 Screens: 200, 100, 50 seats

Formats: 35mm, 16mm, Beta SP, DVD, VHS, SVHS, slide projection and data projections

For bookings: Robert Walker or Karen Welboum at events@watershed.co.uk.

CINEMA CHAINS

The largest of the chains listed below – Odeon, Vue, Cineworld, National Amusements and Empire Cinema – now account for most of the cinema business in the UK.

Apollo Cinemas

Houston House, 12 Sceptre Court, Sceptre Point, Preston, Lancs PR5 6AW
tel (01772) 323544 *fax* (01772) 323545
website www.apollocinemas.co.uk

13 sites across the UK.

Artificial Eye

14 King Street, London WC2E 8HN
tel 020-7420 5353 *fax* 020-7240 5252
website www.artificial-eye.com

Company has 2 sites in London: Renoir and the Chelsea. Primarily screens own distributed work.

Cineworld Cinemas

Paver Road Studios, Paver Road, Chiswick
tel 020-8987 5880
website www.cineworld.co.uk
Head of Film Buying Andrew Turner

Cine-UK run Cineworld – a fast-growing chain of independent cinemas with 78 sites comprising 812 screens. Cineworld screens primarily show studio and mainstream features, but also have a number of initiatives to screen arthouse and independent work; part of the Digital Screen Network.

City Screen (Picturehouses)

Hardy House, 16-18 Beak Street, London W1F 9RD
tel 020-7734 4342 *fax* 020-7734 4027
email enquiries@picturehouses.co.uk
website www.picturehouses.co.uk

Independent chain of cinemas which place an emphasis on arthouse, world and independent programming. The chain includes 20 Picturehouse sites:

Arts Centre, Haverhill
Broadway, Letchworth
Campus West Theatre, Welwyn Garden City
Chelsea Cinema, London
Cinema City, Norwich
Curzon Mayfair, London
Curzon Soho, London
David Lean, Croydon
Dukes, Lancaster
Electric, Notting Hill
Electric, Birmingham
Everyman, Hampstead
Filmhouse, Richmond
Grosvenor, Glasgow
Hyde Park Leeds
Maltings Cinema, Ely
Phoenix, East Finchley
Renoir, London
Richmond Filmhouse, Surrey
Ritz Cinema, Belper
Rex, Berkhamsted
Tyneside Cinema, Newcastle
Soho, Charlotte St and Covent Garden Hotels

Hollywood Screen Entertainment

Anglia Square, Norwich, Norfolk
tel (01603) 621903
website www.hollywoodcinemas.net
Managing Director Trevor Wicks

Small chain with 6 sites.

Independent Cinema Office – see Independent Cinema Office.

The ICO works in partnership with a range of film exhibitors, helping them to create unique, commercially viable programmes that appeal to the most diverse possible range of local audiences. ICO clients range from the internationally acclaimed Watershed Media Centre in Bristol to local authority-run cinemas such as Hull Screen, to arts centres such as Street's hugely successful Strode Theatre (which boasts one of the highest screen averages in the UK). Current ICO clients include:

- Bristol Arnolfini
- Bristol Watershed
- Caernarfon Galeri
- Consett Empire Theatre
- Dartington Barn
- Derby Metro Cinema
- Hull Hull Screen
- Leicester Phoenix Arts
- London Broadway Theatre (Catford)
- Ludlow Assembly Rooms
- Luton Hat Factory
- Northampton Forum Cinema
- Nottingham Broadway
- Saffron Walden Saffron Screen
- Sheffield Showroom
- Stanley Lamplight Arts Centre
- Stockton-on-Tees Arc
- Stoke Stoke Film Theatre
- Street Strode Theatre

Mainline Pictures (Screen Cinemas)

37 Museum Street, London WC1A 1LP
tel 020-7242 5523 *fax* 020-7430 0170
website www.screencinemas.co.uk
Company Director Tony Bloom, *Programmer of Cinemas* Roger Austin

Independent chain; owns and operates 7 cinemas including: The Screens on Baker Street, Islington Green and Haverstock Hill in London, and Screens at Oxted, Winchester, Walton and Reigate. The Mainline cinema programmes include the best in independent, arthouse and quality mainstream. Hosts regular events and film premieres and masterclass events at London locations. Private hire enquiries should contact Tony Bloom. Cinemas can screen most formats and are part of the Digital Screen Network.

Merlin Cinemas

Savoy Cinema, Causeway Head, Penzance, Cornwall
tel (01736) 363330
email www.merlincinema.co.uk

Small chain with 5 cinemas in Cornwall.

Movie House Cinemas

Yorkgate Leisure Complex, 100-150 York Street, Belfast BT15 1WA
tel 028-9074 1404
(Accounts) *tel* (028) 9035 5717 (Marketing)
fax (028) 9074 1360

Chain with 5 sites in Belfast. Available for corporate and private hire.

National Amusements (Showcase Cinemas)

Showcase Cinema, Redfield Way, Lenton, Nottingham NG27 2UW
tel 0115-986 2508
email ukcs@national-amusements.com
website www.showcasecinemas.co.uk
Film Buyer Marie Bunker

One of the UK's major chains with 19 sites.

Northern Morris Associated Cinemas

Eller Howe Farm, Lindale, Grange Over Sands, Cumbria LA11 6NA
tel (015395) 35735
website www.nm-cinemas.co.uk

6-site chain with cinemas in Leeds and the Lake District. Most sites are in historical buildings.

Odeon Cinemas

54 Whitcomb Street, London WC2H 7DN
tel 020-7321 6240 *fax* 020-7321 0357
website www.odeon.co.uk
PA and Booking Assistant to the Film Booking Director Wendy Scott

The UK's largest cinema chain with 100 cinemas, also one of the oldest cinema chains in the world. Sales account for nearly a third of all cinema-going.

Reeltime Cinemas

Carlton, Westgate-on-Sea Kent, St Mildred's Road CT8 8RE
tel (01843) 834290
website www.reeltime-cinemas.co.uk

9 cinemas based in the South of England.

Vue Entertainment

10 Chiswick Parke, 566 Chiswick High Road, London W4 5XS
tel 020-8396 0100
email filmbuying@vuemail.com
website www.myvue.com

One of the UK's 5 major chains with 58 sites. Email address is for screening invitations only.

Resources

FILMMAKERS' ORGANISATIONS, SOCIETIES, GUILDS

These organisations offer services which will be useful to a range of professionals working in the film industry. Even if you are not eligible for membership, some of the members' organisations and guilds offer resources such as courses, practioner/members' contacts, and in some cases, professional advice on their area of expertise.

Academy of Motion Picture Arts & Sciences (AMPAS)

8949 Wilshire Boulevard, Beverley Hills, CA 90211, USA
tel + 1 310 247 3000 *fax* + 1 310 859 9619
website www.oscars.org

The Academy of Motion Picture Arts and Sciences is a professional honorary organisation of more than 6000 motion picture professionals, and was founded to advance the art and science of motion pictures. Their biggest activity each year is staging the Oscars (also see page 288).

Advertising Association

7th Floor North, Artillery House,
11-19 Artillery Row, London SW1P 1RT
tel 020-7340 1100 *fax* 020-7222 1504
email aa@adassoc.org.uk
website www.adassoc.org.uk

A non-profit-making organisation that represents the mutual interests of the diverse UK advertising industry.

Advertising Standards Authority (ASA)

Mid City Place, 71 High Holbern,
London WC1V 6QT
tel 020-7492 2222 *fax* 020-7242 3696
email enquiries@asa.org.uk
website www.asa.org.uk

Independent body set up by the advertising industry to police the rules laid down in the advertising codes to protect consumers, and to create a level playing field for advertisers. The Committee of Advertising (CAP) offers free pre-publication advice on non-broadcast advertising material. Contact the CAP Copy Advice Team on 020-7492 2100.

AIM (All Industry Marketing for Cinema)

47 Dean Street, London W1D 5BE
tel 020-7478 4370 *fax* 020-7287 6695
email info@allindustrymarketing.com
website www.allindustrymarketing.com

Established in 1984, AIM is the All Industry Marketing coalition set up to promote cinemagoing throughout the UK. The membership is made up of organisations across the film industry.

American Film Institute

2021 North Western Avenue, Los Angeles, CA 90027, USA
tel ++ 323-856-7600 *fax* ++ 323-467-4578
website www.afi.com

AFI is a national institute providing quality screen education for new filmmakers, and celebrating excellence in the art of film, television and digital media. Core activities include: maintaining a catalogue of American feature films; running the AFI Film Festival (see page 266); and the AFI Conservatory (see page 23).

ASIFA

email president@asifa.net
website www.asifa.net
President Nourreddin Zarrinkelk

International alliance of organisations and festivals specialising in or promoting animation. Site has a calendar of international animation festivals (though not exhaustive) with deadlines and dates.

Association for Media Education in Scotland (AMES)

c/o Des Murphy, 24 Burnett Place,
Aberdeen AB24 4QD
tel (01224) 277113
email d@murphy47.freeserve.co.uk

The Association aims to advance all aspects of media education in the Scottish Educational system at all levels, and to encourage media education throughout the public at large. The Association publishes the *Media Education Journal* (ISSN 0268-1941) twice a year.

Association of Independent Film Exhibitors

c/o Cornerhouse, 70 Oxford Street,
Manchester M1 5NH
tel 0161-200 1510
Contact Dave Moutrey

Authors' Licensing & Collecting Society

Marlborough Court, 14-18 Holborn,
London EC1N 2LE
tel 020-7395 0600 *fax* 020-7395 0660
email alcs@alcs.co.uk
website www.alcs.co.uk

ALCS represents the interests of all UK writers, and aims to ensure that writers are fairly compensated for any works that are copied, broadcast or recorded.

BARB (Broadcasters' Audience Research Board)

2nd Floor, 18 Dering Street, London W1R 9AF
tel 020-7529 5531 *fax* 020-7529 5530
email enquiries@barb.co.uk
website www.barb.co.uk

Provides in-home TV viewing measurement for the UK.

The British Council

Film Department, 10 Spring Gardens,
London SW1A 2BN
tel 020-7389 3051 *fax* 020-7389 3175
email film.department@britishcouncil.org
website www.britfilms.com
Head of Film Department Paul Howson

Founded in 1934, the British Council is the UK's lead organisation for international cultural relations. It has offices in 110 countries and its work covers the arts, education, science, English teaching, sport and governance and human rights. Although funded by a government grant, it operates at arms'-length from government.

The aim of its Film Department is to broaden and build international audiences for new work from Britain, and to encourage mutually beneficial partnerships with individuals and institutions in other countries. Its activities include: organising prints and guests for international film events (festivals, seminars, workshops, masterclasses, showcases); acting as a clearing-house for UK shorts seeking international festival screenings; providing a features preview service for programmers from major international festivals; providing grants to enable British filmmakers to attend international events; organising British stands at key market events, such as the Berlinale and Clermont-Ferrand; and running the website **www.britfilms.com**, which provides a wide range of information on the UK film industry. The Council works with a wide range of organisations including the *bfi*, The Script Factory, Documentary Filmmakers Group, UK Film Council, and film schools and regional screen agencies. It does not finance film development or production.

British Academy of Film and Television (BAFTA) – see page 287.

Supports, develops and promotes the artforms of the moving image, by identifying and rewarding excellence, inspiring practitioners, and benefiting the public. With an expert industry membership of nearly 6500 individuals globally, BAFTA focuses attention through awards ceremonies on the highest achievements of films, video games and television programmes shown in the UK each year in order to motivate and inspire those who make them, and to educate and develop the taste of those who watch them.

Holds a range monthly events and screenings. Membership ranges from £200 to £300 a year. Full eligibility criteria are available on the website.

British Association of Picture Libraries and Agencies

18 Vine Hill, London EC1R 5DZ
tel 020-7713 1780 *fax* 020-7713 1211
email enquiries@bapla.org.uk
website www.bapla.org

UK trade association for picture libraries with more than 400 members. Website includes a searchable online database of images.

British Board of Film Classification (BBFC)

3 Soho Square, London W1 3HD
tel 020-7440 1570 *fax* 020-7287 0141
email contact_the_bbfc@bbfc.co.uk
website www.bbfc.co.uk

The BBFC classifies films intended for cinema entertainment on behalf of Local Authorities. All cinema films, whether short or feature length, require a classification either from the Local Authority or the BBFC. The BBFC is the statutory body responsible for the classification of videos and DVDs under the terms of the Video Recordings Act 1984. Fees for classification can be found on the website.

British Broadcasting Corporation (BBC)

Television Centre, Wood Lane, London W12 7RJ
tel 020-8743 8000 *fax* 020-8749 7250
website www.bbc.co.uk

BBC commissioning

The BBC has 5 major programming divisions: Radio & Music; Drama; Entertainment & CBBC (Children); Factual & Learning; Sport; and News. If you wish to submit an unsolicited programme idea to one of the divisions, then refer to the details of their commissioning process published on **www.bbc.co.uk/commissioning**.

BBC resources for filmmakers

The BBC also has a website devoted to identifying and developing new talent (**www.bbc.co.uk/talent**). On the website it publishes calls for submissions, and provides details on BBC production schemes, as well as general information about the various media industries in the UK.

Also very useful is its magazine-style website for filmmakers, **www.bbc.co.uk/filmnetwork**; this has a filmmaking guide, a large library of short films, which can be viewed online, and interviews with filmmakers, producers and programmers.

Also see page 133.

British Cinema and Television Veterans

22 Golden Square, London W1F 9AD
tel 020-7287 2976
email bctv.veterans@btopenworld.com

Association for people who have worked in the cinema and television industries for more than 30 years.

British Copyright Council

29-33 Berners Street, London W1T 3AB
tel (01986) 788122 *fax* (01986) 788847
email thesecretary@britishcopyright.org.uk
website www.britishcopyright.org.uk

The BCC is a national advisory body that represents the interests of copyright-owners in the UK. It lobbies the British Government, the European Commission and Parliament, and international bodies such as the World Intellectual Property Organisation on matters of copyright.

British Educational Communications and Technology Agency (BECTA)

Milburn Hill Road, Science Park,
University of Warwick, Coventry CV4 7JJ
tel 024-7641 6994 *fax* 024-7641 1418
email becta@becta.org.uk
website www.becta.org.uk

Promotes the use of communications technolgies in education.

British Federation of Film Societies (BFFS)

Unit 315, The Workstation, 15 Paternoster Row,
Sheffield S1 2BX, UK
tel 0845-603 7278
email info@bffs.org.uk
website www.bffs.org.uk
Administrator Ros Hill

BFFS is a national body which promotes non-theatrical film exhibition and represents the interests of film societies through training and advice, equipment loans, publicity materials and representation with distributors and funding bodies.

British Film Institute

21 Stephen Street, London W1T 1LN
tel 020-7225 1444 *fax* 020-7436 7950
website www.bfi.org.uk
Director Amanda Nevill

World-renowned national body established in 1933. Exists to promote understanding and appreciation of cinema and television, and of Britain's film and television heritage in particular. Core activities include:

• running the the *bfi* Southbank (formerly National Film Theatre), arguably the world's finest cinema, which screens more than 1000 films a year from the broadest international range of new and classic titles (see page 338);
• publishing a series of books on cinema and television, and the monthly film magazine *Sight and Sound* (see page 234);
• maintaining the National Film and TV Archive;
• hosting the London Film Festival and the London Lesbian and Gay Film Festival (see page 261);
• running the *bfi* national library, which has the world's largest collection of materials on film and TV;
• releasing selected films theatrically and on DVD and video;
• promoting media literacy by producing training materials for teachers and hosting confereneces and educational programmes.

British Screen Advisory Council (BSAC)

13 Manette Street, London W1D 4AW
tel 020-7287 1111 *fax* 020-7287 1123
email bsac@bsacouncil.co.uk
website www.bsac.uk.com

Independent agency which identifies key areas of importance to the UK audiovisual industries, and lobbies government for change as necessary. Also hosts events and interviews with major players in the audiovisual industries.

British Video Association (BVA)

167 Great Portland Street, London W1W 5PE
tel 020-7436 0041 *fax* 020-436 0043
email general@bva.org.uk
website www.bva.org.uk

Trade association representing the interests of the home-entertainment sector.

Broadcasting Press Guild

Tiverton, The Ridge, Woking, Surrey GU22 7EQ
tel (01483) 764895 *fax* (01483) 765882
email rl@broadcastingpressguild.org
website www.broadcastingpressguild.org

Association of journalists specialising in written media.

Campaign for Press and Broadcasting Freedom

2nd Floor, 23 Orford Road, Walthamstow,
London E17 9NL
tel 020-8521 5932
email freepress@[NOSPAM]cpbf.org.uk
website www.cpbf.org.uk

Carlton Screen Advertising

12 Golden Square, London W1F 9JE
tel 020-7534 6363 *fax* 020-7534 6464
email enquiries@carltonscreen.com
website www.carltonscreen.com

Central Office of Information (COI)

Hercules Road, London SE1 7DU
tel 020-7928 2345 *fax* 020-7928 5037
website www.coi.gov.uk

Cinema & Television Benevolent Fund (CTBF)

22 Golden Square, London W1F 9AD
tel 020-7437 6567 *fax* 020-7437 7186
email info@ctbf.co.uk
website www.ctbf.co.uk

The CTBF is the British trade charity of the film, cinema and commercial television industries, including cable and satellite. Around 250,000 people work behind the scenes in these industries. The CTBF provides care and financial support to those who have fallen on hard times, from providing support to those struck down with illness to helping struggling young filmmakers break into the industry. All applications for help will be considered from those who have worked, salaried or freelance, for 2 or more years in UK film and TV. Examples of applications might include: struggling to make ends meet on a low salary; illness, accident or redundancy; or students in need of financial help to get through college.

Cinema Advertising Association (CAA)

12 Golden Square, London W1F 9JE
tel 020-7534 6363 *fax* 020-7534 6227
website www.adassoc.org.uk

Cinema Exhibitors Association (CEA)

22 Golden Square, London W1R 3PA
tel 020-7734 9551 *fax* 020-7734 6147
email cea@cinemauk.ftech.co.uk

Trade association representing over 90% of the cinema exhibitors in the UK.

Cinema Theatre Association

44 Harrowdene Gardens, Teddington, Middlesex TW11 0DJ
tel 020-8977 2608
website www.cinema-theatre.org.uk

Commonweath Broadcasting Association

17 Fleet Street, London EC44 1AA
tel 020-7583 5550 *fax* 020-7583 5549
website www.cba.org.uk

Founded in 1945, CBA strives to support and encourage quality broadcasting throughout the Commonwealth, through project development and travel bursary funds for broadcast producers, training and awards programmes.

CBA also provide bursaries for UK and Commonwealth producers to travel for training and conferences. See the website for details of its Programme Development Fund (for programmes intended for UK broadcast). Can support development of the project up to a maximum of £10,000.

Critics' Circle

51 Vartry Road, London N15 6PS
email info@criticscircle.org.uk
website www.criticscircle.org.uk

Critics' Circle is an organisation made up of 300 critics who work in the arts. The film section hosts an awards ceremony each year (see Critics' Circle Film Awards).

Deaf Broadcasting Council

Woodlands Farm, Wiston, Haverfordwest, Permbrokshire SA62 4PJ
fax (01437) 731566
website www.deafbroadcastingcouncil.com
Contact Anthony Kent

A consumer organisation representing deaf, deafened and hard of hearing television viewers.

Defense Press and Broadcasting Advisory Committee

Floor 1 Spine H 21 MOD, Main Building, Whitehall, London SW1A 2HB
tel 020-7218 2206 *fax* 020-7218 5857
email dnotice@hotmail.com
website www.dnotice.org.uk

Department for Culture, Media and Sport (DCMS)

2-4 Cockspur Street, London SW1Y 5DH
tel 020-7211 6200
email enquiries@culture.gov.uk
website www.culture.gov.uk
Minister with Responsibility for Film Shaun Woodward

The DCMS is responsible for Government policy on the arts, sport, the National Lottery, tourism, libraries, museums and galleries, broadcasting, creative industries (including film and music), press freedom and regulation, licensing, gambling and the historic environment.

Department for Education and Skills (DfES)

Sanctuary Buildings, Great Smith Street, London SW1P 3BT
tel 0870-000 2288
email info@dfes.gsi.gov.uk
website www.dfes.gov.uk

Agency responsible for Government policy on education (including provisions for media education), with a remit to "create opportunity and release potential in everyone".

The Directors' and Producers' Rights Society

20-22 Bedford Row, London WC1R 4EB
tel 020-7269 0677 *fax* 020-7269 0676
email info@dprs.org
website www.dprs.org

European Captioning Institute

First Floor, Holborn Tower, 137 High Holborn, London WC1V 6PL

tel 020-7430 5800 *fax* 020-7430 5801
email sales@ecisubtitling.com
website www.ecisubtitling.com

The Feminist Library

5 Westminster Bridge Road, London SE1 7XW
tel 020-7928 7789
email info@feministlibrary.org.uk
website www.feministlibrary.org.uk

Film Archive Forum

c/o British Universities Film & Video Council (BUFVC), 77 Wells Street, London W1T 3QJ
tel 020-7393 1508 *fax* 020-7393 1555
email luke@bufvc.ac.uk
website www.bufvc.ac.uk

Film Distributors' Association (FDA)

22 Golden Square, London W1F 9JW
tel 020-7437 4383 *fax* 020-7734 0912
email info@fda.uk.net
website www.launchingfilms.com
Chief Executive Mark Batey

FDA is the trade association for UK theatrical film distributors. It offers an evolving range of services both to UK film distributors and to the UK's national and regional film journalists. Serves as the principal forum whereby film distributors meet, and offers a voice for distribution to advocate the pivotal role of distributors in the UK's film economy.

FDA provides a comprehensive, up-to-date list of forthcoming film releases, with their release dates, for journalists; it also provides a very useful booklet detailing how the UK distribution sector works. These can be accessed via the website.

Membership is open to any operating theatrical film distribution company in the UK. Current membership accounts for approximately 97% of UK cinemagoing.

Film Education

2nd Floor, 21-22 Poland Street, London W1F 8QQ
tel 020-7851 9450 *fax* 020-7439 3218
email postbox@filmeducation.org
website www.filmeducation.org

The Film Office

The Old Town Hall, Patriot Square, Bethnall Green, London E2 9NP
tel 020-8980 8771 *fax* 020-8981 2272
email info@thefilmoffice.fsnet.co.uk
website www.filmoffice.co.uk

First Film Foundation

9 Bourlet Close, London W1P 7PJ
tel 020-7580 2111 *fax* 020-7580 2116
email info@firstfilm.demon.co.uk
website www.firstfilm.co.uk

FOCAL International Ltd (Federation of Commercial Audio-Visual Libraries)

Pentax House, South Hill Avenue, South Harrow, Middlesex HA2 0DU
tel 020-8423 5853 *fax* 020-8933 4826
email info@focalint.org
website www.focalint.org
Commercial Manager Anne Johnson *General Manager* Julie Lewis

A not-for-profit professional trade association providing: footage and content sales of clips, archive footage, stock shots, stills, audio; footage researchers with professional skills to find and deliver the material within budget, and with rights cleared; footage consultants; facilities to store, restore or deliver the material on any format; and media lawyers specialising in media and copyright issues. Focal also offers a free Footage Finder, which will email your request to all libraries in one hit. Holds an annual awards ceremony to recognise the best uses of footage in anything from historic boradcast programmes to commercials and films.

Gaelic Media Service – Seirbheis nam Meadhanan Gaidhlig

Taigh Shiphoirt, Seaforth Road, Stornoway, Isle of Lewis HS1 2SD
tel (01851) 705550 *fax* (01851) 706432
email fios@gms.org.uk
website www.gms.org.uk

The Gaelic Media Service has a mandate to fund programme production and development, training, audience research and related activities, and also to seek a broadcast licence with the ultimate aim of the establishment of a dedicated Gaelic television channel. Offers grant-aid funding to television and radio projects that have a UK commissioning broadcaster on board, and which match GMS's funding criteria. Grant-aid funding is available to independent producers or the in-house production arm of broadcasters. Funding levels vary; contact GMS for further details.

German Films Service – UK Office

Top Floor, 113-117 Charing Cross Road, London W2H 0DT
tel 020-7437 2047 *fax* 020-7439 2947
email ordonez@german-films.de
website www.german-films.de

Grierson Memorial Trust

77 Wells Street, London W1T 3QJ
tel 020-7580 7526
email awards@griersontrust.org
website www.griersontrust.org

Hollywood Foreign Press Association

646 N Robertson Blvd, West Hollywood, CA 90069, USA
tel ++1 310 657-1731 *fax* ++1 310 657-5576
email info@hfpa.org
website www.hfpa.org

The Hospital

24 Endell Street, London WC2H 9HQ
tel 020-7170 9110 *fax* 020-7170 9102

email studio@thehospital.co.uk
website www.thehospital.co.uk/studio

The Hospital was the vision of Paul G Allen – co-founder of Microsoft – and Dave Stewart, musician and producer. It opened in 2003 and houses a Private Members' Club, a Gallery, TV & Music Recording Studios, and Origin Bar & Dining Room. The long-term aim is to create a club, and a wider international community of mutually supportive artists and media professionals. Also see page 185.

IAC (Institute of Amateur Cinematographers)

Global House, 1 Ashley Avenue, Epsom, Surrey KT18 5AD
tel (01372) 822 812
email admin@theiac.org.uk
website www.theiac.org.uk
Chairman Linda Gough

The IAC supports amateur cinematographers and moviemakers. It has around 300 affiliated clubs, as well as a couple of thousand individual members. Arranged in 7 regions, with many clubs as well as individual members in all parts of the country. These regions and clubs usually have their own annual events, often including a movie competition and festival where non-commercial films are shown to their best advantage. The IAC also organises an International Movie Festival every year, which moves around the UK. Membership is £36-£50 and all are eligible.

Imperial War Museum Film and Video Archive

Lambeth Road, London SE1 6HZ
tel 020-7416 5291/2 *fax* 020-7416 529
email filmcommercial@iwm.org.uk
website www.iwmcollections.org.uk
Head of Production Office Paul Sargent

Film archive; also preserves and makes accessible official film records from the beginning of the 20th century. Can supply images in any standard or format. For details on the screening room, see page 247.

Incorporated Society of British Advertisers (ISBA)

Langham House, 1b Portland Place, London W1B 1PN
tel 020-7291 9020 *fax* 020 7291 9030
email info@isba.org.uk
website www.isba.org.uk

Independent Cinema Office – see page 298.

Institute of Practitioners in Advertising (IPA)

44 Belgrave Square, London SW1X 8QS
tel 020-7253 7020 *fax* 020-7245 9904
email info@ipa.co.uk
website http://www.ipa.co.uk

Intellect

Russell Square House, 10-12 Russell Square, London WC1B 5EE
tel 020-7331 2000 *fax* 020-7331 2040
website http://www.intellectuk.org

International Association of Broadcasting Manufacturers (IABM)

PO Box 2264, Reading, Berkshire RG31 6WA
tel 0118-941 8620 *fax* 0118-941 8630
email info@theiabm.org
website www.theiabm.org

International Federation of the Phonographic Industry (IFPI)

IFPI Secretariat, 54 Regent Street, London W1B 5RE
tel 020-7878 7900 *fax* 020-7878 7950
email info@ifpi.org
website www.ifpi.org

International Institute of Communications

Regent House, 24-25 Nutford Place, London W1Y 5YN
tel 020-7323 9622 *fax* 020-7323 9623
email enquiries@iicom.org
website www.iicom.org

International Intelligence on Culture

4 Baden Place, Crosby Row, London SE1 1YW
tel 020-7403 7001
email enquiry@intelCULTURE.org
website www.intelculture.org

ITV Network Ltd

200 Gray's Inn Road, London WC1X 8HF
tel 020-7843 8000 *fax* 020-7843 8158
email info@itv.com
website www.itv.co.uk
Managing Director (Granada) Mick Desmond
Managing Director (Carlton) Clive Jones *Director of Programmes* Nigel Pickard

Comprises 16 independent regional TV licensees, broadcasting across 15 regions of the UK. Commissions and schedules its own programmes and from independent production companies, shown across the ITV network. ITV's 4 channels are set up as follows: ITV is the main terrestrial channel, with a programme budget of almost £1 billion and with mixed-genre programming; ITV2 is aimed at a younger audience but also has a mix of programming and is available on freeview digital; ITV3 shows the best of ITV drama; and ITV4 is intended for more challenging programmes.

IVCA (International Visual Communication Association)

19 Pepper Street, Glengall Bridge, London E14 9RP
tel 020-7512 0571

website www.ivca.org

Promotes good business practice in communications industries.

Kraszna-Krausz Foundation

122 Fawnbrake Avenue, London SE24 0BZ
tel 020-7738 6701 *fax* 020-7738 6701
email info@k-k.org.uk
website www.k-k.org.uk
Administrator Andrea Livingstone

Created in 1985 by Andor Kraszna-Krausz, the founder of Focal Press. It exists to further the understanding and development of the art and science of photography and the moving image (film, TV and their derivatives). Seeks to encourage high standards, by offering financial support in the form of grants to assist in the development and completion of new or unfinished projects in the fields.

Funding can be for projects, works or literature (including CD-Rom) where the subject matter directly relates to the art, history, practice or technology of photography or the moving image. All must make a significant contribution to the understanding, appreciation or application of these media. Grants are between £1000 and £5000, and are intended for work which could not otherwise be finished, but for which the grant means they will be completed. Applications are considered twice a year, with deadlines on 1st May and 1st October. Final decisions are made by trustees at July and December meetings.

Lux

3rd Floor, 18 Shacklewell Street, London E8 2EZ
tel 020-7503 3980 *fax* 020-7503 1606
email info@lux.org.uk
website www.lux.org.uk

A not-for-profit organisation that supports and promotes contemporary and historical artists' moving-image work, and those who make it, through distribution, exhibition, publishing and research.

Mechanical-Copyright Protection Society (MCPS)

Copyright House, 29/33 Berner Street,
London W1T 3AB
tel 020-7580 5544
website www.mcps.co.uk

MCPS, the Mechanical-Copyright Protection Society, is a not-for-profit organisation that ensures its 17,000 composer, songwriter and music publisher members are paid royalties when the music they have created is recorded on CDs, DVDs, downloads, computer games and everything in between. Works in an operational alliance with PRS – the Performing Right Society (the MCPS-PRS Alliance).

Media Ed

email info@mediaed.org.uk
website www.MediaEd.org.uk

A site for teachers, students and anyone interested in media and moving-image education in primary, secondary, further and informal education in the UK. The website includes resources for teaching Media & Film Studies and news; it is funded by *bfi* Education.

Mediawatch-UK

3 Willow House, Kennington Road, Ashford,
Kent TN24 0NR
tel (01233) 633939 *fax* (01233) 633836
email info@mediwatchuk.org
website www.mediawatchuk.org
Director John Beyer

Organisation founded by the late Mary Whitehouse, concerned with maintaining standards of taste and decency on television and radio. Open for membership to people who agree with and support aims. Membership fees are £15 p.a.

Mental Health Media

356 Holloway Road, London N7 6PA
tel 020-7700 8171 *fax* 020-7686 0959
email info@mhmedia.com
website www.mhmedia.com

Metier

EQ, Suite E229, Dean Clough, Halifax HX3 5AX
tel (01422) 381618 *fax* (01422) 380719
email www.thinkeq.org.uk
website www.thinkeq.org.uk

A national equality and diversity agency working in the creative industries.

Moonstone International

67 George Street, Edinburgh EH2 2JG
tel 0131-220 2080 *fax* 0131-220 2081
email info@moonstone.org.uk
website www.moonstone.org.uk
Managing Director Fiona Kinsella

The Museum of Television and Radio (California)

465 N Beverly Drive, Beverley Hills, CA 90210, USA
tel ++ 1 310 786-1000
website www.mtr.org

The Paley Center for Media

25 West 52nd Street, New York, NY 10019, USA
tel ++ 1 212 621-6600
website www.paleycenter.org

Formerly The Museum of Television & Radio, New York, the organisation now recognises that the media landscape is a dramatically different one; its new name better reflects this institution's evolving and expanding role. Convenes media leaders and the public for programmes that illuminate the immense impact of media in all its forms on lives, culture and society. The inspiration for the new name is founder, industry pioneer and former CBS chairman William S Paley.

Music Publishers Association Ltd
3rd Floor, 20 York Buildings, London WC2N 6JU
tel 020-7839 7779 *fax* 020-7839 7776
email info@mpaonline.org.uk
website www.mpaonline.org.uk

National Association for Higher Education in the Moving Image (NAHEMI)
Sir John Cass Department of Art,
London Metropolitan University,
59-63 Whitechapel High Street, London E1 7PY
tel 020-8840 2815
email yossibal@aol.com

National Campaign for the Arts
1 Kingly Street, London W1B 5PA
tel 020-7287 3777 *fax* 020-7287 4777
email nca@artscampaign.org.uk
website www.artscampaign.org.uk
Director Louise de Winter

The UK's only independent lobbying organisation representaing al the srts, seeking to ensure they are recognised and resourced as a key element of our national culture. The NCA is a membership organisation whose members shape and inform its campaigns work.

National Film Trustee Company Limited (NFTC)
4th Floor, 66-68 Margaret Street, London W1W 5SR
tel 020-7580 6799 *fax* 020-7636 6711
email info@nftc.co.uk
website www.nftc.co.uk
Managing Director Louisa Bewley

The NFTC is the foremost film revenue collection and monitoring agency in the UK. Holds money on trust, giving producers and financiers protection from insolvency of any of the parties or changes in ownership. The organisation disburses revenue in the order agreed by all parties to the collection agreement.

National Union of Journalists
Headland House, 308-312 Grays Inn Road,
London WC1X 8DP
tel 020-7278 7916 *fax* 020-7837 8143
email info@nuj.org.uk
website www.nuj.org.uk

Nielsen EDI
Sixth Floor, Endeavour House,
189 Shaftesbury Avenue, London WC2H 87J
tel 020-7170 5200 *fax* 020-7170 5201
website www.entdata.com

Nielsen is a global data research and measurement company for the motion picture industry and captures box office figures in more than 14 countries and 50,000 screens.

Ofcom
Riverside House, 2a Southwark Bridge Road,
London SE1 9H
tel 020-7981 3000 *fax* 020-7981 3333
email mediaoffice@ofcom.org.uk
website www.ofcom.org.uk

Ofcom is the independent regulator and competition authority for the UK communications industries, with responsibilities across television, radio, telecommunications and wireless communications services.

Office for Fair Trading
Fleetbank House, 2-6 Salisbury Square,
London EC4Y 8JX
tel 0845-722 4499
email enquiries@oft.gsi.gov.uk
website www.oft.gov.uk

Office for National Statistics
Customer Contact Centre, Room 1.015,
Office for National Statistics, Cardiff Road,
Newport NP10 8XG
tel 0845-601 3034 *fax* (01633) 652747
email info@statistics.gov.uk
website www.statistics.gov.uk

The Official UK Charts Company
4th Floor, 58/59 Great Malborough Street,
London W1F 7JY
tel 020-7478 8500 *fax* 020-7436 8519
email darren@theofficialcharts.com
website www.theofficialcharts.com

Pearl & Dean
3 Waterhouse Square, 138-142 Holborn,
London EC1N 2 NY
tel 020-7882 1100 *fax* 020-7882 1111
website www.pearlanddean.com

Cinema advertising company.

Performing Right Society (PRS)
29-33 Berners Street, London W1T 3AB
tel 020-7580 5544
website www.prs.co.uk

PRS collects and distributes performance and broadcast royalties for artists.

The Photographic Phonographic Industry Ltd (BPI)
25 Saville Row, London W1X 1AA
tel 020-7851 4000 *fax* 020-7287 2252
email general@bpi.co.uk
website www.bpi.co.uk

Producers' Alliance for Film and Television (PACT) – see page 96.

Radio, Electrical and Television Retailers' Association (RETRA)
Retra House, St John's Terrace, 1 Ampthill Street,
Bedford MK42 9EY

tel (01234) 269110 *fax* (01234) 269609
email retra@retra.co.uk
website www.retra.co.uk

Raindance Ltd – see page 359.

The Research Centre for Television and Interactivity

4th Floor, 227 West George Street, Glasgow G2 2ND
tel 0141-568 7113 *fax* 0141-568 7114
website www.researchcentre.co.uk

Works with broadcasters, producers and others in the creative industries to develop business and talent in the sector. Primary activities include: training for researchers, and a talent database.

The Royal Photographic Society

Fenton House, 122 Wells Road, Bath BA2 3AH
tel (01225) 325733
email info@rps.org
website www.rps.org

Royal Television Society

5th Floor, Kildare House, 3 Dorset Rise,
London EC4 8EN
tel 020-7822 2810 *fax* 020-7822 2811
email info@rts.org.uk
website www.rts.org.uk

Shooting People

website www.shootingpeople.org
Founders Jess Search, Cath LeCouteur

Shooting People is a unique filmmaking service. Made for and by filmmakers, it is a dynamic online community of more than 34,000 filmmaking members. This network brings together people from all over the UK through daily online bulletins and regular events to get their films developed, created and distributed.

Founded in the UK, Shooting People now operates as well in NY, San Franscisco and LA. The organisation is "a passionate believer in both original, creative filmmaking and in the power of filmmakers to learn from each other and help each other out".

Shooting People also runs a distribution label – Shooting People Films (see page 300), and a publishing arm which has released a number of invaluable books for filmmakers.

Skillset

Prospect House, 80-110 New Oxford Street,
London WC1A 1HB
tel 020-7520 5757 *fax* 020-7520 5758
email info@skillset.org
website www.skillset.org

Skillset is the Sector Skills Council for the Audio Visual Industries (broadcast, film, video, interactive media and photo imaging), with the responsibility for dispensing funds from the Lottery and the industry for media training and development.

– see page 52.

Talent Circle

website www.talentcircle.co.uk

A free online community noticeboard with jobs, casting, resources and industry news for those working in indie film or production. Aimed at film professionals, filmmakers, production staff, actors and film talent, Talent Circle allows you to create a personal profile and receive daily bulletins.

UK Post – see page 162.

Variety Club of Great Britain

Variety Club House, 93 Bayham Street,
London NW1 0AG
tel 020-7428 8100 *fax* 020-7428 8123
email info@varietyclub.org.uk
website www.varietyclub.org.uk

Children's charity which occassionally stages premieres.

The Video Standards Council

Kinetic Business Centre, Theobald Street,
Borehamwood, Herts WD6 4PJ
tel 020-8387 4020 *fax* 020-8387 4004
email vsc@videostandards.org.uk
website www.videostandards.org.uk

Voice of the Listener and Viewer

VLV Librarian, 101 King's Drive, Gravesend,
Kent DA12 5BQ
tel (01474) 352835 *fax* (01474) 351112
email info@vlv.org.uk
website www.vlv.org.uk

Represents citizen and consumer interests in broadcasting, and speaks for listeners and viewers on the full range of broadcasting issues.

Women in Film and Television (UK)

6 Langley Street, London WC2H 9JA
tel 020-7420 4875 *fax* 020-7379 1625
email info@wftv.org.uk
website www.wftv.org.uk
Chief Executive Jane Cussons

A membership association open to women with at least 1 year's professional experience in the television, film and/or digital media industries. Offers a range of events – including an annual awards ceremony – and a monthly publication for members. Also runs Directing Change, a mentor programme for women newly working in the film industry.

Filmmaking degrees

If you cannot find a programme in your area listed below, or in the subsequent section on short courses, refer to the British Film Institute's online database of all the media courses available in the UK (**www.bfi.org.uk/education**).

UK

Bournemouth University

The Media School, Bournemouth University,
Fern Barrow, Poole, Dorset BH12 5BB
tel (01202) 965950
email media@bournemouth.ac.uk
website www.bournemouth.ac.uk

University of Bradford

Electronic Imaging and Media Communication,
Bradford University, Bradford BD7 1DP
tel (01274) 234001 *fax* (01274) 233727
email ugadmissions@inf.brad.ac.uk
website www.eimc.brad.ac.uk

Housed in the School of Informatics, EIMC runs a range of media and new media-related degrees and has a strong research profile. It is a cross-disciplinary department covering all aspects of media, from games and photography to film theory and practice. Contact Admissions for full details.

Subjects include: Media, Technology & Production; Animation & Games; New Media.

Cardiff University

Cardiff School of Journalism,
Media & Cultural Studies, The Bute Building,
King Edward VII Avenue, Cardiff CF10 3NB
tel 029-2023 8832 *fax* 029-2087 4000
website www.cardiff.ac.uk/jomec

Offers a BA in Journalism, Film & Media, with diplomas and MA programmes in a number of Journalism and PR specialisms.

University of Central England

University of Central England in Birmingham,
Perry Barr, Birmingham B42 2SU
tel 0121-331 5719 *fax* 0121-331 6501
email media@uce.ac.uk
website www.mediacourses.com

Courses include: BA (Hons) Media & Communication; MA Media Enterprise; MA Media Event & Exhibition Management; MA Media Production; and MA Media & Communication (theory).

Central Saint Martins College of Art and Design

Information Office, Central Saint Martins,
Southampton Row, London WC1B 4AP
tel 020-7514 7022 *fax* 020-7514 7254
email info@csm.arts.ac.uk
website www.csm.arts.ac.uk

CSM offers a Postgraduate Diploma in Character Animation, which trains animators in 2D and 3D animation through a programme of industry-based mentoring. Also runs an extensive programme of short courses for film and television professionals (see page 357.

University of East Anglia

UEA, Norwich NR4 7TJ
tel (01603) 456161 *fax* (01603) 458553
email eas.admiss@uea.ac.uk
website www.uea.ac.uk

Courses include: BA (Hons) Film & American Studies; BA (Hons) Film & English Studies; BA (Hons) Film & Television Studies, BA (Hons) Film Studies & Art History; BA (Hons) Media Engineering; MA in Creative Writing: Scriptwriting; MA in Film Studies; MA in Film Studies with Film Archiving; and MPhil and PhD in Film Studies or Television Studies.

Goldsmiths College (Department of Media and Communications)

Lewisham Way, New Cross, London SE14 6NW
tel 020-7919 7615
email media-comms@gold.ac.uk
website www.goldsmiths.ac.uk

Goldsmiths runs practical and theory courses on all aspects of filmmaking, including feature film, documentary, short film, animation, television and digital imaging.

Courses include: BA (Hons) Anthropology & Media; BA (Hons) International Media; BA (Hons) Media & Communications; BA (Hons) Media & Sociology; BA Media & Modern Literature; MA in Digital Media: Technology & Cultural Form; MA in Feature Film; MA in Filmmaking; MA in Screen Documentary; MA in Scriptwriting; MA in Television Journalism; MA in Transnational Communications & Global Media; MPhil and PhD in Media & Communication; and MRes in Media & Communication.

University of Kent at Canterbury

School of Drama, Film & Visual Arts,
Rutherford College, Canterbury, Kent CT2 7NX
tel (01227) 764000 *fax* (01227) 827846
website www.kent.ac.uk

Courses include: BA (Hons) American Studies (Art & Film); BA (Hons) Film Studies; BA (Joint Hons) Film Studies and another subject; MA in Film Practice as Research; MA in Film Studies; MDrama (Hons) Drama & Theatre Studies (undergraduate Honours programme).

LCC (London College of Communication)

University of the Arts London, School of Media, Elephant and Castle, London SE1 6SB
tel 020-7514 6800 or 020-7514 6828
fax 020-7514 6848
email a.heath@lcc.arts.ac.uk
website www.lcc.arts.ac.uk

A full-time BA in Film & Video over 3 years integrates theory and practice with history. Students build experience through practice workshops and varied practical 16mm film, television studio and digital video projects. They build creative partnerships and learn to collaborate through crewing and practice-based learning. In the third year, students specialise in a major practice area: sound design, editing, cinematography, production or direction. Fees are £3070; overseas: £10095 (plus materials).

LCC also offers other degree courses, including: an MA and PgDip in Interactive Media; an MA in Documentary Research; and an MA in Screenwriting. Runs an extensive programme of short courses.

Leeds Metropolitan University – see entry under page 24.

Courses include: BA (Hons) Film & Moving Image Production; BA (Hons) Media & Popular Culture; BSc (Hons) Creative Music & Sound Technology; BSc (Hons) Multimedia Technology; BSc (Hons) Music & New Media; Foundation Degree and Cert in Film and Television Production; HND in Multimedia Technology, Leeds Metropolitan University; MA and PgDip in Film & Moving Image Production.

London Film Academy

The Old Church, 52a Walham Grove, London SW6 1QR
tel 020-7386 7711 *fax* 020-7381 6116
email info@londonfilmacademy.com
website www.londonfilmacademy.com
Joint Principals Daisy Gili, Anna MacDonald

Established in 2002, LFA aims to prepare multi-skilled, adaptable and innovative filmmakers and apprentices for work in the industry. The programmes also aim to equipt students with knowledge of all roles in the filmmaking process, and emphasise the importance of collaboration.

Courses include: Filmmaking Diploma (1 year); Filmmaking Certificate (1 month, full-time); and Panico Foundation (6 Saturdays or Sundays). Also runs a range of weekend filmmaking workshops. Qualification includes Diploma or Certificate. Prices range from £150 to £13,100, depending on course.

London International Film School

24 Shelton Street, London WC2H 9UB
tel 020-7836 9642 *fax* 020-7497 3718
email info@lfs.org.uk
website www.lfs.org.uk
Director Ben Gibson

Oldest established film school with a practice-based programme that teaches all areas of the filmmaking process to each student. School offers an MA in Filmmaking, an MA in Screenwriting, and a programme of craft specialisms. Over 75% of the student intake is from outside the UK.

London Metropolitan University

Central House, 59-63 Whitechapel High Street, London E1 7PF
tel 020-7320 1000
email e.pierson@londonmet.ac.uk
website www.londonmet.ac.uk
Undergraduate Admissions Tutor Elaine Pierson *BA Course Leader* Peter Hewitt *MA Course Leader* Charlotte Worthington

Founded in 2002, when London Guildhall and North London Universities merged. Undergraduate and Postgraduate programmes combine cultural and critical theory with film and video practice; students develop skills through hands-on production experience. Emphasises single camera and location shooting. BA programmes have standard entry requirements and entry to MA programmes is by portfolio and interview.

London South Bank University – see page 353.

In addition to a Media Writing BA, LSBU also offers the following undergraduate film degrees: BA Digital Film & Video – gives practical production experience in digital video formats and across a range of film and TV genres, including factual programming and documentary as well as the short feature and original drama; and a BA in Film Studies course – aims to give students a firm foundation in film theory and history through a mixture of lectures, student-led seminars and weekly film screenings (this is not a practical filmmaking course).

Middlesex University (Department of Film)

Middlesex University, Media Arts, Cat Hill, Barnet, Hertfordshire EN4 8HT
tel 020-8411 6706
email p.phillips@mdx.ac.uk
website www.cea.mdx.ac.uk

Courses include: BA (Hons and Joint Hons) Film Studies; BA (Hons) Film, Video & Interactive Arts;

BA (Hons) Media & Cultural Studies; BA (Hons) Television Production; BPhil, MPhil and PhD in Video &/or Film; MA and MSc in Design for Interactive Media; MA in Electronic Arts; MA in Film & Visual Cultures; MA in Media & Communications Management; MA in Scriptwriting; MA in Video; MPhil and PhD in Contemporary Cultural Studies & Media Studies; and MPhil and PhD in Electronic Arts.

Napier University – see page 35.

Courses include: BA Media Arts; MA Producing Film & Television; MA Documentary by Practice; MA Screenwriting for Film & TV (retreat programme).

National Film and Television School

Beaconsfield Studios, Station Road,
Beaconsfield HP9 1LG
tel (01494) 671234 *fax* (01494) 674042
email admin@nftsfilm-tv.ac.uk
website www.nftsfilm.ac.uk

The UK's national centre of excellence for vocational training in film and TV programme-making. Courses cover all aspects of the practical film- and programme-making process and include MA, BA and short course programmes.

Newport School of Art, Media and Design – see page 25.

In addition to its BA in Cinema Studies & Scriptwriting, the University also offers the following media courses: BA (Hons) Animation; BA (Hons) Computer Games Design; BA (Hons) Documentary Film & Television; BA (Hons) Film & Video; BA (Hons) Performing Arts; MA Animation; and MA Film.

Northern Media School, Sheffield Hallam University

Postgraduate Office, Sheffield Hallam University,
Psalter Lane, Sheffield S11 8UZ
tel 0114-225 4648 *fax* 0114-225 2603
email chris.dawson@shu.ac.uk
website www.shu.ac.uk/media/nms/
Postgraduate Administrator Chris Dawson

The Northern Media School is a leading provider of production-based postgraduate media education in the UK. It is part of Sheffield Hallam University, which also has an extensive undergraduate programme in film and media studies and production. A high proportion of graduates go on to work in the industry as journalists, directors, producers, cinematographers, editors, sound recordists and production personnel both in the broadcast and independent sectors.

The MA in Film & Media Production lasts 18 months and students may specialise in Directing, Scriptwriting, Post-Production, Cinematography, Sound Design and Producing. Specialisms are agreed at the time of entry.

Fees: home and EU £6150; overseas £9735

University of Reading

Department of Film, Theatre & Television,
Bulmershe Court, Woodlands Avenue, Earley,
Reading RG6 1HY
tel 0118-931 8878 *fax* 0118-931 8873
email film.drama@reading.ac.uk
website www.rdg.ac.uk/FD

Courses include: BA (Combined Hons) Film & Theatre with English, German, Italian or History of Art; BA (Hons) Film & Theatre; BA (Hons) Italian with Film Studies; MA in Italian Cinema; MA in Film Studies by Research.

Royal Holloway – see page 25.

In addition to the Feature Film Screenwriting MA, Royal Holloway also offer MA programmes in Screen Studies, Producing for Film & Television, and Documentary by Practice.

University of Stirling

Department of Film & Media Studies,
Stirling FK9 4LA
tel (01786) 467520 *fax* (01786) 466855
email stirling.media@stir.ac.uk
website www-fms.stir.ac.uk

Courses include: BA (Hons) Film & Media Studies; BA (Hons) Journalism Studies; BA (Joint Hons) Film & Media Studies in combination with 1 other subject; BA Film & Media Studies; MLitt and PhD in Media Studies; MRes in Media Research; MSc and PgDip in Media Management; and MSc and PgDip in Public Relations.

University College for Creative Arts

(The Surrey Institute of Art & Design)
University College, Falkner Road, Farnham,
Surrey GU9 7DS
tel (01252) 722441
email info@ucreative.ac.uk
website www.ucreative.ac.uk

BA Hons Film Production; BA Hons Digital Screen Arts; MA Film & Video.

University of Wales, Aberystwyth

Department of Theatre, Film & Television Studies,
Parry-Williams Building, University of Wales,
Aberystwyth, Penglais Campus, Aberystwyth,
Ceredigion SY23 3AJ
tel (01970) 622828 *fax* (01970) 622831
website www.aber.ac.uk/tfts

Aberystwyth offers many courses designed to prepare students for work in the film and television industries.

Courses include: MPhil and PhD in Television Studies; MA in Film Studies; MA in Screenwriting for

Radio & Screen; MA in Audience & Reception Studies; BA (Hons) Film & Television Studies; and BA (Hons) Media & Communication Studies. Students also have the opportunity to do Joint Honours in Film & Television and most other subjects.

University of the West of England, Bristol – see page 221.

University of Westminster

The School of Media, Arts & Design, Watford Road, Northwick Park, Harrow, Middlesex HA1 3TP
tel 020-7911 5944 (main department)
fax 020-7911 5943
email mad@wmin.ac.uk
website www.wmin.ac.uk
Course Director Stephen May

Courses include: BA Film & Television Production; MA Film & Television: Theory, Culture & Industry; BA Contemporary Media Practice; MA in Screenwriting & Producing (see page 25). Fees are £4000 for home students and £8000 for overseas students.

OVERSEAS

These are widely regarded as the top non-UK-based international film courses.

American Film Institute

Conservatory, AFI, 2021 North Western Avenue, Los Angeles, California 90027, USA
tel + 1 323 856 7600 *fax* ++1 323 467 4578
email shardman@AFIonline.org
website www.afi.com

AFI is a national institute providing leadership in screen education and the recognition and celebration of excellence in the art of film, television and digital media. It has a major education programme designed to train the next generation of filmmakers at its world-renowned Conservatory; maintains America's film heritage through the AFI Catalogue of Feature Films; and explores new digital technologies in entertainment and education through the AFI Digital Content Lab and K-12 Screen Education Centre.

Australian Film, Television & Radio School (AFTRS)

PO Box 126, North Ryde, NSW 2113, 1670 Australia
tel ++ 1300 131 461 *fax* ++ 61 02 9887 1030
email infonsw@aftrs.edu.au
website www.aftrs.edu.au

The Australian Film Television and Radio School (AFTRS) is the national centre for professional education and advanced training in film, television and radio. The aim of AFTRS is to recognise and develop new and emerging talent; to provide industry professionals with opportunities to gain additional skills; and to assist them in their creative and professional development. Training is directed towards those people with demonstrated creative potential, clear ability and commitment.

AFTRS accepts around 100 students each year in its full-time postgraduate programmes, with a further 5000 students undertaking courses in the national short course programme. Part-time attendance for the postgraduate programmes is also available. Courses are organised around 13 specialist teaching departments: Cinematography, Design, Digital Media, Directing, Documentary, Editing, Producing, Radio, Screen Business, Screen Composition, Screen Studies, Screenwriting, and Sound and Television. The teaching staff is drawn from experienced industry practitioners. Professional associates of visiting film, television and radio programme-makers, critics, theorists and other relevant specialists also contribute to the teaching programme and to the assessment of students' work.

Please note that full-time courses are open only to Australian citizens and permanent residents of Australia.

California Institute of the Arts

School of Film/Video, 24700 McBean Parkway, Valencia, California 91355-2397, USA
tel ++1 661-255-1050
email admiss@calarts.edu
website film@calarts.edu

The School of Film/Video is one of the USA's leading colleges for studying the art of the moving image. It is singularly devoted to filmmaking as a personal, independent art form. The school is especially unique in that it promotes the studies of all major types of filmmaking: dramatic narrative, documentary, experimental live-action, character-based animation, experimental animation, multimedia, and installation. It offers 4 programmes, each one with its own specialised curriculum focusing on specific areas in filmmaking. At the same time, all share an ethos in combining rigorous practical training with theoretical inquiry, hands-on production with aesthetic reflection.

The Programme in Film & Video provides artists with a dynamic laboratory for producing new forms of narrative, documentary and experimental work in both film and video. Internationally renowned Programmes in Experimental Animation and Character Animation give students an excellent foundation in both technique and creative thinking, and prepare them to produce work at the very forefront of animated filmmaking. The Film Directing Programme focuses on the fundamentals of dramatic storytelling and theatre practice, but also calls for innovative approaches to staging drama for the screen.

Graduates of the School of Film/Video have distinguished themselves in every area of independent and commercial filmmaking. Their work has been represented extensively at major festivals and museums around the world as much as it has been in the film, television and animation industries.

Columbia University – see page 23.

National Film School of Denmark

Theodor Christensens Plads 1,
DK-1437 Copenhagen, Denmark
tel +45 32 68 64 00 *fax* +45 32 68 64 10
email infoz@filmskolen.dk
website www.filmskolen.dk/english

A state school, financially supported by the Danish Ministry of Cultural Affairs; founded in 1966 by Theodor Christensen and situated on the small island of Frederiksholm in the harbour of Copenhagen. There are 4 study programmes available: Film, TV, Scriptwriting and Animation Directing – each offered in 4-year programmes, except the scriptwriting course which is 3 years.

The school is an art school, but practical knowledge is also very important. The teaching programme is a mixture of theoretical and practical training and includes a large number of exercises and productions. The students' final project is a film produced on a professional level and presented to the public on national TV. No diploma or former education is in itself a guarantee of admission. All students must pass an entrance test, including both practical exercises and interviews.

University of California at Los Angeles (UCLA)

School of Theater, Film & Television,
405 Hilgard Avenue, Box 951361, Los Angeles, California 90095-1361, USA
tel +1 310 825 5761 *fax* +1 310 825 3383
email webmaster@emelnitz.ucla.edu
website www.tft.ucla.edu

The only university in the USA where the study of theatre, film, television and digital media is integrated within a single professional school. Located in Los Angeles – the entertainment capital of the world – TFT draws on industry leaders for its faculty, advisers and mentors.

TFT's talented alumni have won Oscars, Emmys, Tonys and nearly every other meaningful artistic accolade in the performing and visual arts. Its strong academic programmes are enhanced by exceptional resources, such as the UCLA Film & Television Archive – the largest university-based film and television archive in the world; also The Geffen Playhouse, one of Los Angeles' most prestigious performance venues. TFT annually attracts the finest students from around the world, and competition for admission is intense.

New York University, Tisch School of the Arts

721 Broadway, 12th Floor, New York, NY 10003, USA
tel + 1 212 998 1517
email special.info@nyu.edu
website www.nyu.edu/tisch

Offered through Tisch School of the Arts' Kanbar Institute of Film & Television, the MBA/MFA Dual Degree in Producing is designed to bridge the gap between the "creatives" and the "suits"; a new dual-degree graduate programme that gives aspiring film producers and studio executives the knowledge to navigate the fast-changing landscape of financing and filmmaking today. The joint MBA/MFA degree is a partnership between NYU's Stern School of Business and Kanbar Institute of Film & Television at Tisch School of the Arts, both highly regarded in their fields.

International Film School of Paris

(Ecole Internationale de Création Audiovisuelle et de Réalisation)
50, avenue du Président Wilson,
Batiment 136 – BP 12, 93214 La Plaine Saint-Denis, France
tel ++ 33 1 4998 1111 *fax* ++ 33 1 4996 0007
email international@eicar.fr
website www.eicar.fr

The International Film School of Paris brings together students from all over the world to collaborate as filmmakers. In addition to BFA and MFA programmes, the school offers 2- and 3-week summer courses and a 1-year fast-track programme, all taught in English. EICAR teaches the full process, from screenwriting and directing to shooting and editing. Students create several short films on all formats, including Digital HD, 16mm and 35mm.

Polish Film School Lodz

Państwowa Wyższa Szkoła Filmowa,
Telewizyjna i Teatralna, ul.Targowa 61\6390-323, Łódź
tel +48 42 634 58 20 *fax* +48 42 674 81 39
email swzfilm@filmschool.lodz.pl
website www.filmschool.lodz.pl/english

University of Southern California (USC)

School of Cinema-Television,
University Park Campus, Los Angeles, California 90089, USA
tel +1 213 740 8358
email admissions@cinema.usc.edu
website www-cntv.usc.edu/

Since its founding in 1929, the School of Cinematic Arts has served as a dynamic hub where students and faculty transform their dreams into the new philosophies, technologies and artistic movements that influence how we entertain, educate and express ourselves. Across its hundreds of different programmes, the school provides a one-of-a-kind opportunity for a diverse range of students from across Europe, Asia, Africa and the Americas, to explore and expand their creative potential. It focuses on instructing students using the latest techniques and methodologies, as well as the history and lore that anchor the art form.

Vancouver Film School

198 West Hastings Street, Suite 200, Vancouver, British Columbia V6B 1H2, Canada
tel +1 604-685-5808 *fax* +1 604- 685-5830
email admissions@vfs.com
website www.vfs.com

VFS is a post-secondary entertainment arts school which offers a comprehensive education balancing theoretical instruction and hands-on production taught over a single year.

SHORT COURSES IN FILMMAKING

Film degree courses offer a practical way to learn your trade. In addition, they can often give you a 'leg up' in the industry, as you meet other filmmakers who may become collaborators in the future and teachers who are often professionals themselves. However, they also represent a major investment of both time and money.

If cost proves prohibitive, a short course can be a relatively inexpensive opportunity to hone your craft skills, learn how to use a new piece of media software or create work for your portfolio.

BKSTS – The Moving Image Society

email training@bksts.com
website www.bksts.com

– see page 160.

Runs a range of highly regarded short courses for film and television professionals, including a Film Foundation course which covers production basics; projectionist training; and an 8-week Digital Technologies course.

Brighton Film School

Brighton Film Studios Ltd,
The Brighton Business Centre, 95 Ditchling Road, Brighton BN1 4ST
tel (01273) 602070
email franz@brightonfilmschool.org.uk
website www.brightonfilmschool.org.uk
Director & Senior Lecturer Franz von Habsburg MBKS

BFS offers a 1-year part-time course which starts in September. This is a technical course designed for those who want to work in professional film production. Thus, all aspects of production are included, from screenwriting and directing through to cinematography and editing. Essential technical theory and practical tuition by a variety of lecturers in all disciplines are combined with film company visits. Entry is restricted to a maximum of 12 applicants who are divided into 2 film crews; the crews will then work side by side throughout the course – following intensive tuition – to script, plan, shoot and edit several productions using 35mm, 16mm and DV. The course costs £3500 (including all materials). Course participants also receive a number of other benefits.

Cardiff Centre for Lifelong Learning

Senghenydd Road, Cardiff CF24 4AG
tel 029-2087 0000
email learn@cardiff.ac.uk
website www.cardiff.ac.uk/learn

Cardiff offers a 12-week part-time short course in Digital Video Production. The course has no prerequisites and costs £231.50. Contact General Enquiries on the number above for further details.

Central Saint Martins College of Art and Design (Short Courses)

University of the Arts London, Short Course Office, 10 Back Hill, London EC1R 5EN
tel 020-7514 7015 *fax* 020-7514 7016
email shortcourse@csm.arts.ac.uk
website www.csm.arts.ac.uk

Short courses cover a wide range of film and creative media skills, such as: Art Direction for Film; Storyboarding for Film; Video and Animation; and Directing for the Camera. Also offers a range of screenwriting and acting courses. Fees vary.

Connections Communications Centre

Palingswick House, 241 King Street, London W6 9LP
tel 020-8741 1766
website www.cccmedia.co.uk

Founded in 1982, Connections Communications Centre is a registered charity dedicated to promoting cultural diversity and new opportunities in the media industry. Provides training, mentoring and job assistance to help open doors to the media industry for those excluded through lack of training and economic or social deprivation.

European Film Academy Master Class

European Film Academy, Kurfürstendamm 225, 10719 Berlin, Germany
tel ++ 49 30 887 167-0 *fax* ++49 30 887 167-77
email masterclass@europeanfilmacademy.org
website www.europeanfilmacademy.org

Besides getting an insight into the working principles of successful and experienced filmmakers, the EFA Master Classes provide participants with contemporary theory and procedures in the rapidly evolving field of international film production. Also assists young filmaker talents to build up European networks.

Course Contents: EFA Master Classes cover Directing; Acting; Cinematography; Production Design; Production; Marketing; Distribution.

Applicants: Mainly intended for European Filmmakers who have completed at least one feature or several short films. A maximum of 16-20 participants guarantees intense working conditions.

Selection: Selection is by Master of the workshop based on pre-selection by a European Film Academy committee. Applicants should submit CV, filmography, letter of motivation, and DVD/Video of latest work.

Venue: EFA Master Classes take place across Europe often in local film studios.

Programme: Retrospectives of the Master's films and/or panel discussions take place alongside training.

Fees: Range from 500-800 EUR.

Film Skills Training Ltd

Pinewood Studios, Pinewood Road, Iver Heath, Buckinghamshire SL0 0NH
tel (01753) 656851
email sue@filmskills.org
website www.filmskills.org

Offers art department short courses, such as Introduction to VectorWorks V12 and Working in Wardrobe. Costs vary according to course.

Light House

The Chubb Buildings, Fryer Street, Wolverhampton WV1 1HT
tel (01902) 716055 *fax* (01902) 717143
email peter@light-house.co.uk
website www.light-house.co.uk

See page 338 for details on the venue. Light House is an award-winning media centre which offers a range of services, including production and post-production resources, training, talks and festivals, and a film club as well as a 2-screen cinema.

Lighthouse Arts and Training Ltd

9-12 Middle Street, Brighton BN1 1AL
tel (01273) 384222 *fax* (01273) 384233
email info@lighthouse.org.uk
website www.lighthouse.org.uk

Lighthouse is a media arts facility and training resource in Brighton.

Courses include: Intensive Introduction to Screenwriting; The Producer's Clout – A Course for Emerging Film Producers; Write Moves – For Experienced Writers New to Screenwriting; and Digital Media Arts PG Dip.

Lighthouse also has post-production facilities and camera equipment for hire.

London College of Communication (LCC) – see entry under page 353.

Offers an extensive range of short courses across most aspects of film and video production and post-production.

Moonstone Filmmakers Lab – see page 349.

The Filmmakers' Lab is open to directors with a developed screenplay. It is a residential programme run over 17 days, at which participants rehearse, shoot, edit and screen key scenes from their projects in collaboration with professional actors, composers and crews, and under the guidance of an award-winning director. Advisers are selected from the Sundance Institute and throughout Europe. Experienced directors with feature scripts may apply; participants are selected on the originality and viability of the project, and their track record. Costs are £2000 + VAT.

Neil Gorton Prosthetics Studio Ltd – see page 188 for courses in special FX make-up and prosthetics.

no.w.here

14 Kingsgate Place, London NW6 4TA
tel 020-7372 3925 *fax* 020-372 3925
email courses@nowhere-lab.org
website www.nowhere-lab.org

no.w.here is an arts centre for artist film production, which gives public access to film facilities at low cost. Technical courses and workshops cover traditional analogue filmmaking practices, but with an artistic focus; included are techniques such as optical printing, animation and drawing on film, and super 8 shooting and hand processing. No formal experience is necessary for courses. Apply through email above.

Northern Visions Media Centre

23 Donegall Street, Belfast BT1 2FF
tel 028-9024 5495 *fax* 028-9032 6608
email info@northernvisions.org
website www.nvtv.co.uk www.northernvisions.org
Programmes Director Marilyn Hyndman

Northern Visions is an access media arts centre in Belfast offering training and resources in digital video, television and new media. The provision of skilled support services offers opportunities for artists, filmmakers, community and cultural organisations to realise high-quality production. The centre is committed to offering opportunities to people marginalised by mainstream media or denied self- and/or collective expression. Community media and grassroots activities promote and support the drive to create an inclusive information society. Broadcasting through NvTv is a natural progression for all those using Northern Visions resources and support to communicate and engage with the wider public.

Courses include: Media arts and literacy programme; 1- and 2-day intensive workshops in film and television; community television journalism school; active citizenship programme with training and mentoring; Irish language broadcast trainee programme; and other projects such as youth production unit when funds made available. Qualifications offered when courses are accredited, such as OCN.

International Film School of Paris – see page 356.

Raindance Ltd

81 Berwick Street, London W1F 8TW
tel 020-7287 3833 *fax* 020-7439 2243
email info@raindance.co.uk
website www.raindance.co.uk
Founder Elliot Grove

Raindance is dedicated to fostering and promoting independent film in the UK and around the world. Activities include: Raindance Film Festival, Training Courses, Raindance Kids Film Festival, and Raindance Film Productions. Also hosts the increasingly prestigious British Independent Film Awards (BIFAs) in London (see page 287). The courses aim to give individuals the tools to start shooting their film, and include courses on writing, directing, producing and editing. Also offers a number of Diploma courses in the same subjects. Raindance Membership costs £50 and includes discounts on courses, Festival Passes, and tickets to the British Independent Film Awards.

Short Courses @ NFTS

Beaconsfield: National Film & Television School, Beaconsfield Studios, Station Road, Beaconsfield, Bucks HP9 1LG
tel (01494) 677903 *fax* (01494) 678708
email shortcourses@nfts.co.uk
website www.nfts.co.uk

A leading training provider of high-quality, cost-effective, professional standard courses specifically aimed at people already working in the film and television industries. All courses are intensely practical and tutored by leading professionals working in film and television. With the industry undergoing a series of rapid changes, the organisation monitors skills shortages and offers an innovative course programe that continually evolves to meet industry needs. Courses cover a wide range of skills and specialisations, offering attendees the chance to build on existing knowledge as well as learning new skills.

Straight Curve

Burnhill Business Centre, 50 Burnhill Road, Beckenham, Kent BR3 3LA
tel 0845-021 4000 (Workshops)
tel 0845-021 3000 (General)
email info@straightcurve.co.uk
website www.straightcurve.co.uk
Contact Tina Lockett

A young company offering a variety of filmmaking workshops at weekends: Scriptwriting for Absolute Beginners; Script Development Intermediate; Studio Lighting for DV; Location Shooting for Absolute Beginners; Intensive Location Sound Recording; Health & Safety; and Studio Music Recording. Also runs a unique short movie-making experience, dry hires the latest final cut pro editing suite, provides video recording facilities for corporate training and seminars, and offers video film workshops for schools and colleges.

PUBLISHERS

These publishers all release film-related titles. If you have a great idea for a film book you would like to pitch, here's where to start!

bfi Publishing

British Film Institute, 21 Stephen Street, London W1T 1LN
tel 020-7255 1444 *fax* 020-7636 2516
website www.bfi.org.uk
Head of Publishing Rebecca Barden

Founded in 1982. Film, TV and media studies; general, academic and educational resources on moving image culture. Titles include: *The Cinema Book* (Pam Cook); *Stars* (Richard Dyer); and the highly regarded *bfi Film Classics* and *bfi TV Classics* series. Proposals welcomed by email, and should include project outline, sample material and author CV. See website for full guidelines.

Marion Boyars Publishers Ltd

24 Lacy Road, London SW15 1NL
tel 020-8788 9522 *fax* 020-8789 8122
email catheryn@marionboyars.com
website www.marionboyars.co.uk
Directors Catheryn Kilgarriff, Rebecca Gillieron (Editorial)

Publishes a range of works, including film and cinema titles aimed at students, filmmakers and general film fans. Titles include: *Dogville vs. Hollywood*, *Quintessential Tarantino*, and *Writers at the Movies.*

Welcomes unsolicited ideas for books. Contact by email according to information on website.

Cameron & Hollis

PO Box 1, Moffat, Dumfriesshire DG10 9SU
tel (01683) 220808 *fax* (01683) 220012
email sales@cameronbooks.co.uk
website www.cameronbooks.co.uk
Directors Ian Cameron, Jill Hollis

Produces and publishes a range of serious film criticism books, together with books on contemporary art. Previous titles include: *English Hitchcock* and *Ealing Studios*, both by Charles Barr; and *Katharine Hepburn* by Andrew Britton. The company welcomes unsolicited manuscripts – writers should submit by mail with a one-page synopsis in the first instance.

Crescent Moon Publishing

PO Box 393, Maidstone, Kent ME14 5XU
tel (01622) 729593
email cresmopub@yahoo.co.uk
website www.crescentmoon.org.uk
Director Jeremy Robinson *Editors* C Hughes, BD Barnacle

Publishes cinema and media (general films study and cinema buffs), plus cultural studies and feminist works. Submit 2 sample chapters – not complete works – with sae. Titles include: *The Sacred Cinema of Andrei Tarkovsky*, by Jeremy Mark Robinson; and *Disney Films, Disney Lands, Disney Business*, by Daniel Cerruti.

The Exeter Press

Reed Hall, Streatham Drive, Exeter, Devon EX4 4QR
tel (01392) 263066 *fax* (01392) 263064
email uep@exeter.ac.uk
website www.exeterpress.co.uk
Publisher Simon Baker

Small scholarly and academic press specialising in the humanities, including film history and performance studies. Target market is student, academic and cinefile.

Titles include: *The World According to Hollywood*; *The Great Art of Light and Shadow: Archaeology of the Cinema*; and *The Beginnings of the Cinema in England 1894-1901* (5 Volumes). Submit proposal document by post or email.

Faber and Faber Ltd*

3 Queen Square, London WC1N 3AU
tel 020-7465 0045 *fax* 020-7465 0034
website www.faber.co.uk

High-quality general fiction and non-fiction, drama, film, music and poetry. Editorial Director Walter Donohue runs the film department, which has published some of the best film titles in the last decade, such as: *Spike, Mike, Slackers and Dykes*, *The Sleazy History of British Cinema*, *Projections 1-13*, and *Screenwriters' Masterclass*, as well as many contemporary film scripts.

Faber does not accept unsolicited submissions or book ideas.

Flicks Books

29 Bradford Road, Trowbridge, Wiltshire BA14 9AN
tel (01225) 767728
email flicks.books@dial.pipex.com
Partners Matthew Stevens (Publisher), Aletta Stevens

Founded in 1986. Cinema, TV, and related media.

Samuel French Inc

45 West 25th Street, New York, NY 10010, USA
tel 212 206 8990 *fax* 212 206 1429
email samuelfrench@earthlink.net

Play publishers and authors' representatives (dramatic).

Icon Books Ltd

The Old Dairy, Brook Road, Thriplow, Cambridge SG8 7RG
tel (01763) 208008 *fax* (01763) 208080
email info@iconbooks.co.uk
website www.iconbooks.co.uk
Directors Peter Pugh (managing), Simon Flynn (publishing), Duncan Heath (editorial), Andrew Furlow (marketing)

Publishers of popular, smart non-fiction titles including cultural and cinema studies, such as: *Cinemas of the Mind – A Critical History of Film Theory*, and *Irony and Crisis: A History of Postmodern Culture*.

Manchester University Press

Oxford Road, Manchester M13 9NR
tel 0161-275 2310 *fax* 0161-274 3346
email mup@manchester.ac.uk
website www.manchesteruniversitypress.co.uk
Chief Executive David Rodgers *Head of Sales & Marketing* Ben Stebbing *Head of Editorial* Matthew Frost

Founded in 1904. Works of academic scholarship: literary criticism, cultural studies, media studies, art history, design, architecture, history, politics, economics, international law, modern-language texts. Textbooks and monographs.

New Playwrights' Network

10 Station Road Industrial Estate, Colwall, Nr Malvern, Herefordshire WR13 6RN
tel (01684) 540154 *fax* (01684) 540154
email simonsmith@cressrelles4drama.fsbusiness.co.uk
Publishing Director Leslie Smith

General plays for the amateur, one-act and full length.

Oberon Books

521 Caledonian Road, London N7 9RH
tel 020-7607 3637 *fax* 020-7607 3629
email info@oberonbooks.com
website www.oberonbooks.com
Managing Director Charles Glanville *Publisher* James Hogan *Editor* Dan Steward

New and classic play texts, programme texts and general theatre and performing arts books. Founded 1986.

Pandora Press

144 Hemingford Road, London N1 1DE
tel 020-7607 0823 *fax* 020-7609 2776
email ro@riversoram.com
website www.pandorapress.co.uk
Directors Elizabeth Rivers Fidlon (managing), Anthony Harris

Feminist press. General non-fiction: biography, arts, media, health, current affairs, reference and sexual politics.

Phaidon Press Ltd

Regent's Wharf, All Saints Street, London N1 9PA
tel 020-7843 1000 *fax* 020-7843 1010
email enquiries@phaidon.com
website www.phaidon.com

Visual arts, including fine art, art history, photography, architecture, design, decorative arts, music, fashion and film; now also publishing illustrated cookery, children's and travel books.

Film books are aimed at students, filmmakers and general cinema lovers and include: *Cinema Today*, *The Movie Book*, *Hitchcock at Work*, and *Stanley Kubrick: Drama and Shadows*. Editorial submissions should be made in writing; full details are available from the website.

Plexus Publishing Ltd

25 Mallinson Road, London SW11 1BW
tel 020-7924 4662 *fax* 020-7924 5096
email plexus@plexusuk.demon.co.uk
website www.plexusbooks.com
Directors Terence Porter (managing), Sandra Wake (editorial)

Film, music and popular culture releases, with many celebrity biographies such as: *James Dean: A Biography*, *Peter Jackson: From Gore to Mordor*, and *Johnny Depp: A Modern Rebel*.

Polity Press

65 Bridge Street, Cambridge CB2 1UR
tel (01223) 324315 *fax* (01223) 461385
website www.polity.co.uk

Publishes media and cultural studies texts, including works by Derrida, Benjamin and Zizek, and titles such as: *New Wave Shakespeare on Screen*, and *A Social History of the Media: From Gutenberg to the Internet*.

Reaktion Books

33 Great Sutton Street, London EC1V 0DX
tel 020-7253 1071 *fax* 020-7253 1208
email info@reaktionbooks.co.uk
website www.reaktionbooks.co.uk
Publisher Michael R. Leaman

Publishes books on fine arts, design, architecture, cultural studies and film studies. Film books are primarily serious academic film study. Proposals should be sent by post to the Editorial Director, with synopsis, sample chapter and sae.

Titles include: *Death 24 x a Second* (Laura Mulvey); *Mad, Bad & Dangerous?: The Scientist and the Cinema* (Christopher Frayling); *Chris Marker* (Catherine Lupton); *Andrei Tarkovsky* (Robert Bird); *War and Film* (James Chapman); *Film Music* (Peter Larsen); and *Photography and Cinema* (David Campany).

Reynolds & Hearn Ltd

61A Priory Road, Kew, Richmond, Surrey TW9 3DH
tel 020-8940 5198 *fax* 020-8940 7679
email enquiries@rhbooks.com
website www.rhbooks.com
Directors Richard Reynolds (managing), Marcus Hearn (editorial), David O'Leary, Geoffrey Wolfson

Film, TV, photography, music, media. Established 1999.

Media titles include reference tie-ins, yearbooks, biography and screenplays. Credits include: *The Prisoner Scripts* and *Film Review Annual*. Welcomes enquiries with ideas for publications, but no unsolicited manuscripts; email an outline or project proposal.

Routledge

2 Park Square, Milton Park, Abingdon,
Oxford OX14 4RN
tel 020-7017 6000 *fax* 020-7017 6699
website www.routlege.com

Publisher whose output includes quality film, media and cultural studies books. Titles include: *British Queer Cinema*, and *East European Cinema, Technology and Culture*.

Book proposals must demonstrate the audience for the book and how it is different from competing publications. Detailed proposal guidelines are available from the website.

Taschen UK Ltd

5th Floor, 1 Heathcock Court, 415 Strand,
London WC2R 0NS
tel 020-7845 8580 *fax* 020-7836 3696
email contact-uk@taschen.com
website www.taschen.com

Art, architecture, design, film, lifestyle, photography, popular culture, sex. Founded 1980.

Film titles include: work on directors such as Kubrick, Truffaut and Wilde; erotic cinema; and film noir. Does not welcome unsolicited manuscript ideas.

Titan Books

144 Southwark Street, London SE1 0UP
tel 020-7620 0200 *fax* 020-7620 0032
email editorial@titanemail.com
website www.titanbooks.com
Publisher & Managing Director Nick Landau, *Editorial Director* Katy Wild

Founded in 1981. Graphic novels, including *Simpsons* and *Batman*, featuring comic-strip material; film and TV tie-ins and cinema reference books. No fiction or children's proposals, no email submissions and no unsolicited material without preliminary letter. Email or send large sae for current author guidelines. Division of Titan Publishing Group Ltd.

Wallflower Press

6a Middleton Place, Langham Street,
London W1W 7TE

tel 020-7436 9494
email info@wallflowerpress.co.uk
website www.wallflowerpress.co.uk
Editorial Director Yoram Allon

Founded in 1999. Cinema and the moving image, including TV, animation, documentary and artists' film and video – both academic and popular. Writers with proposals should make contact by email; a fully detailed proposal may then be requested, along with sample chapters.

Titles include: *Remapping World Cinema*, *Sex and the Cinema*, and *The Cinema of Spain and Portugal.*

Internet

While many of the companies listed in *Filmmakers' Yearbook* have sites you may find informative, here is a list of additional Web resoures we find useful.

SCREENWRITING

There are innumerable sites for screenwriters on the Internet, featuring everything from magazine-style articles on craft and interviews with professionals, to downloads of produced screenplays. With the help of The Script Factory, we list below a small selection of some of our favourite sites.

Script downloads

www.scriptpimp.com
Has an extensive database of scripts, as well as a number of other useful resources for writers who aspire to work in the US industry.
www.dailyscript.com
Great site with film, TV and a 'script of the day'.
www.gutenberg.org
Project Gutenberg is an online library of more than 18,000 books – and many classic plays – which have gone out of copyright in the US. Also a growing collection of music recordings and scores.
www.simplyscripts.com
www.script-o-rama.com
A real labour of love from a film fan – includes cult classics and anime.
www.imsdb.com
Internet movie script database which claims to have the largest collection of movie scripts on the Web.
www.scriptfly.com
A good all-round resource for screenwriters, this site features script downloads with a broad selction of US indies. Also invites screenwriters to upload their own 'spec' scripts into a section of the site, which industry execs can access.

Information on treatments and formatting

www.writingtreatments.com
Site dedicated to the art of the Treatment, which includes downloadable examples from produced films illustrating just how varied these documents can be.
www.wordplayer.com
Good general site by writers for writers, featuring an article by Terry Rossio (*Shrek*) on 'Proper Treatments': this uses three examples to show different ways in which you can approach your own.

General writing sites

www.writing.org.uk
Humourous site from writer Robin Kelly with excellent resources for writers, including formatting information for stage, screen and radio.
www.alcs.co.uk

Site for the Authors' Licensing & Collection Society which exists to help ensure that writers are paid properly for their work.

Books, software, DVDs

www.thescreenwritersstore.net

Excellent online resource sellling books, DVDs, audio and software for filmmakers and screenwriters specifically.

www.amazon.co.uk

www.virgin.net

PRE-PRODUCTION

Producers' Resources

www.cftpa.ca

Canada's national producers' organisation provides a comprehensive online guide to the Canadian industry.

www.pact.co.uk

UK producers' organisation with useful dowloadable research documents for sale.

www.fiapf.org

Website for the International Federation of Producers, with links to extensive resources as well as news on politics and policy which affect international filmmakers.

Casting/crewing sites

www.castingnetwork.co.uk

Casting calls and information for actors.

www.mandy.com

Mandy posts casting calls for actors for film.

www.pcrnewsletter.com

PCR publishes calls for cast and crew from casting directors, filmmakers and production companies.

www.shootingpeople.org

Shooting People distributes a daily email bulletin with casting information to actors through its 'Casting Network'; also circulates crew information via its 'Filmmakers' Network'.

www.uk.castingcallpro.com

Casting information for members who must all be trained or experienced actors.

Storyboarding assistance

www.exposure.co.uk

Its online 'Eejets Guide to filmmaking' includes useful storyboarding tips.

www.skillset.org

Skillset has produced a useful beginners' guide to the film industry, which includes information about storyboarding and planning.

PRODUCTION AND POST

Production and tech sites for filmmakers

www.ascmag.com

Site of *American Cinematographer*, a journal of film and digital production techniques. Includes selected articles and interviews from the magazine.

www.dvinfo.net
The Digital Video Information Network is a site of linked message boards for DV camera users. It has boards for DV and HDV, with a P2 Series board in the works. Users can exchange information and ask technical questions of other users. The site also has related techincal articles.
www.filmmaking.net
Includes forums for filmmakers on very specific subjects, and extremely helpful FAQs pages with information on all aspects of pre-production, production and post-production.

PROMO/PUBLICITY

Trailers

The following sites host trailers for hundreds of studio and independent feature films.
www.darkhorizons.com
www.apple.com/trailers
http://film.guardian.co.uk/trailerpark/
www.comingsoon.net/trailers/

Posters

Buy and download film posters here:
www.filmsite.org/posters.html
http://moving-print.com/
www.carltonscreen.com/htm/aboutus.php
www.filmbank.co.uk/visionbank.asp

Stills

These sites host stills collections for new and upcoming releases and festivals.
www.image.net
www.picselect.co.uk

DISTRIBUTION/EXHIBITION

Box-office statistics and analysis

Nielsen (www.nielsenedi.com/charts)
Tracks box-office data for all films for all distributors across the UK, Ireland, and in international territories.
Cinema Business (www.cinemabusiness.co.uk)
Specialist magazine website which contains box-office data (as supplied by Nielsen EDI) and analysis.
UK Film Council, UK Film Box Office (www.ukfilmcouncil.org.uk/cinemagoing/box-office/)
The UKFC's statistics department provides weekly UK box-office information.
UK Film Council, research and statistics (www.ukfilmcouncil.org.uk/information/statistics/)
Originates and gathers data on films and the film industry to contribute to evidence-based policy and strategic development.

Distribution funding and support

UK Film Council distribution and exhibition funding (www.ukfilmcouncil.org.uk/cinemagoing/distributionandexhibition/)

Information on digital equipment funding, and small capital investment in cinemas.

Arts Council (www.artscouncil.org.uk/funding/index.php)

Information on grants for the arts for individuals, arts organisations and other people who use the arts in their work.

Reel Solutions (www.reelsolutions.co.uk)

Support and guidance for the independent cinema industry. Suitable if you are looking to set up your own local independent cinema, organise a film-based event or need help with programming.

Trade issues for exhibitors

BBFC (www.bbfc.org.uk)

Designed to keep the public and the industry informed about the work of the BBFC, this website includes: up-to-the-minute information about classification decisions; the policies and guidelines used by the BBFC when classifying a work; how to submit a film, DVD or video game for classification; and information about the BBFC.

Film Distributors' Association (www.launchingfilms.com)

Information about releases, cinema and distribution stats, plus excellent essays on current issues (piracy, digital distribution and exhibition, etc.).

Technology and digital

Arts Alliance (www.artsalliance.co.uk)

Leading provider of digital technology to the theatrical market.

UK Film Council – Digital Screen Network (www.ukfilmcouncil.org.uk/cinemagoing/distributionandexhibition/dsn/)

The UKFC-funded network of digital screens.

BKSTS (www.bksts.com)

Useful site with training, discussion about cinema and media technology.

Venues and programming

British Federation of Film Societies (www.bffs.org.uk)

News and information about existing societies, plus information about establishing new ones.

Independent Cinema Office (www.independentcinemaoffice.org.uk)

Excellent site packed with useful information related to the Independent Cinema Office, which develops and supports independent film exhibition throughout the UK.

OTHER

General film information and news sites

www.brightlightsfilm.com

This online journal includes academic publications on world cinema. Great resource for theorists and researchers.

www.bfi.org.uk/filmtvinfo/gateway

The *bfi*'s Film Links Gateway is a selective collection of film and TV weblinks with an emphasis on specialised cinema. Links are organised by category.

www.britfilms.com

Very helpful site published by the British Film Council; includes a catalogue of completed British films and information about ones in production.

www.filmfestivals.com

This is an extremely useful site listing all film festivals with their deadlines. You may search for festivals by deadline or country. The site also posts festival news, such as press announcements and festival award winners.

www.imdb.com

So obvious as to almost not warrant a mention ... arguably the most important movie site on the Web, both for fans and for professionals. Site includes information on virtually every film ever made, including titles in production and pre-production. Each title includes links to external reviews where they exist, and it has reasonably reliable cast and crew listings, as well as hyperlinks to all related people or companies. Once discovered, you will use it daily.

www.indiewire.com

Excellent online magazine, which covers business and creative news in independent world cinema. Includes blogs, festival news and interviews with independent filmmakers. Bookmark it!

www.screendaily.com

Free daily news e-bulletin for the global film industry, published by Screen International.

www.shadowsonthewall.co.uk

Good e-zine with current and forthcoming UK releases, and info on festivals plus industry production gossip.

Watching short films online

The following sites tend to provide a more curated selection of short films:

Atom Films (www.atomfilms.com)

Biggest online short film library. Unusual in that filmmakers are paid by Atom for exhibition.

BBC film network (www.bbc.co.uk/filmnetwork/)

All British short films with some very high-quality shorts.

British Film Institute (www.bfi.org.uk/filmdownloads.html)

Films from the BFI archive, including rare clips.

Encounters short film festival (www.encounters-festival.org.uk)

Films from previous programmes.

Dazzle Films (www.dazzlefilms.co.uk)

Short film sales agent's own site.

First Light (www.firstlightmovies.com)

Short films from young filmmakers.

FourDocs (www.channel4.com/fourdocs)

Download good-quality documentary shorts.

The Lux (www.lux.org.uk)

Primarily screens artist's film and video.

Shorts International (www.britshorts.com)

Short film sales agent's own site.

File sharing and user-upload broadcast

www.uthtv.com

Youth TV is a P2P file-sharing site aimed at young people who want to self-distribute work – video, blogs, artwork, music – directly to the user.

www.ukscreen.com/screen

British filmmakers share their films on this site.

www.videoegg.com

Groundbreaking website that turns everyone into a moviemaker! The free site allows you to upload, edit and share video files by linking to sites like **myspace** or **blogger**.

www.youtube.com

Like **videoegg**, **youtube** allows users to share video files.

Culture and cinema

www.bbc.co.uk/dna/collective/

Great BBC site for film, games, books, arts and music lovers. Aimed at a hipper readership than most culture mags and includes good reviews, news and and generally smart member comments.

www.flavorpill.net

Arts, music and culture online magazine with email zines that go out to readers in London, San Francisco, Chicago, LA and NYC. Includes film reviews for smaller, video and film artist releases and festivals.

www.kultureflash.net

Weekly e-newsletter with info about interesting cultural events in London – gigs, films, exhibitions.

Index